W9-AOH-645

MASTERPLOTS II

African American
Literature
Series

MASTERPLOTS II

AFRICAN AMERICAN LITERATURE SERIES

2

He-Po

Edited by

FRANK N. MAGILL

SALEM PRESS

Pasadena, California   Englewood Cliffs, New Jersey

∞ The paper used in these volumes conforms to the
American National Standard for Permanence of Paper
for Printed Library Materials, Z39.48-1984.

Library of Congress Cataloging-in-Publication Data
Masterplots II: African American literature series/edited
by Frank N. Magill
    p. cm.
    Includes bibliographical references and index.
        1. American literature—Afro-American authors—
Stories, plots, etc. 2. Afro-Americans in literature. I.
Magill, Frank Northen, 1907-   . II. Title: Master-
plots 2. III. Title: Masterplots two.
PS153.N5M2645   1994   93-33876
810.9'896073—dc20   CIP
ISBN 0-89356-594-6 (set)
ISBN 0-89356-596-2 (volume 2)

PRINTED IN THE UNITED STATES OF AMERICA

LIST OF TITLES IN VOLUME 2

MASTERPLOTS II

AFRICAN AMERICAN
LITERATURE
SERIES

A HERO AIN'T NOTHIN' BUT A SANDWICH

Author: Alice Childress (1920-   )
Type of work: Novel
Type of plot: Social criticism
Time of plot: The early 1970's
Locale: Harlem, New York
First published: 1973

> ### Principal characters:
> BENJIE JOHNSON, a thirteen-year-old heroin addict
> ROSE JOHNSON, Benjie's mother
> CRAIG BUTLER, a struggling maintenance man who wants to
>   marry Rose Johnson

The Novel

A Hero Ain't Nothin' but a Sandwich traces the devastating effects of drugs on its principal character, Benjie Johnson, his family, and society. Born into a poor family in the ghetto of Harlem, Benjie wanders aimlessly into the jaws of destruction. Benjie has been taught never to be "chicken," so when he is challenged into taking drugs, he responds by showing his friends that he can take heroin without becoming a casualty. The issues of identity and the quest for wholeness that surround Benjie's motivation for taking drugs become significant in light of the fact that the novel is set in the period immediately following the Civil Rights movement of the 1960's. *A Hero Ain't Nothin' but a Sandwich* mirrors urban ghetto life, depicting blacks who seem fragmented and alienated because of race, gender, and class barriers.

The novel opens with Benjie trying to convince himself that he is not a junkie and that he can give up heroin at any time. He suffers from depression because his mother loves Craig Butler, a struggling but dignified maintenance man whom Benjie feels has replaced him as head of the house. While Butler tries to act as a positive role model and strong stepfather for Benjie, the youth moves to discredit and to enrage him at every turn.

Benjie copes with feelings of displacement by associating with gang members, who influence him to experiment with drugs. Benjie smokes marijuana until one day he finds himself in the company of young men who have moved from marijuana to heroin. Benjie proves to the gang that he is not afraid of drugs by taking heroin. Childress portrays Benjie as an arrogant teenager who believes he has to prove something to the world while simultaneously depicting him as a hurting, confused, sensitive youth who craves love and security.

Before Benjie is aware of what is happening to him, he becomes a junkie. He finds himself demanding that Tiger, a small-time pusher, introduce him to a "connection" who has easy access to heroin. Tiger introduces Benjie to Walter, a callous pusher who cares only about money. Walter sells Benjie heroin and later involves him in the sale of drugs.

Benjie soon crumbles under the pressure of drugs and school. Two of his teachers notice that Benjie is inattentive in class. Once a bright young student, Benjie nods daily or skips school. His teachers report him to his parents, and he is placed in a detoxification center.

Benjie's treatment is short-lived; within a week after treatment he steals to get a fix. His stealing is connected to his resentment toward Butler's relationship with his mother. Benjie sets out to prove that Butler, like Benjie's father, can be made to leave. He succeeds in provoking Butler by selling his suit and overcoat to buy drugs. Butler moves because he fears he will physically abuse Benjie.

Although Butler has good cause to abandon Benjie, he does not. When Benjie steals a toaster from the boardinghouse where Butler lives, he chases him to throttle him. During the chase, Benjie tries to leap over rooftops and finds himself hanging on to the edge of one. He begs Butler to let him die, to end his misery, but his stepfather saves him.

The novel concludes with Butler waiting in the cold for Benjie to appear for a counseling session. Childress leaves the reader haunted about whether Benjie, who claims to be drug-free, has chosen to seek another fix.

The Characters

Benjie Johnson searches for love to fill the void left by his biological father, who abandoned him. He is angry, frustrated, distrusting, manipulative, and rebellious. He experiments with drugs because he believes that taking drugs will make him a man, especially in the eyes of his wayward friends. Childress suggests that without proper nurturing, Benjie and others in his predicament are on their way to becoming statistics.

Alice Childress' use of multiple narrators in *A Hero Ain't Nothin' but A Sandwich* vivifies the trauma, uncertainty, and dangers experienced by a poor, young black male growing up in the ghetto, where, as Benjie says, "a chile can get snatch in the dark and get his behind parts messed up by some weirdo." The myriad narrators help to illuminate Benjie's real problem: insecurity. Each of the narrators sheds light on a young man who is in dire need of someone to give him a sense of self. He deliberately tries to alienate everyone who offers him help because he does not see himself as a drug addict but only as an occasional drug user. Benjie's perceptions of reality are countered by his mother, his teacher, his friend Jimmy Lee, his doctor, and his stepfather.

Rose Johnson and her mother are presented as women who head the Johnson household but who are powerless to help Benjie. He sees his mother and grandmother as nervous women who make him nervous in turn. His inability to relate to them is exacerbated by their going to a conjure woman/fortune teller to secure a potion meant to steer Benjie from drugs. With these two women, Childress suggests the ineffectuality of the efforts of women trying to teach boys how to be men in a society that strangles. While these women love Benjie dearly and make sacrifices for him, he seems to need something more, something they cannot give him.

Childress clearly suggests that in many cases black men are better suited to nurture black boys. Benjie's teacher Nigeria Greene, a black nationalist, tries to instill self-esteem in Benjie. He spends hours with Benjie, trying to shield him from the destructiveness of the streets. When Benjie comes to class in a daze and with needle marks in his arm, Nigeria turns him over to the principal and subsequently to the authorities for drug rehabilitation. He tells Benjie that it is "nation time," a time for black people to save one another.

Benjie distances himself from his drug-free friends, especially Jimmy Lee. It is from Jimmy Lee that the reader learns that Benjie started experimenting with heroin as a result of peer pressure. When Jimmy Lee tells Benjie to straighten up because heroin will kill him, Benjie merely dismisses Jimmy Lee as a would-be social worker.

Another character Childress uses to suggest that black men can and must take responsibility for other black men is the doctor. Benjie's doctor, in a fatherly manner, tries to give Benjie hope. He tells him to start over, noting that "the world ain't perfect" but, nevertheless, "Hard as it is, life is still sweet." It is these words of encouragement that Childress places strategically to anchor Benjie. The doctor is a significant character because he represents for Benjie the possibility of survival and success for black men.

While Benjie has Nigeria Greene, Jimmy Lee, and the doctor to bolster his self-esteem, it is Craig Butler who comes closest to saving Benjie. Butler accepts Benjie as his son, even though Benjie berates him and steals from him. Benjie resents Butler for loving Benjie's mother. Benjie feels displaced. The harder Benjie tries to push Butler away, though, the more his stepfather demonstrates that he will not abandon him. When Benjie is hanging from the rooftop and Butler risks his own life to save him, Benjie comes to see that he is loved and that he can feel secure in his relationship with Butler. As the novel ends, Butler is waiting outside the rehabilitation clinic for Benjie to show up for a counseling session.

A Hero Ain't Nothin' but a Sandwich offers a portrait not just of Benjie Johnson but of a whole generation of young black boys who could be swallowed up by the ghetto. Childress makes it clear that the responsibility for these young black men rests primarily with older black men. She calls to black men to accept the challenge of "nation time."

Themes and Meanings

Benjie Johnson is a haunting character. At the novel's conclusion, the question of whether he will survive his drug use goes unanswered. Benjie is appealing because he is a typical American boy. In some respects, he resembles Oedipus Rex, whose tragic flaw, his pride, leads to great suffering.

Like Oedipus, Benjie is troubled about his parents. While Benjie has never known love from his biological father, he is constantly reminded that he is the son of Big Ben. His mother tells him often that he looks exactly like his father. Benjie has low self-esteem because of his father's irresponsibility; he wonders how anyone could really love him when his own father abandoned him. This scar only worsens when his mother falls in love with Craig Butler. Fortune deals Benjie a serious blow by placing in his life a stepfather who dares to want to nurture and love him. Like Oedipus, however, Benjie determines to triumph over fate. Benjie spends countless hours thinking up ways to unseat his stepfather.

Each time Butler tries to reach out to Benjie, the young man recoils. Benjie is especially annoyed that Butler wants to help him with his drug problem. When Butler tells Benjie that he can make something of his life if he tries, Benjie ridicules Butler for calling himself a "maintenance man" and reminds him that he is merely a janitor. Benjie tells Butler not to offer him advice, because he does not see where opportunity has come for Butler.

As Benjie moves from marijuana to heroin, his resentment grows. Benjie becomes more and more alienated from his friends and family. When Butler tries to lend Benjie support, Benjie tells him to stop trying to be a hero.

Benjie's feelings for Butler are compounded by his relationship with his mother. The closer Rose and Butler become, the more Benjie seeks drugs to dull his feelings. He feels as if his mother has abandoned him, too. Childress links Benjie to Oedipus in her characterization of him as an adolescent perhaps too attached to his mother and too resentful of her relationship with his stepfather. He is exceptionally sensitive about his mother's pain when she and Butler begin to argue over his drug addiction. He is angry that his mother loves Butler, but he aches when he sees her crying after Butler moves out of the house.

Benjie's guilt about his mother is exacerbated when he learns that his mother, in a state of desperation, has gone to a fortune teller to find a way to end his addiction. While she bathes him in indigo water, Rose cries about Benjie's problems and about her arguments with Butler. Benjie's response to his mother's crying is to wonder why someone thirty-three, essentially an old woman, is carrying on about some man. He cannot understand why she is not satisfied with simply being a mother.

Later in the novel, however, the young man comes to understand why his mother loves Butler, who is truly a hero. The day Butler risks his life to keep Benjie from falling from the rooftop is the day that Benjie realizes that he does, indeed, have a father. Childress uses a near-death experience to shock Benjie into a new level of growth, one that allows him to accept his mother and stepfather as parents. Childress leaves the reader guessing about Benjie's future. She suggests that the power of love may not be enough to reclaim him from the throes of drug addiction.

A Hero Ain't Nothin' but a Sandwich delves into the complexity of parenting in a society where humans dull their senses with drugs instead of finding ways to heal themselves. The novel also examines a host of other issues. Poverty, for example, is a major theme in the novel. Childress portrays life in the ghetto of Harlem, where poor people struggle to survive in a stifling environment. She calls attention to the fact that children suffer the most from poverty and other ills such as drug addiction.

Childress' novel also addresses racism, sexism, and ageism. Butler, in particular, seems to be the spokesperson for Childress' views on racism. Essentially, Childress links poverty experienced by blacks to racism. The world of her novel shows the have-nots as people who are doubly victimized because of their race and class.

Childress' Mrs. Ransom Bell embodies the author's belief that sexism and ageism run as rampant as racism and classism in America. Mrs. Bell, the mother of Rose and grandmother of Benjie, is an old, black, poor female. She recalls her days in the South before she came to the North looking for a better life. She points out that there were only two ways in her day for black women to survive: by doing housework for whites or by getting married. Childress, however, illustrates that the narrow, pre-scriptive roles for black women only empowered many of them to struggle harder to achieve against the odds. Mrs. Bell becomes a shake dancer, earning a living by shivering every part of her body at once or each part separately. She tells that she became a shaker because she promised never to let anyone starve her off the face of the earth. Even after her marriage, Mrs. Bell was not free from hard times. She tells of her husband's inability to get a job because he did not belong to the all-white brick-layer's union. Childress depicts a world where black people suffer but remain optimistic and confident in their own will to survive and succeed.

Childress' treatment of the theme of ageism is perhaps one of the most passionate in contemporary literature. She demonstrates clearly that it hurts to be old. Mrs. Bell complains that her family treats her as if she is senile. Even more disrespectful are the young people who mug her and other elderly people in their Harlem neighborhood, robbing them of money, groceries, and dignity. Mrs. Bell sums up the misery of old age when she says that maybe old is more than pain; it is the loneliness that occurs when the mind goes one way and the body goes another. Childress speaks of the strangeness of living in a society that places no value on the wisdom that comes with age. Nowhere is Childress' point more evident than in her depiction of Benjie, who is an anomaly to his grandmother because he does not see her for the resource that she could be in helping him survive adolescence.

Critical Context

A Hero Ain't Nothin' but a Sandwich, Childress' first novel, drew recognition for her in a way that her plays had not. Childress began her writing career in 1950 as a playwright. Her play *Trouble in Mind* (1955) won an Obie Award. Childress' *Wedding Band* (1966) was broadcast nationally on ABC television, and *Wine in the Wilderness* (1969) was presented on National Educational Television. Her plays are as saturated with alienated, fragmented, poor people as are her novels, which include *A Short Walk* (1979), *Rainbow Jordan* (1981), and *Those Other People* (1990), and her book-length collection of vignettes, *Like One of the Family: Conversations from a Domestic's Life* (1956).

A Hero Ain't Nothin' but a Sandwich gave high visibility to Childress as a skilled author of adolescent fiction. For the first time in her writing career, she was able to reach the masses. Childress, who was born into a poor South Carolina family and reared in Harlem, writes about poor people who struggle with dignity.

Childress' novel is a milestone because it treats, sensitively and perceptively, life in the ghetto for black Americans. Unlike many of her contemporaries, moreover, Childress creates a loving, sensitive, generous, black man, Craig Butler, taking responsibility for his family. She portrays African Americans who struggle to survive in a world that often turns a deaf ear to them and captures both the pain and the beauty of being African American.

Bibliography

Brown-Guillory, Elizabeth. *Their Place on the Stage: Black Women Playwrights in America.* Westport, Conn.: Greenwood Press, 1988. One-third of the book focuses on Childress' plays and contributions to the American stage. This study represents the most comprehensive research available on Childress' writings.

_____. *Wines in the Wilderness: Plays by African-American Women from the Harlem Renaissance to the Present.* Westport, Conn.: Greenwood Press, 1990. Contains substantial biographical information and analysis of Childress' plays.

Bullins, Ed. Review of *A Hero Ain't Nothin' but a Sandwich*, by Alice Childress. *The New York Times Book Review*, November 4, 1973: 36-40. A highly laudatory early review from a noted playwright. Bullins praises the book for offering a "suggestion of hope" while still presenting "the unconcealed truth."

Childress, Alice. Interview. In *Interviews with Contemporary Women Playwrights*, edited by Kathleen Betsko and Rachel Koenig. New York: Beech Tree Books, 1987. Childress comments on her fiction and drama and discusses attempts to ban *A Hero Ain't Nothin' but a Sandwich* from some school libraries.

Draper, James P., ed. *Black Literature Criticism: Excerpts from Criticism of the Most Significant Works of Black Authors over the Past Two Hundred Years.* Detroit: Gale Research, 1991. Contains a thorough overview of Childress' life and writing. Includes well-chosen excerpts from relevant criticism.

Elizabeth Brown-Guillory

HIGH COTTON

Author: Darryl Pinckney (1953-   )
Type of work: Novel
Type of plot: Bildungsroman
Time of plot: The early 1960's through the end of the 1980's
Locale: Indianapolis, Indiana; New York City; parts of the American South; London, England; and Paris, France
First published: 1992

Principal characters:
> THE NARRATOR, never given a name and determined to escape any pigeonhole, racial or other, into which others might be tempted to place him
> GRANDFATHER EUSTACE, a graduate of Brown and Harvard who, after several business failures, becomes a minister of the Congregational church
> AUNT CLARA, the narrator's mother's aunt, obsessed with blood mixture
> UNCLE CASTOR, a jazz musician who has fallen on hard times
> JESSE, a security guard at Columbia University
> JEANETTE, an alcoholic singer the narrator comes to know in Harlem
> DJUNA BARNES, a writer, an actual historical figure
> BARGETTA, like the narrator a member of the Also Chosen, his friend in college and his guide to Paris

The Novel

"If you're chopping in high cotton you've got it easier." The narrator and protagonist of this novel has certainly had it easier than many of the black men of his generation. He is a member of the Also Chosen, a product of that educated black middle class that, according to W. E. B. Du Bois, would yield the "Talented Tenth," the gifted minority who would lead the black race along the path of progress.

The narrator makes no claim to racial leadership. In fact, he rarely makes much of a claim to racial identity. Never an Africanist, he is for much of his life an Anglophile. When he finally flies to England for the first time, following his graduation from a predominantly white high school in a suburb of Indianapolis, Indiana, he has already affected an accent that makes him sound like a cross between Cary Grant and Katherine Hepburn.

He has, to be sure, not been left quite untouched by the momentous historical events of his time. In the early 1960's, he participates in a civil rights march in Indianapolis. Of course, he is a child, his parents have brought him, and the whole thing reminds him of milling around on the lawn after church on Sunday. He is briefly, and ludicrously, involved with the Heirs of Malcolm, a minor, more-righteous-than-thou variation on the Black Panther Party, while a student in a suburban junior high school. Branching out politically while in England, he wanders into a gathering of radicals but discovers that political commitment involves getting up too early in the morning, especially if one happens to be hung over.

Returning to the United States, he studies at Columbia University. This brings him into contact with Harlem, but the contact remains very much on his terms. He hangs out one summer at a Harlem bar not on the customary Columbia students' circuit. When Jeanette, a woman he has come to know, confides her fear as she awaits the result of medical tests, he is not prepared to provide the emotional support she obviously needs. No one, he reflects, has to know that he sets himself apart.

He passes through a series of meaningless jobs, the lax standards of performance of which he consistently fails to meet. He sets out to sink into the lower classes, managing to reach the level of handyman. In this capacity, he is for a time employed by Djuna Barnes, whose novel *Nightwood* (1936) is a minor classic of literary modernism. They part on unfortunate terms when she does not quite succeed in stopping herself from a racist comment.

By 1978, the narrator has his first real job, in a publishing house. His tenure is brief. A sojourn in Paris follows. There he enjoys the company of Bargetta, a striking black woman who has been his friend since college. In college, she refused to be answerable to the Soul Sisters of Barnard. She knew very well who she was; she was not going to tell anyone else. In Paris, the narrator sees Bargetta drifting into obsession as her relationship with an untalented white artist falls apart.

In these and other episodes, the protagonist's position is often passive, more observer than agent. He is also primarily an observer in relation to his family, whose most memorable figure is Grandfather Eustace, a university graduate, sometime educator, failed businessman, nonevangelical preacher in the Congregational church, and formidable presence in the life of the narrator. Grandfather seems determined to hold the protagonist to standards the protagonist will not meet, even though Grandfather himself cannot point to a life of impressive achievement. After failing in business, he entered the church for want of somewhere else to go. Even as a preacher, he was never exactly a success. One episode of the novel deals with Grandfather's dismissal from his church in Louisville, Kentucky.

As a teenager, the narrator comes to regard his grandfather as a shattered idol. He recognizes how compromised the old man is in his relations with whites. He sees through Grandfather's refusal to face the ugliness that is an essential part of American racism. He is even critical of Grandfather's indifference to the past, especially to the African past, in his exclusive concern for the future advancement of the race. By the end of the novel, the narrator has come to a more precise appreciation of his grandfather, who has died, as a man who knew the real but loved the ideal.

When the narrator attends a Black Muslim meeting at the Felt Forum in New York City, he feels himself still to be a detached observer rather than a participant. He has, it seems, come to realize that his story, while very much his own, has also been the story of a black man of his generation. His racial identity is not all there is to him, but it is not something he could escape even if he wanted to. What he cannot know, as the novel closes, is whether in setting himself apart for so long he has squandered some opportunity to live authentically the life of a black man in his time. He is sorry, he says, that he went to such lengths not to be of use to himself, solely so that no one would be able to ask anything of him. To have nothing to offer, he now sees, was not the best way to have nothing to lose.

The Characters

The unnamed narrator is the elusive protagonist of this novel. Although the novel follows him through adolescence and young manhood, readers discover nothing about his sex life, apart from an allusion to someone he is not reconciled to losing and a reference to the nights of the wide bed, now over. Such evasions are characteristic of his presentation of self throughout the novel. If he seems in such respects to evade the reader of the novel, it may be that he is following a project of evasion throughout the novel itself. As a young black man, he finds that others, black and white, are always ready to define him, and he is unwilling to live within the limits of other people's definitions. He sometimes turns others' compulsion to define to his own interest, as when he slips into a role prescribed by one of society's scenarios, but he never commits himself to any role he tries on. Ironically, his determination to distance himself from stereotypes, for example by ostentatiously carrying a highbrow journal when he rides the subway, threatens to distance him as well from any possibility of developing an authentic self. His recognition of this irony and his acceptance of what his elusiveness may have cost him indicate the level of maturity he is approaching as the novel comes to an end.

What this narrator does best is to observe, but his powers of observation are for some time baffled by his grandfather, who is second in importance only to the narrator himself in the design of the novel. The narrator brings to his observation of his grandfather his usual ironic detachment. He sees through the proud old man's defenses and deceptions. Irony proves inadequate as a key to one who is such an intimate presence in the narrator's psychological and moral life. The narrator cannot understand his grandfather by distancing himself from the old man, because by so distancing himself he risks missing the essential truth of their closeness. Like the narrator, his grandfather is obsessed with racial scenarios, although, like the narrator, he is unwilling to play a prescribed role in one. He becomes a minister, but he does not offer the "heart religion" of the stereotypical black preacher. His choice of the Congregational church, the tiniest of black denominations in the South, places him out of the mainstream of African American spiritual life but firmly in the tradition of New England rectitude—at least until he is dismissed by his congregation. Like the narrator, Grandfather struggles with the problem of vocation: To what life, if any, is he called? If the answer is that he is called to none, where can he look for meaning? Like the narrator, Grandfather is obsessed with the presentation of self. He lives in terror of being mistaken for a welfare client. As the narrator sets himself apart from Harlem, Grandfather sets himself apart from Dorchester, from Roxbury, and from the Rutherford Street projects. With the cruelty of adolescence, the narrator at one point sees in his grandfather a shattered idol. The truth toward which he moves, and it is a truth that may set him free, is that Grandfather Eustace is more like his spiritual twin.

Themes and Meanings

The central theme of any *Bildungsroman* is the education and formation of its protagonist. Understanding *High Cotton* is to a considerable extent a matter of following the process that leads the narrator to the level of self-understanding he has reached by the end of the novel. The issue with which he must contend, in spite of his gift for evasion, is how to deal with the questions of race and status that confront him as one of his generation of the Also Chosen. Spokesmen such as W. E. B. Du Bois have defined the responsibilities that go with the advantages he enjoys, and Grandfather Eustace relentlessly enunciates the theme of advancing the race.

The narrator's instinctive strategy can be described as one of refusal. As a child, he withdraws from his environment into his Anglophile fantasies. In his adolescent flirtation with the militancy represented by the Heirs of Malcolm, he assumes briefly a role that asserts his racial identity, but in a form deviant from the calling of the Talented Tenth. Although he seems for a time to immerse himself in the life, or a corner of the life, of Harlem, spiritually he is there as a visitor: No one has to know that he sets himself apart. His deliberate descent into the lower classes seems to be an unsuccessful attempt to deny the status into which he was born; it is an irony that he finds himself employed as handyman by a writer he might have studied at Columbia.

If refusal were all, however, there would be no education. The narrator's efforts at refusal are all, at another level, forms of engagement. It is finally clear that the spirit of Grandfather Eustace lives on in his grandson, just as it is clear that his grandson is not merely a later version of Grandfather Eustace. In living out his individual story, the narrator has been living out what could only be the story of an African American man of his generation and his background. He has escaped nothing, even if it has often seemed that the defining events of modern African American history have occurred at several removes from his life. His individual story cannot help being part of the story of what it means to be black in the United States. A question that may be implicit here is whether it is equally true that any story of what it means to be black in America must be an individual story. Are there as many ways to be black in America as there are black Americans? Or is this a question that may arise more easily out of the experience of the privileged minority than out of the agony of the inner cities? At any rate, the narrator of *High Cotton* seems finally to arrive at a black identity in his own way.

Emphasizing the education and formation of the protagonist is an appropriate way to examine the meaning of this novel considered as *Bildungsroman*. The meaning of so rich a novel as this one, however, is scarcely exhausted by a single approach. For some, *High Cotton* works above all as a fascinating portrait gallery, offering in Aunt Clara, Uncle Castor, Jesse, Bargetta, and the others a display of the vitality and diversity, if also of the pathos, of African American life and of the life that surrounds it in the second half of the twentieth century. Still other readers respond most intensely to the qualities of style and voice that mark the novel. Each of the major characters has a distinctive voice, and the voice of the narrator gives to the novel as a whole a unifying style.

Critical Context

Of the black male children born in the United States during the "Negro Nadir," the period of the ascendancy of Booker T. Washington and his eloquent espousal of vocational training for black people and the strict separation of the races in all things social, how many attended Brown University? How many attended Harvard University? How many were graduated from both? Reflection on these questions makes clear what a tiny minority within the African American community is represented in the family of the narrator of *High Cotton*. Drawing, it seems, on his own family history, the author is exploring a subject matter that has hitherto been largely neglected in African American literature.

He is also clearly distancing himself from the tradition of protest in African American fiction. This is not to say, of course, that Pinckney is in any way an apologist for racism and the injustices generated by racism. For him, art is not propaganda, and the novel is not a weapon. Every black American man must learn what it is to be black, American, and a man, and must study how, indeed whether, these three components of the self can relate to one another. A novel such as *High Cotton*, apart from the formal satisfactions it may offer, can make some contribution to understanding these questions.

Of the African American novelists who have preceded him, Pinckney seems closest in spirit to Ralph Ellison, whose *Invisible Man* (1952) also features a slippery and anonymous narrator who undergoes a process of education and formation through a series of episodes that bring him from childhood to manhood. Like Pinckney's narrator, Ellison's goes through a number of identity shifts on his way to defining himself. Both novels have marked autobiographical elements, and both make a theme of the riddles of racial identity. Finally, both are characterized by an allusive and virtuosic verbal style, reflecting in each case the author's delight in the possibilities of language itself and his eagerness to place the African American experience in the widest possible frame of cultural reference.

Before writing *High Cotton*, Pickney had already established himself as an independent and provocative critic of African American literature. His essays have appeared in *The New York Review of Books* and *Granta*, and his treatment of writers such as Alice Walker, Jean Toomer, Zora Neale Hurston, Langston Hughes, James Baldwin, and Countée Cullen has been characterized by his refusal to reiterate orthodox pieties. *High Cotton* extends, rather than inaugurates, his importance as an African American writer.

Bibliography

Als, Hilton. "Word!" *The Nation* 254 (May 18, 1992): 667-670. By not naming the narrator, Pickney implicitly asks whether an African American can be different from that monolith, "The Negro." The apparent independence of the individual episodes is deceptive; the novel moves within a strict narrative line.

Bell, Pearl K. "Fiction Chronicle." *Partisan Review* 59 (Spring, 1992): 288-291. Pinckney struggles to convey the confusion and uncertainty about race and status that someone born into the black elite in the 1950's had to try to sort out. At the end, the narrator is fiercely honest about the understanding he has reached regarding his blackness and about himself as an individual in relation to his race.

Mars-Jones, Adam. "Other People's Identities." *The Times Literary Supplement*, August 14, 1992, 17. The narrator is one of the least self-revealing in literature. The novel shows a pattern of too little experience and too much analysis. Pinckney, or his narrator, seems to suffer from a morbid fear of direct statement.

White, Edmund. "Black Like Whom?" *The New York Times Book Review* 97 (February 2, 1992): 3. Djuna Barnes's *Nightwood* is a model for *High Cotton*. Unlike Barnes, Pinckney has a subject, that of race. He treats his theme with excruciating honesty and a total freedom from restraint.

Wood, Michael. "Living Is Easy." *The New York Review of Books* 39 (March 26, 1992): 13-14. The narrator and Grandfather Eustace are the novel's dubious but memorable heroes. The narrator does not deny his blackness but cannot accept the drastic simplifications that acknowledgment of blackness seems to imply. One's color, the novel implies, is not who one is, but it is something one cannot fail to have.

W. P. Kenney

HIS OWN WHERE

Author: June Jordan (1936-   )
Type of work: Novella
Type of plot: Psychological realism
Time of plot: The mid-1960's
Locale: New York City, particularly the African American community of Bedford-
    Stuyvesant
First published: 1971

> *Principal characters:*
> BUDDY RIVERS, the protagonist, a sixteen-year-old boy living
>   alone
> ANGELA FIGUEROA, Buddy's companion, the oldest of five
>   children, with three brothers and a sister
> MRS. FIGUEROA, Angela's mother, a nurse
> MR. FIGUEROA, Angela's father, a cab driver who is often angry
>   about his life
> MR. RIVERS, Buddy's father, an essentially unseen but powerful
>   presence, confined to a hospital bed with serious injuries
>   suffered in a traffic accident
> MRS. RIVERS, Buddy's mother, who has left before the narration
>   begins but remains in Buddy's memory

The Novel

His Own Where covers several months in the life of Buddy Rivers, a student at Boys
High School in Brooklyn who is at a point at which he realizes that he must assume
complete responsibility for his decisions and choices. He has been living with his
father in a house in the heart of the African American community of Bedford-
Stuyvesant in the borough of Brooklyn, a house that they have been personally reno-
vating so that it reflects their sense of who they are. Buddy's mother has returned to
the Caribbean, discouraged by her inability to order her life as she wishes. Buddy is
devastated when his father is seriously injured in a traffic accident shortly before the
action of the novel begins. The book is set in the mid-1960's, a time when ideas of
black pride and black power were capturing the minds and spirits of many African
Americans. Buddy's journey toward independent existence is an expression of a communal aspiration and is marked by the same difficulties that most black people had
to confront.

The narrative action, revealed almost entirely from within Buddy's mind and expressed as a series of thoughts and images as Buddy realizes them, is framed by a
scene in a cemetery, a symbol of loss and isolation but also of spiritual sanctuary. As
the book opens and closes, Buddy and Angela, a girl he meets in the hospital where
his father is and where her mother works, are separated from the world and together

with each other, a nascent "family" creating a space that is theirs alone, their "own place for loving" at the beginning of "a new day of the new life" they are attempting to build. The first chapter shifts back slightly in time to show Buddy and Angela on a kind of first date. Buddy leads Angela to his private place of refuge from the din of the streets, a reservoir in a wooded glen in the heart of the city. Buddy tells Angela about his father. There is another shift, back further in time, to describe how Buddy meets Angela's mother while maintaining his nightly vigil at his father's bedside. He sees Angela for the first time and is attracted to her "coolness." He overcomes his shy politeness with strangers to speak for Angela when her mother launches into a tirade against her. As Buddy learns about Angela's life with her restrictive parents, he begins to dream about giving her the freedom and space she needs to grow and of sharing the house he and his father have "made simple" but functional and comfortable, an extension of their desire for a clean, uncluttered, carefully crafted home.

Angela's parents cannot see Buddy's positive qualities, regarding him as a threat because of his youth. Her father, in a drunken rage, beats her badly enough so that Buddy must rush her to the emergency room. From there, she is sent to a shelter while the police investigate the situation. Buddy believes that he has been blamed. He transfers his irritation with unfeeling authority to his high school, where he organizes demonstrations against useless exercise in gym class and against the prison-style seating in the cafeteria. His high spirits and spontaneous organizing instincts give the regimented and sullen student body, as well as the cafeteria staff, a moment of joyful release that amuses even the police. The school principal, Mr. Hickey—whose name suggests an Irish American background not exactly suited to his job overseeing an African American student body—suspends Buddy, effectively placing both Buddy and Angela outside the formal social structure of the community. Their exile is effectively irreversible, since Buddy's parents, who are unavailable, would have to intercede for him at school, and Angela has been moved to a Catholic home for girls north of the city.

Buddy recognizes that he must act if Angela and he are to remain in contact. After a practice drive in his father's car, extending the range of his experience beyond the neighborhood he is familiar with, he drives to the home for girls (actually a kind of prison) and overwhelms the nuns (guards), rescuing Angela from what he regards as a sexless, soulless unnatural state. In high spirits, he proclaims their liberation, announcing, "Jesus was a one hundred percent, hip to the living, female-loving dude." Angela visits her parents and then joins Buddy in his house. He has carefully prepared the setting, trying to make it as special for her as it is special for him. They spend a tender night together but realize that the nuns, the police, and Angela's parents will be in pursuit of them. They depart for the retreat/refuge of a park department utility shed near the reservoir. With sparse furnishings they have brought and some supplies they have purchased, they establish a new home, minimal but planned and decorated together. There, they both dream of possibilities. Although aware of the temporary state of their "home," they are fortified by their mutual resolve, their commitment to each other, and their dream of a life together.

The Characters

June Jordan's conception of character presentation is the fundamental component in her development of the narrative in *His Own Where*. To present the mind and heart of protagonist Buddy Rivers as intensely as possible, she has written the book almost entirely from his perspective, using primilary present-tense narration in the form of a stream-of-consciousness projection of his thoughts at the moment that they occur. Jordan alters the conventional rules of syntax to concentrate on the most appropriate word-clusters to express Buddy's emotions and to illustrate the process of his thinking at the moment each thought is formed. The structure of each sentence—or, more appropriately in many cases, each line, since the separate units of meaning often resemble lines in a contemporary poem—is determined by the logic of his understanding of a situation rather than conventional rules of grammar. For example, in a description of a family dinner, Buddy's reactions to the surroundings are presented in a catalogue of sensory stimuli and his responses to them.

> The perspiration smell of toilet water. Buddy, helping carve, he feel the swarm of aunts and uncles cousins. Feel them sweaty near, amazing and predictable. And rhinestones and the wellmade gray-plaid special suit. The hugging and the jokes. The sudden ashtrays and his mother in a brandnew apron serving. Serving and remote. Retreating to the kitchen sink excuse from laughter where the family relax drink rum to celebrate another year survival.

Buddy's point of view is so central to the narration that even when Jordan describes him from the outside, the language she uses is consistent with his speech and thought patterns. Because he is present at almost every instance of the narration, his understanding of who is speaking eliminates the necessity for an authorial intrusion in the form of "He said" or similar attributions. The other characters are seen almost entirely from his perspective, so that each tends to be reduced in complexity to a single, dominant trait. Angela is the only real exception, as she is so significant an element in Buddy's world. Buddy also recalls his father with a surge of feeling that tends to make him, even in the limited and fragmentary way in which he is seen, a person whose life suggests a depth and resonance beyond the fleeting glimpses of Buddy's recollections.

The contrasts between the couples in the book—Buddy and Angela, Mr. and Mrs. Rivers, and Mr. and Mrs. Figueroa—are designed to emphasize the pain and loss of the older generation, the instinctive apprehension of the younger one, and most significant, the vitality and promise of the younger one. Buddy's linguistic facility is an expression of his creative imagination, an exciting capacity for a metaphoric vision that can conceive of the entire city as a hospital with people caring for each other, a dreary building as a warm home, a ragged garden as a private Eden, and a public school as the scene of a rock party. Buddy's warmth, energy, decency, intelligence, and determination contribute to his attractiveness as a character, while the style of Jordan's presentation defines the distinctive, individual nature of his personality.

Themes and Meanings

June Jordan has argued that Black English is "an endangered species . . . a perishing, irreplaceable system of community intelligence," and that its extinction means "the extinguishing of much that constitutes our own proud and singular identity." Survival of what she regards as "our own voice" is threatened when "white standards control our official and popular judgements of verbal proficiency and correct, or incorrect, language skills, including speech." As a poet whose own voice skillfully blends many of the forms of Black English with a complete control of "white standards" and traditional poetic forms, Jordan has demonstrated the aesthetic potential of what Gwendolyn Brooks has called a "blackening" of the language. In *His Own Where*, Jordan attempted to capture the full range of possibility of Black English in an extended, frequently poetic, narrative written entirely in that form of discourse.

Jordan faced the challenge of constructing a narrative that did not require a return to "standard" English to explain phrases and terminology that might be unfamiliar to the reader. She also chose to avoid giving the media-fostered impression that Black English is composed primarily of profane street slang. Buddy Rivers is depicted through the emerging pattern of his thoughts, and as the characterization is defined, the logical system of his mind—which is easy to understand and to follow, operating according to familiar suppositions and assumptions—functions as the syntactical frame that provides the structure for his language. Within this structural arrangement, Jordan demonstrates the rich, poetic power of Black English, frequently employing devices with precedents in the traditional literature of Great Britain and the United States. For example, Angela is overwhelmed by her first impression of Buddy's refuge in the cemetery. Jordan expresses her reaction in a line reminiscent of Dylan Thomas, describing Angela as "blinded by the light wiggles blinding in the silent waterfills her eyes." When Buddy looks at the feast prepared for a holiday, the string of adjectives he uses recalls many poems of Allen Ginsberg, and the description of Buddy's mother that builds on the conceit of her "hungering" as an emblem of need is not unlike poetic usages reaching back at least to the seventeenth century.

Jordan makes the central focus of the book the enthusiasm and appreciation for life that both Buddy and Angela exhibit. The inadequacy of conventional institutions to appreciate or encourage this valuable trait is demonstrated conclusively by the stilted, cramped letter that Angela writes as she tries to work with the techniques she has been taught in school. It is so clearly unlike her that Buddy thinks she has been brain-damaged by her father's blows or that it has been censored by the sisters at the shelter. A striking contrast is a poem she writes, one that is an explicit statement of linguistic facility and sensitivity. The dreams Buddy and Angela have near the end of the story, surrealistic projections of desire shaded by fears engendered by their tenuous situation, give full range to their capacity for imaginative thinking. Angela's dream is a Whitmanic vision of a pluralistic America in which people share a spirit of communal cooperation and mutual respect. This is the place, the ultimate "where," of the title *His Own Where*, now also "her own" space. Buddy's "where" ironically is situated in a cemetery, underlining the disparity between the aspirations of young African Americans and the reality of their lives in the late twentieth century.

Critical Context

His Own Where was a finalist for the National Book Award in 1972, but it has not been the subject of much critical attention partly because of the hybrid nature of its form. Although described as a novel by its publishers, it is closer in length, at ninety pages, to a novella, and it resembles, in its structure, a poetic cycle or a series of poetic tableaus. Some uncertain librarians have placed it in the young adult section, possibly because of its consideration of teenage and premarital pregnancy. Jordan conceived of the book as a tribute to and an evocation of the spirit, resilience, and humanity of its young protagonists. She used all of her skills as a poet and her own experiences in urban settings to render the psychological mood of the generation of African Americans born after World War II. Reliance on the rhythms of popular music and the speech patterns and styles of the black community give the book an impressive authenticity. Although its audience has been somewhat limited, its poetic power remains undiminished and it has in no way become dated by social changes since its publication.

Bibliography

Christian, Barbara. *Black Feminist Criticism: Perspectives on Black Women Writers.* Elmsford, N.Y.: Pergamon Press, 1985. Discusses Jordan in the context of other contemporary African American female writers.

Jordan, June. *Civil Wars.* Boston: Beacon Press, 1981. Jordan's first collection of personal/political essays, one of the first such books written by an African American woman in the United States.

_____. *Living Room: New Poems, 1980-1984.* New York: Random House, 1985. A collection indicating the direction of Jordan's poetry.

_____. *On Call: Political Essays.* Boston: South End Press, 1985. Carries Jordan's concerns with poetry, politics, her personal experiences, and Black English into the 1980's.

_____. *Technical Difficulties: African-American Notes on the State of the Union.* New York: Pantheon, 1992. Jordan's incisive commentary on Martin Luther King, Jr., Jesse Jackson, Clarence Thomas, Anita Hill, and Mike Tyson, as well as responses to the political state of the American nation in the last decades of the twentieth century.

_____. *Things That I Do in the Dark: Selected Poems, 1954-1977.* New York: Random House, 1977. Gives a sense of Jordan's range during the first three decades of her career as a poet.

Tate, Claudia. *Black Women Writers at Work.* New York: Continuum, 1984. Conversations and interviews with many of Jordan's peers and fellow artists. Provides a context for Jordan's work.

Leon Lewis

HOME TO HARLEM

Author: Claude McKay (1889-1948)
Type of work: Novel
Type of plot: Social realism
Time of plot: Immediately following World War I
Locale: Harlem, New York and Pittsburgh, Pennsylvania
First published: 1928

> *Principal characters:*
> JAKE (JACOB BROWN), the protagonist, a tall, brawny black army
>   deserter
> RAY, a Haitian immigrant to the United States
> FELICE, a high-priced Harlem prostitute
> CONGO ROSE, an entertainer at the Congo nightclub
> AGATHA, a beauty-parlor assistant
> ZEDDY PLUMMER, a compulsive gambler who threatens to report
>   Jake as an army deserter
> BILLY BIASSE, the operator of a longshoremen's gambling parlor

The Novel

The title *Home to Harlem* suggests that the famous New York "Black Belt" is the place to which African Americans return when they want to find true comfort and harmony, when they want to be among their "family" and friends, even though, like most of the characters, they have migrated from elsewhere—from Haiti, from Virginia, from Maryland (as in the cases of Ray, Jake and Zeddy, and Agatha). The novel is essentially an account of life in Harlem as seen through the experiences of Jake, who (though not a native New Yorker) has come to regard Harlem as his hometown and is constantly comparing it with other places in his experience. Though the brief sojourn of Jake gives a linear development to the plot, *Home to Harlem* is actually a cyclical novel, for it is apparent that Jake has opened and closed one episode of his life in Petersburg, Virginia, another in Europe (with the Army), and a third in Harlem, before entering on yet another in Chicago with Felice.

The story opens with Jake working as a stoker aboard a freighter en route from Cardiff, Wales, to New York. He had joined the Army with patriotic motives, but when he was assigned to carrying building materials for barracks, he became disillusioned, donned civilian clothes, and went to London, where he worked on the docks and lived in the East End. He was horrified by the race riots of 1919, so he shipped out for America, for Harlem, for brown lips "full and pouted for sweet kissing. Brown breasts throbbing with love." His London mistress was now just "a creature of another race—of another world." It is this antithesis of the white and black cultures that informs the whole novel: McKay emphasizes the difference between the controlled, puritanical behavior of white society and the free, spontaneous, libidi-

nous life of the black ghetto, in which sex, drugs, alcohol, knives, guns, unemployment, and poverty are pervasive. The several chapters are essentially episodes in
Jake's life that describe his contacts with these aspects of Harlem life.

Back in Harlem, Jake visits saloons, restaurants, and a cabaret, the Baltimore,
where he meets Felice, a young prostitute, and he spends the night with her. As her
name suggests, she is the personification of happiness—in herself and for Jake—
and is instinctively warm and responsive. Jake also meets Zeddy Plummer, a "stocky,
thick-shouldered, flat-footed" former Army buddy who knows that Jake deserted
and advises him to be circumspect. Zeddy's life is saved by Jake during a fight with a
loan shark, but Zeddy later threatens to inform the police that Jake is an Army
deserter, proving his contention that in Harlem friendships are often temporary and
unreliable—a fact that the novel demonstrates amply.

Searching for Felice (and, ultimately, for happiness itself), Jake visits the Congo,
a popular nightclub, where he meets Congo Rose, who wants him as her "sweetman"—a role he deprecates, since he feels that men should not live off women.
Nevertheless, he moves in with her, even though he feels no love, or even deep
desire, for her; he agrees "simply because she had asked him when he was in a fever
mood for a steady mate." This sexual imperative is the basis of most of the relationships in *Home to Harlem*, though occasionally some are dictated by economic necessity. Signs that Rose has other sex partners, and her clear masochism, impel Jake to
take a job on the Pennsylvania Railroad as a waiter.

It is while working for the railroad that Jake meets Ray, a serious-minded Haitian
immigrant who aspires to be a writer and who is intent on introducing his colleagues
to literature, politics, and black achievements in the world. Ray is himself introduced to the black subculture of flophouses, drugs, and easy sex and becomes a
close friend of Jake, through whom he meets Agatha.

After a series of adventures in the nightlife of Harlem, Jake meets Felice again,
and they decide to leave for Chicago, where, they believe, they will be free of the
problems of Harlem and will be able to make a new life.

The Characters

As in almost all of his fiction, Claude McKay offers in *Home to Harlem* characters who represent the polarities that he attempted to bridge: the intellectual and the
emotional, the potent and the impotent, the hardworking and the indolent, the caring and the carefree, the permanent and the transient. (All these were ultimately
fused in Bita Plant, the protagonist of McKay's 1933 novel *Banana Bottom*.)

Jake, having been separated from black women for two years while in Europe, is
keen to resume his physical contact with them upon his return to Harlem; however,
he is not one of the unthinking, faceless men of the crowd. Rather, he is a hardworking man with leadership qualities (as demonstrated by his leading a longshoremen's
team), with a keen sense of duty (as he shows by enlisting in the Army), with a
quick perception of being deceived (as he shows when he is made to lug lumber
instead of being given front-line combat duty), with a sense of self-esteem (he is

unwilling to be kept as a sweetman), and with a desire to improve his lot within the existing social and political system. That is, he is generally conservative yet ambitious; he is not a reactionary and not a progressive. He bonds well and readily with other blacks, yet he is not dependent; he listens and learns and has confidence in being able to cope and to endure. In many ways, he is a most admirable character: He is resilient and resourceful, adaptable and yet not flaccid.

Ray, on the other hand, is a lonely adventurer, and his principal trait is his inability to come to terms with the existing social situation. He is an intellectual, a reader (while stopping over in Pittsburgh, he buys and reads four regional black newspapers; he quotes William Wordsworth's sonnet on Toussaint Louverture verbatim; and he alludes to works by Johann Wolfgang von Goethe, Sherwood Anderson, D. H. Lawrence, Henri Barbusse, and other important writers, both contemporary and classic), and a cultured person (he frequently speaks in French). He is proud of the black cultural heritage and is anxious to teach his railroad companions about their social and cultural background, although he is often regarded as somewhat eccentric, especially for someone in his line of work. Yet because he enters the novel so late and leaves Harlem (with its possibility of at least reasonable comfort in the company of Agatha, who is roughly his equivalent in respectability and achievement) for continued vagabondage in a lowly occupation, he does not become a character to be admired: His actions are less admirable than his ideas. While he has an interest in befriending other black men, it is a passing interest; and he is unable, it seems, to establish a true interest in women, whether from a physical or an intellectual motivation. In these respects, he is a true foil to Jake. Jake leaves Harlem with a goal (a new life with Felice); Ray leaves Harlem only to escape. Ray is, in fact, little more than a voice for McKay's social and political opinions and a vehicle for displaying the author's own intellectual interests. He is pessimistic: "Civilization is rotten," he says on one occasion; on another, he tells Agatha, "The more I learn, the less I understand and love life." As most critics have pointed out, Ray is fundamentally an authorial self-portrait.

The other characters are representatives of the Harlem underworld. Zeddy Plummer, Jake's razor-wielding Army buddy, is an informer, a sweetman, a strike-breaker, a gambler, a heavy drinker, and an inept hustler. Billy Biasse (whose name also serves to characterize him) is prejudiced and is interested in small-time racketeering, yet he is also a realist eking out an existence in a rough-and-tumble, dangerous environment. The many minor female characters are generally presented as admirable in the sense that they are hardworking (whether as beauty-parlor technicians or as prostitutes) and are prepared to be the breadwinners for their unemployed sweetmen; even if these women are exploited and preyed upon, they are able to survive rather well. Only Felice, however, seems capable of warm and instinctive responses; the other women have been deprived of true affection and simple love.

Themes and Meanings

Home to Harlem is essentially a story without a plot. There is no story line in the strict sense; Felice is lost for a time and then found by chance. Everything else in the novel is introduced to let the reader know what life is like in Harlem, and this the book does with noteworthy verisimilitude. The story is not linear, because life in the Black Belt is not shown to proceed in a logical, cause-and-effect fashion; rather, it is depicted as serendipitous, often unfair, and certainly unpredicatble and dangerous. Ray's participation in the life of Jake is short-lived and fundamentally ineffective. In this way, McKay seems to suggest that there is no possibility of amelioration from the outside and from would-be saviors who are transient and not from within the social structure.

On the other hand, Jake, who is part of Harlem and who has become accustomed to its harshness and brutality, can see the possibility of finding love, affection, and even self-satisfaction and self-improvement by leaving it all behind. Prostitution, he seems to suggest, is nothing to hold against a woman if society has forced her into it for survival.

McKay was a longtime resident of Harlem after he migrated from Jamaica (which he saw as Edenic), and he thought of Harlem as dehumanizing in the extreme. His attitude is reflected in Ray's comment that if he married Agatha he soon "would become one of the contented hogs in the pigpen of Harlem, getting ready to litter little black piggies." It is this image that McKay presents throughout the novel: Where people are overcrowded and treated like animals, they become animals. In this respect, *Home to Harlem* is a noteworthy piece of social realist fiction; it is hard to find a more detailed and reliable eyewitness account of this section of 1920's New York.

It is the pervasive contrast between Jake and Ray that gives *Home to Harlem* its principal thematic development. Jake is forthright, versatile, optimistic, and persevering; he comes in contact with Ray, who is deliberate, cynical, pessimistic, and unpredictable. Jake is impressed by the intellect and interests of Ray, yet he discerns that a person made "impotent by thought" is irrelevant to the lives of Harlem's masses. Jake is principled: He will be unemployed rather than be a strikebreaker; he will live with a woman, but he will not be a kept man; he sees that the white world is one of materialism and opportunism, but he does not want to participate in it; he sees that the lives of the black folk are difficult, but he does not succumb to the blandishments of purported prophets and saviors. Nevertheless, he feels that he can survive and perhaps even succeed in life. The dialectic permeates the novel.

The two nightclubs that are foregrounded in the novel are likewise of symbolic interest. The Congo is "an amusement place entirely for the unwashed of the Black Belt," but the Baltimore, with which Jake and Felice identify, is more restrained and even polite—though not refined and sedate. The Congo is for sweetmen, the Baltimore for men.

Whenever McKay is writing about the quick action of nightclubs, rent parties, and similar social entertainments, he uses a staccato style—short sentences, short words, parallel structures—and a close approximation to the dialects of Harlem. His narrative passages and transitions are more leisurely and even-paced, yet nowhere is the "purple passage" commonplace. Ellipses are frequent, but they serve to suggest tension and the hesitancy that is common in situations involving social inequalities, illegitimate propositions, and indecisiveness.

Only occasionally does McKay allow his own political and social views to intrude explicitly. The black-white issue that absorbed him in his journalism is never directly introduced, though it can be discerned by implication. The authorial voice is to be seen in what both Jake and Ray say, for they represent the two sides of McKay himself: They represent the body and the mind.

Critical Context

The initial reception of *Home to Harlem* was extraordinary. The novel was praised by white critics and condemned by most black ones. It was the first book by an African American to receive the gold medal of the Institute of Arts and Sciences. It was praised by *The New York Times* for the verisimilitude of the speech of the characters and by *The Bookman* for the accurate transcription of Harlem slang and dialect, as well as for its evocation of the terror lingering in the streets and apartments of the Black Belt. The *New York Herald-Tribune* commended McKay for his stark realism, for his ability to present sordid truths about black life in New York "with the same simplicity that a child tells his mother" of what has happened.

Yet many readers, especially black ones, thought that McKay was merely trying to present the life of Harlem in a manner that would be of interest to white readers. The high-minded W. E. B. Du Bois, the leading voice of the black intelligentsia at the time (and a cultivated mulatto who spent his summers in Paris) attacked *Home to Harlem* in *The Crisis*, his influential magazine. In the June, 1928, issue, Du Bois wrote: "*Home to Harlem* for the most part nauseates me, and after the dirtier parts of its filth I feel distinctly like taking a bath. . . . It looks as though McKay has set out to cater to that prurient demand on the part of the white folk for a portrayal in Negroes of that licentiousness which conventional civilization holds white folk back from enjoying." Alain Locke, perhaps the principal philospher of the Harlem Renaissance and a protégé of Du Bois, also attacked McKay. Both Locke and Du Bois, however, were far removed from the life of the multitudes of Harlem and were keen to address themselves to the social advancement of the "Talented Tenth" that occupied much of Du Bois's thought. Both Du Bois and Locke were anxious to publicize the academic and cultural achievements of African Americans and had little in common with the unemployed, the exploited, the tenement dwellers who made up the bulk of the black community in the United States. More recently, Richard A. Long has questioned the reliability of McKay's depiction of Harlem life, and Nigel Thomas has argued that *Home to Harlem* should never have been published. Thomas suggests that too much of McKay's material is presented in summary form, that scenes in the book are often lacking in artistic unity, that there are too many debates between Jake and Ray, and that the tone of the novel is too overwhelmingly brutal.

By way of rejoinder to these objections—and specifically to those of Thomas—Hope McKay Virtue, the author's only child, has made the point that the novel was the first of its kind and that it depicts a time and community with which its detractors have been unfamiliar. Historically, *Home to Harlem* is important as the first African American novel published by a white publisher in the United States to receive widespread critical attention and recognition. Moreover, the book helped to establish the tradition of social realism long favored by black writers, and it helped to pave the way for the politically significant writers of the Black Arts movement of the 1960's and 1970's. The success of *Home to Harlem* also allowed McKay to devote his time to writing fiction; without this apprentice piece, his much greater subsequent novel *Banana Bottom* might never have been written.

Bibliography
Bone, Robert A. *The Negro Novel in America.* Rev. ed. New Haven, Conn.: Yale University Press, 1965. Argues that the "Harlem School" of novelists portrayed the distinctive culture of black America in a distinctive language, which included slang and dialect. Bone argues that Jake represents instinct, while Ray is the inhibited, overcivilized thinker, a figure for McKay himself.
Cooper, Wayne F. *Claude McKay, Rebel Sojourner in the Harlem Renaissance: A Biography.* Baton Rouge: Louisiana State University Press, 1987. This prize-winning study is the authoritative source of information on the writer's life. Almost every article on McKay is considered, and the documentation is authoritative and exhaustive.
Giles, James R. *Claude McKay.* Boston: Twayne, 1976. A useful introduction to the life, poetry, fiction, and general prose that stresses McKay's early life in relation to his later religious, social, and political beliefs. McKay's *Gingertown* (1932) receives sustained analysis and evaluation.
Pyne-Timothy, Helen. "Perception of the Black Woman in the Work of Claude McKay." *College Language Association Journal* 19, no. 2 (December, 1975): 152-164. Asserts that the black woman in McKay's works sustains the needs of the black man and defines the future of the race. These women manage to survive even though many are exploited and betrayed by the men they have attempted to help. Notes that McKay openly opposed marriage between black men and white women.
Ramchand, Kenneth. *The West Indian Novel and Its Background.* London: Faber, 1970. Notes that McKay was absorbed by the "Negro Question," by vagabondage, and by the urge to be a famous writer. Ramchand argues that McKay's characterization of the "primitive Nego" runs close to the white stereotype; that his polemics tend to weaken the imaginative vitality of his novels; and that his celebration of racial self-esteem acted to diminish the possibility of an integrated society in America.

A. L. McLeod

THE HOMEWOOD TRILOGY

Author: John Edgar Wideman (1941-   )
Type of work: Two novels and a collection of short stories
Type of plot: Social and psychological realism
Time of plot: The 1920's-the 1980's, with flashbacks to the nineteenth century
Locale: The Homewood section of Pittsburgh, Pennsylvania
First published: 1985: *Damballah*, 1981; *Hiding Place*, 1981; *Sent for You Yesterday*, 1983

Principal characters:

JOHN FRENCH, the patriarch of the central Homewood family

FREEDA HOLLINGER, his wife, the great-granddaughter of a slave, Sybela Owens, who fled north out of slavery to Pittsburgh to found this family

JOHN, the persona of the author, a black writer

TOMMY, John's brother, whose part in an attempted robbery and murder is central to several story lines

BESS, the great-great-aunt of Tommy, representing history in the novel as the granddaughter and thus the direct link to Sybela Owens

ALBERT WILKES, a piano player who disappears for seven years after killing a white policeman

CARL FRENCH, the son of John French, the source of many of the Homewood stories the Wideman persona learns in different works of the trilogy

BROTHER TATE, Carl's friend, a man who maintains silence for sixteen years

LUCY TATE, Carl's occasional lover for several decades

DOOT, at times a narrator, the nephew of Carl French who returns to Homewood and tries to understand the complex history of his community

The Novels

The three volumes of what is known as the Homewood trilogy were originally published as separate Avon paperbacks. The novel *Hiding Place* and the short-story collection *Damballah* were published in 1981, and the novel *Sent for You Yesterday* in 1983. Following the critical success of the three works—*Sent for You Yesterday* won the prestigious PEN/Faulkner Award for Fiction—Avon Books reissued them in a paperback titled *The Homewood Trilogy* (1985). The University of Pittsburgh Press published a hardback edition of the three works in 1992 as *The Homewood Books*.

In his preface to the 1992 edition, John Edgar Wideman explains the trilogy's evolution—the three different works were written simultaneously, he says—and its significance:

> The three books offer a continuous investigation, from many angles, not so much of a physical location, Homewood, the actual African-American community in Pittsburgh where I was raised, but of a culture, a way of seeing and being seen. *Homewood* is an idea, a reflection of how its inhabitants act and think. The books, if successful, should mirror the characters' inner lives, their sense of themselves as spiritual beings in a world where boundaries are not defined by racial stereotypes or socioeconomic statistics.

Wideman's goal in the three volumes, he declares in this preface, "is to celebrate and affirm."

Damballah, the volume that opens the trilogy, is a collection of twelve stories that have a unity of place. The setting in nearly all the stories is Homewood, a predominantly black section of Pittsburgh. Wideman begins *Damballah* with three separate prefaces: an epigraph "to robby," his brother, that begins "Stories are letters"; a passage called "damballah: good serpent of the sky," from a book on Haitian voodoo; and "a begat chart" that lays out the family tree underpinning so many of these stories. The family tree begins with a slave, Sybela Owens, who fled north in the nineteenth century, and ends with John, the persona of the author, born in 1941. The three elements of so many of Wideman's stories are in these prefaces: distinctly biographical foundations, roots in African American folklore and myth, and communicative function as personal "letters," to family, friends, and readers.

The title story, "Damballah," opens the collection. It is a brief narrative of a black slave named Orion who was killed in 1852. The story that closes the collection, "The Beginning of Homewood," is the history of Sybela Owens. Between these two historical/biographical bookends are ten stories, many of them about Homewood, with recurring characters, incidents, and themes. Wideman's stories in *Damballah* weave in and out of a lived neighborhood, and the best stories capture the texture and past of this place.

Hiding Place and *Sent for You Yesterday* are novels that expand on the characters and situations touched on in the short stories of *Damballah*. Because the three works were written simultaneously, they can illuminate each other when read in the same way. *Hiding Place*, for example, extends the situation described in the short story "Tommy" in *Damballah*. Tommy, whose partner killed someone in a robbery attempt, escapes to the isolation of Bruston Hill, where his great-great-aunt Bess lives. In their thorny interaction of a few days, they help each other, although Tommy is killed by the police in the end. Bess tells the family history that underpins this community, reconnecting Tommy and herself to it:

> You Lizabeth's son, Thomas. Your grandmother was my sister's girl. You wasn't even close to born when my sister Gert died. Freeda was her oldest. And some say the prettiest in her quiet way. John French your granddaddy. Strutting around in that big brown hat like he owned Homewood. Hmmph. Tell me I don't know. Know you coming and going.

Sent for You Yesterday is an even more complex and less linear fiction, a novel containing several stories. "The Return of Albert Wilkes" centers on that character's reappearance in Homewood seven years after killing a white policeman. Wilkes is gunned down by the police as he sits playing the piano. In "The Courting of Lucy Tate," the next generation—Carl, Lucy, and Brother Tate—enter the novel as friends, relatives, and lovers. The final section, "Brother," concerns a recurring dream that Brother Tate has, but it ends with Carl, Lucy, and Doot—the Wideman persona in this work—eating and drinking together and sharing stories. These stories, concerning the death of Brother Tate's son Junebug in a fire, Brother Tate's own mysterious death some sixteen years later, his wife's hospitalization, the legend of Albert Wilkes, and the love affair of Carl and Lucy, are parts of the myth of Homewood that Doot is learning.

To describe the plots of the Homewood trilogy is to attempt to make linear what is decidedly recursive fiction. Even the short stories of *Damballah* carry Wideman's distinctive fictional style. Much of the narration takes place inside the minds of Wideman's characters, in their own personal language. Dialogue is equally difficult to follow, for Wideman never uses quotation marks and rarely identifies speakers in any traditional manner.

The author cares less for story in the conventional sense than for the effect of character and place on each other. Like James Joyce and William Faulkner before him, Wideman depicts the consciousness of a people, in this case the African American consciousness of the twentieth century. In any one fictional work, he may mix several points of view and several different narrative voices. Similarly, there are often jumps between incidents and ideas that are not easy to follow, a narrative stream of consciousness that readers may find surreal. The difficulties in the Homewood trilogy are their own reward, however, for John Edgar Wideman renders twentieth century African American life in all of its linguistic richness and tragic fullness.

The Characters

Characters in the Homewood trilogy are three-dimensional with a vengeance, but readers may not always be able to fathom their depth. Because several central characters exist in each of the works, they can be comprehended from multiple perspectives. Wideman's focus is on the interior life, the thoughts and feelings of characters struggling to get through their lives. Action and incident are incidental to the interior experiences of characters caught up in them.

Tommy in *Hiding Place*, for example, is a man on the run, not only from the police but also from his responsibilities as husband and father. Much of the novel takes place in his head as he struggles with his past and tries to figure out a future. Likewise, Brother Tate in *Sent for You Yesterday* has been silent since the death of his son Junebug and remains so until his own violent death sixteen years later. He is rendered in multiple viewpoints through thought, memory, and dream. Throughout the trilogy, family members appear and disappear, shedding light on each other and themselves. As Doot muses about himself in *Sent for You Yesterday*, trying to get a handle on his own family history,

> Carl's sister Lizabeth's first child. John French's first grandson. John French my first daddy because Lizabeth's husband away in the war. By the time Carl and my father returned from the Pacific, I was big enough to empty the spittoon which sat beside Daddy John French's chair.

The most problematic character, but the one who is the key to the rest, is the persona of the narrator, the multiple John Edgar Wideman character who appears at various times in the three works as Doot, John, and others. He is the writer brother of Tommy who—like Wideman himself—has fled the violent urban East for the relative security of Wyoming. In the course of the three works, he returns and discovers the values of his family and community. One of the central themes of the Homewood trilogy is this reconciliation of the John/Doot character with his family home.

Themes and Meanings

There is no simple meaning to the Homewood trilogy. On one hand, these are three separate works that have been put together because they are set in the same locale, but on the other hand each has its own individual subjects. Calling them a trilogy does not cancel out their differences as three individual works of literature.

Still, they share certain meanings. On the most obvious level, the three volumes depict the life and history of one black neighborhood, a district that has all the dangers and all the potential strengths of any inner-city neighborhood. It is a geographical area of neighborhood bars, such as the Bucket of Blood and the Velvet Slipper, a neighborhood in which crime is common, drugs are taking over, and characters will be killed. It is an area with a history, but also an inner city where that history is slipping away. As Lucy says at the end of *Sent for You Yesterday* of characters like Brother Tate and John French,

> They made Homewood. Walking around, doing the things they had to do. Homewood wasn't bricks and boards. Homewood was them singing and loving and getting where they needed to get. They made these streets. That's why Homewood was real once. Cause they were real. . . . Just sad songs left. And whimpering. Nothing left to give the ones we supposed to be saving Homewood for. Nothing but empty hands and sad stories.

These stories obviously represent something vital to Wideman. The neighborhood provides myths and meanings that can be sustaining to his characters. Doot, in *Sent for You Yesterday*, is—like his persona in the other works—coming back to Homewood and only now beginning to understand its richness and meaning. The community, its history, its music, and its language, provide a cultural safety net for its residents. As Wideman writes in the epigraph to that last novel,

Past lives live in us, through us. Each of us harbors the spirits of people who walked the earth before we did, and those spirits depend on us for continuing existence, just as we depend on their presence to live our lives to the fullest.

The stories encapsulate this history and heritage, and they provide the friendship, family, and community that are the antidotes to the isolation and alienation of so much of twentieth century American urban life. The stories of Mother Bess, of Brother Tate, of Sybela Owens—these are part of a living past that Wideman wants his readers to acknowledge and celebrate.

Critical Context

The Homewood trilogy occupies several important places in black culture. It reveals a major African American writer wrestling with his own history. The story of the persona in the Homewood books is also the story of John Edgar Wideman, who grew up in this neighborhood but who left in more ways than one. The trilogy reveals his return and his rediscovery of the values and strengths that underpin this community's past and the past of his family. Like Alex Haley's *Roots: The Saga of an American Family* (1976), the Homewood books show African American writers a way back to their own heritage.

The trilogy also represents the resolution of the conflict between black and white literary values. In Wideman's first three novels before the Homewood trilogy, his method was clearly postmodernist, and even his style seemed closely modeled on T. S. Eliot and James Joyce. In the Homewood books, readers watch Wideman working out a way to use all that he has learned about aesthetics to render a black community, to forge, as it were, a black postmodernist discourse. He was successful, as the PEN/Faulkner Award for Fiction for *Sent for You Yesterday* demonstrates. His works have as much complexity and depth as those of any writer working in the last quarter of the twentieth century. Again and again in these three works, Wideman draws upon black history and folklife to find his motifs and meanings. Even his style, using such forms as call-and-response and the blues, reflects that search. Like Toni Morrison, Ernest J. Gaines, and other contemporary black writers, Wideman has bridged the literary and cultural chasms of the twentieth century and come up with complex and beautiful celebrations of African American life.

Bibliography

Bennion, John. "The Shape of Memory in John Edgar Wideman's *Sent for You Yesterday.*" *Black American Literature Forum* 20 (Spring/Summer, 1986): 143-150. Observes that the nontraditional form of this concluding volume in the Homewood trilogy involves "a structuring of reality which balances past and present, consciousness and subconsciousness, memory and actuality, life and death."

Berben, Jacqueline. "Beyond Discourse: The Unspoken Versus Words in the Fiction of John Edgar Wideman." *Callaloo* 8 (Fall, 1985): 525-534. Critique of the complex structure of *Hiding Place*, a novel that juxtaposes "the harsh world of poverty with the realm of dreams and fantasies."

Coleman, James W. *Blackness and Modernism: The Literary Career of John Edgar Wideman.* Jackson: University Press of Mississippi, 1989. Explains how Wideman has used modernism and postmodernism to bring his characters out of their isolation and into contact with the needs, concerns, and traditions of black people. The volume includes a 1988 interview with Wideman.

_____. "Going Back Home: The Literary Development of John Edgar Wideman." *College Language Association Journal* 28 (March, 1985): 326-343. Finds in the Homewood trilogy the creation of a myth of family history and the history of the community that Coleman believes will sustain both Wideman and his characters.

Rushdy, Ashraf H. A. "Fraternal Blues: John Edgar Wideman's Homewood Trilogy." *Contemporary Literature* 32 (Fall, 1991): 312-345. A detailed analysis of the process by which Wideman's narrator in the Homewood trilogy achieves a "blues voice" that allows him to depict the complex interconnections among community, family, and the individual, particularly between brothers.

David Peck

THE HOUSE BEHIND THE CEDARS

Author: Charles Waddell Chesnutt (1858-1932)
Type of work: Novel
Type of plot: Social realism
Time of plot: The Reconstruction era
Locale: North Carolina and South Carolina
First published: 1900

Principal characters:

ROWENA (RENA) WALDEN, the protagonist, a strikingly beautiful
  mulatto woman
JOHN (WALDEN) WARRICK, Rena's brother and a friend of her
  fiancé
GEORGE TRYON, Rena's white fiancé
MOLLY WALDEN, the mother of John and Rena
FRANK FOWLER, a dark-complexioned, honest, loyal man who
  adores Rena
JEFF WAIN, a lecherous and deceptive mulatto

The Novel

The House Behind the Cedars is a story about the efforts of two mulattoes to pass
for white in the post-Civil War South. Through John and Rena Walden, Charles
Chesnutt depicts both a successful and an unsuccessful attempt at "passing."

John's adventure into the white world is successful. As a child, the light-skinned
John decides that he is more white than black and, therefore, has the right to enjoy
all of the privileges of a white man. After serving as an apprentice lawyer in Judge
Straight's office and after reviewing the laws regarding miscegenation in the South,
he and Judge Straight decide that South Carolina is the best place in the South for
John's new identity. Thus, a few years before the Civil War, the eighteen-year-old
John Walden gets money from his mother, Molly, kisses his little sister Rena good-
bye, and leaves his hometown of Patesville, North Carolina, for Clarence, South
Carolina. There, he takes the name John Warrick and begins his life as a white man.

Because of his fair skin and patrician manners, John encounters little difficulty.
He escapes serving in the Confederate Army; instead, he manages the plantation of
a wealthy Southerner who has left his wife in order to fight for the Confederacy.
When the plantation owner is killed, John marries his widow, who is the descendant
of a wealthy South Carolina family. Hence, through his marriage, John is connected
with one of the leading families of the region. He continues his upward mobility by
becoming a well-established lawyer whose clientele consists of well-to-do whites.
After ten years of living in the white world, John returns to Patesville to visit his
mother and sister. Observing Rena's beauty and intelligence, he persuades Molly to
let Rena go back to South Carolina with him. He believes that by crossing the color
line she, too, will enhance her social and economic opportunities. John is convinced

that Rena, if she remains in Patesville, "must forever be a nobody." Throughout the novel, John retains his stature as a well-to-do southern gentleman.

Rena's success at passing, unlike her brother's, is short lived. Although her sojourn in the white world is spectacular enough, she is eventually rejected. Having spent a year in a boarding school in Charleston, schooling that prepares her to be "a lady," Rena is chosen Queen of Love and Beauty at a tournament reenacting chivalric scenes from Sir Walter Scott's 1819 novel *Ivanhoe.* This event is the town's major social function; hence, Rena's capture of the coveted title is proof of her successful debut in the white world. Her position as a white woman is strengthened by the attention that she receives from George Tryon, a young aristocrat who is chosen the valiant knight of the tournament. Soon, the two become engaged, and a wedding date is set.

Rena's blissful state changes when she receives a letter from her mother informing her that she is ill. Leaving a note for George but omitting her destination, Rena hastens to her mother's house in Patesville. Coincidentally, George travels to Patesville and discovers Rena's true identity. Although the couple does not speak to each other during the discovery, Tryon's facial expressions reveal his rejection of Rena: "When Rena's eyes fell upon the young man in the buggy, she saw a face as pale as death, with staring eyes, in which love, which once had reigned there, had now given place to astonishment and horror." Discerning no "love," "sorrow," or "regret" in Tryon's visage, Rena is totally devastated. She faints in his presence, and afterward she despairs over her lost love.

Rena's reentry into the black world reveals both her commitment to her people and her innocence of the perils confronting her. After recuperating from Tryon's rejection of her, Rena decides to remain among her own people and close to her mother. Consequently, she refuses her brother's offer to return to South Carolina or to relocate in the North, where both of them are unknown. Eventually, persuaded by Jeff Wain, a visitor to Patesville, and her mother, Rena accepts a teaching position at a black school in another county.

Rena becomes so absorbed in her teaching that she barely notices Jeff Wain's attempts to seduce her. After several of his unwanted advances, she moves out of Wain's boardinghouse into the home of a couple living near the school. In the meantime, Tryon learns that Rena's school is only a short distance from his mother's home, where he has been residing since the broken engagement. As a result of much inner conflict and self-deliberation, Tryon decides that he loves Rena and is determined to see her again, even if it is against her will. Therefore, the climax of the story occurs when both Jeff Wain and George Tryon appear unexpectedly as Rena leaves school. Startled and confused but determined to avoid both men, Rena flees into the nearby woods. Elder Johnson, her landlord, discovers her, but the experience and the exposure to inclement weather damage Rena mentally and physically. One night while the Johnsons are asleep, Rena wanders back into the woods. This time she is discovered by Frank Fowler, who takes her home to her mother. Before her death, Rena calls Frank to her bedside and acknowledges his long, faithful friendship. "You loved me best of them all," she tells him with her last breath.

The story ends with George Tryon's final effort to contact Rena. He decides to hasten to Patesville and declare his love to her. Unfortunately, he arrives just in time to observe a woman tying a funeral ribbon on the door of the house behind the cedars. He learns that the ribbon is for Rena.

The Characters

Rena Walden is an admirable character, despite her "tragic mulatto" trappings. Instead of bewailing her black blood, as do many mixed-blood heroines in the fiction of the period, Chesnutt's Rena has no strong desire to pass for white. She is thinking of becoming a teacher when her brother and mother decide that she should cross the color line. A kind heart, common sense, and high morals are Rena's outstanding assets; her compassion and lack of snobbery are evident throughout the novel. Truly committed to her ailing mother and to her race, Rena demonstrates common sense and moral fortitude by refusing her brother's offer to "pass" a second time and by rejecting both suitors, the dishonorable Jeff Wain and the well-intentioned George Tryon. Although Rena's decision never to marry and her commitment to her people are traits common to many "tragic mulatto" characters, Chesnutt lays the groundwork for Rena's transformation to take place naturally. She grows from a passive victim of other people's decisions to a thinking woman of remarkable courage.

John Walden is a rational and businesslike lawyer who makes no apologies for his decision to pass for white. To him, passing is not a moral issue but a sensible way for mulattoes, "the new people" of the South, to claim their inalienable rights. John functions as Rena's guide and decisionmaker while she remains in the white world. Therefore, he is crucial to the structure of the novel. When Rena decides not to pass, illustrating the ability to think independently, John is no longer essential to the plot; consequently, he remains a static character.

On the other hand, George Tryon evolves from a narrow-minded youth hampered by traditional customs to an understanding man shaped by his own conscience. Realizing that he has fallen in love with a black woman, Tryon listens to custom first and his heart later. The narrator emphasizes his willingness to forgive any fault in Rena except her "racial impurity." George is prepared to forgive illegitimacy or poverty, but he cannot bring himself to marry anyone with one drop of black blood. At first, even the thought of such an act is devastating to the aristocratic George. Nevertheless, the loss of Rena's companionship causes the young man to review his thinking. He decides that he had been deceived not by Rena but rather by his own blindness. After all, he reasons, she had given him a clue to her racial identity when she compared herself to a black nurse; moreover, John had said that he and Rena were "new people" with no impressive ancestors. With this revelation and the belief that his love for Rena supersedes Southern custom, Tryon resolves to seek Rena's forgiveness. Tryon's evolution from arrogance to humility represents Chesnutt's faith in a new South, tolerant of racial differences.

Other characters show the complicated social structure of the South and provide a backdrop for the action. Molly Walden is the perennial mulatto of the old South who believes in the sanctity of whiteness. Jeff Wain is the typically depraved mixed-blood character depicted in much white plantation fiction; he is a liar, a brute, and a seducer. Although Frank Fowler is a foil to Jeff Wain, he does not rise above the stereotype of the childlike black who is loyal to his mistress. Judge Straight represents the few rational liberals in the white South, and Dr. Green exhibits the archconservatism found in the region. His views about blacks and miscegenation suggest the reasons why passing becomes an attractive alternative to Rena and John.

Themes and Meanings

Chesnutt's overriding theme in *The House Behind the Cedars* is the problem of passing and its effects on both blacks and whites in the South. Because of the book's emphasis on color and caste, separation, alienation, and lost and recovered identity are closely connected themes.

If John Warrick, who is recognized among whites as a "big bug" and a gentleman, is to keep this identity, he must remain separate from his immediate family and alienated from both blacks and whites. This point is illustrated by John's return to Patesville at the beginning of the novel. Observing familiar landmarks in the old town, Warrick recognizes an old woman who had befriended him during his childhood, but he does not reveal his identity. Warrick behaves similarly when his morning walk leads him to his mother's house behind the cedars. Even though the object of the trip is to visit his mother, he must resist the temptation to stop there in broad daylight, since he would then be recognized by people who know him. The chapter's title, "A Stranger from South Carolina," is ironic, for John is familiar with the town and its residents; the title, however, suggests John's estrangement from his people. In chapter 7, "Amid New Surroundings," the narrator not only reveals Rena's adjustment to her new home but also comments on John's loneliness in and alienation from the white world: "There was a measure of relief in having about him one who knew his past, and yet whose knowledge, because of their common interest, would not jeopardize his future. For he had always been, in a figurative sense, a naturalized foreigner in the world of wide opportunity." Chesnutt depicts the world of the mulatto as one filled with opportunity but plagued by secrets and insecurities as well.

The theme of alienation is further revealed by both John's and Rena's predicament after her racial identity is discovered and her engagement is broken. John knows that "the structure of his own life has been weakened" by his sister's plight. George's knowledge of the secret is a threat to John's career and ambitions. He must forego his political dreams, because his private life cannot stand scrutiny. John must relegate himself to a life of obscurity and "spiritual estrangement." Realizing his position, he suggests to Rena a solution that will separate them even further from family, friends, and region: The two will leave the South and begin yet another new life as white people. Rena's denouncement of this plan for herself brings into sharp focus another moral issue raised by the practice of passing: Should a mulatto forsake dependent parents, siblings, and children to pursue personal ambitions? Obviously,

Chesnutt's answer to that question is no, for the reader applauds Rena's response of fidelity to her mother. Having learned the hard way about the perils of passing and the sacrifice of one's true identity, Rena chooses family and race over a fraudulent life-style.

Chesnutt reinforces his view of the fraudulent aspect of passing by beginning his novel with a discussion of time, which, he says, "touches all things with a destroying hand." Although this passage applies directly to the physical setting of the novel, it symbolically foreshadows the discovery of Rena's fake identity. Time related to passing is mentioned, specifically, during and after the ball at which the queen of love and beauty is crowned. Rena is relieved when the ball is over. Believing that her good fortune is only a dream, Rena makes a direct reference to time and circumstance when she declares, after the ball, that "I am Cinderella before the clock struck." Alluding to Cinderella conjures up all sorts of social imagery. Rena and the reader realize that the protagonist is like the queen of the fairy tale who has to return to an abject state at midnight. Rena's time as queen of the white aristocracy, symbolized by the ball, is limited. Chesnutt thus uses Rena to warn all "passers" that the idea of crossing the color line without consequences is a fairy tale. The author suggests that a passer's make-believe identity, good only until its hour of discovery, can relegate the victim to alienation and despair.

The tragic effect of passing is not confined to Chesnutt's black characters. George Tryon, too, is a victim of Rena's plight. He suffers as a result of their broken engagement, but, like Rena, emerges from it with a better understanding of himself. Tryon concludes that Southern custom demanding separation of the races is "tyranny," and he decides to forsake the world and marry Rena. Rena dies before George reaches her; nevertheless, he has decided on an admirable course of action that would put him at odds with Southern tradition, represented by Dr. Green.

Critical Context

By 1900, Charles W. Chesnutt had earned a considerable reputation as a writer of short stories with such collections as *The Conjure Woman* (1899). He hoped that *The House Behind the Cedars* would raise some commotion on the question of miscegenation, a controversial topic at the turn of the century. In 1890, Chesnutt wrote that he had conversed with a "well-bred gentleman" who "considered a mulatto an insult to nature, a kind of monster that he looked upon with infinite distaste." Chesnutt feared that this attitude was widespread, and he therefore wished to write realistically about mulattoes and other blacks, portraying them as humans proud of their race. Chesnutt also criticized the portrayal of blacks in literature by popular white writers of the day, and *The House Behind the Cedars* represented an attempt to refute the character types such writers created.

Modern critics value *The House Behind the Cedars* as the first novel to present objectively the pros and cons of passing. Rena and John possess a certain dignity not found in other mulatto characters of nineteenth century fiction; caught between two worlds, they react to their social environment sensibly, rather than sentimentally.

Both characters are prototypes emulated in later works on the subject of passing. John anticipates the hero of James Weldon Johnson's *The Autobiography of an Ex-Coloured Man* (1912), and Rena resembles the heroine of Nella Larsen's *Quicksand* (1928). Despite its groundbreaking nature, however, *The House Behind the Cedars* did not sell well. Chesnutt published two subsequent novels, *The Marrow of Tradition* (1901) and *The Colonel's Dream* (1905), and both dealt with controversial race-related topics; when neither proved popular, Chesnutt largely abandoned his literary career.

Bibliography

Andrews, William L. *The Literary Career of Charles W. Chesnutt.* Baton Rouge: Louisiana State University Press, 1980. The chapter on *The House Behind the Cedars* explores the genesis of the novel as it relates to Chesnutt's literary ambitions. Examines the work according to its features of nineteenth century realism.

Chesnutt, Helen K. *Charles Waddell Chesnutt.* Chapel Hill: University of North Carolina Press, 1952. A biography of Chesnutt by his daughter. The work contains letters pertaining to *The House Behind the Cedars* and other works by Chesnutt.

Gayle, Addison, Jr. *The Way of the New World: The Black Novel in America.* Garden City, N.Y.: Anchor Press, 1975. *The House Behind the Cedars* is discussed in chapter 2. The study focuses on Rena and Molly Walden, and notes that Chesnutt created them to plead the cause of the mulatto.

Harris, Trudier. "Chesnutt's Frank Fowler, A Failure of Purpose?" *College Language Association Journal* 23 (March, 1979): 215-228. Examines the role of Frank Fowler in *The House Behind the Cedars* in respect to Chesnutt's stated literary goals. Fowler's failure to rise above the plantation stereotype is attributed to Chesnutt's own racial prejudice toward dark-skinned blacks.

Keller, Frances Richardson. *An American Crusade.* Provo, Utah: Brigham Young University Press, 1978. The best biography of Chesnutt. Reviews Chesnutt's life and writings in a social context.

Render, Sylvia Lyons. *Charles W. Chesnutt.* Boston: Twayne, 1980. A critical interpretation of Chesnutt's fiction. Emphasizes Chesnutt's handling of such elements as irony, imagery, theme, and point of view.

Ernestine Pickens

HURRY HOME

Author: John Edgar Wideman (1941-   )
Type of work: Novel
Type of plot: Psychological realism
Time of plot: 1964-1968
Locale: Chicago, Illinois; Spain; Paris, France; and North Africa
First published: 1970

> *Principal characters:*
> CECIL OTIS BRAITHWAITE, the second African American to be
>   graduated from the law school he attended
> ESTHER BROWN, Cecil's long-suffering wife
> CHARLES WEBB, an expatriate American whom Cecil meets in
>   Spain
> ALBERT, an itinerant expatriate from Southern California who
>   latches onto Cecil at a kiosk in Spain and is searching for
>   Webb's son
> ESTRELLA, a whore whom Cecil patronizes after meeting her
>   through Albert
> ANNA, the black woman who is the mother of Webb's son; she
>   does not appear in the novel except through her letters to Webb
> UNCLE OTIS, Cecil's uncle

The Novel

The 180 pages of *Hurry Home* are divided into three sections. The point of view shifts frequently from third to first person, sometimes even taking notebook form. The jumpy narration, lacking transitions to aid the reader, is extremely difficult to follow. Despite the clues tucked away casually at points throughout—dates and place names thrown in almost in passing—putting events in a logical and coherent order demands constant attention. This storytelling style, apparently meant to be in a high modernist mode, but an ineffective employment of it, combines with often-shaky prose and a spattering of merely decorative literary allusions to turn the story of the protagonist, Cecil Braithwaite, into a mere puzzle too much of the time.

The ordeal of Cecil Braithwaite commands attention, for it presents an intelligent man striving for high achievement and succeeding against considerable odds. Cecil is only the third African American to have been admitted to his law school and is only the second to be graduated. Cecil has to cope with poverty, work, and the distress he suffers from his girlfriend Esther's stillborn birth of the son they had already named Simon.

The novel opens on November 14, 1968. November is the month in which bad things always happen to Cecil, the month that he can get through only by going to bed with a bottle. He had been graduated from law school and married Esther in

1964, spent three years abroad, and returned to Esther in 1967. In 1968, he is working as a janitor at the Banbury Street Arms, enduring life as best he can. Why he is not practicing law is not explained, but he apparently is in a state of spiritual sloth.

Cecil's state of mind is dramatized in the opening scene. As he cleans a stairwell, he picks up a tin can, crushes it, and drops it five stories to the basement. The echoing racket rises to the fifth floor, where a woman—red-haired S. Sherman, thirty-two years old—opens her door and asks him why he dropped the can. They have been aware of each other's presence for a year. The result of their meaningful stares is that Cecil and S. Sherman expend in sex the tensions, hungers, and frustrations of their crippled lives.

The scene switches abruptly to the laundry room at the Banbury Street Arms, where Esther toils. She is suffering from a severe headache, and her misery is evoked in two pages of naturalistic description. The brief interlude depicting the hopelessness of Esther's life fades out as her Aunt Fanny comes to help her, only to be banished by the martyred Esther.

Another narrative jump presents Cecil in a meditative mood on the night of both his commencement and, later in the day, his marriage. He arises from bed, dresses, and slips out the door, not to return for three years.

Cecil appears next in an unknown city, dozing in its public library over a volume of the works of painter Hieronymus Bosch, in which he has been searching out black figures in the paintings. The remainder of the first section is a series of brief scenes: Cecil recollecting making love to S. Sherman while tormenting himself with thoughts of Simon, Cecil at the barbershop, Cecil in an altercation over paying for a shoeshine. In all these scenes it is difficult to determine whether the narrative is in present time or flashback, but they apparently all are the recollections of Cecil after his flight from Esther's bed.

The second section opens with Cecil on an ocean liner headed to Europe. The scene shifts abruptly to a conversation Cecil has with Charles Webb in a cafe near the Alhambra in Spain. A significant topic of their talk is Bosch's painting *The Adoration*, which impressed Cecil strongly. Notes from a visit to The Prado, the museum home to *The Adoration*, then follow. Vignettes substitute for any sustained narrative throughout the section: Cecil talking with Albert, the expatriate from California who forces himself on Cecil; Cecil with the whore Estrella; Cecil apparently recollecting a cafe brawl that lands him in a Spanish jail cell "with a bunch of gypsies." He calls himself "El Moro"—the Moor, or black one—in the episode of the cafe brawl. This section concludes with a boat crossing to Ceuta, the small portion of Spain situated anomalously across the Strait of Gibraltar in North Africa. It has been a difficult exile for Cecil, but it ends with him throwing away his last half-empty bottle of Felipe Segundo, a Spanish rotgut, in a decisive act that precedes his hurrying home.

The third section opens not with Cecil but with a ten-page excursus on her life with Cecil written by Esther on April 19, 1967. The passage turns out to be an answered prayer, as Cecil returns to her that same day. The rest of the section, culminating in Cecil's homecoming, is a series of excerpts from Cecil's diary, beginning with him in Paris making a vow that "Nothing will take me back to her [Esther's] world, to the Banbury Arms."

The Characters

The only fully developed character is Cecil, and even the picture of him is fragmented. What one can say directly of him is that he is a very intelligent and sensitive young African American who is troubled by his situation in a racist culture and haunted by the death of Simon. What readers do not know is why, four years after receiving his law degree and a year and a half after returning to his wife, Esther, he is still working as a janitor at the Banbury Street Arms when the novel opens.

Several things are bothering him on November 14, 1968, when his story begins. November is a month that always brings him bad news: He is now plagued by hemorrhoids; his dead son, Simon, had been conceived in November; and Esther's Aunt Fanny had come to live with them in November. There is no clue about what has happened to Cecil in the eighteen months since his return from his European exile. Certainly a man with a prestigious law degree would be expected to have a better job than one as janitor at the Banbury Street Arms. There are no clues to this mystery, and the reader is left with a sense that Cecil has become an invisible man because of his skin color.

When Cecil first appears, he is collecting trash in the Banbury Street Arms: "Five floors, fifteen apartments each left their bundles on the back stairs for Cecil to carry away." He picks up an empty Carnation evaporated milk can, crushes it in his hand, and drops it five floors to the basement. The racket brings S. Sherman to her doorway, asking "Why did you do it?" What follows between these two people who have been aware of each other for months but have kept each other at length is a sexual coupling that raises several questions.

Why does this red-haired, presumably white, woman offer herself spontaneously to this black janitor? Perhaps it is some fundamental hunger for the touch of another human being, a hunger fueled by her recognition in Cecil of a need, a disappointment in life, that matches her own. Their urgent copulation then spells out a kind of ancient rite in which sex becomes the best revenge on life, a direct and intense existential grappling to seek out and engage another self.

During their brief respite from life, S. Sherman, thirty-two years old, rebukes Cecil for dropping the can and confesses that she has never done this sort of thing before. A scene ensues that is intended to be profoundly moving but may strike some readers as banal. As Cecil lies in postcoital repose with his head on S. Sherman's breast, he stares through a triangle created by her uplifted thighs, joined at the knees by the calf of one leg, and imagines a series of common domestic intimacies with Simon at their center.

While this erotic encounter plays itself out, Esther is coping with a headache and the laundry. This is all that readers are given of Cecil and Esther's life after his return from Europe. What appears at first to be a scene from the middle of the action meant to introduce characters and setting turns out to be the end of Cecil and Esther's story.

Themes and Meanings

It is hard to say what meaning is supposed to be derived from Cecil's frenetic behavior. His grief over Simon is understandable, but does it, by itself, justify his actions—especially his callous treatment of Esther?

It is difficult to admire Cecil in the novel's introduction to him, as he couples meaninglessly with a stranger while Esther toils in the basement. He emerges no more sympathetically during his extended moratorium from life's demands. His activities in Europe have no substance. The two expatriates with whom he temporarily takes up bring out nothing in him. Webb, the man looking for his son, becomes a useful guide to the art treasures of The Prado but does not prompt Cecil to assert himself in any way that reveals substantial character traits. Hieronymous Bosch's paintings open up to Cecil the grim, lurking horror of human existence, but no defiant gesture against evil ensues. Whatever moral credit accrues from a fleeting aesthetic shiver is certainly too slight to build a sympathetic character.

The overwhelming impression left by Cecil's three-year absence is of an abandonment to debauchery. He may be anguishing over Simon or struggling with unresolved identity crises, but his actions suggest little more than self-pity. When he finally decides to return home to Esther, the stage is set for a happy ending, but that ending has already been undercut in the novel's opening pages in the scene with S. Sherman. Apparently Esther is more of a burden to Cecil than a relief. He had been pleased to have Esther's Aunt Fanny come to live with them because it gave him an excuse to move out. Cecil's problem may be that of a man trapped in marriage out of a sense of responsibility, and this marital imprisonment may emblematize his situation as a black man in the United States. Cecil remains a puzzling figure and a difficult man with whom to sympathize, a victim of his own bad faith.

The paintings by Bosch and others are useful in characterizing Cecil, but most of the literary allusions are mere decorations. Cecil thinks frequently of Ernest Dowson's *fin de siècle* lyric poem in which the poet professes "I have been faithful to thee, Cynara, in my fashion." This may be intended as an apology to Esther for Cecil's own "madder music" and "stronger wine," and therefore has some thematic relevance. Several allusions to T. S. Eliot's Prufrock and other allusions to Wallace Stevens, John Keats, Othello, Oedipus, and Alexander Pope only create a bogus "literary" style. The punning lines in the fashion of James Joyce (for example, "Pipers piping. Gloom pipes. Down from heel and hills pied piper and plague of worms. Bitches hide wombs. Batches fried grooms.") will probably annoy readers and certainly contribute little to the history of modernism.

Critical Context

Hurry Home perhaps suffers from being Wideman's second novel, a step in a writer's career that often proves difficult. Scholars who have written on Wideman generally find little to say about *Hurry Home* and, even worse, betray uncertainty even about what is happening in the novel. The reservations about *Hurry Home* should probably be seen in the light of two facts. First, it is the work of a young man who has just enjoyed an intensely literary education (Wideman was a Rhodes Scholar). Second, its author is still searching for his own voice and subject matter, both of which he found, very successfully, in *The Homewood Trilogy* (1985).

It could be claimed that the techniques of the great modernists in which Wideman is so well versed were not appropriate for him but represented a phase that he had to work through until he had put these literary fathers behind him. That is why *Hurry Home* is so clearly an apprentice work, with bits and pieces of his education sticking out in the narrative without being assimilated. It is significant that his first novel, *A Glance Away* (1967), features a central character much like Eliot's Prufrock, who is alluded to half a dozen times in *Hurry Home*, but that his third novel, *The Lynchers* (1973), is told more straightforwardly and with far less literary allusion. From then on, even though he reverts to stream-of-consciousness narrative in *Hiding Place* (1981), Wideman seems to have arrived at a mature style that serves his thematic purposes well.

Bibliography

Coleman, James W. *Blackness and Modernism: The Literary Career of John Edgar Wideman.* Jackson: University Press of Mississippi, 1989. Of the seven chapters in this book, one is devoted to *Hurry Home* and is subtitled "The Black Intellectual Uncertain and Confused." The black intellectual's alienation is stressed, and much is made—though not to much point—of the modernist narrative method. An interview recorded in 1988 makes an excellent appendix.

_____. "John Edgar Wideman." In *African American Writers*, edited by Valerie Smith. New York: Scribner's, 1991. A useful survey of Wideman's career, but only brief comments on *Hurry Home*.

Rushdy, Ashraf H. A. "Fraternal Blues: John Edgar Wideman's Homewood Trilogy." *Contemporary Literature* 32 (Fall, 1991): 312-345. No discussion of *Hurry Home*, but Rushdy's detailed commentary on Wideman's themes and subjects is excellent. Perhaps the most perceptive analysis of Wideman's work. Excellent bibliography.

Samuels, Wilfred D. "Going Home: A Conversation with John Edgar Wideman." *Callaloo* 6 (February, 1983): 40-59. An interview that elicits some interesting insights from Wideman. Should be read along with Coleman's interview.

_____. "John Edgar Wideman." In *Afro-American Fiction Writers After 1955.* Vol. 33 in *Dictionary of Literary Biography*, edited by Thadious M. Davis and Trudier Harris. Detroit: Gale, 1984. Although published seven years before the similar piece by Coleman listed above, this is still a useful introduction to Wideman's career prior to the 1980's.

Frank Day

I GET ON THE BUS

Author: Reginald McKnight (1956-   )
Type of work: Novel
Type of plot: Psychological realism
Time of plot: The 1980's
Locale: Senegal
First published: 1990

> *Principal characters:*
> EVAN NORRIS, the protagonist and narrator, an alienated African
>   American who has left the United States for two years to teach
>   in Senegal for the Peace Corps
> WANDA WRIGHT, Evan's stateside girlfriend, with whom he
>   persistently fails to communicate
> AMINATA GUEYE, a student, Evan's Senegalese girlfriend
> AFRICA MAMADOU FORD, a native of Oakland, California, and
>   resident of Senegal
> LAMONT SAMB, Aminata's Senegalese fiancé, a former teacher of
>   French in Wales

The Novel

Building on some of the territory identified by the author in his first work of fiction, the prize-winning collection of stories *Moustapha's Eclipse* (1988), and on his experiences as a teacher in West Africa, *I Get on the Bus* is a compelling meditation on the state of blackness in the closing years of the twentieth century. Given the novel's background and the innumerable manifestations of Senegalese life, culture, language, and environment that it contains, it is tempting to regard the work in an autobiographical light. Although the work itself does not intentionally dismiss such an approach, its use of a first-person narrator paradoxically makes that approach unsustainable, since by virtue of the terms of reference of his narrative, the protagonist becomes a representative and problematic case and not a distinct, ego-centered "I." Evan Norris is a condition rather than a person; or rather, because of the type of person he is, he becomes a condition.

That condition issues from the involvement of Evan's perceptive and alert intelligence with a culture that is articulated in unfamiliar and unassimilable terms. Evan's intelligence, the critical character of which has been honed by his education, speaks essentially of the individual's autonomy. His decision to leave the United States and a complicated but potentially rewarding situation with his girlfriend, Wanda Wright, confirms his individuality and autonomy. His individuality leads Evan to reject his position with the Peace Corps. It is not clear, however, that he rejects the Peace Corps as such, since to do so would place him in an analytical mode and thus undermine the peculiar forms of impotence that color his Senegal experience.

By resigning his Peace Corps position, Evan in effect submits to a different order of experience, one that produces visceral rather than cerebral reactions. One of the ways in which he progresses through the world of the novel is by recounting a range of physical symptoms, most revealingly intense pains in his head. This order of experience intensifies some of the feelings of disorientation from which he has suffered, both in the United States and as a teacher supposedly identifying with a benevolent mission. This intensification is expressed in ways over which Evan has no control and which are manipulated, for their own inscrutable purposes, by the various other characters with whom he becomes involved.

The forms of expression that make Senegalese experience distinct and impossible for Evan to fathom appeal to areas of himself with which he has little experience. His Senegalese world is one of spirits, some of which are disembodied forces while others are what might be termed re-embodied. The reality and force of these unhuman entities, and of the means whereby they attain human agency, is undoubted by all but Evan. Understandably, he is at a loss to know what to make of the jinni and the demms who evidently hold his existence in thrall. It is this condition and his lack of command over it that constitute the disjointed but ultimately overwhelming plot line of *I Get on the Bus.*

The obscure maneuvering of the plot, with a problematic basis in various versions and interpretations of events that predate Evan's arrival in Senegal and in the painful physical and hallucinatory mental state to which he succumbs while there, seems ultimately to demonstrate how Evan, although ostensibly in a state of transition, is a prisoner with three options. The first and most compelling of these is represented by the joint forces of Aminata Gueye, his Senegalese girlfriend, and Lamont Samb, her fiancé. Were Evan to align himself with their forces, he would of necessity become the enemy of Africa Ford. Africa, however, represents a second condition that Evan might attain, that of an African American who assents to the spiritual and cultural code of the host nation while retaining enough of his Americanness to prosper as a vendor on the streets of Dakar, the Senegalese capital. The third possibility is to resist both of these options, which is what Evan, with his occidental orientation, wonders if he wants to do, particularly since that orientation has to be filtered through his relationship with Wanda Wright. The very assumption that such an orientation is feasible defines Evan's troubling and troublesome condition. He finds himself prey to the various cultural structures of others, whose invitation to him to identify with those structures is both irresistible and essential to resist. Whether Evan succumbs is moot, since in either case he loses his integrity.

The Characters

The identification of Evan as a character at a crossroads in his life is emphasized by the fact that he encounters a confluence of external forces. Evan's passivity, indecisiveness, and erratic judgment are brought home to him by his headaches, paranoid imaginings, and profound sense of cultural dislocation. These sufferings are not merely the fabrications of Evan's own distressed state of mind. They have their sources and their power in the ways in which he is perceived by the characters who come into close contact with him.

This quartet of characters consists of two Senegalese, Aminata and Lamont, and two Americans, Africa and Wanda. They establish the terms of the conflict that besets Evan, although to see the novel strictly in terms of the framework they provide is too schematic. The author is sufficiently attentive to the texture of the world he is creating to ensure that the scaffolding of imaginative logic that these four characters support is adequately concealed. In addition, many of the minor characters, both Senegalese and American, make distinctive contributions to the novel's overall effects, even if the value of this contribution derives from the manner in which it augments the central issue of Evan's psychological and cultural travail.

The combination of Aminata and Lamont represents, at different but interrelated levels, the seductive power of Senegal. Their sleek appearance, the supple manner in which their minds work, and their ability to negotiate Anglophone and Eurocentric mindsets while retaining an alert sense of their native culture give their presence a potency that Evan finds irresistible. Evan's attraction to this formidable couple is the very thing that undoes him. Aminata's curative and restorative powers, together with Evan's strongly developed sense of her sexuality, provide him with a viable and willed attachment to his foreign surroundings. It is largely as a result of Aminata's intervention that Evan is motivated not only to feel well but to discover what has been poisoning not only his body but also his consciousness.

Assenting to Aminata as a source of revitalization, however, eventually leads Evan to Lamont. The latter embodies at an intellectual level the seductive promise of the rehabilitation that Aminata provided at the physical level. Once the connection with Lamont has been made, Evan finds it impossible not to become preoccupied with, and then implicated in, the plot that seems to be the joint property of Lamont and Aminata. Belief in this plot, and acceptance of its consequences, requires Evan to become a creature of the spirit of Senegal, with its mystery, jeopardy, and overtones of animism. Captured by this spirit, he will implicitly surrender the American component of his Africanness.

On the other hand, this American component does not put Evan in his element. His attempt to dissociate himself from his Americanness, signified by flashbacks to some white, aging, hippie friends, is complicated by the fact that he has not been able to find an alternative to it. Wanda, with whom Evan is living and whom he will perhaps marry, is recalled a number of times, indicating that it is with the African ingredients of being an African American that Evan should identify. No model of how this might be accomplished is available, however, and Wanda herself is recollected as an embodiment of pragmatism and a self-improvement ethic that seems to underline the power of the dominant culture in the United States to condition even those who seem to reject it. Wanda argues for her rejection of Americanness along racial lines, a line of argument Evan finds unpersuasive on grounds that it does not describe the terms on which he desires to relate to the world, terms that would articulate the double burden of the African and the American experience.

Something of what this burden entails and how it might be borne is suggested by Africa Ford. In a number of ways, however, his position is more a complement to Wanda's than a model for Evan. Africa's Senegalese experiences may be a prototype for Evan's, even to his bewitched involvement with the Gueye family. Ford identifies with those experiences, internalizes them, processes them, adopts the terms upon which they have been conceived, and assimilates them into himself, with the aid of a marabou as powerful and as resourceful as Aminata's father. None of these accomplishments prevents him from selling American T-shirts on the sidewalks of Dakar, as though he still retains not only his native country's business ethic but the class level at which he knows that such an ethic can work for him. Evan is not from the lower classes, nor does he think of himself as the "homeboy" that Africa calls him. There is no home for Evan, largely as a result of his declining to be anybody's boy.

Themes and Meanings

The reiterated references to loss, disorientation, lack of understanding, self-deception, disruption, and dislocation that stitch together the comparatively limited narrative material of *I Get on the Bus* seem to suggest that its themes are plainly stated and their meanings somewhat obvious. As suggested by the novel's title and the present tense in which the narrative is told, there is no denying the protagonist's unsettled and transitional state. The novel's themes are not necessarily so straightforward, and its meanings not quite so forthcoming. Given the character of the novel's grounding in the cultural anthropology of Senegal, its obvious interest in the status of folk religion as a complex map of the fears, longings, ambitions, and inhibitions to which everybody is susceptible, it is not surprising that the reader shares some of Evan Norris' perceptual uncertainty.

At certain points in *I Get on the Bus*, such as when Evan imagines himself to be a woman, there is no doubt as to the hallucinatory character of the action. For the most part, however, such certainty is difficult to substantiate. Early in the novel, Evan thinks that he kills a crippled beggar. It is not until much later that he learns that his having done so is all but impossible. When, in introducing himself to the reader, Evan says that he believes he is coming down with something, something that without a doubt is malaria, since he has not been taking his quinine tablets, there are no grounds to disbelieve him. Visceral as the accounts of his physical condition are, it is also quite possible that these disturbances are the function of his deranged and fretful consciousness.

This frame of mind drives his inability either to accept what he is told by those he meets, whether Peace Corps colleagues, Senegalese, or Americans, or to find a reliable form whereby he can convey his own reading of what he encounters. The combination of his excessive visibility, by virtue of which he becomes, like any solitary foreigner, an object of intense scrutiny, and his incapacity to know where he stands in relation to the versions of himself that his foreignness engenders makes it tempting to regard *I Get on the Bus* as an intriguing revision of Ralph Ellison's classic novel *Invisible Man* (1952).

The restlessness and dislocation with which Evan becomes synonymous are economically represented by the novel's title phrase. That phrase also has, like the rest of the work, a marked hallucinatory undertone, the presence of which makes *I Get on the Bus* resemble the magic realism of certain South American writers, notably Gabriel García Márquez, the difference here being that the magic is black. The title phrase, taken in conjunction with the heightened, dread-laden experiences that take place on board the bus, readily conjures up contemporary connotations of taking a trip. Evan's nonnaturalistic endurance of a mundane social activity establishes the pattern of his reactions to all the social and personal transactions he undertakes.

Evan not only is a free man but also acts in the name of that freedom by rejecting his life with Wanda, his Peace Corps position, life in Senegal on the terms proposed by Aminata and Lamont, and life in opposition to them as lived by Africa Ford. The freedom to which Evan is so firmly attached seems no more than an indecisive drift, lacking the counterbalance of any sense of responsibility. Evan thus resembles the existential heroes of postwar novels. Much more to the point, however, is that he identifies his malaise as part of the legacy of the post-civil rights generation of African Americans, a generation whose troubled voice and uncertain condition is clearly recorded in *I Get on the Bus.*

Critical Context

Cultural relations between Afro-America and Africa have a long history and have gone through a number of phases, seeking expression in a number of artistic and social forms. Despite the importance and significance of this area of African American culture, the transition from one environment to another and from one form of historical conditioning to another has given the intercontinental connections a limited, tentative, and frequently picturesque character. Not the least interesting aspect of *I Get on the Bus* is the manner in which it enacts some of the tensions in the connections. It recognizes within the disordered sensibility of Evan Norris the problems that even beginning to account for the consequences of the black diaspora must bring into being.

Although the author has good and sufficient personal reasons for setting the novel in Senegal, the choice of country helps to crystallize some of the cultural and historical problems. As one of France's African possessions, this country has had a cultural development somewhat different from that of the countries that were under British rule. One of the consequences of this difference can be seen in the fact that it was the Senegalese poet and political leader Leopold Senghor who was one of the creators of the term "negritude." The word is not merely a term coined to emphasize the cultural and humanistic significance of blackness but is rather an ethic of difference. The cultural history of modern Senegal is excluded from *I Get on the Bus,* which is set in the less inspiring time of Senghor's successor, David Diop. It is not difficult, however, to see the novel's protagonist struggling to articulate his difference in an attempt to find a means of reconceptualizing his blackness that will provide him with a measure of self-respect and integrity at the same time.

The crisis of consciousness Evan enacts, and which the novel shows penetrating every fiber of his being, is one that arises directly from his citizenship of the United States. Evan is a product of the upward social mobility experienced by the expanding African American middle classes after the Civil Rights movement—a movement in which buses were not unknown, as perhaps the author punningly wishes to remind the reader—and the institutional advantages, notably educational, this mobility entailed. The result for him is a more than proportionate decline in authenticity. This dimension of *I Get on the Bus* provides the novel with a greater sense of urgency than the more distant and academic Senegal dimension can provide. Despite its color and interest, Senegal is effectively the medium of loss as Evan experiences it. His life in the United States, however, is the source of that loss. The urgency that arises from this state of affairs is related to the confusing, inconsistent, and typically one-dimensional images of black maleness sponsored by contemporary American culture. In its cogent and subtle representation of this issue, explicitly related to the influence of culture on psyche in the protagonist's Senegal experiences, *I Get on the Bus* documents a critical context for the author's generation.

Bibliography
Brailsford, Karen. "I Get on the Bus." *The New York Times Book Review*, September 16, 1990, 22. A review of the novel, giving a sense of its main features.
Giddings, Paula. "Reginald McKnight." *Essence* 21 (March, 1991): 40. A profile of the author, providing relevant background information.
Larson, Charles R. "Cultures in Collision." *Washington Post Book World*, June 17, 1990, 1, 11. Review of *I Get on the Bus*, focusing on its treatment of the identity theme.
McKnight, Reginald. *Moustapha's Eclipse*. Pittsburgh: University of Pittsburgh Press, 1988. The author's prizewinning first book, a collection of stories that provide relevant introductory material to some of the themes, issues, and locales of *I Get on the Bus*.
Vaillant, Janet G. *Black, French, and African: A Life of Leopold Sedar Senghor*. Cambridge, Mass.: Harvard University Press, 1990. A biography of the Senegalese poet and politician whose work raised fundamental issues relating to interconnections between race, identity, and literature. *I Get on the Bus* should be evaluated in the context of these interconnections.

George O'Brien

I KNOW WHY THE CAGED BIRD SINGS

Author: Maya Angelou (Marguerite Johnson, 1928-   )
Type of work: Autobiography
Time of work: 1931-1945
Locale: Stamps, Arkansas; St. Louis; San Francisco
First published: 1970

> *Principal personages:*
> MARGUERITE JOHNSON, the author, whose name becomes "Maya"
>   in early childhood, when her brother calls her "Mya sister"
> BAILEY JOHNSON, JR., the author's brother and beloved
>   companion, one year older than she
> ANNIE HENDERSON, the author's maternal grandmother, who helps
>   to rear Maya
> WILLIAM Johnson, the author's "Uncle Willie," Annie
>   Henderson's older son
> BAILEY JOHNSON, SR., the author's father, Annie Henderson's
>   younger son
> VIVIAN BAXTER JOHNSON, the author's mother, the daughter of an
>   influential black St. Louis couple
> MR. FREEMAN, the boyfriend of Maya's mother
> BERTHA FLOWERS, a black woman who brings Maya out of an
>   emotional trauma by affectionately teaching her the beauty of
>   the poetic use of her voice

Form and Content

In this first of five volumes of autobiography, Maya Angelou tells the story of her life from age three, when her divorcing parents sent her and her brother to live with their maternal grandmother in Stamps, Arkansas, to age sixteen, when, reunited with her mother in San Francisco, she gave birth to her son. Thus her story begins with semi-orphanhood and ends with motherhood. Interpreting her quest for freedom and self-affirmation as representative of that of many African Americans and American women—especially black American women—she presents incidents from her life that illustrate conditions faced by many persons. In her case, these conditions result, after much struggle, in a moment and message of hope.

Angelou begins her narrative with a painful incident that she does not date but that seems appropriate to age six or seven. In a church recitation, Maya cannot bring herself to remember the lines of an Easter poem beyond the first two, which seem to her to express her constant state of temporariness as a displaced orphan and humiliated outcast. Her dream of being beautiful, understood, and accepted—all of which she has imagined in terms of being white—is shattered, and her mind is occupied with thoughts of persecution, impending death, and imperative self-restraint. She feels about to burst; her means of release, the socially unacceptable one of urinating in her pants, merely reinforces her predicament.

After this introduction, Angelou turns to her arrival in Stamps at age three and proceeds by chronicling her emotional development, with reflection upon the implications of her experiences for understanding racism, sexism, and the general human condition. Her story is divided into four parts that take place in three settings: in Stamps with her grandmother (whom she called "Momma") and Uncle Willie, from age three through seven; in St. Louis with her mother and her mother's parents, brothers, and boyfriend, while she was eight; back in Stamps from age nine to thirteen; and in California with her mother, to age sixteen. Her brother was her constant companion during all but the last year.

The Johnsons in Stamps and the Baxters in St. Louis were relatively well-off black families, featuring strong and influential women. In Stamps, Momma owned properties that she rented to poor whites and owned and operated the Wm. Johnson General Merchandise Store, which served as a lay center for the black community. Her family attended the Colored Methodist Episcopal Church. The sensitive, curious, and thoughtful Maya was in a position to observe a wide range of black experiences, roles, character types, and patterns of expression. She tells, for example, of bone-weary cotton pickers caught in economic enslavement within the general impoverishment of blacks; a threat to Uncle Willie's life by the Klan; the complete segregation in Stamps, with its resulting ignorance and prejudice on the part of both whites and blacks; a confrontation between Momma and some racially insulting children of her tenants; and the antics of enthused parishioners during services, in contrast to Momma's more reserved role and behavior.

For Maya, all of this was happening in the context of protection by Momma's loving and authoritative competence and Bailey's loving companionship. Family life in the store included disciplined study of arithmetic; leisurely reading of novels, poetry, and Shakespeare; and lessons on deportment and avoidance of trouble with whites.

Taken suddenly at age eight to live in St. Louis, Maya found her mother, whom she had known only as someone who had abandoned her and who probably was dead, to be a wonder of light-skinned beauty and hurricane energy, in constant social demand. Grandmother Baxter, whose features would not identify her as black, had connections with the St. Louis underworld, with the police, and with local politicians, and her uncles were the terror of the black community. Experiencing neglect by her mother, Maya fought against considering St. Louis her home, but nevertheless suffered nightmares (Bailey developed a stutter). She felt sorry for Mr. Freeman, her mother's boyfriend, who suffered similar neglect; when he began to abuse her sexually, an abuse at first accompanied by gestures of affection, she fantasized that at last she had found her real father. At his trial for rape, she denied any earlier contact; when Freeman, briefly out of jail, was kicked to death, she believed that her lie had caused his death and that her speaking might bring death to others. She stopped talking, except to Bailey, and when the Baxters could no longer tolerate what they took to be her impudence, they sent her and Bailey back to Stamps.

Back in a community environment of quiet resignation, Maya could relax, but for a year she did not talk, and she suffered from memory loss and dulled senses. Then Momma introduced her to Bertha Flowers, a beautiful and educated black woman who brought Maya out of her cocoon by giving her special attention that focused on love of the human voice in the recitation of literature. By age ten, Maya had gained sufficient self-esteem not only to converse normally but also to work in a white woman's home and, furthermore, to retaliate when that woman made a racist assault upon her name. Shortly thereafter, she met a girl like herself, with whom she was finally able to be girlish and to share speculations about romance.

In Stamps, however, Maya and Bailey were again surrounded by racists. Even their religious experiences, in church, revival tent, and home, focused on the community's and Momma's teachings about inequality, persecution, and justice. As the children grew older, they increasingly came under attack. When Maya was graduated from the eighth grade, a white speaker made it clear that the graduates had no legitimate intellectual ambitions. When Momma desperately took Maya to a white dentist to whom Momma had given a loan, he viciously turned them away. Then, when fourteen-year-old Bailey was ordered by a white man to help carry the corpse of a lynched man into the jail, Momma decided that the children must rejoin their mother, now living in San Francisco.

In California, Maya found her mother just as beautiful and active, but more attentive; the man she had married made a good stepfather, and life in the city, with its fluidity and diversity, was exactly to Maya's liking. She performed well in school and took evening classes in drama and dance. When, at age fifteen, she went to spend the summer with her father, several experiences quickened the pace of her maturation. With her drunken father asleep in the back seat, she commanded a bucking automobile down a mountain road out of Mexico. Then, after a fight with her father's girlfriend, Maya ran away and lived for a month in an automobile junkyard with an interracial group of homeless children. By the time she returned to San Francisco, she had been initiated into self-reliance, social self-confidence, and human brotherhood; and there, after a determined campaign, she became the city's first black female streetcar conductor. Her growing independence and awareness also precipitated a final crisis of her youth. When anxiety about her sexuality led her to experiment, she became pregnant. Angelou ends her story with the birth of her son, Guy, and her discovery, with her mother's help, that she can trust herself to care for her child.

Analysis

Angelou's title alludes to the poem "Sympathy" by the African American writer Paul Laurence Dunbar, in which a bird wounds itself against the bars of its cage and yet sings when it returns to its perch. Dunbar identifies the bird's song as a prayer or plea to heaven for release. His title implies that he is singing this poem as both his own prayer and his declaration of sympathy for others like him. Angelou's title, a line repeated in the poem, establishes her tone of compassionate protest and provides her central theme and metaphor. It leads prospective readers to wonder what such an unnatural life as that of an imprisoned bird would be like for humans, what forms such a "cage" might take in human life, how such a life could produce song, whether freedom would be possible, and what Angelou can tell, from her experience and sympathetic imagination, about the answers to these questions.

Angelou identifies the bars of the "cage" as racism, sexism, and the powerlessness of their victims, whose disabling responses of "fear, guilt, and self-revulsion" merely become additional bars. Whole communities and classes of humans are thus restricted from being fully themselves. Yet Angelou shows how this imprisonment, exactly because it is so unnatural, also naturally produces the response of "song," in the form of struggle, survival, self-affirmation, and at last freedom.

Like Dunbar, Angelou suggests that, by nature, humans are freely expressive. Yet she illustrates many restrictions that are placed on expressive selfhood by acts of injustice committed because of self-centeredness and prejudice. When these injustices are experienced during childhood, Angelou explains, persons internalize patterns of understanding that may last for life. For example, because blacks in Stamps were "people whose history and future were threatened each day by extinction," they lived lives of resignation (with occasional exceptions such as revival meetings, where the theme would be God's system of justice). Angelou remarks on her own tendency, even as an adult, to feel rage, paranoia, and dread of futility.

Using herself as illustration, Angelou shows how resignation and rage are produced by all-encompassing racist oppression, by omnipresent sexist stereotyping that diminishes the value of any female who does not meet its standards of feminine beauty, and by neglect or violence within families. Describing her sense of temporariness and homelessness (felt even in church, where the congregation often expressed the same feelings about themselves in this world), Angelou tells of having fantasized that her beauty in a white woman's throwaway dress would evoke understanding and appreciation of her worth, thereby awakening her from her "black ugly dream"; instead, she experienced only frustration, humiliation, and fear that she would die. Her early chapters suggest the fairy tale of the Ugly Duckling; and although it seems that Maya intuited that she was a swan, she nevertheless suffered a crippling loss of self-esteem. Her frequent suspicions that she might be a changeling made her so emotively vulnerable that, for example, she at first thought that a sexual abuser might be her real father, because his attentions gave her a sense of having a real home. Again, though her dream became a nightmare, again she was misplaced and displaced, and again she was imprisoned in misunderstanding, fear of death, and guilt-ridden silence. Throughout her childhood, Angelou blamed herself for life's injustices.

Yet if Angelou's girlhood odyssey through deathlike psychological depths took her into an underworld (sometimes literal as well as figurative) of race, gender, and family disempowerment, it was in these same areas that she was empowered to seek self-affirmation. The black community of Stamps, although oppressed, gave her a rich culture of language, story, song, religious vision, and faith and brought her together with individuals whose unselfishness and wisdom ensured her survival and growth. Although she was damaged by family experiences of abandonment, neglect, and violence, her family life with Momma, Uncle Willie, and Bailey in Stamps and with her mother in San Francisco also provided the love that sustained her quest. Although her mother and grandmothers sometimes acted in ways that reinforced Maya's confusion and ambivalence toward life, these same women, and Bertha Flowers, provided not only daily support but also the role models of competent and effective womanhood that Angelou celebrated in her book and emulated in her life.

Angelou's effectiveness as a writer is based on her ability to tell stories well. The story of her girlhood is composed of many vignettes; her memory when writing them was so vivid and complete that she fills her reader's imagination with sensory details, images, character sketches, poignant remarks, revealing conversations, typical gatherings and goings-on, and many people's points of view (especially Bailey's, with its special relation to her own). Meanwhile, the reader gathers meaning from the double perspective of the child whose immediate survival is at stake and the adult who can interpret and evaluate with compassion, moral outrage, self-criticism, or humor because of her greater safety as well as greater wisdom. Because the adult's viewpoint dominates, Angelou's artistry graces her telling with a lyrical style that often transforms her prose into a song—whether sorrow song or praise song—of her faith in the beauty and resilience of the human spirit.

Critical Context

When at age forty, in response to the urging of literary friends, Maya Angelou wrote the story of her girlhood, she had achieved an international reputation as a singer, dancer, actor, journalist, civil rights activist, and lecturer. Her readers would know that they were reading about a girl who had triumphed, but only Angelou knew that the victory had been won against great odds.

As an artist, she knew that she was joining a long line of African American women and men who had written within a major literary tradition of American autobiography, and an even longer line of anonymous black bards and storytellers within the oral tradition, whose poems and stories were becoming known by contemporary readers because of the interest in African American history and culture that had been generated by the Civil Rights movement of the 1960's. Contemporary black authors also were being widely read as a result of the Civil Rights movement and the Black Arts movement. Writing by African American women was still comparatively neglected, but by 1970, the women's movement was generating interest in women's lives and art generally.

It is not surprising, then, that *I Know Why the Caged Bird Sings* was quickly discovered by the public and by reviewers. Angelou's very readable story has continued to move and enlighten readers because she has explained the struggle, offered hope of victory, and affirmed the dignity of individuals who live by a multiplicity of identity roles simultaneously.

As the historical conditions of black American life have become generally known, scholars studying Angelou's autobiography have turned their attention to the psychological dimensions of the life that she has recorded and to the artistic devices by which she presents them. The resulting understanding of her story has revealed an even more complex and more deeply human struggle and triumph than was seen by early readers, and this understanding has further enhanced her effectiveness as an artist, educator, and role model.

Bibliography
Angelou, Maya. "An Interview with Maya Angelou." *The Massachusetts Review* 28 (Spring, 87): 286-292. Remarks on the art of autobiography, including the narrative voice, the selectivity of memory, and the effects of the writing process.
Arensberg, Liliane K. "Death as Metaphor of Self in *I Know Why the Caged Bird Sings.*" *College Language Association Journal* 20 (1976): 273-291. Asserts that Angelou's narrative of her girlhood is empowered by tension between quest for a life-affirming identity and obsession with annihilation. In order to adapt to the early threat of breakdown of identity, she developed a self-defense of mutability, of which the pervasive metaphor is death. The birth of her son brings about Maya's psychological rebirth into a woman who can trust herself to be life-giving, nourishing, and protecting.
Braxton, Joanne M. *Black Women Writing Autobiography: A Tradition Within a Tradition.* Philadelphia: Temple University Press, 1989. Argues that Angelou uses the child's vision as principle of selection and the protecting mother as primary archetype, bringing to fruition certain themes of black female autobiography: the importance of family and of rearing one's children, resistance to a hostile environment, sympathy, and self-definition.
Kent, George E. "Maya Angelou's *I Know Why the Caged Bird Sings* and Black Autobiographical Tradition." *Kansas Quarterly* 7, no. 3 (1975): 72-78. Kent asserts that Angelou presents an emerging self equipped with an imagination that can successfully engage intransigent institutions, perceive both the beauty and absurdity of life in black communities, and create its own coherence.
MacKethan, Lucinda H. "Mother Wit: Humor in African-American Women's Autobiography." *Studies in American Humor* 4 (Spring/Summer, 1985): 51-61. Notes that empowerment through the acquisition of language and the development of verbal humor is a unifying theme in Angelou's autobiography.
McMurry, Myra K. "Role-Playing as Art in Maya Angelou's *Caged Bird.*" *South Atlantic Bulletin* 41, no. 2 (1976): 106-111. Angelou shows that individuals and groups can artistically humanize static, institutionalized roles to facilitate interrelationship and affirm self.
Tate, Claudia. "Maya Angelou." In *Black Women Writers at Work.* New York: Continuum, 1983. Angelou talks of the special need of black American women to make images of themselves and to have positive role models. Also discusses her responsibility as a writer and her writing process.

Tom Koontz

IF HE HOLLERS LET HIM GO

Author: Chester Himes (1909-1984)
Type of work: Novel
Type of plot: Social criticism
Time of plot: During World War II
Locale: Southern California
First published: 1945

> *Principal characters:*
> BOB JONES, the narrator and main character, a young black man
>   struggling with the second-class status afforded him by white
>   America
> ALICE HARRISON, Bob's well-to-do girlfriend
> MADGE PERKINS, a middle-aged white woman who becomes a
>   focal point of Bob's efforts to gain mastery over a hostile white
>   world

The Novel

If He Hollers Let Him Go is an account of five days and nights in the life of Bob Jones, a bright young black man who has risen to a leadership position in the Atlas Shipyards during the height of World War II. As the book's narrator, Bob gives an intense account of his anxieties, rage, love, and confusion as he deals with life in a country that proclaims freedom and equality but that practices racial discrimination.

The novel opens with Bob having a series of anxiety dreams. Upon waking, he realizes that his position of authority (he is a crew leader at the shipyards) has heightened his sense of insecurity as a black man in a white-dominated world. Struggling to maintain his self-respect and confidence, he leaves for work; once there, Bob is criticized by his supervisor, Kelly. Madge Perkins, a middle-aged white woman who works at the plant, is assigned to work with Bob, but she refers to him with a racial slur; Bob, in turn, calls her a "slut." Madge lodges a complaint, and Bob is demoted from his position as crew leader. Bob is later sucker-punched by a white worker after he wins big at a lunchtime game of craps. Unconscious, Bob is robbed of his winnings.

From this point on, Bob is obsessed with recovering his self-respect. His strategy is basically three-pronged. He plans to crash the color line at a posh restaurant with Alice Harrison, his upper-class, light-skinned black girlfriend. He also plans to avenge himself against his two white antagonists, sexually in the case of Madge, violently in the case of the white worker who punched him.

None of these plans works out. Bob takes Alice to the restaurant, but the two of them run short of defiance and are unable to enjoy their meal in the hostile surroundings. Bob is able to threaten the worker who punched him, taking some satisfaction in the fear that comes into the man's eyes, but he is unable to go through with the killing. Finally, he does seduce the powerfully ambivalent Madge; when she cries out for him to rape her, however, he is revulsed, and he leaves without completing the sexual act. On top of all this, Bob's replacement, a boorish white man, wins over Bob's crew by getting cushy assignments that Kelly had refused to give to Bob.

Rebuffed on every front, Bob agrees to follow Alice's advice that he make peace with the white world around him, accommodating himself to inequality rather than fighting it. He plans to marry Alice and attend college with the goal of becoming a lawyer. These plans are ruined when Madge falsely accuses Bob of having raped her, and he is beaten by white coworkers. Rape charges against Bob are dropped in return for his enlistment in the Army. Too exhausted to argue his innocence, Bob agrees. The novel ends as he goes off to defend a country in which he no longer believes.

The Characters

Bob is tormented by severe racial anxiety. When he is awake, he shares with the reader his obsession with the treatment he receives at the hands of white people, ranging from his supervisors and policemen to coworkers and waiters. This narration presents a man at war with his society, wavering between uncontrollable fear and boundless rage. Bob is at war with himself as well, not knowing whether he wants to accommodate himself to the injustices of a discriminatory society or exist in a permanent, perhaps self-destructive state of social rebellion.

Bob's dreams help to convey the psychological depth of his anxiety. In his dreams, he and other blacks are constantly being tricked and trapped by diabolical whites, sometimes fighting back but never winning, never quite beating the system. These dreams express Bob's anxiety in a series of haunting images and also indicate its inescapable nature. Even sleep provides no refuge.

Together, Bob's waking narrative and dreams portray a bright, ambitious, and confused young man. Although intelligent and articulate, Bob is ravaged by fear and indecision. He is made cynical by his very idealism and by the failure of his country to live up to its professed ideals.

The other characters are conveyed through Bob's eyes. Alice clearly recognizes Bob's talent and spirit. Her love seems sincere, but she believes that Bob's failure to accommodate himself to America's racist (but improving) social order is a disastrous course. She wants no part of him if he insists on confronting the system. Himes's portrayal of Alice is evenhanded; one can readily empathize with her.

Madge is more difficult to fathom. Unlike Alice, she is inarticulate and vulgar. Himes makes it clear that she has been scarred by unpleasantries in her own life. With regard to Bob, she expresses, through physical gestures and limited dialogue, a combination of revulsion and sexual attraction. She clings to the fiction of her racial superiority, her badge of worth in an otherwise paltry existence. On the other hand, she is drawn to Bob sexually expressly because of his race. This manic reaction to Bob is hinted at, somewhat awkwardly, almost from the start of the novel. Madge comes across as real; she is Bob's bane not because of diabolical intent but because of a perverse confluence of circumstances that she herself does not understand.

The book's minor characters are portrayed rather economically. Kelly, Bob's supervisor, consistently keeps Bob waiting, once while he finishes telling a racial joke. Herbie Frieberg, Bob's union shop steward, is an instantly recognizable Jewish character who responds to Bob's demotion with annoying detachment. Overall, Himes does a good job of making characters recognizable, yet not quite stereotypical. One character, however, remains a mystery: Don, the apparently sympathetic white supervisor who assigns Madge to work with Bob and who later gives him her address. Don's motivation is never quite made clear. Is he being helpful? Is he being a troublemaker? Bob wonders about these questions but does not come to an answer.

Themes and Meanings

If He Hollers Let Him Go is rife with themes. Most obvious is the theme of how different the American experience has been for black Americans. One part of Bob's experience is accepted universally by his fellow black characters: the indignity, essential inequality, and hypocrisy of America's treatment of black people. No black character in the book argues that America is fair. Even Alice, who disagrees radically with Bob's solution to the problem, never disputes his diagnosis.

Most of the book's white characters, on the other hand, act to reinforce the subordinate status of black Americans. They are at best oblivious or mildly sympathetic to the plight of black people, at worst very pleased to remind Bob that he is black and therefore of a lower status.

The theme of racial disparity is made particularly poignant by two subthemes. First, Bob's peculiarly intense feelings of anger and despair are linked closely to his belief in the principles of American democracy. Bob supposes that these principles apply to black as well as white Americans; the reality he confronts, however, is that American ideals are expressed in universal terms but are applied selectively—and certainly not to black people, no matter how bright, hardworking, or ambitious they might be.

A second subtheme increases the weight of this realization. The United States is at war, the ultimate test of ideals and allegiance. The situation is an uncomfortable one for Bob and many other black Americans, since they are asked to be patriotic in a country that has betrayed their hopes and dreams. The book's conclusion, with Bob entering the military, thus presents a final, bitter irony.

Related to the theme of racial alienation is the novel's portrayal of class status within black America. The black men and women with whom Bob works come, for the most part, from modest socioeconomic backgrounds. Most are minimally educated. Alice, on the other hand, comes from a privileged background; her father is a doctor who travels in exclusive circles. She also has many white friends. Not unconnected with this is the fact that Alice is light-skinned enough so that she is tempted, at times, to pass for white.

Unlike Bob, the black men and women from these two broad classes seem relatively well-adjusted to their situations. They have adopted different, but equally workable, strategies for coping with racial discrimination. Bob, however, is in between classes. He identifies with his fellow workers but, unlike them, has elaborate ambitions for a formal education and career in the law. On the other hand, he does not want to escape his roots and make humiliating concessions, as Alice and her family have done.

By far the most controversial themes raised by Himes deal with the perverse sexual byproducts of American racism. The relationship between Bob and Madge is both frightening and sexually compelling. For Bob, Madge is a symbol of whiteness. To experience her sexually is a way for him to gain equality with or, temporarily, mastery over white America. To Madge, Bob is forbidden fruit, made more attractive by the taboo against interracial sex. Thus, she desires to be "raped" by Bob. In that way, Madge can experience the ecstasy of sex with Bob while maintaining her superior virtue. The result is a sexual dynamic that is psychologically and physically compelling and completely loveless. Certainly, Himes does not suggest that all interracial relationships operate along these lines; he simply makes clear that racial separation and domination have led to some unedifying psychosexual consequences.

Finally, there is the theme of latent violence. While Bob suffers rather than perpetrates nearly all the violence in the novel (the one exception occurs when he loses his temper with a minor character who is black), he is constantly fantasizing about evening the score through violence. Though he never quite gives in to the urge, Bob is forced to deal with the fact that white America has truly put murder in his heart.

Critical Context

If He Hollers Let Him Go was a commercial failure and drew a mixed response from critics. The critical reception was in marked contrast to that given to Richard Wright's *Native Son*, published only five years earlier. Though *Native Son*, too, was by a black author and explored sensitive racial themes, it drew a surprisingly large readership and was widely applauded.

The reasons for the tepid response to Himes's novel are unclear. To be sure, *If He Hollers Let Him Go* is far from flawless. The book seems contrived at times, and Himes sometimes repeats himself and belabors certain themes. On the other hand, Himes displays extraordinary narrative powers and clearly covers ground that Wright and other black authors had yet to explore. The explanation may lie in a combination of factors. Himes's novel is more difficult to categorize than Wright's; while *Native Son* is unabashedly violent and tragic, *If He Hollers Let Him Go* manages to end ambiguously—indeed, the ending is anticlimactic. Moreover, Bigger Thomas, the protagonist of *Native Son*, is a kind of primitive innocent, highly identifiable by his dialect and lack of sophistication. Bob Jones, on the other hand, is very like the first-person narrators of contemporary "hardboiled" literature by such white authors as Raymond Chandler and Jim Thompson.

The timing of the novel's publication may also have worked against Himes. In 1945, Americans were still locked in war with the Axis Powers. It may well be that a message such as Himes's was less welcome in the midst of a unified effort against racist foes. This may explain why some critics dismissed *If He Hollers Let Him Go* as a mere "protest" novel. (In later paperback printings, the novel was sensationalized for its theme of interracial sex, helping to diminish its literary reputation.)

Himes's next few books also were commercially unsuccessful, though they did win him a critical following. In 1953, Himes emigrated to Europe, where the French reading public was far more appreciative of his work. It was a series of mystery-suspense novels featuring two Harlem police detectives, "Coffin" Ed Smith and "Gravedigger" Jones, that brought Himes to the attention of American readers. Originally written for a French publisher between 1958 and 1971, the Harlem detective novels have gone through several American printings and served as the basis for three films.

This success, though, did not spark much interest in Himes's earlier work. By the 1970's, *If He Hollers Let Him Go* was out of print, and it remained so until 1986, when it was reissued along with *Lonely Crusade* (1947), Himes's second novel. By that time, Himes's more serious novels and his extraordinarily rich autobiography had begun to draw renewed attention. The result has been a growing awareness of Himes as an important pioneer, one whose work remains fresh and inspiring.

Bibliography

Himes, Chester. *The Autobiography of Chester Himes.* 2 vols. Garden City, N.Y.: Doubleday, 1972, 1976. These candid and detailed volumes are notable for their passionate objectivity. Himes is abundantly self-critical and frank about his shortcomings. The work reveals strong ties between Himes's life and his books, helping to throw light on various themes as they developed over his career.

Hughes, Carl Milton. *The Negro Novelist: 1940-1950.* 1953. Reprint. New York: Citadel Press, 1990. Explores Himes's first two novels as part of a general discussion of black novelists from 1940 to 1950; other authors discussed include Richard Wright, Ralph Ellison, and Zora Neale Hurston. Describes the 1940's as a breakthrough decade for black literature.

Littlejohn, David. *Black on White: A Critical Survey of Writing by American Negroes.* New York: Viking Press, 1966. Places Himes in the context of other prominent African American authors. Discusses a number of common themes, but also introduces readers to the uniqueness of Himes's literary voice.

Lundquist, James. *Chester Himes.* New York: Ungar Books, 1976. A standard biography. Covers Himes's imprisonment for armed robbery, his early writing career and literary influences, his experiences in the defense industry in California during World War II (experiences that inspired *If He Hollers Let Him Go*), his expatriation to Europe, and his subsequent career.

Margolies, Edward. "Race and Sex: The Novels of Chester Himes." In *Native Sons: A Critical Study of Twentieth Century Negro American Authors.* Philadelphia: J. B. Lippincott, 1968. Examines the sexual consequences of racial tension as they are played out in Himes's novels. Sensibly argued and convincing.

Milliken, Stephen. *Chester Himes: A Critical Appraisal.* Columbia: University of

Missouri Press, 1976. A thorough, authoritative analysis of Himes's life and work that does an excellent job of describing the raw power of Himes's racial commentary. Also shows the continuity between different phases of Himes's literary career.

Yarborough, Richard. "The Quest for the American Dream in Three Afro-American Novels: *If He Hollers Let Him Go, The Street,* and *Invisible Man.*" *MELUS* 8 (Winter, 1981): 33-59. Focuses on the disparity between American ideals and the realistic expectations of African Americans at about the time that Himes wrote *If He Hollers Let Him Go.*

Ira Smolensky

IN THE CASTLE OF MY SKIN

Author: George Lamming (1927-   )
Type of work: Novel
Type of plot: Bildungsroman
Time of plot: The 1930's and 1940's
Locale: Creighton's Village, Barbados
First published: 1953

> *Principal characters:*
>> G., the narrator, a young Barbadian, nine years old when the
>> novel opens, seventeen and on the verge of emigrating to
>> Trinidad when it ends
>> TRUMPER, a teenage friend of the narrator who emigrates to the
>> United States and returns on the eve of the narrator's own
>> departure
>> BOB, a friend of the narrator and Trumper
>> BOY BLUE, a friend of the narrator and Trumper
>> G.'S MOTHER, a strong, disciplinarian village woman
>> MA, an elderly woman in the village
>> PA, Ma's husband
>> MR. SLIME, a teacher in the village school at the beginning of the
>> novel
>> THE SHOEMAKER, a villager who appears throughout the novel
>> MR. FOSTER, a villager who appears throughout the novel

The Novel

In the Castle of My Skin is an autobiographical novel by a young native of Barbados living in England. The novel's plot covers the years from the time of a great flood when the narrator is nine years old to the eve of his departure for the larger island of Trinidad at the age of seventeen.

The virtually unnamed narrator, G., clearly is a surrogate for the author, though Lamming's narrative strategy of alternating first-person and third-person narrators has the effect of submerging G.'s identity beneath the larger collective identity and situation of the inhabitants of Creighton's Village. The larger intended effect of the occasionally confusing alternation of narrators is that two mutually reinforcing stories are told within one narrative frame. The first is the story of the ostensible protagonist's coming of age and the dawning of his political awareness. The second story concerns the great social upheavals that occur over the years, especially following the sale of the village by Mr. Creighton, the landlord, to a group of men including Mr. Slime, the populist leader who betrays the villagers' trust.

In the Castle of My Skin begins during a rainstorm on G.'s ninth birthday, a reference to an actual flood that afflicted Barbados when Lamming was a child. The early scenes of G.'s disappointment and his mother's response (she "put her head through the window to let the neighbour know that I was nine, and they flattered me with the consolation that my birthday had brought showers of blessing") effectively establish the setting as well as the sense of collective identity, awareness, and suffering that are crucial to the novel's purpose. The first-person narrator makes this explicit as he describes his mother visiting with two neighbor women:

> Miss Foster. My mother. Bob's mother.
> It seemed they were three pieces in a pattern which remained constant. The flow of its history was undisturbed by any difference in the pieces, nor was its evenness affected by any likeness. There was a difference and there was no difference.

In the domestic geography of the village, he conveys a naturalness and innocence that surely will not last to the book's end:

> In the corner where one fence merged into another, and the sunlight filtering through the leaves made a limitless suffusion over the land, the pattern had arranged itself with absolute unawareness.

The important third chapter, written in the third person, achieves a skillful segue from a general depiction of a boy's school and a Queen's Birthday celebration to a subtly crucial plot element involving a potential scandal for a teacher, Mr. Slime, who resigns and later becomes a populist leader. The short fourth chapter features a discussion by Ma and Pa, an emblematic, choruslike elderly couple, of Mr. Slime's new projects, the Penny Bank and the Friendly Society. Referring to the migration of many West Indians early in the twentieth century to Panama to work building the canal there, Ma says: " 'Tis a next Panama we need now for the young ones. I sit there sometimes an' I wonder what's goin' to become o' them, the young that comin' up so fast to take the place o' the old. 'Tis a next Panama we want, Pa, or there goin' to be bad times comin' this way."

Much of the heart of the novel is nearly plotless, though not purposeless. The narrator and his friends Trumper and Boy Blue engage in adolescent ruminations on the beach. Many of the ideas expressed by the three boys, about the sadness and loss of growing up, about sexual awakening, about their place in the village and their wonder at the opportunities of the outside world, are hardly specific to the Caribbean. These universal themes establish *In the Castle of My Skin* squarely in the tradition of the *Bildungsroman*.

The narrator goes off to the High School, establishing an unwanted distance between him and his friends. A riot—like the flood, the fictional counterpart of a historical event in Barbados—jars the villagers into an uneasy awareness that times are changing. Trumper emigrates to the United States. He returns just in time to tell the narrator about that country. The novel ends with the narrator on the verge of leaving for Trinidad and the community on the verge of ruin from the landlord's sale of its land to a group including the apparently treacherous Mr. Slime. Mr. Slime's complicity in the land sale is not narrated explicitly but can be supposed from strong hints.

The Characters

In the Castle of My Skin is a very oddly structured novel. Its alternation of first- and third-person narrators seems undisciplined (the author was, after all, only twenty-three years old when he began writing it) but is, in fact, a bold and considered device for conveying a sense of the village's communal identity while simultaneously narrating G.'s coming of age and his eventual, inevitable emigration. Lamming, using the first-person narrator, the ostensible protagonist, as his surrogate, intends the same effect in this novel as in his collection of autobiographical literary essays *The Pleasures of Exile* (1960). Critic Sandra Pouchet Paquet's remark about *The Pleasures of Exile* could be said with equal justice about *In the Castle of My Skin*: "Autobiographical values are determined by the narrator's acute and pervasive sense of participating in a great historical moment. His valuable life surrenders its meaning in a gesture of collectivity."

In the novel, then, as in the book of essays, the unusual, unexpected main character is the community at large. This fact establishes Lamming's political and social values and sympathies. The tragedy of the land sale near the novel's end is the community's communal tragedy. At the same time, the individual protagonist, the first-person narrator G., is separating himself from the community by emigrating to Trinidad. Although he does not yet know it as he prepares to leave, his emigration is preparatory to the writing of the narrative.

G. is not well prepared for the outside world. His academic achievements are modest and disappointing to his mother, who is tenacious and fiercely ambitious for him. "She would talk about pulling through; whatever happened she would come through, and 'she' meant her child." At the same time, by virtue of his education at the High School, he no longer belongs in the village. He is caught between two worlds. Of his friends he writes: "Whether or not they wanted to they excluded me from their world just as my memory of them and the village excluded me from the world of the High School. . . . It was as though my roots had been snapped from the centre of what I knew best, while I remained impotent to wrest what my fortunes had forced me into."

Trumper, Bob, and Boy Blue, G.'s friends, serve to throw the narrator's predicament into relief. Ma and Pa, the old couple, are wise, sad commentators on the changes taking place. Other characters, such as the Shoemaker, Mr. Foster, Miss Foster, and Bob's mother, are given individual identities, though always carefully within a structure that limits their awareness of the world and their own roles to those of villagers. The outside world impinges on the novel through Trumper's departure for and return from the United States and through the narrator's later awareness, as he writes, of the political and historical significance of events such as the riot, the land sale, and his own emigration.

Themes and Meanings

Character, theme, and point of view are inextricable in *In the Castle of My Skin*. As already noted, the alternation of first- and third-person narrators is the author's crucial device for conveying the communal identity of his protagonist and his concern with the fate of the community as a literary and moral question.

The novel's autobiographical framework is a strategy for narrating the larger story of the village's demise. *In the Castle of My Skin* clearly is not merely an autobiographical novel or a standard *Bildungsroman*. At the same time, the narrator's awareness of the community's plight, increased between the time of the events recounted and the time of writing, is a crucial element. As Sandra Pouchet Paquet writes about *The Pleasures of Exile*, though again her remarks apply equally well to the novel and to G. as its "author," "His dissenting voice is personal and collective. As colonial subject, Lamming offers himself as a representative text to be read and as a privileged interpreter of his own historical moment." That is, Lamming unabashedly uses his own subjective, autobiographical understanding of events and relationships to correct, in his view, earlier "imperialist" versions of his island's and region's history.

Lamming allows his narrator to comment on the characters in such a way as to emphasize individuals' importance as parts of the communal identity. Possibly because of his relative youth when he wrote the novel, he eschews subtlety in favor of explicit insistence which, nevertheless, is effective in its repetition. "Three, thirteen, thirty" is a phrase he uses several times in the first two chapters to refer to representative village women. He later expands the phrase's use to refer to collectivity in general.

> Three, thirteen, thirty. It does not matter. They come and go to perpetuate the custom of this corner. Once a week, black pudding and souse. The pattern has absorbed them, and in the wood where the night is thickest it has embraced another two in intimate intercourse.

The middle chapters, in which the three boys ruminate on cosmic questions, serve as a bridge from G.'s childhood to the cataclysmic events at the novel's end. In a symbolic scene, G. frets about having lost a pebble from the beach that he had arbitrarily decided he must not lose, and which he hid for safekeeping. It is a scene and a sentiment familiar to anyone who has gone through adolescence.

> It had become one of those things one can't bear to see for the last time. . . . I selected the spot and placed the pebble under the leaf on the even slope. A day had passed. There was no change in the weather, and the waves were as quiet as ever on this side of the sea. . . . But the pebble had gone. The feeling sharpened. It had really started the evening before when I received the letters, and now the pebble had made it permanent. In the evening I had read the letters and it seemed there were several things, intimate and endearing which I was going to see for the last time.

In the Castle of My Skin is, classically, a novel about losing innocence and gaining self-awareness.

Critical Context

The important African American novelist Richard Wright wrote, in his introduction to the first American edition of *In the Castle of My Skin*, "One feels not so much alone when, from a distant witness, supporting evidence comes to buttress one's own testimony." Wright went on to refer to "Lamming's quietly melodious prose." This was high praise coming from a very distinguished voice very early in Lamming's career. Sandra Pouchet Paquet writes that "The novel was very well received and has held its own as a classic of modern Black writing."

Having written five other novels and *The Pleasures of Exile* by 1993, Lamming achieved recognition as the most important novelist to have emerged from the English-speaking Caribbean, perhaps barring V. S. Naipaul. C. L. R. James, the patriarch of West Indian writers, said in 1972, "I do not know at the present time any country writing in English which is able to produce a trio of the literary capacity and effectiveness of Wilson Harris, George Lamming, and Vidia Naipaul." James was prone to effusiveness and bold remarks, though not to irresponsible claims. Critic Daryl Cumber Dance asserts that in making such a sweeping assertion James "was guilty neither of exaggeration nor of nationalism."

Ian H. Munro, in a summary of Lamming's career and the critical reception of his books, quotes novelist Ngugi wa Thiong'o as calling *In the Castle of My Skin* "a study of colonial revolt" and "one of the great political novels in modern 'colonial' literature." Munro notes that "Much of both the praise and the criticism of Lamming's novels after *Castle* revolves around his obvious preoccupation with showing his characters and their actions as a product of historical forces outside their ken. Lamming's works are all symbolic to some degree: his characters frequently embody themes and act out roles appropriate to their place in the symbolic scheme." This tendency of Lamming's is obvious in *In the Castle of My Skin*. As Munro also stated, "the political goals and issues of the novel ultimately bulk larger than the individual life of its characters."

Bibliography

Buhle, Paul. "C. L. R. James, West Indian: George Lamming Interviewed by Paul Buhle." In *C. L. R. James's Caribbean*, edited by Paget Henry and Paul Buhle. Durham, N.C.: Duke University Press, 1992. An interview with Lamming by the biographer of C. L. R. James, the first important West Indian to publish abroad, and in later life an influence on radical activists and critics of society in Britain and the United States, as well as on younger Caribbean writers, including Lamming. The interview concerns the subject of James's influence on Lamming.

Dance, Daryl Cumber. *Conversations with Contemporary West Indian Writers.* Leeds, England: Peepal Tree Press, 1993. A collection of interviews with West Indian writers, including Lamming. Other subjects include the Caribbean literary and political patriarch C. L. R. James, the Nobel Prize-winning poet Derek Walcott, and the prominent female novelist Jamaica Kincaid.

Lamming, George. *The Pleasures of Exile.* Ann Arbor: University of Michigan Press,

1992. A collection of autobiographical, interrelated essays on the perspective and concerns of the postcolonial writer, specifically in the West Indian context. Lamming discusses his own fiction and poetry as well as William Shakespeare's *The Tempest* (1611) and C. L. R. James's classic history of the Haitian revolution, *The Black Jacobins: Toussaint Louverture and the San Domingo Revolution* (1938). The Ann Arbor Paperbacks edition includes a helpful, lucid foreword by Lamming scholar Sandra Pouchet Paquet of the University of Pennsylvania.

Munro, Ian H. "George Lamming." In *Fifty Caribbean Writers*, edited by Daryl Cumber Dance. New York: Greenwood Press, 1986. A biographical and critical essay on Lamming and his work, with helpful citations of critical studies of *In the Castle of My Skin* and Lamming's other books.

Paquet, Sandra Pouchet. Foreword to *In the Castle of My Skin*. Ann Arbor: University of Michigan Press, 1991. An excellent discussion of the novel, most fruitfully read after having read the novel.

_____. *The Novels of George Lamming*. London: Heinemann, 1982. The first book-length study of Lamming's work.

Wright, Richard. Introduction to *In the Castle of My Skin*. New York: McGraw-Hill, 1954. An enthusiastic introduction to the novel's first edition, by one of the most prominent African American novelists.

Ethan Casey

IN THE WINE TIME

Author: Ed Bullins (1935-   )
Type of work: Play
Type of plot: Naturalism
Time of plot: The early 1950's
Locale: A side street in a large Northern industrial city
First produced: 1968, at the New Lafayette Theatre, New York City
First published: 1969

>   *Principal characters:*
>   CLIFF DAWSON, an unemployed Navy veteran
>   LOU DAWSON, Cliff's wife, who is three months pregnant
>   RAY, Lou and Cliff's nephew, a quiet, good-hearted, sensitive boy

The Play

The play begins with a moderately long prologue, which may be likened to a soliloquy, spoken years later by the adult Ray. This device provides a context that distances the action that follows, sets the urban scene, gives a wistful tone, introduces the special, inward, and sensitive personality of Ray, and establishes his experience and point of view as the focus of attention and meaning. In poetic prose, Ray shares his memory of what for him has turned out to be the most meaningful event of his last "wine time" summer, his daily, brief meetings with a mysterious girl with whom he fell in love. By the end of that summer, she had moved away, and he had turned sixteen and joined the Navy.

The three acts of the play then take the form mainly of dialogue between family members and friends in a working-class neighborhood; the characters are entertaining themselves with large quantities of talk and wine after another trying day. Men and women talk to one another about their relationships, men talk with men about women, and women talk with women about men. The audience senses the hidden agendas in these conversations. Themes emerge, such as the ways in which lives are molded by the pressures of poverty and racism, the nature of true manhood and the ways in which it might involve women and family, and potential and loss.

The action takes place mostly on the Dawson family's stoop, but sometimes the stage lighting shifts the scene to "the Avenue," where a mirroring subplot takes place. Act 1 tells the audience what it needs to know about Cliff and Lou Dawson and their adopted nephew, Ray, and presents some options that might be available for Ray. It also presents the conflicts between and within Cliff and Lou. These conflicts are echoed and aggravated by conflicts between these characters and various minor characters. In act 2, the option of "the girl" is presented along with the conflict within Ray, and the earlier established conflicts are heightened. In act 3, the conflicts and themes are quickly brought to a crisis that is just as quickly resolved by violence.

The action all takes place on a single hot summer night. As usual, Cliff, Lou, and

Ray are out on their stoop, talking and drinking cheap wine. From time to time, they are joined by friends and acquaintances. Their neighbors are also out on their stoops, frowning on Cliff, whom they consider loud and crude. Cliff is equally annoyed by his neighbors, whom he considers snobbish, pretentious, and small-minded. The Dawsons are comparatively new arrivals on Derby Street, and from the beginning of their time there, Cliff has felt rejected and insulted by his neighbors, who think it suspicious and disgraceful that Cliff is a college student, and unemployed, while Lou rears a teenaged boy. In his bitterness, Cliff frequently entertains himself by making a nuisance of himself, shocking his neighbors by drunkenly shouting obscenities and insults. Lou somewhat shares his attitude toward their neighbors, but she is more understanding of their viewpoint and is uncomfortable with her husband's displays, as well as with his roughness toward her. To some extent, she shares and enjoys his roughness; she feels proud of his strength and superior vitality, and she is proud of herself for having saved him from a worse fate in the Navy by marrying him. Cliff is not entirely satisfied with his landlocked domestic life. Although he knows that he has had his time of adventure and must put that behind, he still takes out his frustration in quarrels with his wife, sometimes with only partly mocked violence. Yet he loves, respects, and even admires his wife for her sensitivity and high principles, which he has found to be rare.

When Ray expresses his desire to join the Navy when he turns sixteen, in just a week, Cliff encourages him and promises to sign his enlistment papers. Lou, though, says that Ray is a year too young. While Lou is indoors washing her hair, Ray and Cliff talk about the opportunities for a more meaningful life that the Navy would offer Ray, especially regarding women. Cliff learns that Ray is more experienced sexually than he had thought, although he has known about Ray and his girlfriend, Bunny.

In the context of these thoughts about women and Ray's future, Ray mentions a new girl, beautiful and mysterious, probably somewhat older than he, whom he sees at a certain time every day on the Avenue. Each day she smiles at him and hums what has become their song. Cliff has not witnessed these trysts, but he immediately sees the threat that they present to the escape into a good life in the Navy that he has projected for Ray. He thus does what he can to disillusion Ray about the girl.

On this night, meanwhile, Bunny has been up the Avenue with her girlfriend and two young men, one of whom, Red, is making an obvious play for her attentions. While Cliff and Ray are gone to buy more wine, Bunny, Red, and other friends and neighbors, with their jug of wine, gather at the Dawsons' stoop. Tension rises, especially because of Red's provocations; and after Cliff and Ray return with a new jug, which is already half empty, the mood grows steadily darker. Ray drinks himself into a near stupor, but he is able to understand when Bunny informs him that she is Red's girl now. Red urinates into an empty jug and hands it to Ray. As Ray raises it to his lips, Bunny knocks it away, smashing it on the sidewalk. Ray punches her in the face, and Red jumps on Ray. Knives are drawn, and fighting swirls around the stoop and into the alley. Cliff runs out of the house and into the darkness. When he emerges, he announces that he has killed Red. A policeman arrives and places Cliff under arrest.

Themes and Meanings

"Wine time" is a summer evening in a black or mostly black neighborhood of a city. It begins approximately at the end of suppertime, when residents come out of their homes into the cooler but still-hot air, and lasts until bedtime, which may be far into the night. It is named for the large amount of cheap wine that is consumed by the people on the sidewalks and stoops that line the streets. In the context of this play, "wine time" suggests a social ritual, marked by conviviality, sexuality, intoxication, and relaxation, among the neighbors, young and old. At the same time, it suggests a lapse in social constraints, a fluidity of action, enhanced desire, and lowered inhibitions, with revelations of felt truths that are hidden during the day. It is a time-out, a break from the pressures of the day. There is a weariness to be rested, there is also a release and an excitement. Anything can suddenly happen, good or bad. Life is still hopeful and troublesome and must be lived, hour by hour; people fall into patterns, repeating their feelings, their talk, and their nightly acts. "Wine time" also suggests a time of youth, with its accompanying inexperience, ignorance, and uncertainty, but also with its potential for discovery, decision, and growth—or for mistake and a slip into oblivion. The term also suggests romance, actual or imaginary or something in between.

These motifs are established, or hinted at, in the poetic, prose prologue to the play. In the mixture of comfort and discomfort, satisfaction and dissatisfaction, love and hate that Ray remembers, the audience begins to perceive that time is a series of passages, through momentary meetings to impossibility and separation, in a search that is never completed. As the action of the play unfolds, the characterizations of three couples—Ray and "the girl" (actually a young woman, at least several years older than he), Cliff and Lou, and Red and Bunny—present variations on the theme of the relationship between a man and a woman and, especially regarding the restless Cliff and the proudly competent Lou, the theme of true manhood and how it relates to family.

The play does not offer a final word about manhood, but it suggests that manhood is often misunderstood by men as being a state of complete independence, freedom from responsibility, and exercise of control over women for the sake of self-gratification. The play also suggests that poverty and racism reinforce this misunderstanding. In the figure of Ray's dream girl, who is mature, independent, self-possessed, loving, and wise—a fantasy, yet all too real for the youthfully naïve Ray—the play offers a glimpse of a possibility that a man might find himself at last, and fulfill his life in a loving relationship. As the play proceeds, however, Ray increasingly adopts Cliff as his model, suggesting that Ray's future is more likely to hold violence and unfulfillment. The play suggests that some black men do not want to grow out of their "wine time," or are too late in understanding that it must be left behind. But such a time, and failure, are also universal themes.

Critical Context

In the Wine Time was the first of a cycle of twenty plays, with characters linked by kinship or association, projected by Bullins about the black American experience in the twentieth century. It was also his first full-length play. Before it was first produced in 1968, critics had acknowledged the talent Bullins had displayed in his one-act plays, but *In the Wine Time* was not widely noted in its first production; it has, however, come to be considered to be one of his most important plays. Along with Amiri Baraka, whom Bullins has said "created me," Bullins led the black theater movement of the 1960's.

From the beginning, Bullins has been interested primarily in his plays' reception not by critics but by black audiences. His purpose, he has suggested, is to provide black theatergoers with fresh insights as they consider the weight of their own lives. His passionate conviction is that black playwrights can and should contribute a vision for tomorrow, thereby building not only a new black theater but also a black nation and future. With this commitment and audience, Bullins has found it artistically possible to present anything he envisions for the judgment of that audience, free from the constraints of white publishers and critics. Furthermore, while the problem of racism is often present and meaningful in his plays, its presence need not be central or blatant, because he is not bringing it to the attention of white theatergoers or explaining it to them. Therefore, too, his plays can be free from ideology and political or revolutionary rhetoric.

Still, Bullins writes for change. As the critic Don Evans has pointed out, the mirror that the plays hold up to the audience shows black people their ugliness. Indeed, Bullins' early plays were rejected by some critics for their obscene language, unconventional style, and violent, unflattering pictures of black life. Bullins, however, has remarked that he was a conscious artist before he was a consciously revolutionary artist, and that he is thus able to act as an agent for change in the black community. Bullins' plays force black audiences to look at those parts of their communities that trouble themselves, and to examine their own choices, dreams, evasions, and self-delusions.

In the Wine Time suggests that persons may dream the right dreams of peace and union but may be too naïve, unimpassioned, or misled to realize them. The play also explores how persons may try vainly to bring dead dreams back to life or may dream the wrong dreams and make choices that restrict their own freedom. Whether the dream be the American Dream or an individual's personal dream, it is ambiguous and fragile, and may suddenly turn into a nightmare.

Bullins has remarked that his characters are, like most persons, many dimensional and ever-changing in an ever-changing universe, like points in a dreamlike vision. This sense of the dreamlike quality of the universe and of persons' lives and visions crosses with Bullins' naturalistic dramatic techniques to influence the way he structures his plays. Some critics have faulted his plays for lack of conventional form and focused point of view; some have, upon greater reflection, discovered an unconventional form in the plays; some have found a free form that is vigorous and delightful, exhibiting artistic freedom and assurance; and others have explained that the plays are structured by an awareness of space and by quasiritualistic patterns that are recognized by black audiences as reflections of their own experiences and community patterns.

Bibliography

Anderson, Jervis. "Profiles." *The New Yorker* 49 (June 16, 1973): 40-44. Presents the complexities of the artist in the context of his personal background, the Black Arts movement, and the New Lafayette Theatre.

Andrews, W. D. E. "Theater of Black Reality: The Black Drama of Ed Bullins." *Southwest Review* 65 (1980): 178-190. Asserts that, in contrast to Baraka's "Messianic" theater, Bullins offers an "Orphic" descent into ghetto depths. Notes that the abstract sense of menace in his plays is like that found in the plays of Harold Pinter.

Cook, William. "Mom, Dad, and God: Values in the Black Theatre." In *The Theater of Black Americans*, edited by Errol Hill. Vol. 1. Englewood Cliffs, N.J.: Prentice-Hall, 1980. Compares Bullins' portrayal of family members, especially the father figure, to Lorraine Hansberry's and James Baldwin's. Argues that Bullins' characters do not fear sex or feel religious inhibitions; they celebrate the possibilities in ghetto street life, with a stoic acceptance of those few pleasures that life affords.

Evans, Don. "The Theater of Confrontation: Ed Bullins Up Against the Wall." *Black World* 23 (April, 1974): 14-18. Claims that Bullins is not pessimistic about the struggle of black men, but he must show the frustrating impotence that they feel.

Sanders, Leslie. "Ed Bullins." In *American Playwrights Since 1945*, edited by Philip C. Kolin. New York: Greenwood Press, 1989. A survey of sources, information, and major ideas about Bullins' work.

Smitherman, Geneva. "Everybody Wants to Know Why I Sing the Blues." *Black World* 23 (April, 1974): 4-13. Examines how, from the oral tradition of black literature, Bullins brings the trickster figure and the blues motif. Notes that as a bluesman, he reexamines black experience and moves to transcend its brutal aspects.

Steele, Shelby. "White Port and Lemon Juices: Notes on Ritual in the New Black Theater." *Black World* 22 (June, 1973): 4-13, 78-83. Argues that Bullins' use of symbols, characterizations, themes, and language styles establishes a ritual pattern that is recognized by black audience members as reaffirming their values.

True, Warren R. "Ed Bullins, Anton Chekhov, and the 'Drama Mood.'" *College Language Association Journal* 20 (June, 1977): 521-532. Compares Bullins to Chekhov with regard to their uses of naturalism of settings and passivity of characters who are trapped by social and environmental forces.

Tom Koontz

INCIDENTS IN THE LIFE OF A SLAVE GIRL

Author: Harriet Jacobs (1818-1896)
Type of work: Autobiography/slave narrative
Time of work: 1818-1861
Locale: North Carolina, Philadelphia, and New York City
First published: 1861

> *Principal personages:*
> LINDA BRENT, a slave and the narrator; "Linda Brent" is a
>   pseudonym for the author
> AUNT MARTHA, Linda's grandmother
> ELLEN and BENNY, Linda's two children
> WILLIAM, Linda's brother
> DR. FLINT, the pseudonym for Dr. James Norcom, Jacobs'
>   "master" and tormentor
> MRS. FLINT, a character representing Linda's other "master,"
>   Mary Matilda Hornblower Norcom
> MR. SANDS, a white man with whom Linda has her two children
> MRS. BRUCE (FIRST), a white woman in New York who employs
>   Linda
> MRS. BRUCE (SECOND), who married Mr. Bruce following the
>   death of his first wife

Form and Content

   Incidents in the Life of a Slave Girl was long believed to be a fictional account of slavery. Through extensive research, however, scholars have documented its authenticity as an autobiography by Harriet Jacobs, and it is now considered one of the most important antebellum slave narratives. No doubt the author's decision to use pseudonyms for herself and her characters and the "novelish" nature of the autobiography (with its plot, dialogue, and episodic chapters) led some literary critics and historians to question the historical authenticity of *Incidents in the Life of a Slave Girl.* Possibly, too, the relative lack of access to written modes of expression by black women of the early nineteenth century also inspired some of this skepticism.

   The issue of authenticity is, in fact, central to the whole tradition of African American slave narrative. *Incidents in the Life of a Slave Girl*, like other narratives, was written as testimony on behalf of and documentation for the antislavery cause. As such, it represents a highly activist literature, one in which the express purpose was political. Jacobs participated in the abolitionist movement and was assisted in her literary efforts by other abolitionists.

   As was the case with many other slave narratives, *Incidents in the Life of a Slave Girl* is accompanied by letters attesting its authenticity: the first by Amy Post, a white Quaker abolitionist, and the second by George Lowther, a free black man in Boston. This tradition of advocacy letters arose in response to early skepticism inside and outside the white abolitionist movement about the authenticity of slave narratives in general. Were these stories of the horrors of slavery really true? How could their authenticity be proven?

In essence, the question became "Who will be allowed to speak?" and "In what terms?" Harriet Jacobs, like several other leading black abolitionists, had disagreements with white abolitionists such as Harriet Beecher Stowe over the best way to present her story. *Incidents in the Life of a Slave Girl* was edited by white abolitionist editor Lydia Marie Child. The involvement of white antislavery activists in the publishing of some slave narratives has inspired some literary critics to wonder if the literary voice of slave narrative represents authentic black experience or instead has been cultivated according to the purposes and perspectives of white editors and readers. Other critics argue that black authors exercised definitive control over the form and content of their voices. This controversy illustrates the interesting and complex nature of slave narrative as a literary genre and invites a rigorous exploration of the complexity of American abolitionist history. Harriet Jacobs' autobiography provides an important voice in that history.

Incidents in the Life of a Slave Girl recounts the early childhood through middle adulthood of Linda, the pseudonym of author Harriet Jacobs. Born into slavery in North Carolina in approximately 1818, Linda loses both parents at an early age and forms a primary and essentially maternal bond with her grandmother, Aunt Martha, a free black. Yet Linda's life is controlled by her master and mistress, Dr. and Mrs. Flint. In fact, Linda's life story is structured as a response to Dr. Flint's predatory sexual pursuit, which begins in her early adolescence and continues, in varied forms, until his death. In response to Flint's constant harassment and Linda's fear that he will eventually rape her, she chooses to bear two children with another white man in the community, Mr. Sands. She agonizes over this decision, believing that she has compromised her own morality. She also subsequently suffers her grandmother's wrath and judgment in response to this decision, which threatens her emotional security. Linda's hope is that Flint will see her relationship with Sands as a break from his influence and will abandon his pursuit. When this strategy fails, Linda decides to escape, hoping that in his exasperation over losing her Flint will sell her children to their father and thus allow them a measure of protection from the evils of slavery. Linda escapes but is unable to flee the area, and she is hidden in the homes of sympathetic neighbors until the risk in doing so becomes too great. She is then compelled to hide in a tiny space above her grandmother's shed. Incredibly, Linda spends seven years cramped away in this room, watching the world and her children from a small peephole cut in the wood.

Eventually, arrangements are made for her escape to the North, first to Philadelphia and then to New York. Still enraged at Linda's refusal of his advances and obsessively unwilling to relinquish his legal authority over her, Flint pursues her, both through letters and expeditions north. Before her own escape, Linda had arranged for her young daughter, Ellen, to be sent north to live with her father's family. Once in New York, she also sends for her son, Benny. Protected by her sympathetic white employer, Mrs. Bruce, Linda is able to elude capture for several years, even after the notorious Fugitive Slave Law of 1850 makes the North perilous for escaped slaves. Flint dies, and his heirs continue to pursue their "property." In the closing chapter of the autobiography, the second Mrs. Bruce buys Linda's freedom from Flint's family. Although ambivalent about having to receive a purchased freedom, Jacobs closes her story with Linda's celebration of her liberation from slavery.

Incidents in the Life of a Slave Girl is divided into forty-one short chapters, each recounting an episode from the story of Jacobs' life. She constructs dialogue between her characters to allow a range of perspectives to appear in the story and occasionally uses chapters to address broader issues directly: "The Church and Slavery," "The Fugitive Slave Law," and "Prejudice Against Color," for example.

Analysis

An intriguing question arises immediately when considering *Incidents in the Life of a Slave Girl*: Why did Jacobs use pseudonyms for herself and other historical people? Why would she choose to distance herself in this way from her own autobiography, especially considering that slave narrative, as a genre, builds upon the authority of the speaker's own experience to pose a direct political challenge to slavery?

One obvious reason would be as a protective device. Jacobs, like other slave-narrative authors, may have chosen to mask the historical identity of her family in order to protect their privacy and the safety of those slaves still bound in her former community. Like other slave narratives, *Incidents in the Life of a Slave Girl* provides only sketchy details of its protagonist's actual escape and refrains from naming many of her accomplices. This also, no doubt, stems from a desire to protect them. The fact that Jacobs does not name the actual Dr. Flint and his family can be understood as a tactic to prevent more violence or abuse by them toward members of her family or her former friends in Edenton, North Carolina, the actual community of her birth and the location of the early portions of *Incidents in the Life of a Slave Girl*.

There is another possible explanation for Jacobs' decision to use pseudonyms, however, and this reason gets to some of the unique characteristics of the book as autobiography and as slave narrative. Harriet Jacobs directly confronts the sexual abuse that constantly confronted many female slaves. She offers herself as "evidence" in this sense, but she does so through her own voice and in her own terms. Her terms in this case include an apparent psychological and emotional ambivalence about her own actions in response to this abuse. Ultimately, she makes a clear claim for the legitimacy of her choices given the continued threat of rape by Flint. Jacobs challenges the moral absolutism of her readers, and perhaps of herself, by clearly presenting the context within which her seemingly immoral choice to have children with Sands is made. Lacking the legal options of marriage and the freedom to control her own life, she does her best to protect herself and her children. It seems entirely understandable, given this subject matter and the social realities of nineteenth century American society, that Jacobs would protect herself with a pseudonym as she made public such deeply traumatic and personal experiences.

Incidents in the Life of a Slave Girl offers a critique of slavery rooted in female experience. In addition to exposing the vulnerability of female slaves to sexual exploitation, Jacobs focuses on her roles as mother, (grand)daughter, and seeker-of-home. She develops her attack on slavery from within an intricate network of family relations—not the solitary heroine here, but a woman so committed to her children that she spends seven years in a suffocating cubicle in order to protect them. In the broader context of the African American experience of slavery, children and family (and the ability to keep and develop those bonds) become symbols and actual expressions of liberation and freedom. This "family" framework, in addition to Jacobs' portrayal of the special suffering of female slaves, adds important texture from black women's experience to the body of slave-narrative literature.

In addition, *Incidents in the Life of a Slave Girl* addresses themes that are common in other slave narratives. First, a deeply personal quest for freedom is also understood as representing the desires of the entire slave community. In other words, the quest is not only for individual freedom but for the end of slavery and the freedom of all enslaved African Americans as well. In the story, Linda crosses water to reach Philadelphia—a biblical metaphor for liberation—but her crossing represents liberation not only for herself but also, symbolically, for all slaves. After she reaches the North, her gaze is constantly back toward those she has left behind. Her autobiography thus uses one life as a symbol for the liberation of a whole people.

Like many other slave narratives, *Incidents in the Life of a Slave Girl* is infused with religious reference and poses a scriptural challenge to slavery. The role of religion in slave communities and in African American history is complex. There exists a range of opinion about the influence (or lack of it) of white slaveholding Christianity on the religious self-understanding of recently arrived African slaves as well as on later generations of African Americans. Religion is integral to most early nineteenth century black literature and oratory, and the role played by diverse religions in early black activism is rigorously debated by scholars. Harriet Jacobs constructs her story within an explicitly religious framework; she directly condemns slaveholding Christianity by claiming the validity of a more genuine Christianity. Her own religious views show some interesting internal conflicts that illustrate how difficult it was for enslaved Christians to embrace such traditional Protestant precepts as submission and self-denial.

Unlike some authors of slave narratives, Jacobs does not dwell on her efforts to acquire literacy, which is often a metaphor for freedom in slave autobiography. Yet the importance of her own literacy is expressed in two ways: Her ability to read the Bible helps keep her sane during her long confinement, and her literacy allows her to write *Incidents in the Life of a Slave Girl*. This literary independence gives her the power to control her story and to speak to a relatively broad audience in her own terms.

Critical Context

Harriet Jacobs published *Incidents in the Life of a Slave Girl* herself just prior to the formal outbreak of the Civil War. Although initially reviewed by the abolitionist press and fairly well distributed, the book soon faded into obscurity, only to be resurrected with the mid-twentieth century revival of interest in African American women writers. Jacobs continued her abolitionist efforts during the war and wrote occasionally for the abolitionist press. After the war, she worked during Reconstruction in the South.

Jacobs' autobiography stands among thousands of other written and oral slave testimonies and shares with many of them the themes of bondage, suffering, self-definition, self-assertion, and escape to freedom. In *Incidents in the Life of a Slave Girl*, Jacobs speaks her own life in her own voice. Prior to the appearance of slave narrative, the black abolitionist press, and the first black-authored fiction, African American experience was most often portrayed in literature as an objectified "problem" by white writers. In her autobiography, Jacobs takes the subjective stance of a black woman defining her own experience from a viewpoint deeply rooted in the black slave community. In doing so, she poses a sophisticated and fundamental challenge to white slaveholding American culture.

Bibliography
Andrews, William L. *To Tell a Free Story: The First Century of Afro-American Autobiography, 1760-1865*. Urbana: University of Illinois Press, 1986. A valuable exploration of African American autobiography and slave narrative. Includes a long section on *Incidents in the Life of a Slave Girl* that places Jacobs' work in relation to other African American autobiography.
Foster, Frances Smith. *Witnessing Slavery: The Development of Ante-bellum Slave Narratives*. Westport, Conn.: Greenwood Press, 1979. A useful history of the development of the slave-narrative genre.
Harding, Vincent. *There Is a River: The Black Struggle for Freedom in America*. New York: Vintage Books, 1983. A passionate, scholarly, and detailed study of early African American history (to 1865). Excellent source for understanding *Incidents in the Life of a Slave Girl* in the broader context of antebellum black activism. Includes an excellent bibliography and thorough documentation.
Jacobs, Harriet. *Incidents in the Life of a Slave Girl*. Edited by L. Maria Child and Jean Fagan Yellin. Cambridge, Mass.: Harvard University Press, 1987. An excellent source for several reasons. Yellin provides a substantive historical and analytical introduction to the text, with an interesting feminist critique. She has extensively documented the historical facts, chronology, and personages in *Incidents in the Life of a Slave Girl* and provides samples of Jacobs' correspondence and photographs.
Williams, Kenny J. *They Also Spoke: An Essay on Negro Literature in America, 1787-1930*. Nashville, Tenn.: Townsend Press, 1970. Chapter 3 discusses the structure of the slave narrative.

Sharon Carson

INFANTS OF THE SPRING

Author: Wallace Thurman (1902-1934)
Type of work: Novel
Type of plot: Satire
Time of plot: The mid-1920's
Locale: Harlem, New York
First published: 1932

> *Principal characters:*
> RAYMOND TAYLOR, the protagonist, a young black writer
> PAUL ARBIAN, a writer and painter, one of the most daring
>   characters in the novel
> STEPHEN JORGENSON, a student from Copenhagen, for a short
>   while a roommate to Raymond
> SAMUEL CARTER, another white character, a liberal missionary
>   with a goal of "saving" black people
> EUSTACE SAVOY, a would-be classical singer who disavows all
>   interest in Negro spirituals
> PELHAM GAYLORD (GEORGE JONES), a would-be portrait artist
> EUPHORIA BLAKE, the owner of "Niggeratti Manor," where many
>   of the characters live
> LUCILLE, Raymond's confidante and sometimes girlfriend

The Novel

Infants of the Spring is a satire of the temper and of the major and minor figures of the Harlem Renaissance. As such, the novel details a number of artists and their struggles to be faithful to their artistic visions, along with their knowledge that what they produce has consequences for African Americans as a group. Efforts to maintain artistic integrity while promoting social causes produce individuals who are often culturally confused and display divided loyalties.

The characters who live at Niggeratti Manor, a fictional Harlem brownstone that has a real-life counterpart, are mainly younger artists trying to arrive on the literary, artistic, and music scenes. Many of them perceive a mission to produce a counter-movement to the ideology advocated by the Harlem Renaissance's more notable and older members.

Raymond Taylor, the central consciousness, is one of the manor's more talented writers and offers a running commentary on action at the manor. The plot of the novel moves forward when Raymond meets Stephen Jorgenson, a graduate student from Copenhagen, Denmark, who has come to New York to study for a Ph.D. at Columbia University.

Raymond and Stephen become instant friends. When they become roommates, the two are constantly together, so that when Raymond comments on what is happening at the manor, he and Stephen spend long hours discussing it. Moreover, Stephen is initially fascinated with black people, their culture, and their struggles for racial equality and artistic integrity. Soon, though, Stephen's Scandinavian upbringing, coupled with an interest in Raymond that he cannot explain, causes him to judge the residents of the manor. He tires of their drunken escapades, their attacks on the missionary Samuel Carter, and their inability to get anything done. His talks with Raymond become tinctured with a veiled acidity that sours their relationship. Before this rupture in their friendship, a number of events take place at the manor that move the plot forward and showcase the odd cast of residents.

Paul Arbian constantly tries to shock people with overt discussion of his bisexual nature. He even brings to one of the parties a young man who, he promises, will disrobe for the crowd at a designated time.

Eustace Savoy, in his failure to accept his black musical heritage of Negro spirituals, disgusts Raymond, Stephen, Paul, and others. Most believe that his hatred of his culture and his desire to express European classical music is a symptom of what is wrong with the ideology of the leaders of the Harlem Renaissance.

Pelham Gaylord, who has little talent as a portrait artist, is arrested for raping a teenage girl who lives on the third floor of the manor with her mother. His arrest brings a certain amount of scandal to the manor that Dr. Parkes (Thurman's satirical treatment of Alain Locke) thinks is detrimental to what the older generation of black leaders has been trying to accomplish.

Dr. Parkes's control over the Harlem Renaissance's acceptable forms of creative expression is captured in a scene at the manor. Several recognized artists join the manor's usual crew for a "distinguished salon," with Dr. Parkes presiding. Dr. Parkes comments that African Americans' future depends on what these artists create and how they carry themselves. Much dissenting discussion ensues. This and other similar events spell the demise of Niggeratti Manor, and it is not long before Euphoria Blake, the landlord, gives all the artists eviction notices. She concedes that her experiment has failed.

At the novel's end, most of the manor residents have retreated from their earlier lofty and unrealistic goals of creating art that makes a difference. Paul Arbian, in his final effort to both shock and to create something new, commits suicide, with the pages of an experimental novel he has written all around his body. Only Raymond seems destined to create the kind of work the others had wanted to.

The Characters

As a satirist, Thurman has some help in his creation of characters, for many of them follow closely the known traits of their real counterparts. This is especially true in his depiction of major players of the Harlem Renaissance who are only minor characters in *Infants of the Spring*. During the scene in which Dr. Parkes presides over his "distinguished salon," numerous artists are presented, and each conveys a sense of the person on which he or she is modeled.

Sweetie May Carr (Zora Neale Hurston) is a short-story writer who, the narrator

records, is known more for her outrageous and ribald behavior than for any significant literary production. She is depicted as acting in the manner preferred by her
patrons—she is primitive and agreeable, and she tells earthy "darky" stories as a
way to dupe her patrons out of money.

Tony Crews (Langston Hughes) is already a standout of the movement, having had
two volumes of poetry published. White critics loved his work. Most black critics
did not, because of his honest treatment of black urban life that included such subject matter as gambling, prostitution, and rent parties. He is quiet, always smiles,
and maintains a sense of mystery.

DeWitt Clinton (Countée Cullen), already praised by the older black leaders of
the Harlem Renaissance as the poet to emulate, basically took black themes and
used traditional Romantic poetic forms to express them. When he arrives at the
salon, he is accompanied by his ever-faithful male companion.

The major characters of the novel demonstrate Thurman's ability, within satire, to
create original fictional people. Most are highly individualized. Some, including
Paul, had never appeared in African American literature before this novel.

Raymond, as the novel's protagonist and central consciousness, is the most fully
realized of all the characters, and he, like other characters, shares an affinity with a
real-life personage of the Harlem Renaissance, namely Wallace Thurman. Raymond
develops as a character through Thurman's use of the third-person omniscient point
of view and through the abundance of dialogue that helps to sustain the novel's
structure. Quite simply, Thurman's characters talk a lot.

Raymond is variously portrayed as moody, impatient, a complainer, a literary
snob (he thinks André Gide and Thomas Mann are the only living writers of any real
merit), secretive, a first-class bohemian, and a conservative, a man not in control of
his feelings but still deeply reserved. This duality extends to other areas of his life.
He has yet to develop a satisfying heterosexual relationship with Lucille, his girlfriend. They talk, have dinner, and go to films, but they are not intimate with one
another. He has made it clear to Lucille that he does not want their relationship to
move to that level, yet he is jealous when she tires of his antics and begins to date
Bull, a man who will treat her as a woman.

When his friendship develops with Stephen, he is aware of how meaningful it is,
but he does not consider an analysis of it that might suggest all the reasons why he
and Stephen are so compatible. Stephen, however, has considered the possibility that
he is in love with Raymond. Lack of encouragement from Raymond is as much a
reason for his departure from the manor as is his discontent with the other residents.

Raymond fares better in his analysis of the arts movement itself, with its rigid
proscriptions for artists. Raymond is not sure if he can or should create art that is
meant to improve the social conditions of African Americans. He is not sure if his
art is to be political or aesthetic, and like Thurman, he alternates between the two,
perhaps favoring the "art for art's sake" ideology.

Paul, on the other hand, seems less concerned with what others might think of his
paintings and drawings, even though he is always demanding an audience. Rather

than spending much effort analyzing what he might do, Paul does. He is always working, even if he is drunk. He, more than any of the other characters, directly and consistently challenges Dr. Parkes's way of thinking. Some of Paul's characterization, and how he creates his art, relates to his sense of himself as the "other." In acknowledging his bisexuality, Paul achieves a freedom that both assists him in his development as an artist and defeats him. His kind of freedom has few outlets in Harlem of the 1920's. His need for attention and his final creation, his own death, capture his alienation and his uniqueness.

Themes and Meanings

Infants of the Spring is Thurman's bold attempt to invigorate the Harlem Renaissance with new vision and new energy. As a satirist, his task is to make clear what needs to change and why it is wrong. In his creation of the artists who live at Niggeratti Manor, he presents their frustrations with the limits of the movement and criticizes their own lack of talent or vision to see alternatives. He creates characters and situations that demand recognition by the movement's leaders.

Dr. Parkes and Eustace Savoy personify what is wrong with the Harlem Renaissance. Dr. Parkes and his importance in securing patrons, publishing contracts, auditions, and exhibitions for the younger artists cannot be overlooked. He has made a career of guaranteeing to white people of affluence and influence that if they support black art, that art will not be inflammatory against them, will not disrupt the status quo, and will show that black artists can create in the genres peculiar to America's European traditions. Those black artists who have made reputations for themselves have usually fulfilled Dr. Parkes's expectations of them.

Eustace Savoy is one artist who would like to follow in that tradition. He abhors anything black and thinks that Negro spirituals are beneath him. Instead, he wants to be a classical singer. When Raymond and Paul criticize him, they do so knowing that they also struggle to keep from selling out.

Finding alternative visions is extremely difficult when there are no models. This idea is captured in Raymond's struggle to write his novel. How can he create art, as a black man, when society as a whole, as announced by what the white patrons want from black artists and what black leaders want from black artists, has put him into a pigeonhole and tries with all its might to keep him there?

His struggles to extricate himself from a cultural prison are seen in his relationship with Stephen, a friendship that transcends most societal scripts for black and white interaction, and in his discussions at the manor with other artists. What come from the discussions are new ways of envisioning artistic expression, but with those come the price the individual artist must pay for such expression. Even more important, Thurman suggests that only a great artist has a chance of overcoming cultural hegemony. This idea is presented through the large number of artists at the manor who, by the novel's end, have been defeated in one way or another. Eustace is carted off to a mental hospital. Pelham is in jail. Bull has disappeared. Aline has opted to pass for white. Paul is dead.

Only Raymond, who follows his artistic integrity and who has the talent to realize it, remains as a witness to the Niggeratti Manor experiment. Through his own writing, he can rectify, if in only a small way, the errors of those who charted the limited direction for the expression of black artists. With such an ending, *Infants of the Spring* is a harbinger of the demise of the Harlem Renaissance.

Critical Context

Thurman's second novel, *Infants of the Spring*, is part of a body of African American literature, written during the Harlem Renaissance and after, that is as critical of black people as it is of the conditions that black people struggle against. Like his contemporaries Richard Bruce Nugent, Aaron Douglas, Nella Larsen, and Langston Hughes, for example, Thurman often turned his critical eye on black leaders and black middle-class society.

Thurman's attempts to offer alternatives for black artists, especially the younger ones who had something new to say, are contained in *Fire!!*, a literary journal he founded and edited, and *Harlem*, a more general and less bold periodical. Furthermore, in his first novel, *The Blacker the Berry* (1929), he castigated the black middle-class community for its negative treatment of darker-complexioned African Americans and its adherence to white middle-class values that often had little to recommend them.

Thurman's criticism of the leaders of the Harlem Renaissance makes its most significant argument by exposing the ways in which the movement prevented younger artists from doing their work. He notes a contradiction when leaders such as Dr. Parkes (Alain Locke) insist that the movement intends to bring freedom and equality to black people but who then block the avenues through which artists might find access to an audience. Artists who challenge authority have little place to turn and no freedom to express creativity. This is disturbing to Thurman. His exposé of the temper of the cultural renaissance of the 1920's is his resistance to cultural authority.

Most initial reviewers of *Infants of the Spring* either liked it or hated it. Those who applauded it thought Thurman captured a reality that was lacking in other works of the period. Those who despised it thought it was wrong of him to present dissension among black artists and leaders to the general public.

Infants of the Spring is a faithful account of one of the twentieth century's most productive times for black artists and an account of the movement's effects on some artists who wanted to be different.

Bibliography

De Jongh, James. *Vicious Modernism: Black Harlem and the Literary Imagination.* Cambridge, England: Cambridge University Press, 1990. Examines major historical and literary events that made Harlem a culture capital. Suggests that Harlem as a cultural center is the main theme in *Infants of the Spring.*
Gayle, Addison, Jr. *The Way of the New World: The Black Novel in America.* Garden

City, N.Y.: Anchor Press, 1976. General overview of the development of the African American novel. Sees Thurman as an important dissenter among writers of the 1920's and 1930's.

Lewis, David Levering. *When Harlem Was in Vogue.* New York: Oxford University Press, 1989. Good readable general discussion of the contexts and people that made the Harlem Renaissance so important to black culture. Significant discussion of Wallace Thurman.

Perkins, Huel D. "Wallace Thurman, Renaissance 'Renegade'?" *Black World* 25 (February, 1976): 29-35. Sees Thurman as an instigator of new thought and direction during the 1920's.

West, Dorothy. "Elephant's Dance, a Memoir of Wallace Thurman." *Black World* 20 (November, 1970): 77-85. A reflection on who Wallace Thurman was, by a woman who was a part of the Harlem Renaissance.

Charles P. Toombs

THE INTERESTING NARRATIVE OF THE LIFE OF OLAUDAH EQUIANO, OR GUSTAVUS VASSA, THE AFRICAN

Author: Olaudah Equiano (1745-1797)
Type of work: Autobiography/slave narrative
Time of work: c. 1750-1789
Locale: West Africa, Virginia, and the Atlantic Ocean
First published: 1789

Principal personages:
OLAUDAH EQUIANO, an African kidnapped into slavery
RICHARD BAKER, a fifteen-year-old American sailor
DANIEL QUEEN, a well-educated sailor about forty years of age
THOMAS FARMER, a benevolent English captain

Form and Content

The Interesting Narrative of the Life of Olaudah Equiano, or Gustavus Vassa, the African is considered the first major slave autobiography in American literature. It served as the prototype for the numerous fugitive slave narratives used in the fight against slavery by the abolitionist groups during the period prior to the Civil War.

In the mid-1750's in West Africa, the eleven-year-old Olaudah Equiano and his sister are kidnapped and sold into bondage. After serving for a short time as a slave in Africa and being separated from his sister, he is purchased by European slave dealers. Equiano undergoes the worst terrors of the Atlantic crossing known as the Middle Passage, an experience shared by countless Africans tightly packed in slave ships sailing to the New World and to a life of cruel servitude.

The slave ship takes Equiano to Barbados, where he is put up for sale. He is not purchased there, however, and soon the frightened and bewildered youth is sent to Virginia. Eventually, a British Royal Navy captain purchases Equiano and puts him aboard a trading vessel.

Equiano is called Gustavus Vassa, the name of a Swedish freedom fighter, and the young slave spends the next ten years working on various ships plying the Atlantic between England and the Americas. Thus, he is spared a crueler existence on a Caribbean or an American colonial plantation. He is befriended by two sailors, Richard Baker and Daniel Queen, who introduce him to religion and reading. Queen provides fatherly instruction and arouses Equiano's desire for freedom. Of the several captains Equiano must serve, he becomes closest to Thomas Farmer, and it is Farmer who urges Equiano's master to allow the young slave to purchase his freedom.

Because of his enterprising activities, Equiano saves enough money to buy his liberty on July 10, 1766. Thereafter, he works as a free man on commercial vessels and at times sails on scientific expeditions to regions in the Arctic and in Central America. He also becomes a Christian convert and learns how to read and write.

Finally, he settles in England, where he becomes involved in the controversial and disastrous plan to transport poor black men and women to the African colony of Sierra Leone. In the late 1780's, the crusade to abolish the slave trade begins in Great Britain, and Equiano decides to write his two-volume autobiography, a harsh indictment of the institution of slavery.

Analysis

The long personal story of Olaudah Equiano established the slave-narrative genre in literature. Equiano takes the form of the spiritual autobiography that Saint Augustine used in his fifth century religious conversion work *Confessiones* (c. 400; *Confessions*) and adds to its pattern a new dimension—that of social protest. The spiritual conversion account follows a three-part structure in describing a life of sin, a conversion experience, and the emergence of a new religious identity. Equiano relates his spiritual undertaking in that manner, but he also parallels his battle to free himself from a life of sin with his struggle to escape from the physical bonds of slavery.

The prose style of *The Life of Olaudah Equiano* alternates between a florid, lofty tone typical of many eighteenth century works and a plain and graphic manner of writing. The latter style is the one Equiano uses effectively to describe his personal experiences and dangerous adventures.

Equiano presents himself in the early part of his narrative as a picaresque figure who is both fearful of and awe-stricken by the technical marvels of the white world. He allows himself to enter into the cultural life of the West, but he never becomes blind to the defects of that world. His personal experience with slavery and his fond, vivid memories of his African homeland impel him to reveal the truth about the evils of human bondage and to give an accurate account of the laws, religion, and customs of the African society.

In a remarkable manner, Equiano also presents himself in his work as an enterprising and heroic character. He relates how he labors hard after his slave duties are done so that he can save funds to buy his freedom. This act, of course, is important to Equiano, and he shows this by including his manumission paper in the middle portion of his autobiography. From that point on, he writes about his life in a more exuberant and authoritative tone. He confidently describes how he takes on many different and challenging roles until he finds the one in which he feels he can do the most good—that of a fighter in the struggle against slavery.

Much of Equiano's autobiography is based on his extensive reading in the travel and antislavery literature of his day. He relies on the popular primitivistic works of the travel writers who paint Edenic or idealistic pictures of remote areas of the globe. Equiano uses these descriptions of Africa and mixes them with his own recollections of the country of his youth. Despite his reliance on what he reads, he is always careful to present the true condition of the Africans, many of whom he sees as suffering under the corrupting influences of the white world's technology and materialistic practices. Thus, he describes how Europeans introduce instruments of warfare on the African continent while they stir up animosities and greed to implement their trafficking in human cargo.

Equiano's work is the first slave narrative that details the horrors of the slave-ship crossing from Africa to the West Indies. This terrible ordeal is indelibly impressed upon the mind of the young slave, who witnesses men and women packed in the suffocating hold of the ship and experiencing filth, stench, disease, tortures, sexual abuse, and near-starvation. In a reversal of Western notions about native savages, Equiano views the white slavetraders as cannibals and depicts his fears of being eaten by these strange-looking, longhaired, red-faced dealers in human flesh.

As he writes his narrative, Equiano attempts to erase several misconceptions that his white readers possess about black men and women. The best way he believes he can accomplish this is by demonstrating through the account of his life that a black person is as much a human being as a white person. Thus, Equiano's life achievements stand for the abilities of all blacks to fulfill themselves as members of the human race if they are allowed their physical and spiritual freedoms. He stresses through his own experiences that these dual freedoms are necessary for the attainment of a person's proper role in life. Equiano shows that slavery degrades him but that his freedom permits him to succeed in many areas in which he can employ his talents and industrious habits. He strongly proves his point by depicting himself surmounting all types of obstacles, from his youthful slave days to his successful mature years, through much hard work and dedication. In this manner, he resembles his contemporary Benjamin Franklin, who climbed from rags to riches by means of the American free-enterprise spirit of self-reliance, diligent work, and frugal practice.

Critical Context

When Olaudah Equiano's two-volume autobiography was published in 1789 in Great Britain, it was presented to members of Parliament and leaders of the antiabolitionist movement. The great founder of Methodism, John Wesley, had it read to him on his deathbed. Many of the important personages in England were listed as subscribers to the former slave's work, which is believed to have played a major part in the eventual abolition of the British slave trade. The remarkable narrative was published in the United States in 1791 and soon became a popular autobiography on both sides of the Atlantic. It was translated into several European languages and ran through many editions until well into the nineteenth century.

Equiano's work is the prototype of the slave narrative, which became the chief instrument of the antislavery crusade. The former slave created a new literary genre when he combined the form of the spiritual autobiography with the story of the slave's escape from bondage. This pattern can be observed in the fugitive-slave works of the nineteenth century. The most notable are *Narrative of the Life of Frederick Douglass, an American Slave* (1845) and Harriet Ann Jacobs' *Incidents in the Life of a Slave Girl* (1861). Influences of the design can be seen also in Harriet Beecher Stowe's fictional slave book *Uncle Tom's Cabin* (1852) and in many nonfiction and fiction works of twentieth century literature such as Richard Wright's *Black Boy* (1945), *The Autobiography of Malcolm X* (1965), and Toni Morrison's *Beloved* (1987).

Critics see Equiano's narrative as following not only a spiritual but also a secular pattern of autobiographical writing. The secular manner was popularized by Benjamin Franklin's *Autobiography* (1791), in which the emphasis is on character development and material success. In like manner, Equiano is careful to make his point that a black person can develop and become materially successful through personal enterprise. Equiano, however, also stresses the fact that spiritual, personal, or material achievement can only be realized when a man or woman is given the freedom to accomplish all of this.

Bibliography

Andrews, William L. "Voices of the First Fifty Years, 1760-1810." In *To Tell a Free Story: The First Century of Afro-American Autobiography, 1760-1865.* Urbana: University of Illinois Press, 1986. Explains how Equiano's unique slave experience permitted him to lead a bicultural life as a person who belonged to two worlds. Because Equiano understood the realities of both the Western and African ways of life, he was able to force the reader to examine cultural values concerning race and morals.

Costanzo, Angelo. "The Spiritual Autobiography and Slave Narrative of Olaudah Equiano." In *Surprizing Narrative: Olaudah Equiano and the Beginnings of Black Autobiography.* Westport, Conn.: Greenwood Press, 1987. Analyzes the text's position in the tradition of spiritual and secular autobiographical writing. Demonstrates how Equiano employs many of the literary devices that autobiographers use, such as the creation of a strong character type, the before-and-after contrast of an individual's life, and the journey motif, which depicts a person undergoing experiences on the road from innocence to maturity.

Edwards, Paul. "Three West African Writers of the 1780's." In *The Slave's Narrative*, edited by Charles T. Davis and Henry Louis Gates, Jr. New York: Oxford University Press, 1985. Discusses the importance and popularity of Equiano's autobiography and explains the difficulties that the former slave encountered in his experiences with the white society. Describes how even a few members of the British abolitionist group revealed their racist attitudes toward Equiano when he assumed a significant position in the political struggle to end the slave trade.

Foster, Frances Smith. *Witnessing Slavery: The Development of Ante-bellum Slave Narratives.* Westport, Conn.: Greenwood Press, 1979. A useful study of the development of the slave-narrative genre.

Williams, Kenny J. *They Also Spoke: An Essay on Negro Literature in America, 1787-1930.* Nashville, Tenn.: Townsend Press, 1970. A history of African American literature from Equiano's time through the Harlem Renaissance.

Angelo Costanzo

INVISIBLE MAN

Author: Ralph Ellison (1914-   )
Type of work: Novel
Type of plot: Social criticism
Time of plot: The 1940's and early 1950's
Locale: The Deep South and New York City
First published: 1952

Principal characters:
THE NARRATOR, the canny, unnamed voice of the story
DR. A. HERBERT BLEDSOE, president of the college the narrator attends
MR. NORTON, a New England financier and college benefactor
BROTHER JACK, the leader of The Brotherhood, a revolutionary group
TOD CLIFTON, a Harlem activist
RAS, THE DESTROYER, a militant Rastafarian

The Novel

Having spoken in the prologue of his need to come out into the light, to surface from a building that has been "rented strictly to whites" and "shut off and forgotten during the nineteenth century," the narrator gives immediate notice that he is telling not a single but a typological, or multiple, story. Everything that has happened to him bears the shadow of prior African American history. He vows, however, that all past "hibernation," all past "invisibility," must now end. It falls to him to "illuminate"—that is, literally and figuratively to write into being—the history that has at once made both him and black America at large so "black and blue" and yet which has been a triumph of human survival and art.

To that end, he steps back into Dixie and into a "Battle Royal," a brawl in which a group of blindfolded black boys fight for the entertainment of whites. The scene gives a crucial point of departure for the novel. In fighting "blind," the boys illustrate an ancestral divide-and-rule tactic of the white South; the boys' reward is money from an electrified rug. Equally, when a sumptuous white stripper dances before the townsmen, an American flag tattooed between her thighs, the ultimate taboo looms temptingly yet impossibly before the black boys. Literally with blood in his throat, the narrator thanks his patrons and leaves, having received a scholarship to a Tuskegee-style college. He thinks, too, of his grandfather's advice, that of a slavery-time veteran of black mimicry, who tells him to "overcome 'em with yeses, undermine 'em with grins, agree 'em to death and destruction"—the words of the trickster as seeming "coon" or "good nigra" whose every act of servility in fact derides his white oppressors. Nor can the narrator be unmindful of a dream in which mountains of paper contain a single, recurrent message: "Keep this Nigger Boy Running."

At the college, he believes himself to be in a black version of an ideal Dixie. His life, however, undergoes a major reversal when he shows Norton, a white philanthropist, the incestuous "fieldnigger" family of the Truebloods, thus reawakening Norton's own sexual hankerings after his recently deceased daughter. In order to find medical help for the overcome Norton, the pair moves on to The Golden Day, a black brothel for army vets, and there, to his greatest discomfort, the narrator recognizes in the patients caricatures of the self-same black bourgeoisie he most aspires to join—doctors, teachers, lawyers, and businessmen. His resulting expulsion from the college, even so, produces more paper promises, in the form of supposed letters of recommendation to likely employers in New York.

These letters, too, prove false, Bledsoe's revenge on a disciple who has strayed from the appointed path. The son of the aptly named Mr. Emerson reveals the deception and guides the narrator to the Liberty Paints factory. Put to work making "Optic White," he inadvertently adds "concentrated remover," as if to insist upon his own blackness within the all-white grid of America. Moved on, he begins work in the factory's paint process section. The machinery explodes, however, and in the factory hospital, he overhears himself being talked about as a likely candidate for lobotomy.

Signing a release, he heads back to Harlem, taking part almost by chance in a spontaneous outcry at an eviction. Immediately, The Brotherhood draws him into its ranks, making him their Harlem spokesman and using him to organize black Manhattan into a political wedge against the ruling order. Yet he also finds himself mythified into a sexual stud by one of the white "sisters." Increasingly, too, he comes up against Ras's fervid black nationalism. Most of all, he is held responsible for the disappearance of Tod Clifton, another activist; the narrator later sees Clifton on a street selling Sambo dolls and witnesses his death at the hands of the police. The narrator's trial by The Brotherhood for conspiracy and "petty individualism" follows immediately, a species of witchhunt and black "black comedy" culminating in the spectacle of Brother Jack's eye falling out of its socket.

The narrator takes to wearing dark glasses, with the result that a variety of Harlemites mistakenly think him to be Bliss Proteus Rinehart, a numbers man, lover, clergyman, and politician. Yet the impersonation, which he comes to relish, proves inadequate when Harlem erupts. In the melee, he encounters a band of looters who plan to burn their tenement slum building; he then meets Ras himself, in the garb of a black Don Quixote, and finally runs into a pillaging, panic-driven crowd that pushes him underground into a nearby manhole. There, he burns all his past "papers," a briefcase full of false promises and impedimenta, prime among them his high school diploma, one of Clifton's dolls, and the slip that contains his Brotherhood name.

So "freed," he endures a massive castration fantasy, and he resolves to abandon his assumed hibernation and to speak—to write down—this "nightmare." If, indeed, his has been the one story, his own, it has throughout also been that of the African American community itself. He even suggests still wider human implications, and in such a spirit, "torturing myself to put it down," he bows out by asking in the epilogue: "Who knows but that, on the lower frequencies, I speak for you?"

The Characters

Foremost in the novel is the unnamed figure of the narrator. His is the voice through which the entire panorama of *Invisible Man* is reflected, a life begun in the Deep South and brought north to Harlem as America's premier black city-within-a-city. In language full of richly oblique double-meanings and nuance, often bluesy and vernacular, he speaks of writing "confession," of implying from within his specific case history that of an altogether wider, historic black America. He also serves as Ellison's own surrogate, from start to finish cannily and reflexively aware of his literary "performance." In both the prologue and the epilogue, and at each turning point in his career—the Battle Royal, the Trueblood "quarters," the Golden Day, the Liberty Paints factory, The Brotherhood, his incarnation as Bliss Proteus Rinehart, the Riot, and his final "hibernation"—he functions as both the subject and the object of his own story, both the teller and, as it were, the tale. Few novels have created a subtler autobiographical self.

The narrator's encounter with Bledsoe, the president of the black college to which he wins his scholarship, introduces the first of a line of characters marked out by splits and self-division. In one guise, Bledsoe plays the perfect Uncle Tom, fawning and grateful, and dancing to the tune of Norton, the white philanthropist from Boston. In another, he plays the black despot, the college's administrative tyrant known to the students as "Old Bucket-head." Ellison so fashions him as a kind of harlequin, one self hidden within the other.

Norton ("Northern," as his name implies) in turn acts out his double game. He can flatter himself that his "destiny" lies in helping black students to become dutiful mechanics and agricultural workers. Yet when he encounters the incestuous True-bloods, impoverished black sharecroppers living in The Quarters, he reveals his own hitherto unacknowledged dark longings for his dead daughter. In the Golden Day brothel, Ellison has the veterans, ironically to a degree, associate him with a roll-call of other white would-be American messiahs, among them John D. Rockefeller and Thomas Jefferson.

The narrator subsequently hears the sermon of the Reverend Homer Barbee on returning Norton to the college. This blind "Homer" preaches a truly parodic Emersonianism, a message of uplift at odds with the life actually led by black Americans within a fearful, racist white Dixie.

On arrival in Harlem, the narrator meets one of the strong female presences in the novel, Mary Rambo. She takes him in, mothers him, and typifies a standard of black community care. He also meets in Brother Jack, the leader of The Brotherhood, another of Ellison's deft caricatures. Patronizingly, Jack appoints the narrator "the new Booker T. Washington," his personal apparatchik. He also speaks the language of "scientific terminology," "materialism," and other quasi-Marxist argot. When he leads a witchhunt against the narrator, only to have his "buttermilk" glass eye pop out, he grotesquely reveals himself for what he is, a half-seeing—or truly one-eyed—Jack.

Tod Clifton, the Harlem youth leader, is the novel's martyr figure. Pledged to fight black joblessness, the color line, and (at the outset) black nationalism, Tod is shown to move increasingly into a fascination with Ras's Caribbean "Africanness." That he ends up peddling Sambo dolls, then shot by a white policeman, and finally the name at the center of the Harlem riot that ensues, points to Ellison's interest in the black activist as both individual and icon.

In this, Tod links perfectly to Ras, The Destroyer, the militant Rastafarian whose politics recall the back-to-Africa nationalism of Marcus Garvey. Yet if Ras derides The Brotherhood as a white-run fraud serviced by deluded black lackeys, he himself becomes a figure derided, an anachronistic Don Quixote replete with horse and shield. The novel thus returns in the aftermath of the riot to the narrator as once more the presiding "character" of *Invisible Man*, each figure he has put before the reader part real, part mythic.

Themes and Meanings

Invisible Man tells an African American *Pilgrim's Progess*, a modern black rite of passage. In part, its story could not be more literal, a South-to-North, Dixie-to-Harlem journey that recalls the movement of black Americans from the postbellum South to the Northern cities. In equal part, however, the story operates as a kind of fantasia, a "dream" history, which serves as both the narrator's past and that of most of his black American cocitizenry. As he looks back from his "border area" manhole, lit with 1,369 light bulbs illegally running on electricity from a company named "Monopolated Light & Power," he declares himself to be "coming out," no longer either invisible nor, as it were, uninscribed and wordless.

In this respect, he offers himself as both an actual man and as a key figure from African American folklore, a "man of substance, of flesh and bone, fiber and liquids" and a Jack-The-Bear whose time of "hibernation" has come to its appointed end. Dipping into blues and jazz, street talk and rap, he promises in the prologue to "irradiate"—that is, in every sense to seek to throw light upon—his own story and that of the larger American black-white encounter. Inevitably, the touchstones involve slavery, Reconstruction, the Jazz Age, the Depression, and interwar Harlem, with hints of the coming 1960's Civil Rights and Black Power movements.

Ellison's narrator in *Invisible Man* ranks as one of the most canny, daring characterizations in modern literature. Every action he takes, every transition in his life, almost everything he says, carries a double or emblematic implication without becoming simply or reductively allegorical. His role in the Battle Royal scene calls up the stereotype of the black male as pugilist, from slave fighter to Joe Louis. As a student, the narrator might well imagine himself as a would-be Booker T. Washington, but his goals are preset and accommodationist. In Trueblood and The Golden Day, he begins to see the "true" image white America holds of him and his community, that of either permanent inferior, sexual spectacle, or, at best, token professional.

In the North, equally, he can work at Liberty Paints, but only in the basement, as a support figure for a white, one-color, America. In The Brotherhood, his party membership again rests less in his own gift than in his willingness to follow the committee's dictates, the white-set political line. If he speaks on women's rights, various of the white sisters fantasize him as a sex fiend, a stud. Even in his role as con man, he betrays his true inner self. Finally, forced by the riot to an "underground" self-reckoning, once again both literal and fantastical, he "sees" and in turn demands to be "seen" in a manner beyond myth or stereotype. His own black selfhood and that of his African American community at last, thereby, emerge on terms undetermined by others.

This same doubling, or multiplication, applies to the other key presences in *Invisible Man*. Bledsoe incarnates a historic past gallery of "separate but equal" leaders, in one face "putt'n on ol' massa" and in another acting the part of mean, self-serving authoritarian. Norton, likewise, imagines himself all good intention, but he is in fact the embodiment of condescending white liberal racism. In the North, Mr. Emerson proves less the reformer implied in his name than another white betrayer. Brother Jack, with his "political science," proves as inadequate to the narrator's needs as Ras, with his "Mama Africa" Rastafarian black nationalism. Tod Clifton, especially, moves from activist to figure of despair, as sad and ultimately self-destructive as the Sambo dolls he takes to peddling in the street. These and lesser figures—from Mary Rambo, a warm, transplanted black Southern woman who befriends the narrator in Harlem, to Dupre, an arsonist-looter—in Ellison's always inventive fashioning serve as both individuals and types, the one always in a teasing imaginative balance with the other.

Undergirding the whole of *Invisible Man* lie Ellison's organizing metaphors and tropes—invisibility and sight, vision and blindness, blackness and white, underground and above—a complex, supremely adroit creation of texture. If H. G. Wells's science fiction classic *The Invisible Man* (1897) hovers behind the title, so, equally, do a host of other eclectic sources from Dante to T. S. Eliot. At the same time, and throughout, Ellison calls upon his intimacy with the treasury of African American music and folklore. Citing, typically, the old Louis Armstrong version of "What Did I Do to Be So Black and Blue?," the narrator, and Ellison behind him, answers with *Invisible Man*, storytelling with all the feints and improvisational riffs—and at the same time all the overall discipline—of a great jazz composition.

Whether read as "confession" or as "history," the book fuses its "high" references with those of black, vernacular culture, verbal and musical, its seriousness of purpose with a winning talent for humor and well-taken irony. Best of all, perhaps, it manages to transpose, brilliantly, inventively, the black and white of America's racial makeup into the black and white of the written page.

Critical Context

Invisible Man quickly gained recognition as a landmark of African American, and American, literature on publication in 1952. Together with James Baldwin's *Go Tell It on the Mountain* (1953), it was taken to signal a black literary renaissance, a breakthrough from supposed "Negro protest fiction" such as Richard Wright's *Native Son* (1940), Ann Petry's *The Street* (1946), or Chester Himes's *Lonely Crusade* (1947). Supported by writers such as Saul Bellow as well as by a host of fellow black writers, Ellison won, among other major prizes, the National Book Award for *Invisible Man.*

There has long been agreement that the novel represents a pinnacle of African American literary achievement, with perhaps Jean Toomer's *Cane* (1923), *Native Son*, *Go Tell It on the Mountain*, and Toni Morrison's *Song of Solomon* (1977) as matching companion pieces. Its rich, startling ventriloquy, command of image, and skillful use of vernacular ensure a rare feast of narration. Such qualities have carried over into Ellison's essay work, too, as collected in *Shadow and Act* (1964) and *Going to the Territory* (1986). Occasionally, well-meant talk has arisen of a "School of Ellison," composed, among others, of such writers as Leon Forrest, Toni Morrison, John Wideman, Clarence Major, Ishmael Reed, and James Alan McPherson. Yet Ellison remains, as always, resolutely his own man, and *Invisible Man* remains the upshot of a uniquely endowed imagination.

Bibliography

Bell, Bernard W. "Myth, Legend, and Ritual in the Novel of the Fifties." In *The Afro-American Novel and Its Tradition.* Amherst: University of Massachusetts Press, 1987. Proposes that *Invisible Man* begins in medias res, moves simultaneously in linear, vertical, and circular directions, and offers, in its use of blues, jazz, wry humor, and a mythic death and rebirth motif, a "paradoxical affirmation and rejection of American values."

Bone, Robert. "Novels of Negro Life and Culture." In *The Negro Novel in America.* New Haven, Conn.: Yale University Press, 1958. Argues that Ellison repudiates naturalism in favor of "postimpressionism." The whole novel is angled to render "blackness visible," a "laughing-to-keep-from-crying" blues, which depicts in its black narrator's story the route out of illusion into understanding.

Byerman, Keith E. "History Against History: A Dialectical Pattern in *Invisible Man.*" In *Fingering the Jagged Grain: Tradition and Form in Recent Black Fiction.* Athens: University of Georgia Press, 1985. Sees *Invisible Man* as "a crucial text for contemporary black fictionists." In each of the novel's major phases, the college, the move to Harlem, and The Brotherhood, Ellison carefully undermines all fixed, cause-and-effect versions of history.

Callahan, John F. "The Historical Frequencies of Ralph Waldo Ellison." In *Chant of Saints: A Gathering of Afro-American Literature, Art, and Scholarship*, edited by Michael S. Harper and Robert S. Stepto. Urbana: University of Illinois Press, 1979. Asserts that *Invisible Man*'s narrator learns the essential conditions of American life to be "diversity, fluidity, complexity, chaos, swiftness of change," anything but one-dimensionality—be it racial or otherwise. History in *Invisible Man* thus means metamorphosis, "many idioms and styles," rather than the received writ of any one version.

Gayle, Addison, Jr. "Of Race and Rage." In *The Way of the New World*. Garden City, N.Y.: Anchor Press, 1975. Suggests this "picturesque novel" to be a four-part history of the "black man's trials and errors in America." Argues that the book's prologue and epilogue add up to a depiction of "soul," "the richness and full- ness" of black heritage. Argues that *Invisible Man*, however, is to be faulted for its final assimilationism, the flaw of believing in "the path of individualism instead of racial unity."

Ostendorf, Berndt. "Ralph Waldo Ellison: Anthropology, Modernism, and Jazz." In *New Essays on "Invisible Man,"* edited by Robert O'Meally. Cambridge, En- gland: Cambridge University Press, 1988. Interprets *Invisible Man* through three frames: as a series of ritual transformations, as a work of modernist tactics, and as a jazz improvisation.

A. Robert Lee

IOLA LEROY
Or, Shadows Uplifted

Author: Frances Ellen Watkins Harper (1825-1911)
Type of work: Novel
Type of plot: Social criticism
Time of plot: The last months of the Civil War through early Reconstruction
Locale: North Carolina, Mississippi, Georgia, Northern states
First published: 1892

> *Principal characters:*
> IOLA LEROY, a mulatto who refuses to pass into white society
> ROBERT JOHNSON, Iola's uncle
> DR. GRESHAM, a white physician
> DR. FRANK LATIMER, a black doctor from the South
> TOM ANDERSON, a heroic former slave
> AUNT LINDA, a matriarch of the black community

The Novel

  Iola Leroy: Or, Shadows Uplifted, a novel set at the close of the Civil War, is a tale of racial uplift loosely developed around the fortunes and misfortunes of the title character. The opening chapters focus on conversations among the slaves and highlight the masking in which they engage around whites to conceal their joy as they follow the progress of the Union Army. Robert Johnson, the most literate of the slaves, provides leadership and counsel as the Union Army approaches and the folk prepare for their lives of freedom. When the army arrives, Robert, Tom Anderson, and many others join in the fight for freedom. After Iola's rescue from slavery, she is assigned to the field hospital as a nurse. Iola refuses Dr. Gresham's proposal that she marry him and move to the North as his white wife.

  Harper follows these chapters with a flashback to nearly twenty years before the war. Iola is the daughter of Eugene Leroy, owner of a large plantation, and Marie Leroy, his former slave. When her father dies of yellow fever, Iola learns that she is black. She is sold into slavery along with her mother. After the war, Iola, in keeping with her sense of duty, opens a school for the freed, later destroyed by fire, and discovers that Robert Johnson is her uncle. They unite forces in their search for lost family members. During their search, they meet with the folk from the former plantations and learn that they are all thriving. Aunt Linda, a former cook, comments on the need for education, temperance, and moral training. All of Robert and Iola's family members are eventually reunited, and with the exception of Iola's brother Harry, who remains in Georgia, they move north to live with Robert.

  Harper uses their time in the North as an opportunity to comment on the racial prejudices existing there. Both Robert and Iola have difficulty finding places to stay, and Iola is fired from her job once it is learned that she is black. It is also in the North that the characters engage in a "conversazione," a forum for presenting key areas of concern among black intellectuals: emigration, patriotism, education of women, and the moral progress of the race. The texts of some of Harper's own speeches are incorporated into these discussions. Iola meets Frank Latimer, a black doctor from the South. They soon develop an attraction for each other and marry. A romance also develops between Harry Leroy and Lucille Delany, a schoolteacher from the South, who have both come north to visit.

At the close of the novel, all the key characters return to the South and settle in the same area where many were once slaves. Dr. Latimer sets up a medical practice, and Iola becomes a Sunday school teacher. Harry and Lucille marry and return to Georgia to head a large school. Robert purchases a large plantation and resells it to his people as small homesteads. Thus, all the major characters devote their lives to the educating, healing, and training of the members of their race; they devote their lives to the "grand and noble purpose" of racial uplift.

The Characters

The protagonist, Iola Leroy, is light-skinned enough to pass as white, but she refuses to do so, choosing instead to devote her life to the improvement of conditions for all African Americans. Iola is the daughter of a Creole plantation owner and one of his former slaves. Iola is sent to school in the North, but when she returns to the family estate, she discovers that her father has died suddenly of yellow fever, that her sister Gracie is near death, and that she and her mother have been reduced to the status of slaves. Iola is rescued from slavery by Union soldiers and becomes a nurse at a field hospital. After the war, Iola and her uncle search for their lost family, which is eventually reunited and moves to the North. Her experiences with discrimination even in the North, however, heighten her awareness of the race problem, and after she marries Frank Latimer, she chooses to return to the South with him to continue the struggle for racial uplift. Her steadfast refusal to pass as white and her devotion to the causes of African Americans are clear indications of the strength of her character.

Robert Johnson, Iola's uncle, emerges as a leader in the novel's first chapter, when, as one of the few literate slaves on the plantation, he provides information about the progress of the war. Robert joins the Union Army and becomes a lieutenant in a "colored company"; like his niece, he refuses to pass as white. Robert is an exceptionally admirable character; after the war, he sells his property and purchases a large North Carolina plantation, which he converts into a community of homesteads for the poor.

Dr. Gresham, the white New England physician with whom Iola works in the field hospital, is a likeable character who helps to illuminate Iola's integrity. He falls in love with Iola and proposes marriage to her on the grounds that she not reveal her race. She rejects the proposal, and when he encounters her again after the war, he accepts her final rejection lovingly and with respect for her fortitude.

Dr. Frank Latimer, an African American doctor from the South who meets Iola in the North, succeeds where Gresham does not. Like Iola, Latimer is offered a life of ease (in his case, by a grandmother) if he will consent to pass for white. He refuses, giving many of the same reasons Iola gives to Gresham when she rejects his proposal. Their shared convictions make them a perfect match, and they marry and work together for the cause of racial uplift.

Tom Anderson is among the first liberated slaves to join the Union Army, and he appeals to the post commander for the release of Iola. Although he lacks the literacy of Robert, Tom is well aware of the events unfolding around him and is eager to serve the cause of freedom. Tom dies as honorably as he has lived, saving a boat filled with Union soldiers by exposing himself to enemy fire.

Aunt Linda, a former cook on the Johnson plantation, becomes the matriarchal leader of the local black community after the war. She furthers the idea of community among the newly freed, chastising those who sell their votes or drink excessively. Her entrepreneurship allows her to purchase property. As a successful woman, she introduces feminist ideas among the folk.

Themes and Meanings

Harper's purpose in writing *Iola Leroy*, as expressed by the title character, was "to do something of lasting service for the race." This purpose manifests itself in the novel's prevailing theme: the imperative of placing racial uplift above all other goals, including passing for white or marrying solely for love or physical attraction. Four of the main characters in the novel are presented with the appealing option of bettering their fortunes by living as white persons, and all refuse to abandon their commitment to the race, voluntarily acknowledging their racial kinship.

Iola decides to identify with her mother's race in her rejection of Dr. Gresham's proposal. She also rejects later opportunities to pass as white when she seeks employment and boarding in the North. Robert Johnson, Iola's uncle, also makes this choice. When Robert escapes to the Union Army, a young officer suggests that he join the regiment as a white man, thereby improving his chances for promotion. Robert, without hesitation, rejects this idea, declaring his intention to remain in the black unit where his leadership is needed. His decision is based on duty rather than personal advantage. Harry Leroy, Iola's brother, having spent part of his life as a white man, exhibits some reluctance to join ranks with his race. He learns of his racial connections and the demise of his family while attending school in Maine. When he declares his intention to enlist in the Union Army, the school principal suggests that he join the white regiment. Yet Harry decides, as did Robert, to link his fortunes with the black race because of his desire to assist in its elevation and to find Iola and his mother. The last character faced with this decision is Frank Latimer, the grandson of a Southern aristocrat, whose mother had been a slave. After he is graduated from medical school, his paternal grandmother offers to better his fortunes if he will forsake his racial heritage. He refuses her offer, explaining his decision later to Iola as one based on duty.

Iola is also an early feminist, expressing the view that the woman who is able to support herself is stronger and happier and makes a better marriage companion than one who cannot. She herself seeks employment shortly after she moves north to live with Robert. This independence also is reflected in her determination to make a significant contribution to the cause of uplift by establishing a school and in her intention to write a book.

The plight of the folk is another theme running through the novel, exemplified particularly through the character of Aunt Linda. Using dialect to signal their presence, Harper portrays the folk as intelligent, if not literate, and fully aware of what needs to be done to correct past ills, but they look to those who have the benefit of education for leadership. It is also primarily through conversations with the folk that the reader learns of the prevalence of hypocritical religious practices.

In addition to using the experiences of various characters to develop themes, Harper uses the narrative device of the "conversazione" and informal gatherings to air contrasting solutions to the "Negro problem"; these solutions range from emigration to moral progress. Commentary addressing these issues appears throughout the novel, establishing and reinforcing its didactic tone.

Critical Context

William Still, in his introduction to the first edition of *Iola Leroy*, admitted his initial concern that Harper would ruin her good reputation by writing on the subject of slavery, but he asserted that after reading the manuscript his fears were allayed. *Iola Leroy*, Harper's first and only novel, was written when she was sixty-seven and had already enjoyed a distinguished career as a poet, essayist, and lecturer. Her decision to write a novel was based on her prevailing drive to do all she could in lasting service for her race. Originally conceived as a book to be used in black Southern Sunday schools, the novel has much broader appeal as an extension of Harper's rhetorical career. She spent much of her early life giving lectures on many of the same issues raised in the novel: abolition, temperance, education, women's rights, and general racial uplift. *Iola Leroy* is important as one of the earliest attempts in African American literature to address this combination of issues in fictional form. One might claim that the novel is essentially a lecture dressed in a thin fictional garment. Harper's purpose never changed, whether she was writing poetry, delivering speeches, or producing fiction. With such a strong didactic agenda, it should surprise no one that *Iola Leroy*'s primary purpose in the context of Harper's life and the prevailing social exigencies was, in Harper's own words, to "awaken in the hearts of our countrymen a stronger sense of justice and a more Christlike humanity in behalf of those whom the fortunes of war threw, homeless, ignorant and poor, upon the threshold of a new era."

Bibliography
Carby, Hazel V. " 'Of Lasting Service for the Race': The Work of Frances Ellen Watkins Harper." In *Reconstructing Womanhood: The Emergence of the Afro-American Woman Novelist.* New York: Oxford University Press, 1987. Discusses

Iola Leroy as a logical extension of Harper's political activism rather than an aberration. The novel can be viewed as a continuation of Harper's lifelong crusade against slavery, racism, and the suppression of black women. An examination of her speeches reveals that all the issues raised in *Iola Leroy* have already been addressed in her earlier speeches and poetry. Thus, the novel should not be evaluated in formal literary terms but in terms that locate it squarely within the political debates of Harper's time.

Christian, Barbara. "Shadows Uplifted." In *Black Women Novelists: The Development of a Tradition, 1892-1976.* Westport, Conn.: Greenwood Press, 1980. Focuses on the contradiction between Harper's public life as a lecturer and the concerns of the novel. After the war, Harper traveled extensively throughout the South, lecturing to and about impoverished black women, yet the novel centers on a refined and educated octoroon who advocates the right of women to work. For most black women, work was necessary for survival. This contradiction could be a consequence of the author's attempt to write a novel that would help to break down the numerous stereotypes associated with black women.

Foster, Frances Smith, ed. *A Brighter Coming Day: A Frances Ellen Watkins Harper Reader.* New York: Feminist Press, 1990. Provides the literary, social, and biographical context out of which *Iola Leroy* and Harper's other writing emerged. Harper's literary canon begins with her poetry and extends to lectures, letters, essays, speeches, and finally a novel. By the end of her career as a writer, she was optimistic that, because of such intellectual activities, the race was experiencing progress.

Washington, Mary Helen. "Uplifting the Women and the Race: The Forerunners— Harper and Hopkins." In *Invented Lives: Narratives of Black Women, 1860-1960.* New York: Doubleday, 1987. Focuses on the pressures under which black women at the turn of the century wrote, as they responded to the prevailing negative images of blacks and women. The characters in the novel are given political rather than emotional or social roles. In all instances, their choices are based on the extent to which those choices enable them to articulate a political position.

Watson, Carole McAlpine. " 'I Have Woven a Story . . .': Uplift and Protest, 1891-1920." In *Prologue: The Novels of Black American Women, 1891-1965.* Westport, Conn.: Greenwood Press, 1985. Identifies *Iola Leroy* as a novel with strong emphasis on the courage, intelligence, and morality of African Americans that exhorts readers to engage in activities designed to improve the conditions of black people. Sees Harper as offering numerous positive images of blacks who unselfishly work for the betterment of their race.

Shirley W. Logan

JAZZ

Author: Toni Morrison (1931-   )
Type of work: Novel
Type of plot: Psychological realism
Time of plot: 1926, with flashbacks to pre-Civil War times
Locale: Harlem, New York, and Virginia
First published: 1992

> *Principal characters:*
> THE NARRATOR, never identified; she sees, hears, and knows
>   everything
> VIOLET TRACE, a woman born in rural Virginia, the third of five
>   children whose mad mother drowned herself in a well and
>   whose father visited the family occasionally
> JOE TRACE, Violet's husband
> DORCAS MANFRED, Joe's girlfriend, whom Joe shoots after he
>   discovers that she has another boyfriend
> ALICE MANFRED, Dorcas' aunt, who reared her
> FELICE, Dorcas' best friend, who becomes part of that
>   "scandalizing threesome on Lenox Avenue" with Joe and
>   Violet three months after Dorcas' death

The Novel

Jazz is an account of both the personal and the historical. While focusing on the lives of Joe and Violet Trace, the novel also provides an account of African American life in the South from the mid-nineteenth century through the Great Migration that brought millions north beginning in the 1870's and continuing in a steady stream into the twentieth century. The story of the Traces' move in 1906 from Virginia to Harlem is part of the African American story.

The novel opens and closes with the puzzling relationship of Joe, Violet, and Felice. The narrator, a strong and critical voice throughout the book, has access to the information readers will need to understand a fifty-year-old man who "fell for an eighteen-year-old girl with one of those deepdown, spooky loves that made him so sad and happy he shot her just to keep the feeling going" and his wife, who cut the dead young girl's face at her funeral. Like the Greek chorus, the neighborhood busybody, or perhaps more accurately the tribal storyteller who must get the story right because she is the only channel of truth and history, the narrator explains not just Joe and Violet, Dorcas, and Felice but the forces that brought them together in Harlem in 1926 and brings all African Americans together as a people. Although not presented in neat chronological order, the novel taken as a whole provides a fairly complete account of the characters' and African Americans' lives. As the narrator observes at the end of the novel, "Busy, they were, busy being original, complicated, changeable—human, I guess you'd say."

Joe and Violet are orphans seeking mothers and love, acceptance, and validation. Violet's life is informed by the suicide of her mother, Rose Dear, after her husband left for a subversive fugitive political life and after her family was turned out by creditors. "Violet never forgot Rose Dear or the place she had thrown herself into— a place so narrow, so dark it was pure, breathing relief to see her stretched in a wooden box." Violet's youth is permeated with Grandmother True Belle's stories of Baltimore and the beautiful blond child, Golden Gray, of her mistress, Miss Vera Louise Gray, and a local slave boy. When handsome Joe Trace falls out of the walnut tree under which she was sleeping and she chooses him, he is a substitute for that golden boy.

Joe Trace is reared by the Williamses, a kind local couple who treated him just like one of their own six children. "That 'like' I guess it was made me ask her," Joe says, "where my real parents were." Mrs. Williams' reply leads to Joe's first remaking of himself: "O honey, they disappeared without a trace. The way I heard it I understood her to mean the 'trace' they disappeared without was me." He thus chooses "Trace" as a surname. He changes again when selected "to be a man," to be taught everything a man needs to survive in the woods and in the world by the best man in the county, the "Hunter's Hunter," Henry LesTroy. He learns well enough to track the elusive woman that Henry intimates is his mother and to track Dorcas across Harlem.

Twenty years in "the City" find Violet silent and Joe longing to rediscover the feeling of young love. Although their circumstances have improved since stepping off the Southern Sky train that took them north in 1906, Joe moving from night-shift fish cleaner to hotel waiter to door-to-door cosmetics salesman and Violet progressing from domestic work to "unlicensed" beautician, their relationship disintegrates: "they were still a couple but barely speaking to each other." Violet says, "Before I came North I made sense and so did the world." The narrator warns that "the streets will confuse you, teach you or break your head" because the City "makes you do what it wants, go where the laid-out roads say to. . . . You can't get off the track a City lays for you." The track Violet finds herself on takes her at the age of forty to a "mother-hunger" that makes her almost steal a child, hold dolls at night rather than her husband, and feel like such a divided self that one of those Violets cuts Dorcas' dead face with a butcher knife hidden in a birdcage.

The City leads Joe only one place, as the narrator notes: "you always end up back where you started: hungry for the one thing everybody loses—young loving." Having spotted Dorcas at the drugstore and again at her aunt's apartment, Joe chooses her, an opportunity he has never had before. With her, he can talk about things— Vesper County, his mother, his changing selves—that he never told anyone. As the narrator notes, "That girl had been his necessary thing for three months of nights" until she left him for young men, dancing, jazz, and gin. He did not mean to kill her, but he needed to hold on to the "alive love" he felt for her. Such a love for Violet has faded and scabbed over. It is gone until Felice enters their apartment looking for the opal ring she had lent Dorcas the night of her murder. Her presence ironically renews the Traces' marriage. As the narrator observes: "It's nice when grown people whisper to each other under the covers," when the "body is the vehicle, not the point." Joe has killed Dorcas; Violet has killed those warring selves inside her, along with the image of Golden Gray that caused her so much self-hatred and disappointment. When Felice asks what remains, Violet responds, "Me." Joe, Violet, and Felice are all at peace with themselves and comfortable once again in the City.

The Characters

Morrison chose to present the story of Joe, Violet, and the others through a narrator who is seemingly all-knowing though by no means objective. She is in everybody's business not simply because she is nosy or wants to interfere but because she needs to understand people, their past, their circumstances, and their relationships. She tries to reveal the truth. She will also admit when she has had to imagine the truth, when she has fallen short in presenting it, and when she has failed. An individual's truth is not easily discernible, and it is not apparent all at once. It also contradicts. Therefore, the narrator's explanation of the events dominating the lives of a few people on Harlem's Lenox Avenue during the first three months of 1926 requires an account of recent history, music, magazines, newspapers, and hairstyles.

Although Joe Trace is a murderer, he is drawn sympathetically. The neighborhood women trust the door-to-door cosmetics salesman to come into their homes, to escort them home at night, and to warn the young ones of city dangers. He is their neighbor, their friend. Everyone knows that Joe killed Dorcas, but because no one saw him do it, because Dorcas' aunt, Alice Manfred, knows the futility of calling white policemen to investigate a black girl's murder, and because Joe has suffered so, he goes unprosecuted. Joe Trace does not conform to the violent urban stereotype. His strong back and keen knowledge of nature helped him survive in rural Virginia and gave him and his wife a poor but happy life. In coming to the City, Joe climbed the rungs of the ladder available to African American men. His desire to regain young loving and to fill the void left by his mother, who refused to touch his hand in the Vesper County woods, and by his silent wife, causes him to lose control of himself and his life.

Understanding Violet is just as difficult. The fifty-year-old woman the reader sees at the novel's beginning, one who drinks malteds laced with Dr. Dee's Nerve and Flesh Builder in an attempt to regain her long-lost hips and who is called "Violent" for having cut a dead girl's face, is fragile, fragmented, and silent. She is a woman who wonders what exactly Joe found in Dorcas and hopes to discover it by studying the girl's photograph, placed prominently on the apartment mantelpiece. The narrator observes that Violet was not always "cracked" or divided. "I call them cracks because that is what they were. Not openings or breaks, but dark fissures in the globe light of the day" that led her to almost steal a child, to sit down in the middle of the street for no reason, and to say totally inappropriate things. She had once been strong enough to drive a team of horses, strong enough to claim Joe Trace when he fell out of a walnut tree. After Dorcas' death and Joe's sorrow, after she released her parrot that said "I love you," and after "*that* Violet" had cut Dorcas' face, she demands from Alice Manfred, "Tell me something real. Don't say I'm grown and ought to know. I don't. I'm fifty and I don't know nothing." Morrison provides glimpses of that orphaned girl haunted by her suicidal mother. She leaves the reader with a woman who finds comfort under the covers with her husband of all those years, delighting in her new parakeet and the regular visits of a young girl.

Dorcas, the murder victim, does not appear as victimized as one might expect. Although Violet wanted to love her, she proclaims her "ugly inside and out." Felice denies that characterization but admits that "she used people. . . . Dorcas was cold." Even the narrator, who can empathize with Dorcas' need to explore, does not like her: "I always believed that girl was a pack of lies." Dorcas loves an old man to appease her own sexual desires and leaves him for the same reason. She lets herself die with the feel of a young man's arms around her, the taste of sweet liquor in her mouth, and the sound of jazz in her ears.

Morrison's narrator does not know everything. What she has not observed, she invents: the thoughts and feelings of characters, and events and people from their past. She is also self-corrective at times. When she thinks she has not portrayed Golden Gray as justly as she should, she admits it: "What was I thinking of? How could I have imagined him so poorly?" Taking a deep breath, she begins again. "Now I have to think this through, carefully, even though I may be doomed to another misunderstanding. I have to do it and not break down." What she produces, for all her self-censure, is a comprehensive portrait of intriguing people who surprise even her: "It never occurred to me that they were thinking other thoughts, feeling other feelings, putting their lives together in ways I never dreamed of." She gives the truth.

Themes and Meanings

For African Americans to survive, first, and then to thrive, Morrison insists, they must be at once creative and conforming, innovative and traditional. They must build upon what came before while imagining a new way. The jazz that emanates from the streets of Harlem and is the novel's recurring motif embodies such qualities.

Joe Trace, while wary of the rhythms he hears in doorways and from the rooftops, uncertain of what to make of the "sooty" guitar music played by the blind twins that could be contributing to Dorcas' restlessness, knows what saved his forbears: "Those old people, they knew it all. . . . [B]ack then, back there, if you was or claimed to be colored, you had to be new and stay the same every day the sun rose and every night it dropped. And let me tell you, baby, in those days it was more than a state of mind." Being new and remaining the same is exactly what jazz is about. The riffs are newly invented with each performer and performance, but the underlying beat can be traced way back and is the common force holding a culture together.

Alice Manfred fears the power of such music. The drumbeat she hears on Fifth Avenue in 1917, as frozen black faces march past her and her young niece, draws her in, providing her with "a rope cast for rescue" from the alienation and distance from everyone that she has felt since her husband left her for another woman many years ago. That music, like that of the church, sustains, but jazz is dangerous, smells of flesh, and reminds her of "the life below the sash." She believed the ministers and editorialists who claimed "it wasn't real music—just colored folks' stuff: harmful, certainly; embarrassing, of course; but not real, not serious." Such music lures Dorcas to Joe Trace, nightclubs, parties, young men, and death. From such powerful forces, Alice eventually flees.

The primary significance of jazz is the strength it provides and the positive force it represents. The narrator ends the novel with an affirmation of Joe and Violet Trace, insisting that "they are real. Sharply in focus and clicking." This "clicking" can be heard in "the sound of snapping fingers under the sycamores lining the streets." It is in the ankles and hips of young girls, in "the eyes of the old men who watch these girls, and the young ones who hold them up." It is in response to the records playing on Victrolas.

The characters in Morrison's *Jazz* are all listening for that clicking. They sense an absence and try to fill it by searching for mothers, fathers, young love, love lost along the way, or children they thought they did not want. When some finally hear the clicking in a parade drumbeat or sitting in windowsills fingering horns, life does not change dramatically. It is simply real. A fifty-year-old couple shares dinner and a warm bed, entertaining a young girl as they all enjoy her latest jazz recording. A new parakeet will not sing until they take it to the roof "where the wind blew and so did the musicians in shirts billowing out behind them. From then on the bird was a pleasure to itself and to them."

Critical Context

Jazz is Toni Morrison's sixth novel. *The Nation*'s John Leonard has remarked, "Novel by novel, Toni Morrison reimagines the lost history of her people, their love and work and nightmare passage and redemptive music." Having won the 1988 Pulitzer Prize for *Beloved*, Morrison was not content to repeat a successful formula; rather, she continued to take stylistic risks. Although some critics complained that Morrison's experimentation in *Jazz* had resulted in characters who are more distant and less empathetic than those in her previous works, the book's reception was broadly favorable. Morrison's receipt of the 1993 Nobel Prize in Literature provided dramatic proof that her evolving approach was continuing to touch readers worldwide.

Bibliography

Gates, David. "American Means Black, Too." *Newsweek* 119 (April 27, 1992): 66. A review of *Jazz* that maintains that the novel is not just about the story and characters but also about "the process of its own creation."

Leonard, John. "Her Soul's High Song." *The Nation* 254 (May 25, 1992): 706-714. A thorough critical examination of all of Morrison's novels. Excellent short survey of her works, characters, and key themes.

McDowell, Deborah A. "Harlem Nocturne." *The Women's Review of Books* 9 (June, 1992): 1, 3-4. Maintains that Morrison intends to animate "the dry and disconnected bones of the black historical past." Sees a direct connection between *Jazz* and *Beloved*, especially between characters.

Miller, Jane. "New Romance." *London Review of Books*, May 14, 1992, 12. Insists that "*Jazz* is a love story, indeed a romance" of older women and African American culture.

O'Brien, Edna. "*Jazz.*" *The New York Times Book Review*, April 5, 1992, 1, 29-30. Admires the worlds of Harlem and the rural South evoked by Morrison but misses "the emotional nexus" provided by other writers such as William Faulkner and James Joyce in creating their own vivid worlds.

Rubin, Merle. "Morrison's Poignant Harlem Novel." *The Christian Science Monitor* 84 (April 17, 1992): 13. Claims that the novel "demonstrates once again that [Morrison] is one of the most brilliant and inventive American novelists writing today." Admires the novel's musical quality and compelling characters.

Laura Weiss Zlogar

JOE TURNER'S COME AND GONE

Author: August Wilson (1945-   )
Type of work: Play
Type of plot: Psychological realism
Time of plot: 1911
Locale: Pittsburgh, Pennsylvania
First produced: 1986, at Yale Repertory Theatre, New Haven, Connecticut
First published: 1988

> *Principal characters:*
>   SETH HOLLY, the owner of the boardinghouse which is the play's
>   principal setting
>   BERTHA HOLLY, Seth's wife, five years his junior
>   BYNUM WALKER, a conjure man who claims the power to "bind"
>   people to each other
>   RUTHERFORD SELIG, a peddler known for his ability to find missing
>   people
>   HERALD LOOMIS, a man searching for a wife he has not seen for
>   ten years

The Play

Many of the characters in *Joe Turner's Come and Gone* are searching for something. This motif thus provides an important organizing principle for a play that does not aspire to tightness of structure. The story the play tells finds its center, however, in Herald Loomis' search for Martha, the wife he has not seen in ten years. This search brings Loomis, with his eleven-year-old daughter Zonia, in the fall of 1911 to the boardinghouse in Pittsburgh owned by Seth Holly and his wife Bertha.

Bynum Walker, one of the two boarders in residence, tells Loomis that the man to see if he wants to find his wife is Rutherford Selig, a peddler known as the "People Finder." Loomis has just missed Selig, but he will be back next Saturday. Loomis resolves to wait.

Bynum himself has asked Selig to find someone Bynum calls the "shiny man," whom Bynum met only once, years before. The shiny man, as Bynum's father explained to him, is the "One Who Goes Before and Shows the Way." It was Bynum's father who showed Bynum how to "find his song"; according to Bynum's father, if Bynum ever sees a shiny man again, he will know that his song has been accepted and that he has made a mark on life. Bynum's song is the Binding Song. Like glue, he sticks people together—but, he knows, "You can't bind what don't cling."

Mattie, a woman in her twenties, comes to Bynum for help. Her man, Jack Carper, has walked out on her, and Bynum is known as a rootworker, a conjure man, a man who can fix things. Will he use his powers to bring her man back? Jeremy, another boarder, not long from the country, offers to be Mattie's man, at least for a while.

Seth Holly's watchful eye makes sure there is no carrying on in the boarding-house, and his observations now tell him who Loomis' wife is. Zonia bears a strik-ing resemblance to a woman Seth and Bertha know as Martha Pentecost, a former resident of the boardinghouse. Seth, though, says nothing to Loomis, because he senses that there is something not quite right about him. Moreover, Seth, who runs the boardinghouse, makes pots and pans for Selig to peddle, and tries to get backing to set up a business, has enough on his mind without getting involved in other peo-ple's affairs.

By Sunday morning, Mattie has decided to move in with Jeremy. Before the day is over, another young woman, Molly Cunningham, has rented a room for a week, and Jeremy is immediately attracted to her.

While waiting to hear from Selig, Loomis continues to act in ways that do not seem right to Seth. He goes too far, in Seth's view, when he interrupts the juba dance that is a Sunday night ritual at the boardinghouse and collapses after uttering a vision involving bones walking on water.

For Seth, this amounts to "carrying on," and over Bertha's objections, he tells Loomis that he will have to leave the following Saturday. Other residents will also be leaving soon. Jeremy has been fired, and he and Molly decide to travel together.

That evening, Bynum sings "Joe Turner's Come and Gone" as he and Seth play dominoes. When Loomis insists that Bynum stop singing the song, Bynum replies that Loomis seems to him to be a man who has forgotten his song. Each person has a song, Bynum believes, and a man who forgets his searches for it until he realizes he has had it with him all along. Bynum has realized that Loomis is one of "Joe Turner's niggers."

Provoked by Bynum, Loomis tells his story. In 1901, he was caught by Joe Turner, who hunts men as another might hunt possum, and was forced to serve seven years as an indentured servant. By the time he was free, his wife had gone. He has been searching for her ever since, sure that the sight of her face will give him the starting place he needs to begin the life that must take the place of the one taken from him by Joe Turner.

What, Loomis asks, does Joe Turner want? He wants your song, Bynum explains. That is why, for seven years, Loomis could not let himself sing it. After all that time, he forgot how; but, says Bynum, Loomis' song is still with him. "You one of them bones people," Loomis says to Bynum.

Bertha's attempts to console Mattie after Jeremy's defection are only partly suc-cessful, but Mattie does respond to Loomis when he asks her to be with him. She hesitates, though, because the power she senses in Loomis frightens her. "You'd use me up too fast," she tells him. When Loomis tries to touch Mattie, he finds that he cannot. "I done forgot how to touch," he says.

On Saturday morning, Selig brings Martha to the boardinghouse. "I been looking for you," she tells Loomis. She came to the North, she explains, because the trouble that black people were having in the South led her pastor to decide to move the church. Not knowing what might happen on the journey, Martha left Zonia with

Martha's mother, who would keep her safe. She is, then, anything but a woman who simply walked away from her man and abandoned her child; she has been looking for them ever since she learned that Loomis had taken Zonia. During Loomis' time away, however, she had to accept that he had died to her. She has mourned him and moved on.

Loomis tells Martha that he has wanted to say his goodbye to her and to reunite her with her daughter. Loomis says he has done all he can for Zonia, who he says needs her mother.

Loomis then angrily accuses Bynum of having bound him to the road. Drawing a knife, Loomis shouts that no one is going to bind him. Bynum says Loomis has it wrong; he did not bind Loomis to the road. "I bound the little girl to her mother," he states.

Concerned for Loomis, Martha urges him to have faith. Loomis replies that Jesus Christ is merely a white man "with a whip in one hand and a tote board in the other." When Martha tells him that Jesus bled for him, Loomis replies that he can bleed for himself. Using the knife with which he threatened Bynum, he draws his own blood. With this act of self-assertion comes the realization that he is standing free on his own; he has found his song. Joe Turner has finally gone. Now Loomis can move on. Mattie follows him out the door. Looking after them, Bynum sees that Loomis is "shining like new money."

Themes and Meanings

Joe Turner's Come and Gone is set in Pittsburgh in the fall of 1911. Slavery is almost half a century in the past, but it lives vividly in the memory of African Americans. The end of slavery, moreover, has not meant the end of enslavement. There is still Joe Turner. In exploring such realities of history and memory, the play powerfully develops the themes of movement, stability, and permanence, especially as these engage the relation of the individual struggle for personal freedom and meaning to the promise of community and heritage.

The enslavement of Herald Loomis by Joe Turner has both metaphorical and literal significance. As metaphor, Loomis' enslavement refers to the African American experience of slavery. Loomis is torn arbitrarily from his family, as countless Africans were torn from their communities and forced into slavery and as many slaves were torn from their families. Loomis' search for Martha recalls the quest for reunion that was the story of many African American families in the years following emancipation.

At the literal level, Loomis' experience underlines the limits to African American freedom in a society that had theoretically abolished slavery long before. He is a victim of an arbitrary power that can turn against any African American of his generation, especially, but certainly not exclusively, in the South.

At both levels, Loomis' story expresses the sense of rupture and disorientation arising from the experience of enslavement. The slaves at emancipation had been robbed of their African heritages; Loomis, three years after the end of his time as an indentured servant, or latter-day slave, still seeks a starting place.

The boardinghouse to which his quest has brought him is not merely a neutral setting for the action. It is a rich, though unobtrusive, symbol. In addition to Loomis and Zonia, three other residents pass through in the course of the play. Others have come and gone before these, among them Martha Pentecost, the woman for whom Loomis is looking. The boardinghouse, then, suggests an image of people in transit, searching, restless, moving forward on hope.

Yet the boardinghouse itself suggests stability as well as movement. Certainly, it represents stability to Seth Holly. The son of free Northern parents, Seth has property and a sense of who he is and where he belongs. Yet his attachment to his property, his obsessive accounting for time and money, threaten, in spite of Bertha's softening and humanizing influence, to harden into a posture of reaction and indifference. He is unable to see, for example, the limits on his own freedom imposed by the indifference, hostility, and contempt of the white men to whom he turns for loans. He does not seem to understand the full implications of his business association with Rutherford Selig, whose forebears were also "People Finders"—finders of runaway slaves for slaveowners.

Bynum's situation is different still. His residency at the boardinghouse seems to be permanent, and it is perhaps permanence, rather than mere stability, that he represents. He is a conjure man, and, while Seth regards his activities as mere mumbo jumbo, Bynum stands for the survival of the African heritage that the slaveholders had thought to suppress. In one sense, at least, he is most certainly a binder, a binder of the present to the past. Thus it is fitting that Bynum leads the juba, one of the many rituals of ultimately African origin with which he is associated. It is also fitting that Bynum, through a pattern of call and response, leads Loomis through the enunciation of his vision. The vision of bones walking on water offers a complex recapitulation of the experience of being brought into slavery, a kind of memory that reaches back beyond the individual's personal memory. When Loomis recognizes Bynum as one of the "bones people," he is acknowledging in Bynum the incarnation both of the experience of slavery and of the triumph over that experience through the workings of the spirit.

If Bynum represents a link between past and present in the African American community, he is also instrumental in Loomis' finding again the song he has lost, enabling Loomis to affirm at last his personal freedom. As Loomis thus breaks the inner grip of slavery through his act of self-assertion, Bynum sees that Loomis is "shining." As Bynum knows, Loomis' shining implies the vindication and justification of Bynum's life. Given what Loomis has been through, his shining also confirms the healing and creating power of the heritage to which Bynum gives flesh and blood presence.

Critical Context

When *Joe Turner's Come and Gone* opened on Broadway in the spring of 1988, August Wilson's play *Fences* (pr., pb. 1985) was still in its Broadway run, putting

Wilson in the unusual position of having two plays running on Broadway at the same time. Both plays won the New York Drama Critics Circle Award, as had Wilson's earlier play *Ma Rainey's Black Bottom* (pr. 1984, pb. 1985). *Fences* also won a Tony Award and a Pulitzer Prize. By the end of the decade, Wilson had clearly established himself as the most honored American playwright to emerge in the 1980's.

Set in 1911, *Joe Turner's Come and Gone* is one entry in Wilson's long-term project of writing a play exploring each decade of African American struggle in the twentieth century. He writes as a self-proclaimed black nationalist, but his mature plays are enthusiastically received by racially mixed, "mainstream" audiences.

Indeed, Wilson's nationalism does not manifest itself in overt denunciations of white racism, although an awareness of the history of the oppression and exploitation suffered by African Americans certainly plays a significant part in his work. In *Joe Turner's Come and Gone*, the figure of Joe Turner unmistakably symbolizes the white oppressor, and Rutherford Selig engages in small-time exploitation of Seth and of those who use his services as a "People Finder." Moreover, the white men who refuse to back Seth's efforts to set up a business take their place in a pattern of white racism. Similarly, in *Fences*, the white baseball owners who have denied Troy Maxson and others their opportunity to play in the big leagues, and the sanitation department officials who reserve the preferred driving jobs for whites only, combine to impose limits on black aspirations. Ma Rainey and the other musicians are also victims of white exploitation in *Ma Rainey's Black Bottom*.

Yet Wilson, in a move of genuine artistic, ethical, and political affirmation, refuses to grant the oppressors and exploiters a place at the heart of African American life. Beyond question, they often define limiting external conditions on that life. Wilson, though, is concerned not with the surrounding conditions of African American life but with the life itself. The tensions, tragedies, and triumphs depicted in *Joe Turner's Come and Gone* and in Wilson's other plays arise from within the African American community, out of the needs, hopes, and struggles of African American people. African Americans have, in Wilson's eyes, their own identity, their own dignity, their own significance. They are not defined by their relation to the white world. Thus, Joe Turner can make a captive of Herald Loomis, but it is Herald Loomis, finding strength in reestablishing ties to his personal and racial past and to the African American community, who finally must set himself free.

In his first successful play, *Ma Rainey's Black Bottom*, Wilson celebrated without sentimentality the genius of African American music. In *Joe Turner's Come and Gone*, he gave dramatic life to the belief that, in a cultural heritage ultimately African in inspiration, the African American can find an inexhaustible source of strength and renewal.

Bibliography

Brown, Chip. "The Light in August." *Esquire* 111 (April, 1989): 116. Explains that Wilson has found a way to formulate his politics in his art; he emphasizes black life on its own terms, not in confrontation with the white system.

Freedman, Samuel G. "A Voice from the Streets." *The New York Times Magazine* 136 (March 15, 1987): 36. Notes that most of Wilson's plays concern the conflict between those who embrace their African past and those who deny it. The plays reflect a positive sense of racial identity Wilson received from his mother.

Harrison, Paul Carter. "August Wilson's Blues Poetics." In *August Wilson, Three Plays.* Pittsburgh: University of Pittsburgh Press, 1991. Discusses how *Joe Turner's Come and Gone* operates outside the restraining logic of naturalism. Argues that Wilson has reclaimed the blues voice as the vehicle for black narratives and has reaffirmed the potency of the African continuum as a repository of values.

Poinsett, Alec. "August Wilson: Hottest New Playwright." *Ebony* 43 (November, 1987): 68. Poinsett examines how Wilson excavates much of his dramatic material from the blues. The song in *Joe Turner's Come and Gone* is a metaphor for a cultural heritage African Americans should retain and celebrate.

Reed, Ishmael. "August Wilson: The Dramatist as Bearer of Tradition." In *Writin' Is Fightin': Thirty-seven Years of Boxing on Paper.* New York: Atheneum, 1990. Reed asserts that Wilson is a "tradition bearer," one who knows the old stories and reveres the styles in which they are rendered. Values such as self-reliance and family are among his major concerns. Wilson's characters, Reed observes, are heirs to the disaster that occurred during the nineteenth century, when the gains of Reconstruction were forfeited. Reed also notes that more than Wilson's earlier plays, *Joe Turner's Come and Gone* contains elements of the supernatural.

W. P. Kenney

JONAH'S GOURD VINE

Author: Zora Neale Hurston (1891-1960)
Type of work: Novel
Type of plot: Social realism
Time of plot: The post-Civil War period through the early twentieth century
Locale: Alabama and Florida
First published: 1934

> *Principal characters:*
> JOHN PEARSON, a minister and carpenter
> LUCY POTTS PEARSON, John's first wife
> JUDGE ALF PEARSON, a wealthy white landowner suspected of
>   being John's father
> AMY CRITTENDEN, John Pearson's mother
> NED CRITTENDEN, John's stepfather
> HATTIE TYSON, John Pearson's second wife
> SALLY LOVELACE, John's third wife

The Novel

Jonah's Gourd Vine is a thinly disguised biography of Zora Neale Hurston's parents, whose names she barely veils in the novel. The story focuses on John Pearson's rise from a poor, illiterate Alabama sharecropper to the powerful, well-to-do moderator of the Florida Baptist Convention, to his subsequent fall from power and grace, to his painful resurrection and death.

The narrative opens on a sharecropping farm near the Songahatchee River in Alabama several years after the emancipation. Amy and Ned Crittenden and their three sons, including John, whom Amy had before marrying Ned, live the typically dismal life of the Southern black sharecropper—poor, perpetually in debt, ill-fed, ill-clothed, and generally hopeless. These difficulties, coupled with Ned's heavy drinking and his near hatred of his wife's mulatto son, make their domestic life a tragedy from which the sixteen-year-old John flees after he knocks Ned down for beating Amy.

John finds employment and an entirely new way of life on the plantation of Judge Alf Pearson, who, the reader soon realizes, is John's father. John is given considerable responsibility while in the judge's employ; he is also given the opportunity to go to school. It is also while at Judge Pearson's that John becomes involved in several of his many affairs with women.

It is the fiery, petite Lucy Potts whom John vows to marry, which he does eventually, although his numerous extramarital affairs do not stop. During one of these affairs that has kept John away from home for several nights, Lucy's brother, Bud, comes to collect a debt from John and, finding no money, takes the bed that Judge Pearson had given John and Lucy for a wedding present, dumping Lucy and her newborn baby on the floor in the process. When John does return, he whips Bud within an inch of his life and must flee to escape prosecution and possible lynching.

Subsequent years find John and his family in Eatonville, an all-black town in central Florida, where John has prospered under Lucy's careful direction. He has become a successful carpenter, a property owner, the popular pastor of neighboring Sanford's Zion Hope Baptist Church, and the powerful moderator of the Florida Baptist Convention. Likewise, his weakness for other women has increased, and his sexual escapades threaten his security in the church, but Lucy is always there as a constant strength and defender. Lucy dies prematurely, however, from a body weakened by the ravages of tuberculosis, too many years of rapid childbirth, and increasing concern, worry, and aggravation over John's philandering.

Lucy's death proves to be John's undoing, as he soon marries the selfish, self-centered Hattie Tyson, who destroys virtually everything John and Lucy have built together. John not only loses his children, his wife, and his congregation, but he also loses his power, his influence, and his dignity. Finally, John leaves the ministry and Eatonville, convinced that he is mostly misunderstood and that distance is the best cure for his social illness.

The last leg of John Pearson's journey finds him in Plant City, Florida, where, with the help of his third wife, the saintly Sally Lovelace, he puts his life back together: He regains a full measure of dignity and prosperity, and he accepts the call to become pastor of the Pilgrim Rest Baptist Church, an even larger congregation than the one he left in Sanford. For a while all is tranquil, but during a visit to Sanford, John gives in to his sexual urges. In a guilt-laden stupor, John is struck and killed by a train as he rushes back to Sally in the new Cadillac she has bought for him. His death is mourned statewide, and in the end, John Pearson is remembered for the good things he had done.

The Characters

In *Jonah's Gourd Vine*, Hurston takes a stock figure from African American literature and lore, the folk preacher, and imbues him with real human characteristics in a successful effort to show the character as a human being, subject to the same strengths, weaknesses, and shortcomings of other human beings rather than as a godlike being who is unaffected by human frailties. Also, because Hurston relies heavily on details from her personal experience—*Jonah's Gourd Vine* is loosely based on her parents' biographies—the characters are all the more real and compelling.

The characters are presented in a more or less straightforward narrative manner; there are few if any experimental techniques. The central characters, John Pearson and his wife Lucy, are presented as complex, wholly believable characters with tragic flaws that prove, especially in John's case, to be their undoing.

The plot is likewise developed in a linear fashion. Although the ending—with John's death after he is struck by a locomotive—seems gratuitous and melodramatic, it is nevertheless believable within the context of the story.

John Pearson is presented as a man with many conflicts; however, it is his uncheckable tendency to be a "man amongst women" that is presented as so incompatible with his role as pastor of a Baptist congregation. His inability, perhaps his refusal, to control his sexual appetite leads to his downfall. Pearson has the makings of a successful man, however: He is physically strong, he is a talented carpenter, he possesses a superb singing voice, and he is an exceptionally powerful preacher of the gospel. These traits seem to suit Hurston's narrative strategy quite well, as she explores the adage "the bigger they come, the harder they fall."

Similarly, Hurston's portrayal of the petite Lucy Pearson is designed to contrast directly to John's character. Lucy is physically small, yet she is a paragon of goodness and propriety. She, too, sings superbly, but she lives the life she sings about, and for that reason she emerges as a wholly sympathetic character who is victimized by her philandering, hypocritical husband.

Hurston's greatest strength is her depiction of her native Florida and most especially of the folk who populate the all-black town of Eatonville and its surroundings. Her characterizations in *Jonah's Gourd Vine* are a tribute to her talent for portraying folk characters in a realistic, uncondescending manner. The dialect of the characters is superbly drawn, as are their appearances, habits, and even their naming processes. Several characters are true stereotypes—Hattie Tyson, the "bad woman," is one example—but they nevertheless fit well in this archetypal examination of the fall of man.

As such, Hurston presents a realistic and compassionate picture of black life in a small Southern town. As in most of her fiction, whites appear only on the periphery; racial strife is mostly insignificant in Hurston's world. Rather, she shows with great skill and consummate artistry the day-to-day struggles of black folk in this native setting.

Themes and Meanings

Much of *Jonah's Gourd Vine* is focused on the character of John Pearson, perhaps the best portrayal of the black folk preacher in African American literature. John Pearson is depicted as a powerful preacher, called of God, but he is also shown in the human dimension, as a man subject to the same urges, weaknesses, and faults as ordinary men. It is this tension between the godlike qualities and the human elements around which the novel revolves.

For example, the reader is presented with the central question, "How can a man propose to lead a Christian congregation when he is guilty of the same sins he preaches against in others?" This question puzzles John's wife, Lucy, members of John's congregation, and even John himself. As John's philandering continues, his relationships with his wife, church, and community deteriorate. Yet John Pearson is a powerful preacher, and when he is in this element, he and his congregation can enjoy, together, the ecstasy of the Holy Spirit. With his powerful singing and preaching voice, John is able to swell the membership of Zion Hope Baptist Church from fewer than three hundred to nearly a thousand members and to become the moderator of the Florida Baptist Convention, a high religious post that carries with it many luxuries.

John Pearson's relationships with women are also central to the novel. For example, when he is in the presence of virtuous women—Lucy Potts and Sally Lovelace—John prospers. These women encourage him, and he strives; they motivate him, and he achieves; they design, and he builds; they support him, and he accomplishes. Conversely, in the absence of these women, John falters, as is clearly seen following Lucy's death; he falls into a cycle of drinking, domestic violence, and social disintegration. Likewise, when John is separated from Sally toward the end of the novel, his weaknesses overtake and engulf him once again. Further, there are the nonvirtuous women who serve as vehicles for John's destruction—Hattie Tyson chief among them. These women, as the author portrays them, are interested only in their own gain and are not concerned about others. In the case of Hattie Tyson, the reader sees her vindictiveness as well: She helps John's detractors kick him when he is already wounded.

Finally, John Pearson is like the biblical Jonah, who tried to run away from God and from his responsibilities. Early in the novel, John compromises himself by doing things that are expedient rather than right; this often entails flight from trouble or responsibility. John leaves home after a fight with his stepfather; he moves to another state to avoid prosecution after a fight with his brother-in-law; he goes to Tampa because he cannot bear to witness his young daughter's life-threatening illness; he leaves his church when expulsion seems imminent; and when he is struck and killed by a train, he is running away from yet another affair. In short, John Pearson never learns to accept the responsibility for his actions, and this makes the various consequences all the more difficult for him to face.

One important feature of *Jonah's Gourd Vine* is Hurston's presentation of life among the black folk that she knew, loved, and appreciated so much. The author gives glimpses of the social life, the domestic life, and the religious expression in all-black Eatonville. She does not concern herself very much with the relationships between whites and blacks; rather, she examines the dynamics of the black community and how black people interact. The use of language is instructive in that Hurston writes not only in dialect but also in the folk idiom—what she often called "a Negro way of saying" things. The effect is a realistic picture of black people in their native setting.

One of the most illustrative examples of the language and drama of black life is John's final sermon at Zion Hope, "The Wounds of Jesus." The sermon is full of the powerful drama, the sharp imagery, the overpowering delivery, and the unmistakable style and technique usually associated with black preaching. These aspects provide interest and depth to Hurston's portrayal of Reverend Pearson; they also combine with other elements of John Pearson's personality to create an astounding climax as he walks away from the pulpit, out of the church, and finally out of the town itself. Pearson's sermon is the actual transcription of a sermon Hurston had heard in Eau Gallie, Florida, during one of her many folklore-collecting trips. Its authenticity further strengthens the realism Hurston wanted to establish in *Jonah's Gourd Vine*.

Critical Context

Hurston published *Jonah's Gourd Vine* in 1934, thirteen years after she had published her first short story, nearly a decade after she had become established as an award-winning writer, and several years after she had established herself as an important American folklorist whose specialty was black life of the American South and the Caribbean. Naturally, there was considerable interest in her first novel. Few were disappointed in her craft, although writers and critics with socialist leanings were disturbed that Hurston refrained from writing much protest fiction in favor of writing stories that celebrated the culture and values of black communities in the South. *Jonah's Gourd Vine* was generally well received, and its publication was the beginning of Hurston's most fruitful and rewarding period of writing that included *Their Eyes Were Watching God* (1937), *Moses, Man of the Mountain* (1939), and the award-winning *Dust Tracks on a Road: An Autobiography* (1942).

With the revival of interest in Hurston's canon that began in 1973 after two decades of general neglect, critics have looked favorably upon *Jonah's Gourd Vine* as a novel important not only for its artistic value but also for its folkloric value. In addition, this first novel shows the development of its author as a craftsperson who had perfected the short story and then gone on to master the longer genre of the novel.

Bibliography

Hemenway, Robert. *Zora Neale Hurston: A Literary Biography.* Chicago: University of Illinois Press, 1977. The most complete study of Hurston's life and works. Includes biography, textual analyses, and a general wealth of information suitable for any student of Hurston.

Holloway, Karla F. *The Character of the Word: The Texts of Zora Neale Hurston.* Westport, Conn.: Greenwood Press, 1987. An important study of Hurston's use of language to delineate and differentiate character. The author provides a number of interesting readings and rereadings of Hurston's characters.

Lupton, Mary Jane. "Zora Neale Hurston and the Survival of the Female." *Southern Literary Journal* 15 (Fall, 1982): 45-54. Explores an all-important and all-encompassing theme of Hurston's work. While much of the focus is on *Their Eyes Were Watching God*, there is considerable information that is useful for the study of all Hurston's work, including *Jonah's Gourd Vine*.

Newson, Adele S. *Zora Neale Hurston: A Reference Guide.* Boston: G. K. Hall, 1987. A valuable resource for scholars of Hurston. This reference book catalogs all the Hurston criticism up to the time of the book's publication.

Walker, Alice. "Zora Neale Hurston: A Cautionary Tale and a Partisan View." In *In Search of Our Mothers' Gardens.* San Diego: Harcourt Brace Jovanovich, 1983. An interesting essay by one of Hurston's leading champions.

Warren J. Carson

THE JOURNALS OF CHARLOTTE FORTEN GRIMKÉ

Author: Charlotte L. Forten Grimké (1837-1914)
Type of work: Diary
Time of work: 1854-1892
Locale: Boston, Massachusetts; Philadelphia, Pennsylvania; St. Helena Island, South Carolina; and Jacksonville, Florida
First published: 1988 (portions published in 1953 as *The Journal of Charlotte L. Forten*)

> *Principal personages:*
> CHARLOTTE FORTEN GRIMKÉ, the bright, ambitious, but overly self-critical daughter of Robert Bridges Forten
> ROBERT BRIDGES FORTEN, Charlotte's father, a dedicated abolitionist
> JOHN GREENLEAF WHITTIER, a celebrated poet, essayist, and abolitionist who was a friend of the Forten family
> WILLIAM LLOYD GARRISON, the renowned antislavery speaker, essayist, and editor of *The Liberator*
> THOMAS WENTWORTH HIGGINSON, a prominent white abolitionist from Cambridge, Massachusetts, who became the commanding officer of the First South Carolina Volunteers
> SETH ROGERS, a physician who was also an active abolitionist
> ELLEN MURRAY, a fellow teacher of freed slaves with Charlotte on St. Helena Island
> FRANCIS GRIMKÉ, Charlotte Forten Grimké's husband, whom she married in 1878

Form and Content

Although Charlotte Lottie Forten Grimké was a teacher as well as a minor essayist, poet, and translator, it was her personal journal, which she started keeping at the age of sixteen, that proved to be her most lasting contribution to African American letters. She began her journal in May, 1854, beginning with a preface that explains her intention to use this journal to chart her own intellectual growth. The first dated entry, from May 24, is typical of her early diary in that it begins with her expressing disapproval that by awakening at 5 A.M., she let the sun rise several hours before she did; this, she declares, is an advantage she will not let the sun have over her again any time soon. She goes on to note that she has just begun reading Charles Dickens' *Hard Times* (1854) and is certain that she will enjoy it. Her first entry, like many of the entries to follow, reveals her absolute drive that she must work incessantly to improve herself. Growing up at a time when slavery was still an active institution in Southern states, and when inferiority of African Americans was assumed by many white Americans, including many of Charlotte's fellow Northerners living in and around Philadelphia and Salem, Charlotte was driven not only by the need to develop her own talents and abilities but also by the need to prove, through her example, the talents and abilities of black Americans.

Born in Philadelphia on August 17, 1837, as the daughter of Robert Bridges Forten and Mary Virginia Woods Forten, Charlotte Lottie Forten grew up in one of the most active black antislavery families in Philadelphia at the time. In November of 1853, she was sent to Salem to continue her schooling. While there, she stayed with Charles Lenox Remond and his wife Amy Matilda, both black abolitionists and friends of the Forten family. They were well connected to the abolitionist movement in and around Salem. It was the intellectually and emotionally stimulating environment of being part of a movement dedicated to eliminating slavery and improving conditions for Northern free blacks that excited the intellectually thirsty Charlotte during her teenage years and that infuses the early entries of her diary.

The second dated entry in Charlotte's diary, from May 25, 1854, concerns the arrest of Anthony Burns, an escaped slave who was arrested off the streets of Boston for return to slavery in the South. In the days that followed, his case became celebrated as antislavery activists demanded his release. On June 2, Charlotte reports in her diary that he had been sent back to slavery. As disheartening as this news was to Charlotte, it was to have a more personal implication. Her father, tired of striving against the ever-present racism in Philadelphia and looking to relocate, decided because of this case that moving his family to Massachusetts, where his daughter already was, would be no improvement. Instead they moved to Canada in the autumn of 1855.

A desire for her father's approval was certainly one of Charlotte's motivations for working so hard on the program of self-improvement recorded in her journal. In her early entries, there are repeated references to her hopes that her father and the rest of her family will join her eventually, and it was quite a disappointment for her when they did not. Her father's financial support of her ceased during her final year as a student at the Salem Normal School, quite probably because of financial hardships of his own. She found herself forced to go into debt to her hostess, Amy Remond, to support herself. Upon graduation, Charlotte was offered a position at the Epes Grammar School in Salem. She accepted in the hope that this would ensure her ability both to support herself and to live among the active abolitionists of Massachusetts whom she found so stimulating. In her first term as a teacher, though, the health problems that were to hound Charlotte for the rest of her life forced her to miss several days of teaching. In June, 1857, again suffering ill-health, she retreated to Philadelphia for six weeks to recover from a respiratory ailment. Over the next few years, she was forced to resign several teaching posts for similar reasons.

Against such pressing realities, Charlotte's continued dedication to self-education (including studying French, German, and Latin) and to the abolitionist cause shows Charlotte's spirit. Reading the works of great authors—her favorites included Elizabeth Barrett Browning, whom she refers to several times as "the priestess of poetry"; Harriet Beecher Stowe; John Greenleaf Whittier; and Ralph Waldo Emerson—was for her a worthy end in itself, but she was always particularly pleased when she read a writer such as Whittier or Stowe whose talent she respected and who dealt directly with her constant concerns of eliminating slavery and confronting racism.

Although living in a free state, Charlotte was keenly aware of the prejudice directed at her as a black woman. Her September 12, 1855, entry deals with her happiness upon returning to school but immediately turns to her acknowledgment of being looked down upon by her classmates. "I wonder that every colored person is not a misanthrope," she muses, and asks several rhetorical questions: "When, oh! when shall this cease?" "Is there no help?" "How long oh! how long must we continue to suffer—to endure?" Partly as a response to this alienation from her classmates, she persuades her one friend from school, Sarah Brown, to join the Female Anti-Slavery Society with her. It was an integrated group that sponsored antislavery lectures and talks, and it continued to help Charlotte focus her intellectual life around the abolitionist cause.

Despite some early literary publications, including several poems in William Lloyd Garrison's antislavery newspaper *The Liberator*, Charlotte's own high standards, as well as her frustrations at her ill-health, caused her to be overly critical of herself. Birthdays tend to be days on which she reflected on how little she had accomplished. Between May, 1859, and June, 1862, there is only one entry. Shortly after she returned to her daily journal keeping, John Greenleaf Whittier suggested that she (using him as a reference) apply for a post teaching on the South Carolina Sea Islands. After being rejected by the Boston Education Commission, the members of which tell her that they are not seeking female teachers, she moves back to Philadelphia, where another contingent of teachers is being organized. On October 21, 1862, she learns that she has been accepted and will ship out the next day.

Charlotte's students were to be the so-called "contraband" slaves of the Sea Islands off the South Carolina coast, where the Union had established a military outpost. At the time, slaves from plantations under Union control were considered the contraband of war and thus under the direction of the Union. Because the Emancipation Proclamation officially freed all slaves living in confederate states on January 1, 1863, Charlotte's students all became officially free slightly more than two months after Charlotte arrived.

The effort to provide a basic education to the newly freed slaves living on the Union-controlled South Carolina Sea Islands is sometimes referred to as the Port Royal Experiment. Secretary of the Treasury Salmon P. Chase saw in this population of former slaves a chance to disabuse many of the common prejudices among white Americans that stated that African Americans were inherently inferior. A successful experiment, he recognized, would help serve as a model for programs that could be set up during the Reconstruction period.

Because Charlotte's students brought little educational background with them to her classroom, and because many of them spoke Gullah, a heavily African-influenced English dialect, Charlotte's job was to give them basic instruction. She launched into the work with all the energy and enthusiasm she had, though not without some trepidation and not without recurring bouts of ill-health. On her first day of teaching there, November 5, 1862, she frankly records in her journal her dismay at how much work has to be done and how unprepared her students are for school. Her disappointment, however, is constantly tempered by her loving fascination with the people she is meeting, her sympathy for their plight, and not least of all, her appreciation of the strange (to her) natural beauty of her surroundings.

It is also in the South Carolina entries that she records what is evidently a romantic impulse toward a man, Dr. Seth Rogers, a married white surgeon who had treated her before the war and who volunteered as a surgeon for the First South Carolina Volunteers, a regiment of black soldiers. Both are careful to keep their relationship within proper bounds, and though their attachment is to all appearances romantic, Charlotte does record that he asked her to think of him "as a brother."

During the summer of 1863, poor health and the heat impelled Charlotte to take a vacation from her teaching. She traveled north for the summer. Upon her return, she recorded several sporadic entries. Her fourth journal ends abruptly with a May 15, 1864, entry that mentions that the last few months have had some happy and some painful events. Among the painful ones, left unmentioned by her, was the death of her father on April 25, 1864, of typhoid fever scarcely six weeks after he had joined the Union forces as a sergeant-major.

Her fifth journal is by far her shortest. It covers the period from November 15, 1885, to July, 1892. Entries are sporadic: Gaps of months or years between entries are not uncommon. Nevertheless, a composite picture emerges of Charlotte Forten Grimké as a mature married woman. She married the Reverend Francis Grimké on December 19, 1878, and remained married to him until her death in 1914. During these years, ill-health was a constant companion, not an occasional visitor. Nevertheless, she remained busy and committed to her literary pursuits as well as to the larger goal of equality. Her final entry, dated July, 1892, three years later than the previous one, briefly summarizes her life being busy but on the whole happy, with the greatest drawback being her constant poor health.

Analysis

When Ray Allen Billington first published Grimké's journals in 1953, he omitted large sections covering the years 1854-1862 on the grounds that her musings on friends, family, and literature would not be of much interest to the general reader. The complete journals, published as part of the Schomburg Library of Nineteenth Century Black Women Writers and edited by Brenda Stevenson, restores these missing passages and also includes much of Charlotte Forten's early poetry in the footnotes.

The result is that a much fuller portrait of a young woman emerges. The entries reprinted by Billington from Charlotte's teenage years show a young woman deeply committed to the abolitionist cause and widely interested in the great ideas of her day. The complete journals also show her to be a young woman who was a constant victim of deep self-doubts and who craved the community of support she found among her abolitionist friends in Salem. Further, in her recurrent careful considerations of literature, readers can see the development of a young writer trying to train herself for her lifelong pursuit of creating literature.

The South Carolina entries, in Charlotte's third and fourth journals, may be the section of the most enduring historical interest. As a writer, Forten becomes more mature and assured during this period, as well as more intimate in some ways. She frequently addresses her journal directly, calling it "A," creating the impression that she is using the journal to replace the company of friends. The entries during this period are longer, and there is less of the self-criticism that marks her earlier journal entries. This section of her journals seems to be informed by the assurance that the work she is doing, helping to educate African Americans newly freed from slavery, is of lasting worth. The values and skills that she has carefully been developing, as shown in the earlier years of her journal, all contribute to her daily work.

Because the opening pages of Grimké's fifth journal are missing, it is impossible to determine if she intended it as a continuation of her earlier journal or if she had some other goal in mind. Whereas the earlier journal was begun as an attempt to track and encourage her intellectual development, the later journal is more a simple record of some events in her life. The demanding need for constant self-improvement, so evident in her earlier journal, is tempered by a mature acceptance of herself. Even the frustration at her constant ill-health is tempered by a level of acceptance. The later journal does make it clear that in her late middle age, as in her teenage years, Charlotte Forten Grimké continued to see her life as a project under construction.

Critical Context

A 1985 American Playhouse production, "Charlotte Forten's Mission: Experiment in Freedom," helped revive interest in Forten's South Carolina experience. Until the publication of the complete *The Journals of Charlotte Forten Grimké* in 1988, Grimké was most widely known through the abbreviated diary edited by Ray Allen Billington, which emphasized her relationship to the abolitionist movement and her work with the Port Royal Experiment. Her journals were widely considered to be primarily of historical interest, providing one young woman's account of important people and events before and during the Civil War.

The publication in 1988 of both an essay by Joanne Braxton, "Charlotte Forten Grimké and the Search for a Public Voice," and the complete journals helped to change that perception. Braxton argues that in the complete journals, a reader can see a young African American female writer who is trying to find literary models that will be useful to her as well as trying to make established European-American models meaningful to her own life and writing.

In her own lifetime, Grimké received praise for her literary talents, most notably from William Wells Brown, the former slave and noted abolitionist, and John Greenleaf Whittier, both personal friends. The judgment of history on her literary production other than her journals has been rather cool. Her journals stand as her most significant literary work by far. As Ray Allen Billington said in his introduction to her journals, Grimké's "bequest to humanity was a journal which could reveal to a later generation her undying belief in human decency and equality."

Bibliography
Billington, Ray Allen. Introduction to *The Journal of Charlotte L. Forten*. Edited, with an introduction, by Ray Allen Billington. New York: Dryden Press, 1953. Reprint. New York: Norton, 1981. Billington's introduction to his heavily edited edition of Forten's journals remains an essential source for those interested in placing Forten's work with the Port Royal Experiment in its historical context. This edition also contains helpful maps.

Braxton, Joanne M. "Charlotte Forten Grimké and the Search for a Public Voice." In *The Private Self: Theory and Practice of Women's Autobiographical Writings*, edited by Shari Benstock. Chapel Hill: University of North Carolina Press, 1988. An analysis of Grimké's complete journals, based on Braxton's archival research and personal appreciation of the journals. This article maintains that Charlotte, as a young woman, used her journal to try out different poetic voices.

Brown, William Wells. "Charlotte L. Forten." In *The Black Man, His Antecedents, His Genius, and His Achievements*. New York: Thomas Hamilton, 1863. An attempt by a leading abolitionist to publicly recognize Forten's talents while she was still a young woman.

Sherman, Joan R. "Charlotte L. Forten Grimké." In *Invisible Poets: Afro-Americans of the Nineteenth Century*. Urbana: University of Illinois Press, 1974. A consideration of Grimké's poetry. Concludes that although she was a minor poet, her skills and sensitivity were above the ordinary.

Stevenson, Brenda, ed. Introduction and notes to *The Journals of Charlotte Forten Grimké*. New York: Oxford University Press, 1988. A thorough introduction to Grimké's life and work. Includes a chronology of events in Grimké's life as well as a key to persons mentioned in her journals. The complete journals themselves, as reprinted in this volume, have become the definitive text.

Thomas Cassidy

JUBILEE

Author: Margaret Walker (1915-   )
Type of work: Novel
Type of plot: Historical realism
Time of plot: The 1840's to 1870
Locale: Dawson, Georgia; Abbeville, Troy, Luverne, and Greenville, in south-central
   Alabama
First published: 1966

> *Principal characters:*
>   VYRY BROWN, the protagonist, the daughter of a slave and her
>   white owner
>   RANDALL WARE, a free black man and a landowner who marries
>   Vyry in a slave ceremony
>   INNIS BROWN, a former field hand who befriends Vyry and her
>   children during the Civil War and becomes her first legal
>   husband
>   JOHN MORRIS DUTTON, Vyry's father, a rich Georgia planter
>   SALINA DUTTON (BIG MISSY), John Dutton's wife
>   ED GRIMES, Dutton's "slave driver"

The Novel

   Jubilee tells a story of slavery, the Civil War, and the Reconstruction period from
the point of view of the black people who were often both victims and pawns in a
struggle that convulsed an entire nation. Just as *Gone with the Wind* (1936) is the
story not just of a period but of a woman, the indomitable Scarlett O'Hara, so the
narrative power of *Jubilee* derives from its protagonist, the slave Vyry, modeled after
Margaret Duggans Ware Brown, the author's great-grandmother. The book was inspired by the stories told to Margaret Walker at bedtime during her childhood by her
grandmother, Elvira Ware Dozier, who is Vyry's daughter Minna in the novel. Thus,
as Walker points out in her book *How I Wrote Jubilee* (1972), the novel has a solid
basis in oral tradition, which was later amplified with the extensive study of slave
narratives. In her attempt to ensure the accuracy of her work, Walker invested a solid
ten years in research, checking not only the historical background but also minute
details of everyday life.
   Walker's novel is divided into three sections, each of which represents a distinct
historical period as well as a separate segment of Vyry's life. The first, "Sis Hetta's
Child—The Ante-Bellum Years," is the account of Vyry's childhood as a slave. It
begins when Vyry is two years old and her mother, Sis Hetta, is dying in childbirth.
Although she is only twenty-nine years old, Sis Hetta has given birth to fifteen children, many of them the offspring of her white master, John Dutton. Although he

does not acknowledge Vyry or his other slave children, his wife Salina Dutton, or "Big Missy," is painfully aware of their existence. Because Vyry looks so much like her own daughter, Lillian Dutton, Salina vents her anger toward her husband by mistreating Vyry on every possible occasion. Vyry cannot expect any help from her father. When she asks permission to marry Randall Ware, Dutton refuses his permission, thus making it clear that, despite his facile promises, he has no intention of ever setting Vyry free, either during his life or after his death. The section ends with Vyry's attempt to flee to freedom and to her husband, whom she married in a slave ceremony. Because she is encumbered by her two young children, Vyry is easily captured, and then is punished by being given seventy-five lashes. Like her scars, the memory of this beating remains with her for life.

In the section that follows, " 'Mine Eyes Have Seen the Glory'—The Civil War Years," Vyry continues to act in keeping with her nobility of character. Even though she cannot share in her white family's belief that theirs is the best of all possible worlds, she takes care of both the women who are left when the men march away and the wounded men who return to die. Even after she has been freed and, having given up hope of Ware's return, has decided to leave the plantation with her new husband, Innis Brown, she delays her departure until she has found someone to care for Lillian, who has lost her mind.

The last part of the novel, set in the turbulent period after the war, traces Vyry's progress westward through Alabama as she and Innis Brown, along with their growing family, search for a place to make their home. Recalling the biblical story of the Hebrews, who escaped from slavery in Egypt only to wander in a hostile desert, Walker entitles this section " 'Forty Years in the Wilderness'—Reconstruction and Reaction." Vyry's wilderness is southern Alabama, where, Innis has been told, there is abundant land to which no one has title and that can therefore be claimed by the newly freed slaves. Unfortunately, the family is forced out of one place after another. Floods and fever drive them out of a fertile lowland. At their next stop, they unwillingly become tenants, virtual slaves to a dishonest landowner. Finally, in Troy, they are burned out by the Ku Klux Klan. After this last disaster, Vyry for the first time despairs. When the family reaches Greenville, she refuses to let Innis put up a house. Then providence seems to take a hand. As she is passing through a white neighborhood, Vyry hears cries for help and, reacting instinctively, she goes to the aid of a young woman in labor. The grateful family and their friends later promise Vyry their protection if she will stay in Greenville as a midwife. When she agrees, her white neighbors gather to build the Browns a house.

The only problem that remains is that of Jim, Vyry's son by Randall Ware. He loathes farm work and as a result dislikes Innis Brown, who he thinks works him like a slave. Some time after an eruption in which Innis beats Jim, again providence seems to come to Vyry's aid. Randall Ware appears, and although Vyry can see that her own life is now tied to that of Innis, she is happy to send Jim with his father so that Jim can receive the education he desires. The novel ends with reconciliation, not only between whites and blacks but among the members of Vyry's own family.

The Characters

Margaret Walker's preoccupation with crafting a story that, above all, tells the whole truth can be seen in her approach to characterization. In *Jubilee*, even the most oppressive whites are shown as individuals, with their own frustrations and their own griefs. The overseer Ed Grimes, for example, resents the fact that he must spend his days in the fields with the slaves while his wealthy employer indulges his own whims. Grimes's sense of social inferiority and his fear of the slaves under his control help to explain his willingness to join with Big Missy in torture and murder.

As for Salina herself, Margaret Walker once commented in an interview that those readers who called the woman a "monster" misunderstood the story. Given her upbringing as a young Southern lady, an upbringing that denied her any knowledge of sex, Salina was conditioned to react as she did when confronted with the realities of marriage. Moreover, it is not surprising that Salina hates her husband's offspring by another woman, slave or not. Unfortunately, the institution of slavery gives her the opportunity to vent her wrath upon the innocent child Vyry.

Although Walker wants her readers to understand the motivations of her unsympathetic characters, she also believes that one can choose to rise above a corrupt society, as Vyry manages to do. Readers who find *Jubilee* to be one of the most memorable historical novels set in this period often point to the spiritual grandeur of its central character. Even if Walker had not so fully revealed her protagonist's feelings, the facts of her story alone would have shown how consistently Vyry repays injury with forgiveness. Rejected by her father, tortured by his wife, and brutally beaten after her attempt to follow her husband to freedom, Vyry has every reason to hate the white race. On occasion after occasion, however, when white people meet adversity, she aids them.

It is appropriate that at last Vyry is rewarded, that her family finds a permanent home as a result of one of her many acts of kindness. Although it is obvious that throughout the story Vyry is always motivated by her Christian faith, in *How I Wrote Jubilee* Walker also gives some credit to her character's practical good sense, which shows her that hatred will hurt no one but herself.

Walker shows Randall Ware, too, as both a product of his background and a person who thinks for himself. Because he was born free, Ware has not had Vyry's long training in subservience, and normally he asserts his worth, no matter who questions it. He can also be practical. When he has no other choice, he gives up some of his property to predatory whites. When he is evicted from the legislature, he turns his attention to education, which he reasons must be a source of empowerment or whites would not be so anxious to deny it to blacks.

Walker uses the privilege of an omniscient narrator to describe Randall Ware's experiences when he is away from Vyry, but she does not penetrate Ware's consciousness as fully as she does that of her heroine. Generally, the author simply relates Ware's adventures, leaving the reader to deduce what Ware is feeling. When he reveals his opinions in dialogue, as he does, for example, in the final chapters of the novel, it appears that he is important primarily as the spokesman for black militancy as an option for his people.

Like Vyry and like Ware, Innis Brown is to some degree a product of his environment; therefore, his indifference to education and his anger with his stepson Jim are understandable. As a field hand, he had no glimpse of the kind of life with which house servants such as Vyry were familiar. In owning his own land and his own house, he has achieved all that he could ever hope for. One can only guess at the bewilderment that Innis felt when Vyry sided with Jim and at his apprehension when Ware suddenly appeared to reclaim his wife. In the dramatic final pages, it is Vyry's feelings that Walker reports; both Ware and Brown are left to speak for themselves.

The fact that Walker does not permit her readers a glimpse into the hearts and souls of characters so important and so sympathetic as Ware and Brown might be considered a defect in the novel. On the other hand, it may well have been a deliberate decision by the artist. By presenting everyone else somewhat hazily, Margaret Walker placed her noble heroine in a clearer focus.

Themes and Meanings

Among the themes that can be traced through *Jubilee* are the centrality of folklore, myth, and music in the black heritage, the roles of black women as preservers and transmitters of the cultural identity of their people, and the importance of black Christianity in the struggle for freedom. It is also rewarding to look at *Jubilee* as a book about illusion and reality.

As Walker has pointed out, her perspective on history is not that of whites, either Northern or Southern, but that of African Americans. In the conversations among slaveowners in her novel, and in their speeches to the slaves, it is evident that the white masters have deluded themselves into believing that their motives for keeping slaves are noble, that the slaves are well treated and happy, and that any hopes of freedom they might cherish are simply proof of their childlike ignorance.

Because, as Walker shows, such justifications for the suppression of African Americans did not disappear with the Emancipation Proclamation, the discussions between Innis Brown, Vyry, and Randall Ware at the end of the book are all related to another major theme in the novel, that of the struggle for freedom. Given the blindness of whites, Walker seems to be asking, how can blacks progress beyond nominal freedom to full equality?

Each of the three main characters has a different answer. Innis Brown takes a passive approach. Despite his experiences with oppression, both during slavery and since his emancipation, he thinks, or perhaps he wants to think, that if he works hard and stays away from whites, he and his family will be safe. His attitude is explained partly by the fact that by owning his own land, he has achieved his highest goal.

Vyry, on the other hand, has had a glimpse of greater possibilities. She knows that her children have the capacity to move upward in society. She also realizes that if they are to do so, they must acquire education. Isolation on the farm is no answer, because even to get schools established, blacks will have to associate with whites.

Vyry pins her hopes for change on persuasion, supplemented by prayer.

Randall Ware represents a third point of view, that of the black separatists and militants. He has already tried political action and been thrown out of the office to which he was elected. Convinced that whites will do everything they can to suppress blacks, he sees education as the major weapon giving blacks a chance in the inevitable conflict ahead.

Although in this work Walker does not clearly commit herself to one position or another, it is obvious that any answer to the problems of blacks must depend on the destruction of the illusions so long held by whites. For this reason, the theme of freedom is intertwined with the theme of the pursuit of truth. Exploration of these themes must be perceived as one of the author's major purposes in writing *Jubilee*.

Critical Context

From the standpoint of literary history, *Jubilee* is of importance as the first realistic novel about slavery, the Civil War, and the Reconstruction period to be written by a black author. Although it was a popular success, the activists of the 1960's considered the book too moderate and Vyry too forgiving. In other words, Walker's novel was politically incorrect. Unlike her more militant poetry, *Jubilee* was largely ignored by critics until the late 1970's, when it was discovered that many of the themes and motifs then being identified as of major importance in black literature and history had already been introduced in *Jubilee*. Moreover, Vyry was seen as one of those strong black women who, although powerless to change their society, had succeeded in preserving their culture.

Walker is considered a writer of more than historical importance. Her reputation is based not only on her poetry, collected in *This Is My Century: New and Collected Poems* (1989), but also on this novel, so long neglected by critics but assuming its rightful place as one of the masterpieces of historical fiction.

Bibliography

Bell, Bernard W. "The Contemporary Afro-American Novel, 2: Modernism and Postmodernism." In *The Afro-American Novel and Its Tradition*. Amherst: University of Massachusetts Press, 1987. An excellent essay with detailed analysis of such matters as the importance of the epigraphs in the forward movement of the book. Although Bell admires the character of Vyry, he argues that because her interests are limited to the welfare of her own family she cannot be seen to represent black women of the present day.

Carby, Hazel. "Ideologies of Black Folk: The Historical Novel of Slavery." In *Slavery and the Literary Imagination*, edited by Deborah E. McDowell and Arnold Rampersad. Baltimore: The Johns Hopkins University Press, 1989. An interesting comparison of Margaret Mitchell and Margaret Walker, emphasizing the different ways the two writers used the oral histories on which their works were based. Urges that *Jubilee* be given more critical attention.

Goodman, Charlotte. "From *Uncle Tom's Cabin* to Vyry's Kitchen: The Black Female Folk Tradition in Margaret Walker's *Jubilee.*" In *Tradition and the Talents of Women*, edited by Florence Howe. Urbana: University of Illinois Press, 1991. Defends *Jubilee* against criticism that it is bogged down in detail, arguing that the elements of everyday life mentioned by Walker are "signifiers" of the folk tradition that enabled black women to preserve a sense of community despite exile, slavery, and oppression.

Pettis, Joyce. "Margaret Walker: Black Woman Writer of the South." In *Southern Women Writers: The New Generation*, edited by Tonette Bond Inge. Tuscaloosa: University of Alabama Press, 1990. Walker's concerns with contemporary issues justify her placement in "the new generation." *Jubilee* is significant as the first realistic historical novel about slavery and the Civil War to be written by a black writer.

Traylor, Eleanor. "Music as Theme: The Blues Mode in the Works of Margaret Walker." In *Black Women Writers, 1950-1980: A Critical Evaluation*, edited by Mari Evans. Garden City, N.Y.: Anchor Press/Doubleday, 1983. Shows how Vyry's songs not only "articulate progressive stages in her life" but also "amplify its meaning," uniting her story with that of her people and her place and time. An illuminating study.

Walker, Margaret. *How I Wrote Jubilee.* Chicago: Third World Press, 1972. A detailed description of the process through which *Jubilee* took shape. Invaluable.

_____. Interview by John Griffin Jones. In *Mississippi Writers Talking*. Vol. 2. Jackson: University Press of Mississippi, 1983. An important interview. Walker refers explicitly to *Jubilee* in pointing out various responses of African Americans to racism. Also discusses why the battle against sexism has not been the same for black women as for white women.

Rosemary M. Canfield Reisman

JUST ABOVE MY HEAD

Author: James Baldwin (1924-1987)
Type of work: Novel
Type of plot: Psychological realism
Time of plot: Approximately 1950 to 1978
Locale: New York City; the Deep South; Paris, France; and London, England
First published: 1979

> *Principal characters:*
>> HALL MONTANA, the narrator, a middle-aged African American
>> who has been successful in many different business enterprises,
>> including advertising and publishing
>> ARTHUR MONTANA, Hall's younger brother, a gifted gospel singer
>> who becomes an international celebrity
>> JULIA MILLER, a beautiful black girl who first appears as an
>> eleven-year-old child prodigy achieving spectacular success
>> as an evangelist; she later becomes a prostitute and a fashion
>> model
>> JOEL MILLER, Julia's father, a selfish man who is happy to exploit
>> his daughter for his own financial gain
>> JIMMY MILLER, Julia's brother, two years her junior
>> ALEXANDER "PEANUT" THEOPHILUS BROWN, a close friend of both
>> the Miller and Montana families
>> CRUNCH HOGAN, another close friend of both the Miller and
>> Montana families

The Novel

Just Above My Head is narrated by Hall Montana and deals with his memories of his beloved brother Arthur as well as of friends and other relatives. There is a deliberate contrast between the life-styles and attitudes of the older generation of African Americans, consisting of the parents of Hall and Arthur Montana and Julia and Jimmy Miller, and those of the younger generation. Though still stigmatized by racial prejudice, the young people have better opportunities to achieve financial success and self-realization. Hall's memoirs mainly concern the struggles of Arthur, Julia, and himself to survive and grow in a white-dominated society.

The story begins two years after Arthur's death but immediately flashes back to the days of his and Hall's childhood, at the beginning of the Korean War. All the young men in the story live under the shadow of the draft. Hall is eventually drafted and loses touch with the other characters while he is serving in Korea.

One of the most important people in the lives of Arthur and Hall is Julia Miller, who at the age of eleven is inspired by the Holy Ghost and is in constant demand as a preacher at black fundamentalist churches. The book is flavored with many excerpts from Julia's sermons as well as abundant quotations from traditional gospel hymns. Baldwin attempts to give his work the feeling of a musical composition, thereby suggesting that music has played a large part in the survival of African Americans in a hostile environment.

Arthur sings in churches and soon becomes recognized for his outstanding voice and impassioned delivery. Throughout the novel, Arthur's fame increases. He is an international celebrity by the time of his death.

When the "Freedom Movement" begins in the South, Arthur and his young colleagues are asked to appear at political rallies, most of which are held at churches because these are the only relatively safe places to hold such meetings. Many pages of the book are devoted to descriptions of the religious-political meetings in rural churches surrounded by hostile white mobs and law enforcement officials who are indifferent at best. On one of these tours, Arthur's friend Peanut mysteriously disappears. He is never heard from again; he has probably been abducted and murdered in some isolated field in the dead of night.

At the age of fourteen, Julia is brutally raped by her father and thereafter forced to live in incest. These incidents occur at a time when she has lost her religious faith and no longer desires to preach. With the help of Crunch Hogan, she breaks away from her father. Later, she has a love affair with Hall. Her beauty and personality enable her to succeed as a fashion model in the competitive milieu of Manhattan. She is chronically dissatisfied, however, and goes to North Africa for an extended period to try to find herself through tracing her roots.

Arthur's career skyrockets when he begins a love affair with Julia's brother Jimmy, illustrating one of Baldwin's key ideas, that people find themselves or destroy themselves through love. Arthur and Jimmy travel the world together and live together for many years. Arthur's guilt about his homosexual tendencies is responsible for his heavy drinking. The hard itinerant life he leads as a musician causes him to die prematurely of a heart attack in a London pub.

The Characters

At least four of the characters in *Just Above My Head* are projections of the author himself. Hall Montana is Baldwin the novelist. Hall is a conservative heterosexual who works at conventional jobs and becomes a devoted father to two children. At one time in his life, Baldwin seriously considered getting married and trying to overcome his homosexual tendencies through leading a conventional life involving marriage and a steady job. He decided that such a course would be unfair to himself and to any woman he married. He could not continue to deny his homosexuality and he could not indenture himself to the routine job and financial responsibilities that marriage would entail. Instead, he moved to Paris and led a precarious existence for many years as a freelance writer.

Arthur Montana, the gospel singer, is Baldwin the homosexual artist and has Baldwin's middle name as his first name. Like Baldwin, Arthur is an acknowledged homosexual who has no intention of leading a conventional heterosexual life. Like

Baldwin, Arthur goes to Europe and finds himself happier and more creative in the artistic world of Paris. Baldwin moved to Europe early in his career because the stigma of being black in the United States made him so angry and humiliated that he felt unable to be creative. He lived in France for most of his life and eventually was honored by being appointed a member of the Legion of Honor, the highest honor that can be given an artist in France.

Julia Miller, the most intriguing character in the book, is Baldwin the preacher. As a child, Baldwin acquired considerable fame in Harlem as a child evangelist. He suffered exactly the same loss of religious faith at approximately the same age as does Julia. The fact that Julia is a girl does not really make her different from Baldwin himself, because he had pronounced feminine tendencies from early childhood, when he served as a substitute mother to his younger brothers and sisters. He saw himself in some ways as a woman and wished he had been born a woman. Like Julia, Baldwin turned to carnal love when he became disillusioned with the spiritual love he had preached as a child. Julia's abusive father, Joel Miller, was modeled after Baldwin's own stepfather, who was subject to violent rages and would beat young Baldwin sadistically.

The character of Jimmy Miller has been given Baldwin's own first name. Like Baldwin, Jimmy has a loving nature and considerable social charm. Jimmy represents the loving, dependent side of Baldwin's nature. Jimmy wants to find a strong man who will love and protect him; he finds that person in Arthur Montana to whom he remains devoted for many years. Jimmy and Arthur are both talented musicians, and in this respect they are also projections of Baldwin, who was a lifelong music lover and at one time considered a career as a jazz pianist.

It is a sign of Baldwin's genius that he was able to project himself into so many different characters. Many novelists create characters who are alter egos, but the typical novel contains only one such character, who is the hero and viewpoint character. Baldwin has displayed his versatility by projecting himself into Hall, Arthur, Julia, and Jimmy as well as by modeling other characters after his own friends and relatives. *Just Above My Head* is Baldwin's autobiography in disguise.

Much of the characterization is effected through Hall Montana's narration. He has strong feelings about all these characters and writes about them with extreme sensitivity. Through the character of Hall, Baldwin is able to express his own opinions and feelings without being that most annoying type of novelist, the "intrusive author" who violates the verisimilitude of his fictitious creation by interjecting his own comments.

Themes and Meanings

The most important theme in *Just Above My Head* concerns homosexuality. Baldwin was plagued throughout his life by guilt about his openly acknowledged homosexual nature. One of the reasons he moved to Paris was that Europeans were much more tolerant of such proclivities at a time when homosexuals were treated like vicious criminals in the United States. Through the character of Arthur, Baldwin attempts to show that homosexuals deserve understanding because they can be valuable contributors to society. In several places in his novel, Baldwin provides lengthy and detailed descriptions of sexual behavior between two males, including sodomy, fellatio, and mutual masturbation. Some readers might find these descriptions offensive; Baldwin, however, believed that genuine love between two individuals of the same sex was just as beautiful as heterosexual love.

The meaning of the title *Just Above My Head* does not become clear until the end of the book. Baldwin's description of Arthur's death contains the following sentence:

> He starts down the steps, and the steps rise up, striking him in the chest again, pounding between his shoulder blades, throwing him down on his back, staring down at him from the ceiling, just above his head.

Just Above My Head was the last important work Baldwin penned, and he died eight years after it was published. Throughout the novel he implies that the shadow of death is hovering over his own head and that, furthermore, it hovers over all of us. As fellow mortals, we should be tolerant of each other's faults and differences. This admonition also applies to the views on race relations described in the novel: People should be tolerant of racial differences as well as all other kinds of differences that exist between one human being and another.

Baldwin was fervently religious as a youth and never got over his instinctively religious perception of the world, even though he gave up being an evangelist at the age of fourteen. Baldwin came to see sexual love as equivalent to the spiritual love preached by Christianity, provided that the sexual love was genuine. His novel implicitly teaches that the solution to America's racial problem lies in love. This is reinforced by his descriptions of homosexual love between white and black men. Baldwin thought he had conquered racial prejudice; many of his friends and lovers were white. He disapproved of black protest literature and in his novels attempted to show that differences between whites and blacks were purely illusory.

The successful professional careers of the three most important characters—Hall Montana, Arthur Montana, and Julia Miller—are intended to symbolize changing times. African Americans still had an uphill battle to fight but had won important victories through such activities as the Freedom Movement. They could succeed in any field of endeavor if they refused to allow themselves to be psychologically crippled by the disease of racism.

Baldwin also felt guilty because he was so successful and because he lived a comfortable, bohemian existence in Europe rather than being in the midst of the civil rights struggle in the United States. These feelings are projected onto Arthur Montana. He attempts to show that Arthur's success does not compensate him for his unhappy itinerant existence.

Critical Context

Just Above My Head was on the best-seller list of the *Washington Post* for thirty-seven weeks but did not make the best-seller list of *The New York Times.* The novel received widespread critical attention because Baldwin was one of the most famous writers of his day. Most reviewers were respectful but unenthusiastic. Darryl Pinckney, for example, wrote a long review of the book for *The New York Review of Books*, calling it "flat and didactic" but acknowledging that Baldwin was, as always, effective in describing "the maddening halfway house that the black man finds himself in in late-twentieth-century America."

The consensus seemed to be that the book did not fulfill its ambitious design. It was too long, but it did not seem complete. One of the major problems frequently pointed out concerned its complex structure. The whole story is supposedly told from the point of view of Hall Montana, the narrator, yet he frequently describes events at which he was not present, including the most intimate sexual encounters between a man and a woman or between two men. How is Hall supposed to know what other people had been thinking and feeling in such situations? In several places Baldwin tried to explain away this obvious flaw by having Hall say that he was only imagining what went on, but if he was only imagining what went on in some situations, how is the reader to know when his narration is reliable and when it is not?

The importance of *Just Above My Head* is that it serves black authors as a model for a kind of novel different from that often associated with black novelists. Baldwin's novel might be called a "black protest novel against black protest novels." He believed that there were too many novels written in the spirit of Richard Wright's *Native Son* (1940) and Ralph Ellison's *Invisible Man* (1952). Baldwin wanted to demonstrate that black novelists could, and should, have more to say than that African Americans were victimized by white Americans. It was Baldwin who, more than any other black novelist, tried to forge a new kind of fiction in which African Americans were shown as unique individuals rather than as sullen, stereotyped victims of white oppression. Through dialogue, narrative, and example, Baldwin emphasized one of his most ardent beliefs, that racism is a double-edged sword that injures white Americans every bit as much as it does black Americans.

Bibliography

Campbell, James. *Talking at the Gates: A Life of James Baldwin.* New York: Viking Penguin, 1991. A well-written biography that focuses on how Baldwin was influenced by the world and how he influenced that world. Discusses his relations with contemporary authors such as Richard Wright, William Faulkner, Norman Mailer, and William Styron.

Clark, Kenneth B. *The Negro Protest.* Boston: Beacon Press, 1963. Consists of interviews with three of the most prominent black leaders of the period: James Baldwin, Malcolm X, and Martin Luther King, Jr. Clark gets them to talk about one another and then discusses the differences and similarities among these three dynamic individuals who shaped American history.

Kollhofer, Jakob J., ed. *James Baldwin: His Place in American Literary History and His Reception in Europe.* Frankfurt am Main, Germany: Peter Lang, 1991. A collection of essays, by American, French, and German experts, evaluating Baldwin's contribution to literature. Especially interesting in revealing the extent of Baldwin's reputation in Europe and the European viewpoint on race relations in the United States.

Stanley, Fred L., and Nancy V. Burt, eds. *Critical Essays on James Baldwin.* Boston: G. K. Hall, 1988. Contains essays on Baldwin's works in general as well as on his fiction, his nonfiction, and his plays. An essay by Eleanor W. Traylor focuses on *Just Above My Head.* Many other references to that novel throughout the book are listed in the index.

Troupe, Quincy, ed. *James Baldwin: The Legacy.* New York: Simon & Schuster, 1989. Produced in commemoration of Baldwin's death in 1987, this book is a collection of interviews and memoirs. It is illustrated with many photographs of Baldwin at various stages of his life and contains a valuable bibliography.

Weatherby, W. J. *James Baldwin: Artist on Fire.* New York: Donald Fine, 1989. An entertaining and illuminating biography based on conversations and interviews with more than one hundred people who knew Baldwin at different stages of his life. Weatherby himself was personally acquainted with Baldwin for more than twenty-eight years.

Bill Delaney

KINDRED

Author: Octavia E. Butler (1947-   )
Type of work: Novel
Type of plot: Fantasy
Time of plot: 1976 and the early 1800's
Locale: Los Angeles and Maryland
First published: 1979

> *Principal characters:*
> DANA FRANKLIN, a twenty-six-year-old African American writer
> RUFUS WEYLIN, the son of a slaveowner
> KEVIN FRANKLIN, Dana's white husband, a writer in his mid-
> thirties
> ALICE GREENWOOD, the Weylins' slave and Dana's ancestor

The Novel

Kindred traces the emotional and physical dilemmas Dana faces as a twentieth century African American woman periodically transported back to the antebellum South. In portraying the experiences of a 1976 woman who must readjust to life during the slavery era, Butler dramatizes important themes: the continuing relevance of the past to the present; the horrors of slavery, which have lost their reality for many, including Dana and her white husband, Kevin; and the ways in which the development of racist attitudes and behavior are a product of societal conditioning.

Dana's time-travel experiences begin, ironically, in 1976, the year of the American Bicentennial, a celebration of American freedom and independence. Dana's fantastic experiences begin on an ordinary day: While Dana and Kevin are unpacking cartons in their new home in Los Angeles, she is overcome by nausea and dizziness. She then finds herself at a riverbank at which she hears the cries of a drowning white child. After reviving him by giving him artificial respiration, she is attacked by the boy's mother, who thinks she has tried to kill him. As a man points a gun at Dana, she once again feels sick and faints. Dana immediately finds herself back at home in Los Angeles, yet she is covered with the mud of the riverbank. This episode contains elements that recur when Dana is transported to the past and then back to the present: She is sent back to the past when the life of Rufus Weylin, the son of a slaveowner, is in danger, and she is transported back to the present when her own life is in danger.

As a result of her second trip to the past, Dana learns more about the significance of the past to her own life. She learns that Rufus is an ancestor of hers who must live long enough to father a child named Hagar with a slave named Alice. Without the birth of Hagar, who initiates Dana's family line, Dana will not exist. Dana must, therefore, ensure the survival of Rufus, who has a tendency to find himself in life-threatening situations, in order to ensure her own existence. In addition, Dana takes an emotional interest in Rufus: from her second meeting with him, she wants to try to prevent him from accepting and practicing the racism that is a part both of his family and of the antebellum South. Thus, Dana feels that she needs to protect Rufus on both physical and psychological levels.

Though Dana's being transported back to the past by any danger to Rufus' life seems to ensure his physical survival, her ability to ensure his moral survival is undermined by the dual time level of the past and the present. During Dana's trips to the past, only a few minutes or hours go by in 1976; yet these short time spans can equal months in the alternative time of the antebellum South. The result is that when Dana returns to her life in the present for even a short time, years go by for Rufus. Consequently, Dana is gone from Rufus' life for too long for her to have a lasting influence on his racist attitudes.

Another central element of the plot arises as Dana's husband, Kevin, is transported back to the plantation with her after he holds her as she is called back to the past. The initial gap between Kevin's and Dana's perceptions of the antebellum South is central. At first, Kevin does not realize how badly slaves are treated. Also, he initially thinks that the nineteenth century would be a fascinating era during which to live. Yet after Kevin and Dana become separated and he spends five years in the antebellum South, Kevin's witnessing the abuse of slaves causes him to help some of them escape. Kevin's involvement in the lives of slaves makes the antebellum South appear as cruel and unjust to him as it does to Dana.

Meanwhile, Dana becomes more involved in the lives of the Weylin slaves and especially of Alice, to whom Rufus becomes more and more attracted as the years go by. Dana points out that Rufus' attitudes toward Alice make obvious that she has failed to prevent Rufus from becoming an abusive bigot. Rufus' assertion to Dana that he will have no qualms about raping Alice if she does not willingly become involved with him brings home to Dana that Rufus has internalized the racist and sexist attitudes of his family and of white society. His decision to rape and impregnate Alice both affirms his power and, ironically, ensures the birth of Hagar, who will initiate Dana's family line and ensure Dana's existence.

The climax of the action of the book comes when Dana is called back to the past on July 4, 1976, the day of the American Bicentennial. Dana finds that Alice has killed herself as a result of Rufus' threat to sell their children (a threat he makes to force Alice to stay with him). Moreover, Rufus makes clear his intention to rape Dana. Consequently, both Dana and Rufus are in danger, which reminds the reader that danger to Rufus makes Dana stay in the past and that danger to Dana transports her back to the present. Thus, the result of Dana's stabbing Rufus as he attacks her has an appropriate, though disfiguring, complication: She loses her left arm—it is literally lost in the past as Rufus clings to her—as she is transported for the final time to the present. The epilogue affirms that Dana and Kevin, reunited permanently in the present, can be free of Rufus. Yet they will always retain the knowledge of the personal meaning of the past to their lives.

The Characters

The book is told from the first-person point of view of the heroine, Dana. Consequently, the reader is exposed firsthand to Dana's reactions to being transported to the antebellum South; to Dana's evaluations of the nature of her white ancestor, Rufus; to her feelings about the initial naïveté of her husband concerning the oppression of blacks and American Indians in the nineteenth century; and to her growing understanding of the perils and strengths of blacks in general and slaves in particular.

Since the novel is told from Dana's point of view, the reader can clearly empathize with her reactions both to her extraordinary experiences and to the brutality of the slavery era. One can readily identify with Dana's feelings of powerlessness, since she must return to the antebellum South whenever Rufus' life is endangered. Dana's resultant inability to live normally in the present—her inability to drive a car, for example—becomes a vivid alteration in her life. Similarly, Dana's first-person narration makes vivid for the reader the cruelty and hardships blacks faced in the antebellum South. Seeing slaves beaten, for example, makes Dana (and the reader) aware that the beatings and abuse slaves suffered were much more shocking in reality than they seem through presentations on television and in films. Thus, Butler's use of Dana as narrator enlivens the book's subject matter.

Other characters are also brought vividly to life. Rufus develops from a boy who bonds with Dana into a complete racist who tries to rape her. Dana's desire to protect Rufus from such a decline makes the reader disappointed as he becomes the racist his society molds him to be. Another character whose development is enlivened by Dana's reactions is Kevin. For example, Kevin's naïve assumption that the nineteenth century would be a great time in which to live seems especially ridiculous in light of Dana's observations about the oppression of slaves and of Indians. The growth in Kevin's character is shown in a later conversation with Dana in which he tells her of his risking his safety to help slaves escape after he is separated from Dana and is left behind in the past. Butler uses Dana's conversations and experiences with other characters to show the dynamic nature of those characters.

Butler's use of Dana as the first-person narrator, therefore, does not create a myopic narrative style that makes everyone but the narrator seem static and flawed. Instead, Dana's narration highlights the development and complexity both of Dana and of *Kindred*'s other characters.

Themes and Meanings

Butler's portrayal of the two main characters, Dana and Rufus, conveys many of the novel's complex themes. The depth of the characterizations is contingent upon the narrative technique: By making Dana the first-person narrator, Butler makes the reader not only understand but also empathize with her psychological and physical dilemmas as she lives in the slavery era. Moreover, the empathy that Dana has for the slaves marks her narration, enhancing the reader's knowledge of the brutality they suffered.

One of *Kindred*'s central themes is the role of environment in shaping people's attitudes and personalities. Moreover, Butler makes clear her belief that environment and training shape one's self-image and, thus, one's feelings toward one's own and others' power or powerlessness. Butler's principal concern regarding these themes is the development and acceptance of racism. Similar to the main plot of Mark Twain's *The Tragedy of Pudd'nhead Wilson* (1894), these themes are enacted in Rufus' development, for Dana realizes that from childhood Rufus is being steadily trained to assume both his position as master and the related racist attitudes and behaviors. Kevin sums up this theme when he discusses Dana's hopes to prevent Rufus from becoming more racist as he grows up:

> After all, his environment will be influencing him every day you're gone. And from what I've heard, it's common in this time for the master's children to be on nearly equal terms with the slaves. But maturity is supposed to put both in their 'places.'

Another central theme is the relation of both race and gender roles to privilege and power. This theme is especially striking when one compares Rufus' and Kevin's experiences with Dana's and Alice's. Rufus asserts more and more boldly that racial superiority and abuse of African Americans, including his sexual abuse of Alice, are a part of his power and privilege as a white man. In comparison, Kevin's initial belief that it would be fun to live during the slavery era shows the racial naïveté and insensitivity afforded by his position as a white man who has lived free from oppression. In contrast, Butler portrays the sexism, sexual exploitation, and abuse that are symbolized especially by Alice's treatment at the hands of Rufus. Factors of race and gender are central to the oppression and exploitation Dana experiences, again mostly at the hands of Rufus.

Thus, while Butler does not underestimate mistreatment and exploitation of African American males, Dana's experiences in the antebellum South particularly make clear that the gender and racial privilege enjoyed by such vastly different white men as Rufus and Kevin negatively affect both the characters of these men and the lives of African American women.

Critical Context

Kindred, especially on its initial publication, was seen as a significant departure from the science fiction "Patternist" series, of which Butler's first three novels, *Patternmaster* (1976), *Mind of My Mind* (1977), and *Survivor* (1978) are a part. Yet as criticism on Butler has grown, critics have analyzed *Kindred* as embodying several of the important themes of the Patternist novels, particularly emphasizing the themes of power and of oppression as unifying topics. In addition, *Kindred*, as a result of its creative use of elements of the slave narrative, earned Butler increasing attention as an innovative interpreter of important themes of the history and literature of slavery in a genre not used by many African American writers. Thus the book has proved important to scholars who specialize in science fiction as well as to those who concentrate on African American literature. Moreover, Butler's emphasis on

Dana's strength and survival skills has resulted in an appreciation by critics who value the feminist aspects of the novel. Consequently, the feminist, science-fiction, and African American themes in *Kindred* have attracted a widening number of diverse readers and scholars.

Bibliography

Butler, Octavia. "Black Women and the Science Fiction Genre: Interview with Octavia Butler." Interview by Frances M. Beal. *Black Scholar* 17 (March/April, 1986): 14-18. An interview that gives insights into Butler's beliefs as a science-fiction writer and her thoughts on the relevance of the genre to the African American experience.

Govan, Sandra Y. "Connections, Links, and Extended Networks: Patterns in Octavia Butler's Science Fiction." *Black American Literature Forum* 18, no. 2 (Summer, 1984): 82-87. Identifies and compares recurring themes in Butler's novels, emphasizing power as a central topic in Butler's work. In addition, Govan discusses how power affects male-female relationships in Butler's fiction. Govan also discusses how Butler's characters endure hardship by using coping mechanisms and adaptability.

Salvaggio, Ruth. "Octavia Butler and the Black Science-Fiction Heroine." *Black American Literature Forum* 18, no. 2 (Summer, 1984): 78-81. Though this essay focuses on Butler's Patternist heroines, it identifies many themes and feminist characteristics that are also central to *Kindred*. Also discussed are the heroines' assertions of independence and power as they confront racism and sexism.

Washington, Mary Helen. "Meditations on History: The Slave Woman's Voice." In *Invented Lives: Narratives of Black Women, 1860-1960*. Garden City, N.Y.: Doubleday, 1987. Analyzes the ways in which African American women recounted their experiences as slaves. Gives readers insights on the literary representation of female slaves' lives.

Weixlmann, Joe. "An Octavia Butler Bibliography." *Black American Literature Forum* 18, no. 2 (Summer, 1984): 88-89. Presents a thorough bibliography on Butler's works.

Jane Davis

KWAKU
Or, The Man Who Could Not Keep His Mouth Shut

Author: Roy A. K. Heath (1926-   )
Type of work: Novel
Type of plot: Tragedy
Time of plot: The second half of the twentieth century
Locale: Guyana
First published: 1982

> *Principal characters:*
> KWAKU CHOLMONDELEY, the protagonist, an orphan who has been
>   reared by his uncle
> BLOSSOM DEAN, Kwaku's "lifelong friend and conscience," the
>   village bookworm
> MISS GWENDOLINE, Kwaku's wife through an arranged marriage
> MR. BARZEY, Kwaku's neighbor, a faith healer
> KWAKU'S UNCLE, who rears him after his mother dies and his
>   father disappears, and who has little affection for his nephew
> PHILOMENA, Kwaku's favorite daughter, who grows up to be a
>   flirtatious teenager
> RONA, Miss Gwendoline's favorite daughter

The Novel

   Kwaku focuses on the life of its protagonist, who, despite the fact that he is orphaned, bowlegged, and seemingly incapable of staying out of trouble, manages to rise from being a humble shoemaker in C village to becoming a famous healer in New Amsterdam, a large Guyanese city. A series of events, including an ill-advised promise he makes, plunges him and his family into poverty, alcoholism, and violence.

   Even when he is a child, Kwaku's desires for glory and fame lead him into a series of comic misadventures. He is not malicious: "The only flaw in himself was a weakness for letting his tongue run away with him." The boasts he makes and the stories he invents render him an outsider in his own village, where he is generally viewed as being unreliable. The low opinion that others generally hold of him does not prevent him from having high expectations for himself, however, so that when he wishes to marry, he feels entitled to give his matchmaking uncle a long list of specifications for his bride, including profession, height, degree of literacy, and even style of table manners.

   His arranged marriage to Gwendoline, a woman from far outside the village who is unaware of his bad reputation, transforms Kwaku into a reliable member of the community. He works hard as a shoemaker's apprentice, and as his family grows, he stays devoted to his wife. When his vanity drives him to seek the assistance of his next-door neighbor, the one-toothed Mr. Barzey, in ridding himself of gray hairs, he begins to develop artistic yearnings. Mr. Barzey's photographs offer Kwaku a window into a larger world, and he becomes "lost in a dream of far-away places."

Kwaku's tenuous hold on respectability, and his livelihood itself, is threatened when a plague of locusts attacks C village and destroys the coconut palms on which many of the villagers depend, directly or indirectly. The poverty that all but the government employees suffer affects his family, forcing him to send two of his children away to be cared for by relatives. An offer of help from Blossom Dean, Kwaku's lifelong friend, inflames Gwendoline's jealousy. The situation is worsened when Kwaku manages to breach the village conservancy and flood the cultivated fields. Although he is given temporary asylum by Blossom and her boyfriend Wilfred, he is eventually captured by the police, only to be released when Mr. Barzey confesses to the crime. The hunger of his children convinces Kwaku that it is time for him to seek his fortunes in the wider world.

Upon his arrival in New Amsterdam, Kwaku, after some initial difficulty, manages to apprentice himself to a shoemaker. After curing a neighbor's heart condition with garlic, he acquires a reputation as a healer and is able for the first time in his life to dress well, to send ample money home to his family, and to rise in the world. His fame as a healer grows, and with it "some unquenchable urge to be rich." Although he recognizes that this is not natural to him, he is driven by it. When he returns to C village for a visit, "the man who could not keep his mouth shut" once again gets himself into trouble with his tongue. His promise to a local fisherman that he can get his wayward daughter to return through his healing powers goes unfulfilled. In revenge, the fisherman places an obeah curse on Gwendoline to strike her blind. As Kwaku works in New Amsterdam to support his family for the next two years, she gradually loses control over her family. In order to reestablish order, Kwaku returns to his village, but he is unable to find any clients for his healing practice. By the time he finally returns to New Amsterdam with his family, he finds that he has been supplanted by another healer. He and his family gradually slip into poverty. At the close of the book, he and his family have been evicted from their home and are once again living with the shoemaker to whom he was apprenticed during his early days in the city. His twins have become brutal and wild, to the point where they beat up their father. Gwendoline has become an alcoholic, and Kwaku is reduced to digging through trash cans to find scraps to sell for pig fodder. Philomena, his favorite daughter, has given birth to an illegitimate child, and his sons are spending all of their time in a Rastafarian commune. The novel ends as Kwaku dances in a rum shop for pennies to buy cheap liquor and Gwendoline dreams of the village in which she was reared.

The Characters

Kwaku Cholmondeley fits into the tradition of the comic hero. He is resourceful, absurd, and full of dreams of glory. He is, however, more than a lovable idiot bumbling his way through a series of adventures. His loyalty to his family makes him a deeper, richer character, and the contrast between his dreams and the harsher reality that he experiences lends a poignancy to the work.

The two strongest female characters in the book, Miss Gwendoline and Blossom, are jealous of each other and are similar in their relationships to Kwaku. Both are strong allies of his, each bears at least one of his children, and both attempt to moderate his ambitions and keep him grounded in the world in which he lives. Both women struggle with their jealousy for each other. Neither is simply a killjoy, attempting only to tame a rebellious male spirit; each is a complex character in her own right. Some of the most painful scenes in the book occur as Gwendoline, once a vibrant, competent, intelligent woman, becomes increasingly isolated after losing her sight and finds her relationships with her beloved children fraying.

Mr. Barzey is one of the most complicated characters in the book, in that he embodies conflicts between tradition and technological advancement and between family and the desire to break free. His artistic endeavors set him apart from other characters, yet the art form that he has chosen, photography, is a means of capturing a world that may soon be lost. Although photography is an art form requiring modern equipment, his original purpose in taking photographs was to capture on film the spirits he saw as a child. His family is unsympathetic to his ambitions: His daughter-in-law uses his darkroom sink to wash dishes. These conflicts finally make life impossible for him, but before his death, he passes on his precious album of photographs to Kwaku, the man who is perhaps closest to him.

It is the myriad secondary characters, both villagers and residents of New Amsterdam, who provide the novel's texture. Practitioners of obeah, humorless members of Guyana's ruling party, lascivious women, uncomprehending bosses, and sarcastic village farmers all contribute to a varied portrayal of Guyanese life.

Themes and Meanings

There are several interconnected themes in *Kwaku*, among them the struggle for individual expression in a communal society, the conflict between the desire to live in a fictive world and the desire to live honorably and loyally, and the pull of modernity in a traditional culture. Throughout the novel, characters find their lives deeply affected by traditional methods of healing, even when that healing proves ineffective. Kwaku's relationship with Mr. Barzey develops in the context of the older man's futile attempts to treat his graying hair yet ends up by centering on the modern art of photography. Later on, Kwaku makes his fortune as a traditional healer. He loses that fortune when the exigencies of the marketplace—the appearance of a rival healer—force him out of the business. Emphasizing the traditional nature of these characters' lives is the language, sprinkled with Guyanese patois, Heath uses to narrate his story.

Against the backdrop of these traditional beliefs, Heath subtly invokes the economic difficulties created by the modern Guyanese state. Although the novel is not overtly political, there are references to the difficulties of living with an omnipresent ruling party in a country that seems to be on the verge of collapse. Kwaku's own gradual collapse seems to mirror that of his country, which like him is gradually sinking under the weight of its debt. There are rumors that spare parts and cars will no longer be imported into the country. There are people whose traditional occupations have been destroyed by new regulations, such as Kwaku's dead uncle, a cooper, who was put out of business by the introduction of the Pure Water Supply Scheme. A chance remark that Kwaku makes leads to his being paid a visit by two government officials, who sternly admonish him against disparaging the Party. Within this context, in which rumors abound, the truth is hard to determine, and the struggle for survival requires a great deal of ingenuity, storytelling becomes an important means of constructing an identity.

In *Kwaku*, truth is a commodity with fluctuating value. At times, lying can be a noble act, as when Mr. Barzey incriminates himself to protect Kwaku. At other times, lies provide the novel with a vehicle for comic relief. Kwaku is not the only liar in the book, but he is certainly the most active one. His lies are rarely designed to harm others; rather, they are his means of preserving hope in a world that sometimes offers him few opportunities for optimism. For example, when he first moves to New Amsterdam, he writes letters home describing his life in glowing terms, although he is in fact eking out an existence as a shoemaker's apprentice. He sees his lies as "additions to the dull fare of day-to-day living, like casreep to pepper-pot, or coconut to cook-up rice." Some of his lies get him into comic predicaments, such as his childhood boast of having witnessed an accident that he in fact never saw. That boast lands him in court to testify, a task that turns out to be time-consuming and troublesome. Although much of the novel's comic force is derived from the contrast between Kwaku's lies and the truth, by the novel's end Kwaku's lies have taken on tragic overtones. Rather than being jokes that the reader can enjoy, Kwaku's glowing accounts of his terrible existence come to seem both pathetic and brave: pathetic because transparent, and brave because imagination is ultimately the only means he has of exerting any kind of control over his life.

The reader's paradoxical experience of Kwaku as being both a brave and a foolish figure is reinforced by the narrative distance Heath maintains from his character. Kwaku's actions are often described at an almost sociological remove. Heath's clinical descriptions of his character's comic failures are interspersed with passages in which the reader is allowed a sympathetic entree into Kwaku's mind and allowed to experience fully his pains and joys.

Critical Context

Like Heath's five novels preceding it, *Kwaku* was reviewed favorably in British and American periodicals. Reviewers applauded the novel's verve, comic spirit, rich use of the vernacular, and undercurrent of tragedy. A Guyanese-born writer living in England, Roy Heath has had his work compared to that of V. S. Naipaul. Unlike Naipaul, Heath has not yet attracted a great deal of serious academic attention, perhaps because, as Charles R. Larson notes, he has "abandoned the overt element of protest so common in the works of so many third world writers."

Despite its emphasis on issues of family, home, and village, however, *Kwaku* is deeply concerned with the political issues of its time. As Heath has noted, Guyana's declaration of independence in 1966 was a formative event for him in his quest to be a writer. The political chaos of Guyana forms a powerful backdrop to the events of the novel. Perhaps even more important to the novel, however, are the Guyanese stories and folktales that Heath recalls having heard as a child. Although these stories have found their way into all of his fiction, they are particularly important in shaping the narrative of *Kwaku*, in which myths, fables, and storytelling itself take on great importance. Kwaku both survives and, often, embroils himself in improbably difficult situations through his love of storytelling, and this provides the novel with much of its comic energy. Equally important, however, and perhaps more moving are the scenes in which Kwaku, the loving father and husband, regales his family with folktales, stories that bring them together not only as a family but as members of a larger community. Ultimately, the reader joins this community, a fellowship based on a love of language and of narrative.

Bibliography

Bold, Alan. "The Good Shoemaker Schweik." *The Times Literary Supplement*, November 12, 1982, 1243. Views *Kwaku* as belonging to the comic tradition of Czech writer Jaroslav Hašek's *The Good Soldier Schweik* (1921-1923), the protagonist of which is also a "village idiot" who survives through creative stupidity.

Booklist. Review of *Kwaku: Or, The Man Who Could Not Keep His Mouth Shut*, by Roy A. K. Heath. 80 (October 1, 1983): 223. Sees *Kwaku*, despite its comic surface, as a tragic metaphor for the hopelessness and desperation of contemporary Guyanese life.

Larson, Charles R. "Metamorphoses and Other Shenanigans." *The New York Times Book Review* 89 (January 15, 1984): 11. Praises Heath's vivid portrayal of Guyanese village life, his sense of the irreverent, and his innovative language as well as the way he, in making a sudden shift from a comic to a tragic tone, challenges reader expectations that Kwaku will remain a lovable buffoon.

McWatt, Mark A. "Tragic Irony—The Hero as Victim: Three Novels of Roy A. K. Heath." In *Critical Issues in West Indian Literature*, edited by Erika Smilowitz and Roberta Q. Knowles. Parkersburg, Iowa: Caribbean Books, 1984. Provides a general discussion of Heath's literary technique, which McWatt identifies as a distancing from the terrible events he narrates. Sees this conjunction of the tragic and the ironic, and the position in which Heath's characters are thus placed, as an important commentary on the condition of West Indian people.

—————————. "Wives and Other Victims: Women in the Novels of Roy A. K. Heath." In *Out of the Kumbla: Caribbean Women and Literature*, edited by Carole Boyce Davies and Elaine Savory Fido. Trenton, N.J.: Africa World Press, 1990. Views all Roy Heath characters as victims of larger forces, with women being especially oppressed by their circumstances. Sees the domestic settings of Heath's novels functioning as re-creations of the slavery under which previous generations of Guyanese were forced to exist.

Laura Browder

LADY SINGS THE BLUES

Author: Billie Holiday (Eleanor Fagan Holiday, 1915-1959), with William Dufty
  (1916-   )
Type of work: Autobiography
Time of work: 1915-1956
Locale: The United States
First published: 1956

Principal personages:
  BILLIE HOLIDAY, one of the greatest jazz and blues singers of all
      time
  SADIE FAGAN, Holiday's mother, a powerful influence in her life
  CLARENCE FAGAN, Holiday's father, a traveling jazz musician who
      taught her to love music
  LOUIS MCKAY, Holiday's domineering and sometimes abusive
      husband, to whom she was slavishly devoted
  LESTER "PREZ" YOUNG, Holiday's close friend and frequent
      accompanist, one of the greatest jazz saxophonists
  COUNT BASIE, a famous African American bandleader who
      featured Holiday for many years
  LOUIS "SATCHMO" ARMSTRONG, a famous African American jazz
      trumpeter and bandleader who influenced Holiday's style
  BENNY GOODMAN, a famous white bandleader of the 1930's and
      1940's who helped Holiday in her early career
  ARTIE SHAW, another famous white bandleader of the same era
      who was instrumental in advancing Holiday's career

Form and Content

Lady Sings the Blues is a very loosely constructed autobiography arranged in chronological order but leaving many gaps. It is based on Billie Holiday's reminiscences as told to collaborator William Dufty, and as such is largely anecdotal. Holiday had a highly sociable, extroverted nature, and all her reminiscences are about the people she knew. Although her anecdotes are about other people, they reveal her own affectionate, generous, emotional personality. She did not relate to people in an impersonal manner: She either loved or hated them. Although she is considered to be one of the greatest and most influential jazz artists of all time, she devotes little attention to discussing technical aspects of her own music or that of her contemporaries. She is not a critic but an artist.

The book is divided into twenty-four short chapters, many of which bear the titles of popular songs. Readers familiar with Holiday's beautiful renditions of such songs as "Good Morning, Heartache," "Travelin' Light," "I Must Have That Man," and

"God Bless the Child" can imagine her inimitable voice singing a background accompaniment to the text.

The early chapters deal with Holiday's impoverished childhood in Baltimore, Maryland. Her mother was a housemaid and her father, who was seldom at home, was a musician. Her great-great-grandmother had been a slave and had borne sixteen children by her white master, so Holiday was one-eighth white.

Holiday's introduction to sex was early and traumatic. She was raped at the age of ten, and by the age of thirteen she was working as a prostitute. Her attitude toward prostitution was pragmatic: She preferred it to the alternative of hard, underpaid domestic labor. She had acquired a love for music from her talented father, but she did not realize that she had musical talent until someone asked her to sing at a nightclub. Although her vocal range was limited, she put her heart and soul into everything she sang. She had unerring timing, a sensual voice, and a unique ability to improvise variations on melodies the way a jazz musician would.

Musicians respected Holiday as much more than a vocalist. She truly understood music and could communicate back and forth with musicians while they were performing. She became famous as a New York City cabaret entertainer and soon attracted the notice of such influential white bandleaders as Benny Goodman and Artie Shaw. In the 1930's and 1940's, racial segregation was so rigorous that there was little social contact between blacks and whites except in nightclubs.

Holiday went on the road with Artie Shaw. Her main impressions of that period were of the prejudice she encountered everywhere she went. It was considered revolutionary for a black singer to appear with a white band. Throughout her book, Holiday describes how black musicians suffered financially from racial prejudice. Jazz, blues, and swing were all primarily black inventions, but white musicians were capitalizing on them because it was nearly impossible for black bands to get engagements in nightclubs, hotels, and theaters that paid good wages.

Holiday's career is connected with most of the greatest popular musicians and vocalists of her time, and she mentions many of them in her book. The names include Charlie Parker, Count Basie, Duke Ellington, Louis Armstrong, Bessie Smith, Ella Fitzgerald, and many others who shaped jazz into an art form of international prominence. Her best friend in the music world was the gifted saxophonist Lester Young, with whom she made many records. Holiday flatly denied rumors about their supposed ongoing sexual relationship.

Holiday had started smoking marijuana before the age of thirteen. She quickly acquired other bad habits. She was a heavy drinker and claims that at one time she smoked nearly a carton of cigarettes a day, regardless of the effect they might have on her delicate voice. Eventually she had her first introduction to hard drugs such as opium and heroin. Like many other jazz musicians, Holiday soon became a heroin addict. In 1937, she was arrested and sent to prison. Lesbianism was common in the women's prison where she served her sentence; she evidently had some experience with female lovers, although she does not go into detail. She was haunted by rumors of her lesbian tendencies, rumors she stoutly denied, for the rest of her life.

The truth about Holiday, which can be read between the lines, is that her early traumatic experiences with sex left her apathetic toward physical sex. What she wanted was real love and affection, and these seemed impossible for her to find. She began making as much as $2,000 a week, but she could never keep money because she allowed both men and women to exploit her. Her craving for cigarettes, liquor, and drugs reflected a craving for affection. She became involved with men who had vicious reputations. She appeared to like being brutalized by strong, ruthless men, perhaps because she felt guilty for going against the moral indoctrination she had received from her mother.

Holiday describes several of her trips to Europe, where she was widely acclaimed because of her recordings. Like many other black jazz performers, she found that Europeans gave her more respect as an artist and as a human being than she received at home. Europeans also exhibited a much more civilized attitude toward narcotics addiction, treating it as an illness rather than as a crime.

In the United States, law enforcement officials continued to hound her, possibly because they disapproved of the example she set as a role model. She describes an arrest for drug possession on February 23, 1956. Her book ends abruptly with her heading back to New York City on a bus without even enough money to buy anything to eat. After making a fortune as an entertainer and achieving international fame, she was as poor as when she scrubbed steps in Baltimore as a teenage girl.

The last three years of Holiday's tragic life are not recorded in *Lady Sings the Blues*. They were a downhill spiral because she had ruined her delicate voice with hard living and had also lost her perfect timing. She lived on her reputation, making appearances in second-rate nightclubs accompanied by second-rate musicians. She died of heart failure, cirrhosis of the liver, and kidney infection on July 17, 1959.

Any complete study of Holiday must include listening to her records. Anyone who listens to the jazz recordings of her youth and then turns to the blues recordings she made at the end of her career can hear her whole story in her voice. Fortunately, many albums are readily available at record stores and libraries. She is better known after her death, and is known to a wider international audience, than she was during her tempestuous, tragic lifetime.

Analysis

Lady Sings the Blues is a patchwork quilt of anecdotes with no consistent thesis holding it together. One of the major themes has to do with the difficulties of being a black jazz artist in America. White musicians such as Benny Goodman and Artie Shaw, as well as a host of others, were able to capitalize on an art form invented by African Americans and with roots in Africa. Black musicians were barred from many clubs and theaters because of racial prejudice. They found it nearly impossible to tour the United States, and in the 1930's and 1940's, touring the country was a prerequisite to financial success. Holiday describes this phenomenon with ironic humor rather than the bitterness that was expressed by many black jazz musicians in the 1960's and later decades.

Another important theme concerns drugs. Few people have had more experience with illicit drugs than Holiday, and she presents drug addiction as the worst form of hell on earth. The tragedy of this great artist is that her career was cut short by drugs, and the strongest moral to be drawn from her life is that using drugs is equivalent to committing suicide. She says explicitly:

> If you think dope is for kicks and for thrills, you're out of your mind. There are more kicks to be had in a good case of paralytic polio or by living in an iron lung. If you think you need stuff to play music or sing, you're crazy. It can fix you so you can't play nothing or sing nothing.
> The only thing that can happen to you is sooner or later you'll get busted, and once that happens, you'll never live it down. Just look at me.

She also believed that the American government's policy toward drug addicts was medieval:

> Imagine if the government chased sick people with diabetes, put a tax on insulin and drove it into the black market, told doctors they couldn't treat them, and then caught them, prosecuted them for not paying their taxes, and then sent them to jail. If we did that, everyone would know we were crazy. Yet we do practically the same thing every day in the week to sick people hooked on drugs. The jails are full and the problem is getting worse every day.

That was written in 1956, when the drug problem was minuscule compared to what it has since become. Many people came to advocate the decriminalization of narcotics as the only feasible solution to a problem that threatens to destroy society.

Many of the anecdotes in the book concern jails and law enforcement officers. Holiday's descriptions make it appear that the justice system in the United States was bigoted and corrupt. She claims that she was framed on at least two occasions by overzealous officers who planted incriminating evidence.

Holiday also talks at considerable length about the pleasures she had in life. Her life was not all suffering and tragedy; she enjoyed life to the fullest. She talks about the interesting people she was able to meet because of her fame as an entertainer. Her greatest pleasure, of course, was music. She learned to love music as a child and was absorbed in music all of her life. In connection with various performances of famous songs such as Cole Porter's "Night and Day," she describes her approach to singing: She had to believe in the words she was singing or else it was impossible for her to sing at all.

She was understandably proud of her rags-to-riches success. Throughout her autobiography, she brags about the big money she made as a performer and all the celebrities she met. The reader senses that she had to keep reassuring herself that the whole thing was not a dream that might melt away. This theme of emotional insecurity runs like a thread throughout the book and sheds light on her substance abuse. She mixed liquor, tobacco, barbiturates, marijuana, and heroin for much of her life. It is hardly surprising that she died at the age of forty-four.

As the title suggests, another major theme of *Lady Sings the Blues* is the blues form itself. The blues are a means of turning grief into joy, pain into pleasure, ugliness into beauty—of conquering despair. That seems to have been the overriding purpose of Billie Holiday's life and art. Her best records are as beautiful and as meaningful as when they were first created with many of the legendary accompanists of the jazz world.

Critical Context

Lady Sings the Blues sold many copies in the United States and abroad because of Billie Holiday's fame as a singer. The book received mixed reviews. Gilbert Millstein's review in *The New York Times*, for example, was extremely favorable. Millstein said that the personality of Billie Holiday emerged whole—"colloquial, bitter, generous, loving, foolish and tragic." On the other hand, Ralph J. Gleason was extremely unsympathetic and even antagonistic in his 1956 review of the book in the *San Francisco Chronicle*. Holiday had recently received much adverse publicity in that city following a drug arrest. According to Gleason, *Lady Sings the Blues* is "a story packed with self-pity and biased by Miss Holiday's view that she was blameless in everything that happened to her and was the unending victim of prejudice."

It is unfortunately true that few great artists are fully appreciated until after their deaths, and Holiday's autobiography was published while she still had three painful years left to live. Since her death, biographers and musicologists have tended to treat her book with respect, although they generally concur that it glosses over many unpleasant facts and usually tries to present the singer in the best possible light.

The anecdotes about sexual promiscuity and drug use were shocking at the time. *The New Yorker* called the book "as bitter and uncompromising an autobiography as has been published in a long time," and *Time* said that "*Lady Sings the Blues* has the tone of truth." The truth that many people did not wish to hear was that racial prejudice was rampant in the United States and that poverty, crime, prostitution, and substance abuse among African Americans were induced in part by the economic and psychological affliction of being black in a predominantly white society.

Billie Holiday's book, published only a few years before the first Civil Rights Act and the revolutionary 1960's, was particularly effective in drawing public attention to the race problem because she was not only well known but also widely admired and even loved. The book helped to make African Americans aware of the economic exploitation that was a principal motivation behind racial prejudice. Black jazz musicians began in the 1960's to develop a more ethnocentric attitude toward their art. No longer were they content to see their music "ripped off" by white bandleaders, orchestrators, and performers who could capitalize on it while the black musicians themselves were confined largely to ghetto nightclubs or were forced to work for starvation wages. Holiday's feisty, forthright attitude, expressed in her daily life and in the pages of her autobiography, was an inspiration to black entertainers in particular and to African Americans in general.

Lady Sings the Blues is a short work of only 229 pages. It skips over many years—

even whole decades—of Holiday's life. Collaborator William Dufty toned down much of Holiday's profanity and invective because the book was to be published by a major white New York publisher and was intended to appeal to a large and predominantly white audience. Language in the book that was considered shocking in 1956 is now heard every night on television sitcoms. Many facts about Holiday's sex life and substance abuse were deliberately suppressed or considerably softened. Nevertheless, the book had a powerful impact because of the singer's reputation. Like *The Autobiography of Malcolm X* (1965), whose militant subject was strongly affected by Holiday's memoirs of her life experiences, it was one of the earliest autobiographies to attempt to change public awareness by telling the bitter, angry, shocking truth about the condition of African Americans at the time.

Bibliography

Chilton, John. *Billie's Blues: Billie Holiday Story, 1933-1959.* New York: Da Capo Press, 1975. The focus of this biography is on Holiday's development as an artist. The author personally interviewed or communicated with dozens of people and examined much of the material available in magazine and newspaper files. An excellent source of periodical references containing four chapters discussing her many recordings.

De Veaux, Alexis. *Don't Explain: A Song of Billie Holiday.* New York: Harper & Row, 1980. A fictional biography of Holiday that parallels the events described in *Lady Sings the Blues.* The entire story is told in poetic black English. It highlights the origin of the song "Don't Explain," which was created by Holiday while she was grieving over a faithless lover.

Kliment, Bud. *Billie Holiday: Singer.* New York: Chelsea House, 1990. This biography is part of the "Black Americans of Achievement" series. Kliment emphasizes the negative effects of racism on Holiday's life but also candidly discusses her self-destructive tendencies. Contains many excellent photographs.

Mezzrow, Milton. *Really the Blues.* New York: Random House, 1946. This highly entertaining book is a minor classic written by a musician who was active in the jazz world during the 1920's and 1930's. Mezzrow vividly describes the precarious lives of jazz musicians and discusses in knowledgeable terms the many different types of blues.

O'Meally, Robert. *Lady Day: The Many Faces of Billie Holiday.* New York: Arcade, 1991. This biography focuses on Holiday's development as a creative artist. Richly illustrated with photographs of Holiday from childhood to just before her death as well as photographs of all the people who were important in her life.

White, John. *Billie Holiday: Her Life and Times.* New York: Universe Books, 1987. This biography, first published in England, presents a different perspective by focusing on Holiday's early years in Baltimore and her pioneering role as the first black woman to sing with an all-white orchestra in segregated regions. The last chapter contains an illuminating evaluation of all of her recordings.

Bill Delaney

LAWD TODAY

Author: Richard Wright (1908-1960)
Type of work: Novel
Type of plot: Naturalism
Time of plot: February 12, 1936
Locale: The South Side of Chicago
First published: 1963

Principal characters:
> JAKE JACKSON, the protagonist, a narrow, frustrated, and
>   prejudiced postal worker
> LIL, Jake's long-suffering but stubborn wife
> ALBERT "AL" JOHNSON, a fellow postal worker and friend of Jake
> ROBERT "BOB" MADISON, a divorced postal worker and friend of
>   Jake
> NATHAN "SLIM" WILLIAMS, the third of Jake's friends from the
>   post office
> "DOC" HIGGINS, an older man who owns a barbershop
> DUKE, an idealistic young man
> BLANCHE, a seductive, light-skinned prostitute
> BLUE JUICE, a pimp

The Novel

Lawd Today is the story of one day in the life of Jake Jackson, detailing his daily routine from dawn into the early hours of the next morning. The story is cyclical, opening and closing in the Jackson apartment with conflict between husband and wife. Jake's day is periodically interrupted by radio broadcasts celebrating the annual holiday for the birthday of Abraham Lincoln, February 12.

The story is divided into three sections of descending length. The first and longest section, "Commonplace," describes Jake's morning from his waking until he goes to work. Angry at being awakened by the radio from a dream involving the climbing of an endless stairway, Jake picks a fight with his wife Lil over her chatting with the milkman and her doctor bills. After he beats Lil into submission, Jake dresses himself and reads the paper, making bigoted comments on contemporary world events. Jake admires the power of Adolf Hitler and of gangsters, empathizes with the misfortunes of millionaires, and criticizes communists, President Franklin D. Roosevelt, and Albert Einstein.

Leaving the house, Jake begins his busy morning by sorting through the mail, showing his interest in farfetched money-making schemes and patent medicines. He loses two dollars playing a popular lottery game at the Black Gold Policy Wheel when he bets three "sure win" symbols from his dream. Then, after admiring a picture of a blonde girl on an adventure film poster, he goes for a haircut and heart-to-heart at Doc Higgins's Tonsorial Palace. Doc listens to Jake's marital troubles and agrees to help him if Lil lodges another complaint at the post office about his wasting money and beating her. Meeting Bob, Slim, and Al for a game of bridge, Jake enjoys some good-natured kidding with his friends. Later, they all admire the knowledge of the patent medicine man and the pomp of the "generals" of the "Supreme Imperial War Council" in the Back-to-Africa parade.

The second section, "Squirrel Cage," deals with Jake's eight-hour shift at the main Chicago post office. Before his shift begins, Jake tries to get a loan from the paymaster, Jones. Jones refuses him and advises him to see the Board of Review about the status of his employment. They are prepared to fire Jake, since Lil has filed a third complaint, but through the timely intervention of Doc Higgins, Jake is able to keep his job, after which he is able to borrow a hundred dollars at high interest from Jones.

The eight-hour shift is a seemingly endless series of tedious, repetitive tasks involved in sorting and processing mail, all performed under close supervision to assure maximum efficiency of the workers. While hand-stamping mail after lunch, Jake and his three friends have a long conversation that ranges over topics that include sex, how to dominate women, the benefits of the National Guard, and a cynical analysis of race relations.

The third and shortest section, "Rats' Alley," describes the leisure activities of Jake and his friends, which begin after work and continue well past midnight. After being seduced and set up by Blanche, being robbed of his borrowed money, and getting beaten up by Blue Juice at a nightclub, Jake staggers home drunk. There, he has a final fight with Lil, and she knocks him out with a piece of a broken mirror. He collapses in a pool of his own blood.

The Characters

Jake is a frustrated member of the black lower-middle class who has become a bigot and a domestic tyrant. Jake is a living stereotype and a negative reflection of white, working-class prejudices. A stock character who does not develop, Jake has not learned either to deal with the limitations of his world or to imagine an alternative.

When his ambition is frustrated in his dull, dead-end job, Jake puts his faith in unrealistic ways to change his life such as get-rich-quick schemes and gambling. He sees Lil as one of the forces arrayed against his success, and he feels that he must dominate her in order to affirm his own value. Disappointed with his family life, he seeks male companionship, excitement in drinking, and sexual satisfaction from prostitutes. The closest Jake comes to self-affirmation is the drunken realization that, even though he has been beaten and robbed, at least he has no one to blame for his troubles but himself. Stumbling home from "Rats' Alley," Jake yells, "BUT WHEN I WAS FLYING I WAS A FLYING FOOL!"

Lil Jackson is an embattled housewife, terrorized and dominated by her husband, who must fight for dignity and financial support. Having previously been fooled by

Jake into having an unnecessary abortion that has left her with a tumor requiring repeated treatments and operations, Lil must rely on him to pay her recurring doctor bills. When she is not trying to get money for medical and household expenses, threatening to complain of Jake's violence to the post office, or fending off physical attacks, Lil turns for comfort to religious magazines.

Jake prefers the easy camaraderie of male companionship to the responsibility represented by Lil. Despite Al Johnson's high blood pressure and heart condition, Jake envies his swaggering good cheer and National Guard membership and even agrees to join the Guard after Al's sales pitch. Jake and Al constantly compete for dominance in the world of the four friends.

Bob Madison and Nathan "Slim" Williams are sickly counterparts to Jake and Al whose bad health shows the consequences of fast living in the ghetto. Jake's friendship is of doubtful benefit for these two. Jake practically pours whiskey down Bob's throat, even though it will aggravate Bob's inflammation, while Slim's tubercular coughing disgusts and frightens Jake more than its fills him with sympathy.

Doc Higgins is a hypocrite who hides his own self-interested behavior under an appearance of helping his community. A small-business owner who preaches a philosophy of self-help, Doc relies on his political connections to help him get ahead. Rejecting any politics of change, he believes that "we colored folks ought to stick with the rich white folks." While seeming to be Jake's friend and helping him out of a difficult situation, Doc takes advantage of Jake's trouble with the post office for his own monetary gain. After the Review Board agrees not to fire Jake, Doc charges him $150 for his assistance, double the amount upon which they had agreed.

Blanche represents the seduction and danger of unmarried, free women. She is the unattainable object of desire for Jake. Blue Juice is a powerful black man who, like Doc Higgins, is better able to control his environment than Jake is and who takes advantage of Jake's naïveté.

Themes and Meanings

Unlike other African American works that depict the power of racism and the squalid life of the urban ghetto, *Lawd Today* focuses on a black villain-hero who is largely responsible for his own condition. The narrative presents Jake naturalistically, through description and through his own speech and actions, without making any explicit criticism. Yet his fate as a prisoner of his own prejudices against various groups and his unrealistic beliefs about how to improve his life become clear in the failure of all of his attempts at personal liberation.

Jake is an example of how black men from the South are left without moral guidance when rural folk ties begin to erode in Northern cities. Without benefit of family and tradition to validate and affirm black identity against the forces of racist society, men such as Jake have no alternative to the bigotry of the media and the cheapness of consumer culture.

While Jake's situation is particular to a black man, it also shares some of the problems of the American workingman in general. Because he believes what he reads in the papers and hears on the radio, Jake accepts the common bigotry of the unenlightened. His commentary on the newspaper headlines demonstrates that he accepts the worst prejudices of white society against Jews, foreigners, communists, and reform in general. For this reason, he can imagine no alternative to materialism and the pursuit of status based on money and power—what Wright elsewhere called American society's pursuit of trash.

An alternative to everyday life that Jake admires but does not pursue is African American nationalism. While the Back-to-Africa movement seems to offer some hope of racial pride to dispirited urban blacks, its promise of liberation is false. The proud, uniformed generals of the fictional African empire represent how the movement has borrowed the worst aspect of white imperialism, the love of power and its trappings, despite all of its claims about promoting the "Brotherhood of Man, Sisterhood of Woman and the Fatherhood of God."

Juxtaposed to the story of Jake's day is the periodic radio chatter about Lincoln's birthday. The platitudes about the glory of the Civil War and the emancipation of the slaves contrast with the country's failure to reach the goals of racial equality more than seventy years later. This failure is represented by conditions in Chicago's segregated ghetto and by the failure of all of Jake's attempts to better his condition and affirm his identity as a black man.

In *Lawd Today*, the only way for men to define themselves as independent beings is against black women. Men such as Jake see only two kinds of women, mothers and whores, and each type exerts a different kind of control over black men. Mothers represent rural, folk, Christian, and family values. Having left his own rural family milieu to achieve personal independence, Jake tricks Lil into the abortion to prevent her from playing the full mother role, and he beats her to assert his authority. Blanche, the prostitute, offers the promise of an escape from drab everyday life. She uses her sexual power over Jake to trick him out of his money and deprives him of his masculine power.

Critical Context

Since *Lawd Today* was finally published in 1963, critics have debated its merits. Some have argued that the book is a flawed early novel and cite Wright's inability to publish it during his lifetime as evidence of its shortcomings. Wright wrote, revised, and sent out the novel several times from 1931 to 1937, but it was uniformly rejected by publishers. Published after Wright's death, *Lawd Today* has never received the critical attention accorded Wright's autobiographical *Black Boy* (1945) or his other novel about the Chicago ghetto, *Native Son* (1940).

Lawd Today has been criticized as an apprentice novel far inferior to Wright's later work and as an unoriginal text that relies too heavily on borrowings from John Dos Passos, James T. Farrell, and other white writers. Critics have rejected it as dull, unimaginative, and full of unconnected, hackneyed episodes that fail to come together in a compelling plot. Some critics have asserted that the novel is offensive because it relies on so many negative black stereotypes.

Nevertheless, *Lawd Today* has been praised for anticipating Wright's later work. The unlucky antihero Jake Jackson seems to be a model for the more tragic Bigger Thomas. Some have argued that *Lawd Today* even surpasses Wright's later stories and novels in its skillful use of satire and humor that is not threatened by sensational incidents. Wright's first novel has been praised for its structure and balance and for the coherence of its imagery as well as for its use of experimental writing techniques. The radio broadcasts of Lincoln's birthday in the background contrast the emancipation of the slaves with Jake's failed attempts at emancipation, and the melting together of the voices of Jake, Al, Bob, and Slim during the post office dialogue produces a nameless and typical workingman's voice, trapped in unoriginal thought.

The relationship between *Lawd Today* and Wright's activity in the Communist Party during the Depression is complex. The novel echoes communist criticism of capitalist society in its focus on corruption, racism, and the dullness of repetitive, supervised labor. Yet *Lawd Today* does not offer an alternative to Jake's existence, and its spokesman for the communist position, Duke, is restricted to a few statements that are rejected by Doc Higgins and Jake at the barbershop.

Bibliography

Burrison, William. "Another Look at *Lawd Today*: Richard Wright's Tricky Apprenticeship." *College Language Association Journal* 29 (June, 1986): 424-441. Both positive and negative assessments of *Lawd Today* have failed to present a detailed, comprehensive analysis of the text itself. The novel is organized according to the comic pattern of the fool/trickster tale; Jake is a version of the tragic fool. The irony of Jake's position is expressed through complex patterns of colors and numbers and through the use of Lincoln's birthday as background for Jake's unlucky day.

Fabre, Michel. *The Unfinished Quest of Richard Wright.* 2d ed. Translated by Isabel Barzun. Urbana: University of Illinois Press, 1993. The standard biography of Wright. Details his childhood in the South, his role in the literary scenes of Chicago and New York, his relationship with the Communist Party, and his final years among American writers in Paris. Includes interpretation of his novels and summaries of their reception. Fabre explains how *Lawd Today* is autobiographical, since the story of Jake is based on Wright's own experience working in the main Chicago post office during the Depression.

Hakutani, Yoshinobu. "Richard Wright's Experiment in Naturalism and Satire: *Lawd Today.*" *Studies in American Fiction* 14, no. 2 (Autumn, 1986): 165-178. Neither simply naturalism nor satire alone, Wright's novel is an experiment at combining the two types of plot to suggest that the foibles of Jake are those of human nature.

Leary, Lewis. "*Lawd Today*: Notes on Richard Wright's First/Last Novel." In *Critical Essays on Richard Wright*, edited by Yoshinobu Hakutani. Boston: G. K. Hall, 1982. Though *Lawd Today* is an apprentice novel, showing the influence of such writers as John Dos Passos, Gertrude Stein, and James T. Farrell, Wright's creation of Jake as a caricature of the white world is original.

Margolies, Edward. "Foreshadowings: *Lawd Today.*" In *The Art of Richard Wright.*

Carbondale: Southern Illinois University Press, 1969. Because of its subtle indirect social criticism, *Lawd Today* is in some ways more sophisticated than his most famous work, *Native Son*. Themes of the black man as both villain and hero, black nationalism, the erosion of folk ties in Northern cities, and the similarity of the hero's failed strivings to the absurdity of the existentialist hero anticipate major themes of Wright's later work.

Mootry, Maria K. "Bitches, Whores, and Woman Haters: Archetypes and Typologies in the Art of Richard Wright." In *Richard Wright: A Collection of Critical Essays*, edited by Richard Macksey and Frank E. Moorer. Englewood Cliffs, N.J.: Prentice-Hall, 1984. Argues that Jake's quest in *Lawd Today* is the quest of all Wright's heroes: the pursuit of freedom and manhood against the barriers of racism and the power of black women.

Erik D. Curren

THE LEARNING TREE

Author: Gordon Parks (1912-   )
Type of work: Novel
Type of plot: Domestic realism
Time of plot: The mid-1920's
Locale: Cherokee Flats, a small town in Kansas
First published: 1963

Principal characters:

NEWTON BUCHANAN WINGER, the protagonist, a young boy
SARAH WINGER, Newt's mother, the keystone of the Winger family
JACK WINGER, Sarah's husband and Newt's father, willing to do
   whatever work is necessary to keep his family together
ARCELLA JEFFERSON, Newt's first love
JEFFERSON CAVANAUGH, a white judge, the pillar of the community
   of Cherokee Flats
MARCUS SAVAGE, a slightly older contemporary of Newt

The Novel

   The Learning Tree relates two crucial years in the life of Newt Winger. It opens
with a terrible tornado that causes death and destruction in the small Kansas town of
Cherokee Flats and leads to Newt's sexual awakening as he is comforted during the
storm by Big Mabel. The novel concludes with the deaths of Newt's mother, Sarah,
and of Marcus Savage, whose last act before his own death is his attempt to murder
Newt in revenge for Newt's testimony against Marcus' father.

   Although death plays an ever-present role, *The Learning Tree* is also about growing up in small-town America in the early part of the twentieth century. Cherokee
Flats, with a population of six thousand, is home to both blacks and whites. Although blacks cannot compete with whites in athletic events or eat in the same ice
cream parlor, black and white children often play together. The high school is integrated, but the lower grades are not.

   Some experiences transcend racial boundaries. The rural nature of Cherokee Flats
gives Newt and his companions the opportunity to hunt, swim, and experience the
joys and sorrows that befall all children. Like most mothers, Sarah encourages Newt's
academic pursuits. She dreams that he will eventually find a better life. She expresses her faith that the next generation of African Americans will make a new
world for themselves, a world different from that of their parents. Sarah, a strongly
religious woman, impresses upon Newt that good people and bad people come in all
colors, and that all, regardless of color, have the possibility of experiencing redemption, even Marcus Savage, who was sentenced to reform school for beating up a local
white farmer, and even Clint, her drunken son-in-law, who constantly threatens to

kill his wife. Although Sarah hopes that Newt will eventually get away, she notes that the town is like a fruit tree, with good fruit and bad fruit, and "you can learn just as much here about people and things as you can learn any place else. . . . No matter if you go or stay, think of Cherokee Flats . . . till the day you die—let it be your learnin' tree."

Newt's first love is Arcella Jefferson. She is to be the only love of his life. Arcella, however, turns from Newt to Chauncey Cavanaugh, an older white boy whose father is Judge Cavanaugh, an important figure in the community. Arcella never explains her decision, but Newt ruminates that it might have been Chauncey's money or his automobile. Perhaps she might even have liked Chauncey. Whatever the reason for her change of affections, the "only thing wrong with her for Chauncey was her color." Chauncey gets her pregnant.

Rural Kansas is not the Deep South, but racial differences still matter. Newt fears death and worries that interracial violence might destroy the black community. His fear culminates in the murder of Jake Kiner, a white farmer, by Booker Savage, Marcus' father, who then places the murder weapon in the hands of a drunken white man, Silas Newall. Newt, who had been working for Kiner, secretly observes the killing, but he remains silent, concerned about what might happen if he reveals that a black man had murdered a white in Cherokee Flats. His conscience compels him to confide in his mother. At Silas Newall's trial, Newt courageously relates what he witnessed. Booker, in the courtroom at the time, attempts to flee. Some whites threaten to lynch Booker, who commits suicide rather than surrender.

Marcus, Booker's son, blames Newt for his father's death and vows revenge. Sarah, who had been in failing health for some time, dies first. Her last action is to calm her drunken son-in-law Clint, who had threatened to shoot his wife and anyone else who got in his way. Before she dies, Sarah gives her blessing to Newt, who is to move to Minnesota to live with one of his older sisters. His mother's last words to Newt are to make a man of himself and do the right thing. On her deathbed, Sarah sees Minnesota as Newt's promised land.

In the novel's conclusion, Marcus Savage steals a gun and attempts to kill Newt in revenge for Newt's testimony. In the resulting fight, Newt, who is winning, lets Marcus flee as the police close in. Newt secretly hopes that Marcus will escape, but there is no escape. The novel begins with death in a tornado and ends with Marcus' death in a fall down a cliff. Newt considers hunting for Marcus' body but instead heads for home and a new life in Minnesota.

The Characters

The Learning Tree is written in the third person, but the tale is related primarily through the eyes of Newt Winger. It is Newt's life the reader experiences, and it is through Newt that the world of Cherokee Flats comes alive. Gordon Parks, a famous photographer, has the literary ability to allow the reader to "see" that world through his words. Newt is both typical and atypical. With his young friends Beansie, Jappy, Skunk, and Earl, he loves to hike, to hunt, to swim, and even to steal fruit from a local farmer's peach trees.

Newt is more reflective than any of the other characters. Possibly this is because it is Newt's story, told mainly through his experiences. Hunting, swimming, and even stealing peaches were part of many boys' experiences in the small towns of early twentieth century America, but other aspects of Newt's character are unique. One of his ambitions is to go to college, an unusual goal for an African American in the 1920's. Chosen to make the graduation speech at his all-black grade school, Newt asserts that "We are proud to be black. . . . Our class does not expect life to be easy. We only expect it to be better, and we are determined to help make it so by contributing something to it ourselves." It is not easy to be an African American in Cherokee Flats. Once, while Newt is selling brooms door to door with his blind uncle, who populates his unseen world with people of all different colors, a white boy refers to Newt as "nigger." When Newt hits him in retaliation, the boy's mother cries to Newt, "You are a nigger! . . . Nigger! Nigger! Nigger!" On another occasion, a circus comes to town and the promoter puts on a round-robin fight featuring Newt, several of his friends, Marcus Savage, and two Mexicans. The audience is largely white, and during the fight Newt hears taunts about "niggers," "greasers," and "Sambos," even from small children. There is no escaping the significance of color.

Most of the other characters are not so well developed and are more stereotypical. Marcus Savage is so offended by the white world that when visited in reform school by an African American minister, Marcus cries, "You and your white God, git the hell out'a here!" There is little redeeming in Marcus' character other than his wish to avenge his father's death. Newt's father, Jack, is something of a stock figure, never understanding his talented son, always in awe of his wife's ability to handle crises, but nevertheless a noble and solid citizen. Even Sarah, Newt's mother, while more developed as a character, is also predictable. She is the strong African American woman who is the engine that drives the family onward and upward. In Newt's world, Sarah is the *deus ex machina*, the earth mother who will solve the problems besetting her world by comforting and motivating Newt, disarming her drunken son-in-law, and preventing the segregation of the high school. Her almost self-sacrificing death allows Newt to leave Cherokee Flats for Minnesota, a land Sarah and he hope offers greater opportunity.

The characters portrayed in *The Learning Tree* are not complicated. They are predictable, and in their predictability they reflect the perception of a young boy such as Newt. Parks's novel, even with its many adult aspects, is an adolescent boy's story.

Themes and Meanings

Gordon Parks, born in Fort Scott, Kansas, is one of the twentieth century's true Renaissance men. He is not only a novelist and writer but also a photographer, filmmaker, and musical composer. Born in 1912, Parks would have been about Newt's age at the time at which the novel is set. Parks's mother died when he was sixteen, and he moved to Minnesota. *The Learning Tree* is thus broadly autobiographical.

One major theme in the novel is that of the adolescent boy discovering his world, dreaming his dreams, playing with friends, and exploring love and sex. Newt's story is very much in a long tradition of American fiction featuring small-town boys and the joys and pains of growing up. Parks treats that boy's world with obvious nostalgia. It was his own life he was recapitulating, and there were many idyllic moments.

The theme of death is also at the heart of the novel. It is sometimes said that adolescents believe themselves to be immortal, but this was not true of Newt. He experienced death, and feared it. The tornado that opens the novel causes the death of a neighbor. Later, Newt is traumatized when forced to view a dead body in the local mortuary. A number of the characters die in the course of the story. Big Mabel, Newt's first sexual partner, dies in an auto accident, Jake Kiner is murdered by Booker Savage, Booker commits suicide, and Booker's son Marcus falls down a cliff attempting to escape from the police. Sarah's long decline lay like a shadow over Newt and the rest of the Winger family. It is only after Sarah's death that Newt is able to escape his fears. The night before Sarah's burial, Newt forces himself to lie on the floor in the room with the casket, and in time he is able to fall asleep. Death no longer has the same sting.

The Learning Tree is also the story of an African American in a predominantly white world. The violence endemic to the novel is largely racial in origin. If Judge Cavanaugh is the honorable white man, perhaps because he had lived with the Wingers as a child, the local policeman, Kirky, personifies the redneck white authority figure. Although he is not an inherently evil man, Kirky's racial prejudices invariably determine his actions. Sarah, because of her strong moral and religious beliefs, has some influence in Cherokee Flats, even on Kirky, but ultimately the white judge, the white policeman, and the white superintendent of schools have the power. Sarah tells Newt that Cherokee Flats should be his learning tree, and he learns that color matters in that world. In his graduation speech, he notes that "Our race is not the best liked in the world." That belief is reinforced immediately, when he and Arcella are unable to sit down and eat their ice cream in Sampson's drugstore. Only whites have that right.

Cherokee Flats might be suitable as a learning tree, but one must move on, must escape. A railroad running through town is a symbol both of prison and of freedom. Hall, the high-school principal, a white man who sympathized with Newt's college dreams, told him the story of Curtis Mathews, an African American who was the valedictorian when Hall graduated from college. Years later, Hall came across Mathews working as a redcap porter in a railroad station. Mathews' talents had been insufficient to overcome society's bigotry. The railroad through Cherokee Flats also went to Chicago, Seattle, and New York, lands of dreams and opportunity. Newt's brother-in-law, Clint, dreamed about escape, but his dreams never materialized. They remained firmly lodged in his bottles of alcohol. One day Newt and one of his friends, Earl, are riding in an automobile. Earl, the driver, races an onrushing train to a crossing, and in the resulting crash he loses his foot. Earl stays in Cherokee Flats. At the end it is Newt who will leave on the train.

Critical Context

The reviews of *The Learning Tree* were supportive but not enthusiastic. Whitney Balliett called it an old-fashioned melodrama, but with an African American rather than a white hero. Comparing it to Harper Lee's *To Kill a Mockingbird* (1960), Balliett complained about excessive "blood, blood, blood." David Dempsey also noted the melodramatic nature of the novel. Arguing that it was too much an adventure story, Dempsey disapproved of the plot. He found the significance of *The Learning Tree* in its portrayal of a time when African Americans were more concerned with their personal problems than with racial justice. Another reviewer, Nat Hentoff, called it a book for boys, not adults. Placing it in the literary tradition of works about small-town life by such writers as Mark Twain, Sherwood Anderson, and Thomas Wolfe, he noted the moralistic nature of the work and its characters, contrasting that with the moral ambiguities portrayed by Ralph Ellison and William Faulkner.

The reviewers reflected their own time. When the book was published in 1963, the Civil Rights movement was fighting racism on many fronts. Parks's portrayal of African Americans in the different world of the 1920's did not strike a familiar chord with the literary and social critics of a later time. The author writes of a society and a family in which traditional religious and moral values were accepted without question. By the 1960's, much had changed.

The Learning Tree has had little impact upon later African American writers, and later critical commentaries rarely discussed its significance as a work of art. Nevertheless, it has remained in print almost continuously since it was first published, and in 1969 it was made into a successful film directed by Gordon Parks, who became the first African American to direct a major Hollywood film. If not widely praised by critics, then or since, the novel has been read avidly by more than one generation of Americans.

Bibliography

Balliett, Whitney. Review of *The Learning Tree*, by Gordon Parks. *The New Yorker* 39 (November 2, 1963): 209. Calling Parks's novel an old-fashioned melodrama, Balliett wishes that it had focused more on the Wingers' home life rather than on the violent incidents that too often confronted young Newt.

Dempsey, David. "Witness to a Killing." *The New York Times Book Review*, September 15, 1963, 4. Dempsey's review of *The Learning Tree* was the most negative of the major reviews. His comments reflect the militant idealism of the Civil Rights movement, and he implies that art should serve politics. Parks was found lacking in this respect.

Hentoff, Nat. " 'Sorta Like Fruit.' " *New York Herald Tribune*, August 25, 1963, p. 6. Hentoff believed that boys would get more from the novel than would adults. He urged that *The Learning Tree* be placed on high-school reading lists, claiming that white children could learn much from Newt Winger's story and that black youths could identify with it more than with some other required literary works.

Moore, Deedee. "Shooting Straight: The Many Worlds of Gordon Parks." *Smithson-*

ian 20 (April, 1989): 66-77. A general article about Parks and his many accomplishments, written shortly after Parks was awarded the National Medal of Arts by President Ronald Reagan, an award that suggests the magnitude of the changes that took place during Parks's lifetime.

Yoder, Edwin M., Jr. "No Catch for the Hawk." *Saturday Review* 49 (February 12, 1966): 40. Yoder favorably reviews Parks's *A Choice of Weapons* (1966). Not disguised as fiction, this work tells of the barriers Parks faced after leaving Kansas. The reviewer called it an excellent introduction to what it meant to be black, poor, and ambitious in the years between the two world wars.

Eugene Larson

A LESSON BEFORE DYING

Author: Ernest J. Gaines (1933-   )
Type of work: Novel
Type of plot: Social realism
Time of plot: 1948
Locale: Southern Louisiana
First published: 1993

> *Principal characters:*
> JEFFERSON, a barely literate twenty-one-year-old black man
> GRANT WIGGINS, a university-educated schoolteacher, the
>   reluctant choice to teach Jefferson the lesson he must learn
>   before dying
> MISS EMMA, Jefferson's godmother
> TANTE LOU, Miss Emma's friend and Grant's aunt

The Novel

In the year 1948, in rural southern Louisiana, Jefferson, a barely literate black man of twenty-one, has been sentenced to death because he had the misfortune to be a bystander at a shooting that resulted in the death of a white man. The action of the novel covers the period between sentencing and execution. That the sentence will be carried out is never in serious doubt. The question the novel explores is the terms on which Jefferson will confront his own death.

The issue that organizes the novel arises from the plea a desperate defense attorney made to the jury at Jefferson's trial. Recognizing that an acquittal was impossible, he made it his goal to save Jefferson from the electric chair. A man, argued the attorney, can and should be held accountable for his actions. But when you look at Jefferson, he asked, do you see a man? To execute someone so simple, he concluded, would be like putting a hog in the electric chair.

The strategy did not work, but its effects are still felt, not by the jurors, but by Jefferson and those who care about him. His aged godmother, Miss Emma, accepts that Jefferson must die, but he must not die in the belief that he is no better than a hog. Before he dies, Jefferson must learn the lesson of his own dignity and humanity.

For this lesson, a teacher is required. Miss Emma, with the cooperation of her friend Lou, turns to Lou's nephew, Grant Wiggins. A product, like Jefferson himself, of the black quarter, Grant is a university graduate who now teaches the children of the quarter between the months of October and April, when the children are not working in the fields. At first, Grant resists the call. He has plenty on his mind, including the complexities of his relationship with Vivian, a schoolteacher in the nearby town of Bayonne who is in the process of getting divorced from her husband. Moreover, Grant is a man whose allotment of hope is just about used up. He cannot bring himself to believe that his work with the children can possibly make a positive difference in their lives. What, then, can he do for Jefferson? Who am I, Grant wants to know, to say what a man is, or how a man should die? It is hard enough to figure out how a man should live.

Even with Grant's reluctant participation, other obstacles remain, notably that represented by the local white power structure. Miss Emma can claim a right to special consideration because of the services she has rendered to powerful white families over the years. Her claim is acknowledged by the white people she has to convince, yet they remain dubious. For one thing, it is hard for a member of the white community, in this time and this place, to understand a project the purpose of which is to affirm the humanity of a black man, especially one under sentence of death. They want the execution to go smoothly and quietly. They are afraid that what Miss Emma proposes may stir up trouble, especially as it involves this educated black man, Grant, whose correct grammar strikes some of them as a provocation. For Emma's sake, they give their grudging consent to the undertaking.

Grant is not the only one involved in the attempt to do something for Jefferson. Grant and the Reverend Ambrose, the preacher from the quarter, often find themselves at cross purposes. For the Reverend Ambrose, what matters is not whether Jefferson affirms his human dignity but whether he finds salvation. Tensions between the Reverend Ambrose and Grant threaten to break out into conflict at any time.

The most challenging obstacle to the success of the project is Jefferson himself. He heard what his attorney said, he understood what he heard, and he is tempted to accept it. He has known few possibilities in his life, he has had very few choices, and now a freakish combination of circumstances has determined that he must die. Is this what it is to be a man? At one point, he even goes down on all fours and, hog-fashion, pushes his snout into his food dish.

At first, Jefferson resists all of Grant's efforts, and Grant, who was never enthusiastic about the project, is prepared to admit defeat. Miss Emma and Tante Lou, however, expect him to try—even more, they expect him to succeed—and Vivian adds her voice to theirs. In a situation he would never have chosen to become involved in, Grant must commit himself to the effort. The struggle begins to pay off when Jefferson agrees that he does not want to cause further pain to his godmother. In thus concerning himself with another, in the shadow of his own death, Jefferson begins to sense his place in the human family. He is touched by a gift from the schoolchildren, and he is grateful for the radio Grant brings to him. As he lets himself know these emotions, he begins to recognize that he is indeed a man.

Grant himself is by no means untouched by what is happening. In the commitment he found it so difficult to make, and in thus opening himself to the pain of sharing Jefferson's agony, he has begun to move toward a new realization of his own humanity.

The law takes its course. At the time designated by the state, Jefferson dies in the electric chair. Paul, a white jailer who has treated Jefferson and Grant with sympathy and respect, is able to tell Grant that Jefferson was the bravest man in the room. He also brings the diary that Jefferson has been keeping at Grant's suggestion. Capitalization is erratic, the spelling is weak, the punctuation is uncertain, and the style is inelegant, but the message of Jefferson's diary is clear: "tell them im a man." Paul and Grant, white man and black man, realize that Jefferson has indeed taught them a lesson before dying.

The Characters

The strong will of two women provides the energy that sets the action of *A Lesson Before Dying* in motion. The tension between two men who both have something to learn about what it is to be a man provides the central structural principle of the novel.

Miss Emma and Tante Lou are old women in 1948, the year in which the action of the novel takes place. Both were born not long after emancipation, and both have been servants in the homes of white people. They have learned the practice of humility, as required by their position in a racially ordered society, and they also know the deeper humility that is part of their Christian faith. They also know their own worth, and they know how important that knowledge is. That is, in part, what motivates their determination that Jefferson will not go to his death thinking himself less than a man. They know what they can claim for themselves within the place society has defined for them. They employ this knowledge when they present their project to Henri Pichot, whose influence in the region makes his approval a necessity. He must acknowledge that Miss Emma has a right to ask for special consideration, for even this insane social system has its rules, but the women must in turn ask in the tones required by their position within the system. Fortunately, Miss Emma, Tante Lou, and Henri Pichot know how the game is played.

Grant and Jefferson form at first glance an obvious contrast. Grant is an educated man who has known the world beyond the quarter, while Jefferson may seem to represent Grant's worst fears of what the quarter may normally be expected to produce. The design of the novel demands that these two touch each other at a very deep level, and that can happen convincingly only if it becomes evident that the two men share some quality that will permit that touching to occur. What both men need, as gradually becomes clear, is a recognition and acceptance of their own humanity. The circumstances of Jefferson's life and of his impending death make this immediately evident in his case. Grant, however, lives in a psychological prison. He is helpless to bring about a satisfactory resolution to his relationship with Vivian, and he is convinced that his efforts to educate the children of the quarter are an exercise in futility. That he is required by social convention to conceal the signs of his own education when talking to white people intensifies his sense of hopelessness. He lives therefore from moment to moment, in a constant, barely repressed awareness of his impotence. What he does not at first recognize is that his call to teach Jefferson will allow him to find his own dignity and humanity. Thus, he and Jefferson share a lesson, the lesson, perhaps, all people must learn before dying.

The interaction among these principal characters is enriched by an abundance of sharply drawn minor characters, both black and white. As is customary in Gaines's work, there are no stereotypes or caricatures to be found in this novel. He treats all of his characters, even those of whose conduct he must disapprove, with imaginative sympathy and generosity.

Themes and Meanings

Given the dramatic situation at its center, it is inevitable that a major theme of *A Lesson Before Dying* must be that announced by the questions that trouble Grant: What is a man? How must a man live? How must a man die? The word "man" here must be understood in two senses. One of these is the inclusive sense, according to which "man" is synonymous with "human being." This usage has become suspect as sexism in language has become an issue. In this case, in a novel in which this issue arises in an especially poignant way for a male character, the word "man" obviously speaks to the human condition as such. At the same time, "man" is also to be understood in its gender-specific sense. Certain of the issues raised in the novel touch on what is specifically expected of a male human being in a particular context, the context of southern Louisiana in 1948.

It would be too much to expect that a single novel could provide final answers to questions that go as deep as these. What readers can expect is that a novel that raises such questions as insistently as this one does will at least illuminate some aspects of what the answers might be.

The possibility of change, and of positive change, has been a frequent theme of Gaines's fiction. That possibility propels the action of his two best-known novels, *The Autobiography of Miss Jane Pittman* (1971) and *A Gathering of Old Men* (1983). That theme is present here as well. It is the possibility of change, of development, of transcendence that comes from within, from an awareness of self, that defines the humanity of both Jefferson and Grant. The inner action of the novel can be described as the gradual coming to recognition of this possibility in both characters. The way to this recognition may vary, but for both Jefferson and Grant it seems to involve openness to others and acceptance of the responsibilities that this openness entails. Jefferson accepts that he may be responsible for Miss Emma's pain and becomes resolute through that acceptance. Grant accepts as his own the responsibility initially imposed on him by Miss Emma and Tante Lou and thereby becomes capable of moving beyond his earlier acquiescence in futility. Jefferson must stand for the possibilities and potentials that Grant previously has been unable to see in his pupils.

The meaning of the novel rests as well on the psychological truth of its observations. For all the novel's emphasis on transcendence, it also shows, especially in most of the white characters, the strength that can be embodied in the struggle against change, whether individual or social. Henri Pichot seems related to characters found elsewhere in Gaines's work: white men (they usually are men) who are aware at some level of the inevitability of change but who refuse to be the agents of change. The transcendence that occurs in Jefferson and in Grant comes in tiny increments; there is for neither man a privileged moment of awakening.

The possibility of transcendence found in the individual human being may point to possibilities for the human community as well. Much of the interaction of black and white characters in this novel is based on conventions established over generations; the power of the past is strongly felt. The relationship of Paul to Jefferson and Grant suggests that the past may be transcended, a suggestion consistent with the thematic emphases of Gaines's earlier novels.

In its attention to social interaction, to the casual injustices of the period, and to the nuances of interaction, *A Lesson Before Dying* manifests the concerns associated with social realism. Social realism, however, tends to define character as a social product: We are what society makes us. In depicting characters who transcend social determinism, the novel moves on to the psychological, or, as some might say, to the spiritual.

Critical Context

Because critics had waited ten years for a new novel by Ernest J. Gaines, it is not surprising that interest in *A Lesson Before Dying* was high. Widely reviewed, the novel has been received very favorably by most critics, some of whom regard it as Gaines's finest work. Critics have especially called attention to those features of the novel most characteristic of Gaines's work in general: the absence of melodrama in treating a situation that might lend itself to melodramatic excess; the consistent avoidance of the propagandistic; and, more positively, the broad and generous humanity felt everywhere in the novel. Other forms of recognition include a nomination for the Southern Book Award for 1993. In June of 1993, it was announced that Ernest Gaines was a recipient of the prestigious MacArthur Grant, sometimes called the "genius grant," in recognition of his work over the years.

In *A Lesson Before Dying*, Gaines is true to the concerns and qualities manifested in his fiction throughout his career. He has always been a reflective, rather than an "angry," writer, and he has always been sensitive, as he is here, to the nuances of behavior, especially in the social interaction between different races and different generations. This attention to nuance has led some critics to find his fiction too gentle, too forgiving in its portrayal of characters who might easily be seen as villains. It is nevertheless impossible to question the integrity and moral consistency that characterize his work. Few critics have failed to note the quiet assurance of his art.

Readers familiar with the masterworks of African American fiction may be tempted to find in *A Lesson Before Dying* an intriguing relationship to Richard Wright's novel *Native Son* (1940). Most African American fiction writers to emerge since World War II have been aware of Wright's shadow, and some, such as James Baldwin, have apparently found it necessary to attempt to topple this giant as they struggle for their place in the sun. Gaines has rejected Wright as an influence, finding *Native Son* too urban to serve as a model for his own fiction. There is an interesting parallel between *A Lesson Before Dying* and the last section of *Native Son*. Both involve a character awaiting execution and the attempt of another character to establish some kind of communication with the condemned man. This is not the place for a detailed analysis of Wright's masterpiece, but the communication, or communion, that occurs between Grant and Jefferson might be read as Gaines's humanistic answer to the majestic bleakness of Richard Wright's vision.

Bibliography
Babb, Valerie Melissa. *Ernest Gaines.* Boston: Twayne, 1991. Although completed too early to contain a discussion of *A Lesson Before Dying*, this remains a useful general study of the author and his work. One of Babb's main themes is that Gaines's writing, while true to the African American experience, ultimately transcends that experience to voice the concerns of humanity.
Gaudet, Marcia, and Carl Wooton. "Looking Ahead." In *Porch Talk with Ernest Gaines: Conversations on the Writer's Craft.* Baton Rouge: Louisiana State University Press, 1990. In an interview, Gaines discusses *A Lesson Before Dying* as a work in progress. Comparisons of his comments and the finished work provide valuable insights into the processes of creation and revision.
Larson, Charles R. "End as a Man." *Chicago Tribune Books*, May 9, 1993, 5. More than any other novel of African American life, *A Lesson Before Dying* is about being a man in the face of adversity and about the morality of connectedness, of each individual's responsibility to his community.
Shepard, R. Z. "An A-Plus in Humanity." *Time* 141 (March 29, 1993): 65-66. The novel reflects Gaines's dramatic instinct for conveying the malevolence of racism and injustice without the usual accompanying self-righteousness.
Yardley, Jonathan. "Nothing but a Man." *The Washington Post Book World* 23 (March 28, 1993): 3. Gaines reflects the breadth and depth of mind to understand that generalizations are always suspect, that one must look at individual human beings instead of stereotypes if there is to be any hope of understanding. The real lesson in the novel is learned not by Jefferson but by others.

W. P. Kenney

LET ME BREATHE THUNDER

Author: William Attaway (1911-1986)
Type of work: Novel
Type of plot: Naturalism
Time of plot: The 1930's
Locale: The northwestern United States
First published: 1939

> *Principal characters:*
> ED, the narrator, a young white man in his twenties, a migrant worker
> STEP, a young white man in his twenties
> HI BOY, a nine-year-old Mexican boy abandoned by his family
> SAMPSON, the owner of Four Mile Farm, an apple and sheep ranch
> ANNA SAMPSON, a blonde teenage girl who likes film magazines; she falls in love with Step
> MAG, a fifty-three-year-old black woman, a former prostitute who owns a brothel
> COOPER, Mag's companion

The Novel

Let Me Breathe Thunder is a terse tale of three hobos in the western United States during the Great Depression. William Attaway's novel quickly builds to its tragic climax of racial brutality by depicting the social and economic desperation of the times. Step, Ed, and Hi Boy ride the rails looking for work and adventure. They sleep outdoors, travel both by day and by night, and eat when and where they can. They are at the mercy of the elements, the train "bulls," and the town police, who harass migrant workers.

Step and Ed have traveled the Southwest and West for years. Like thousands of other unemployed men during the Depression, they know no other life. A week before the novel starts, they meet up with Hi Boy, a Mexican boy who has ten dollars and does not speak English. Step takes the money. They travel to Seattle, where Step gets drunk, fights with a bartender over a woman, and knocks the man out. They flee from the town, buying tickets with the last of Hi Boy's money. Uncomfortable in the train, Step insults the conductor and other passengers. They eat in the dining car but cannot pay for the meal. As they are about to jump from the train to avoid their bill, a stranger pays for their food. The stranger, Sampson, offers them a job on his farm in Yakima. Step laughs at first at the job offer, but they follow the farmer after Step flips his lucky dog tail to decide whether to accept it.

They travel in a boxcar with three other hard-luck drifters with no jobs or homes, two of them white and one black. The hobos talk of wandering desperately in search of work and discuss their inability to settle down. Whites and blacks suffer the same indignities and poverty of the unemployed. Step gets angry at Hi Boy for complaining about the rain and cold, since such complaints violate the "code of toughness."

In Yakima, they visit Step's old friends, the black couple Mag and Cooper. Hi Boy gets a gun and punctures his hand with a fork to prove his courage to Step. At Sampson's farm, they get jobs and a place to sleep. Anna, Sampson's young daughter, likes Step, but Step sees all women as trouble. Ed warns Anna away from Step, but she pays no attention.

The farm sits in the cool clear air of the mountain desert. A family of rattlesnakes lives under the front porch, and wild pheasants feed with the chickens. Mount Rainier towers over the landscape, and thunder cracks on its snowy head even in clear weather. According to Indian legend, a trapped wandering spirit breathes thunder at its loss of freedom. Step and Ed castrate lambs and cultivate apples, but apples are left to rot on the trees because there are no buyers for them. Sampson begins to think of guns and revolution. His four sons died in World War I, and his wife died from her grief over their deaths.

Ed hints to Step about staying on the farm, but Step, afraid of growing soft, makes fun of him. Ed fears Step's control over Anna and forces Step to promise not to touch her. After Hi Boy's hand becomes infected, they go into town to see the doctor. The climax of the novel occurs rapidly as Step, Anna, Ed, and a girl he picks up get drunk at Mag's house. Step sleeps with Anna, who is destroyed by the loss of her virginity. Ed wants to run, but Step brings Anna home and lies to Sampson.

They decide to stay until payday. Sampson wants Hi Boy to remain. Step and Ed prepare to leave Hi Boy, and they try to evade Anna. Anna sneaks into town to say goodbye to Step. At Mag's house, she is attacked by Cooper and mistakenly shot in the arm by Mag. Anna is rescued by the white townspeople, who return to lynch Cooper. Cooper flees on the same train as Ed, Step, and Hi Boy. Ed saves Cooper from Step's wrath. They ride in an open boxcar at night in the freezing rain. Hi Boy's infection gets worse; he passes into a coma and dies. Ed and Step hide the body in a train heading for the Southwest. Lost in darkness, not sure where to go next, Ed and Step watch the train's lights disappear over the horizon.

The Characters

The characters in *Let Me Breathe Thunder* are described in simple, direct language. The hard-nosed Step fights his desires and often acts kindly. His affection for Ed and Hi Boy is subtle, in contrast to his tough exterior. He keeps an old dog tail for good luck. Step wants to be good, but his basic desires and economic conditions prove his undoing. With no past and no future, Step lives for the moment.

Ed is the narrator and principal character. He tells his tale in plain, everyday English. He does not reveal his age, background, or family history. Ed and Step live for the road. As traveling buddies, they share a past of trains and jobs and an affection stronger than any in the novel. At one time they had a dog named Butch that was killed by a train. They are irresponsible and happy until they run into Hi Boy, a Mexican boy whose family has been arrested for breaking into a train to steal food.

Hi Boy tries to fit into their wandering life, but Step thinks the boy is not tough enough to make it on the road.

Ed, Step, and Hi Boy go to Sampson's farm and confront the issues of family, work, and responsibility they had neglected for so long. Sampson's loneliness is relieved by the presence of the boys, and Step and Ed fall into a routine. Anna falls for Step and shatters the calm. Step is torn between sexual desire and fear of commitment to Anna. Ed gets Step to promise to leave Anna alone, but Step breaks his promise. After sleeping with Anna, Step wants to flee immediately but stays to get his paycheck and meet his fate. Anna sneaks away from the house and runs to Mag's to meet Step.

Ed fears that the wandering life will destroy him, the way it destroyed the three hobos they met in the dark rail car. The fact that one of the hobos is black and that Mag and Cooper, old friends of Step, are black does not register negatively on either Ed or Step. Step had saved Mag from being run out of town by outraged whites years before. Mag claims that the West is more tolerant than the South. Until the final racial incident, Ed and Step seem remarkably free of prejudice for white men of this period. Step has told Ed about Mag but never mentioned that she was black. This integrated balance is shattered when everyone thinks Cooper raped Anna.

Ed is attracted to Mag. He respects her strength, her independence, and the fact that at the age of fifty-three she still wants a man. He is impressed by her business sense and her property. Even though Mag and Cooper's life is far from easy, it offers the prospect of a settled existence. Mag is the strongest character in the novel because she does not live a life of illusion. Her generosity and deep understanding of human needs represent the power of folk people. The union of Mag and Cooper is destroyed when dormant racial hatred shatters the peaceful town. Even Step succumbs to insane racial rage against his old friends.

Sampson tries to maintain order, but all of his good luck symbols are destroyed. The high mountain breathes thunder into the clear sky, implying the coming forces of fate. None of the characters can change behavior soon enough to avert disaster. Cooper pretends to be attracted to Anna to make Mag jealous. He does not hurt or rape her, but Mag overreacts and shoots at Cooper, wounding Anna. Townspeople believe that there has been a rape, and Mag's carefully balanced existence is destroyed. Step and Ed rip Hi Boy out of the only home he might have. Everyone acts against his or her best interests, caught in a tragic vise of social, economic, and biological conditions.

Themes and Meanings

Let Me Breathe Thunder is a simply told story of migrant workers on the road caught in a predetermined universe of tragic proportions. Naturalistic in style and execution, the novel emphasizes a psychological connection between the characters and their environment. The deceptively naïve qualities of the text mask complicated symbols of forces beyond the characters' control. Economics, class, race, and biology determine their fates. Thus Hi Boy's tragic death and the burden of his character is implied by the name of the town, Las Cruces (the crosses), where Ed and Step find him. The towering mountain represents an unforgiving natural environment. Naturalism suggests that human beings are driven by the sexual, social, and economic structures that dictate their fates.

Migrant workers with no money and ranchers who let fruit rot on the ground are both products of larger economic forces. The inexorable machine of war eats up Sampson's four children, and the economic depression destroys his farm. Sampson believes in elemental human kindness and tries to appeal to Ed and Step's better side, but characters such as Step and Ed have been created in the forge of inhumane social conditions. Civilized feelings are brutally damaged by the sexual and economic powers that control them. Step and Ed's lack of personal history suggests disintegrated families. They have only each other and Hi Boy. They are restless, driven by cultural dislocation and economic deprivation, unable to take control of their lives.

Underneath their toughness, they are kindhearted, but each of their attempts to find happiness ends in failure because they have no power. First-person narration reveals the conflicts complicating their lives. Step's flirtation with Anna threatens the stability of Ed and Step's relationship. Ed feels responsible for Anna because of her father's kindness.

Perpetual movement and lack of commitment are pitted against the inherent human need for community and stability. This sense of community is offered by the Sampsons, but Step and Ed are more drawn to the black life-style of Mag and Cooper. These two worlds are segregated in Yakima, but Step and Ed bridge the gap. Mag is kind and friendly to everyone. Her folk skills save Anna, who runs to Mag's house to try and find Step. Until the final confrontation, racial prejudice is cleverly hidden. Once Cooper attacks Anna, racial hatred erupts in all of its absurd fury and reveals itself as a powerful social determinant.

The human frailty of the characters is overshadowed by the two great monoliths of the novel. The Great Depression is an economic and social entity driving lives in unseen ways, and the towering Mount Rainier represents the power of the natural order that controls the vicissitudes of human existence. The inevitable cycle of social and biological determinism results in destruction. The tragedy of human existence cannot be assuaged through symbolic offerings and good luck charms. Caught in the terrible grip of determinism, the characters play out their tragic fates against the backdrop of an unfeeling universe.

Critical Context

William Attaway is best known for his novel *Blood on the Forge* (1941), a novel with black characters about migration to the industrial North. *Let Me Breathe Thunder* shares many of the themes of proletarian struggle and economic determinism demonstrated in his later work. Most critics comment on the oddity of a black author writing what some call a derivative novel with white characters. Certainly, the influence of John Steinbeck's *Of Mice and Men* (1937) can be seen in the work.

Let Me Breathe Thunder contains three African Americans and one Mexican, who share a merciless fate with the poor white characters. Attaway demonstrates an understanding of both white and black consciousness and shows through the final climax the power and destruction of racial hatred. Written from the viewpoint of a white character, the book shows how white prejudice lies waiting to attack. The central theme of social and biological determinism applied to a novel about migrant workers establishes a democracy of the lost driven by race, class, and economic dysfunction. *Let Me Breathe Thunder* belongs to the proletarian novel tradition exemplified by such novels as Jack Conroy's *The Disinherited* (1933) and Tom Kromer's *Waiting for Nothing* (1935).

Let Me Breathe Thunder is a novel that can stand on its own. As a first novel, it successfully produces a compelling tension between characters both black and white, and environment. Its hard-bitten style is suggestive of the work of Ernest Hemingway and of the popular hard-boiled detective genre. Its blend of psychological and symbolic detail creates a moving depiction of characters swept up in forces beyond their control. The despair of characters locked in dark cattle cars hurtling through the night to nowhere resonates as an apt metaphor for Depression-era angst.

The motivations of and scenes between characters, both black and white, show an acute sense of human behavior. The plot structure tends toward the melodramatic, but the bleak tragedy of the characters' existence provides a sweeping indictment of America's cultural and economic state during the Great Depression. The novel shows a powerful authorial voice with an understanding of the complicated interactions of America's class and racial systems. Black critics of the period such as Ralph Ellison and Ulysses Lee urged the author to apply this understanding to a novel addressing African American themes. Attaway responded with *Blood on the Forge*, one of the most powerful novels about black migration and black working conditions ever written. Unfortunately, Attaway's achievement was overshadowed by the publication of Richard Wright's *Native Son* in 1940. Attaway was a member of the Federal Writers Workshop, which aided unemployed writers in the 1930's. He went on to write for film, radio, and television and published important work on black music from Barbados.

Bibliography

Bell, Bernard W. "Richard Wright and the Triumph of Naturalism." In *The Afro-American Novel and Its Tradition.* Amherst: University of Massachusetts Press, 1987. Bell illuminates the naturalist tradition in terms of black writing and analyzes Attaway's writing closely in terms of class and race consciousness. Sees the roots of Attaway's work in the interplay between Freudian psychology and Marxist social analysis. Stresses the biological and socioeconomic conditions that control Attaway's naturalistic style and theme. Bell also outlines the historical and political themes of the early part of the twentieth century, including the Great Migration, the Depression, Communism, and the Chicago School of Sociology.

Bone, Robert. *The Negro Novel in America.* New Haven, Conn.: Yale University

Press, 1958. Examines Attaway's connection to the Federal Writers Workshop. Sees the novel as unoriginal and too closely based on Steinbeck, making no new contribution to the proletarian novel of the 1930's. Gives Attaway only a small place in the annals of black writing during the Depression.

Margolies, Edward. Introduction to *Blood on the Forge*, by William Attaway. New York: Collier Books, 1970. Critical and biographical survey of William Attaway, concentrating on Attaway's second and last novel. Provides valuable information about the black migration from the South to northern urban areas that began in the 1890's. Traces the influence of World War I and its need for war armaments and munitions in giving work to many blacks, who fled from the repressive South only to end up entrapped in another kind of living hell. Sketches Attaway's life and demonstrates that the author's own hobo existence provided much background for his novels.

Yarborough, Richard. Afterword to *Blood on the Forge*, by William Attaway. New York: Monthly Review Press, 1987. Biographical and critical essay on William Attaway, with a generous review of *Let Me Breathe Thunder* that places it in its literary and historical context. The statistical analysis of the Great Migration and the black working class helps to orient the reader to Attaway's underlying themes. The first novel seems a likely start for a writer with Attaway's history of work on ships and his wanderings as a migrant worker and hobo.

Young, James O. *Black Writers of the Thirties.* Baton Rouge: Louisiana State University Press, 1973. Describes the novel as a picaresque proletarian novel that is naïve and sentimental in its search for universalities among the alienated working class. Attaway has a firm position in the ranks of black writers of the period because of his understanding of African American themes in relation to race, class, and working-class conditions.

Stephen F. Soitos

LET THE CIRCLE BE UNBROKEN

Author: Mildred D. Taylor (1943-   )
Type of work: Novel
Type of plot: Social criticism
Time of plot: The 1930's, during the Great Depression
Locale: Rural Mississippi
First published: 1981

> *Principal characters:*
> CASSIE, one of four children in the Logan family
> PAPA (DAVID LOGAN), Cassie's father
> HARLAN GRANGER, a powerful white landowner
> T. J. AVERY, a young black friend of the Logans
> WADE JAMISON, T. J.'s white attorney
> SUZELLA RANKIN, the Logans' second cousin
> STACEY, the Logans' eldest son
> MAMA, Cassie's mother

The Novel

Let the Circle Be Unbroken recounts one family's struggle against prejudice and poverty as seen through the eyes and experiences of Cassie, the main character. The Logans battle the Great Depression, powerful, greedy, white landowners of rural Mississippi, segregation, and domestic tragedies that threaten to destroy the family at every turn. They maintain their dignity, pride, and faith, however, and keep the family together.

The novel begins with friends and neighbors preoccupied with the tragedy that has struck T. J., Joe Avery's son, and the effects of the Depression on rural Mississippi. T. J. and his two white friends, R. W. and Melvin Simms, had broken into the Barnett's Mercantile and stolen a gun. In their scuffle to escape, Melvin fatally had shot the owner, Jim Lee Barnett; Papa Logan had set his field ablaze to prevent a white vigilante group from lynching T. J. for the murder. T. J.'s arrest and impending execution greatly distress the Logans, who have no faith in the white judicial system and view the trial as only a legal way to lynch a black boy. In fact, the prosecution, the judge, and the all-white jury are so eager to hang the "nigger" that neither Justice Overton's testimony linking R. W. and Melvin to the murder nor the holes that the defense bores into Mrs. Barnett's testimony that she saw "niggers" murder her husband is enough to forestall the jury's guilty verdict. Cassie and her brothers, Christopher-John and Little Man (who steal away to the courthouse to observe the trial), witness firsthand racism and segregation at work in legal garb and must fight to maintain their self-esteem.

Back on the farm, Papa and Mr. Morrison, a friend, repair tools and broken fences in preparation for crop time, which ends the short school year by drawing everyone to the fields. They are wary of the crop-reduction officer, Mr. Handsworth, but must also resist Harlan Granger, who wants to forge Papa Logan's subsidy check—which the AAA has given him in return for destroying his cotton crop—and run him off his duly purchased property. Only a few blocks away, Moe Turner's family, friends of the Logans who, like many other poor peasants, have been sharecropping on the Montier plantation since the mid-1880's, are threatened with starvation through persistent poverty. Concurrently, Miz Lee Annie Lees, a sixty-year-old neighbor hard hit by segregation and the Depression, memorizes large sections of the Mississippi constitution and dreams of improving conditions for blacks through the ballot before she dies.

The scene changes as Cassie and her brothers learn that their family's tradition has been violated by Cousin Bud, who has married a white woman from New York. The family's resentment over his action runs very deep, so he must leave prematurely after promising to take his daughter to visit with the family. Yet this is only one of Cassie's worries, because conditions have worsened on the farm, and Papa must leave home in search of work. Cousin Bud returns with Suzella, his mulatto daughter, who also antagonizes the Logans by considering herself white. Cassie's turbulent relationship with Suzella reaches a breaking point when Suzella attempts to befriend white boys in the neighborhood. While the family feud goes on, the local farmers' union is busted by big planters who continue to prey on the poor sharecroppers, more neighbors are forced off the land, and Stacey and Moe run away to Louisiana.

With Stacey and Moe's departure, T. J.'s execution, Papa's working far away from home, and the Depression taking its toll on family relations, Cassie loses control and vents her frustration on her classmates. Christmas morning arrives, however, and family members greet one another warmly. They gather in a circle around the fire to sing a song, "Will the Circle Be Unbroken?" Afterward, they all go to church. This brings Cassie and her younger brothers a feeling of warmth but does not eliminate the pain they feel, for Cousin Bud has returned to take Suzella (now their friend) back to New York. When Cassie tries to escort them as far as a friend's place, Suzella is assaulted by three white boys, who earlier had wanted to date her but then discovered that her father was black. Stripping Cousin Bud in the presence of Suzella and Cassie, they attempt to lynch him for marrying a white woman, but Mr. Morrison intervenes. Cassie and Suzella are horrified.

Cassie, who has become interested in reading the Mississippi constitution, gets yet another lesson in segregation at the registrar's office when she goes to see Miz Lee Annie register to vote, but she is subjected to insults and called a foolish nigger meddling in white business. At the same time, Mama and Papa Logan, who accompanied Cassie to Strawberry, find themselves surrounded by a large demonstration by poor union farmers, and Harlan Granger exploits their presence for his own ends. This tragic episode ends in a comedy of errors, as Wade Jamison assists the Logans in securing the release of Stacey and Moe from police custody, and the family rejoices. The circle remains unbroken, and Cassie, Stacey, Christopher-John, and Little Man have reason to look to the future with optimism.

The Characters

Cassie is old enough to understand segregation and the realities of African American life in 1930's Mississippi. She is bright and curious, characteristics reflected in her desire to learn about the Mississippi constitution. Proud of her race, she despises her mulatto cousin who thinks of herself as white. Yet the execution of her friend T.J., her brother's running away from home, the racial hostility she experiences, and the problems of the Depression take an emotional toll on her. Her parents' nurturing of her pride and self-respect and her close family ties, however, give her the strength she needs.

Papa, Cassie's father, is an old-fashioned disciplinarian but also a hardworking and considerate father. He tries to support his family by working on their small farm, but he is faced with a constant struggle against poverty. He is forced to take out-of-town work, but he manages to stay two steps ahead of Harlan Granger, who is determined to annex the Logan property through deception.

Mama, Cassie's mother, is the daughter of a sharecropper who was once a schoolteacher. She lost her teaching job because she supported a boycott against the Wallaces, who ran the store on the Granger plantation. Mama assists students with evening lessons, works hard to help sustain the family, and runs the farm in Papa's absence.

Stacey, the Logans' eldest son, is devastated by T.J.'s execution; his father's departure from home further depresses him. Stacey is not able to deal with his emotional problems as effectively as his sister does, and he runs away, leaving his family to undertake a long search for him.

Harlan Granger, the Logan family's chief antagonist, is the most powerful of the four major white landowners in the county. He thrives in an environment of segregation and prejudice, gets special treatment from the sheriff, and is hated by the poor people of the county. He is envious of the Logan's property, and he makes repeated, dishonest attempts to annex it to his own much larger estate.

Themes and Meanings

As a sequel to the Newbery Medal-winning *Roll of Thunder, Hear My Cry* (1976), *Let the Circle Be Unbroken* shows the work of a careful craftswoman mastering the art form of African American story in fiction. With vividness, persuasion, and wit, Taylor demonstrates that pride, independence, and determination can sustain a family against segregation and economic disaster. Through Cassie, her lead character, Taylor wants younger Americans to understand the level of discrimination, disfranchisement, and hard times that two earlier generations fought under segregation.

High on Taylor's list of concerns is what she sees as an unjust judicial system designed for whites only and supported by a vicious vigilantism against which blacks are defenseless. The child T. J., for example, is found guilty of murder only because of the color of his skin; his friends, Stacey and Moe, are arrested and detained only because they are black; Dube Cross, an impoverished sharecropper, is singled out in a racially mixed union action for severe punishment because he is a "nigger." Additionally, blacks who attempt to register to vote can still be lynched or lose their property. R. W. and Melvin Simms are allowed to bear witness against a black friend for a crime that they themselves committed, Mrs. Barnett does not have to see the color of a criminal to know that he is black, and an attorney cannot prevail in a Mississippi court of law defending a black person against whites. All whites are not set against blacks, however; Jamison gives the Logans sound advice, and white peasants join with blacks to fight the injustice of big planters.

The novel mirrors the miserable conditions under which post-Reconstruction sharecroppers lived in the South and the genesis of their displacement from rural areas to poor urban centers. During the Depression, neighborhoods were destroyed by powerful, greedy landowners who forced thousands of poor, landless sharecroppers to live at their mercy or flee the plantations. The scene with the Crosses and the Turners is very moving. The former is fatherless and reduced to mendicancy, but that is too degrading for proud Dube Cross, the teenage breadwinner, so he joins the union to fight for change. Moe Turner is optimistic that each year his family will escape the vicious cycle of poverty and indebtedness to the plantation, but they are wiped out by the Depression, so Moe runs away in search of work. Propertied blacks also walk a treacherous road under segregation. Their dogged determination to be self-supporting contradicts their status as defined in a segregated economy: black, poor, landless, dependent, and ignorant. Only the black church provides a source of strength and hope, and family moral values and tradition keep blacks from total deprivation.

At every turn of the novel, Taylor exposes her readers to the psychology and degradation of segregation, especially through the feelings of the children. The Suzella episode underscores the fact that a light complexion could earn a girl automatic acceptance among whites until a taint of blackness was found in her. Cassie and her brothers must be subservient to their white counterparts, and vigilantes lynch blacks for marrying whites. Just as degrading is the fact that Papa and Mama are required to bow to whites and address them as "sir" and "madam," even when those whites are young enough to be their grandchildren, while whites call them "boy" or "nigger" and treat them as subhuman.

This crafty demonstration of the impact of segregation and the Depression on a black family seems almost biographical. Taylor gives readers invaluable insights into the crisis of existence for African Americans under segregation. She does this with such savoir faire and controlled power that it takes a perceptive reader to suspect that Taylor's own family, two post-Reconstruction generations, is ensconced behind some of her fictitious characters. Perhaps only Cassie's tender age, given her vocabulary, raises doubts about this biographical hypothesis. Behind the fiction is personal experience in Jackson, Mississippi (Taylor's hometown), and a knowledge of black history that make her work authentic and powerful. With great skill, Taylor takes an otherwise dull and dolorous subject and brings it to life through compelling characterization.

Critical Context

When it first appeared in 1981, *Let the Circle Be Unbroken* found a receptive audience and an established literary tradition. Mildred D. Taylor's first book portraying the Logan family, *Song of the Trees* (1975), was awarded the Council on Interracial Books Award in the African American literature category and hailed as the outstanding book of the year by *The New York Times*. Her second novel, *Roll of Thunder, Hear My Cry*, won the Newbery Medal and laid the critical foundation for *Let the Circle Be Unbroken*. Together, they received the Coretta Scott King Award in 1982 as an authentic interpretation of aspects of the African American experience during the Depression. *Let the Circle Be Unbroken* received a positive review in *The Times of London*, in 1982, and by 1989 had already gone through its ninth printing, having fetched good ratings from *The Horn Book Magazine, Publishers Weekly, The Christian Science Monitor*, and other distinguished publications. Having published also *The Golden Cadillac* (1987), Taylor has established herself as a prolific writer and an engaging interpreter of twentieth century African American history.

Bibliography

Fogelman, Phyllis J. "Mildred D. Taylor." *The Horn Book Magazine* 53 (August, 1977): 410-414. Gives a brief account of Taylor's early life and discusses the influences on her first two books.

Harper, Mary Turner. "Merger and Metamorphosis in the Fiction of Mildred D. Taylor." *Children's Literature Association Quarterly* 13, no. 1 (Summer, 1988): 75-80. Analyzes the communal oral tradition in Taylor's novels. Describes Taylor's work as "an imaginative blending of history, cultural traditions and practices."

Rees, David. "The Color of Skin: Mildred Taylor." In *The Marble in the Water: Essays on Contemporary Writers of Fiction for Children and Young Adults*. Boston: The Horn Book, 1980. A comparative study that recognizes that Taylor "comes closer than anyone else to giving us a really good novel about racial prejudice."

Taylor, Mildred D. "Newbery Award Acceptance: Address." *The Horn Book Magazine* 53 (August, 1977): 401-409. Taylor describes the origins of her prize-winning novel, which she says is "about human pride and survival in a cruelly racist society."

_____. *Song of the Trees*. New York: Dial Press, 1975. Taylor's first novel about the Logan family. Selected by *The New York Times* as one of the outstanding books of 1975. Followed by the Newbery Medal-winning *Roll of Thunder, Hear My Cry*.

N. Samuel Murrell

LET THE DEAD BURY THEIR DEAD

Author: Randall Kenan (1963-   )
Type of work: Short stories
Time of work: Primarily the twentieth century
Locale: Tims Creek, North Carolina
First published: 1992

Principal characters:

CLARENCE PICKETT, a young boy who passes on advice from
    dead residents of the town to living residents
JOHN EDGAR STOKES, an old black man who has a showdown
    with local white bigots
HENRIETTA WILLIAMS, an older black woman who, after her
    grandson's death, invites her grandson's male lover to stay
    with her for a few days
AARON STREETER, a spoiled and very self-conscious man
MABEL PEARSALL, a spiritually and physically tired schoolteacher
BOOKER T. WASHINGTON, a fictionalized version of the influential
    black educator
DEAN WILLIAMS, a white homosexual man hired to seduce and
    help blackmail a wealthy black man
LENA WALKER, a recently widowed middle-aged black woman
REVEREND BARDEN, a minister who delivers a eulogy for a dead
    young woman with whom he had a sexual affair
IDA PERRY, the widow of a judge; she is haunted by the spirit
    of a young black man beaten to death by her husband
REGINALD KAIN, the imaginary editor of the title story
PHARAOH (MENES), the leader of a possibly apocryphal slave
    revolt

The Stories

Let the Dead Bury Their Dead is a series of loosely related short stories all set in Tims Creek, North Carolina, the fictional predominantly black rural town Randall Kenan first explored in his novel *A Visitation of Spirits* (1989). Besides being linked by a setting, the characters in these stories are also linked by a vague search for meaning, particularly in spiritual beliefs and, not infrequently, in sexual desire. Because many of these characters have lived lives that have forced them to suppress any personal search for spiritual or sexual understanding or fulfillment, they are often surprised to the point of near total disorientation when they find themselves forced to attain some new level of understanding in either realm.

The short stories in this volume are perfectly comfortable with what has often been called magical realism. There are important apparently supernatural elements in these stories, but the stories themselves do not give themselves over to the realm of fantasy. Although the magical elements are always meaningful and sometimes astonishing, the meaning of them is by no means always clear, certainly not to the characters in the stories. Furthermore, sexual desire is presented as an element that is in almost every way magical. It too is meaningful, and it can be spiritually redemptive, but it also can be lost or misinterpreted easily.

The lead story, "Clarence and the Dead," one of the most refreshingly original stories in the collection as well as one of the best, shows how surprising the link between the spiritual and the sexual realms can be. Clarence Pickett is a preschool-age boy who suddenly gains the ability to serve as a medium for the dead residents of the community in speaking to their living loved ones. The town responds by ostracizing Clarence, especially as his spirit talk is increasingly shown to be reliable. Ellsworth Batts, however, a man who has never recovered from his wife's death years earlier in a fire, sees the possibility of redemption when Clarence begins talking in the voice of Ellsworth's dead wife, Mildred. He forms an attachment to Clarence that quickly becomes viewed by the town as an "unnatural affection" between a man and a boy, especially when he begins to apparently court Clarence and later tries to sneak into Clarence's room at night. Ellsworth dies when the town, revolted by his behavior, tries to run him out of town, and Clarence dies shortly thereafter. "Clarence and the Dead" serves as a wonderful introductory story to this volume not only because it introduces many of the main themes but also because it demonstrates the connection between sexual desire and spiritual fulfillment as sometimes necessary but ambiguous and possibly dangerous as well.

Sexual desires that are socially forbidden or at least problematic play a key role in a number of the stories. "Cornsilk" focuses on a young man remembering an incestuous affair he had with his stepsister. "The Strange and Tragic Ballad of Mabel Pearsall" tells of a schoolteacher who becomes obsessed with the idea that her husband fathered an infant she sometimes babysits. "What Are Days?" tells of a middle-aged widow, Lena Walker, who learns both to grieve and to live through an affair with a teenager who mysteriously disappears after they spend a passionate weekend together. "Ragnorak! The Day the Gods Die," one of the most powerful stories in the collection, tells of Reverend Barden saying a eulogy over the dead body of a young woman with whom he had an affair. Her death forces him to face the emptiness of his own life.

Several of the stories focus specifically on the social unacceptability of male homosexual love, including "The Foundations of the Earth," in which a grandmother tries to come to terms with her dead grandson's male lover, and "Run, Mourner, Run," in which a young white man who had been hired to seduce and help blackmail a wealthy black man finds himself falling in love with the man who was supposed to be his mark. Among the recurring themes that Kenan explores in these stories is the dialectical paradox of personal desire; that is, desire can seem to transcend the public sphere altogether and create a personal sphere which, for a while, seems complete. Ultimately, though, that personal sphere must answer to the public one, sometimes to be crushed by it. Kenan's stories examine how that can happen, and what happens next.

The final story, "Let the Dead Bury Their Dead," is close to a novella in length and serves as a coda to the entire volume, in that it picks up most of the thematic strands of the other stories. Presented as a folk history assembled by James Malachi Greene (one of the central characters in *A Visitation of Spirits*) and edited by Reginald Kain (who shares Kenan's initials) in the year 2000, the story takes the form of an oral history interspersed with letters and diary entries. It even includes extensive pseudoscholarly footnotes, including one that mentions a supposed 1996 publication by Randall Kenan, *Go Curse Your God, Boy, and Die: Stories.*

A conversation between Ruth and Ezekiel Cross—James Greene's great-aunt and great-uncle—and assorted letter and diary fragments tell the story of the founding of Tims Creek, North Carolina. The town was first called Tearshirt and was founded by escaped slaves led by a black man known as Pharaoh to Ezekiel Cross but referred to as Menes in the written records of Rebecca Cross and her son, Phineas Cross. In her diary, Rebecca Cross wonders if her husband, Owen Cross, has a homosexual attachment to this slave. The account that Ezekiel Cross gives of the slave/master relationship also suggests this possibility. Three years after Menes escapes with eighteen other slaves, Phineas Cross encounters their hidden settlement on land owned by Owen Cross, an encounter Phineas describes in great detail in a letter to his male lover living in England. Although most aspects of Ezekiel's story are rebutted either by the editor or by Ruth Cross, Phineas' letter does help to establish the reality of a community of escaped slaves led by one who had been a favorite of Owen Cross. The portion of Ezekiel's tale that gives the short story its title, though, is more fabulous. After the Civil War, and after Pharaoh's death, a preacher comes into town who calls the dead back to life to attack the living people of Tearshirt. Although the people are saved by a miraculous reappearance by Pharaoh, Pharaoh himself, in his disgust, calls fire down on Tearshirt. The few survivors who rebuild the town rename it Tims Creek.

Ezekiel Cross makes no claims of absolute truth for his story; he simply claims that it is the story he heard. Read allegorically, this story of a rebellion of the dead and the destruction of the town in flames might be a folkloric version of an attack by the Ku Klux Klan on this town, or more generally of the failure of the post-Reconstruction era to make good on the promises of equality. None of the various storytellers, however, presents evidence to support an allegorical reading. Instead, the reader is left with the fact that this story is told about the town's history because it is a good story, and having a good story is reason enough to tell it. Further, being a story about storytelling but also about rebirth, the story seems to imply both that storytelling is fundamentally about spiritual rebirth and that rebirth can be frightening but can make for awfully good stories.

Themes and Meanings

More than in many short-story collections, the stories in *Let the Dead Bury Their*

Dead are unified by several common themes and ideas. In many of these stories, there is an implicit acceptance of the supernatural world as a real one that sometimes affects the world of everyday reality. This supernatural world is often linked to sexual passion, to spiritual searching and spiritual passion, and to storytelling itself. All these forces are presented as being possibly transformational but also unreliable and disruptive.

The story "Let the Dead Bury Their Dead" begins with several quotations including one by the Russian critic Mikhail Bakhtin from *The Dialogic Imagination* (1981) that identifies the fantastic in folklore as a "realistic fantastic" that Bakhtin associates with "those eternal demands" of men. This quotation is followed by a shorter one from Zora Neale Hurston: "Now you are going to hear lies above suspicion." The implication is that the fantastic is used in a similar way by Kenan in his own stories, and that the reader should not worry too much about what could "realistically" have happened but instead should ask how the fantastic is used in the stories.

In the story "Things of This World," John Edgar Stokes encounters a Chinese man named Chi, whose name in an African tongue means "personal god" and who seems literally to have fallen from the sky. After facing down some local white bigots, Stokes says to Chi, "I could die right now—content." With that, he dies and Chi disappears. Chi seems to be an earthly manifestation of Stokes's personal god. Chi, however, does nothing fantastic; as the title implies, he only helps Stokes move on to the next world content, after wrapping up the things of this world. In this story, the fantastic serves to highlight the everyday world.

Although spiritual searching is an important element in a number of stories, it emerges as a main theme in "The Foundations of the Earth" and "Ragnorak! The Day the Gods Die." In both stories it is brought into apparent conflict with sexual passion. In "The Foundations of the Earth," Henrietta Williams invites Gabriel, the male lover of her deceased grandson, Edward, to Tims Creek for a visit. For her, the visit is a process of learning to accept that her grandson was a homosexual. When members of her church are outraged that a neighbor, on a Sunday, is plowing fields on land he leases from Henrietta, she slowly comes to believe that perhaps there is no split between the transcendent spiritual world and the everyday world. She advises the farmer to do what he has to do. Implicitly, she can now begin to accept that her grandson's sexuality was not unholy. "Ragnorak! The Day the Gods Die" goes inside the mind of Reverend Barden, a recurring character in these stories who is also present in *A Visitation of Spirits*. He says a eulogy over the body of Sarah Tate, a woman with whom he had an affair. While she was alive, he had been satisfied to see their lovemaking as something of almost holy worth; with her death, he must face the spiritual emptiness of his life.

That sexual passion can have a spiritual force is a theme running through many of these stories. Aaron Streeter, the young man in "Cornsilk," makes his memory of a sexual relationship with his half-sister, Jamonica, an obsessional focus in his life. This is in part a way of forestalling the true implications of his own spiritual laziness, which he shows an awareness of in the self-reflection in which he glibly engages. Sexual passion, because it can make one person care about another, seems to work as a spiritually redemptive force in Dean Williams' life. He falls in love with Ray Brown, the wealthy black man he has been hired to seduce and betray. By itself, it is not enough. Because Dean achieves no spiritual clarity, he ignores his impulses not to betray Ray. In "What Are Days?," however, being passionately, sexually loved by a teenager who then mysteriously disappears serves as an intermediate step for a widow, Lena Walker, not only to begin loving herself again but also to grieve for the dead husband toward whom she still has some unresolved anger. In all the other stories that focus on sexual passion, such desire is presented as something that can transform one morally and spiritually but is not by itself a sufficient guide.

The first and last stories, "Clarence and the Dead" and "Let the Dead Bury Their Dead," are the two in which elements of the supernatural are most prominent. In both, the supernatural is part of a more general folkloric context. Both stories are also finally about the importance of a community having a story to tell. "Clarence and the Dead" is told from a first-person-plural point of view, by a narrator who seems to represent the town itself. The narrator is careful to note that this story is pieced together from accounts that people in the town reported to each other, often long after the events, making it clear that there has been plenty of time for this story of a young boy who speaks in the voices of the dead to grow in the retelling. The narrator, however, is rather unconcerned by the possibility that these fantastic events may have been exaggerated, or for that matter that they may not have been real. The narrator's main concern is that this story—which is not much spoken of any more—iould be known.

By contrast, "Let the Dead Bury Their Dead" is a story that revels in all the distorting effects of folklore. By placing Ezekiel Cross's account of Pharaoh's slave revolt and of the later revolt of the dead side by side with contrasting and supporting evidence, this story calls attention to the distortion that takes place in all stories. A point the story makes is that stories cannot be judged by their fidelity to "reality." Ezekiel Cross's tale might transform the story of the founding of Tims Creek into an apocalypse of biblical proportions, but it keeps the tale lively and interesting. Stories, too, prove to be potentially transformational, but not accurate, guides to absolute truth.

Critical Context

In his short stories, Randall Kenan shows himself to be not only a fine writer but also an active student of literature. *Let the Dead Bury Their Dead* shows the influence of a wide variety of writers but does not let these influences interfere with the enjoyment of the text. In the best tradition of artistic influence, Randall Kenan has borrowed ideas and techniques both broadly and widely to fashion a series of short stories that are highly original.

Using a series of interconnected short stories to tell the story of a town is a form pioneered by Sherwood Anderson in *Winesburg, Ohio: A Group of Tales of Ohio*

Small Town Life (1919) and developed by Anderson's African American protégé, Jean Toomer, in *Cane* (1923). Like both Toomer and Anderson, Kenan uses the form to reveal the hidden and half-hidden passions of members of the town. Kenan's stories, however, are much fuller than the short sketches in *Winesburg, Ohio* or *Cane.* Although he is sometimes satisfied with presenting only a fleeting glimpse, he tends to make his reader look long and hard at each person.

In his interest in history, his playfulness, and his deep concern with ideas that are of spiritual importance to people, Kenan also shows a definite affinity to a more contemporary writer, Charles Johnson, author of *Middle Passage* (1990) and *The Sorcerer's Apprentice* (1986), among other works. Kenan's first novel, *A Visitation of Spirits*, had a plot similar to the title story of *The Sorcerer's Apprentice*; in both stories a young black man calls on magical powers that he is then unable to control. Among the ideas that Kenan shares with Johnson is the conviction that ideas themselves are important to people and thus should be important to fiction; therefore, one finds in both of these writers an interest and willingness to ruminate over ideas. Additionally, both writers are willing to present magic in their writing as it is presented in folklore—that is, as something that sometimes works and can affect people's lives but is only a small part of a larger reality.

The two most apparent influences on Kenan's work are James Baldwin and Toni Morrison. Kenan shares in common with Baldwin a willingness to explore the importance people place on sexual desire in all of its manifestations and an understanding that sexual desire can be charged with a spiritual fervor. With Morrison, Kenan seems to share some of his recurring moral vision. Morrison has written extensively on the importance in African American literature of both the community and ancestor figures in the community. One of the changes in direction that is evident between Kenan's first book and *Let the Dead Bury Their Dead* is that the reader gets much more exploration of Tims Creek in the later book. Further, although *A Visitation of Spirits* certainly was concerned about the role of community elders, the stories in *Let the Dead Bury Their Dead*—especially the title story, but also "Ragnorak! The Day the Gods Die" and "Cornsilk"—explore more richly the problematic interaction between younger members of the community and their elders.

Bibliography
Johnson, Charles. *Being and Race: Black Writing Since 1970.* Bloomington: Indiana University Press, 1990. A major statement on black writing by a writer whose influence on Kenan is noticeable. Of particular importance to a reader of Kenan are Johnson's comments on Jean Toomer and Henry Dumas.
Miner, Valerie. "Carolina Dreamin'." *The Nation* 255 (July 6, 1992): 28-29. A review by a female novelist of *Let the Dead Bury Their Dead.* Focuses largely on Kenan's treatment of women and finds much to praise.
Morrison, Toni. "Rootedness: The Ancestor as Foundation." In *Black Women Writers, 1950-1980: A Critical Evaluation*, edited by Mari Evans. Garden City, N.Y.: Anchor Press/Doubleday, 1983.

——————. "Unspeakable Things Unspoken: The Afro-American Presence in American Literature." *Michigan Quarterly Review* 28 (Winter, 1989): 1-34. Though not about Randall Kenan, these two articles by Toni Morrison do give a good overview of recurring themes and values in African American literature. The importance of the community and of ancestor figures in African American literature are particularly relevant to Randall Kenan.

Mosher, Howard Frank. "The Ghosts on Main Street." *The New York Times Book Review* 97 (June 14, 1992): 12-13. An early but quite enlightening and very favorable review of *Let the Dead Bury Their Dead.*

Thomas Cassidy

LIKE ONE OF THE FAMILY
Conversations from a Domestic's Life

Author: Alice Childress (1920-   )
Type of work: Novel
Type of plot: Social realism
Time of plot: The early 1950's
Locale: New York City
First published: 1956

> *Principal characters:*
> MILDRED JOHNSON, a thirty-two-year-old domestic worker
> MARGE, Mildred's best friend
> MRS. M., a well-meaning but obtuse employer
> MRS. C., an employer who tells her guests that Mildred is "like one of the family"
> MRS. L., Mildred's favorite employer

The Novel

Although it is classified as a novel, *Like One of the Family* does not have either the movement of plot or the change in character usually associated with that genre. Instead, Alice Childress' work is a series of monologues, each of which is independent, even though all involve the same speaker and the same listener. This format can be explained by the fact that these monologues originally appeared separately, some of them in the newspaper *Freedom*, where they were called "Conversations from Life," and others in the *Baltimore Afro-American*, under the heading "Here's Mildred." Sixty-two of the monologues were assembled for publication in book form, but there seems to have been no principle governing the order in which they were printed, other than an effort to vary the subject of discussion from one chapter to the next.

While it is not structured conventionally, *Like One of the Family* has its own kind of unity, achieved primarily through the use of a single voice. In each chapter, Mildred Johnson relates her experiences to Marge, her downstairs neighbor in a Harlem apartment building. Almost all these conversations take place either in Mildred's three-room apartment or in Marge's. Whatever the location, the pattern is almost always the same. One of the women stops in at the end of the workday or in the evening, and the two sit down, usually in the kitchen, make a pot of coffee, and visit.

In the chapter "All About My Job," Mildred explains why this friendship is so important to her. She is black and she is a domestic worker. These two facts alone, Mildred says, "ought to be enough reason for anybody to need a friend." She continues, "I do believe I'd lose my mind if I had to come home after a day of hard work, rasslin' 'round in other folks' kitchens if I did not have a friend to talk to when I got here." Because the two friends are the same age and do the same job, and because both were reared in the South, Marge can understand what Mildred is talking about.

With Marge, Mildred can be her own person, as she can never be with her white employers. Even when she rebukes them, Mildred maintains a logical, restrained manner, in sharp contrast to the passion and anger she feels free to reveal to Marge. Although she occasionally annoys her friend and although she sometimes has to apologize for her more extravagant comments, Mildred does not feel the need to watch her words when she talks to Marge. With a white employer, Mildred must be aware of the fact that if she shows the extent of her anger, she will certainly be dismissed. Thus the action of the novel concerns not merely the incidents that Mildred describes but also the ebb and flow of Mildred's emotional life, which follows a pattern of repression and release.

At the end of *Like One of the Family*, Mildred's character and her situation are the same as they were at the beginning of the book. She is still working by the day, because in that way she can be more independent; when she investigates a weekly position with a single employer, she discovers that such a job would be little better than slavery. She still hopes that the civil rights battle will soon be won; however, she does not expect her own life to become very different as a result. The one change Mildred anticipates is a personal one. Throughout the novel, she has been analyzing the men she meets. In the final chapter, Mildred tells Marge that she has decided to marry Eddie, a salesman whose paychecks are uncertain but whose kindness and decency make him, in her eyes, a much better husband than many so-called good catches.

The Characters

Like One of the Family is dominated by the character of Mildred Johnson, not just because she is the only person whose thoughts are presented firsthand but, more important, because of the quality of her mind. It is this which produces the suspense in a book that has no real plot; one is drawn from paragraph to paragraph, page to page, simply to find out what Mildred will say next. For example, in one of the few chapters set outside of the apartment building, "Ridin' the Bus," Mildred surprises Marge by insisting on riding in the back of the bus, as blacks had so often been forced to do. In the observations that follow, Mildred produces a brilliant discussion of freedom as the principle that enables both blacks and whites to ride where they like. She then gives a definition of an ideal society as one in which people not only sit where they like but also choose their seats without even noticing the race of others. In every chapter, there are similar illustrations of Mildred's intellectual abilities, her skill in analyzing and synthesizing, her genius at seeing the profound implications of the simplest action.

Mildred's friend Marge is also essential to the novel. It is Marge, the accepting and trustworthy listener, who permits Mildred to speak with perfect freedom, whether she is indulging in fantasy, such as her dream of a Christmas of real peace, or exploring controversial subjects, such as the idea of a union for domestic workers, complete with demands, strikes, and pickets. Moreover, although she is never quoted, Marge does come to life through Mildred's comments and reactions. For example, the reader learns that Marge is plump but has beautiful hands, that she gets depressed after an exhausting day of domestic work, that she throws herself enthusiastically into cooking meals and planning outings, and that she frequently dissolves in laughter, especially when Mildred is acting out one of her adventures.

The other characters in *Like One of the Family* are all presented in a straightforward fashion, with Mildred serving as omniscient author, reporting their words and their gestures, while delivering her own perceptive analyses of their underlying motives. In "More Blessed to Give . . .," for example, she describes how a child attending a party was reluctant to accept a box of candy and then, when it was pressed upon her, insisted on presenting it to one of the hostesses. Mildred explains the child's conduct to the other adult visitors, and later to Marge, by stating that everyone has a need to give, as well as to receive. Because Childress has established Mildred as a reliable authority, such character analyses are clearly meant to be taken at face value. Throughout the novel, then, it is Mildred who functions as the authorial voice, defining and evaluating character.

Themes and Meanings

For the themes of *Like One of the Family*, one need look no further than the explicit statements of Mildred Johnson. A compulsive educator, Mildred is bent on pointing out deficiencies in society and in individuals to everyone with whom she comes in contact. Mildred's intention may be simply to inform her listeners, as when she explains the facts of black history to young children, or to reform them, as when she lectures her minister or one of her employers. Whatever the audience, whatever the situation, Mildred's lessons are based on the three principles she values above all: integrity, respect for oneself and for others, and the need to work for a better future.

Mildred loathes dishonesty, hypocrisy, and pretension. It is this that so annoys her when Mrs. C. tells her visitors that Mildred is "like one of the family"; it is this which she finds offensive at Mrs. H.'s cocktail party, where the guests prove their sophistication by calling everything "wonderful" or "amusin'." Yet it is not only white employers whose superficial values draw Mildred's fire; she is equally annoyed with the snobbery of prosperous blacks who boast about their wealth and their material possessions.

Because Mildred's values are not superficial, she can be proud of who and what she is. Therefore, when she goes to a church function where only the supposedly prestigious occupations are praised, Mildred points out the value of her own job. Behind the doctors and lawyers, she says, are people like herself, whose hard work at low wages makes it possible for their children to rise in the world. The same ideas are stressed in "The 'Many Others' in History" when, at a meeting honoring famous African American leaders, Mildred pays tribute to the hardworking but unknown heroes and heroines in her own family. On the other hand, she is appalled that black children know so little about the leaders of whom they should be proud; in "All About Miss Tubman," Mildred gathers the children in her apartment building for a badly needed lesson. She comments that "you youngsters are starved in more ways than one."

It is this sense of her own worth that enables Mildred to stand up to her employers. As a professional, Mildred refuses to put up with demeaning comments such as Mrs. C.'s or with the personal questions that Mrs. M. thinks it her right to ask. She is offended when one employer clutches her pocketbook all the time that Mildred is in the house, displaying a lack of trust, or when another asks for a health card, implying that Mildred may be carrying diseases. It is also this insistence on being given respect that impels Mildred to go on a picnic, although she knows she and her friends may be attacked by whites, and to encourage a friend's son to go to the South and work for civil rights, even though she realizes he may be jailed or killed.

Despite experiences that could well have turned her bitter, Mildred remains an optimist. Her dream is not a dream of black power but of a color-blind society in which people will live in peace. Such ideas cause her to reproach some of her fellow blacks, who are forming a "benevolent club" that will exclude everyone who is not black. In "A New Kind of Prayer," Mildred points out that the main function of churches seems to be to pray to overcome someone else. Instead, in what another African American calls a "dangerous prayer," Mildred asks for "Peace, Love and Plenty" and vows to work for those goals—not just for her people, but for all people, as long as she lives.

Critical Context

Until recently, Alice Childress' reputation has depended primarily on her achievements in the theater. With *Gold Through the Trees* (pr. 1952) and *Trouble in Mind* (pr. 1955), Childress became the first black woman to be recognized as a major American playwright. Therefore, critical discussions concentrated on those plays and on later works such as *Moms: A Praise Play for a Black Comedienne* (pr. 1987). Comments about her fiction often were limited to discussion of *A Hero Ain't Nothin' but a Sandwich* (1973), which has even been mistakenly referred to as Childress' first novel; by the 1970's, *Like One of the Family* had long been out of print and was difficult to obtain. It was not until the reissue of *Like One of the Family* in 1986 that this novel, originally published thirty years before, began to receive the attention it deserved.

Like One of the Family is now seen by critics as a work of inherent value and of historical importance. In Mildred, critics have noted, Childress created a kind of independent, assertive African American woman who in the 1950's was new to fiction. Moreover, by drawing upon her own experiences as a domestic worker, in *Like One of the Family* Childress presented the first accurate description of the lives of a large group of women who had long been ignored.

Admittedly, *Like One of the Family* has flaws, such as the sermon-like quality of the less dramatic chapters and the lack of a structural plan for the book as a whole. It has also been argued that Mildred's high success rate in converting her employers is implausible and that the novel is thus somewhat less realistic than it might have been.

Despite such minor shortcomings, however, *Like One of the Family* is now considered an outstanding work. Despite the book's often comic tone, Childress' opinions, delivered through Mildred, have a solid philosophical foundation. Furthermore, Mildred herself is more than merely an interesting and sympathetic character; she represents the "many others," the heroic black women, unnamed in history books, who have for centuries transmitted a sense of self-worth to later generations.

Bibliography
Austin, Gayle. "Alice Childress: Black Woman Playwright as Feminist Critic." *Southern Quarterly* 25 (Spring, 1987): 52-62. Sees elements of feminist criticism in Childress' dramatic work—for example, in her refusal to accept traditional polarities, her insistence on the need for social justice, and her refutation of the stereotypical images of black women in literature written by men.
Childress, Alice. "Alice Childress: A Pioneering Spirit." Interview by Elizabeth Brown-Guillory. *SAGE: A Scholarly Journal on Black Women* 4 (Spring, 1987): 66-68. Childress discusses the childhood influences that directed her toward a literary career, particularly those of her grandmother and one of her teachers. Also traces her theatrical career.
_____. "Knowing the Humán Condition." In *Black American Literature and Humanism*, edited by R. Baxter Miller. Lexington: University Press of Kentucky, 1981. A paper delivered by Childress at a 1978 conference. Argues that much criticism of film, drama, and fiction is deficient because the critics themselves do not understand "the human condition." For African American writers, Childress argues, this problem is particularly troubling, since white critics typically look not for realism but for what they consider appropriate images.
Gibbs, Sandra E. "Black Novels Reissued." *New Directions for Women* 16 (July, 1987): 17. A review written after *Like One of the Family* was reissued, expressing delight that the work would once again be available. Finds Mildred's comments as applicable in the 1980's as they were in the 1950's. States that Mildred represents those real people in the black community who are "common-sense" advisers and who transmit "a strong sense of self and Black American history."
Harris, Trudier. *From Mammies to Militants: Domestics in Black American Literature.* Philadelphia: Temple University Press, 1982. A thorough, well-written book that places *Like One of the Family* and other novels in a sociological and literary context. Two introductory chapters provide an excellent background for later discussions of specific works. In "Beyond the Uniform," Mildred is seen as rejecting the limitations generally placed on black domestic workers and, similarly, as challenging the assumptions inherent in stereotypical language. Concludes that Mildred represents a bridge between maids "who espouse freedom of mind" and

"the revolutionary maids who exhibit freedom of action."

_____. "'I Wish I Was a Poet': The Character as Artist in Alice Childress's *Like One of the Family.*" *Black American Literature Forum* 14 (Spring, 1980): 24-30. Argues that Childress combines traditional literary devices with "audience attention, participation, and response" from the black oral tradition. Notes that Mildred is a skilled artist, always conscious not only of Marge but also of the black domestic servants who are responding to her words.

Killens, John O. "The Literary Genius of Alice Childress." In *Black Women Writers, 1950-1980: A Critical Evaluation*, edited by Mari Evans. Garden City, N.Y.: Anchor Press/Doubleday, 1983. Observes that throughout her works, Childress uses humor and satire to expose hypocrisy and notes that she is dedicated to the causes of African Americans. Killens admires Childress for maintaining her artistic integrity despite pressures from "the white racist publishing establishment."

Troutman-Robinson, Denise. "The Elements of Call and Response in Alice Childress' *Like One of the Family.*" *MAWA Review* 4 (June, 1989): 18-21. Discusses parallels between Childress' book and the collaborative relationship between preacher and congregation in black evangelical churches. Concludes that, like so many other African American writers, Childress has been strongly influenced by the oral tradition.

Rosemary M. Canfield Reisman

LINDEN HILLS

Author: Gloria Naylor (1950-   )
Type of work: Novel
Type of plot: Social criticism
Time of plot: The early 1980's
Locale: A suburb of a Northern city
First published: 1985

> *Principal characters:*
> WILLIE MASON, an idealistic young African American poet
> LESTER TILSON, a poet and dropout
> LUTHER NEDEED, a wealthy fifth-generation mortician
> WILLA PRESCOTT NEDEED, Luther's wife

The Novel

Two journeys are at the heart of *Linden Hills.* The first is that of Willie Mason, living from hand to mouth, who fears becoming a forty-year-old grocery-bagger. He wonders whether he has made a mistake and should follow the dream of material success. He welcomes a suggestion that he and Lester Tilson seek holiday jobs in Linden Hills, even though an ominous cry from the Hills chills him. What he finds there convinces him that he is doing the right thing, that in the Hills the wrong dream is followed.

At Lester's home, Willie learns that Mrs. Tilson's desire for money drove her husband to work two jobs until he died from a heart attack. Willie perceives the ill feeling within the Tilson home and recognizes Lester's hypocrisy when he mocks his sister.

The next day, they find work at the wedding reception of Winston Alcott, who marries a woman he does not love because marriage is what Luther Nedeed and Linden Hills expect. Only Willie recognizes that Winston's best man is also his former lover. Later, Willie stares at a centerfold of a black nude and is appalled because he sees exploitation, not sex, in the chains against which she struggles. Another man calls this photo an example of progress for African Americans: "Today *Penthouse* . . . tomorrow the world."

At the home of a nervous widower, Willie and Lester are spirited upstairs to prepare the dead wife's room for a new bride; at the same time, a wake is held downstairs at which the guests discuss the danger of a proposed low-income housing development too close to Linden Hills. Only Willie seems to understand the ghastly funeral dinner, at which guests devour "brown and bloody meat" that seems to represent the lives of the less fortunate.

Hired to deliver supplies to the church where the dead woman will be buried, Willie realizes that the Reverend Hollis, a man whom he has admired for years, is an alcoholic and a liar. After the funeral, Willie senses something unclean in the way

Nedeed caresses the lid of the woman's coffin. Willie is the one who runs to the body of Laurel Dumont, who had dreamed of being the first African American Olympic swimmer but who instead commits suicide by diving into her empty pool. When Willie turns her over, she is faceless.

Plagued by nightmares that are a direct result of these encounters, Willie struggles to put his experiences into perspective. Finally, at Nedeed's home, where he and Lester are to trim the tree on Christmas Eve, Willie instinctively recognizes the missing Willa as she emerges from the basement carrying her dead child. When an accidental fire engulfs the house and its inhabitants, the people of Linden Hills stand at their windows to watch, but in spite of Willie's pleas they refuse to help. Willie resolves to leave and never return.

Willie's physical journey parallels Willa Nedeed's psychological journey. She begins as a woman with no name or face, imprisoned without food or available water in a basement that was once a mortuary, her dead son in her arms. It is her cry of grief that Willie has heard. Ultimately, she looks for something with which to wrap her child's body. Rummaging through a trunk, she finds a faded wedding veil to shroud the child, and she also finds the Bible of Luwana Packerville, the slave wife of the first Luther Nedeed. From Luwana's writing on the blank pages, Willa discovers that this woman, who had been purchased by her husband, had remained a slave even after their two-year-old son had been freed. Willa identifies with Luwana's loneliness and anguish as she reads about how Luwana's child had been taught to abandon her.

Willa discovers the recipe books of Evelyn Creton Nedeed, so frustrated by her husband's coldness that she had mixed aphrodisiacs into his food, purged herself with laxatives, and committed suicide on Christmas Eve by eating vanilla ice cream laced with roach poison. Willa identifies with her emptiness as well.

She finds Priscilla McGuire Nedeed's photo album and notes how the shadow of her young son gradually had grown to eclipse her face, until Priscilla's face in the photos had become only a blurred spot. Willa feels her own face and is surprised to find it there. She looks in a pan of water and sees herself mirrored. No longer a faceless Nedeed wife, Willa remembers her name. She realizes that she willingly walked down the basement steps and that she can walk back up. She reclaims herself as the homemaker and mother she is, tidies the basement, still holding her child, and then goes purposefully up the stairs. Willa has rediscovered herself, just as Willie has validated himself.

The Characters

Although Naylor uses an omniscient point of view, much of the novel is presented through the alternating characters of Willie and Willa. Willa's perceptions and experiences are separated visually from those of Willie and the others by the use of a different typeface. This device works particularly well to signal the dream linkages and unconscious bond between Willa, locked in the basement with her dead son, and Willie in the world above ground. Each character serves to reinforce the other.

The distinctive typeface disappears only when Willa emerges from the Nedeed basement to confront her husband in the final chapter.

Naylor deliberately invests her characters with allegorical traits in order to parallel figures in the works of Dante Alighieri. The characters are sometimes wrenched in order to fit Dante's mold, however, and their allegorical qualities make it more difficult to view them realistically. Although both Willie and Lester are made unlikely poets so that they can represent Dante and Vergil touring the Hell of Linden Hills, their characters are two-dimensional, and their dialogue often seems forced.

Luther Nedeed is a perverse and powerful figure who is reincarnated through five generations. What the Nedeeds do is to destroy people's sense of the past and history: "A magician's supreme art is not in transformation but in making things disappear." Everything begins with the present in Linden Hills, which is corrupted by materialism. Even so, Nedeed's cruelty to Willa and his son is not entirely credible. Nothing really justifies his murder of the child by starvation except the fact that the Nedeeds represent evil; but pure, unregenerate evil does not translate well into human form. The allegorical symbolism is sometimes labored, as when Nedeed leaves triangular footprints in the snow.

The allegorical requirements can also interfere with character motivation. Laurel Dumont, the would-be champion swimmer, is supposedly stripped of her identity and lease when her husband files for divorce, but her suicide is not adequately motivated; she simply inhabits the level of Hell where those who commit violence against themselves dwell.

Real energy is found in Naylor's minor characters. Luwana Packerville Nedeed is sympathetically revealed through the notations in her Bible, although the number of times she speaks in one year, recorded by 665 scratches on her body, seems forced. Another wife, Priscilla McGuire Nedeed, possesses a social life of her own and an intelligence, and she is known by her first name until her face is eclipsed by the shadow of her son. On the other hand lie the strength and powerful love of Laurel's Southern grandmother, Roberta Johnson, or Lester's Grandma Tilson, one of the very few who are not afraid to stand up to Nedeed.

Another clearly drawn minor character is the Reverend Michael T. Hollis, alcoholic and heretic. Beyond his symbolic significance, he is a real man who was once inspired to choose a religious vocation, although it was the power emanating from the pulpit that attracted him, not religious devotion. Even Maxwell Smyth, climbing the corporate ladder, becomes a bitterly comic character in his anal-retentive denial of his blackness.

Themes and Meanings

Some critics have praised Naylor for avoiding stereotypes and didacticism in this novel; others have argued that she attempts to draw too many characters who cannot be fully explored, and that Willie and Lester, who are central to the novel, are her weakest characters. Nevertheless, they have agreed that Naylor draws vivid, unforgettable minor characters. Her strongest characterizations are of Willa and the vague

Nedeed wives, who gradually come into focus through tangible reminders of their lives.

Naylor's characters struggle with skin color and history. Many people in the Hills seem to deny their own blackness by attempting to erase or mask it, and Naylor suggests that this ambivalence is part of their spiritual sickness. Lester's sister, who idolizes Eleanor Roosevelt and Diana Ross, "paid her dues to the Civil Rights Movement by wearing an Afro for six months and enrolling in black history courses in college," but now she employs bleaching cream and hair relaxer and wants a "good" marriage in Linden Hills. The Reverend Hollis, leading a conservative Baptist church, has lost the power flowing from congregation to pulpit that first attracted him to the ministry in the storefront churches of his youth. Maxwell Smyth, in his management job at General Motors, has achieved perfect physical control of himself and his environment. With rigid self-discipline, he never sweats or is cold, needs only three hours of sleep each night, and spends "every waking moment trying to be no color at all."

Swimmer Laurel Dumont has dived into a corporate career and neglected the roots that could nourish her, symbolized by her grandmother and the blues of Bessie Smith. The earlier Nedeed wives, chosen for their pale skin and lack of African features, are doomed to unhappiness: Luwana rejects the white god who has left her with nothing; Evelyn tries first to lighten her already pale skin, then to darken it in an attempt to attract her husband. These women are not mad, but they are beaten; only Willa finds strength by learning their histories, their pasts. Even the dead child Sinclair Nedeed, with his African features and white skin, is denied his rightful place.

The Nedeed men, in looking ahead, negate their own past. Luther's great-grandfather recognized that "the future of Wayne County . . . was going to be white." Luther himself sees Linden Hills as successful, not as black. The Nedeeds' fatal mistake is to try to emulate white materialistic society. They buy into the dream too well.

It is important to recognize the novel's intentional parallels with the work of Dante Alighieri. Linden Hills, like Dante's Hell, is an inverted cone, wide at the top and narrow at the bottom, with each of its eight circular drives representing a circle of Hell. Luther Nedeed (whose name is a play on "Lucifer de Eden"), self-styled ruler of this false paradise, has built his house at the bottom of the hills at 999 Tupelo Drive, the ninth and deepest circle of Hell. Because "up means down in the Hills," Nedeed's house number is really 666, the biblical mark of the beast. Thus, Willie and Lester's journey through Linden Hills is a symbolic descent into the Inferno like that of Dante and his guide Vergil. Just as Dante discovers sinners on his journey, a lost soul is found on each circular drive, beginning with the Tilsons in Limbo, or the first circle (First Crescent Drive), and moving down to the Nedeeds in the ninth circle of betrayers, where, as in Dante's work, the cold is bitter and accompanied by ice and snow. Naylor's Hell, however, is not theological but is a death of the soul; the false success of white materialism is the trap that destroys these African Americans, who have given up their identity for status.

Other themes include invisibility or facelessness, a recurring topic in African American literature. Willa's absence is noted and even "tasted" by Willie long before he knows who she is. The dead Laurel Dumont is faceless, like the Nedeed wives (especially Priscilla McGuire, whose photographs become faceless), and Willie dreams that he has no face. Mirror imagery also appears frequently. Willie and Willa can be seen as alter egos, or opposing selves, mirroring each other. This becomes particularly evident when Willie dreams of something that Willa is experiencing; the words "Will he eat it?" that Willa reads in a recipe book become, in Willie's nightmare, "Willie, eat it." In a number of key scenes, the characters view their own images, as when the Reverend Hollis dresses before his mirror. In a sense, Willie and Lester mirror each other as well.

Critical Context

Naylor has said that her subject is always the lives of African American women, and in *The Women of Brewster Place* (1983), which received the American Book Award for best first novel, and *Mama Day* (1989), she reaffirms the importance of female bonding. *Linden Hills* comments indirectly on the lack of and need for sisterhood by examining an upper-middle-class African American suburb in which women are largely exploited or invisible and in which men have, in the course of upward mobility, sacrificed their racial identity and their essence. Willie, the sensitive protagonist, expresses Naylor's belief that people do have choices in life and that those choices matter.

Naylor has skillfully employed a classical European framework for her modern Inferno and has given it the richness of many characters and backgrounds. She continues to reject the concept of "the" African American experience, as if there were only one; this novel, like her others, presents the multiple experiences of her men and women. Critics agree that Naylor, like Toni Morrison and Alice Walker before her, brings a strong new voice to African American literature.

Bibliography

Andrews, Larry R. "Black Sisterhood in Gloria Naylor's Novels." *College Language Association Journal* 33, no. 1 (September, 1989): 1-25. Explores the bonds between female characters in Naylor's first three novels. The upper-middle-class women of *Linden Hills* seem most isolated, having modeled their lives too closely on the dominant view of success—to marry "well." Although two older characters are intuitive and compassionate, communication and support between and within generations seem to fail until Willa, through her identification with the Nedeed wives, finally gains choice and the power to leave the basement.

Collins, Grace E. "Narrative Structure in *Linden Hills.*" *College Language Association Journal* 34, no. 3 (March, 1991): 290-300. Focuses on the parallel journeys from ignorance to knowledge taken by alter egos Willie and Willa. Willie's physical journey through Linden Hills and Willa's psychological journey into the past are "hell-journeys" that mirror each other in plot and theme and illustrate the need to reclaim or verify one's self in the materialistic culture of the American Dream.

Gomez, Jewelle. "Naylor's Inferno." *The Women's Review of Books* 2, no. 11 (August, 1985): 7-8. Argues that *Linden Hills* too often seems like a literary exercise. Although Gomez praises Naylor's talent, she is critical of her treatment of characters and emphasis on skin color, charging that Naylor has merely accepted the traditional symbolism of blackness (the dark-skinned Nedeeds) as evil rather than challenging it.

Jones, Robert. "A Place in the Suburbs." *Commonweal*, May 3, 1985, 283-285. Centers on the universal loss of innocence and grace. Naylor rejects nihilism because memory offers the hope of salvation: "Self-knowledge is made possible only by memory. . . . Memory sets you free." Jones examines from a Christian perspective the lives of those characters who have reached for the American dream of success and found themselves bitterly disappointed.

Naylor, Gloria, and Toni Morrison. "A Conversation." *Southern Review* 31, no. 3 (July, 1985): 567-593. Naylor's philosophy of writing; early influences, especially Morrison's *The Bluest Eye* (1970); her interaction with characters in *Linden Hills*. She confirms that a study of Dante triggered the form that she chose for the novel.

Ward, Catherine C. "Gloria Naylor's *Linden Hills:* A Modern *Inferno.*" *Contemporary Literature* 28, no. 1 (Spring, 1987): 67-81. A detailed and excellent reading of Dantean symbolism that links the circular drives of Linden Hills with the corresponding circles of Hell. Ward admires the risks Naylor takes in writing "an allegory about moral accountability" with a mythic scope that embraces African American and European sensibilities, the oppression of women, and the importance of cultural history. The novel demonstrates a faith in the power of individual choice and self-recognition illustrated by Willa and Willie.

Joanne McCarthy

THE LONELY LONDONERS

Author: Samuel Selvon (1923-   )
Type of work: Novel
Type of plot: Social realism
Time of plot: The early 1950's
Locale: London, England
First published: 1956

Principal characters:

MOSES ALEOTTA, a Trinidadian immigrant to England; a factory
worker who is a father figure to younger West Indian
immigrants

HENRY OLIVER, a Trinidadian immigrant nicknamed Sir Galahad,
a factory worker befriended by Moses

CAPTAIN, a Nigerian immigrant nicknamed Cap, a close
acquaintance of the West Indian characters

TOLROY, a Jamaican immigrant, a factory worker who has to settle
his newly arrived family

TANTY, a Jamaican immigrant, Tolroy's aunt

The Novel

Although it depicts in realistic terms the lives of West Indian immigrants newly
arrived in England, the terms in which it does so are so lyrical in language and
lighthearted in attitude that *The Lonely Londoners* seems less a conventional novel
than a cavalcade of humors and manners, a Mardi Gras of misadventure or, to use
one of the novel's own terms, a "fete." Its structure is episodic, possibly a result of
the author's well-known ability as a short-story writer and radio dramatist. This
structure has the effect of making the work's sense of time seasonal rather than
social. The characters do not have the space in which to develop. In addition, the
novel is written for the most part in the English of the author's native Trinidad,
reverting to standard usage only at points when some conceptual dimension needs to
be invoked in order to clarify a character's state of mind.

Instead of limiting the work's appeal, however, these features subtly convey the
implications of the title. Even the unfamiliar constructions of the author's English
are rich in cultural undertones of various kinds, while remaining for the uninitiated
reader quite easy to understand. The attempt to preserve the character of the uncertainty, vitality, and foreignness that the immigrants bring, along with the addictive
attractions and possibilities of London life, fuels *The Lonely Londoners*, making it
more a fascinating document with strong ethnographic tendencies than a well-made
novel in the conventional mode.

Despite the author's clear understanding of the economic, racial, and political
components of his characters' social existence, the sense of the social that emerges
is that which derives from leisure activities and the pursuit of happiness, particularly

the variety that, it is believed, the female form embodies. This emphasis does not overlook other, more pressing, areas of immigrant experience. Subjection to prejudice by employers, labor unions, landlords, and various other social structures is deftly but inescapably sketched. The immigrants' bemused incomprehension of England and the English is constantly close to the surface of their experiences. Even the English climate seems prejudicial. As the novel's title suggests, the immigrants' lives embody an economic and social dead end. Nevertheless, despite their less than modest status, options, and future, and despite a variety of attitudes on the part of individuals, they are seldom demoralized and dwell only fleetingly on the vicissitudes of their situation.

Their faith in life, their articulation of liberty, and their pursuit of happiness, or at any rate, a good time, is relentless, spirited, and essentially optimistic. Such orientations are expressed through a fondness for fashionable and, relative to the wearers' economic wherewithal, expensive clothing; trips to the cinema and restaurants in the West End, preferably with white girls on their arms; and organizing a fete, a dance featuring traditional music provided by a traditional steel band.

Much of the time, however, the characters are found with time on their hands. This too is expressive of the quality of life of the immigrants, as opposed to being a documentary record of a given set of actual immigrants' lives. The amount of time spent "coasting a lime," the American equivalent to which is "hanging out," forms a sober contrast to the images of themselves as lovers and fashion models that constitute their conception of successful participation in the society of what they call, with ambivalent affection, "the old Brit'n." The novel's episodic structure reflects the lack of structure in the characters' social existence, a lack underlined by their working the night shift, this being the form of employment they can obtain with any degree of regularity and ease. Even the episodes that occur outside their single rooms and hostels, episodes in such well-known London venues as Piccadilly Circus and Speaker's Corner in Hyde Park, show the immigrants to be marginal, detached, and engaged in activities that, though very human, are essentially inconclusive.

The manner in which the immigrants abbreviate the names of the West London locales in which they settle—"the Water" for Bayswater, "the Gate" for Notting Hill Gate, "the Grove" for Ladbroke Grove—represents their desire to familiarize themselves with their surroundings. This desire, also expressed in reference to "the Circus" and "the Arch," the latter referring to Marble Arch, remains at the level of intention. Nothing in *The Lonely Londoners* indicates that the immigrants will be able to relieve the loneliness or become Londoners in the fully accepted sense of the term. This state of affairs makes all the more noteworthy the spiritedness that the characters bring, naïvely perhaps, to their various adventures, amatory and other. Were it not naïve, that spirit might not be so persistent. The author's identification and recapitulation of his characters' energies by means of their patois is an act of loyalty and fond, if slightly ironic, homage that lends them a viability and distinctiveness not otherwise accorded to their presence or to the social status upon which that presence is based.

The Characters

Unlike the conventional novel, *The Lonely Londoners* has no protagonist. Moses Aleotta, to whom the reader is initially introduced, has a certain status, but this derives not from his social position, his special resources, or his extraordinary experiences. It derives instead from the length of time he has been in London. Seniority gives Moses an authority and significance in the eyes of the group that has formed around him. In the eyes of newcomers, Moses is a vital mentor, guide, and informant. Such a view makes Moses increasingly conscious of the human cost of his immigrant status, as revealed in his rather embittered and nostalgic conversation with the younger, fresher Galahad toward the end of the novel. Although none of the characters is immune from the loneliness of the novel's title, it is Moses who is the most complete embodiment of unsensational, unsentimental isolation.

Galahad, on the contrary, makes a much more obvious effort to enter English society in his pursuit of white women. His date with Dolly, however, is not exactly what either partner expects; Galahad is somewhat disappointed by the girl's grade of culture, while she is unaccustomed to his standard of hospitality. The conflicts that are gently implied in this episode are repeated in various ways throughout the novel. They are most obviously in evidence in the area of sexual relations, but they also exist between West Indian family members, as in the case of Tolroy's brother and sister-in-law, and between members of the West Indian community generally, as the pretentious behavior of the impresario Harris demonstrates. These remain conflicts without issue. Dolly appears and disappears. What she is thought to represent remains poorly defined, elusive, unsettling, and symptomatic of being unsettled.

Cap, however, seems to be the exception required to prove the rule. His unpredictable and vaguely anarchistic way of life, driven by his opportunistic momentum, represents in extreme form the unorthodoxy of the immigrant presence. Cap's ways of dealing with money, with women, and with lodgings are fraught with irregularity and improvisation. The fact that he proceeds unscathed by his experience seems to render him invulnerable to the loneliness that informs West Indian lives. Cap's experience also places him beyond the fringe of society, giving his behavior an egotistical vehemence entirely lacking from the ambitions and adventures of Moses and fellow countrymen.

On the contrary, what characterizes the experience of the vast majority of the characters in *The Lonely Londoners* is its harmlessness. It would be too facile to say that the journey that Tanty makes from the Harrow Road to Great Portland Street, from her restricted domicile to the world of work and white people, is symptomatic in its straightforwardness and potential trauma of the passage from home to England that is a continual source of reflection in the novel. Nevertheless, the singularity of Tanty's trip is a reminder of West Indian guilelessness, as represented by the author. It is true that the Barbadian nicknamed, on account of the darkness of his complexion, Five Past Twelve, does smoke marijuana at the fete. Another of the novel's numerous minor characters bets on the football pools, a form of legalized gambling on the results of soccer games. This is the extent of their vices. Unlike other members of immigrant groups, these characters do very little drinking, and in only one case is sporting expensive cigarettes part of a character's style.

In this way, and also by the text's consistent emphasis on the characters' desire for gainful employment both as an economic matter and as a matter of dignity, the author tactfully but explicitly calls attention to his people's fitness for full citizenship and counteracts the stereotypes frequently imposed on immigrants, on black people, and on black immigrants. It may be that readers encountering *The Lonely Londoners* long after it was first published may find themselves impatient with the simplicity of the characters and the general lightheartedness that informs their lives. Part of the function of such strategies of representation, however, is disarming, intended to render an assimilable depiction of the immigrants that neither belittles them nor threatens the host society.

Themes and Meanings

There is no protagonist in *The Lonely Londoners.* Although some characters are more engaging than others, are more sharply drawn than others, or are given to more outrageous behavior, none is superior. For the most part, they share very similar backgrounds, and their situations are uniform in all important respects. Their futures also have a sameness. The author is careful to arrange the text so that no character's stories take precedence over another's. By this means, the organization of the material in *The Lonely Londoners* is a facsimile of the fragile community that its characters constitute, a fellowship held together by memories of the past, various experiences of rejection in the present, and some elementary forms of male bonding whereby they attempt to project a future for themselves.

The communitarian ethic that underlies the novel's lack of a protagonist reveals the condition the immigrants share to be essentially a holding operation. They find themselves with no alternative but to live for the day, and they are prepared to live that way with a will. The lack of a protagonist also means the absence of a plot. This absence is not necessarily to be regretted, since *The Lonely Londoners* is a novel shaped by the spirit of its material rather than by the letter of precedent and the tradition of the English novel. The absence of plot, however, expresses the absence of a particular scheme of action, with the promise of productive activity, instructive encounters, and a specific outcome. None of these possibilities is pertinent to the lives of Samuel Selvon's characters.

The nonexistence of two of conventional fiction's most fundamental structuring elements is an indication of how a sense of loss permeates *The Lonely Londoners.* The attachment that the characters have for one another arises out of a need for protection, a need to adhere to representatives of a known world. There is no indication that once the attachment has been formed it can be used in an activist manner, either to redress or at least protest against discriminatory practices, or more modestly to allow the immigrants to be recruited for or join a cricket team, an area of experience in which West Indian expertise has been universally acknowledged, even in England. The reason these options are not available is that it is the ordinariness of his immigrants that the author wants to stress—the fact that they have no particular qualifications or aptitudes and possess, as the various references to clothing and Galahad's first appearance suggest, only what they stand up in.

They exist in the cultural nakedness of their mere blackness. Their education offers them no protection, they have no special skills to give them the illusion of indispensability, and they are not sufficiently talented to avail themselves of the spurious assimilation of a career in show business. They are as devoid of religious feeling as they are of criminal tendencies. In view of such lacunae, the characters are deprived of access to the world at large, the world of cultural codes and sublimated energies. As in the case of the novel's ostensible structural deficiencies, these deprivations and omissions instruct the reader as to the author's inescapable emphasis. The sense that he conveys of his characters is that of their insistent and inescapable physical presence, a presence conveyed by their blackness, by their capacity for laboring work, by the affectation of fashionable wardrobes, and by their unrepressed sexuality.

The undeniability of the characters' maleness, and their understandable incapacity to forgo it, is not introduced solely for prurient reasons. On the contrary, it crystallizes the cultural conflicts that underlie the immigrants' experience and that have no issue in *The Lonely Londoners*. The abortive, inconclusive, and anticlimactic pursuit of white women is less a trope of sexuality than, as its provocative potential indicates, a cultural trope. To date a white woman is regarded as an obvious proof of the existence of a color bar and of the immigrant's ability to cross it. Although recognition of this ability is culturally conditioned and couched in clichés of display and other elements of machismo, nevertheless it articulates a fundamental component of humanity. By emphasizing the human needs and aspirations of his characters, Selvon reinstalls what society at large has tended to deface.

Critical Context

Conditions in England in the immediate postwar period were conducive to substantial immigration from the colonies. The amount of rebuilding that needed to be carried out, the shortage of workers caused by the war, and various other complicated demographic and social factors led to the tapping of a large pool of black labor from the West Indies. Neither party to this arrangement was quite prepared for the effects that it would have. In particular, English society, proverbially private, insular, and elaborately stratified, was ill-equipped at both the structural and cultural levels to consider the new workers as equal partners in the rehabilitation of the social fabric.

Inevitably, the immigrants found themselves in a variety of economic, social, and cultural ghettos. These were all the more palpable since they did not have an explicit geographical equivalent. Although it is true that the Brixton section of South London became synonymous with West Indian immigrant families, *The Lonely Londoners* is a telling account of the first wave of immigrants, which consisted largely of single men. The single rooms in which they lived were to a considerable extent confined to the area of West London delimited in the novel. This area did not, however, constitute a ghetto in the sociological sense, with the result that there was continual problematic interaction between white and black residents. These conditions culminated in the first serious postwar English race riot, at Notting Hill in 1956. This context conditions the sense of conflict, alienation, foreignness, and taboo that forms the understated subtext of *The Lonely Londoners* and that gives a particularly complex set of connotations to the ordinary humanity of the term "lonely."

Public recognition of this immigrant influx, in cultural terms, did not occur immediately. Because of this lack, authors such as Samuel Selvon performed an invaluable service both to their countrymen and to their hosts by considering immigrants' conditions and experiences as subjects appropriate for literature. Despite the popular success of novels by white authors dealing with the immigrant situation such as Colin MacInnes's *City of Spades* (1957), were it not for Selvon's novels *The Lonely Londoners* and *The Housing Lark* (1965), and his collection of stories *Ways of Sunlight* (1957), the vivid lives and hard times of the first West Indian immigrants to England might not have been given their due, and one of the migrations symptomatic of postwar relations between the First and Third Worlds might well have had its human component go unrecorded.

Bibliography
Gikandi, Simon. *Writing in Limbo: Modernism and Caribbean Literature.* Ithaca, N.Y.: Cornell University Press, 1992. Using contemporary literary and cultural theory, this work examines the destiny of Caribbean literature in the light of the modernist movement and postcolonial political reality. Selvon's sense of displacement as a central element of West Indian experience is evaluated.

Ramchand, Kenneth. "Sam Selvon Talking." *Canadian Literature* 95 (Winter, 1982): 56-64. An informative overview of the author's career and artistic outlook, containing much that is relevant to establishing a context for *The Lonely Londoners.*

——————. "Song of Innocence, Song of Experience: Samuel Selvon's *The Lonely Londoners* as a Literary Work." *World Literature Written in English* 21 (Autumn, 1982): 644-654. An article that details the artistic elements of *The Lonely Londoners* and sees it in the context of Selvon's other fiction.

——————. *The West Indian Novel and Its Background.* 2d ed. London: Heinemann, 1983. Provides an introduction to the world of West Indian fiction, with particular emphasis on its socioeconomic and linguistic aspects, the latter crucial to any study of Selvon. Contains an extensive bibliography.

Ramjaj, Victor. "Selvon's Londoners: From the Centre to the Periphery." In *Language and Literature in Multicultural Context,* edited by Satendra Nandan. Suva, Fiji: University of the South Pacific, 1983. Establishes a cultural context in which Selvon's literature of immigration can be appreciated. Includes material on *The Lonely Londoners.*

George O'Brien

THE LONG DREAM

Author: Richard Wright (1908-1960)
Type of work: Novel
Type of plot: Naturalism
Time of plot: The 1940's and 1950's
Locale: Clintonville, Mississippi
First published: 1958

> *Principal characters:*
> REX "FISHBELLY" TUCKER, the protagonist, son of a prominent
>   black Clintonville undertaker
> TYREE TUCKER, Fishbelly's father, a leader in the black
>   community
> EMMA TUCKER, Fishbelly's mother, the long-suffering wife of
>   Tyree Tucker
> TONY JENKINS, a friend of Fishbelly
> ZEKE JORDAN, a friend of Fishbelly
> SAM DAVIS, a friend of Fishbelly
> GLORIA MASON, Tyree Tucker's light-skinned mistress
> GERALD CANTLEY, the sheriff of Clintonville and head of a
>   criminal syndicate
> HARVEY MCWILLIAMS, the town's white liberal lawyer and sworn
>   enemy of Gerald Cantley

The Novel

The Long Dream is a combination of naturalistic writing and the *Bildungsroman*, or novel of initiation, concerned with the childhood and adolescence of Rex "Fishbelly" Tucker. Fishbelly is born into a life of comparative privilege and respectability but soon discovers that his father's cooperation with the white authorities cannot protect him from the realities of the Jim Crow, or segregated, South. In a series of dramatic and psychologically revealing episodes, Wright illustrates, through Tyree Tucker and Fishbelly, his thesis that the life of a black man is "a long dream."

The novel begins with a number of experiences from Fishbelly's childhood, the most memorable of which is the lynching of his older friend and sometime mentor Chris Sims. Chris commits the crime of being caught in a hotel room with a white girl. After he is discovered, killed, and mutilated by a white mob, his body is taken to Tyree's funeral home for burial. In a moment of revelation for the young Fishbelly, his father takes him to the funeral home to display to him the badly beaten face of Chris Sims, as a warning and a demonstration of the power the white world has over the black.

Fishbelly grows up to be a respected member of the middle-class black community of Clintonville. After a brief encounter with the police while trespassing on a white property owner's land, Fishbelly manages to avoid any contact with the white world until his sixteenth year. In that year, two things happen: Fishbelly drops out of school, and he later becomes enamored of the near-white girl Gladys, emulating the behavior of his father, whose light-skinned mistress Gloria Mason is the envy of the Black Belt of Clintonville. All of this comes to an abrupt end, however, when the Grove, the bar at which Gladys works, burns during a Fourth of July celebration, resulting in more than forty deaths. When it is revealed that Tyree is a co-owner of the bar, which was in violation of several fire codes, the truce arranged between Tyree and the whites comes to an end.

The remainder of the novel is an object lesson for the embryonic Civil Rights movement. Tyree, though an extortionist and a pimp, maintains some dignity by demanding from Sheriff Gerald Cantley and the whites in authority that they either live up to their business commitments or provide him with a black jury at an upcoming trial. Cantley predictably denies Tyree's request, at which point Tyree decides that he should seek a more socially responsible form of justice. He contacts the town's liberal white lawyer, Harvey McWilliams, and gives him the evidence necessary to convict Cantley. Things fall apart, however, when the evidence is stolen from McWilliams and when Tyree is murdered by Cantley and his operatives.

Fishbelly, heir to the Tucker fortune, is now in a position either to take up his father's role as ally of the white power structure or to break free to experience a new mode of life. He first pursues the former, only to find that Cantley intends to treat him in the same manner as he treated his father. Fishbelly is subsequently set up in a false charge of sexual assault against a white woman. Cantley keeps Fishbelly in jail for more than a year, hoping to convince Fishbelly to relinquish any evidence that he may have against the sheriff, before McWilliams is able to get him free. Upon his release, Fishbelly decides to leave Mississippi for Paris. When he arrives in France, he writes to McWilliams and reveals to him the location of the missing evidence concerning Cantley.

The Characters

Rex "Fishbelly" Tucker is a character whose personality is developed according to the rules both of naturalism and of psychoanalysis. His early life is revealed through a series of episodes that focus on significant moments of what Sigmund Freud called "infantile experience"; these episodes are then shown as having significant effects on his later life. In one example, Fishbelly finds a discarded condom in a vacant lot, and he and his friends naturally turn it into a plaything. They are then told by an older neighbor, Chris Sims, that the thing is dirty and that they should not be seen with it. The boys are shocked to hear from Chris the purpose of the thing and to find out where it had been. This experience has a significant effect on the development of sexual attitudes in each of the young men. When Chris is later lynched for having been found in a hotel room with a white woman, Fishbelly's attraction to and repulsion from sexual behavior become even more pronounced.

Tyree Tucker, Fishbelly's father, also contributes to young Fishbelly's anxiety. Tyree is perhaps the most complex character in the novel; he reveals depth of character unexpected in a seemingly conformist resident of Clintonville's Black Belt. Tyree leads a double life. By day, he is the most respected black undertaker in town; at night he oversees a variety of operations, from slum housing to brothels to juke joints. Wright portrays his character objectively in the first half of the novel but makes Tyree more sympathetic as he comes into conflict with his white "business" partners. Tyree finally decides that he must side with the progressive elements of society and demands a black jury when he is brought up on charges of violating the town's fire codes. He also shows great bravery when facing the entire power structure of the town by threatening to expose the corrupt business practices of the white establishment.

The minor characters in the novel all help to fill in the panorama of small-town Mississippi life. Tony Jenkins, Zeke Jordan, and Sam Davis, Fishbelly's running mates, experience much of the same psychological confusion. They each seek a separate escape or compensation for their problems, ranging from alcohol to promiscuous and possibly dangerous sexual behavior. Gloria Mason, Tyree's mistress, who is light-skinned enough to pass for white, serves as an emblem of the fascination that white society holds for the Tucker family. Tyree comes as close to breaking the sexual taboo as he can, but he does not dare to declare war on Southern customs, benefiting as he does from their preservation.

The two main white characters in the book, Sheriff Gerald Cantley and attorney Harvey McWilliams, represent respectively the forces of reaction and progress in the white community. Cantley extorts half of the profits from Tyree Tucker's illegal operations and provides "protection" for Tyree as long as Tyree plays according to the rules of segregated society. He is the stereotypical Southern sheriff who is interested not in justice but only in preserving the status quo. McWilliams is likewise a common figure in Southern fiction from William Faulkner on. The most developed form of this figure can be seen in the character of Atticus Finch in Harper Lee's *To Kill a Mockingbird* (1960). More militant than Finch, McWilliams vows to keep up the fight until he exposes the corruption in the town.

Themes and Meanings

Richard Wright, in his famous essay "The Ethics of Living Jim Crow," described the psychological as well as the physical restrictions of growing up in the segregated South. *The Long Dream* is a fictionalized version of that essay. Wright uses the combined techniques of naturalism and psychoanalytic theory to develop the insights sketched in the essay. Although placed in a classic naturalistic environment in which the pressure of society threatens to destroy him, Fishbelly Tucker manages to escape, as a result of his traits of psychological resilience, developed during his Jim Crow upbringing.

Fishbelly's psychological development is illustrated through a series of dreams that fit Sigmund Freud's theories introduced in *The Interpretation of Dreams* (1900). Freud explains that dreams are composed of two elements, "infantile experience" and "the day's residues." Fishbelly's dreams, particularly those that occur in the early chapters, are syntheses of traumatic experiences and foreshadow concerns that will be important in the plot. Fishbelly's "locomotive" dream at the end of chapter 3 is a combination of his statement to his father, whose sexual encounter he interrupted, that he sounded like a locomotive, and of Fishbelly's own awakening sexuality. It is also a foreshadowing of Fishbelly's mode of escape from Mississippi: The train takes him to Memphis, from which he leaves the United States for Paris. Likewise, the locomotive again appears in his dream after his older friend Chris Sims is lynched for being caught in a hotel room with a white girl. This time, however, Fishbelly does not remember any of the details of the nightmare; "instinct" told him that "he had to learn how to live with these images of horror."

Linked to the psychological analysis of the dream is the sociological analysis, for which Wright is justly celebrated. The life of the African American male is a long dream, as stated in one passage, a never-ending struggle of learning how to deal with the horrors of segregation, prejudice, and oppression. This second part of the dream is the concern of the majority of the novel, which traces the effects of that oppression through all levels of Black Belt society. Fishbelly encounters the entire range of responses to be found in the Black Belt, which, to paraphrase the narrator, range from alcohol to religion to sex. He and his friends run the entire range of these experiences during their adolescence: one friend, Zeke Jordan, tricks young women into sexual encounters by saying that he is sterile or by using condoms that he intentionally damages; another, Sam Davis, finds a substitute religion by repeating the Black Nationalist rhetoric of his father, a tenant in one of Tyree Tucker's slum buildings. These scenes contribute to the tension that builds until the truce between black and white arranged by Tyree Tucker is broken.

The last section of the novel, "The Waking Dream," concerns Fishbelly and his escape from the Clintonville society that claimed his father's life. Much like Wright himself, Fishbelly realizes that he has no future in the segregated South. As he wakes from a dream, he sees that his only hope for survival is to leave the United States altogether. He spends more than a year in nightmarish circumstances in the Clintonville jail, charged with sexual assault against a woman who does not appear at any of the hearings. After his release, he immediately leaves for Paris to join his friends. He does not, however, completely abandon the dream for those who remain behind in Mississippi. He writes to his attorney and reveals to him the location of documents that implicate the white power structure in corruption. Although his decision to leave Clintonville can be viewed as an escape, it is also Fishbelly's only means of keeping the dream alive.

Critical Context

First published in 1958, *The Long Dream* was a financial failure for Wright, though the reviews of the novel were mixed. Wright was criticized both for being out of touch with black life in the United States after his eleven years of exile in Paris and for underestimating the quality of resistance found in black communities throughout the United States, particularly those in the South. Despite positive reviews of the novel from *The Nation* and *Time* magazines, an aura of failure surrounded the novel and Wright late in his career. An unsuccessful stage adaptation of the novel added to that aura.

The renewal of interest in Wright's work in the 1980's led to a reexamination of Wright's novels of exile, of which *The Long Dream* is the most important. Interest in Wright as a Southern writer brought about a reappraisal of the work as a commentary on his Mississippi childhood. The novel follows closely much of Wright's early naturalistic writing, especially *Uncle Tom's Children* (1938), a collection of works set in Mississippi that includes the short story "Bright and Morning Star" and the essay "The Ethics of Living Jim Crow." In these stories, Wright includes a range of Southern African Americans who resist the ideology of segregation and who are either ground down by the system, like Tyree Tucker, or who manage to escape, like Fishbelly and Big Boy of the story "Big Boy Leaves Home."

The novel is perhaps most important as a continuation of the themes presented in Wright's autobiographical work *Black Boy* (1945). Although the second volume of Wright's autobiography, *American Hunger*, was suppressed until 1977, *Black Boy* enjoyed a wide readership and influence. In it Wright graphically depicts the initiation of a young boy into the nightmare world of segregation and racial violence. In *The Long Dream*, Wright gives the reader both the sketch of the dream and its interpretation.

Bibliography
Fabre, Michel. *The Unfinished Quest of Richard Wright.* Translated by Isabel Barzun. New York: William Morrow, 1973. A thoroughly researched biography of Wright by a French scholar. Unlike many of the early reviewers of *The Long Dream*, Fabre admires the book for the strength of its narrative, comparing it favorably to *Native Son.*
Felgar, Robert. *Richard Wright.* Boston: Twayne, 1980. An introduction to the fiction, nonfiction, and poetry of Richard Wright. Felgar considers *The Long Dream* to be primarily a derivative work, repeating but not improving upon material introduced early in Wright's career.
Gayle, Addison. *Richard Wright: Ordeal of a Native Son.* Garden City, N.Y.: Anchor Press/Doubleday, 1980. An analysis of Wright's career as a writer and his troubled relationship with the Federal Bureau of Investigation and the Central Intelligence Agency, using many released government documents as source material. Gayle associates Wright with Tyree Tucker and not with Fishbelly, as many other critics have.
Margolies, Edward. *The Art of Richard Wright.* Carbondale: Southern Illinois University Press, 1969. An early but extremely thorough analysis of Wright's work. There is an extended essay on *The Long Dream*, despite the author's feeling that the book is a disappointment.
Moore, Jack B. "The View from the Broom Closet of the Regency Hyatt: Richard

Wright as a Southern Writer." In *Literature at the Barricades: The American Writer in the 1930's,* edited by Ralph F. Bogardus and Fred Hobson. University: University of Alabama Press, 1982. Concentrates on Wright's Southern background and on his adaptation of the conventions of naturalism to Southern writing.

Walker, Margaret. *Richard Wright: Daemonic Genius.* New York: Warner Books, 1988. A combination of memoir and literary analysis by the well-known African American author, a close friend of Wright. Special emphasis is given to Wright's early years in Chicago, where the two met. Walker considers *The Long Dream* to be a failure but concludes her book with a quote from the novel.

Jeff Cupp

LUCY

Author: Jamaica Kincaid (Elaine Potter Richardson, 1949-   )
Type of work: Novel
Type of plot: Psychological realism
Time of plot: The late 1960's
Locale: An unnamed city in the United States
First published: 1990

Principal characters:

> LUCY JOSEPHINE POTTER, the protagonist, a young woman who
> has left her home in the West Indies to work as a live-in child-
> care provider
> MARIAH, Lucy's employer, an attractive, wealthy white woman
> LEWIS, Mariah's husband, a wealthy lawyer who falls in love with
> his wife's best friend, Dinah
> DINAH, Mariah's envious best friend and Lewis' lover
> PEGGY, Lucy's best friend, a woman of Irish extraction
> who lives with her parents and works at the motor vehicle
> registry
> HUGH, Dinah's twenty-two-year-old brother, who has traveled to
> Africa and Asia; he becomes Lucy's lover
> PAUL, an artist with whom Lucy has an affair
> MAUDE QUICK, one of Lucy's prudish, mean-spirited relatives
> TIMOTHY SIMON, a photographer who aspires to greatness in his
> field but who photographs food for the cooking sections of
> magazines in order to make a living
> LUCY'S MOTHER, who appears only in Lucy's memories but
> continues to influence Lucy's thoughts and behavior

The Novel

Lucy tells about a year in the life of a nineteen-year-old girl from the Caribbean who has just arrived in the United States. When the novel opens, Lucy is experiencing the shock of adapting to a new culture. Even the weather is deceiving: Although the January sun is shining, Lucy shivers in her thin clothing. She likes her new employers, Mariah and Lewis, and their children, for whom she cares, but she is somewhat homesick. This emotion confuses her because she was so eager to leave her home and begin a new life.

Interspersed with the day-to-day happenings of her life are her memories of home, which revolve around her sexual awakening and her love-hate relationship with her mother. Mariah wants Lucy to see the world through her eyes and love the things that she loves. For example, Mariah loves daffodils and tells Lucy all about them. Mariah's words trigger in Lucy the unhappy memory of being forced to memorize poetry about daffodils at the Queen Victoria School for Girls when she was ten years old. Her anger about daffodils is explained when she finally sees a daffodil and remarks that she had to wait nine years to see a flower that never grew on her island but that she was forced to revere under British rule.

Mariah, although well-meaning, often upsets Lucy by her attitude toward life. Lucy cannot understand how Mariah can be always cheerful and always kindhearted but also always blind to the injustices done to people of color. During a train ride planned by Mariah for the sole purpose of providing a new experience for Lucy, Lucy notices that the other passengers all look like Mariah's relatives and the waiters all look like Lucy's relatives.

Lucy eventually makes friends with Peggy, with whom she has little in common except their thirst for shared experiences. Peggy and Lucy spend their free time together and talk frequently on the telephone. Both dream of living on their own. Mariah disapproves of Peggy because she smokes, uses slang, and generally meets the criteria of "a bad example." She bars Peggy from the house. Otherwise, she does not interfere because she realizes that Lucy needs a friend of her own age.

After about six months, Lucy has become acclimated to American culture and is looking forward to spending the summer at Mariah's family home near one of the Great Lakes. There Lucy meets Hugh, the brother of Dinah, who is Mariah's best friend. Lucy and Hugh become lovers, but neither is looking for commitment. They part in September without regrets.

All the time Lucy has been in the United States, she has been thinking of her life back on the island. She finally admits that she does not read her mother's letters because she knows they will only increase the longing she has for her mother and for her former home. Lucy does not talk of her mother to anyone.

Peggy introduces Lucy to Paul, an artist. Lucy and Paul immediately become lovers, though Peggy tries to discourage Lucy from this course. Peggy and Lucy begin to discuss sharing an apartment, while Mariah and Lewis begin to argue constantly. Mariah's eyes are usually red from weeping. Lewis moves out, but not before Lucy has seen him in a passionate embrace with Dinah.

Lucy continues to live with Mariah. Maude Quick, one of Lucy's relatives, arrives with the news of Lucy's father's death. Lucy then opens the letter from her mother and learns that her father died a pauper. Lucy sends her mother all the money she has, and Mariah contributes twice Lucy's share. Only then does Lucy reveal the reason she feels hatred for her mother. Until the age of nine, Lucy was an only child; her parents then had three sons in the space of five years. Both parents dreamed of their sons' futures, talking about how proud they would be when their sons were graduated from British universities and became important men. Lucy had expected her mother to dream similar dreams for her only daughter, and she was deeply hurt when her mother could only suggest nursing school. Lucy writes one last letter to her mother, giving her a false address.

After leaving Mariah's employ, Lucy moves into an apartment with Peggy and begins working for photographer Timothy Simon in his office. She suspects Peggy and Paul of having an affair, but she really does not care if they are. The novel ends with Lucy's search for identity unfinished.

The Characters

As the narrator, Lucy reveals her personality through her thoughts, dreams, and memories, as well as through her interactions with other characters in the novel. A sensual young woman, she does not love any of the men with whom she involves herself. That her mother is the only person she has ever loved becomes clear as the novel progresses. Lucy sees herself as identical to her mother and works hard to free herself and to find her own sense of self.

Lucy describes and comments on the actions and personalities of the people she meets in the United States. Most suffer from her analysis. For example, although superficially Mariah and Lewis have a perfect marriage, Lucy notices its flaws long before either of the pair notices them. An astute judge of character, Lucy knows that Dinah envies Mariah, that Lewis and Dinah are lovers, and that Lewis is manipulating Mariah so it will seem as though Mariah initiates their divorce.

A genuinely caring person, Mariah tries to understand Lucy's anger and resentment toward her mother and toward British rule of her former home, but her lack of depth makes this an impossible task. The episode in which Mariah attempts to explain to Lucy the beauty of daffodils underscores both Lucy's anger and Mariah's lack of understanding. Mariah's inability to see the world as it is contributes to her downfall. A woman for whom everything has always come easily, she views her life and the lives of the people surrounding her as sunny and cheerful. This view causes her to miss many of the danger signs that appear in her marriage and leaves her extremely vulnerable when her relationship with Lewis falls apart. Mariah's identity, which is directly connected to being Lewis' wife, dissolves under pressure, leaving her a broken and unhappy shell of her former self.

The men in Lucy's life seem almost interchangeable. None has a lasting effect on her, perhaps because Lucy's quest for selfhood does not include finding a husband. Long before leaving her island, Lucy learned that power lies within oneself, that it cannot be transferred from a man to a woman. Her recollections of her father, with his many children born to various women, remind her of the transience of most relationships. She therefore is not shocked at Lewis' behavior; rather, her shock is reserved for women such as Mariah. Lucy cannot understand why Mariah is hurt and baffled by Lewis' behavior.

Although she appears only in Lucy's memories, Lucy's mother continues to play a crucial role in Lucy's life. In many ways, Lucy's mother necessitates the search for independence Lucy undertakes. A strong-willed woman who never doubts that she is always right, Lucy's mother proves to be a formidable obstacle. Lucy has strained against her mother's rules for as long as she can remember. Lucy's name demonstrates the conflict between the two. Lucy recalls asking her mother why she chose to name her as she did. Her mother replied that Lucy is a shortened form of Lucifer, adding that Lucy had always been troublesome. Kincaid has remarked that remembering how Lucy received her name is a key to understanding the novel.

Themes and Meanings

Lucy tells her story in a practical, matter-of-fact way, juxtaposing everyday episodes with anecdotes from the past that illuminate the major themes of the novel. Lucy's alienation from the cultures of the West Indies, Great Britain, and the United States permeates the book. Lucy wishes to block out the past and attempts to do so by not opening the letters she receives from home. So many small details of life in the United States trigger memories of her past that she is unable to free herself completely from it. The major theme in the novel is Lucy's conflicting feelings about her mother and about her surrogate mother, Mariah. At the end, Lucy tries to break off all communications between these women and herself, but their relationships are clearly unresolved.

Lucy's search for identity is an outgrowth of her alienation and of her conflict with her mother and with Mariah. As Kincaid develops this theme, Lucy rejects every female role model offered to her: her mother, Mariah, Dinah, Peggy, and Maude Quick. One of her greatest fears is that she will become like one of these women, none of whom has chosen a life course that appeals to her.

The novel is written in rather short, simple sentences, and its language resembles that of a fairy tale. Such use of language, along with the somewhat abrupt beginnings and endings of chapters, helps convey the overall sense of the novel and provides insight into the central theme of Lucy's conflict with her mother.

The theme of independence occurs in every relationship Lucy has with a man. She does not want to fall in love because that would involve dependency. She has just escaped the possessive love of her mother, and she recoils from any attempt at possession by a man. Even her relationship with Mariah is affected. After Mariah's marriage disintegrates and Mariah becomes possessive, Lucy moves out. An underlying theme that parallels Lucy's search for independence is that of the difficulties experienced by former colonies that must learn to govern themselves.

The theme of the clash of diverse cultures appears early in the novel, when Lucy recounts a dream. The dream involves Lewis and Mariah, who immediately give it a psychoanalytic reading. Lucy excitedly tells them of the dream only to show them that they have become a part of her life. Knowing nothing of Sigmund Freud's work on interpreting dreams, Lucy misses the point Lewis and Mariah try to make. They, of course, lack the cultural background to understand the compliment Lucy believes she is paying them.

Lucy's desire to have the same career options as her brothers demonstrates the theme of inequality between the sexes. Even though Lucy is bright and aspires to a profession, all her family can suggest is that she might become a nurse. No one suggests that she could have a university education and become a doctor or a lawyer. Lucy sees unfairness in such a categorization of women's role in society, and she rebels.

Critical Context

Lucy is the third of Jamaica Kincaid's books of fiction, following *At the Bottom of the River* (1983), a collection of short stories, and *Annie John* (1985), a critically acclaimed novel that was one of three finalists for the 1985 Ritz Paris Hemingway Award. *At the Bottom of the River* won the American Academy and Institute of Arts and Letters' Morton Dauwen Zabel Award. Both *Annie John* and *Lucy* were published in installments in *The New Yorker*, but they did not receive critical attention until their publication as books.

Kincaid's style has changed dramatically from that used in *At the Bottom of the River*, which gave little attention to setting, character development, or chronological sequencing of events. Her two novels provide a much more solid foundation in all three of those areas, making them more easily understood.

Both *Annie John* and *Lucy* are fictionalized accounts of the author's own life. *Annie John* is a coming-of-age novel ending with the title character's departure from the West Indies. Although not a sequel, *Lucy* details the life of the title character at the ages of nineteen and twenty. Many of the incidents in it happened to the author during her first few years in the United States.

Most critics agree that the author has made a strong contribution to African American literature. The renowned African American scholar Henry Louis Gates, Jr., has commented on Kincaid's work:

> She never feels the necessity of claiming the existence of a black world or a female sensibility. She assumes them both. I think it's a distinct departure that she's making, and I think that more and more black American writers will assume their world the way she does. So that we can get beyond the large theme of racism and get to the deeper themes of how black people love and cry and live and die. Which, after all, is what art is all about.

All three books, along with a much-anthologized short piece entitled "Girl," written in 1978 and appearing in *At the Bottom of the River*, have found favor among critics and scholars. In general, Jamaica Kincaid's novels speak to the common desire to break away from the past and become a new person, one who is strong and independent. The difficulty inherent in such a project is clearly represented in these autobiographical works.

Bibliography

Braxton, Joanne, and Andrée Nicola McLaughlin, eds. *Wild Women in the Whirlwind: Afra-American Culture and the Contemporary Literary Renaissance.* New Brunswick, N.J.: Rutgers University Press, 1990. Discusses the contributions of African American women writers, identifying Jamaica Kincaid as a leader in the field of contemporary Caribbean writers.

Cudjoe, Selwyn R. "Jamaica Kincaid and the Modernist Project: An Interview." *Callaloo* 12 (Spring, 1989): 396-411. Cudjoe, the author of *Resistance and Caribbean Literature* (1980), interviewed Kincaid in 1987. The interview focuses on

Kincaid's background, her earlier work, and her affinity with modernism, which she views as much like her own version of reality. Of particular interest are the comments Kincaid makes about her mother and her mother's influence on her career.

McDowell, Deborah. "Reading Family Matters." In *Changing Our Own Words: Essays on Criticism, Theory, and Writing by Black Women*, edited by Cheryl Wall. New Brunswick, N.J.: Rutgers University Press, 1989. McDowell traces the debate about the role of the African American male in the works of contemporary African American women writers.

Mendelsohn, Jane. "Leaving Home: Jamaica Kincaid's Voyage Round Her Mother." *Village Voice Literary Supplement* 89 (October, 1990): 21. This positive review of *Lucy* notes the influence of Kincaid's West Indian upbringing on her novels. Discusses the changes Kincaid's writing has undergone since the 1970's. Also gives a brief overview of her life and compares important incidents with their fictionalized counterparts. Contends that although *Lucy* was probably meant to stand alone, it will undoubtedly be read as a sequel to *Annie John*.

Vorda, Allan. "An Interview with Jamaica Kincaid." *Mississippi Review* 20 (1991): 7-26. Kincaid discusses her childhood in Antigua, her relationship with her mother, and her writing career. Focusing on *Lucy*, she remarks on the autobiographical elements of the work. She explains that Lucy would always identify with the oppressed, rather than the oppressor.

Wall, Cheryl. Introduction to *Changing Our Own Words: Essays on Criticism, Theory, and Writing by Black Women*. New Brunswick, N.J.: Rutgers University Press, 1989. Provides a helpful overview of the reception the work of contemporary African American women writers has received. Commenting on the rising interest of both the general public and literary scholars, Wall pays particular attention to writing of the 1970's and later periods.

Cheri Louise Ross

MA RAINEY'S BLACK BOTTOM

Author: August Wilson (1945-   )
Type of work: Play
Type of plot: Psychological realism
Time of plot: 1927
Locale: Chicago's South Side
First produced: 1984, at the Yale Repertory Theatre, New Haven, Connecticut
First published: 1985

Principal characters:
> MA RAINEY, popularly called "Mother of the Blues," a recording
>   star in the rural, Southern, black folk tradition
> STURDYVANT, a producer of pop music recordings
> IRVIN, Ma Rainey's agent, like Sturdyvant a white man who
>   derives his income from black music
> CUTLER, a guitar and trombone player, the leader of Ma Rainey's
>   backup band
> TOLEDO, a piano player, the only band member who can read
> SLOW DRAG, a bass player
> LEVEE, a trumpeter who is twenty years younger than the other
>   band members

The Play

This two-act play takes place in a recording studio and its adjoining band room. The action opens with a tense conversation between the producer, Sturdyvant, and Ma Rainey's agent, Irvin, two white men anxious because of past experiences with the imperious and unpredictable Ma Rainey. She is late, and no one knows why.

Cutler, the leader of Ma's accompaniment band, and two other members, Toledo and Slow Drag, arrive on time and go down to the band room. They are in their mid-fifties, know each other well, and have played for many years in the South. They too express concern about avoiding the troubles of past recording sessions. Levee, another band member, arrives somewhat late, wearing a new pair of shoes. He is twenty years younger than the other musicians, and although he spent the first ten years of his life in the South, he has since lived, and learned his music, in the North.

For most of the first third of the play, largely because Levee does not want to bother with rehearsing, the four men carry on a conversation, partly for practical purposes but mostly for entertainment while waiting for Ma Rainey. Their talk rambles by free association from topic to topic, but it grows increasingly tense as a pattern emerges of conflict between the older men and Levee. Piano player Toledo and trumpeter Levee are of very different temperaments and viewpoints about life, and they frequently annoy each other. It appears to Levee that Toledo picks on him and that no one shows him the respect that he deserves, so he responds in kind. Toledo writes songs in the new style, which he believes will lift him above the authority of Sturdyvant, Ma Rainey, and musicians of the old style.

When Ma Rainey arrives, she brings immediate and potential tension in the form of her nephew, Sylvester, a young woman named Dussie Mae, and a policeman. On the way to the studio, Ma has been involved in a minor automobile accident and an altercation with a taxi driver. She immediately displays the sweep of her power in such circumstances, but it is also clear that the white men respect only each other and are humoring her.

After Irvin has paid the policeman, the band continues to converse. Tension between the men continues to build until, at the end of act 1, Levee recounts an experience from his childhood that he knows was crucial in forming his personality and outlook on life. At the age of eight, he saw a gang of white men sexually assault his mother because his father owned a piece of good farmland. He tried to defend his mother with a knife but suffered a near-fatal wound. His father moved the family and sold the land to one of those white men, smiling all the while. Soon he returned, killing four of the men before he was captured and lynched. Levee warns the other band members that he knows how hard life is, that he is determined to get what he wants, that he knows how to handle white men like Irvin and Sturdyvant, and that Cutler, Slow Drag, and Toledo had better leave him alone.

As the recording session is about to begin, Levee gets in trouble with Ma, who has already decided not to take him on her upcoming tour through Georgia. He risks more trouble for himself by complaining about Sylvester and coming on to Dussie Mae.

During a break in the session, blamed on Levee, the men in the band continue their talk, beginning with the subject of Levee and Dussie Mae. The conflict is mostly between Levee and Toledo, who tries to teach Levee something about the role of women in a man's life. When the subject turns to the value of life, especially in the light of the history of African Americans, Levee declares that death is more real and impressive than is life, and more powerful than God, who hates black people and will not help them. Cutler feels so offended by such blasphemy that he jumps up and punches Levee. In response, Levee pulls a knife and circles Cutler, all the while challenging God to protect Cutler, concluding with the assertion that God is impotent.

The recording session goes well enough, but Ma, after arguing with Levee about his playing, fires him. Levee then suffers another blow to his self-esteem and his plans. Sturdyvant informs him that the songs that he wrote will not be recorded, although Sturdyvant, who had requested the songs, will be kind enough to buy them, and any future songs, for a very small amount of money.

As the band members, alone in the band room, are packing to leave, Toledo steps on one of Levee's new shoes. To Levee, this gesture seems to sum up the frustration and disrespect with which the world has burdened him. He rushes at Toledo and plunges the knife into his back.

Themes and Meanings

This play presents a representative incident that illustrates and interprets a crucial episode in the history of the African American people: the migration from the Southern farms of their origin to the Northern industrial cities; their emergence into modern life, with resulting transformation and spiritual crisis. It is a story of old ways and new ways, with themes of racism and human suffering. The action of the play takes place on the threshold between old and new, and it is appropriately charged with tension and conflict. The conflicts are not resolved during the play, and the play does not end hopefully. The conflicts include those between old and new, white and black people, Northern urban innovation and Southern tradition, young persons and old, ownership and labor, book learning (print) and folk wisdom (oral), backwoods stomp dance parties and electronic mass media, and community cohesion and individualism. At stake are survival, wisdom, and the opportunity for a good life.

Even the setting of the play reflects dualism and threshold in its division of playing space into a ground-level room for the recording session and a basement room for rehearsal. The audience sees only one room at any time. No white character enters the band room.

The contrasts and conflicts show up in the interactions between characters, notably between Ma Rainey and Sturdyvant and between Toledo and Levee. Sturdyvant, representing the interests of sales and new capital, feels no respect for Ma Rainey, her music, or her musicians. He values them only if he can use them for profit. His control over them is limited only by the extent to which he must placate Ma until she has signed release papers. Ma resists by refusing to cooperate unless he accedes to her wishes and recognizes her stardom.

Blues music is the fulcrum upon which the polarized forces balance. It provides the play with a title, a focus for the dramatic situation, and a vehicle for the themes. It is the glue that binds the characters together and the knife that slices them apart. The audience not only hears talk about this music but also hears the music itself, in fragments or in full song, in conflicting thematic styles, sung and played in spontaneous expression of individual and communal agony and wisdom or performed for impersonal mass distribution, traditional songs or songs in the very process of being composed.

In life and in the play, the evolution of this music participates in, parallels, and expresses the pattern of African American history. Ma Rainey is known as "Mother of the Blues" because she gave it birth as a universally recognized African American art form. She knows, however, that the blues existed before her. She knows, as her white contemporaries do not, that the blues carry so much power of meaning because they are "life's way of talking." She explains to Cutler that "you don't sing because you feel better. You sing 'cause that's a way of understanding life." Cutler adds that with such understanding you have "a grip on life to where you can hold your head up and go on to see what else life got to offer." The two agree that with her singing Ma fills an empty world with something that people cannot do without.

Ma's style of singing expresses the viewpoint and values of the black South, in the oral culture of its rural folk tradition: efficacious talk; storytelling; music and dance that feature adherence to a comparatively simple, passed-down performance style; a tightly knit community that provides the basis for hierarchy and clear understanding of where each individual fits; reverence for fertility and harvest; and a just and merciful God who knows the value of the rich, black, river-bottom land that He created and who cares for His black people, who are on the bottom of the American socioeconomic scale.

The blues of the time stood on the threshold of becoming jazz. Jazz represents a somewhat different way of living and of understanding life, playing old songs in a new way and even composing new songs for the new way. In the fluid world of the North, Levee knows no authority but himself and the potential popularity of his music. He has seen the authority of the white man, having witnessed the brute force on which it is based, but he cannot respect it and believes that he can successfully resist and manipulate it. Cutting himself off from traditional community, he tries to make a virtue of being himself. He does not want to waste time in rehearsal. Caring only about himself, he is willing to sell his soul to the devil in return for success.

The older men, doing their best to make their own adjustments to changing times and believing Levee to be an upstart fool, pressure him to return to the old ways of music, communal identity, and religious belief. They cajole him and order him to conform to what they see as reality. Toledo in particular tries to teach Levee by sharing ideas that he has gleaned from his reading about African culture and the need for African Americans to know the historical forces that determine their position in American society. The men appeal to Levee indirectly, in the African and African American way of talking around a subject, with verbal sparring, wit, snatches of blues lyrics, and rich, exemplifying stories.

Outside the artistry of his music, Levee understands and respects only the most literal of possible meanings in what he hears or sees. It is as if the knife that slashed across his eight-year-old breast shone a light into his mind that blinded him to all but the most straightforward but superficial of meanings. He intends to take what life owes him, what death and the devil have promised, at whatever the cost. He believes himself to be the wave of the future, "the New Negro" of the 1920's. As he puts it, "I've got time coming to me." He is not completely wrong. Ma Rainey, after all, "listens to her heart . . . listens to the voice inside her," and Levee plays the music the way he feels it. When his musical expression is taken from him, his confused feelings overwhelm him, and he betrays his own. His striking out at Toledo is akin to stabbing his people and himself in the back.

Critical Context

Ma Rainey's Black Bottom was August Wilson's first play to reach Broadway. It was an immediate critical success and won the New York Drama Critics Circle Award as the best play of the 1984-1985 season. It was the second play completed of a planned cycle of ten about the black American experience. Taken together, the plays will present a synthesis of the modern history of African Americans. Wilson has explained that his approach is to write about one important question confronting black people in each decade. In connection with this play, he has mentioned the problem of missed possibilities, especially in regard to Levee.

Critics have focused on the problem of how black Americans can keep their cultural identity while benefiting from the marketability of its forms. The immediate and continuing success of this play, among white as well as black audiences, is an illustration of that marketability. Although the play exposes racism—some critics see this as the play's subject—Wilson wrote it not so much in the manner of social protest literature, epitomized by Richard Wright's novel *Native Son* (1940), as in the universalizing manner of Ralph Ellison's novel *Invisible Man* (1952). It seems, furthermore, that the audience that Wilson keeps most in mind is black America, particularly working-class people similar to his characters. Responding to novelist James Baldwin's call for "profound articulation of the black tradition," Wilson attempts to present images of strong—though fallible—black individuals and families, so as to show African Americans that their experiences, feelings, and values are instances of the common human condition. He demonstrates the ability of African American culture to provide sustaining strength for black people and suggests some directions for the future.

Ma Rainey's Black Bottom differs from many plays by black authors in the 1960's that influenced Wilson's political and artistic consciousness as a beginning writer by being less polemical. It is like other plays of the era in featuring working-class black characters in everyday situations in which they do battle against prejudiced whites and with each other.

Wilson has been praised for his compassion and respect for life as well as for the effectiveness of both the humor and the prophetic wisdom of his plays. He has described himself as writing from the zestful part of life. Critics have praised his vivid characterization, lively and authentic dialogue, and poetic qualities of language that result from his passionate attention to the speech of black people.

Bibliography

Ching, Mei-Ling. "Wrestling Against History." *Theatre* 19 (Summer/Fall, 1988): 70-71. The play goes beyond rigid realism by blending Christian and African cosmology in order to explain how problems and obsessions from the past must be exorcised by transforming mundane actions into allegorical rituals.

Freedman, Samuel G. "A Voice from the Streets." *The New York Times Magazine*, March 15, 1987: 36, 40, 49, 70. Sketches Wilson's life, with comments by Wilson, revealing some sources of Wilson's artistic attitudes and themes.

Glover, Margaret E. "Two Notes on August Wilson: The Songs of a Marked Man." *Theatre* 19 (Summer/Fall, 1988): 69-70. Explores the meaning of blues music, as seen in its function in the lives of characters in Wilson's plays, within contexts of black community and white exploitation.

Smith, Philip E. "Ma Rainey's Black Bottom: Playing the Blues as Equipment for Living." In *Within the Dramatic Spectrum*, edited by Karelisa V. Hartigan. Lanham, Md.: University Press of America, 1986. Examines ways in which the play is itself a blues composition of music, repartee, and story. The play provides an understanding of persons living at a time of "failure to understand the relationship of self to history and culture."

Wilson, August. "How to Write a Play Like August Wilson." *The New York Times*, March 10, 1991, section 2, pp. 5, 17. Wilson presents his purposes in writing plays that articulate black history and its contribution to the scheme of common human values.

Tom Koontz

THE MAGAZINE NOVELS OF PAULINE HOPKINS

Author: Pauline Hopkins (1859-1930)
Type of work: Novels
Type of plot: Social criticism
Time of plot: The latter half of the nineteenth century
Locale: The eastern United States
First published: 1988: *Hagar's Daughter: A Story of Southern Caste Prejudice*, 1901-1902; *Winona: A Tale of Negro Life in the South and Southwest*, 1902; *Of One Blood: Or, The Hidden Self*, 1902-1903

> *Principal characters:*
> *Hagar's Daughter: A Story of Southern Caste Prejudice*
> HAGAR, a beautiful woman first married to Ellis Enson, then to
>   John Bowen
> JEWEL, the protagonist, Hagar's daughter
> ELLIS ENSON, a Southern aristocrat who marries Hagar and is
>   attacked and left for dead
> ST. CLAIR ENSON, the major villain who masterminds a scheme to
>   get rich by marrying Jewel
> CUTHBERT SUMNER, a Northern aristocrat framed for the murder
>   of Elise Bradford
> *Winona: A Tale of Negro Life in the South and Southwest*
> WINONA, the daughter of White Eagle and a runaway slave
> JUDAH, a strong, handsome African American who loves Winona
> WHITE EAGLE, an English aristocrat who is falsely convicted of
>   murder
> COLONEL TITUS, the indirect heir to an estate; he kills White Eagle
>   and kidnaps Winona and Judah, forcing them to work as slaves
> WARREN MAXWELL, a handsome, unprejudiced, twenty-eight-
>   year-old English lawyer
> JOHN BROWN, the historical personage known for his abolitionist
>   actions
> *Of One Blood: Or, The Hidden Self*
> REUEL BRIGGS, a medical student who keeps his African
>   American heritage a secret
> AUBREY LIVINGSTON, the false friend of Briggs
> DIANTHE LUSK, a beautiful, talented singer with the Fisk
>   University choir who marries Briggs
> AI, a high priest of the lost civilization of Telassar

The Novels

In *Hagar's Daughter: A Story of Southern Caste Prejudice*, Hagar marries Ellis Enson, and they have a child. Shortly after that, St. Clair Enson, Ellis' cruel, dissolute brother, appears with a slave trader, Walker, to prove that Hagar is of mixed blood. Hagar does not know of her heritage and has been reared as white. After much soul searching, Ellis decides to ignore Hagar's race and to take her and the child to Europe. Upon learning of this plan, St. Clair beats Ellis severely and leaves him for dead. Hagar and her daughter then become the property of St. Clair, who sells them at a slave market. Believing Ellis to be dead and herself to be beyond help, Hagar jumps into the Potomac, carrying her daughter along with her.

Twenty years later, in Washington, D.C., Cuthbert Sumner is charged with the murder of Elise Bradford. Sumner's fiancée, Jewel Bower, marries him as he awaits trial. Her father dies. At Sumner's trial, the identities of various characters are revealed. St. Clair Enson, using the name General Benson, and Walker, using the name Madison, have attempted to bilk the Bowen family out of its fortune. St. Clair, who fathered Bradford's child, murders her to keep her from interfering with his plan to marry Jewel and gain control of her money. Sumner is framed in order to remove him from Jewel's life. Henson, a detective, admits that he is Ellis Enson, and Mrs. Bowen identifies herself as Hagar.

Sumner is acquitted, and St. Clair and Walker are arrested. Ellis and Hagar are reunited, and soon Hagar finds evidence proving that Jewel is their daughter. Sumner rejects her. He overcomes his prejudice too late and learns that she is dead.

In *Winona: A Tale of Negro Life in the South and Southwest*, the title character and Judah live with White Eagle, an English aristocrat who is murdered by Colonel Titus. Warren Maxwell, in search of the heir to a fortune, meets Winona and Judah and hopes to take them to England, but Bill Thomson claims he is their owner and takes them to Missouri. Maxwell finds Winona and Judah working as slaves on Titus' plantation after learning that Titus is the indirect heir to the fortune.

When Winona and Judah are about to be sold, Maxwell helps them to escape to abolitionist John Brown's camp. Soon thereafter, Maxwell is shot by Thomson and narrowly avoids being burned at the stake by a proslavery mob. Titus stops the mob but arrests Maxwell, who, after a mockery of a trial, is condemned to death. While awaiting execution in prison, Maxwell falls ill and is tended by Allen Pinks, who is actually Winona in disguise. After he recovers, she helps him to escape. In a battle, Judah causes Thomson to fall off a cliff. Before dying, Thomson reveals that White Eagle is the missing heir to the fortune. Winona, Maxwell, and Judah go to England, where Winona marries Maxwell and Judah is knighted.

In *Of One Blood: Or, the Hidden Self*, Reuel Briggs, passing as white, goes to a Halloween party, where he sees the supernatural image of Dianthe Lusk. Soon after, Dianthe is involved in an accident and is declared dead. The extraordinary skill of Briggs, a medical student, revives her. She has lost her memory, and he lets her believe that she is white. They fall in love, but Aubrey Livingston, a false friend of Briggs who knows his secret, blocks all professional opportunities for Briggs, except for one that will take him to Africa. Dianthe and Briggs get married the night before he leaves. Briggs leaves Dianthe in Livingston's care.

Livingston, lusting after Dianthe, drowns his own fiancée and withholds Briggs's letters to Dianthe. Briggs never receives her letters. Livingston blackmails Dianthe into marrying him by telling her of her heritage and threatening to tell Briggs.

In Africa, Briggs is part of an expedition looking for treasure hidden in a lost city. Briggs finds the city, Telassar, which turns out to be inhabited. He learns that he is King Ergamenes, whom the civilization has awaited. A birthmark that all members of the royal family have proves this identity. Briggs also learns that Africa was the cradle of civilization. The hidden people of Telassar are highly advanced. Through their technology, he learns the depths of Livingston's depravity. He returns to the United States in time to hold Dianthe for a moment before she succumbs to the poison she had prepared for Livingston but that he had forced her to drink.

Aunt Hannah, an old former slave, explains that Briggs, Livingston, and Dianthe are brothers and sister, all born to her daughter Mira. Hannah had switched Mira's son Aubrey with the dead infant of the master. Under hypnotic suggestion, Livingston kills himself. Briggs returns to Telassar to rule with Queen Candace.

The Characters

In *Hagar's Daughter*, the major female characters all pass for white for part of their lifetimes. Hagar and Jewel do it unknowingly and are at first appalled when they learn of their African American blood. Both are portrayed as the epitome of gracious womanhood, both before and after they become aware of their backgrounds. Submissive, pious, pure, and domestic, they represent the nineteenth century values of true womanhood and femininity.

Aurelia Madison, the sexually vibrant and manipulative daughter of the slave trader Walker and a slave, has none of the above qualities. Although she is an adventuress, mitigating circumstances allow for some degree of authorial approval—she is never punished for her part in the scheme to defraud the Bowens.

The central male characters do not always fare well in *Hagar's Daughter*. Walker and St. Clair Enson are villains, representing greed and inhumanity. The white men who espouse abolitionism, the young Ellis Enson and Cuthbert Sumner, demonstrate the limitations of their liberalism when each initially disavows his wife upon learning of her African American heritage. They do eventually reject their racist views.

Because *Winona* contains so many adventures and life-and-death struggles, its characters are delineated more by their actions and speech than by particular stylistic devices. Winona, of mixed heritage, evinces personality traits associated with nineteenth century concepts of both masculine and feminine roles. Courageous and determined, she risks her life to care for the imprisoned Maxwell. She also fondly remembers the happiness she experienced in her childhood home and dreams of becoming Maxwell's wife.

Judah, Winona's childhood companion, embodies strength, intelligence, and vengefulness. Through his forebearance, however, the identity of the missing heir is uncovered. Winona's eventual husband, Maxwell, is characterized as a principled man whose English birth accounts for his lack of racial prejudice. The villains, Colonel Titus and Bill Thomson, display no redeeming traits.

All the major characters in *Of One Blood* pass for white at some point in their lives. Briggs keeps his African American heritage a secret; Dianthe, after losing her memory, believes she is white until Livingston tells her; and Livingston believes he is white until near the end of the novel, when he learns that Briggs and Dianthe are his brother and sister.

Briggs, the scientific genius, trusts Livingston, who is in truth a villain. Livingston's evil character is hidden behind a mask of kindness and geniality. Briggs only learns of Livingston's cruel and murderous behavior by using the technology at Telassar. All the characters from the United States suffer from racial prejudice. Only in Africa is the value of African American heritage recognized.

In all three of Hopkins' novels, most of the characters are not who they seem to be. Use of outward disguises, along with the practice of passing for white, enables the author to build complex characters.

Themes and Meanings

All three of Hopkins' magazine novels were first published in serial form in *Colored American Magazine*. Each episode was preceded by a synopsis, and each episode ended at a suspenseful point in the narrative. In this volume, the synopses have been omitted; only a line stating that the narrative will be continued demonstrates the original episodic format of these novels.

The first novel, *Hagar's Daughter*, written under the pen name Sarah A. Allen, includes many of the narrative elements used in *Winona* and *Of One Blood*. Complex plotting, adventure, suspense, action, and use of disguises, along with multiple and faked identities, appear in all three novels. The main action of each of the novels occurs within white rather than African American society. In order for Hopkins to situate these novels in white society and create strong African American characters who fit into society as members of the upper classes, she relies heavily on the theme of passing for white.

All three novels deal with relationships between white and African American characters, relationships that challenged the prevailing views of society, focusing on often-unrecognized close blood ties between the races. The issues of heritage and inheritance shape these works. One of the major themes in these novels is the improbability of racial purity. So many generations mixed blood that there is little likelihood of anyone being purely white or having only black heritage.

Mistaken, false, and multiple identities appear not only as themes but also as plot devices. Some characters are ignorant of their true identities for most of their lives, including Hagar, Jewel, Winona, Dianthe, and Livingston. Others take on false identities to escape punishment, including White Eagle, St. Clair Enson, Walker, and Colonel Titus. At times, characters assume new identities in order to help those in need. For example, Winona changes her name and pretends to be a boy in order to nurse Maxwell back to health while he is in prison. Cuthbert Sumner in *Hagar's Daughter* and Judah in *Winona* are the only major characters who have only one name and one identity.

The theme of passing informs both *Hagar's Daughter* and *Of One Blood.* In the first novel, Hagar and Aurelia pass for white, and in the second, Briggs knowingly assumes a white identity for part of the novel.

Winona, the only novel of the three set entirely before the Civil War, involves the quest for freedom. The Underground Railroad provides an important backdrop for the actions of the main characters. Revenge, another important theme, appears in *Winona,* acting as a motivation for Judah. Forced to bear the horrors of slavery, he emerges as a strong hero whose desire for vengeance against his former masters causes the truth of Winona's parentage and inheritance to be revealed.

Of One Blood adds a new theme, that of Pan-Africanism. Through Briggs's discoveries on the archaeological mission, Hopkins makes a case for Africa as the source of civilization and as the place that contains both the history and the future opportunities of African Americans.

Critical Context

These three magazine novels fit into African American literature among the work of the novelist William Wells Brown; Victoria Earle Matthews, who wrote for the story papers in the 1890's; and detective novelist Chester Himes. Hazel V. Carby, a noted scholar of African American literature, views the writings of those three authors and Hopkins as providing the foundation of African American popular fiction in the United States.

As a high-school student, Hopkins won a prize for her essay "Evils of Intemperance and Their Remedy" in a contest sponsored by William Wells Brown and the Congregational Publishing Society of Boston. Later, she wrote musical dramas including *Colored Aristocracy* (1877) and *Slaves Escape: Or, The Underground Railroad* (1879), which were performed on stage. She published her first novel, the historical romance *Contending Forces,* in 1900. Between March, 1901, and November, 1903, she published the magazine novels in *Colored American Magazine,* for which she also served as a strong voice in editorial decisions.

The purpose of *Colored American Magazine* was clearly to attempt the creation of an African American renaissance in Boston. It provided an outlet for poetry, fiction, and art, along with expository prose. Although the magazine fell short of its aims, it prefigured the Harlem Renaissance of two decades later.

Hopkins believed that fiction could change people's lives, particularly if the fiction were published in a mass circulation magazine. In a society that condoned lynchings, Jim Crow laws, and general oppression of African Americans, Hopkins hoped to inform her contemporary readers about their heritage and help them learn to value themselves. Hopkins' work is highly political, and some noted African Americans disapproved of her political stance. When the management of *Colored American Magazine* changed, her fiction lost its outlet. At the turn of the twentieth century in the United States, it was nearly impossible for African American authors to get their work published on their own. Without the backing of *Colored American Magazine,* Hopkins' voice was doomed to silence.

Long out of print, the magazine novels have been collected and published in one volume. This volume has had an important effect on African American studies and on Hopkins' reputation as well, bringing scholarly attention to a long-neglected author.

Bibliography

Ammons, Elizabeth. *Conflicting Stories: American Women Writers at the Turn into the Twentieth Century.* New York: Oxford University Press, 1991. Discusses all three of Hopkins' serialized novels, demonstrating that the author became more experimental with each. Concentrating on *Of One Blood*, Ammons makes the point that the novel centers on the figure of the black female artist. Compares Hopkins' use of the supernatural with that of Toni Morrison.

Baker, Houston A. *Workings of the Spirit: The Poetics of Afro-American Women's Writing.* Chicago: University of Chicago Press, 1991. Situates the work of Pauline Hopkins within the tradition of African American women's writing. Although concentrating on *Contending Forces*, Baker's comments also illuminate the texts of the three magazine novels.

Braxton, Joanne. "Afra-American Culture and the Contemporary Literary Renaissance." In *Wild Women in the Whirlwind: Afra-American Culture and the Contemporary Literary Renaissance*, edited by Joanne Braxton and Andrée Nicola McLaughlin. New Brunswick, N.J.: Rutgers University Press, 1990. Discusses the contribution Hopkins made to twentieth century African American literature.

Carby, Hazel V. Introduction to *The Magazine Novels of Pauline Hopkins.* New York: Oxford University Press, 1988. Provides a brief biographical sketch, focusing on her contributions to *Colored American Magazine.* Also examines Hopkins' three magazine novels, emphasizing their political content.

_____. *Reconstructing Womanhood: The Emergence of the Afro-American Woman Novelist.* New York: Oxford University Press, 1987. This work provides context for the writings of Hopkins. Also discusses her major fiction. Concludes that pan-Africanism informed her later work, particularly *Of One Blood.*

Otten, Thomas. "Pauline Hopkins and the Hidden Self of Race." *ELH: A Journal of English Literary History* 59 (1992): 227-256. Deals with *Of One Blood* and discusses psychological theories prevalent at the time Hopkins wrote the novel. Often posits that Hopkins adopted William James's view, that the hidden self was both conscious and personal, in order to link mysticism to long-held African American ideas concerning the mind.

Tate, Claudia. "Allegories of Black Female Desire: Or, Rereading Nineteenth-Century Sentimental Narratives of Black Female Authority." In *Changing Our Own Words: Essays on Criticism, Theory, and Writing by Black Women*, edited by Cheryl Wall. New Brunswick, N.J.: Rutgers University Press, 1989. Discusses nineteenth century African American attitudes toward marriage and freedom. Concludes that Hopkins' texts are liberating.

Cheri Louise Ross

MAMA

Author: Terry McMillan (1951-   )
Type of work: Novel
Type of plot: Social realism
Time of plot: 1964 to 1984
Locale: Point Haven, Michigan; Los Angeles; New York City
First published: 1987

> *Principal characters:*
> MILDRED PEACOCK, a black mother of five
> FREDA, Mildred's oldest daughter
> CURLY MAE, Mildred's sister-in-law and best friend

The Novel

Mama presents the social, communal, psychological, and individual story of Mildred Peacock and her struggles to achieve a satisfying life for herself and her children. Mildred is a resident of Point Haven, Michigan, an industrial town about ninety miles from Detroit. The novel details Mildred's financial, romantic, and parental problems as she rears five children to adulthood. Though titled *Mama*, the novel is more concerned with showing one woman trying to be the best mother she can be while also trying to be the best person she can be. The opposition of these roles (mother and individual) fuels much of the tension, conflict, humor, and character development that make *Mama* such a success.

Set when the Civil Rights, Black Power, student protest, anti-Vietnam War, and feminist movements made their most significant cultural gains, *Mama* positions its protagonist's struggle within the larger context of a rapidly changing America. Everybody is a little off-balance. The setting emphasizes the turbulence and chaos that mark Mildred's life.

Mildred's children are relatively young during the beginning of the novel, and this period is dominated by Mildred's finding ways to keep a roof over their heads, put food on the table, and keep utilities from being disconnected. Being sole breadwinner is difficult. She works at various times during the 1960's as a waitress, domestic, unskilled laborer, and, with reluctance, briefly as a prostitute. Eventually, she goes on welfare. Motherhood consumes much energy, and Mildred needs diversions; although Mildred is a mother, McMillan insists that she is also an individual, an individual who needs sexual expression and romantic love. Mildred has several sexual affairs. She even marries two more times, but her heart is never quite with the men she marries, so she divorces them.

The 1970's record Mildred's life in Los Angeles, where she is able, because of a new government program, to buy a house in the San Fernando Valley. Her daughters continue to do well in school and in their personal lives. Her son Money still uses drugs and returns to Point Haven, where he is arrested and is in and out of jail for a few years. Mildred likes her house with its pool, but she is largely unhappy, continues to drink too much, and has relationships with men that are only temporarily fulfilling. Her financial troubles—the mortgage, the utilities, money for her daughter's wedding—continue to plague her, and, in a remarkable sense, she is no better off than when she lived in Point Haven. Her move to Los Angeles on a personal level is a failure, but on a maternal level it is a good one: Angel and Doll go to college and develop into intelligent, independent, and productive young women.

It is only when Los Angeles overwhelms her that Mildred decides to return to Point Haven for good. She reasons that who she is and what she wants out of life have little to do with geographical location. In the 1980's, with her children grown and apparently successful (she does not know the mess Freda has made of her life), Mildred has more than enough time to reflect on her life, her choices, and the many problems she has had to face, often alone. She is disturbed by physical changes: her sagging breasts, her weak health. The alcohol and cigarettes diminish her health so much that she has little choice but to give them up. While recovering her health, she rediscovers her self. Most important, Mildred discovers that she has worked exceptionally well within the limits of the role of mother, and she decides that, though she is older (forty-eight at novel's end), her life is not over. She makes plans to enter a community college and make a career for herself, for she knows that having reared her children into successful adults under sometimes horrible conditions, she can do other equally satisfying tasks as well.

The Characters

McMillan ties her development and articulation of major characters in the novel to her protagonist, Mildred Peacock. Mildred's personality, conflicts, defeats, and triumphs influence her children and Curly Mae and announce as well as advance the novel's most significant themes and issues. In this regard, McMillan treats character development as an outgrowth of Mildred's pervasive presence in the novel.

As a mother, Mildred is both conventional and a rebel. Her conventional mothering is seen in her struggles to provide the necessities for her children. Mildred provides for her children in conventional ways when she is married to Crook. Though her husband is abusive and has extramarital relationships, Mildred is usually home making sure that her children eat well, are clothed properly, and do their homework. Although Mildred drinks and goes out to nightclubs, she is usually available to her children.

When, however, Mildred divorces Crook, she begins to provide for her children in less conventional ways. She works inside the system at first. She works at an automobile factory until she is laid off, works as a waitress, and, for a brief period, works as a prostitute. She even, with reluctance, goes on welfare.

In Mildred's struggle to keep a roof over her children's heads and to find some space for herself, McMillan shows Mildred's willingness to make even more daring choices, such as taking in male boarders who have risky or unknown pasts or marrying men she does not love to have financial security. Mildred often rationalizes that, since she has little access to power or even a decent job, it is acceptable for her to operate outside the system to secure her children's comforts.

McMillan makes clear that being poor and a single mother is difficult. Mildred often escapes her financial struggle by excessive drinking and smoking; she is not always aware of what is really happening to her children. The irony in McMillan's presentation of Mildred's unfolding character is clear: The mother who struggles to do so much for her children neglects them in more important ways. It is Mildred's unintentional neglect that helps McMillan to define and shape the portrayals of Mildred's children.

As the oldest child, Freda is more sensitive to her mother's struggles and feels the pain that Mildred is experiencing. At the same time, she does not approve of the ways in which Mildred chooses to meet the family's financial problems. Mildred, for example, has too many barely known adult men coming and going in her house. One of these men almost rapes the teenaged Freda, a fact Freda does not tell her mother. A child who understands her mother's struggle and pain, Freda is also a child who needs her mother's love and does not always feel that she has it. As a consequence of Mildred's struggles to make ends meet, Freda becomes determined to live differently. As soon as she gets the chance, she leaves her hometown in search of a career and love in Los Angeles and, later, New York.

Mildred's other children also have scars from their mother's unintended neglect. Once Crook leaves, Money, as the only boy, feels it is his responsibility to help his mother alleviate her financial woes. He begins stealing, then smoking, drinking, and eventually using heroin. Like Mildred, he lives and operates outside the system, and his illegal activities land him in jail. He tells his sisters that he has always felt alone in the family, which he believes centers around the girls.

Bootsey, like Freda, silently disapproves of Mildred's parenting. She rebels against her mother's choices by becoming extremely conventional. She marries right out of high school to a stable man who works at the local Ford plant, and she begins a life that is financially secure but boring. She spends her time acquiring the right clothes, the right house, and the right appliances for her house.

Angel and Doll, the two youngest daughters, also create life-styles that oppose their mother's. They go to college, marry successful men, and essentially live the suburban experience.

As much as Mildred's daughters deliberately try to live life differently from Mildred, they all have a number of relationships with men that are similar to many of Mildred's. As they grow older and begin having children of their own, moreover, Mildred's daughters come to understand that their mother did the best she could with the little her environment offered.

Themes and Meanings

Brought up in the school of hard knocks, Mildred Peacock has developed a style all her own that either attracts or disgusts most people. She is one of the most original and humorous characters to appear in African American fiction. McMillan creates and sustains Mildred's style primarily through urban black speech patterns, but what she does with that language is all hers. She will say what is on her mind, cursing, shouting, and telling people where to go. Coupled with Mildred's verbal expressiveness are her actions. She is always planning and taking actions to make her living condition better, to keep the eviction notice from going up and the electricity from being turned off. Her actions often pit her against the value system of her community, and in these conflicts her true individuality surfaces. Mildred considers many members of the black community to be hypocrites, for they disdain behavior by others that they readily condone for themselves. Mildred will have none of that; her essential presentation of self is unvarnished.

McMillan's characters are real, funny, sad, sometimes pitiful, prepared to live fully. As the oldest, Freda wants to do something to ease her mother's pain and suffering. She understands the toll the bills take on Mildred, and she knows, too, that Crook and the other men do not appreciate her mother. Freda wants to help her mother, and she wants to help herself. She begins planning early for ways to escape the confines of Point Haven. She experiments with smoking and drinking when she is a child, and this behavior foreshadows Freda's adult problems.

A number of themes provide direction for *Mama*. McMillan emphasizes through Mildred's life and her children's that positive change is possible; black people need not be confined or thwarted by race or class limitations. In telling the complicated but ultimately life-affirming story of Mildred's almost never-ending battle, McMillan insists that one's actions do count for something, that effort and hard work can pay off. Life must be more than struggle. For black women, motherhood is important, but it is not everything. In detailing the life of blacks who hover in or near the underclass in American society, McMillan shows that hope is precious, as long as it is tinged with real effort. Mildred's story is not a fairy tale, is not a rags-to-riches story. Instead, her story is laced with real struggles and obstacles that face African Americans born into poverty.

Equally important, *Mama* gives expression to the communal nature of African American family life. Most actions that Mildred or her children take have something to do with assisting one another. For McMillan, family is most important and is the key unit capable of withstanding social, economic, and psychological forces. From beginning to end, *Mama* records the inside story of an African American family at the crossroads of an American society ripe for change. Because McMillan does not gloss over the pain and suffering her characters experience, their limited triumphs are believable.

Critical Context

Mama fits into two major African American literary traditions: social realism and black women's writing. One hallmark of African American literature is its attention to portrayals of real African American life. Often social, political, and economic institutions that oppress blacks are scrutinized, and how blacks respond to oppressive conditions can be the focus of a literary work or a major part of the work's backdrop. McMillan presents with sensitivity and knowledge the hardships that a number of African Americans experienced during the 1960's and 1970's, a time when America promised much for African Americans but offered little.

Mama shows one family's attempts to better itself while adapting to social change. The Peacock family learns that, regardless of what oppressions lurk outside the home, the family is the point of reference. McMillan's ability to capture the full scope of African American life—the pain, the humor, the triumphs, the earthy and poetic language—dominated initial responses to the novel.

Mama, in giving expression to a number of women characters, articulates and extends the literary tradition of black women. McMillan details Mildred's inside and outside story, the private self and the public self. In this sense, *Mama* looks back to Zora Neale Hurston's *Their Eyes Were Watching God* (1937) and its theme of a woman's journey of self-discovery and self-definition in a world that does not value black women. This theme of a black woman searching for self while trying to fulfill some other role, such as mother or wife, also informs McMillan's *Disappearing Acts* (1989). McMillan's first two novels reveal the beautiful and complex stories of those who live in urban black America.

Bibliography

Henderson, Mae Gwendolyn. "Speaking in Tongues: Dialogics, Dialectics, and the Black Woman Writer's Literary Tradition." In *Reading Black, Reading Feminist: A Critical Anthology*, edited by Henry Louis Gates, Jr. New York: Meridian, 1990. Emphasizes how black female subjectivity helps to structure many texts in the black women's literary tradition. Sees Zora Neale Hurston's *Their Eyes Were Watching God* (1937) as a paradigm for other black women writers.

Hirsch, Marianne. "Maternal Narratives: 'Cruel Enough to Stop Blood.'" In *Reading Black, Reading Feminist: A Critical Anthology*, edited by Henry Louis Gates, Jr. New York: Meridian, 1990. Argues that the presentation of black mothers in contemporary black women's fiction is best understood by analyzing the interactions of daughters in relation to a complicated maternal history.

McMillan, Terry. "Terry McMillan: The Novelist Explores African American Life from the Point of View of a New Generation." Interview by Wendy Smith. *Publishers Weekly* 239 (May 11, 1992): 50-51. McMillan discusses *Mama*, her other fiction, and her place in the publishing industry.

Tate, Claudia, ed. *Black Women Writers at Work*. New York: Continuum, 1983. A collection of interviews with African American women writers.

Wade-Gayles, Gloria. *No Crystal Stair: Visions of Race and Sex in Black Women's Fiction*. New York: Pilgrim Press, 1984. Chapter 4, "The Halo and the Hardships: Black Women as Mothers and Sometimes as Wives," discusses black women writers' creation of mothers. Pays attention to the contrary impulses or allegiances that dominate black mothers' lives: allegiances to family and to self. An acceptance of one may mean the other suffers or is neglected.

                                                                    Charles P. Toombs

MAMA DAY

Author: Gloria Naylor (1950-   )
Type of work: Novel
Type of plot: Psychological realism
Time of plot: 1799 to the present, primarily the 1980's
Locale: Willow Springs, a fictitious island off the coast of South Carolina, and New York City
First published: 1988

Principal characters:

OPHELIA (COCOA) DAY, the protagonist and one of the narrators in the novel

MIRANDA (MAMA) DAY, elderly matriarch of the Day clan and unofficial ruler of Willow Springs

ABIGAIL DAY, Miranda's sister and soul-mate, grandmother to Ophelia

GEORGE ANDREWS, a successful engineer with heart trouble

SAPPHIRA WADE, a distant ancestor of Miranda and a famous conjure woman

RUBY, Miranda's adversary, a jealous, murderous woman

BERNICE DUVALL, a woman desperate to have a child

AMBUSH, Bernice's husband

DR. BUZZARD, a bootlegger, gambler, and herbalist with pretensions of possessing magic

MRS. JACKSON, an administrator at a shelter for boys

DR. SMITHFIELD, a local physician

The Novel

Mama Day proceeds, for the most part, in linear fashion and covers the period from Ophelia's meeting with George in New York to the events occurring prior to and during the storm at the end of the novel. Yet the novel's present is tied to the past, so much so that Naylor provides her readers with a family tree dating back to 1799, when Sapphira Wade was born. Much of the narration is in the form of a conversation between Ophelia and George, who, although dead, communicates with his wife. Their sections involve their feelings, values, dreams, and responses to the events they experience. In addition to the first-person narratives, Naylor uses Miranda as the character through whom the third-person-limited point of view is revealed. From Miranda's perspective, readers learn about superstition, magic, family history, and dreams.

Before the novel's action begins (Naylor has divided the book into two parts, one focusing on New York and the events leading to George's visit to the island, and one concerning the events that occur during his stay), Naylor provides her readers with a first-person prologue in which Miranda discusses the legend of Sapphira Wade, the history of the island, and a young college boy whose studies prevent him from understanding his past. The point of the prologue is to establish the importance of listening with a mind open to a reality at odds with facts and reason.

Part 1 concerns events in both Willow Springs and New York City, two different worlds associated with two different people, Ophelia and George, who have been shaped by their backgrounds. Although Ophelia believes that "those were awful times for a single woman in that city of yours," she learns, with George's help, to see the city as distinct communities and to acknowledge and overcome her own prejudices. Significantly, they are brought together by a letter that Miranda "doctored" with a powder, though George could not allow himself to believe in such things.

As they become more intimate, developments unfold in Willow Springs that lead to the conflict in part 2. Bernice's efforts to have a baby result in her near death and Miranda's intervention. The episode establishes Miranda as a midwife/physician capable of performing a gynecological examination, as a herbalist/pharmacist whose drugs come from a chokecherry tree, and as a conjure woman whose rituals guarantee Bernice's fertility. Ruby's "credentials" are also revealed. She has, according to Miranda, murdered her first husband and is responsible for the death of Frances, who was married to Junior Lee, who becomes Ruby's second husband. Naylor writes that "Junior Lee is getting more than a woman, he's marrying himself an event." At the end of part 1, a jealous Ruby suspects that Junior Lee has designs on Ophelia. Of course, Miranda anticipates the impending trouble.

In part 2, Ophelia brings George to Willow Springs, which he describes as a "paradise"; but despite Miranda's warning, Ruby, after seeing Junior Lee talking to Ophelia, afflicts Ophelia with nightshade and a spell. By unbraiding Ophelia's hair, which contains the nightshade, Miranda solves half of Ophelia's problem. To counteract the spell, however, "It's going to take a man to bring her peace." George, whom they consider a boy, proves to be the man. After putting a spell on Ruby's home, which is subsequently destroyed by lighting, Miranda goes to the "other place," associated with Sapphira.

A terrible storm has washed away the bridge to the mainland, and George, who sees modern medicine as Ophelia's only hope, devotes his energies to rebuilding the bridge. George is eventually persuaded to go to the "other place" to meet Miranda, who has been communing with the spirit of Sapphira. Miranda instructs George to return to the chicken coop at her home. Though he does go to the chicken coop, he suffers a heart attack and dies beside Ophelia, who is healed by his actions.

After George's death, which Miranda had foreseen, Ophelia slowly recovers; in the fourteen years that separate his death from the telling of the story, Ophelia marries again and has two sons, one of whom she names George. She still communicates with George, and she continues to retrace their steps and reevaluate the story as time passes. Miranda, however, has the last word in the novel. In August, she finds Ophelia again, and it is clear that she will succeed Miranda: "A face ready to go in search of answers, so at last there ain't no need for words as they lock eyes over the distance."

The Characters

Mama Day is a novel about women, about a historical sisterhood that spans generations. The novel begins with Sapphira's bill of sale from 1819 and with Miranda's various versions of the legend that establishes Sapphira as the first conjure woman. The title of the novel suggests that its protagonist is Mama (Miranda) Day, a literal descendant of Sapphira and her spiritual reincarnation, but Ophelia, Miranda's successor, is the real protagonist of the novel. All three women are related through legend (Ophelia's story itself assumes legendary status), dreams, roles, and appearance. Early in the novel, Miranda sees the likeness between Ophelia and Sapphira and notes that Ophelia "brings back the great, grand Mother."

Ophelia reveals herself through her narrations to George as a bright young woman who has left Willow Springs for Atlanta and New York but remains "at home" in Willow Springs. She retains her hometown values and beliefs (for example, that the way a man chews his food indicates the kind of lover he will be), but she is ambivalent about superstition and magic—she does not accept the potency of Miranda's powder on the letter she mails to George, for example. From Miranda's perspective, however, Ophelia is Sapphira's spiritual descendant, a woman who, unlike George, will ultimately believe in the efficacy of Ruby's spell.

Although Ophelia is an adult in New York, she continues to be called "Baby Girl" and, later, "Cocoa." It is not until she has matured and is ready to listen that she becomes Ophelia. Her dreams about drowning call to mind her mother's drowning and brings to mind the fate of William Shakespeare's Ophelia in *Hamlet* (c. 160). After she survives her experience at Ruby's hands and recovers, she is ready to take her place as a teller and reteller of stories and to fulfill the promise Miranda saw in her.

George also develops in the course of the novel. Though his is a disciplined life, he is more open than Ophelia in New York; but his urban background, Columbia education, and middle-class trappings do not prepare him for Willow Springs. He sees the surface paradise but cannot see or listen in order to understand. He is, in Abigail and Miranda's words, a "boy," a term Dr. Buzzard also applies to him. Dr. Buzzard tells George that Ophelia's salvation is in Willow Springs, not on the mainland, but George asks, "What do you do when someone starts telling you something that you just cannot believe?"

While George and Ophelia speak conversationally, the sections narrated from Miranda's perspective are quite different. They contain dialogue, but the essence of the material is in Miranda's thoughts, dreams, and memories. In effect, Miranda seems both of this world, in which she is midwife, adviser, and guide, and beyond this world, which she can control to some extent. Bernice even brings a dead child named Little Caesar to Miranda in hopes of effecting a resurrection. Yet Naylor presents Miranda's control ambiguously and comically, noting of her that "when she's tied up the twentieth century, she'll take a little peek into the other side—for pure devilment and curiosity."

Unlike Naylor's two earlier novels, *Mama Day* contains some positively portrayed African American males. George is unique among Naylor's male characters. Even Ophelia's unnamed second husband wins Miranda's accolade of a "good second-best." In Ambush, readers encounter another positive male figure: Bernice's husband is faithful, supportive, and sensitive, so much so that Ophelia uses him as a point of comparison for George. On the other hand, readers encounter stereotypical male characters such as Junior Lee and Dr. Buzzard; Naylor may have altered her portraits of males, but she remains more interested in her women characters.

Themes and Meanings

Much of the world of *Mama Day* is fictitious, even mythical, in a manner reminiscent of William Faulkner's fictional Yoknapatawpha County. Naylor even provides her readers with a map of the offshore island between Georgia and South Carolina, but the island, connected to the mainland by a tenuous bridge, seems otherworldly, a matriarchal paradise. The bridge becomes a passage to a mainland world, which Willow Springs residents distrust: "And we done learned that anything coming from beyond the bridge gotta be viewed real, real careful." The mainland is the source of real-estate developers and education that distances students from reality and truth. Miranda cites the example of "Reema's boy," the African American anthropologist whose university education has rendered him unable to listen and to understand. Naylor's readers face a similar task; they read a story that defies logic and are asked to listen and believe, just like George and Ophelia.

Despite the family tree, the bill of sale, and the map, the story of George and Ophelia changes, not for the readers so much as for the tellers; as Ophelia says, "there are just too many sides to the whole story." As Miranda tells about Sapphira Wade, she includes different versions about the death of Sapphira's husband, Bascombe Wade—Sapphira either poisoned him or stabbed him. Yet there is a core of meaning, just as there is a core of meaning in *Mama Day*, and Naylor invites her readers' acceptance of truths that do not derive from "mainland" history, reason, and facts.

The best storytellers and listeners in the novel are women, the Day women especially. Despite Miranda's belief that "we ain't had much luck with the girls in this family," the strain that passes from Sapphira to Miranda to Ophelia produces strong, nurturing women, as well as storytellers (at the end of the novel Ophelia is telling "myths" to her son George). Ophelia believes that, together, Miranda and Abigail were "the perfect mother." Miranda, the midwife, is known as "Mama" Day, and Bernice's problems having and rearing a child keep the idea of nurturing before the readers.

Mothers nurture so that their children will seek and learn, and the novel suggests that people "gotta go away to come back to that kind of knowledge," knowledge about "the beginning of the Days." Religious imagery pervades the novel, and the reference to "Days" suggests the beginning of time, Creation. The knowledge that Sapphira and Miranda had and that which is promised Ophelia transcends this world and makes of this woman something akin to the conjure woman, the seer, the prophet, and the deliverer of truth.

Critical Context

In *Mama Day*, Naylor has developed some settings, characters, and themes from her earlier novels, *The Women of Brewster Place* (1983) and *Linden Hills* (1985). In each of those novels, she created a fictional world, in the first book an urban and narrowly circumscribed one, in the second, a suburban and more extensive one. Both worlds, however, are consciously created: Brewster Place is the child of developers and politicians, and Linden Hills is created by an African American. Willow Springs, another fictional world, is created by a woman. In fact, Naylor's worlds tend to be matriarchies in which sisterhood is a recurrent theme. Although it is rare for her women of the same age to be "sisters" (Etta and Mattie in *Brewster Place* present a significant exception), "sisterhood" seems more common among women from different generations, as is the case with Miranda and Ophelia.

While Naylor's female characters have remained fairly consistent, there appears to be a softening in her depiction of male African Americans. In *The Women of Brewster Place*, men are portrayed, with few exceptions, as weak, ineffectual drunks, violent fathers and lovers, or brutal rapists. In *Mama Day*, George and Ambush are devoted, sensitive men who are committed to their views. Since Naylor has acknowledged and bemoaned the fact that the men in the first novel were not favorably depicted, her *Mama Day* male characters seem the result of a conscious effort to avoid the male-bashing that some critics have noted in contemporary fiction written by African American women.

Memory and dreams play a large role in Naylor's fiction. In *Mama Day*, Ophelia and George have the same dream about her drowning and his reaching out to her; the dream proves accurate on a symbolic level, because she is floundering and needs his touch to recover. Memory, too, is important because of its role in storytelling, a central concern in *Mama Day*. In the same way that Miranda remembers stories about Sapphira, she remembers and tells readers about Ophelia's legend. Ophelia herself has recast her own story, changing it each time as she remembers a slightly different past. In fact, *Mama Day* seems to be as much about narration as it is about character, which may be another way of recognizing the effect of narration on character.

Bibliography

Andrews, Larry R. "Black Sisterhood in Gloria Naylor's Novels." *College Language Association Journal* 33 (September, 1989): 1-25. Analyzes the development of sisterhood in *The Women of Brewster Place* and *Linden Hills.* Discusses how female power and wisdom are passed from Sapphira Wade to Miranda to Ophelia. Strength of the essay lies in Andrews' linking of the three novels in setting, character, and theme.

Christian, Barbara. "Gloria Naylor's Geography: Community, Class, and Patriarchy in *The Women of Brewster Place* and *Linden Hills.*" In *Reading Black, Reading Feminist,* edited by Henry L. Gates, Jr. New York: Meridian Books, 1990. Though Christian does not discuss *Mama Day,* she does comment at length on several subjects that appear in all of Naylor's novels: the geographical fictional world, the nurturing sisterhood of women, and the effects of patriarchy. She also provides a helpful comparison of Naylor and Toni Morrison.

Pearlman, Mickey. "An Interview with Gloria Naylor." *High Plains Literary Review* 5 (Spring, 1990): 98-107. Suggests that *Mama Day,* like the two earlier novels, concerns space and memory, the created world of Willow Spring and the ties to the past. Sees the relationship between Miranda and Ophelia as one between a mother and daughter.

Saunders, James Robert. "The Ornamentation of Old Ideas: Gloria Naylor's First Three Novels." *The Hollins Critic* 27 (April, 1990): 1-11. Relates the three novels to one another. Focuses on legend and myth, calls attention to the tie between Ophelia and her namesake in *Hamlet,* and notes the symbolic function of names in Naylor's fiction. Sees the power of love transcending the improbable narrative format, which involves two speakers, one of whom (George) is dead.

Wagner-Martin, Linda. "Quilting in Gloria Naylor's *Mama Day.*" *Notes on Contemporary Literature* 18 (November, 1988): 6-7. Argues that Ophelia's request that Miranda and Abigail make her a quilt is a central episode in the novel. Concludes that the quilt, made with pieces of material from all the women in the family, incorporates the lives of all the women, good and bad. Ophelia must deal with choices and decide how to handle her family inheritance.

Thomas L. Erskine

THE MAN WHO CRIED I AM

Author: John A. Williams (1925-   )
Type of work: Novel
Type of plot: Psychological realism
Time of plot: May, 1964
Locale: The Netherlands
First published: 1967

> *Principal characters:*
> MAX REDDICK, the protagonist, a black American novelist and
> journalist
> MARGRIT REDDICK, the protagonist's estranged Dutch wife
> HARRY AMES, a famous black American novelist and expatriate in
> Paris who has died unexpectedly
> LILLIAN PATCH, a black middle-class woman who was deeply
> loved by Max but feared a life of poverty if she married him
> MOSES BOATWRIGHT, a brilliant, Harvard-educated black man
> whom Max interviewed in prison
> BERNARD ZUTKIN, an honest, fiercely independent literary critic
> MARION DAWES, a younger black American novelist who openly
> competes with Harry Ames
> ALPHONSE EDWARDS, a black government agent posing as a writer
> ROGER WILKINSON, a black government agent posing as a writer
> THE REVEREND PAUL DURRELL, a black leader who preaches
> nonviolence
> MINISTER Q, a black leader who preaches self-defense

The Novel

Reading as a picaresque novel of its protagonist's adventures on three continents, a spy novel, and a historical novel, *The Man Who Cried I Am* is a political novel in the large sense of exploring the causes and effects of the actions of persons, organizations, and governments in their relationships with each other. Its plot is woven of the inner and outer aspects of the life of its protagonist, Max Reddick, whose personal history illustrates developments in American race relations between the mid-1930's and the mid-1960's. The story is narrated from the omniscient third-person point of view, but in a voice that often features the dying Max Reddick's reflections upon his present circumstances or his memories that are stimulated by the funeral in Paris of his dear friend and fellow black novelist, Harry Ames, and his meeting in Amsterdam with his estranged wife, Margrit.

The novel's opening and closing scenes take place in an outdoor café in Amsterdam. In the opening scene, Max Reddick sits waiting for Margrit to walk by, on her way home. The day before, after Harry Ames's funeral, Harry's mistress had asked

Max to meet her soon about papers that Harry left for him. Now he muses about sexual attraction, the role of black artists as entertainers for the Dutch, the role of the Dutch in making the first sale of African slaves bound for North America, his rectal bleeding and pain, his impending death, and his feelings about Margrit. When finally he sees and calls to Margrit, he confuses her with Lillian, his first great love and loss, and he feels an unanticipated rush of love for his estranged wife. He hides his illness from her, as he hides it from everyone until nearly the end of the novel. After making a dinner date with Margrit, he goes to his hotel, where he catches a glimpse of Alphonse Edwards, a black man who will be one of his assassins and who was present at Harry's death.

Thus the novel's first few pages introduce its plot situation, main characters and motifs, and narrative technique. During the subsequent three hundred pages, extended memory flashbacks present, with Max's analysis, his development as a black writer; his friendship with Harry Ames and his many lesser friendships and acquaintanceships in the literary world; government, including the White House; journalism; his adventures with women; and his heartfelt, wrenching relationships with Lillian and Margrit. Historical episodes that he experienced or observed as a journalist include the cultural scene in New York City during the 1930's, combat by a black division in World War II, the expatriate scene in Paris after that war, school desegregation, the Civil Rights movement and the influence of Malcolm X, and the beginning of black African independence. All these elements from three decades have combined in one of the "vicious cycles" that history forms for persons and civilizations, bringing Max to his present location, personal relationships, emotional and physical condition, racial knowledge and position, political entanglements, and approaching death.

Meanwhile, as the "plot" unfolds over the next twenty-four hours, Max and Margrit agree to meet again at the café, and Max goes to see Harry's mistress in Leiden. There he finds that Harry's papers reveal the work of a group of nations, including the United States, calling themselves the *Alliance Blanc*, or White Alliance. Considering themselves to be threatened by the possibility of a powerful, united black Africa, these nations have secretly taken steps to prevent that unification. Beyond that, the United States government, with collusion among its branches and major agencies, has drawn up a plan, the King Alfred Plan, for detention of millions of black Americans in concentration camps in the event of coordinated and continuing rebellion. In spite of Harry's warning that possession of this information will bring death, Max chooses to try to make it public. On his way back to Amsterdam, he is killed. In the final scene, Margrit sits waiting for him at the outdoor café.

The Characters

Max Reddick's cry of "I am" echoes those of many characters in American literature, but as a black, male victim of racism, Max most notably echoes Richard Wright's protagonists, Bigger Thomas and Cross Damon, and Ralph Ellison's nameless protagonist of *Invisible Man* (1952). Like the last of those, Max is kept running, by racists and by his pride, but he runs on three continents. After decades of struggle and of growing success as a novelist, journalist, and presidential speechwriter, he sees, with his acute eye for the history that he hates, that his successes have been used by racists and have led him away from himself and to his destruction. In choosing his mode of destruction, however, he is finally able to be true to himself and to strike a blow against the enemies of his blackness and his selfhood. Sitting at the café at the opening of the novel, he knows that he exists because he hurts, physically and emotionally. At the end, on his way back to the café (but actually to his death), he is reminded by Saminone, the voice of his honest if humbling historical black identity, that he is real. Saminone is a trickster figure invented by Williams as a device for characterization.

Another device for characterization that Williams uses to make much the same point is Max's love and loss of two women, one black and one white. In loving Lillian, rather than a white woman, Max affirmed his blackness and his freedom from the symbolic power of stereotyped white womanhood, but he also evaded the problems that would accompany interracial marriage in a racist society. Lillian, however, was more concerned about class. Later, in loving Margrit, at first Max worried that she was a "bleached" substitute for Lillian, or that he was marrying her because she was white. Nevertheless, he made a statement against racism by marrying her. Ironically, then, it was he who damaged their marriage because of racial pressures, while color was not a factor in her love for him. On the way to his death, he finally knows that he loves her for herself, and as himself.

Another device for characterization is Max's friendship, as well as his rivalry, with Harry Ames. Again the ambiguities and ambivalences of selfhood and blackness come into play. Harry is an ambitious and defensive individual who, Max says, packages racial anger as a best-selling commodity. He teaches Max the only valid identity for a black writer in racist America: "I'm the way I am, the kind of writer I am . . . because I'm a black man; therefore, we're in rebellion; we've got to be." In his choice of deaths, Max fulfills Harry's imperative and becomes an integrated and heroic self.

Because one of Williams' purposes in this novel is to offer his observations, from experience, of important facts and cause-and-effect patterns in modern American history, another of his techniques for characterization is to model many of his characters partly upon actual persons. Thus, for example, there are similarities between Max Reddick and both novelist Chester Himes and Williams himself, between Harry Ames and Richard Wright, between the Reverend Paul Durrell and the Reverend Martin Luther King, Jr., and between Minister Q and Malcolm X.

Themes and Meanings

To Williams, life appears to be filled with ambiguity and ambivalence, and time has the last word. History is cyclical, but each ending is therefore a beginning. Max Reddick's cry that he exists might be history's apocalyptic proclamation to American racists that the wheel is turning and black is on its way back up, or it might be

Max's personal assertion that an individual life beats death by choosing a death that affirms the superior value of life as enacted in private passion. History and Max's dedication as a writer, black man, and lover stand toe to toe in dialectic, but only time will tell what the new synthesis will bring. History has its ambiguity, and Max has his ambivalence, until a rare moment of clarity when history chooses Max and Max chooses history.

For Max, the clarity comes in answer to the question posed throughout the novel: Why? On the historical level, the answer finally is that racist whites are in so many positions of power that they control any black life that comes to their attention. On the personal level, the answer is that Max is a man who cares and is driven to write. He must know, and to know is to die. Racism has attacked his life like a cancer, and he has helped it along, with his anal retentive analysis, until finally it has brought him to a loosening of his grasp on life, in readiness to die. It then presents him with a heroic way of dying. It has thwarted him as a writer until finally, because he is a writer, he is at a time and place to strike back. It has thwarted him as a lover until finally, because he loves, he knows the value of the blow to be struck.

The value of the blow that Max strikes—by informing the government that he knows of the King Alfred Plan and then secretly destroying the papers so that the government can never know who has them and might suddenly make them public— is its message to racists in the government that individuals will be willing to die in resistance to implementation of a "final solution." The King Alfred Plan is more than a metaphor for the extremes of racist damage to Americans. It is a living memory of historical fact. The first concentration camps were used by the United States Army to contain the Plains Indians. Camps were used again in the American colonization of the Philippines, where German military observers studied the plans. Extreme acts of violence are not beyond the imagination of racists in America. As a political statement by a black writer, *The Man Who Cried I Am* provides a counterimagination with the power to engage in dialogue with history and with individual readers.

Critical Context

Williams' fourth novel brought him international acclaim for the power of his social thought and his artistry. It is a militant novel that was published during a decade of militancy and urgent questioning of the direction that should be taken by the movement for black liberation. Malcolm X, who represented the position that black Americans should defend and free themselves "by any means necessary," had recently been assassinated by black gunmen who might have been directed by the federal government. Martin Luther King, Jr., who represented nonviolent mass action for redress of grievances, had achieved remarkable early successes but appeared to be losing effectiveness as the backlash by white supremacists gathered momentum.

In this context, Williams offered a double perspective on the pervasive effects of centuries-old patterns of American racism. Through his story of the discovery of the King Alfred Plan, Williams dramatized the secretiveness and desperation of racist collaboration and the necessity of unmasking and unveiling the agents and organizations of racism. He warned of the potentially disastrous extent of the racist threat to black Americans and to democracy. Through his protagonist's life and death, Williams illustrated the perversion by racial prejudice and discrimination of every aspect of private and public life, from individual self-concept and romantic love to presidential politics and international intrigue. He also illustrated the terrible price paid by black individuals for racist behavior by whites. Through his protagonist's attitudes and actions, he espoused the position that black Americans must meet force with appropriate counterforce.

Within its literary context, this novel conducts a dialogue with two African American novels that have received major critical attention: *Native Son* (1940) by Richard Wright and *Invisible Man* (1952) by Ralph Ellison. At the end of Wright's novel (on pages that James Baldwin dismissed in his 1951 essay "Many Thousands Gone"), Bigger Thomas, in prison and facing execution but no longer blind to his own humanity or to his oneness with all humans, cries out to his lawyer, Boris Max: "But when I think of why all the killing was, I begin to feel what I wanted, what I am. . . . I didn't want to kill. . . . But what I killed for, I *am*! . . . I'm all right. For real. I am." Ellison's unnamed protagonist, after half-consciously foiling an attempt by fascist racists to erase his black identity, wolfs down three yams on a street in Harlem and affirms his thought of "I am what I am" by remarking: "They're my birthmark. . . . I am what I yam!" The end of his last yam, however, has been bitten by frost (cold and white), and he is kept running, in vicious cycles, by racists and by his pride and denial, through the remaining half of the novel. At the end, he is neither in prison nor dead, but he is in a hole. He has become a novelist as an act of resistance, and he says that he will soon emerge to take further action.

In the 1960's, many young, militant black writers and readers took sides, pitting what they saw as Wright's realistic, streetwise, violent solution against Ellison's assimilationist, ivory-tower counsel of patience. Williams, by making his protagonist an insider who eventually learns better and steps outside, and by giving his protagonist not only sexual virility without violence but two experiences of committed love, is able to both criticize and affirm both Wright's and Ellison's perspectives on issues such as the value of historical black identity, the damage done by racism, the role of violence in resistance, the common humanity of blacks and whites, democracy, and the possibility of America being a home.

Bibliography

Bryant, Jerry H. "John A. Williams: The Political Use of the Novel." *Critique: Studies in Modern Fiction* 16, no. 3 (1975): 81-100. Williams uses the novel to communicate an accurate picture of racism in America, showing whites the extent of the damage done by discrimination and suggesting how African Americans might overcome it. He also uses the novel to show individual struggle for awareness, clear perspective, and self-knowledge in a world in which the truth is ambiguous, motivations are impure, and feelings are mixed. He draws readers into moments of revelation and ambivalence.

Burke, William M. "The Resistance of John A. Williams: *The Man Who Cried I Am.*" *Critique: Studies in Modern Fiction* 15, no. 3 (1973): 5-14. Max Reddick knows the full horror of cyclical human history. His responses to positive experiences in his personal life and his choice of deaths illustrate Williams' theme of affirmation and dignity achieved through resistance.

Cash, Earl A. *John A. Williams: The Evolution of a Black Writer.* New York: Third Press, 1975. Presents autobiographical elements, historical parallels, and Williams' ongoing themes. An appendix includes informative interviews with Williams.

Gayle, Addison, Jr. *The Way of the New World.* Garden City, N.Y.: Anchor Press, 1975. Max Reddick achieves manhood and self-worth by choosing black and human solidarity when he decides to reveal the existence of the King Alfred Plan.

Henderson, David. "*The Man Who Cried I Am*: A Critique." In *Black Expression: Essays by and About Black Americans in the Creative Arts,* edited by Addison Gayle, Jr. New York: Weybright and Talley, 1969. Presents the historical context for the relevance of Williams' *Alliance Blanc* and King Alfred Plan.

Muller, Gilbert H. *John A. Williams.* Boston: Twayne, 1984. Williams devised a form of narration that moves concurrently within two frames, the events and the reveries of Max Reddick's last hours, to dramatize the lives of individuals caught in the cycle of history.

Starke, Catherine Juanita. *Black Portraiture in American Fiction: Stock Characters, Archetypes, and Individuals.* New York: Basic Books, 1971. Summarizes Max Reddick's development from a token black man who has received social rewards toward being a black avenger figure.

Williams, John A., and John O'Brien. "John A. Williams." In *Interviews with Black Writers,* edited by John O'Brien. New York: Liveright, 1973. Williams talks of the innovations made in the form of the novel by African American writers because of the impossibility of evading social and political issues, the need to write as a way of maintaining one's sense of being a real person, the importance of having a humane concern for people's lives, and the themes of love, guilt felt by black Americans who go to college, and the healing effects of time.

Tom Koontz

MANCHILD IN THE PROMISED LAND

Author: Claude Brown (1937-   )
Type of work: Autobiography/novel
Type of plot: Social criticism
Time of plot: The 1940's to 1960
Locale: Harlem, New York
First published: 1965

> *Principal characters:*
> SONNY, the first-person narrator, a young black man
> MR. PAPENEK, the first adult to recognize potential in Sonny
> SUGAR, a young black girl who grows up with Sonny
> PIMP, Sonny's younger brother
> DANNY, Sonny's friend and mentor in the streets

The Novel

Manchild in the Promised Land is the odyssey of a young black man through the treacherous streets of Harlem and beyond. In the person of Sonny, the book's narrator, Claude Brown tells his own story of growth and survival against all odds. Though some of the book is fiction, this autobiographical novel remains an authentic account of Brown's evolution from tough, hardened streetfighter to a young man on the brink of becoming one of the most powerful writers of the urban African American experience.

By the time he is eleven, Sonny is already a member of a street gang called the Buccaneers; the gang's main objective is to steal as much and as often as possible. After he is arrested for stealing, Sonny is sent to the Wiltwyck School for emotionally and socially maladjusted boys. He joins many of his friends who, like Sonny, have been arrested as minors. He also meets Mr. Papenek, the school's administrator, who plays an important role in influencing Sonny's life. Papenek, though physically unimpressive, commands Sonny's respect through his knowledge, polished demeanor, and overall kindness. For the first time in his young life, Sonny realizes that power can be derived from sources other than the gun, fist, or gang; it can be found within the intelligent, educated mind. Though much time passes before Sonny is strong enough to act on the example Papenek sets for him, he never forgets the faith the older gentleman placed in him. Brown dedicates *Manchild in the Promised Land* "to the late Eleanor Roosevelt, who founded the Wiltwyck School for Boys. And to the Wiltwyck School, which is still finding Claude Browns."

Returned to his home, where his father physically and verbally abuses him while his mother stands by, sympathetic but powerless, Sonny soon gets into trouble again on the streets, dealing drugs and stealing. At thirteen, he is shot while trying to steal sheets from a neighbor's backyard clothesline. After he recovers, he is sent to Warwick Reform School, thus beginning a cycle of crime and reformatory life that lasts for most of his teen years. Sonny is not stupid, however; he learns from his experiences, and he realizes that his crimes will land him in a real jail with a permanent record. This awareness, combined with his growing fear of becoming another Harlem statistic who falls victim to the plague of heroin addiction, forces Sonny into the decision to move out of Harlem and away from his unhealthy home environment and the streets that seduce him with false promises of wealth and escape.

Out of Harlem, Sonny takes on various menial jobs to pay for the classes in which he enrolls. He meets a variety of people who represent to him various alternatives to his former lifestyle, including a white girl with whom he falls in love for the first time. Though her parents soon send her away, Sonny learns not only that he has the capacity for love but also that color lines have lost most of their meaning for him. At the same time, Sonny becomes aware of jazz music and its reflection of African American culture. He begins to explore his roots tentatively through art, first by acquainting himself with various musicians who are passionate about their African heritage and successful in separating art from indulgence, specifically drugs. Sonny learns that when life has meaning, drugs are unnecessary. He then begins to experiment with various spiritual movements. When he hears of the Coptic faith from one of his Harlem friends, Sonny becomes intrigued, not so much by the faith itself as by its insistence on fidelity to African culture and language. His religious involvement gives Sonny a desire to see Africa, although he has never before considered doing anything outside New York. Though his interest in the Coptic faith wears off as he becomes more interested in formal education, Sonny sees the experience as a significant contribution to his growing awareness of self.

A turning point in Sonny's life occurs on one of his visits back to Harlem. While walking down a street one day, Sonny notices a small boy approaching him. The child looks up at him and asks, "What do you do?" Sonny has no answer but asks the child why he wants to know. The boy replies, "I want to be like you." Sonny then decides that he will indeed do something, become something, so that he will have an answer the next time a child looks up to him.

As Sonny is making his decision to return to school and leave Harlem street life behind him forever, his younger brother Pimp is entering the Harlem trap of drugs and crime. Sonny is torn between returning to Harlem in an effort to save his brother and walking away and saving himself. The decision is made for him when he realizes that Pimp can no longer be helped. When Pimp is arrested for armed robbery at the same time one of Sonny's oldest friends dies of an overdose, Sonny's last ties to Harlem are broken, and he leaves New York to attend college.

The Characters

Sonny tells his own story, using a mostly limited point of view that mirrors his attitude at a particular age. For example, young Sonny's explanation to his little brother Pimp of how to recognize a Jew or a "cracker" shows that he really does not know but will not admit it: "That's easy. Just ask me. I'll tell you what they is." Later, when he is sent to Wiltwyck School, Sonny asks to see the director but is shuttled to an assistant instead. "I knew he couldn't help me," Sonny thinks. "He was colored. What could he do for anybody?"

Sonny views his parents with chagrin as backward Southerners. His mother has only a fifth-grade education, his father one year less. Both mistrust words, play the numbers, and believe in the importance of a steady job over dreams. Both, moreover, become meek in the presence of white authority, a fact that Sonny hates.

His mother cannot understand her sons or the street life that Sonny prefers, and she fears for them. Religion offers her some consolation; when Sonny is shot in the stomach, she prays at his bedside. On the other hand, Sonny's father is either violent or indifferent, and on weekends he disappears entirely to seek refuge in alcohol and women. Before Sonny is sent to Wiltwyck, his father plays a shell game with him, warning, "That's jis what you been doin' all your life, lookin' for a pea that ain't there." It is the only bit of fatherly advice that Sonny remembers. Eventually, they do not talk at all.

The book is episodic, a vast canvas as diverse and richly peopled as the Harlem of the 1940's and 1950's. Brown builds his characters by accretion of details, beginning with a brief sketch or an anecdote. As their names consistently reappear, these young and futile lives deepen and become real. Eventually Sonny's friends blend into one another by virtue of their sheer numbers—countless youths in juvenile facilities and prison, girls routinely turning tricks at thirteen or fourteen. Brown's tone here is matter-of-fact and nonjudgmental. This is simply the way it is; this is what happens to real people. As one of his friends says, "Man, Sonny, they ain't got no kids in Harlem. . . . nobody has time for a childhood."

One of Brown's real strengths is dialogue. His keen ear catches the blunt street slang and Harlem dialect as he distinguishes between the accents of his characters. Near the end of the book, long conversations between Sonny and his friends offer insight into their behaviors. Danny talks about the lure of heroin and how he finally has been able to give it up. Sugar tells Sonny what has brought her to the streets. Two others try to convert him to the anger and rising power of the Black Muslims.

The book is, in a way, a lament for "the Harlem of my youth. . . . happy Harlem, Harlem before the plague" of drugs that changed it so markedly, and also a tribute to those who have endured its trials. Heroin cuts a wide swath through the lives of most of the characters. When Sonny buys heroin for Sugar, who is suffering from withdrawal, he "watched the syringe as the blood came up into the drugs. . . . I thought, This is our childhood. Our childhood had been covered with blood, as the drugs had been."

Only a few of Harlem's children seem to escape permanent damage. Sonny is finally attending college. Danny, the addict who taught Sonny how to play hookey, is drug-free, married, and rearing two children. Turk, who was with Sonny when he was shot, goes into the Air Force, learns to box, and becomes a successful light heavyweight. He and Sonny agree they are alive only by luck. "We softened to life," Turk says. "We started becoming people. . . . I guess that's what this maturity thing is about, growing up and being able to face being what you are." Sonny's triumph is that he is able to look at himself and his life without flinching and carry on from there.

Themes and Meanings

Brown ends his introduction to *Manchild in the Promised Land* with the question, "Where does one run to when he's already in the promised land?" The question summarizes the novel's themes of displacement and dreams forsaken. Brown's premise is that since the black man never belonged in the white man's promised land, the promises the land offers must be forfeited for other dreams and expectations. Sonny's Harlem, after all, looks very little like any promised land; it is a forsaken hell in which men, women, and children are devoured by their own vices. The escapes of drugs and crime are merely entrances into a lower level of Brown's inferno, and the white man's promised land shines like tinsel somewhere "out there" in America, the land of opportunity and equality.

Manchild in the Promised Land is the story of one young man's struggle, yet Brown wants his readers to see a certain universality in Sonny and the book's other main characters. The Harlem environment itself is a metaphor for the struggle of an entire race; Harlem is united to the black community as a whole by the empathetic struggle for identity, respect, and basic survival. Sonny's parents represent a defeated generation of blacks who believed it was best to keep one's place, grateful to be allowed to live and work in a place like Harlem. Inside this generation, however, is a seething anger that shows itself both in displaced anger toward the coming generation (Sonny's father beats him out of frustration and confusion) and in the attitude of their offspring. Sonny and his contemporaries are many things—angry, degenerate, self-destructive—but they are not beaten. They do not know where they are headed, but they are moving away from the complacency and decay of their parents into an age that, at the very least, will remember their rage.

Sonny and his friends show their rage in various ways: drugs, crime, gang violence. By the time Sonny realizes what most of his friends will tragically miss—that their fast and furious lives burn quickly and uselessly—he has already left behind his youth. This would be a tragedy in any other context, but Brown makes it clear that childhood is no premium in Harlem. Rather, it is a period of time to be endured, a rite of passage, a harrowing ritual of fear and corruption. Sonny survives a shooting, a terrifying experience with heroin, gang fights, and midnight robberies, only to see his hands empty and his road closed. Sonny is boosted over the wall of the Harlem prison by both his acute (and healthy) fear of what he sees around him and his ability to hope for more. Mr. Papenek feeds this hope by recognizing Sonny's intelligence and potential, and he also shows Sonny the way out, though it will be years before Sonny finally acts upon Papenek's directions. Education, Papenek demonstrates to Sonny, is real power: Unlike fighting ability, drugs, or pimping money, it can never be taken away.

Perhaps the book's central theme is the tension between autonomy and social restraint. Sonny knows that his only hope of escaping Harlem is to take control of his life. For a young, uneducated black man, however, such control is a fantasy: His skin color seems to control his destiny, and poverty keeps him down. When Sonny finally risks the only life and identity he has known to face the social barricades that stand in the way of his search for education and equality, he does so only after realizing that his Harlem, the childlike vision of the dangerous playground, has vanished for all time, leaving behind the ugly realities of urban waste and human misery.

Brown depends heavily on the use of dialect and naturalistic description to paint Sonny's world. He draws Harlem as he remembers it, filled with drugs, crime, and violence, but he also portrays the human hope and warmth that somehow survives. Such tenacity of the human spirit makes it difficult for the reader to turn away from Sonny and his world, even when it is painful to look. Perhaps this is Brown's major accomplishment: to make the reader see the black man's promised land, his America.

Critical Context

When *Manchild in the Promised Land* appeared in 1965, it was hailed as a continuation of the Harlem Renaissance of the 1920's. Its bold use of black dialect, realistic portrayal of the ghetto experience, and searing social criticism attracted critics and readers who were ready for a close look at some of the racial issues that were heating up the political scene of 1960's America. In this regard, Brown's voice had found its proper time. A few critics pointed out that the novel did not offer a didactic scheme for black salvation; the book did not, in effect, provide the roadmap out of the ghetto. Brown responded to this observation by stating that it was never his purpose to illustrate the exact source of Sonny's salvation, which, perhaps, remained a mystery to the author himself.

Manchild in the Promised Land has remained Brown's strongest and most widely read work. His second novel, *The Children of Ham* (1976), was generally poorly received by critics, who noted its sensationalism and an absence of the warmth and humanity so central to the earlier novel. *Manchild in the Promised Land*, however, continues to hold its place in the African American literary canon as one of the first works to portray accurately and honestly the black struggle against a hostile environment and social system.

Bibliography

Brown, Claude. *The Children of Ham.* New York: Stein & Day, 1976. The author's nonfiction account of the life of African American children in New York's ghettos.
Davis, Charles T. *Black Is the Color of the Cosmos: Essays on Afro-American Literature and Culture, 1942-1981.* Edited by Henry L. Gates, Jr. New York: Garland, 1982. Davis contrasts the use of sexuality in novels by Richard Wright, Ralph Ellison, and James Baldwin, using Claude Brown's work as part of his analysis. Davis contends that Brown, when compared to other black writers of his time, may appear as a "raving sensualist" because of his graphic and frequent allusions to the sexual aspect of black culture.
Karl, Frederick R. *American Fictions, 1940-1980: A Comprehensive History and Crit-*

ical Evaluation. New York: Harper & Row, 1983. Karl discusses Brown's work in the context of the "journalistic fiction" of the latter part of the twentieth century. He also examines Brown's motives for working with the first-person narrative and using the author as subject.

Ostendorf, Berndt. *Black Literature in White America*. Brighton, England: Harvester Press, 1982. In an essay entitled "Contemporary Afro-American Culture: The Sixties and Seventies," Ostendorf quotes from Brown in regard to the black literary movement in those two decades, which Ostendorf contends saw an explosive exposure for African American culture. He argues that Brown and others, from musicians such as Otis Redding and Ray Charles to writers such as Gwendolyn Brooks, fed the fire.

Petesch, Donald A. *A Spy in the Enemy's Country*. Iowa City: University of Iowa Press, 1989. Petesch traces the evolution of self and personality in black literature from Frederick Douglass to modern writers. *Manchild in the Promised Land* is included in a discussion of the question of "disappearing selves" in Ralph Ellison's *Invisible Man* (1952), Richard Wright's *Native Son* (1940), and other representative works. Petesch's argument is that the main characters in these works, Brown's included, do not surrender self but rather continue to survive and fight.

Penelope A. LeFew

MARKED BY FIRE

Author: Joyce Carol Thomas (1938-   )
Type of work: Novel
Type of plot: Domestic realism
Time of plot: September, 1951, through February, 1971
Locale: Ponca City, Oklahoma
First published: 1982

> *Principal characters:*
> ABYSSINIA (ABBY) JACKSON, a black girl with an indomitable spirit
> PATIENCE JACKSON, Abby's mother, a queenly, loyal, patient, and
> religious woman
> STRONG JACKSON, Abby's father, a gifted storyteller and owner of a
> barbershop
> MOTHER BARKER, a medicine woman
> TREMBLING SALLY, a deranged woman who trembles and shakes
> LILY NORENE WASHINGTON, Abby's best friend
> BROTHER JACOBS, a church deacon

The Novel

A heavily pregnant woman named Patience looks up from picking cotton and sees a tornado bearing down on the cotton field. Mother Barker, one row over, begins to pray. The tornado picks up speed, destroys cotton in a circle around the workers, and then lifts harmlessly into the sky. That night, Mother Barker brings food to the exhausted Patience, who is alone in her cabin. Her husband, Strong, has not accompanied her to the cotton fields because he can make more money in his Ponca City barbershop.

On the following day, Patience has a baby girl, Abyssinia, while she is working in the field. The birth takes place on cotton sacks between the foreman's fire and the weighing-in bin. A spark flies out of the fire and falls on the baby's cheek, leaving a scar in the shape of a cotton blossom.

While still a baby, Abby begins to hum when the congregation sings at church. She grows up playing with the other children of Ponca City and searching for roots with Mother Barker. In her father's Better Way Barbershop, she hears yarns spun by his male customers. She makes ice cream and plays games with her best friend, Lily Norene.

When Abby is ten years old, she is about to be given an award for reading the most books of anyone in her grade when another tornado strikes. During the storm, the children are safe in the school's basement. When they come out, they see that everything has been leveled. Abby and Lily Norene find a neighbor woman named Miss Sally hiding behind a tree. Her mind seems to be gone, and she trembles constantly. Abby's father, who has lost his barbershop, sits motionless on the vacant lot where it used to stand. Ten days later, he leaves town on a bus.

Abby is devastated by the loss of her father. Not long after his disappearance, she returns some empty milk buckets to a deacon in her church, and he rapes her in his barn. She becomes mute and develops pneumonia while recovering from her injuries. While she is still in bed, Trembling Sally comes into the room and accuses Abby of just pretending to be sick. A few days later, Sally throws a shovelful of wasps at Abby. As they sting her, she regains her speaking voice.

Months later, Lily Norene asks Abby to tell her about the rape. "I felt like I was being spit on by God," Abby replies.

With their breadwinner gone, the Jacksons need financial assistance, but when a social worker calls Abby a "dirty nigger," they refuse help and manage to survive by eating wild greens. Every day, they have a different type of pot herb as their main dish.

At a lunch break during cotton harvest when Abby is fifteen, she tells the workers a story about a girl named Lubelle who never cleaned her room. Lubelle loved a snake, which she kept in her closet. When Lubelle's mother scrubbed out the dirt and killed the snake, the girl sickened and died. They buried her next to where she had buried the snake, and a blackberry vine sprang up on the spot. The girl became the plant's berries and the snake its thorns.

On her way home after work that day, Abby goes swimming in a river. Trembling Sally pushes her under the water three times trying to drown her, but Strong Jackson arrives back home just in time to pull Abby out and force the water from her lungs.

After her parents are reunited, Abby feels whole again. She begins to learn the secret arts of healing with roots and herbs from Mother Barker, who, in anticipation of her coming death, asks Abby to sing "Deep River" at her funeral. When Abby says that she cannot sing, Mother Barker assures her that she has not lost her voice, and that the music is still there. Abby believes her and is able to sing beautifully when the time comes.

By 1970, Lily Norene is married to an abusive man and has five children. She is broken both in body and in spirit. Abby tries to heal her, but fails. When Lily Norene discovers that her husband has taken some of their canned goods to another woman, she has a stroke and dies. While Abby is caring for three of Lily Norene's motherless children, Trembling Sally sets their house on fire. Abby and the children escape, but Sally is burned to death.

Abby takes the children to Healing House, the Barker home, which is now hers. Women come with food and stay to stitch bed covers. They agree with Abby when she says, "The holy water of women can mock the fires of hell." She is twenty and ready to try her wings.

The Characters

In *Marked by Fire*'s people-centered society, characters speak in dialect. They use double comparisons such as "more deeper" to get across a point. Older women rehash the day while rocking on porches in the evening. Men do their gossiping at the barbershop, but people of both sexes seem to know everything there is to know about everyone else. Women help with birth and are involved in the care and discipline of children.

The heroine, Abyssinia Jackson, stands as a symbol of the universality of black experience. Long ago an African kingdom called Abyssinia became known as Ethiopia, a name derived from a root meaning "burned faces." As a newborn baby, Abby was burned by a tiny ember which left a permanent scar on her face. In conjunction with the book's title, her name suggests that all black people carry this mark of fire, even though the scar may not be visible.

Abby is a highly intelligent, musically talented daredevil who often gets into trouble. She watches films and soap operas on television and retells the folktales heard from her elders. Her physical description is somewhat sketchy. She has tiny hands and feet. She is neat, wears French braids in six separate plaits, and is skinny.

Her parents are seen mostly through the eyes of others, and her father takes center stage, even though he disappears for a good part of the story.

Patience, Abby's mother, can pick two hundred pounds of cotton in a day, is an immaculate housekeeper, and is so organized that she hangs related items together on the clothesline to dry. She likes pretty clothes and is a warm, loving person who is sometimes capable of meanness. Toward the end of the novel, her hair is turning gray.

She is a perfect wife for Strong, who is a natty dresser with expressive eyes that are often used to flirt with other women. He is the life of any party because he has a sense of humor and is a good talker. He has a rich, deep laugh and is ambitious, but he abandons his family when tragedy strikes. When he returns to them, all is forgiven, even though they have been destitute in his absence.

Mother Barker is a saintly character, aptly named because she is glib and loud when she talks. She might be called Abby's godmother.

Lily Norene, Abby's best friend, has yellow skin, a broad nose, and soft cupidbow lips. She is a complainer and a follower. Both Abby and Lily Norene are victimized by brutal men, but Abby has the strength of character and the support system to enable her to overcome the trauma.

Evil is personified in three characters: Brother Jacobs, the rapist, Trembling Sally, a deranged woman, and an unnamed female social worker. The social worker and Brother Jacobs are really minor characters, but Jacobs becomes major because of his effect on the heroine. He is a flat character with no personality who is described as a farmer with nappy orange hair.

The social worker is a stereotype. She is hard-hearted. Her eyes are rock blue. She is machine-like, and her smile is automatic; her cheeks are described as pale and pasty.

Another stereotype is the school principal. He is ugly, bald-headed, and short. He frowns perpetually and talks as if he has marbles in his mouth.

Themes and Meanings

Abyssinia is a special child. Marked by fire at her birth, she arises from the ashes like the legendary phoenix. Reborn in youthful freshness, she seems untarnished by childhood traumas.

Women of her community are a support system for her, bringing to mind the chorus of classical Greek drama as they comment on, elaborate, and explain the action. Their responses, however, are African American, rather than Greek, in style. The comments come in a rhythmic flow that may sometimes rise to a pinnacle of emotion. The story's women work through love and through food, which is another language for love. It is this love that enables the characters to surmount obstacles.

Names help to delineate character. The name Abyssinia, with its biblical allusions to ancient Africa, represents the victory of all black persons over force, oppression, and evil—the Deacon Jacobses and Trembling Sallys of the world. Patience and Strong are descriptive names, not only of the protagonist's parents, but also of the race as a whole. Mother Barker's name indicates that she is Abby's second mother. She is also a guide of sorts, as she teaches Abby about herbs, cooking, and healing. Lily's name suggests her light color, her purity, and her fragility. She is Abby's foil, her opposite. Abby is strong, and because of that strength she survives. Lily Norene is too weak and soft to endure what life has parceled out to her; she has a stroke and dies.

Characters frequently emerge through dialogue. For example, Strong tells a story in his barbershop about how he got away from his wife to go to a dance one evening after their baby was born. The story reveals that Patience is queenly and is the color of creamed coffee, but it also gives details about Strong: what he wears, his sense of humor, and his feelings toward his family.

Sometimes a character is rounded out by implied comparisons. Trembling Sally is like a bag lady as she raids garbage cans and puts their contents into a sack. She is compared to a tornado that has no control over its actions as it wreaks its destruction. Several times, her eyes are described as "coals of fire." Evil ghosts of Southern folklore have such eyes. Sally's clothes make her look like a scarecrow. This simile foreshadows that Abby will prevail in their confrontations, because scarecrows may be fearful, but they are essentially harmless.

Tornadic fury and healing roots are oppositions of a sacred, primitive earth. Abby, the main character, is born outdoors, close to the earth. The most important symbols of the work are fire, which both cleanses and destroys; water, which heals and is holy; and the tornado, which is evil because of its terrible destruction. The eye of a tornado is described as being full of red pepper.

Eyes of people are important in the book; eyes are depicted as windows into the soul. Eyes "turn funny" when a person contemplates evil. They collect the sun and pass its healing power on to the sick through stares. Moonstones sparkle in Abby's dark, black eyes when she is a toddler, foreshadowing trouble to come; moonstones are bad luck.

Major strengths of the novel are its character development and its lyrical language, which seems to have been inspired by biblical psalms. The tone is uplifting, and the work is sprinkled liberally with metaphors. Abby is a modern heroine who does not achieve recognition through her relationship to a man but becomes a leader and healer in her community through her own efforts.

During her rape, even though the sky is clear, she hears thunder. In African super-stition, thunder means that God is angry, so Abby is certain that the rape is a punish-ment for something she has done.

Dreams serve to foretell events and to promote healing. Water is also a healing agent. In Abby's first dream after the rape, she swallows the blue sky. Mother Barker has told her earlier that blue is the color of the will of God. In her dream, Abby accepts God's will, so that the stinging wasps are the only stimulus she needs to make her able to talk again.

In *Marked by Fire*, water is holy and can heal. When a flood comes, Abby can walk again. She still cannot sing, because her voice is a gift from God that she does not want to accept. In her mind, each gift must be paid for by a punishment. At this stage of her recovery, she is able to function, but she is not able to participate fully in life.

When Trembling Sally tries to drown her, another cleansing of her spirit occurs. She absorbs the meaning of the story about Lubelle and the snake; the story is a metaphor for rebirth. It says to those who listen that sweetness and thorns go to-gether in life just as they do on a blackberry vine. The rape, one of the thorns in Abby's life, will not completely block her access to joy unless she allows it to do so.

She has a second dream that adds to her wisdom. In it, she is told by a tornado, personified as a black woman, that storms, like people, are children of God. They have no choice but to be the way they are. Since Trembling Sally has been compared to a tornado, Abby begins to understand that the poor woman, like the specter of her dream, cannot help herself. Until this moment, Abby has believed Sally to be meting out harsh, but deserved, penalties for some imagined wickedness. Now, Abby sees Sally's actions for what they really are, the rancorous behavior of a lunatic, and she can take charge of the situation.

Before Sally's third attempt on her life, Abby hears an owl prophesying death. That night, she dreams about running through fire, and she hears Mother Barker shout out her name. When she awakens, she finds Trembling Sally setting fire to Lily Norene's house. This time, Abby does not need her father. She saves herself and the orphaned children with whom she is sleeping. Sally is the one who dies.

Strong's return home is the catalyst for Abby's healing process. With her last dream, in which she stands under a rushing waterfall and hears a child sing, recov-ery is complete.

Marked by Fire is written in short chapters that are dated to give the effect of a diary. Epigraphs precede sections composed of from one to four of these chapters. The setting is rural and old-fashioned. Everyone washes on the same day, keeps chickens, and tends a vegetable garden in the backyard. The book's themes concern the movement from innocence to maturity and the process of rebirth after adversity.

Critical Context

Joyce Carol Thomas was the author of five books of poetry and five plays when she published *Marked by Fire*, her first novel, in 1982. That year, it won the American Book Award for children's fiction in paperback. It was also named a best book of the year by the American Library Association and by *The New York Times*. It was made into a musical called *Abyssinia* (1987) by Ted Kociolek and played Off-Broadway with an all-black cast.

Bright Shadow (1983), a sequel, takes Abyssinia into college and a romance. The story continues in *Water Girl* (1986), which takes place in California. Its heroine is Abyssinia's daughter, Amber, who has been adopted by another family. Thomas has also published two other novels, *The Golden Pasture* (1986) and *Journey* (1988).

Bibliography

Childress, Alice. Review of *Marked by Fire*, by Joyce Carol Thomas. *The New York Times Book Review*, April 18, 1982, 38. A laudatory early review by a noted novelist and playwright. Childress praises Thomas for finding "a marvelous fairy tale quality in everyday happenings."

Randall-Tsuruta, Dorothy. *Review of Marked by Fire. The Black Scholar* 13, nos. 4 & 5 (Summer, 1982): 48. Praises Thomas' "poetic tone" and "fine regard and control of dialogue."

Rollock, Barbara. *Black Authors and Illustrators of Children's Books: A Biographical Dictionary*. New York: Garland, 1988. Gives a useful factual summary of Thomas' career. Discusses her editorship of *Ambrosia*, a newsletter for black women, and her lecturing in Africa, Haiti, and the United States.

Thomas, Joyce Carol. *Bright Shadow*. New York: Avon Books, 1983. The sequel to *Marked by Fire* follows Abby into college. Winner of the Coretta Scott King Award as an outstanding contribution to literature for African American children.

Yalom, Marilyn, ed. *Women Writers of the West Coast: Speaking of Their Lives and Careers*. Santa Barbara, Calif.: Capra Press, 1983. Discusses the central role of women in Thomas' fiction and explores the real-life sources of her characters.

Josephine Raburn

MAUD MARTHA

Author: Gwendolyn Brooks (1917-   )
Type of work: Novel
Type of plot: Psychological realism
Time of plot: The early 1920's to the 1940's
Locale: The South Side of Chicago
First published: 1953

>   *Principal characters:*
>   MAUD MARTHA BROWN, the novel's protagonist
>   HELEN, Maud Martha's sister
>   PAPA, Maud Martha's father, a janitor
>   MAMA, Maud Martha's mother
>   PAUL PHILLIPS, Maud Martha's husband

The Novel

Maud Martha does not have a conventional plot; the thirty-four brief chapters relate a series of fragmentary incidents in Maud Martha's life. Brooks, using the third-person-limited point of view, constructs an episodic story of an ordinary African American woman's life, beginning with Maud Martha at the age of seven and ending with her second pregnancy. Historical events (the Great Depression of the 1930's and World War II) affect Maud Martha's life but are not a major theme.

The novel focuses on the title character's domestic life, first as a child and later as a wife and mother. Maud Martha's relationship to her family is affected both by the black residents of Chicago's South Side and by the larger world of white people. Although the life of a black family is of central interest, white people enter the narrative in several incidents. The reader is always aware of the white world as a controlling political and social presence in the lives of these African Americans.

Young Maud Martha is revealed as shy and studious with a strong need to be "cherished." Her home life is portrayed as loving and secure, with a poetic description of her schoolmates, the recounting of a frightening dream about a gorilla, and her sadness and wonderment at her first experience of death, that of her grandmother.

Underlying the benign surface of these childhood events is a darker theme. Maud Martha is insecure over the impending visit of a white schoolmate who, she fears, will find her house bad-smelling and shabby. She also understands, but forgives, her father and mother for preferring her light-skinned sister, Helen. While Maud Martha has a strong feeling of self-worth, she nevertheless expects to be judged less lovable because of her dark coloring and nappy hair.

Although she dreams of living someday in New York, Maud Martha chooses marriage with Paul Phillips. She imagines that he will always be cramped in this marriage, desiring the love of pretty, light-skinned women, but she believes that he will love her for her goodness and sweetness. It is clear that Maud Martha has adopted the standards of beauty of the white world.

Maud Martha gradually becomes disillusioned with the "grayness" of her married life. Instead of her dream apartment, she must settle for two rooms on the third floor of a run-down building. Within these thin walls, she learns to live with the sounds and smells of the other tenants as well as with the roaches that defeat her constant scrubbing. Although Brooks's description of married life is subtle, even elliptical, it is evident that Maud Martha and Paul are sexually incompatible. Moreover, Paul cannot appreciate her artist's sensibility. He covets membership in the Foxy Cats Club, representing the high life in black society, but he is not accepted. With the birth of her first child, Maud Martha contemplates the meaning of marriage and attempts to establish the family traditions she had known at home, but Paul's life-style and friends defeat her.

Maud Martha's life, however, is not dismal. Her poetic view of the details of everyday life and her appreciation for the resilience of poor blacks in the South Side Chicago neighborhood show her instinctive love of life and her qualities as a survivor. The final episode describes the end of the war and the optimistic announcement of her second pregnancy.

The Characters

Maud Martha Brown is the book's only fully developed character, and it is through her consciousness that the story is told. The third-person narration allows the author the flexibility to enter Maud Martha's mind, to record the dialogue with little comment, and to make ironic observations through the narrator.

Since the novel focuses on Maud Martha's inner life and the effect of external events on her development, other characters are described only briefly. The author, however, gives many of these characters depth and substance through the poetic economy of her description. Occasionally, as in the case of two white women who insult Maud Martha, these characters border on stereotypes.

Maud Martha's immediate family includes Papa, a janitor, a comforting father who offers the family security. Nevertheless, Maud Martha perceives that Papa loves her older sister Helen more because she is attractive and lovable. Mama is outwardly loving but unable to help Maud Martha at one of the crucial moments of her life—the birth of her first child. Helen, two years older than Maud Martha, makes only brief appearances in the novel. As a teenager, Helen attracts boys and scolds Maud Martha for losing herself in her books. Helen eventually marries an older man, a doctor. Through the impersonal narration of the conversation between Maud Martha and her mother, the reader understands that the mother disapproves of Maud Martha's marriage but admires Helen's choice of a husband who will offer his wife material comforts.

At the beginning of the novel, Maud Martha is a child of seven; in the final scene, she is a housewife with a husband and daughter and a second child on the way. In portraying her central character, Brooks concentrates on the precise description of people and objects that characterizes her poetry. As a child, Maud Martha compares herself to dandelions, flowers like "yellow jewels for everyday." Shy and book-loving, she does not want to become famous or have people notice her. Because of her dark coloring and nappy hair, she does not consider herself beautiful.

Maud Martha's dream at the age of eighteen is to have an exciting life in New York City, but she settles instead for marriage to Paul Phillips, a grocery clerk. Paul has lighter coloring than Maud Martha, and, as the events in the novel reveal, has adopted the beauty standards of the white world, desiring light-skinned women. Their first apartment is a crowded, roach-infested building that cramps Maud Martha's spirit but does not defeat her optimism.

By revealing Maud Martha's interior life and by reporting the narrator's view of events, the author creates a portrait of an incompatible marriage. Paul lacks the sensitivity and imagination to share his wife's interest in music and theater, even though he goes along with her to make her happy. Maud Martha, however, like Brooks herself, sees life with the eyes of the artist. Her spirit soars above the dreariness and defeats of her daily life.

Although the story is episodic, with little dramatic action or plot, Maud Martha emerges as a complex, fully developed character. Limited by her environment and her natural reticence, Maud Martha nevertheless surprises herself and the reader. As a black woman of her time, she has been trained not to create a disturbance or call attention to herself. Yet she responds with maternal fierceness when a white department-store Santa Claus tries to ignore her daughter. She also has a secure sense of self-worth, despite her fear of rejection for her dark coloring. When her white employer threatens her integrity, she reacts with quiet courage and dignity in refusing to accept the insult. In the person of Maud Martha, Brooks succeeds in creating both an ordinary young African American woman of her time and a complex, unfinished individual who views her life with hopefulness.

Themes and Meanings

Maud Martha is an incisive portrayal of a young black woman in the white world of the 1930's and 1940's. The novel also expresses a number of themes that Brooks would continue to explore in her poetry. Underlying the surface events of *Maud Martha*, for example, is the theme of "double-consciousness" first defined by W. E. B. Du Bois in *The Souls of Black Folk* (1903). Du Bois believed that blacks played a double role in life as individuals seeking their own identities and as outcast members of a racist society that forced them to act deceptively as a condition of their survival. In Du Bois' view, the black artist was especially torn by this conflict, which could not be resolved until African Americans were accepted as fully participating members of society.

Several incidents in the novel reveal this conflict. When Paul and Maud Martha go downtown to a theater, they must buy their tickets from an usher instead of daring to enter the lobby. Maud Martha enjoys the film for its music and scenes of beautiful places, so unlike her gray apartment. When the film is over, Paul and Maud Martha hope the white people will not notice them. In a beauty shop, a white woman selling lipsticks for black women casually says the word "nigger," apparently unaware of her rudeness. Maud Martha is deeply disturbed that neither she nor the owner of the shop is willing to confront the white woman about the insult.

When Paul is laid off, Maud Martha takes a job as a servant for Mrs. Burns-Cooper, who treats her as a child and is condescending about what she imagines to be Maud Martha's home life. In enduring the insult, Maud Martha understands for the first time how her husband (and, by extension, all black men) feels about the treatment he receives in the working world. Neither Mrs. Burns-Cooper nor Maud Martha quite understands why Maud Martha quits at the end of the day. Brooks herself had worked briefly as a domestic; the incident is a portrayal of the hypocritical relationships between blacks and whites.

Maud Martha's deepest outrage occurs when she takes her young daughter to visit a department-store Santa Claus. The white Santa makes it clear that he wants nothing to do with the black child. In explaining the incident to her daughter, Maud Martha is enraged as she identifies with the pain of her child.

In portraying the lives of black people in Chicago in the 1930's and 1940's, Brooks makes the reader aware that the harshness of their lives is the result of the racism of whites who will not share the good things of life and who restrict blacks to their narrow world of poverty.

Brooks also explores the theme of prejudice among blacks, particularly the preference of African American men for light-skinned women. Maud Martha is dark, with "bad" hair, and feels this prejudice with intense pain. Her father and her male playmates comment about her dark skin and find her less than lovable. Her constant awareness of Paul's preference for light-skinned women is a source of pain and insecurity. In one incident at the Foxy Cats Club dance, Maud Martha, pregnant with her first child, feels a hateful jealousy as Paul dances with a beautiful red-haired woman and leaves her sitting alone.

In *Maud Martha*, Brooks departs from the protest themes characteristic of such authors of the 1940's and early 1950's as James Baldwin, Richard Wright, Ann Petry, and Ralph Ellison. Brooks's novel contains no violence or preaching against racism. Moreover, she avoids the earlier fictional stereotypes of black women: the tragic mulatto (the light-skinned woman who comes to a bad end), the nurturing "mammy" figure, or the exotic creature of Harlem high life. Instead, Brooks portrays, with the vivid poetic imagery that is her hallmark, the vibrant strength of a woman who will fight to find a way to fulfill her potential as an individual with a gift to give to the world. (Brooks intended to write a sequel to *Maud Martha* in which her heroine's husband dies and she goes on to a more fulfilling life without him; one chapter of this projected novel was published in 1955.)

Maud Martha avoids the trap that Du Bois describes of regarding herself only as the white world sees her. As several feminist critics point out, Maud Martha is a black woman with inner strength and resilience who can keep her sense of self-worth even as she suffers the racism of the white world and of the men of her own race. In *Maud Martha*, Brooks created a portrait of black life that went beyond the stereotypes of the protest tradition. Maud Martha and the people of the South Side are oppressed, often outraged, but they are not tragic victims. The characters Brooks creates, like those who people her best poetry, represent the strength and vibrancy of African American urban life.

Critical Context

Gwendolyn Brooks was the first African American to win the Pulitzer Prize for poetry. As she was regarded primarily as a poet, *Maud Martha*, her only novel, received little serious attention from the public or from literary critics and was considered a minor work. Black reviewers were generous but often missed the importance of the novel in the African American tradition. White reviewers emphasized the lyrical quality of the writing as an example of Brooks's poetic gifts and praised its optimistic courage in the face of hardship. In the 1970's and 1980's, however, scholars began to examine more closely the place of *Maud Martha* in the tradition of writing by African Americans.

Some critics view the novel as equal to Brooks's best work in poetry, while others focus on the psychological dilemma of a black woman facing prejudice within a race that adopts a white standard of beauty. Feminist critics, however, see Brooks's heroine as a classic example of a woman repressing rage at the neglect of her individuality and creativity and oppressed by both whites and blacks. In this view, the novel is a direct link between the earlier work of Zora Neale Hurston, most notably *Their Eyes Were Watching God* (1937), and the novels of such black woman writers as Toni Morrison and Alice Walker in the 1970's and 1980's.

Bibliography

Bell, Bernard. "Myth, Legend, and Ritual in the Novel of the Fifties." In *The Afro-American Novel and Its Tradition*. Amherst: University of Massachusetts Press, 1987. Views Brooks's work as a link between the poetic realism of Jean Toomer in the 1920's and the fiction of Toni Morrison and Alice Walker.

Brooks, Gwendolyn. *Report from Part One*. Detroit: Broadside Press, 1972. Autobiography describing events from Brooks's childhood and the lives of her own children. Includes a report of her visit to Africa, photographs of family and friends, and three interviews about her work. Reveals the origin of characters and events in *Maud Martha*.

Christian, Barbara. "Nuance and the Novella: A Study of Gwendolyn Brooks's *Maud Martha*." In *Black Feminist Criticism: Perspectives on Black Women Writers*. New York: Pergamon Press, 1985. A reevaluation of the novel from a feminist perspective as a work of social criticism revealing sexism and racism. With its attention to the uniqueness of the ordinary black woman, *Maud Martha* is not a typical black protest novel.

Davis, Arthur P. "Gwendolyn Brooks." In *From the Dark Tower: Afro-American Writers (1900 to 1960)*. Washington, D.C.: Howard University Press, 1974. Traces

Brooks's development from her beginning as a mainstream poet to her involvement with the Black Arts movement. Pays tribute to her brilliant craftsmanship in poetry and recognizes *Maud Martha* as one of her best works.

Hull, Gloria T., and P. Gallagher. "Update on Part One: An Interview with Gwendolyn Brooks." *College Language Association Journal* 21 (September, 1977): 19-40. Brooks discusses a projected sequel in which Maud Martha's husband is killed and she goes on to live an independent life.

Kent, George E. *A Life of Gwendolyn Brooks.* Lexington: University Press of Kentucky, 1990. Valuable information about the autobiographical content of the novel and the negotiations between Brooks and her editor about the possibility of offending white readers.

Shaw, Harry B. "Maud Martha." In *Gwendolyn Brooks.* Twayne, 1980. Analyzes Brooks's poetry and prose as an expression of social themes that depict the black experience in America. Sees *Maud Martha* as a sociological novel but not as a political statement of the kind expressed in Brooks's later poetry.

Tate, Claudia, ed. *Black Women Writers at Work.* New York: Continuum, 1983. Brooks discusses her identification with black readers, the need to support black publishing houses and her indifference toward critics and biographers.

Washington, Mary Helen. "Taming All That Anger Down: Rage and Silence in the Writing of Gwendolyn Brooks." In *Invented Lives: Narratives of Black Women, 1860-1960.* Garden City, N.Y.: Anchor Press, 1987. Sees Brooks's novel as an expression of the anger caused by a society (both black and white) that has repressed the creative instinct of black women.

Marjorie Podolsky

M. C. HIGGINS, THE GREAT

Author: Virginia Hamilton (1936-   )
Type of work: Novel
Type of plot: Social realism
Time of plot: The 1970's
Locale: Near Harenton, Ohio, in the Cumberland Mountains
First published: 1974

> *Principal characters:*
> MAYO CORNELIUS (M. C.) HIGGINS, a black teenager
> BANINA HIGGINS, M. C.'s mother, a beautiful and talented woman
> JONES HIGGINS, M. C.'s father, a day laborer
> BEN KILLBURN, M. C.'s best friend

The Novel

In *M. C. Higgins, the Great*, the title character, a tall, athletic, thoughtful black teenager who lives in the Cumberland Mountains, must come to terms with conflicting allegiances, to his father and the traditions of his family, on one hand, and to his mother and the younger children in the family, on the other. Faced with a threat to the family that is beyond his control, M. C. learns that being an adult means doing one's limited best in an imperfect world.

Although *M. C. Higgins, the Great* moves chronologically, the author also moves backward and forward in time by tracing the thoughts of her characters. Thus the first chapter introduces the protagonist, M. C. Higgins, who has wakened to watch the sun rise over the mountains where he lives. There is great joy in his communion with nature; there is great pleasure in anticipating the future, when, according to his father, M. C. will own Sarah's Mountain, where the family has lived for generations, where they have died and been laid to rest. As he looks around him, M. C. feels the same sense of attachment to the past that impels his father, Jones Higgins, to insist on remaining where his roots are. Yet, unlike his father, M. C. can face the possibility of a different life, far away from Sarah's Mountain. M. C. cannot help wondering what the outside world is like. More immediately, he is afraid that the unstable spoil heap located higher on their mountain, which was left by irresponsible strip miners, will slide down and bury the Higgins home, perhaps killing the family in the process.

The first chapter of the book takes M. C. through what begins as a typical day. He checks the traps that he sets for rabbits, game for the family table. He seeks out his best friend, Ben Killburn, a slight, gentle boy who must meet with M. C. secretly because the Killburns are distrusted and feared for their "witchy" powers. Together, the boys roam through the woods, swinging from vines and branches, joying in their natural surroundings. Later, M. C. sits on the pole his father had erected for him as a prize after he swam the nearby Ohio River. From his perch on the bicycle seat attached to the top of the pole, M. C. watches out for the younger children, for whom he is responsible when their parents are at work. Sometimes he does dizzying acrobatics, pedaling like a madman; at other times, he sits still, like the king of the mountain, observing everything that is happening in his world.

That world, however, is not as permanent as it appears to be. The strip miners have already intruded, scarring the landscape and poisoning the water. A more innocent intruder is the stranger with a tape recorder, James K. Lewis, who has been wandering through the hills to capture the music of the local people before it is lost or becomes tainted by outside influences. M. C. is watching for him, because he knows that his mother, Banina Higgins, has the most beautiful voice in the mountains, and he thinks that if she could just get a recording contract, the family could afford to flee the mountain before the spoil heap descends. From his pole, M. C. also spots another intruder, Lurhetta Outlaw, who later in the story shares an adventure with him and threatens his friendship with Ben.

The events in this novel fall into two categories: those which, as part of an established pattern, give the mountain people their sense of security, and those which interrupt the pattern, demanding a response or effecting a change, for better or for worse. The Higgins children, for example, can plan on seeing their father pedaling home for a hasty lunch with them and on hearing their mother's distant yodel, then her soaring songs, as she trudges toward them at evening. As M. C. discovers, the Killburns, too, have their rituals, their work in the garden while the children play above them in elaborate safety nets, their careful system of preserving and serving vegetarian foods, and their acts of healing, which even include the laying of hands onto the wounds of the ravished mountainsides.

The most obvious interruption of these patterns has come from strip mining. Because of it, M. C. intends to leave the mountains, if he can just get Lewis to make his mother a recording star. That scheme is blocked, however, first by the fact that Lewis' activities are not commercial in nature, and second by Banina's conviction that if she were singing for money, instead of for love, her music would lose its worth. Some of the changes, however, are more subtle. When the wrestling match between M. C. and Jones becomes not play but a serious test of strength in which the father and the son attack each other, it is clear that the two must work out a new relationship. Other breaks in the pattern force M. C. to rethink what he has been taught, much of it by his own father. For example, when he visits the Killburns, he encounters a different moral code, which brands the hunting and trapping that he considers perfectly natural as inherently evil activities. Although Jones has taught M. C. respect for nature, he has not prepared him for such a difference of opinion. Similarly, he could not prepare his son for his first encounter with sexual attraction, which causes M. C. to risk Lurhetta's life and his own in a foolish daredevil venture, nor for the onset of jealousy when she appears to prefer Ben to him.

When the novel ends, M. C. has learned a great deal about life and about himself. His lessons, however, have taken the form of questions, not of answers, of compromises, not of easy solutions. He is still uncertain about the future. Yet he no longer plans to leave the mountain. Instead, he will work on a retaining wall, which may or may not save his home.

The Characters

Virginia Hamilton's handling of characterization is skillful and subtle. The book title itself is used to show the complexity of the title character. Sometimes M. C. thinks in objective terms, as when he states his name, and sometimes in subjective terms, as when he adds the words "the Great." When he is swaying back and forth on his pole, M. C. can call himself "the Great," but when he is diminished by his father, either physically or emotionally, M. C. can no longer use those words. As she transmits M. C's thoughts, Hamilton moves so quickly back and forth between the objective and the subjective that one is often not aware of the changes, but it is this alternation that gives a true picture of the world M. C. sees and of his feelings about that world.

Since M. C. is both the protagonist and the consciousness through which the story is told, the other characters in the novel are seen through his eyes. M. C. reports their actions and comments about what they do and say. This is particularly significant in the case of Jones, M. C.'s father. Although one may have the impression that the author has recorded Jones's own thoughts and feelings, a careful reading shows that, in fact, M. C. is constantly quoting Jones, often out of context, or ascribing ideas to his father on the basis of his facial expressions. Thus Hamilton uses limited omniscience not to characterize Jones but to characterize M. C. and to define his attitude toward his father, whom he has cast as his antagonist. At the end of the novel, Banina becomes a more trustworthy interpreter of her husband's character, explaining his true motivations and proving to M. C. that he has misjudged his father.

Although M. C. does not exhibit the hostility toward the other characters that he does toward his father, his assumptions can be just as inaccurate. For example, when he describes Lewis' confused progress along the mountain paths and his final exhausted appearance, M. C. suggests that the "dude" is a fool. When Lewis begins to talk about his music project, however, it is clear that in his own area of expertise he is intelligent and perceptive. M. C. learns that though he can mock Lewis' mountain skills, he himself is as ignorant about that other world that Lewis represents as Lewis is about his.

Because Ben and M. C. have so much in common, including their age, M. C. comes closer to giving an accurate evaluation of his friend. When he visits Ben's family, however, M. C. again becomes aware of his own misjudgments. He sees that Ben's peculiar habits, such as his vegetarian diet and his refusal to hunt, have a basis in principle. Like his father, like Lewis, Ben is unchanged; M. C., on the other hand, has learned to distrust his own self-centered assumptions about the nature of other people. By thus illustrating the possibility of error in one person's perception of another, Hamilton relates the process of characterization to one of her major themes, that of alienation, which can be overcome only by understanding.

Themes and Meanings

The central conflict in *M. C. Higgins, the Great* is not between people who appreciate nature and those who ravage it, but between M. C. and Jones. On the surface, this conflict is merely a disagreement about whether or not to leave the mountain. Even more basically, however, it is a struggle between a father who wishes to remain fully in control of his family and a boy who is in the process of becoming a man and making his own judgments. Thus while Hamilton obviously wishes her readers to see the disastrous effects of strip mining, her major emphasis is on the themes of alienation and reconciliation through the growth of understanding.

M. C. already knows that his parents are good people. Triumphing over poverty, they are giving their children a rich life. Banina is teaching them to be gentle, to appreciate beauty, whether in the form of a blossoming tree or of a red carpet, and to love music, which they will undoubtedly always associate with their love for her. Jones is teaching them all of his outdoor skills, along with the virtue of hard work, respect for tradition, and a sense of obligation toward the environment and toward the family. Jones, however, is now facing the adolescence of his eldest son, and he is having difficulty letting go of him. That son, in turn, is troubled about his discovery that his father is not always right, which suggests that perhaps Jones may not be as great as M. C. has always thought.

Fortunately, there is enough common ground so that M. C. and his father can grow into a new relationship. Above all, however, Hamilton is a realist, and she does not pretend that Jones will change from an intensely private man into one who verbalizes his emotions. At the end of the book, when Jones comes to M. C.'s aid in building the retaining wall, when for just a moment he drops his guard and lets his pride in his son show clearly, he has probably come as close to communicating with M. C. as he ever will. It is M. C. who has changed. He has had to forgive his father for being human and fallible. Moreover, he has had to develop the kind of sensitivity that Banina has, which enables one to recognize love and pride even when they are expressed without words.

As he learns to understand Ben, Lurhetta, Banina, and, above all, his father, M. C. also develops a new definition of greatness. It is not swimming the Ohio River; it is not ruling the world from a pole high above it; it is not being a famous recording star; it is not being chosen by a particular girl; it is not being either powerful or infallible. Instead, it is staying the course, doing what has to be done, and accepting the limitations of the world, of others, and of one's own nature.

Critical Context

Virginia Hamilton is considered one of the finest writers of fiction for young adult readers. Although she began winning awards with *The House of Dies Drear* (1968), and continued to build her reputation with *The Planet of Junior Brown* (1971), which was a National Book Award finalist and a Newbery Honor Book and received the Lewis Carroll Shelf Award, it was *M. C. Higgins, the Great* that brought her both the coveted Newbery Medal and the National Book Award.

Although some critics find her literary style too complex for many young readers, Hamilton is admired for her originality and for her skill in characterization. While her themes are universal, African Americans note especially her emphasis on their struggle for freedom and her use of the rich traditions of her people, including black myths and folklore.

Bibliography

Giovanni, Nikki. Review of *M. C. Higgins, the Great. The New York Times Book Review*, September 22, 1974, 8. Summarizes the plot in a breezy style and then settles down to an analysis of Hamilton's appeal, which the reviewer attributes to her realism, her characterization, and her uniting "the forces of hope with the forces of dreams." A brief but perceptive article.

Hamilton, Virginia. "The Mind of a Novel: The Heart of the Book." *Children's Literature Association Quarterly* 8 (Winter, 1983): 10-14. Discusses novels published after *M. C. Higgins, the Great*, emphasizing persistent themes in all of Hamilton's works, such as the importance of place and family. Explains her use of language, nonverbal communication, and dialect. A lengthy section on the importance of Africa in her thought and fiction is especially valuable.

_____. "Writing the Source: In Other Words." *The Horn Book Magazine* 14 (December, 1978): 609-619. Comments on the genesis of her works, emphasizing the importance of the revision process, where Hamilton believes she is at her most creative. Also discusses the various genres that appeal to her, and makes some interesting observations about her works' relationship to black literature in general.

Scholl, Kathleen. "Black Traditions in *M. C. Higgins, the Great.*" *Language Arts* 17 (April, 1980): 420-424. Drawing on scholarly sources, this essay traces in detail the use of folklore, song, and myth in Hamilton's novel. The author's explanation of the setting in which folklore is shared and transmitted is particularly enlightening.

Vassallo, Carol. "A Miscellany: *M. C. Higgins, the Great.*" *Children's Literature: Annual of the Modern Language Association Seminar on Children's Literature and the Children's Literature Association* 4 (1975): 194-195. Points out many excellences in the novel. Argues that the pole has several symbolic uses, including, in its swaying, a movement through time into the past, which is consistent with the fact that its base is sunk into the family graves. An interesting analysis.

Rosemary M. Canfield Reisman

A MEASURE OF TIME

Author: Rosa Guy (1928-   )
Type of work: Novel
Type of plot: Bildungsroman
Time of plot: The 1920's to the 1950's
Locale: Montgomery, Alabama; Cleveland, Ohio; New York City, particularly Harlem
First published: 1983

> *Principal characters:*
> DORINE DAVIS, a saucy, free-spirited, hardheaded woman
> SONNY, a natural hustler and Dorine's great love
> BIG H, a "bookish" club owner and numbers racketeer
> HARRY BRISBANE, a failed West Indian restaurateur

The Novel

A *Measure of Time* chronicles the "education" of the main character, Dorine Davis, against a historical backdrop of race relations in the North and South over four decades. It is a sprawling, episodic narrative blending fictional and real characters and events. The novel is divided into four books.

Book 1 begins with Dorine's introduction to New York in the 1920's, especially the glittering black community of Harlem. Although she hopes to begin a new life with Sonny, Dorine learns that he has spent on himself the money she gave him to find a place of their own in the city. This realization ushers in the novel's first flashback to Dorine's childhood in Alabama and her earliest experiences with money and men; thus, book 1 alternates between Dorine's Harlem present and her past in Montgomery and Cleveland.

Sonny continues to try to exploit Dorine, who is torn between her sexual attraction toward him and her need to keep her money for her own survival. Sonny "punishes" her by disappearing for long periods of time, but Dorine always hunts him down. Finally, he concocts a scheme to free himself from what he sees as her possessiveness, and he arranges for her to entertain one of his clients, an undercover policeman.

Book 2 begins after Tom Rumley, a small-time criminal, has posted Dorine's bail and convinced her that she needs to move on with her life. He teaches her the art of "boosting," or shoplifting, and introduces her to his six-member gang. Using Harlem as her base of operations, the nineteen-year-old Dorine travels the country with this group of professional shoplifters.

This life is interrupted by the death of her sister and Dorine's return to Montgomery. Feeling momentarily guilty for having sent her family money but given them nothing of her time, Dorine eventually asserts her independence by hiring a surrogate mother to take care of her sister's children and her own son; she also promises to finance her brother's higher education.

Back again in New York, Dorine becomes the kept woman of Big H, until, bored by inactivity and frustrated by her lover's inability to satisfy her sexually, she rejoins Tom in a scam involving "selling" the Brooklyn Bridge. Partially because of the success of this operation and Dorine's inability to be discreet about her own contributions, Dutch Schultz and his Bronx gangsters learn of the money to be made in Harlem; they kidnap Big H, who is eventually freed, but this act marks the end of the nonviolent black criminal class in Harlem and the beginning of lethal white mobsterism in the area.

Book 3 takes the reader through the Great Depression. Dorine returns to Alabama because her brother-in-law has had a stroke. While in Montgomery, she and her "booster" friend Ann get caught outside during a night of white vigilantism caused by the Scottsboro Boys incident. Her political consciousness is raised, and she toys with the idea of joining the Communists who have rallied in defense of the "boys," but her need for money prevails, and she continues her shoplifting ways.

Dorine seduces Harry Brisbane and moves him and his two daughters into her Harlem apartment. For two years, they live a life punctuated by her road trips and anxiety over Harry's growing instability. They eventually separate.

At one point, Dorine goes to Tennessee to see her brother's graduation from medical school, only to learn that he cannot legally practice medicine in Alabama. Her brother's unconcern about this situation infuriates her, and she once again asserts that the rest of her family are dreaming of a better day while she is out in the real world making money and supporting everyone.

Book 4 opens as the thirty-six-year-old Dorine is released from a five-year term in prison. Although she still has money in the bank and things in storage, her world has changed since her imprisonment. Harlem is seedier; crime is bigger business. At first aimless, Dorine spends time tending to her natural family in Alabama and her extended family of erstwhile "boosters." She helps her brother get out of Montgomery in the trunk of her car after he angers whites by trying to organize sharecroppers, and she handles the final affairs of two members of her former shoplifting gang.

Back in New York, Dorine invests in Sonny's new bar, with the stipulation that she will get the bar if her loan is not repaid in two years. Reunited with her son, who is ignorant of his true parentage, Dorine hopes to give him a future managing her business ventures. Her son, however, wants to return to the South now that the Civil Rights movement has begun to energize its people. Tom calls to tell her of Sonny's fatal heart attack, and Dorine is left lamenting the deterioration of Harlem and wondering about the identity of someone called Martin Luther King, whose cause her brother has just joined.

The Characters

Some reviewers have argued that the novel has essentially only one real character, Dorine Davis, and that the book's other characters serve merely as foils designed to underscore by contrast her unconquerable vitality and resilience. This, however, is not a weakness but rather a strength. In Dorine Davis, Rosa Guy has created a forceful portrait of a woman pulled between the competing demands of love and personal autonomy.

On one hand, there is her need to be physically close to a man, a longing tempered by distrust. Her first sexual experience is not a positive one. She is raped by her white employer, Master Norton. Her subsequent relationship with Sonny also brings more pain than happiness. No matter how hard she tries to make a home for the two of them, Sonny will not be tied down. These early experiences may account for her sexual aggressiveness in later life. She fears lack of control. It is she who stalks Big H and arouses his interest by performing a seductive dance; it is she who seduces Harry Brisbane in Central Park in a wooded area that she has chosen in advance for the occasion.

At times both complementary and antithetical to her quest for male companionship is Dorine's desire for some control over her own life. This longing is objectified in her approach to personal finances. Even as an eight-year-old girl compelled to work in white people's kitchens, Dorine coerces her grandmother into allowing her to retain ten cents of the quarter she earns per week. That dime gives her self-respect and independence.

Even as an adult, she never relinquishes the purse strings, not even for the men in her life. Dorine always keeps an eye on her money.

In this regard, Miss Fanny, Master Norton's wife and the richest white woman of Dorine's acquaintance, serves as a negative role model. To preserve her marriage, Miss Fanny turns a blind eye to her husband's philandering. "With all her money and a town respecting her," Dorine observes in amazement and disgust, "she still had to stand and take whatever this man had to give." Even though she herself experiences moments of surrender to male dominance, Dorine returns again and again to her own personal strengths for her survival.

This may account for the fact that she develops an abiding kinship with her adopted family of shoplifters, a group that comes to mean almost as much to her as her natural family in Alabama. While her blood relations seem to her to be little better than "dreamers" in a somnolent South, her fellow "boosters" are out making things happen. They are "doers." Through sheer bravado at times, they take charge of a situation and snatch fortune from the jaws of fate. Tom Rumley asserts: "Our risks is double, triple that of white boosters. That's why we don't try to fade into no background. We in the acting business. We calls attention to our black selves. We look rich, big time." This mastery of the moment, even if it is little more than roleplaying at times, appeals to Dorine's sense of personal drama, her view of her life as essentially the struggle of one woman against the world.

Yet even Dorine has her contemplative moments; there are points, especially near the end of the novel, when time in its measured, relentless passage seems to stop her seemingly inexhaustible flow of energy. On her last visit to Alabama, for example, she stops in her car to rest. Upon awakening, Dorine notices what she calls "ivy" on the giant pine trees by the side of the road, "miles and miles of leaves, curtains— delicate green, beautiful to the eyes—deliberately hiding the fact that they were hell-bent on squeezing the life out of those once magnificent pines!" Thus, the parasitic kudzu vine comes to symbolize all those forces of life and nature that tend to slow a person down. For Dorine, it has been her fondness for men, her sense of responsibility to family and friends, the exigencies of her lifestyle, including her term in prison. It is, however, time itself that takes the greatest toll. At forty-two, Dorine is left at the novel's end living more in the past than in the present, measuring time spent rather than time to spend.

Themes and Meanings

In permitting Dorine Davis herself to tell the story of her own life, Rosa Guy has created a compelling fictional voice, revelatory of stubborn pride and indomitable energy. Dorine pursues her goals of acquiring money and the things that money can buy. Her material needs, however, are counterbalanced by her obligation to her family in Alabama; "bad luck dogs a feller who turns his back on family," she asserts. These are the two competing inclinations of her character: the urge to keep moving and the longing to make a home, the impetus to personal freedom and the recognition of family and maternal responsibilities.

Dorine's options for earning the money to finance her personal life-style and still send funds home to her siblings are limited. In her time, she is told, a black woman has only three ways to make money: clean house, become a prostitute, or steal. Dorine tries all three. As the title indicates, her choices are a "measure" of her time.

In essence, the novel is a measurement of Dorine's personal progress through four decades. She is left largely untouched by the political and social forces affecting the larger black population, whom she divides into two categories: the poor and the "sporting," or criminal, class. Dorine allies herself firmly with the latter.

At times, however, the greater world intrudes. When she first arrives in New York, for example, the followers of Marcus Garvey shock her into an uneasy recognition of her African roots; the flight of Charles Lindbergh points out how white people, not burdened by the pressing, daily need to secure subsistence, have the luxury of going after personal glory. "Education comes in drips and drops to a feller who never went to school," Dorine tells the reader.

Yet even though the narrative is full of references to influential historical figures, Dorine's education takes place on an individual level. Illiterate until her life with Harry Brisbane, Dorine learns from people including her grandmother, a brothel owner in Cleveland, her fellow shoplifters, and the various men in her life.

Her own vision of Harlem, from the brilliant black renaissance of the 1920's to the drug-haunted seediness of the 1950's, is colored by Dorine's own passage through life. In her youth, she extols "the gay times. The wild times. . . . And for me, laughing, becoming the best of the best and being young." In her middle age, there remain only "memories slinking around the slums, gliding in and out of broken-down buildings, floating over the fallen bodies of junkies, winos." The image of the city, in Dorine's eyes, is a "measure of time."

Indeed, the whole novel is, for Dorine, an extended lesson in social and moral geography. The Alabama sections of the book, for example, slow the pace of the narrative; until the activist period of the 1950's, the South is viewed by Dorine as a "region of quiet and inertia." Dorine is drawn to the North, where the social mobility complements her restless spirit and quiets her impatience with the social and economic constraints imposed on the lives of Southern blacks. In Harlem, she is free to be "her own black self."

This regional contrast is dramatized most effectively in one pivotal, character-defining episode. On her first trip South since establishing her life in Harlem, Dorine takes the train to Montgomery to visit her sick sister. In the stretch from New York to Washington, she is addressed as "Madam Davis," and she eats in her mink coat in the dining car. Once she changes trains in Washington, however, Dorine is forced into a sooty "Jim Crow" car and left to share an old man's fried chicken from a greasy paper bag. She is alternately stupefied and enraged. Earlier in the novel, Dorine comments that the Statue of Liberty has been mislocated; it should have been in Penn Station to welcome black refugees from the segregated South. Thus, setting is also measured by time.

Another thematic variation on the book's title can be traced to Dorine's belated recognition that "kids ain't as much a measure of their folks as they the measure of their own time." Certainly, this is a novel about generational differences. It ends with a sharp contrast between mother and son: Dorine's lifelong willingness to work outside the system to achieve her goals differs from her son's political commitment to change the system from within. Dorine's statement that she "did the hustling (while) other folks did the dreaming" offers an ironic commentary on Martin Luther King, Jr.'s, famous "I Have a Dream" speech. It is a measure of Dorine's time that hustling equaled empowerment; the measure of her son's time is the promise of political activism.

Critical Context

Rosa Guy's critical reputation rests on her prizewinning works for adolescent readers, novels that treat candidly the subject of black-on-black prejudice, especially the troubled relationship between African Americans and African West Indians.

For Rosa Guy, *A Measure of Time* is a departure in that it is only her second adult novel after *Bird at My Window* (1966). Reviews of *A Measure of Time* in the popular press have been consistently good, but Rosa Guy has not received the careful scholarly attention that she deserves.

Bibliography

Bell, Bernard W. *The Afro-American Novel and Its Tradition.* Amherst: University of Massachusetts Press, 1987. Argues for the placement of Guy's work within the context of traditional realism and particularly of what Bell calls "Afro-American neorealism," which asserts that no discussion of character can occur outside a social and historical framework.

Brown, Beth. Review of *A Measure of Time. Black Scholar* 16 (January, 1985): 54-55.

Acknowledges that Guy has not achieved the recognition that she deserves. Guy's emphasis on the education derived from life on the streets draws comparison to the works of James Baldwin and Chester Hines. By her focus on Dorine's over-bearing pride and her refusal to forgive, according to the reviewer, Rosa Guy gives form to the instinctive force of the ordinary black female.

McHenry, Susan. Review of *A Measure of Time*. *Ms.* 12 (July, 1983): 21. Applauds Guy's novel as an immense, engrossing book that offers the reader a sympathetic view of black American life. Dorine Davis' personality is an engaging blend of healthy assurance and restive pride, of common sense and an unfortunate fond-ness for attractive men.

Schraufnagel, Noel. *From Apology to Protest: The Black American Novel*. Deland, Fla.: Everett/Edwards, 1973. Emphasizes Guy's skill in depicting the psychologi-cal damage that can be caused by racial discrimination.

Wilson, Judith. "Rosa Guy: Writing with a Bold Vision." *Essence* 10 (October, 1979): 14-20. Provides a profile of the artist with special attention to biographical detail that has a bearing on her later composition of *A Measure of Time*. Guy's Alabama stepmother, her West Indian father, her parents' involvement in the Marcus Gar-vey movement, her growing up in Harlem, and her reluctance to showcase only the positive, middle-class black experience are discussed.

S. Thomas Mack

MERIDIAN

Author: Alice Walker (1944-   )
Type of work: Novel
Type of plot: Social criticism
Time of plot: The 1960's
Locale: Georgia, Alabama, Mississippi, and New York City
First published: 1976

>   *Principal characters:*
>   MERIDIAN HILL, a black revolutionary and civil rights worker
>   TRUMAN HELD, a would-be black revolutionary; a civil rights
>   worker, artist, and sometime lover of Meridian
>   LYNNE RABINOWITZ, a white exchange student and civil rights
>   worker who marries Truman Held
>   ANNE-MARION COLES, Meridian's friend in college
>   MRS. HILL, Meridian's mother, frustrated and angry most of the
>   time
>   MR. HILL, Meridian's father

The Novel

Meridian explores a number of cultural legacies important to African Americans. The primary legacy is the meaning of the Civil Rights movement, both to those who were its major players and to future generations. In exploring these ideas, Walker uses characters with the spirit of the movement rather than its actual leaders. A novel ostensibly about the Civil Rights movement becomes one that uses the entire African American cultural and historical experience as both background and foreground. This idea becomes clear upon examination of the structural pattern of the novel. The novel begins after many of the major events of the 1960's have occurred. President John F. Kennedy, Martin Luther King, Jr., and Senator Robert Kennedy are dead. Many of the major leaders and players of the Civil Rights and Black Power movements have opted for other agendas, many having little to do with improving black people's lives.

Meridian Hill is still around, trying to do her part to help her people. The novel's opening scene chronicles Meridian's attempts to keep the spirit of the movement alive as she challenges a Jim Crow practice of allowing black people to see a carnival sideshow only on one particular day. Thrust into this scene is Truman Held's return to the South to seek Meridian.

After establishing in a brief scene what is left of the Civil Rights movement, which is no longer in vogue, Walker begins a process of weaving bits and pieces of information together to account for why Meridian is the way she is and why Truman and other characters are the way they are. This is not an easy story to tell, requiring the piecing together of many parts of recent and distant African American cultural history to create the "crazy quilt" that is the novel's major structure.

The story moves around in time, allowing the reader to see what Meridian was like as a girl, how her family helped to make her the kind of person she is, how as a child she saw herself as an outsider in her own family, and how she observed a number of actions of black people in her community that were not always helpful to black children. Meridian's childhood was problematic for a number of reasons. She always believed that her mother did not love or want her. She remarks that it seemed as if her mother showed affection only in ironing her children's clothes. Meridian also thought that her mother and other adults in the community did not give children, especially girls, information that might ensure passage through the teen years without getting pregnant. Because real sex education was not provided, a number of girls became pregnant, including Meridian.

From her father, Meridian begins to understand the importance of family history and heritage, particularly the American Indian heritage she gets from him. Meridian is upset with her father, however, for spending so much time in the past that he silently allows Mrs. Hill's kind of parenting to prevail.

As Walker weaves the bits of information that are Meridian's married life, her pregnancy, and her decision to give up her child, she exposes problems in the black community. Meridian's husband, Eddie, is childish, and he shows disrespect for Meridian by having affairs with other women. More important, when Meridian's child is born, she discovers that she cannot love him the way she knows mothers are supposed to love their children. When her marriage finally deteriorates, she offers her child to Mrs. Hill, but Mrs. Hill wants no part of her grandchild's life. The decision to give up her child is the most significant one Meridian has made up to this point in her life. She gives him up because she loves him and knows she cannot be the kind of mother he needs.

Once Meridian is by herself, she begins to think about what she is going to do with her life. She is granted a scholarship to Saxon College in Atlanta and enters another major period in her life. In college, she becomes more active in the emerging Civil Rights movement. She encourages black people to register to vote and is arrested for doing so. She discovers that Saxon College, a historically black school, is like her hometown community in that it does things to decrease black people's chances for living healthy lives while trying to help them. The school wanted little to do with the Civil Rights movement and did not want its students to help the poor people of the surrounding black community. Its goal was to produce young ladies with an orientation to the middle class. Meridian challenges the school's philosophy when she befriends a pregnant thirteen-year-old girl known as The Wild Child. She brings the unruly and uncivilized girl to her dormitory for a bath and dinner. When giving her a bath, she contemplates who might have raped the girl and why the surrounding black community did nothing to help. This experience shows Meridian that there is a type of mothering that she can give. When The Wild Child is killed by a car, Meridian arranges for Saxon students to be the coffin bearers. She is determined that The Wild Child's life mean something.

At Saxon, Meridian learns the significance of a large magnolia tree, the Sojourner, and the story of a slave woman, Louvinie, associated with it. Louvinie, a gifted storyteller, had her tongue cut out because her scary stories led to the death of her master's son. In paying homage to Louvinie, Meridian begins to appreciate, learn from, and depend on a heritage of black women.

Meridian even remembers her own maternal history and the sacrifices made by women for their families. Meridian's dilemma is how can she measure up to this great historical tradition of motherhood while maintaining some sense of self. Her active participation in the Civil Rights movement becomes a way for her to mother her people and yet not be restricted and frustrated, as her mother was. It is a balancing act, however, that takes its toll on her body, mind, and spirit. Through patching the fragments of her life to those of her culture, Meridian eventually finds the means to a satisfying life.

The Characters

Meridian is a richly drawn and fully developed character whose creation announced a major shift in black characters in African American literature. Walker created a woman who is part human and part saint and brought the two sides together in such a way that Meridian is always believable. At times, Meridian almost seems possessed in her determination to help black people. She makes a number of sacrifices of self and body as she devotes more time and energy to "her cause."

The first indication that Meridian's physical and spiritual sides are at war comes when she begins fainting after a grueling day of civil rights work, during which she is often beaten and arrested. She also begins to have episodes of loss of consciousness. The more she works for her people, the less she is concerned about earthly or material things. Meridian travels to New York City, where she encounters friends in the Black Power movement. Their rhetoric disturbs her. Anne-Marion, for example, asks Meridian, "Can you kill for the revolution?" Meridian returns to the South to be among the common folk, and once there she continues to help in any way needed. After her return, she begins to stop caring about personal hygiene and even about eating. She does not cook, but she gladly accepts the food the rural folks bring to her.

If a part of Walker's intent in the novel is to show the toll that the Civil Rights movement took on some people, she achieves that intent most clearly in her creation of Meridian Hill. Meridian is real and immediate. She gets pregnant a second time, after the only time in the novel she has sex with Truman. She has an abortion because Truman does not love her and also has her tubes tied so that she will never be a traditional mother. Furthermore, Meridian deals with jealousy aimed at the white female exchange students and with sexual exploitation, both issues that she confronts realistically. It is Walker's portrayal of the process of her confrontations that gives the reader the final version of Meridian, one that is succinctly delineated as a believable character.

Walker's skill in character development is also demonstrated in her creation of

Lynne Rabinowitz. Lynne grows from a northern white liberal out to do good for black folks to a woman who suffers the loss of her child, Camara, a rape by her husband's best friend, and rejection by her husband in favor of a younger and thinner white woman. Equally significant, Lynne grows and learns to appreciate who black people are and what makes up the contours of their lives. An understanding of shared pain, mutual suffering, and shared respect for black people's essential culture allows Lynne and Meridian to forgive each other.

A part of their forgiveness comes from their recognition that Truman is not worthy of either of them. Truman learns that the type of love he had to offer Meridian was not enough and never would be, because Meridian was authentic in ways that he was not.

The novel is peopled with a variety of black characters who are the legacy of a history that Meridian learns to appreciate and who are the contemporary rural black folks Meridian serves. The red-eyed man who annually comes to a church service to honor his martyred son and Miss Margaret Treasure, a seventy-two-year-old who thinks she is pregnant, are examples of the unique secondary characters.

Themes and Meanings

"For it is the song of the people, transformed by the experiences of each generation, that holds them together, and if any part of it is lost the people suffer and are without soul. If I can only do that, my role will not have been a useless one after all." Meridian's final understanding of her role in life is one of the most important themes of the novel.

In *Meridian*, Alice Walker documents one woman's struggle to gain a sense of self and to define her relationship to African Americans. In her struggle, Meridian rejects the popular political rhetoric of would-be black revolutionaries, such as Anne-Marion, who spout epithets tinged with hate, in favor of a philosophy predicated on love and on actions that directly help black people in their everyday lives.

Meridian, moreover, rejects the many constraints that have, in the United States, attached themselves to black motherhood, the principal route by which women express kinship to the tribe. Meridian's story shows that there are many ways to be a mother. By returning to the past—understanding her maternal history—and by doing so much of real value for the rural people of Georgia, Alabama, and Mississippi, Meridian becomes a mother who quite simply loves her black people.

The scene in the novel that showcases Meridian's growth as a new kind of mother is contained in "Camara." In this scene, which occurs in a Baptist church, the focus is on a child, a young man who gave his life for the civil rights struggle, and his father, who lost his mind when his son died. The church service to commemorate the son's death provides answers to questions Meridian has been toiling over for a decade. She realizes that human life is more precious than anything and dedicates her life to preserving black people's life and culture. Meridian thus comes to understand that if black people value each other, they will change the social order that oppresses them.

Critical Context

Meridian is considered by many literary critics to be one of Alice Walker's finest novels, moving in its depiction of the people and events that made up the struggle for civil rights in the 1960's. Important in establishing the social and political contexts of the 1960's is her attention to presenting the story from the perspective of a black woman. The novel fills in the empty space where the black woman should be in many fictional and nonfictional representations of the Civil Rights and Black Power movements.

The novel is a seminal one in bringing critical attention to the black woman's story, which figures prominently in the works of a group of black women writers whose careers were launched in the early and middle 1970's. These writers define a significant part of the African American woman's literary tradition. Walker joins such writers as Toni Morrison, Gayl Jones, Audre Lorde, Paule Marshall, Toni Cade Bambara, Mari Evans, and Sherley Anne Williams, whose works extend the African American story.

Walker's novel of a young woman who struggles to define herself and to discover what role she will play for her people is significant in African American literature, for Walker ties Meridian's development to her understanding of her past. In the novel, Walker describes black people's culture and history in some detail. The novel comments on the Black Arts movement of the 1960's and 1970's, which insisted that black artists use their historical past in the creation of their works, by showing how this critical advice might be accomplished.

Bibliography

Banks, Erma, and Keith Byerman. *Alice Walker: An Annotated Bibliography.* New York: Garland Press, 1989. Collects the major and minor material written on Alice Walker from 1968 to 1986.

Bloom, Harold, ed. *Alice Walker.* New York: Chelsea House, 1989. Major critics discuss the majority of Walker's fiction, nonfiction, and poetry.

Christian, Barbara T. "*Meridian*: The Quest for Wholeness." In *Black Women Novelists: The Development of a Tradition, 1892-1976.* Westport, Conn.: Greenwood Press, 1980. Argues that Meridian's growth into a complete and functioning self is tied to her understanding of what black people and their culture mean. When Meridian discovers the connection between self and the tribe, she also realizes that significant social and political change can occur.

Cooke, Michael G. "The Achievement of Intimacy." In *Afro-American Literature in the Twentieth Century: The Achievement of Intimacy.* New Haven, Conn.: Yale University Press, 1984. Focuses on the African American kinship as the most important part of black people's lives and sees Meridian's final understanding of how she is a part of her people, past and present, as the novel's main theme.

Harris, Norman. "*Meridian*: Answers in the Black Church." In *Connecting Times: The Sixties in Afro-American Fiction.* Jackson: University Press of Mississippi, 1988. *Meridian* is discussed as being a revolutionary novel because of its depiction of alternative ways of struggling for civil rights. Emphasizes Meridian's under-standing of the black church in her personal and racial development.

Nadel, Alan. "Reading the Body: Alice Walker's *Meridian* and the Archeology of Self." *Modern Fiction Studies* 34 (Spring, 1988): 55-68. A structuralist examina-tion of Meridian's relationship to black culture.

Charles P. Toombs

THE MESSENGER

Author: Charles Wright (1932-   )
Type of work: Novel
Type of plot: Psychological realism
Time of plot: The late 1950's and early 1960's
Locale: New York City
First published: 1963

> *Principal characters:*
> CHARLIE STEVENSON, the protagonist, an introspective, twenty-
>   nine-year-old African American veteran of the Korean War
> SHIRLEY, the woman Charlie once hoped to marry
> TROY LAMB, one of Charlie's oldest friends in Manhattan
> MAXINE, a precocious seven-year-old who lives in the same
>   tenement as Charlie
> CLAUDIA (THE GRAND DUCHESS), a "drag queen," the most
>   prominent of an outrageous cast of characters that populates
>   this novel
> RUBY STONEWALL, Charlie's cousin, a promising blues singer in
>   Missouri before she lost her singing voice
> GRANDMA, the maternal grandmother who reared Charlie in a
>   small Missouri town in the 1940's and 1950's

The Novel

The Messenger is the autobiographical first-person narrative of Charlie, a lonely man. The novel is episodic. Each of its forty short, loosely connected chapters recalls an incident from Charlie's past or describes in graphic detail his current situation as a promising writer who makes a meager living as a messenger for Wall Street brokers. In a style that is at times spare and reportorial, and at other times highly lyrical and expressionistic, Charles Wright portrays this young man's slide toward an increasing sense of hopelessness and despair in the segregated borough of Manhattan in the late 1950's and early 1960's. "I grow old in the terrible heart of America," Charlie writes. "I am dying the American-money death."

A number of chapters are devoted to memories of Charlie's childhood in Sedalia, a small Missouri town where he was cared for, primarily, by his maternal grandmother. Other chapters are devoted to memories of his quest for greater experiences in the big cities of the Midwest and California, and to memories of his visit to his hometown in 1958, the year his maternal grandmother died. The majority of the novel, however, is devoted to Charlie's descriptions of his travels through the underbelly of Manhattan, where he encounters gay men, drug addicts, transvestites, prostitutes, and con artists.

Many of the New York City chapters present accounts of Charlie's often-humiliating experiences of cruising bars and Wall Street offices trying to find his own sexual pleasure with men or women, or to offer sex in exchange for money to supplement his meager income. His day job as a messenger allows him entrance into worlds from which his skin color might otherwise exclude him. His "tricks" include a wealthy white woman who takes Charlie back to her home in Long Island, a male Wall Street stockbroker who telephones his wife before taking Charlie to an abandoned office, and a male Ivy League student with a club foot who wants Charlie to "hurt [him] a little" in order to achieve sexual pleasure.

Charlie's experiences with alcohol, pills, and loveless sex among strangers cause him to feel despondent, sometimes to the point of madness. He attempts to transcend the pain of his life in a number of ways. Charlie finds some comfort by remembering aspects of a more idyllic past, when he lived with his grandparents in Missouri. He also recovers buried religious feelings when he hears gospel singing at The Holiness Sundown Church. "Somewhere there was such a thing as peace of mind and goodness," he thinks. Charlie finds his main comfort from visiting friends such as Claudia, a male transvestite whose energy and optimism lift Charlie out of his despair, and Maxine, a little girl whose artistic impulses Charlie encourages.

Charlie also is able to make sense out of his life by reading great literature. He compares his situation to Quentin Compson's in *The Sound and the Fury* (1929), a novel by William Faulkner. Like Faulkner's character, Charlie considers himself to be at the end of a family line. Charlie also finds pleasure through an appreciation of art and music, particularly through listening to jazz and to the blues singing of Billie Holiday. Charlie's aesthetic sensibility and his keen use of poetic language and metaphor allow him, in a number of beautifully written chapters, to describe even the drab streets of New York City on a lonely Sunday morning as possessing a quiet power that touches on his religious impulses:

> Toward the east a ballet of soft, white clouds. The rising sun breaks through shafts of gold. It was as if God had suddenly opened His powerful hand on the world. My heart bows its head in the presence of this force. I am suddenly at peace in this early morning. The sun comforts me; I am swaddled in the folds of those wonderful clouds. Let the rays of the sun touch your body and you will be made holy.

Although the decadence of life in the city has become a part of him, Charlie dreams of an escape from New York. In the last short vignette, Charlie, who has been evicted from his tenement apartment, hocks many of his belongings so that he can buy a ticket to Mexico. This destination promises, at least, further experience and adventure, and, at best, the chance for a new start. The novel ends, however, with Charlie's skepticism about the future: "There was horror in the knowledge that nothing was going to happen to me."

The Characters

Without a traditional plot or an extensive dramatic thread to carry the reader through the novel's many scenes of urban despair, *The Messenger* attains its meaning primarily through Wright's portrayal of the insights and recollections of Charlie, the novelist's autobiographical protagonist and first-person narrator. Although the novel presents a collection of other characters, these characters tend to exist in relation to Charlie. They are significant to the degree that they shed light on aspects of Charlie's personality or experience. The artistic impulses of the little girl, Maxine, and the hopefulness of Charlie's girlfriend, Shirley, for example, present points of contrast to Charlie's life of poverty, hopelessness, and loneliness. His white friend Troy is similarly important to the novel primarily as an illustration of how difficult even the most well-intentioned relationships can be between members of different races in a society not comfortable with integration.

Wright uses the reportorial style often associated with American novelist and short-story writer Ernest Hemingway to depict how Charlie's feelings have become numbed by his exposure to scenes of pain and humiliation. Charlie responds in an almost frozen way to scenes of intensely painful content and heavy emotion. The juxtaposition of this objective style with the scenes of terror being depicted is Wright's method of conveying to the reader Charlie's alienation from the emotional content of his own experience. On one of his journeys as a messenger, for example, Charlie comes to the household of a Puerto Rican woman whose baby remains in her apartment one month after it was brutally murdered by her drunken husband. Charlie describes the scene but erases the devastating emotional content of what he records:

> I went over and examined the bundle. Inside lay a dead PR baby about a month old. He was, naked and his head was turned on his left side. A circle of blood had dried and was caked around his mouth, and his little chubby hands were high above his head. There was a blue-black mark on his right cheek, as if he had fallen against something or had been hit or kicked.

Charlie is not always able to distance himself from an emotional response to his experience through objective reportage. Part of what makes Charlie a sympathetic and well-rounded character is his ability to shape poetry out of his dreary surroundings. His personal integrity is far greater than indicated by the series of one-night stands, failed relationships, and addictions that make up his life. "I look out at the wonders of the sky's black face. A sharp, autumnal breeze circles through this stone Hades, this island on the Hudson," he writes. The differences between this lyrical passage of natural beauty found among the squalor of bums and garbage and the cool tones of the description of the murdered baby exemplify a conflict within Charlie's character. Throughout the novel, Charlie oscillates between exuberance and despair about his life and his future.

Themes and Meanings

Charlie Stevenson is a messenger both in occupation and in the metaphorical sense of someone who carries a warning to members of a society who refuse to attend to the needs of all citizens. He lives as an outcast in a culture unwilling to accept racial differences or differences of sexual orientation. His sense of being an outsider is especially acute because he is marginalized from mainstream society in many different ways. Charlie is a light-skinned African American. His racial identity is, therefore, often in question. "What are you, Puerto Rican or Filipino?" Charlie is asked by a man who picks him up while hitchhiking. "Neither," Charlie answers. "I'm colored."

Charlie's sexual orientation adds to his sense of being an outsider. His sexual practices are ambivalent. At times he is pulled toward Shirley, a woman who wants a love relationship and, possibly, a marriage with him, but he also performs "tricks" with both men and women and with both white clients and African Americans. Because the novel is set before the sexual revolution of the late 1960's, Charlie's sexual practices deepen the theme of alienation from mainstream culture. His story is representative of those persons who do not act in a way that is considered to be normal by the majority group.

A member of the working poor, Charlie is an outsider in a society that often equates wealth with social standing. Although he is in a position to witness the luxurious lives of those who manage the country's economic affairs at the New York Stock Exchange, Charlie is employed in the low-paying, low-prestige job of messenger. He watches huge sums of money change hands, but he is not a beneficiary of a wealthy society. His disillusionment with class distinctions becomes severe when he witnesses the hypocrisy of those who pretend to traditional middle-class lives while indulging in extramarital affairs with him. Although he is known to many persons in positions of economic power, his poverty and despair seem unimportant to those who are willing to take advantage of his body. African American novelist and essayist James Baldwin has written that Wright's story of an outsider whose unusual life and impoverished situation forbid him from entering into mainstream American culture as a peer is representative of the anguish and alienation felt by many others who survive in the anonymity of what Baldwin calls "that awful half-light in which so many people are struggling to live."

Critical Context

Wright's first novel, *The Messenger*, was warmly received by reviewers, sold quite well, and developed a following for Wright. Lucy Freeman called it "a poignant portrait of a young man without a country or even a city." Kay Boyle believed it to be among the most significant of a number of contemporaneous novels presenting "ruthlessly honest" portrayals of "the lonely horror of the junkie and homosexual world of New York." James Baldwin considered the book to be a "happening" that should serve as a warning to "city fathers" that "this is New York, this is the way we live now."

Although these critics endorsed the candor of subject matter and admired the fine writing, some critics found it difficult to distinguish between what was fact and what was fiction in *The Messenger*. This blurring of the boundaries between genres led some reviewers to think the work was wrongly identified as "imaginative writing." In spite of the fact that Wright drew heavily on his own experiences—he supported

himself as a messenger while composing it—the novel, according to Jerome Klinkowitz, deserves its place in the canon of African American literature for shattering
old conventions and presenting the usual "'search for meaning' theme in a radical
new form: imaginative literature, and ultimately fantasy."

Joe Weixlmann has said that the direction open to African American writing in
the 1960's and beyond depends less on prescribed forms and more on the writer's
willingness to mix genres such as realism and fantasy in order to create new hybrid
forms of expression. *The Messenger* stands as an influential example of a novel written with the force and energy of what Charlie calls "the fears, confusion, and pain
of being alive."

Bibliography
Bell, Bernard W. *The Afro-American Novel and Its Tradition.* Amherst: University
of Massachusetts Press, 1987. In chapter 8, "The Contemporary Afro-American
Novel," Bell places Wright among writers of "fabulation and satire," in that Wright
draws on his sense of the ironies and absurdity of the 1960's and 1970's in order to
spread his tragicomic vision of the times.
Byerman, Keith E. *Fingering the Jagged Grain: Tradition and Form in Recent Black
Fiction.* Athens: University of Georgia Press, 1985. Byerman places Wright within
the generation of Ishmael Reed and the early Amiri Baraka (LeRoi Jones) as a
leading experimental writer who has redefined what is possible in African American fiction by tending to emphasize the telling more than the tale.
Klinkowitz, Jerome. *Literary Disruptions: The Making of a Post-Contemporary American Fiction.* Urbana: University of Illinois Press, 1975. This collection of essays
by an important spokesman for avant-garde American writing argues in a chapter
devoted to Wright that Wright is important in the tradition of the African American novel for creating a radical new form and for shattering old conventions of the
"quest" narrative.
O'Brien, John. "Charles Wright." In *Interviews with Black Writers.* New York: Liveright, 1973. A 1971 interview that discusses the influence of the southern writer
Katherine Anne Porter on Wright's sensibility, his estranged relationship to New
York City, the role of fantasy in his work, and other subjects.
Schulz, Max F. "The Aesthetics of Anxiety" and "The Conformist Heroes of Bruce
Jay Friedman and Charles Wright." In *Black Humor Fiction of the Sixties: A Plu-
ralistic Definition of Man and His World.* Athens: Ohio University Press, 1973.
Part of a larger study that places Wright within the multiethnic 1960's movement
of "black humor" that included writers such as Kurt Vonnegut, Joseph Heller,
and Thomas Pynchon.

Daniel Charles Morris

MIDDLE PASSAGE

Author: Charles Johnson (1948-   )
Type of work: Novel
Type of plot: Bildungsroman
Time of plot: 1830
Locale: A slave ship
First published: 1990

> *Principal character:*
> RUTHERFORD CALHOUN, the novel's first-person narrator, a well-
> educated and pleasure-seeking freed slave

The Novel

Middle Passage is Rutherford Calhoun's account of the last voyage of an illegal American slave ship, the *Republic*, and of his personal quest for knowledge of the meaning of his life. When the novel begins, Calhoun is a twenty-one-year-old freed slave from Illinois who supports his life of pleasure in New Orleans by theft and lying. To escape a forced marriage to Boston schoolteacher Isadora Bailey and debts owed black underground leader Papa Zeringue, Calhoun stows away on the slave ship *Republic*, where he meets even greater dangers than he faced on land. As a slave he received a classical education, and since his captain requests that Calhoun write the ship's log, he both records the ship's adventures and ponders their philo-sophical implications.

Calhoun makes the journey with strange mates. Captain Ebenezer Falcon, a fear-some dwarf, wants fame as a world conqueror. First mate Peter Cringle is a New England gentleman with a "core of aloneness." A failed captain of industry, he makes the journey to fulfill his father's wish that he become a captain of commerce. Nathaniel Meadows, a parson-type who looks "Biblically meek," sails the seas to escape punishment for the murder of his whole family. Squibb, the cook to whom Calhoun is made assistant, drinks continually. Indeed, all forty crew members are loners traveling in search of a new frontier, Calhoun decides.

When the ship reaches the Gulf of Guinea, Calhoun's philosophical mooring—in a dualism that accepts the oppression of the weak by the strong and a hierarchy that elevates captain over crew and white over black—loosens. So does his faith in self-centered individualism.

First, Calhoun breaks into Captain Falcon's cabin and discovers a collection of African cultural artifacts, stolen along with slaves. Falcon catches Calhoun and makes him swear a loyalty oath. Next, Calhoun sees the African slave market in action and observes the captain and crew's cruelty to their cargo of black captives, the All-museri. Also, Falcon brings on board a mysterious crate that intensifies the crew's fear of their captain's evil designs. From Ngonyama, an Allmuseri appointed ship-board overseer of the captives, Calhoun hears about Allmuseri culture's ethical basis in sharing and healing. Calhoun is attracted to the Allmuseri. Even as he stands in awe of their aura of mystery, he wonders if these primitive Africans are perhaps the original people, the forebears of humanity.

During the return journey, a storm's wind, like a trickster, turns the ship around, sweeping women and children overboard. Heightened chaos and fear cause some crew members to plan a mutiny. When they ask Calhoun to join them, he seals his loyalty to them. Yet when next he meets Falcon, Calhoun betrays these crew members and again pledges loyalty to the captain. While Falcon is telling Calhoun that his secret crate holds the god of the Allmuseri, Calhoun steals the key to the Allmuseri captives' chains. Thus Calhoun, true to his value of protecting his self-interest, aligns himself with all the possible winners. At the same time, he is drawn by the Allmuseri, who represent all humanity.

Calhoun's confusion grows. When he tells Squibb about the hatred he feels toward his own brother, Squibb replies that Calhoun needs love. Then, helping dispose of a dead Allmuseri captive, Calhoun sees himself in the youth's corpse. Next, he notices also that the Allmuseri, in their brief contact with Americans, are losing something of their African mystery. When the Allmuseri take over the *Republic*, they are as violent and oppressive as the crew had been; they even make the crew into slaves. Finally, Calhoun learns that powerful American capitalists own him, the ship, and its cargo. One owner is black New Orleans mobster Papa Zeringue.

As the ship goes around in circles, Calhoun seeks meaning in chaos. In the midst of the dire illness afflicting all the survivors, Calhoun offers healing and comfort. Taking his turn to feed the Allmuseri god, he spends three days with it, meeting therein his long-lost father and himself. Now white-haired and almost unconscious, Calhoun envisions humanity united and compassionate. When he is rescued from the sea by a ship carrying Papa Zeringue and Isadora Bailey, Calhoun's vision is sealed. Calhoun marries Isadora and sets off for home and reconciliation with his brother.

The Characters

Rutherford Calhoun, the first-person narrator of *Middle Passage*, is a complex protagonist. He is by education a philosopher and by inclination a trickster. Once a slave, he is now free. His roots are in rural Illinois, but he loves the excitement of New Orleans big-city life. When his gambling debts and Isadora, a woman determined to marry him, force him to escape New Orleans and stow away on the *Republic*, a slave ship, he adapts quickly to the vicissitudes of a sailor's life. Calhoun is a survivor because he always puts his own interests first.

Calhoun chooses the words in which he narrates his story from some widely diverse word hoards: formal discourse, African American dialect, lyric poetry, nautical jargon, and slang. This rich voice, in combination with his many masks, is Calhoun's weapon of empowerment in the midst of many adventures, which range from ridiculous to truly life-threatening. The narrator and his voice combine comic and serious tones and speed through language shifts, historical allusions, and zany anachronisms to hold and entertain the reader.

With this wonderful voice, Calhoun invites the reader into his adventures. For example, the *Republic*'s dwarfed, pedophiliac, tyrannic, and paranoid Captain Falcon threatens Calhoun with dire punishment for stowing away. In a short while, however, Calhoun is the captain's best friend, and several times during the voyage the two discuss the meaning of life and the nature of God. The trickster stowaway becomes the source of wisdom. Of course, Calhoun also agrees to inform the captain of the crew's misbehavior; just as easily, Calhoun signs on to two factions of the crew, the mutineers and the loyal sailors. Thus Calhoun's wonderfully mixed vocabulary records in the ship's log his comical and yet life-threatening days and nights.

For all his wondrous vocabulary, it seems that Calhoun lives on the surface of his life. Nothing affects him deeply, nothing changes him. Then he meets the Allmuseri, an ancient African tribe whose members become slave cargo on the ship. As he observes them, reflects on their strange god (a prisoner in the ship's hold), and converses with their leader, Ngonyama, Calhoun faces mystery for the first time. When he is in this presence, and in the presence of the suffering of the slaves, something deep within him is affected.

It is then that Calhoun's voice and his character change. This happens as he listens to the African voice of the Allmuseri. Until then, all of Calhoun is American: out for the individual, looking for material success. Now, however, he journeys from these values, from his goals of individual survival and materialistic pleasures, and from a worldview of winner or loser, master or slave, captain or crew, white or black. Calhoun makes his own "middle passage."

As the ship undergoes mutiny, Calhoun sees first the Allmuseri and then his shipmates as his brothers and sisters. He finds himself reaching out to others to heal them and love them. What he finds when he first hears the African voice is a part of himself that he did not know he had. The protagonist Calhoun who left behind his rural past, and his brother, to make his way up in the world on his own, using others when convenient, discarding them when he was done, comes full circle. He ends his journey back where he began, in his rural home, with an American wife and an African child he has learned to love on his journey. Now he is more than a survivor. He has made meaning out of his life.

Themes and Meanings

Rutherford Calhoun's first-person narrative voice in *Middle Passage* is the key to both the protagonist's character and the novel's integrity. The protagonist is many persons: learned African American former slave, practiced thief and liar, agrarian turned urbanite turned sailor. His voice blends many levels of language: philosophical discourse, nautical terminology, lyrical images of field and ocean, witty slang and worn cliché. In this voice, Rutherford Calhoun narrates his adventures in the underworld of New Orleans and the society aboard the slave ship.

Because Rutherford Calhoun is a freewheeling young man who unexpectedly finds himself on a dangerous sea adventure, and because his first words are the humorous announcement that he, like most men who go to sea, is escaping a woman, his character recalls the naïve and comic Ishmael, first-person narrator of Herman Melville's *Moby Dick* (1851). There are other elements in *Middle Passage* that suggest Melville's narrative as source: a character named Peleg, the mad Captain Falcon, and a cabin boy who loses his mind. Though there are similarities, however, there are differences. Melville's narrator Ishmael is at first a comic character with matching voice, but as the plot changes from youthful adventure to romantic quest, the narrator's voice changes to that of a reflective philosopher. Charles Johnson's narrator Calhoun, on the other hand, maintains consistently a voice that combines comic and serious tones from the beginning to the end of his journal and journey.

This multiregistered voice and its speed hold the reader gripped securely throughout the book's language shifts, historical allusions, altered clichés, and zany anachronisms. The narrative voice safely immerses the reader in the plot elements: the young narrator's moves in and out of trouble; the violent storms and shipboard explosions; the slapstick dialogue and philosophical debates in which Calhoun engages the other characters. So, though indebted in some ways to Herman Melville's young white American narrator in *Moby Dick*, Charles Johnson's young ex-slave narrator Calhoun is both trickster and philosopher throughout his African American experience of coming of age.

The ship named the *Republic* suggests Plato's utopia of philosophical truth, and indeed Calhoun makes the ship a scene of philosophical debate. The ship, however, resembles more the American Republic, for most of the text's historical and literary allusions parody America's mythic illusions and pseudoheroes. Thus Rutherford Calhoun's name recalls two American political leaders, Rutherford Hayes, a president who ended Reconstruction in 1876, and John Calhoun, an ardent defender of American slavery, actions mocked when their perpetrators' names are worn by a former slave. Also, though Captain Ebenezer Falcon might recall the romantic Captain Ahab, Melville's larger-than-life hero-conqueror of the metaphysical gods of evil and death, Captain Falcon is a dwarf-sized entrepreneur whose goal is mere fame.

Johnson's use of historical and literary types might have yielded superficial or wooden characters in a different narrative style. Rendered in all the registers of Calhoun's learned-trickster voice, though, the characters take on fullness. Thus Calhoun describes these characters' appearance and setting, telling for example that Falcon, who sounds like a "genie in a jug," decorates his high-poster-style bed with "valances and knotted dirty sheets." In addition, the narrator's talent for lock picking opens up secrets: Falcon protects himself with booby traps and sits naked while he writes the ship's log. More serious, Falcon sleeps with the cabin boy and, when his dream of fame fails, commits suicide. Finally, because Calhoun loves to philosophize, he talks with his captain, and all his mates, about the nature of humanity and the existence of God. Falcon is thus both parodied type and complex individual, basically venal but somehow even likable.

First Mate Peter Cringle is an aloof New Englander, a well-bred Brahmin and a loner of the Henry David Thoreau or Ralph Waldo Emerson type. He protects the weak, such as the cabin boy, Tommy, but only because he himself is weak. Ironically, it is Cringle who leads the crew in an attempt at mutiny. Just as every character does at some point in the text, Cringle tells Calhoun his heart's deepest secret, his failure to live his father's dream and become a captain of industry, a captain of anything. In Cringle's last act, killing himself so that others may eat his flesh and survive, the mate might be fool or saint. Whichever, through Calhoun's imaginative narrative voice, he lives.

Most significant is the African Ngonyama, for he is a key in Calhoun's own quest for the meaning of life. When Ngonyama speaks, Calhoun hears the one voice in himself that has been silenced, that part of himself that is the same as Ngonyama: African and Allmuseri. Here the tribal name becomes important. It is, perhaps "All" of them and "us" inserted in "A . . . meri[ca]."

Plot reveals a similar theme. Calhoun begins his journey on the traditional American individualistic and linear path to fulfill his dream. When Calhoun leaves Illinois, he is on a one-way, linear journey away from a past he rejects and toward a future of his own, individual making. He is, he thinks, breaking all connection with his past. Likewise, when he departs New Orleans to escape the danger Isadora Bailey presents to his self-centered lifestyle, Calhoun joins a captain and crew all on a one-way path to a new frontier, a new world, with each one taking care of himself.

Through his adventures, Calhoun makes his own "middle passage"—into the gray area between whiteness and blackness, Americans and Africans, enemies and friends, individual freedom and social concern. In the chaos of Calhoun's literal and figurative middle passage, all these opposites, this dualistic worldview, collapse. Calhoun accrues to his American identity and experience his African cultural origins, his African brothers and sisters, and all humanity. This is seen in his adoption of an Allmuseri orphan child, Baleka. When the ship's travails reduce everyone to illness except Calhoun, he finds that he both cares for and wants to serve the others. He begins to think anew of Isadora Bailey's love and his brother's rejection of wealth. Finally, when Calhoun, Baleka, and Squibb are rescued from the sea by the same Isadora Bailey and Papa Zeringue from whom he fled, Calhoun's journey and the plot's structure come full circle.

So Calhoun rejects the linear, dualistic definition of life and human relations for a holistic one. With Isadora and Baleka, he sets out for rural Illinois, his beginning, not alone but in the company of a family. The novel's protagonist, who began as a lone male adventurer, finds his life's meaning in interdependence. The *Republic* has sunk. The reader wonders what might rise from its watery grave.

Critical Context

Although *Middle Passage* is only Charles Johnson's third published novel, it is a powerfully mature exploration of themes that Johnson has touched on in his previous works. Rutherford Calhoun's metaphysical odyssey from selfish individualism to unselfish concern for the welfare of others resembles the quests for self-revelation undertaken by the protagonists of Johnson's previous novels, *Faith and the Good Thing*

(1974) and *Oxherding Tale* (1982). *Middle Passage* is also an allegory that incorporates elements of the supernatural, mysticism, and folk wisdom through the inclusion of the Allmuseri, an African tribe introduced by Johnson in *Oxherding Tale* as well as in two short stories that appeared in *The Sorcerer's Apprentice* (1986).

By using the framing device of the ship's log to record the events of Calhoun's voyage of discovery, Johnson also draws upon the tradition of the slave narrative and the dramatic impact of its eyewitness revelations of brutality and betrayal. At another level, Johnson's philosophical fiction draws upon and wrestles with the rich literary past from which it springs—such literary predecessors as Edgar Allan Poe's *The Narrative of Arthur Gordon Pym* (1838), Herman Melville's *Moby Dick* and "Benito Cereno" (1855), and John Gardner's novella *The King's Indian* (1974). Given the diverse elements it incorporates, it is not unusual that reviewers have found *Middle Passage* difficult to categorize. They have praised the power of the novel's language, the novel's inventive narration and many allusions, and the force of the imagination that drives the plot. Johnson's dedication to his craft was amply rewarded when *Middle Passage* received the National Book Award for fiction in 1990.

Bibliography
Davis, Charles T. Introduction to *The Slave's Narrative*. New York: Oxford University Press, 1985. Discusses the writings of slaves and freed slaves as literature and the influence of these narratives on African American fiction. Provides a useful context for Johnson's novel.
Gleason, William. "The Liberation of Perception: Charles Johnson's *Oxherding Tale*." *Black American Literature Forum* 25 (1991): 705-728. Analyzes Johnson's *Oxherding Tale* (1982) in the context of his theory that African American fiction should not take as its focus American racism and its impact but rather find a new vision, liberate its perception, and focus on moral and philosophical goals.
Harris, Norman. "The Black Universe in Contemporary Afro-American Fiction." *College Language Association Journal* 30 (1986): 1-13. Argues that Johnson's novels, like those of Ishmael Reed and Toni Morrison, move beyond the realism and naturalism of earlier African American fiction. Thus Johnson's protagonists live inside the race's mythic history rather than on the site of racial conflict.
Johnson, Charles. "Being and Fiction." In *Being and Race: Black Writing Since 1970*. Bloomington: Indiana University Press, 1988. Presents Johnson's theory of fiction, useful background material for reading *Middle Passage*. Johnson urges African American writers to build their fictions in ways that reach toward meaning beyond everyday experience.
_____. "Reflections on Fiction, Philosophy, and Film: An Interview with Charles Johnson." *Callaloo* 4 (October, 1978): 118-128. A provocative and wide-ranging discussion of the author's varied fields of interest.

Francine Dempsey

MINTY ALLEY

Author: C. L. R. James (1901-1989)
Type of work: Novel
Type of plot: Social realism
Time of plot: The late 1920's and early 1930's
Locale: A barrack yard in Trinidad
First published: 1936

> *Principal characters:*
>> HAYNES, the protagonist, a twenty-year-old educated middle-class black man
>> MRS. ROUSE, a devout Catholic landlady who also believes in "obeah"
>> BENOIT, the live-in partner of Mrs. Rouse for eighteen years; he plays the role of the highly sexed and irresistible lover of 2 Minty Alley
>> NURSE JACKSON, a thin and very light-skinned woman of mixed blood in her late thirties who works as a private nurse to the rich town people, from whom she steals
>> MAISIE, Mrs. Rouse's very pretty but rebellious seventeen-year-old niece
>> PHILOMEN, Mrs. Rouse's honest, energetic, and hard-working Indian servant

The Novel

Minty Alley is the story of Haynes, a young black educated middle-class man who observes and becomes involved in the daily life of the "ordinary people" of 2 Minty Alley, a barrack yard in Trinidad. Life in the yard is presented from the perspective of Haynes, who is himself transformed in the process of observing and participating in that life.

Beset by financial problems and wanting to escape his sheltered, "monotonous," and "empty" life, Haynes decides, after the death of his overprotective mother, to take up lodging among the working people at 2 Minty Alley. Encouraged by the affable landlady, Mrs. Rouse, he ignores his servant's advice about not living among those who are "not [his] class of people." Shortly thereafter, he begins to regret his decision, until a crack in a board in his room affords him the opportunity to play the voyeur and eavesdrop on the sexual activities of the inhabitants of the yard. Changing his mind, he decides to stay so he can witness the "terrific human drama" unfolding at 2 Minty Alley.

Haynes's observer status is quickly changed into one of participant as he becomes increasingly involved in the lives of the yard occupants. In fact, everyone begins to confide in him, and he is forced to use all of his skills and resources to keep the peace among them. Even though from time to time he announces that he will leave, something always comes up to prolong his stay. Consequently, he is drawn into every conflict.

His involvement begins when the son of Nurse Jackson runs into Haynes's room to escape his mother's brutal beating. Haynes intercedes on behalf of the child and fails. The precedent of going to seek his help has already been set. Subsequently, Haynes is drawn into a romantic sexual triangle involving Mrs. Rouse, Nurse Jackson, and Benoit. Mrs. Rouse asks Haynes to speak to Benoit, assuming that Benoit "will respect what you say" since "you are a gentlemen and you have education." Shortly thereafter, Benoit too confides in Haynes, placing him in an awkward position of having divided loyalties.

Haynes's involvement grows even deeper when Benoit deserts Mrs. Rouse and marries Nurse Jackson, effectively curtailing his assistance to Mrs. Rouse. These tasks are taken over by Haynes, who looks after her business so diligently that she comes to admit that he is "of far more help to her than Benoit had ever been in his life." By this time, he is already considered as "one of the family," "one of them," sharing in their "joys and troubles."

Haynes's involvement reaches its apex when he establishes an intimate relationship with Maisie, Mrs. Rouse's seventeen-year-old niece, who takes on the task of his social education. She removes his timidity toward women and his employer. He becomes more self-confident and self-assertive. Maisie herself has to acknowledge that "when you first come here you couldn't say boo to a goose." The relationship between these two, representing two different social classes, is not destined to last. Maisie, unable to tolerate Mrs. Rouse and unwilling to go along with the social expectations of her role, ultimately leaves on a ship bound for the United States. Thereafter, the end of Haynes's class experiment is in sight, since "he knew that without Maisie No. 2 was no place for him."

The end comes quickly, in a succession of events. Benoit dies, Mrs. Rouse makes arrangements to sell the house, and Haynes, having sent for Ella, his servant, retreats to his dull middle-class existence. Even 2 Minty Alley seems to lose its working-class character as it is occupied by a nuclear family, one of whose members can be seen "sitting at the piano playing a familiar tune from Henry's music book."

The Characters

Like most of the other characters in the novel, Haynes is presented as a type. He is a reflection of the educated black middle class, alienated from the masses but seeking to bridge the gap through involvement in their lives.

This involvement has the effect of transforming Haynes and allowing him to develop. He arrives at 2 Minty Alley shy, naïve, and a little timid. By the time he leaves, his experiences, particularly with Maisie, have turned him into an assertive and world-wise gentleman. Even though Haynes returns to his middle-class existence, the reader is left with the impression that life will never be quite the same for him. He has tasted the joys of friendship, and his sexuality has been awakened.

Haynes's credibility as a character is open to question. In the Trinidadian society of the 1930's it is a bit far-fetched to imagine him as a member of the middle class electing to live among and become involved in the lives of the people of a barrack yard. All the same, the author, himself a member of the black middle class at the time, claimed to have lived in a household similar to the one described in the novel.

However plausible Haynes's character may be, it is clear that he is used primarily as a device for looking at the lives of the "ordinary" people of the yard. It is from Haynes's limited perspective that the other characters and their activities are presented. Characters are seen only through his eyes; they have no independent existence outside what Haynes observes or is told. The author begins with the device of placing Haynes in Minty Alley as a voyeur, that is to say as an observer "peeping" in. He quickly abandons this and makes Haynes a participant, so that the members of the working class can be presented with greater accuracy.

It is to Haynes's, or rather the author's, credit that most of the members of the Minty Alley household, although types, are very human. They are living people. Mrs. Rouse, in her predicament involving Benoit and Nurse Jackson, is not difficult to imagine. The strong, enduring black woman is a very familiar figure. So too is the womanizing Benoit, who loses out in the end.

Maisie's credibility as a character is maintained by having her not become romantically involved with Haynes. Theirs is primarily a sexual relationship, one from which she walks away without so much as a backward glance. "Me, Mr. Haynes. You'll never forget me? You must not say such things." It appears that Philomen, Mrs. Rouse's Indian servant, is there for the purpose of raising racial questions. Her devotion, her loyalty, and her obsequiousness are a bit overdone.

Because the inhabitants of 2 Minty Alley are seen through the eyes of Haynes, himself belonging to a different class, they tend to appear one-dimensional. They undergo very little, if any, development throughout the novel. This is more a case of character revelation.

Themes and Meanings:

In an interview in 1972, C. L. R. James, in a reference to the setting of his novel, declared: "I went to live there, the people fascinated me, and I wrote about them from the point of view of an educated youthful member of the black middle class." There is no doubt that *Minty Alley* is meant to be a realistic assessment of the lives of the working masses from a sympathetic middle-class point of view. Haynes's descent into the barrack yard at Minty Alley parallels the author's own movement and becomes the means by which the joys and sorrows, the struggles, and the trials and tribulations of the masses are reported with honesty and dignity. There is a vitality and a sense of endurance to this life, with its "drab surroundings" and its harsh living conditions.

The novel, however, does much more than explore barrack-yard life from a middle-class perspective. James is much more interested in the relationship between the middle class and the masses, represented by the inhabitants of the yard. The author had always been critical of the Caribbean middle class and its impotence in the face of the working class. *Minty Alley* gives him the opportunity to bring the alienated and dull middle class into contact with the working people. It is an education process that must take place if the society is to be saved.

Haynes's stay at 2 Minty Alley results in extensive learning on his part. In the process, he becomes self-assured and is able to provide some leadership to the inhabitants. "He realized that whatever he said would carry weight with them, and with this realization came a sense of responsibility and increasing confidence." He advises them; they listen to his advice and respect and admire him for his contribution. He becomes "the master of the house," but this is a two-way street.

In return, Maisie helps him to find his own sexuality, helps him to explore his emotions, and teaches him how to deal with his boss so that he can make reasonable demands. James seems to imply that the two classes need each other and that each one has something to teach to and to learn from the other.

The act of having Haynes abandon his surroundings to go to live at Minty Alley is a device to bring the two classes together so that they can find out more about each other. It takes Haynes almost an entire year before he confronts the intolerable conditions in which Mrs. Rouse, the landlady, works to make a living. It is beyond him how "any mortal could stand that for so many hours every day for so many days."

James is mindful of the fact that Trinidad's working class is comprised of East Indians as well, and the harmonious relationship of the two races is critical to the development of the society. The presence of Philomen allows him to explore this theme. To this end, he explores the negative attitude some Trinidadians have toward Indians. When Mrs. Rouse listens to advice from the "obeah" man and parts company with Philomen, who has served her faithfully for nine years without any complaint, James means to criticize the manner in which people can allow a workable racial relationship to be subverted by superstition.

This is a novel about interdependency. The middle class needs the working class and vice versa; the Trinidadian needs the East Indian and vice versa. Alienation is detrimental to this society.

Critical Context

C. L. R. James, who has written volumes on areas as varied as history, political thought, sociology, cricket, literature, and philosophy, refers to *Minty Alley* as coming from a "prentice hand" in his masterpiece on cricket and other subjects, *Beyond a Boundary* (1963). For all this, *Minty Alley*, the only novel written by James and the first of the Caribbean novels written in English to be published in England, is pivotal to the development of the West Indian novel.

Although the novel was published in 1936, it was actually written nine years earlier, before the author had left Trinidad for England in 1932. The novel is a product of the emerging literary movement that the author, together with Alfred H. Mendes, another middle-class Trinidadian writer, intended to stimulate as a way of creating a nucleus for a genuine native literature.

James, in particular, had shown interest in the literary possibilities of barrack-yard life and had in fact written a short story, "Triumph," that dealt explicitly and for the first time with the urban life and experiences of a Trinidad barrack yard where ordinary people live. "Triumph" is similar to *Minty Alley* in plot; it is obvious that the short story forms the basis for this novel.

In its focus on the harsh surroundings of the yard, the social activities of the people, the violence, the use of "obeah," and the dialect of the inhabitants, *Minty Alley* signaled the birth of the Caribbean novel of social realism. In this respect, it foreshadowed the outpouring of talent in the literary movement of the 1950's.

If it was a stroke of boldness and rebelliousness to use the ordinary people of the yard as a fitting subject for his novel, it was even more daring to bring the middle class, in the person of Haynes, to live among the yard people and to involve him in their affairs to the point that they can claim him as "one of the family," "one of us." It must also have offended and shocked the defenders of middle-class propriety to have one of their educated members conduct a sexual relationship with the "lower-class" Maisie, who educates him.

In that sense, the novel had serious social and political implications, even though James, on rereading *Minty Alley* after its republication in 1971, claimed not to have been aware initially of the implications. "I saw," he says, "embedded in the novel a fundamental antagonism in West Indian society between the educated black and the mass of plebeians. . . . When I wrote it down fifty years ago I did not have one iota of feeling that I was posing a social or political situation." It may be somewhat difficult to accept this, coming from one of the twentieth century's most astute political theorists, one who has devoted many pages to analyzing the shortcomings of the Caribbean middle class in its dealing with the ordinary working people. Whatever its implications, *Minty Alley* is an important milestone in the historical development of Caribbean literature written in English.

Bibliography
Birbalsingh, Frank. "The Literary Achievement of C. L. R. James." In *Passion and Exile: Essays in Caribbean Literature*. London: Hansib Publishing, 1988. *Minty Alley* makes a significant contribution to the development of a literary tradition in the anglophone Caribbean. It is one of the first novels to examine important social, cultural, and political issues in the region.
Buhle, Paul. *C. L. R. James: The Artist as Revolutionary*. London: Verso, 1988. An intellectual biography, this study by James's editorial collaborator of long standing draws upon extensive interviews with critics and supporters and many previously unpublished documents. It is a penetrating portrait of the man and his times. Includes James's views on a variety of subjects, from Caribbean literature to pan-Africanism to Marxism to Third World politics. Emphasizes James's understanding and use of ideas.
Gilkes, Michael. "C. L. R. James (b. 1901): *Minty Alley* (1936)." In *The West Indian Novel*. Boston: Twayne, 1981. *Minty Alley* is intended to be a sympathetic exam-

ination of "yard" life of the "despised folk," seen from a middle-class perspective. It also explores the potential for cooperation, and the benefits thereof, between the middle class and the working masses.

Paris, D. Elliott. *"Minty Alley*: C. L. R. James, His Life and Work." *Urgent Tasks* 12 (Summer, 1981): 77-98. Holds the view that *Minty Alley* is a forerunner to the later Caribbean literary movement. Notes that James's sympathy is with the working people. This critique draws out the political implications behind the novel.

Sander, Reinhard W. "C. L. R. James." In *The Trinidad Awakening: West Indian Literature of the Nineteen-Thirties.* New York: Greenwood Press, 1988. *Minty Alley*'s primary achievement lies in its detailed presentation of the life of the working people and in its preoccupation with the coming together of the middle class and the working class.

Roosevelt J. Williams

MONTGOMERY'S CHILDREN

Author: Richard Perry (1944-   )
Type of work: Novel
Type of plot: Magical Realism
Time of plot: 1948-1980
Locale: Montgomery, New York
First published: 1984

> *Principal characters:*
> NORMAN FILLIS, a janitor, thirty-nine years old when the novel
>   begins
> GERALD FLETCHER, a boy enduring repeated beatings from his
>   father
> HOSEA MALONE, a drug dealer who pronounces his name Hose-ee
> JOSEPHINE MOORE, the victim of her father's sexual abuse and her
>   mother's complicit silence

The Novel

In 1948, about one hundred fifty black people live in Montgomery, a town located about two hours north of New York City. The first black people had begun arriving about thirty years earlier. Others had come during the Depression and World War II.

It is one of the oddities of the community that, as of 1948, no black person had ever died in Montgomery. That hint of immortality is but a part of what seems in many ways to be an idyllic existence. The novel picks up the story of Montgomery and its children just as the idyll is about to come to an end.

Construction has just begun on a racetrack about a mile and a half outside town. To make way for it, a forest in its first growth is leveled. Norman Fillis, a janitor who is thirty-nine years old at the time, sees the animals fleeing from the forest.

Soon after, the black community suffers its first death. In the thirty years that death has stayed away, the community has forgotten how to mourn. It must learn again the old lamentations and must reacquaint itself with sorrow.

People will have plenty of opportunity. Norman, for one, goes mad, although it is a madness that has its own kind of lucidity, even a kind of poetry. He communes with animals and birds and finds in trees a proof of the existence of God. One morning, Norman feels a strange weight on his head, but the weight lifts when he has his head shaved at the local barbershop. On this same day, Norman discovers that watching fire, whatever the source, lets him "see." It also fills his heart with peace and his mouth with the taste of pomegranates. There is no harm in peace and pomegranates, and there is no real harm in Norman, but when he begins to appear naked in public, it is inevitable that he will occasionally find himself in an institution.

Norman's madness carries with it a kind of power. His visions are basically true. He sees that troubles are coming, even if he can do nothing to prevent them, and he can fly. At first, he can fly only short distances, but his power increases with practice. He also can pass his power on, if he can find the one meant to receive it.

That one may well be Gerald Fletcher. To Norman, the circle in Gerald's eye, in fact a congenital mole, is a sign. Gerald becomes aware as he grows that he is in some strange way the focus of Norman's attention. In fact, Norman lets Gerald see him fly, but when Gerald finds that even his best friend, Iceman, will not believe that this really happened, Gerald lets himself be talked out of his own experience.

Other troubles visit Montgomery and its children. Hosea Malone deserts his wife Meredith and their seven children, the youngest of whom is blind and deformed. A desperate Meredith kills her youngest child. Norman, unobserved, witnesses her burial of the body. Hosea will learn of this twelve years later, when he returns in 1960 to Montgomery in the company of Alice Simineski, an enormously fat white woman with whom he is involved in dealing drugs. When Hosea confronts Meredith with his knowledge, she confides in the pastor, Melinda Mclain, who keeps the secret but who believes she now knows what brought death to Montgomery back in 1948. Twenty more years will pass before Meredith, now sixty-seven, will feel compelled to confess to the police. In the wake of this decision, one of Meredith and Hosea's grown daughters, meaning to kill her father, shoots and kills Alice by mistake.

Gerald's story is not limited to his significance to Norman. Repeatedly beaten by his father, Gerald falls in love with Josephine Moore, a newcomer to Montgomery. Josephine has been repeatedly raped by her father, while her mother, who must know what is going on, has remained silent. Gerald agrees to help Josephine kill her father, although he is never seriously committed to the plan. Josephine finally kills her father without Gerald's help and is sent to prison for her action.

Others of Montgomery's children also suffer afflictions. Twelve-year-old Jonah Washington drowns. Iceman, Gerald's friend and confidant, is electrocuted while trying to liberate a cat from a tree. A boy named Soapsuds is killed in Mississippi; Jesus Mclain, the son of the pastor, is shot down by the police in Cincinnati, Ohio.

As the story approaches its end in 1980, there are few survivors, and their situation is far from untroubled. Gerald, now living in New York City, is involved in a halfhearted effort to save a crumbling marriage. He and Josephine, who has turned up at his apartment, pay one more visit to Montgomery.

Josephine confronts her mother. It is little surprise that the encounter proves unsatisfactory; it is too late for these two to connect. Josephine does learn that the man she killed was not her biological father. She sets out for Georgia in search of her real father.

Gerald sees Norman once more. Since Gerald has had the mole removed (to him, it was never anything more than an annoying minor disfigurement), Norman no longer recognizes him as the one to whom he should pass on his power. Whatever wisdom or madness Norman might have passed on dies with him as his last flight ends in a fatal crash on the courthouse steps. Nobody noticed Norman flying, and the general understanding is that he has committed suicide.

The Characters

Montgomery's Children is a densely populated novel. Its episodic structure, covering an extended period of time, permits a number of its characters to act in effect as temporary protagonists. Moreover, the characters interact with one another, moving within one another's stories in complex and unpredictable ways. Of the many characters who populate the novel, there are four who seem to assume central importance in determining its structure. These are Norman Fillis, Hosea Malone, Gerald Fletcher, and Josephine Moore.

In the eyes of the world, Norman Fillis is simply crazy, but the world does not see as Norman sees. He enjoys an intimacy with nature that is lost to the community when the forest is destroyed to make way for the racetrack. He has witnessed both of the actions that may have inaugurated Montgomery's reign of suffering: the flight of the animals and the burial of Meredith and Hosea's seventh child. He is a man of vision and power. He can fly, he can teach others how to fly, and he envisions a day when all black people will fly. He has a message to pass on to the right one. In the eyes of the world, he is crazy.

Hosea is not crazy. Hosea has seen into the heart of things and has determined that there is nothing there. Since there is no God, since life is meaningless, there are no standards. Hosea's power is negative. He withholds himself. He abandons Meredith and their children, and he will not give Alice the love she craves. He deals drugs out of moral and emotional indifference. Once he learns that going without a hat cures the headaches that bother him for a while, he escapes pain. Those near him, those who permit themselves to feel his influence, such as Meredith and Alice, are not so lucky.

Gerald and Josephine are linked to each other by their age, by their love for each other, and by their victimization at the hands of brutal fathers. Their ultimate estrangement arises out of their differences. Josephine dares and acts, however destructive her actions turn out to be. Gerald holds back. He entertains the possibility of killing Josephine's father, but he is never committed to the act. He is at one moment on the verge of flight, but he cannot commit himself to that action, either. In the face of his friend's skepticism, he allows himself even to deny the experience itself and, thus, the sense of possibility the experience symbolizes. Growing up for him entails a gradual loss of direction. When he finally asks Norman to give him the message, it is too late.

Themes and Meanings

"According to those given to such inquiry a vast range of experience lies just beyond ordinary vision." This sentence appears on the last page of *Montgomery's Children*, and it might be suggested that "just beyond ordinary vision" is where the novel takes place. Up to a point, the novel reflects ordinary vision. It offers what could be regarded as a realistic, if impressionistic, account of the fortunes and misfortunes of a black community in upstate New York but goes beyond that point. Rather than remaining within the bounds of realism, Richard Perry matter-of-factly blends elements of realism and fantasy. The presence of the fantastic in no way cancels out, or even diminishes, the real, but it may invite readers to expand notions of "reality." This kind of blurring of the distinction between the real and the fantastic is one of the touchstones of Magical Realism.

The title of the novel focuses attention on children, and there are, to be sure, a number of children in the novel. "Children" is a word that easily lends itself to metaphorical extension, as in the familiar assertion that people are all God's children. At any rate, relationships between parents and children, broadly rather than narrowly understood, play a crucial role in the novel.

The linked stories of Gerald and Josephine repeat the theme of a distortion in the parent-child relationship. The weight of responsibility in both cases falls on a brutal father, but in both cases the mother is complicit, at least to the extent of having failed to restrain the father's brutality and having lived in the knowledge of it. Gerald makes repeated efforts to establish a loving relationship with his father (who has repudiated his own father, Gerald's grandfather), but the efforts are fruitless. Josephine has killed the supposed father who violated her, and, when she exits the novel, is still searching for her real father.

Hosea has abandoned his children, and a desperate Meredith has killed their seventh child. That he was a seventh child may associate him with magic, since the number seven carries suggestions of power in folklore. His deformity, a watermelon head, may also be significant. It is a deformity, a congenital wart, that marks Gerald as the one to receive Norman's message, and the normalization of Gerald's appearance breaks the connection. Further, the watermelon head seems associated with Hosea's headaches, which disappear when he stops wearing a hat, and with the strange weight on his head that Norman feels at the beginning of his madness.

Parenting here is clearly not merely a biological function. It turns out that the man who has violated Josephine is not her biological father. Parenting involves caring. It also involves acting as a bearer of tradition. A role of the parent is to pass on to the children the traditions and values of the community. From this point of view, *Montgomery's Children* abounds in examples of failed parenting. A look at the two events that, it is suggested, may have brought about the destruction of the idyllic existence Montgomery had known reveals that one of these—Meredith's killing of her child— represents the ultimate violation of a parent's responsibility. The other imputed cause is the building of the racetrack and the destruction of the forest to make way for it. What is violated here is not the relation between generations but the relation of the community to nature. The two themes are related, though, if one accepts that a reverence toward nature, as in the religions of Africa, is part of the tradition parents are obliged to pass on to their children.

The loss of a sense of tradition is humorously depicted in a conversation that takes place in the local barbershop, on the day Norman has his head shaved to remove the weight from his head. With the exception of the professor, the barbershop's black patrons seem to find it hard to get past the notion that Africans do little beyond swinging from trees. That Africans have built empires is too far beyond their ordinary vision for these children of Montgomery to absorb.

The themes that interact in the novel come together in the person of Norman Fillis, who has left ordinary vision behind. Norman may be without honor in Montgomery, but he is the tradition bearer. He carries the power of the spiritual parent. As the children of Montgomery have cut themselves off from the sources of spiritual energy, Norman represents a hope of redemption. The vital links with the past and with nature are still present in him. His promise of a day when black people will fly again is a powerful image of liberation. To make the connection, though, others must be prepared to move beyond ordinary vision, and even Gerald, the one best hope, grows away from the power to take that step. Norman's death, misinterpreted as suicide, marks the ultimate breaking of the chain. Montgomery's children will have to find whatever redemption they can through labor and pain.

Montgomery's Children, though hardly a protest novel, is not indifferent to the social and political history of African Americans between 1948 and 1980. There are references to the opening of a chapter of the National Association for the Advancement of Colored People in Montgomery, to the appearance of African Americans on the police force, and to integration of the school board. The primary focus of the novel remains on the black community itself.

Critical Context

The term Magical Realism gained currency in American criticism in the context of the rise of North American critical interest in Latin American fiction, but it has been pointed out that the essential elements of Magical Realism existed in African American and African culture long before American critics had a name for it. The easy relationship of realism and fantasy associated with the term is common in the black oral tradition, and a significant part of Perry's accomplishment in *Montgomery's Children* involves his suggesting in print some of the force of the storytelling tradition.

It is a quality of this kind of narrative that readers are encouraged to a more liberal notion of causality than associated with literary realism. Thus, it is here possible that the felling of a forest in Montgomery, New York, becomes part of a causal chain that leads to, say, the killing of a young black man in Cincinnati, Ohio. Readers may simply accept this without question, allowing the narrative the right to establish its own rules. They also may find in the departure from the literal an invitation to readings that emphasize the metaphorical and symbolic, thus perhaps seeing the felling of the forest as marking a rupture between the community and the natural environment, a rupture that must ultimately produce destructive consequences. A further possibility, since realism remains a component of Magical Realism, is to consider magical patterns of causality as one possible explanation while looking simultaneously for commonsense possibilities. Are the many failures in human relationships, especially in variations on the parent-child relationship, caused by phenomena such as the felling of the forest and the flight of the animals, or are these failures themselves the cause of the fragmentation of the community? It is in the nature of a novel such as *Montgomery's Children*, when it succeeds, to invite the reader to entertain such a multiplicity of possibilities. Brought to this state, the reader is then ready to interrogate received notions of reality, part of what Magical Realism is all about.

Montgomery's Children does succeed as a work of literary art, and it received enthusiastic reviews when it was published. Ironically, the review that could have contributed most powerfully to the book's commercial success, the very favorable notice that appeared in the influential *The New York Times Book Review*, appeared too long after the publication date to have much effect, and the book turned up quickly on sale shelves in bookstores. This false start has to some extent limited the recognition *Montgomery's Children* has received. A paperback edition that appeared in 1985 was allowed to go out of print in 1992, but this is the sort of book that delighted readers have a way of finding for themselves. It is likely to gain a permanent place in African American literature.

Bibliography
Bailliett, Whitney. "Upstate." *The New Yorker* 59 (February 6, 1984): 124-125. The novel is concerned with evil and redemption and the ways in which black people weigh upon each other more than with how the white world weighs on the black.
Davis, Thulani. "Books." *Essence* 14 (February, 1984). The town of Montgomery is itself a complex character, speaking in several voices. Perry can be compared to Toni Morrison and Ishmael Reed and, for mastery of Magical Realism, to Gabriel García Márquez.
Kissell, John. "*Montgomery's Children.*" *Los Angeles Times Book Review*, February 19, 1984, 7. The central theme is Gerald's love for his father. Surrounding Gerald is an impressionistic history of African Americans since World War II.
Tate, Greg. "*Montgomery's Children.*" *The Village Voice* 29 (April 17, 1984): 44. The novel is a morality tale about urban black America's fall from the garden of racial quarantine into the dystopia of desegregation. Perry shares Toni Morrison's gifts for psychological as well as pathological insights.
Watkins, Mel. "*Montgomery's Children.*" *The New York Times Book Review* 89 (August 5, 1984): 18-19. The novel, in which comic and surreal are balanced, is about the evils of modernism and the redemptive powers of the spirit.

W. P. Kenney

MOSES, MAN OF THE MOUNTAIN

Author: Zora Neale Hurston (1891-1960)
Type of work: Novel
Type of plot: Allegory
Time of plot: Biblical times
Locale: Egypt
First published: 1939

Principal characters:
MOSES, the protagonist and title character
AARON, an alleged brother of Moses who is pompous and self-important
MIRIAM, an alleged sister of Moses who fell asleep while charged with watching the baby Moses
THE PHARAOH, the ruler of Egypt at the time of Moses' birth
TA-PHAR, a ruler of Egypt and enforcer of Hebrew slavery after his father's death
JETHRO, Moses' father-in-law, a wise priest of Midian who practices monotheism and teaches Moses advanced magic
ZIPPORAH, Moses' second wife and Jethro's daughter
AMRAM, Moses' alleged father, a Hebrew slave
JOCHEBED, Moses' alleged mother, also a Hebrew slave
MENTU, an elderly palace servant who instructs the young Moses in magic spells
JOSHUA, a brave Hebrew who is only a child when he first meets Moses

The Novel

Set in Egypt during the time of the Hebrew captivity, *Moses, Man of the Mountain* opens before Moses' birth. The pharaoh had decreed that all male Hebrew newborns would be put to death. When Jochebed gives birth to a third child, a boy, the family hides him for three months from the secret police. After several experiences when the baby is almost discovered, the parents put him in a basket and set him adrift on the Nile.

Miriam, Jochebed's daughter, is supposed to watch the basket and report the baby's fate to her parents. She falls asleep, and when she awakens, the basket is gone. Before she can comprehend this event, her attention is distracted by the sight of the Egyptian princess and her ladies in waiting. Miriam forgets all about her brother and rushes home to tell her mother about seeing the princess. When she arrives, her mother's frantic questioning reminds her of her original mission. She makes up a story in which the princess rescues the baby and takes him home with her to the palace. Thus, a legend was born.

Both Miriam and Jochebed go to the palace on separate occasions, asking to help care for the baby. They are told that the princess had brought her own son home from Assyria and that their help is not needed. Still, the legend persisted.

At the palace, Moses grows into an intelligent boy, filled with curiosity. He makes friends with Mentu, the elderly stablehand, and learns much about the mysterious ways of animals. Mentu first tells Moses about the deathless snake that guards the book of Thoth, located at the bottom of the river at Koptos. This book holds all the secrets of heaven and earth. Moses also learns many secrets from the palace priests.

When the biannual military contests are held, Moses defeats Ta-Phar, engendering a rivalry that lasts until Ta-Phar's death. As a leader, Moses argues for more rights and better treatment for the Hebrew slaves, but he is opposed by the majority at court, including Ta-Phar. Rumors then start that Moses is a Hebrew.

Moses leaves Egypt when he is twenty-five years old. In Midian, he meets Jethro and his daughter Zipporah. He falls in love with her, and they marry. He learns many secrets from the wise Jethro during the twenty years he lives in Midian. He also visits Koptos and defeats the deathless snake that guards the book; he reads all of it.

Jethro tries to persuade Moses to go into Egypt, convert the Hebrews to monotheism, and lead them out of slavery. At first Moses refuses, but then God speaks to him from a burning bush and tells him to do so. Aaron, who will speak for Moses, brings Miriam to meet Moses and help convince the slaves. Soon Aaron and Moses visit Ta-Phar, the new pharaoh. On a regular basis, Moses performs miracles. He turns water into blood and sends plagues of frogs, lice, flies, boils, hail, locusts, and three days of darkness. Finally, every first-born male in Egypt, excluding Hebrews, is killed. The pharaoh agrees to let the Hebrews go but changes his mind and pursues them with his army. The Hebrews escape because the Red Sea parts for them, but the Egyptians are all drowned.

Moses performs miracles for the Hebrews, sweetening bitter water, providing manna and quail, and causing water to gush forth from a cliff. The Israelites defeat the Amalekites because Moses intervenes.

When the Hebrews approach Midian, Jethro and Zipporah and their servants ride to meet Moses. Miriam's jealousy toward Zipporah causes her to agitate among the Hebrew women against Moses' wife. Moses punishes her by briefly afflicting her with leprosy. She is never the same.

Moses goes up the mountain and stays for forty nights, returning with God's laws. He finds the Hebrews worshiping a golden calf. Those who believe in Moses' God are charged to kill those who do not, and the unbelievers are slaughtered.

Hoping that the Hebrews are ready for the promised land, Moses sends a party into Canaan; they report that all good things grow there. The Hebrews, however, are afraid to fight for their promised land, so Moses realizes that they must stay in the wilderness until the original generation has died. Eventually Miriam and Jethro die.

Moses invites Aaron and his son Eleazar to accompany him to the mountain to hear God's voice. Because Aaron has not accepted that his role is over, Moses kills him, giving the robes of the high priest to Eleazar. Moses chooses Joshua as his successor and returns to the mountain, deliberately faking his death. He disappears down the other side of the mountain.

The Characters

The characters in *Moses, Man of the Mountain* are portrayed through their speech and actions rather than through more indirect methods such as use of symbols. The well-rounded character of Moses dominates the novel. He displays various character traits that are for the most part admirable. He is curious, intelligent, patient, forceful, and clever. He is not portrayed, however, as a perfect man. He demonstrates anger, disappointment, exasperation, and the instinct of a gambler. It is interesting to observe that as he loses his identification with the royal family of Egypt, his speech patterns change. He begins to use the dialect of the slaves, and as the novel progresses, he seems to have completely assimilated the Israelites' speech patterns. Moses, a man of vision, hopes to turn the Israelites into a freedom-loving people. He wants nothing for himself. When they offer him a crown, he rejects it and is disappointed that it was offered. Moses believes that a truly freedom-loving people would not be eager for a king to rule them.

Miriam and her brother Aaron appear to have few redeeming qualities. Miriam, who has been renowned as a prophetess among the Hebrews before the exodus, chafes under the direction of Moses. She thinks that she is an important person and that she does not receive the power and recognition that are her due. Only after Moses smites her with leprosy does she stop her constant complaining and agitating.

Aaron, less intelligent but as ambitious as his sister, fares even worse than she in the novel. Aaron mistakenly thinks that he too has been called by God and does not understand why he cannot be the leader of the Hebrews. The fact that he has no leadership qualities does not appear to enter his mind. For more than forty years, he engages in conflict with Moses, attempting to make trouble and undermine Moses' great plans for the Hebrews. Aaron has no vision of what the future of his people could be. He is interested only in power, glory, fine clothes, servants, and adulation. He is a man who would be king if he were asked; of course, no one asks him. Even at the end, when Moses reminds him that the original slave generation may not enter the promised land of Canaan, Aaron sees himself as an exception. Moses is forced to kill him to prevent him from disobeying God's order.

Ta-Phar and Moses engage in a struggle of wills after Moses returns from Midian. Each time Moses brings a plague upon the Egyptians, Ta-Phar desperately commands his priests to equal or better Moses' power. Moses himself is reluctant to force Ta-Phar to let the Hebrews go immediately because part of him enjoys the rivalry. Moses knows the outcome of their struggle from the beginning, but he wants to prove decisively to Ta-Phar the extent of his power.

Joshua, an eager follower who finally becomes a leader, is portrayed as the only one who deserves the honor Moses bestows upon him. At first known for his skill as a fighter more than for his leadership abilities, he grows into leadership over time.

Themes and Meanings

Moses, Man of the Mountain is foremost an allegory. Hurston retells the biblical story of Moses and the Israelites without changing any of the important elements of this well-known episode. At the same time, her novel is the story of African Americans in white America. Although the author does not declare that the Hebrews stand for African Americans or that the Egyptians stand for white Americans, the way in which African American folklore and folkways permeate the novel leaves no doubt about its allegorical structure. The Hebrews speak in African American dialect, while Moses, at least in the beginning, speaks in the voice of a white American liberal.

The themes of power and the use of political power dominate the novel. For example, both Ta-Phar and his father use power to keep the Hebrews in slavery. The possible loss of political power drives Ta-Phar to continue the Hebrews' bondage and to lead his army in pursuit of them even after he has agreed to let them go.

Moses' power to perform miracles originates in his own personality, in his use of magic, and in God. Born with leadership qualities, he is able, as all good leaders are, to learn whatever will be of use to him. Mentu, Jethro, the palace priests, and the book of Thoth at Koptos provide him with knowledge that he uses to demonstrate his powers. The line between the power God gives him and the power he gains through studying magic is somewhat blurred in the novel.

Once the Hebrews leave Egypt, the ongoing power struggle between Aaron and Miriam against Moses intensifies. Allegorically, Aaron and Miriam stand for the African American upper class, which lacks vision but wants the rewards of freedom. Aaron and Miriam appear to want power in order to distance themselves from the ordinary people.

Another theme, that of the individual against society, also appears. Moses is in conflict first against the Egyptians and then against the Hebrews. Hated and feared by the Egyptians after his return from twenty years of self-imposed exile, he finally overcomes them. His conflict with the Hebrews centers on his vision of freedom and the Hebrews' inability to share his vision completely.

The question of identity appears as a minor theme. Moses is never certain about the circumstances of his birth. Hebrew legend insists that he is the son of Amram and Jochebed. He grew up believing that he was the son of an Egyptian princess and her Assyrian husband. When Moses is a mature man and the woman he knew as his mother has died, he sees that her grave is honored. He tells Jethro that regardless of whether she was his natural mother, she was good to him. Although the question of his identity is never answered definitively, it appears that Hurston has cast him as a mulatto, half Egyptian and half Assyrian.

Humor plays an important role in *Moses, Man of the Mountain*. Never dominating, but nearly always present, the humor derives from the folklore and folkways that Hurston skillfully interweaves within the biblical account.

Critical Context

Moses, Man of the Mountain is Hurston's fifth full-length work, following the novels *Jonah's Gourd Vine* (1934) and *Their Eyes Were Watching God* (1937) and the folklore collections *Mules and Men* (1935) and *Tell My Horse* (1938). At the time Hurston was writing these works, the prevailing attitude among African American authors was that only the protest novel was acceptable as a vehicle for their thoughts. Hurston did not write novels that fit such categorization, and in consequence she lost favor among influential writers and critics of the Harlem Renaissance.

Moses, Man of the Mountain has, however, been read as a veiled protest novel. Because of the close identification of African American slaves with the captive Israelites in spirituals such as "Go Down, Moses," the parallels are easy to draw. Perhaps, as has been suggested by several critics, any novel dealing with Moses' story could be seen as a protest novel, simply for the reason stated above. Hurston does not portray the captive people to be without flaws; their occasional pettiness and lack of understanding prevent them from receiving unqualified pity. The humor in the novel prevents it from becoming a serious sociological study of an oppressed race. That the novel does not fit into a prescribed form has caused it to receive both positive and negative critical readings.

The contemporary reviews of *Moses, Man of the Mountain* were mixed. Since then, many critics have commented on what an ambitious work it is, but most have found it to be flawed.

Hurston published her autobiography, *Dust Tracks on a Road*, in 1942, and the novel *Seraph on the Suwanee* in 1948. Amid personal difficulties, her career as a writer ended, although she lived for twelve more years. Her books out of print and her reputation forgotten, Hurston died in a county welfare home and was buried in an unmarked grave.

In the 1970's, African American novelist Alice Walker rediscovered Hurston's work. Walker located her grave, purchased a marker for it, and led the revival of interest in her life and works. Her books have been republished, critical acclaim has grown, and Zora Neale Hurston has finally been accorded a well-deserved place in African American literature.

Bibliography

Baker, Houston A., Jr. *Workings of the Spirit: The Poetics of Afro-American Women's Writing.* Chicago: University of Chicago Press, 1991. Baker situates *Moses, Man of the Mountain* as a conjure book, emphasizing Hurston's familiarity with hoodoo through her work as an anthropologist. He characterizes Moses as a practitioner of hoodoo, that is, a conjurer, and he attributes most of Moses' miracles to magic rather than Judaism.

Carby, Hazel V. *Reconstructing Womanhood: The Emergence of the Afro-American Woman Novelist.* New York: Oxford University Press, 1987. Carby discusses Hurston's choice to write of African American rural folk rather than of urban city dwellers. She concludes that Hurston's choice did not fit well into the mainstream of the Harlem Renaissance and that the choice probably damaged her career.

Gates, Henry Louis, Jr. *The Signifying Monkey: A Theory of African-American Lit-*

erary Criticism. New York: Oxford University Press, 1988. Gates designates Hurston as using rhetorical strategies to structure her works. Although concentrating on *Their Eyes Were Watching God*, Gates's ideas also illuminate *Moses, Man of the Mountain.*

Hemenway, Robert E. *Zora Neale Hurston: A Literary Biography.* Urbana: University of Illinois Press, 1977. Known as the standard biography of Hurston, this book includes critical commentary on all of her writings. He makes the point that Hurston tried out the idea of *Moses, Man of the Mountain* in a short story called "The Cloud and the Fire," published in *Challenge* in September, 1934. He draws parallels between African Americans during slave times and the Hebrews in captivity that demonstrate the book's allegorical nature.

Howard, Lillie P. *Zora Neale Hurston.* Boston: Twayne, 1980. Howard discusses the events of Hurston's life, along with providing critical analysis of each of her works. Examines Hurston's critical reception and her participation in the Harlem Renaissance. Identifies the changes Hurston makes in the biblical story of Moses, concentrating on Moses' powers. Howard concludes that Hurston gives Moses supernatural skills learned from worldly sources rather than from God.

Jackson, Blyden. Introduction to *Moses, Man of the Mountain*, by Zora Neale Hurston. Urbana: University of Illinois Press, 1984. Jackson provides a brief biographical sketch and critical commentary. He asserts that the novel, although clearly allegorical, is also an investigation of power. On that basis, he compares it to Niccolò Machiavelli's *The Prince* (1532).

Cheri Louise Ross

THE MOTION OF LIGHT IN WATER
Sex and Science-Fiction Writing in the East Village, 1957-1965

Author: Samuel R. Delany (1942-   )
Type of work: Autobiography
Time of work: 1957-1965
Locale: New York City
First published: 1988

Principal personages:

SAMUEL DELANY, a black bisexual science-fiction writer
MARILYN HACKER, Delany's wife, a major American poet
SAMUEL R. DELANY, SR., Delany's father, a major Harlem
    businessman and owner of a mortuary
MARGARET CAREY BOYD DELANY, Delany's mother, a funeral
    director and library clerk
HILDA HACKER, Delany's Jewish mother-in-law
W. H. AUDEN, a major British and American twentieth century
    poet, a dinner guest of Delany and Marilyn Hacker
CHESTER KALLMAN, a writer, W. H. Auden's lover
SONNY, a large ex-convict who is, for a time, Delany's lover

Form and Content

In the introduction to *The Motion of Light in Water,* titled "Sentences," Samuel Delany gives some sense of how the autobiography grew and developed. He writes how his thinking about two major events in his life precipitated writing about what can only be called a fragment of his adolescent and young adult years growing up in New York City and his emergence as a major writer of science fiction. His father died of lung cancer in 1958, when Delany was seventeen. As he thinks about the other events in his life during this time, he keeps reaching a certain impasse. Was he really seventeen? And was it really 1958? Although he later acquires enough information to know that his father died in 1960, when the young Delany was in fact eighteen, he understands that knowledge of both the impression he had of those events and the truth of those events is important to any writing about his life that he might do. Essentially he is concerned with truth, the perception of one's reality, and the ordering that is required to know either. Whether his father died in 1958 or 1960, and whether Delany was seventeen or eighteen at the time, his father died when Delany was on the verge of adulthood and change. It is a series of major changes that marks one line of the autobiography's development.

Delany's autobiographical fragment is an oddity in African American autobiographical writing for a number of reasons. On the surface, Delany only accounts for a short time period, basically the time that corresponds with his emergence as a serious writer of science fiction, with all the details of his life at the time that help to account for this. His autobiography is a record of his early literary life.

Delany's background and class also make his autobiography unique. He does not record a significant amount of racial discrimination or other typical hardships that African Americans faced during the 1950's and 1960's. Instead, as a member of a socially elite black family with a relatively long history of being a part of the middle and upper classes of the black community, Delany has a life-style of privilege and of opportunities usually not available to African Americans. Most of his immediate and extended family members were professionals, owners of property, and recipients of degrees and advanced degrees from prestigious universities. Many of Delany's family members were proud of being examples of what African Americans could achieve if given the opportunity. Delany and his cousins, for example, were members of the Jack and Jill of America, a black social club for middle-class children. Their parents took the extra effort to include programs to give their children even more mainstream educational and cultural opportunities.

It is against this background of opportunity that Delany positions his own growth and development. He attended the Dalton School, a private and progressive elementary school. At Dalton, he was encouraged to engage in all sorts of challenging academic and literary pursuits, such as writing poetry, reading in Latin and Greek, reading all of the American and British literary classics, and planning advanced science projects. His parents even had him attend summer camps where these same sorts of challenging opportunities were available. Delany makes it clear, then, that even if he were not a genius, the opportunities his parents gave him would make anyone think he was.

When he attends public high school, it is the experimental Bronx High School of Science. Students from all of New York City's boroughs competed to be admitted; that is, even when he attends public school, he is among the best and brightest. In the integrated Bronx High School, he begins two major explorations: intellectual and sexual. He is gifted in math and science, along with having the skills of a genius in language and writing. He befriends a number of individuals at his level. He also begins to experiment more overtly with his sexually divided nature. He has a number of "crushes" while in high school, on both boys and girls. In high school, he meets Marilyn Hacker, a girl who is a grade ahead of him but is his age. They begin in high school what becomes a lifetime friendship. Like Delany, she is intellectually precocious.

Delany is a bit more detailed about recording his high school years than he is about his college ones, partly because he does not complete college and partly because he learns that for what he wants to do, a traditional college degree is not required. While in high school, he had already written several novels, though none was good enough to be published. At City College of New York, Delany begins to drift from the academic pursuits that had defined his earlier years and sense of self and begins to explore more earnestly the literary and artistic ones. Marilyn Hacker is a key person in his more serious attention to writing, for she also wants to be a writer. The two talented teens spend most of their time talking about literature and writing.

The time they spend together takes on a new note when the two explore sexual expression with each other. Delany tells Marilyn of his homosexual side, and she apparently does not care. Sexual experimentation soon leads to Hacker's pregnancy. Delany and Hacker decide to get married. Because he is black and she is white, the two must travel to Michigan to be married. This is one of the few times when racism has a major impact on Delany's life. The marriage takes place in August of 1961. Delany marries Hacker more out of honor than because of romantic love. He loves her as a friend, but the passion both need to sustain a marriage is shown from the beginning of the marriage as being largely absent. Nevertheless, for several years the two keep their marriage going, even though for Delany it means that his sexual escapades with men become more frequent and increasingly more detrimental to the marriage. They do not get a divorce until 1975.

During the early years of their marriage, Delany and Hacker create some of their first important literary work. They create even as they struggle to make ends meet on part-time or low-paying jobs and as the tension in their marriage mounts. They live in a tenement, with its share of roaches and rats, on the Lower East Side. Hacker's mother disapproves of the marriage and where they live, and she does her best to exacerbate the young couple's problems. Delany has problems adjusting to Hacker's learning and living style. For example, after he acquires a job at a Barnes and Noble bookstore and works all day, he expects Hacker to have cleaned the apartment or at least to have changed her position since the morning, when he left her reading a book. These small disagreements and misunderstandings put a terrible strain on a relationship in which passion is already problematic.

Delany's problems with Hacker mean that he enjoys being away from home. Delany takes great effort to portray the underbelly of New York City's gay culture during this time. At first, he is a novice at locating the haunts of gay men, but before too long he knows most of the major subway restrooms that cater to gay activity, the truck stops at the end of Christopher Street, and the bars in the Village with gay clientele. He also learns the risks these men from many walks of life take, including police raids, police harassment, and blackmail. In detailing not only the substratum of New York City gay culture but also his own developing sexual quirks and fetishes (he prefers men who bite their nails and who are of the working or lower classes, and he prefers oral sex to any other), Delany creates a realistic and wonderful sense of what it was like to be black, a genius, and gay during this time. His gay experiences are as crucial as anything else in giving him subject matter and perspective to create science fiction works that largely go against traditional notions of what is right or wrong and how people should behave.

Delany tells his story primarily by taking one year at a time, highlighting major events and often juxtaposing them with events that happened later or earlier in his life. He had his first science fiction book, *The Jewels of Aptor*, published in 1962. He writes about what it meant to be able to sell fiction, relating this event to his later development as a writer, noting how his writing and he have changed.

By focusing on the years from 1957 to 1965, Delany in effect writes of his whole life. For example, his attending the Bread Loaf Writer's Conference in Vermont in 1960 and having Robert Frost give him advice had a major impact on his decision to create science fiction in his own way.

Analysis

The Motion of Light in Water is an exploration of how one talented black man used the resources of his particular privileged experience of growing up to become a successful writer of science fiction, a literary genre that has few black voices. Beyond this, the work shows the process through which Delany becomes the sort of man that he is, displaying not only his talent as a writer but the internal markings that distinguish him as an individual. Moving through the shadows of memory, Delany constructs a text that is his life.

Throughout the work, Delany shows his doubts that he will succeed at writing. For example, when W. H. Auden and Chester Kallman have dinner with Delany and Hacker, Delany understands the judgment the men give him when he tells them that he wants to write science fiction. Science fiction was not then considered to be an expression of "high literature," and yet Delany brings to the writing of science fiction a broad-based knowledge of all the great Western literary discourses. In his novels, he attempts to do what had not previously been done in the genre, to make it more than an expression of popular literature. His novels are richly textured with literary and historical allusions that reveal his vast knowledge.

Furthermore, Delany charts the doubts that creep into his goal of writing because he is a black man. It is true that he is a black man who has had most of the advantages of any white middle-class man or woman, but he knows that major publishers will not always be receptive to the idea of a black man writing science fiction, as publishers are always aware of their market. Although Delany brings these doubts and potential obstacles to the forefront of his narrative, he is rarely defeated by them. In fact, any defeats or real setbacks that he promotes in the narrative have far more to do with his own idiosyncrasies. For example, he wonders about his taste in men and what this may do to his future life. He often discusses his interest in men who bite their nails, and he ponders what that says about him. Is there, for instance, some lapse somewhere in his development? Is he peculiar?

Although his writing and his bisexuality take up a great deal of narrative space, so do the other topics and events of his life that have helped to shape him. He tells about a number of family and social events that detail the rich and varied life-style of the black middle class. People of that class have their beaches and resorts, their parties, and their dances. Even as he presents these "society" functions of the black middle class, he reminds the reader how important in his family was the desire to succeed. His family and its class are not so blinded by privilege that they are unaware of what the masses of African Americans face. Social or racial responsibility is an important subtext in the narrative.

Delany conveys the topics and issues that shaped his life from the perspective of a seasoned insider. His voice is one that seems wise beyond his years, even when he records events that happened when he was younger. That is, although his life is presented from the adult perspective, the narrative records an insightful young man. A part of this meshing of the adult and younger voices occurs through Delany's initial discussion that he thinks the perception of what happened in his life and the actual facts of his life are equally important to who he is. From the beginning of his narrative, he creates an atmosphere of trust in the reader by being willing to doubt that which he had believed. Did his father die when he was seventeen or eighteen? Was it in 1958 or 1960? Even in doubt, Delany's voice is authoritative.

His narrative authority is again emphasized when he talks about topics and issues that a less honest writer might avoid. Some of this honesty is revealed in his description of a number of sexual escapades that are not always flattering and certainly are. not romantic. He writes how he was sexually promiscuous, how he acquired gonorrhea, and how he often did not even see the faces of men he was involved with sexually. He tells of numerous affairs with white men—most of his gay lovers were white. Few African American male writers have been so bold and forthright.

Critical Context

Most responses to *The Motion of Light in Water* have emphasized its daring and bold treatment of subject matter usually not a part of mainstream discussions of African American literature. The book fills empty literary space. James Baldwin explored in fiction, in such works as *Another Country* (1962), what Delany does in autobiography and in his science-fiction novels. It would be remiss to think of *The Motion of Light in Water* only as a work that explores black gay experience. The work is equally important for its rendering of black middle-class life-styles and certainly joins a tradition that gained momentum in the 1920's and 1930's, that of the black middle-class fictional explorations of Jessie Fauset, Nella Larsen, and Wallace Thurman. Black middle-class representations also figure prominently in the works of Toni Morrison, Terry McMillan, Gloria Naylor, John Wideman, and August Wilson.

Perhaps the most prominent African American literary tradition to which this book belongs is that of black autobiographical writing, a tradition that extends back to thousands of slave narratives and forward to such writers as Maya Angelou and Audre Lorde. Black autobiographical writing is often the only genre that allows a black writer to explore the subject matter, themes, and style of his or her choice. *The Motion of Light in Water* takes part in that tradition even as it extends it to include subject matter that largely has been ignored. Delany is black, middle class, and gay, and he writes science fiction. Few other black autobiographical works address such dynamics; Audre Lorde's autobiographical writing on being a black lesbian is a notable exception.

Delany's book takes the time to process the development of a gifted black writer and relates to the works of many black writers who have offered explanations regarding their own creative steps. As one of the few black voices in science fiction, Delany may well have offered a seminal text, showing the creative processes of the science-fiction writer.

Bibliography

Fitting, Peter. "Positioning and Closure: On 'Reading Effect' of Contemporary Utopian Fiction." *Utopian Studies* 1 (1987): 23-36. Looks at Delany's creation of utopian worlds and compares those worlds to similar ones depicted in the fiction of Ursula K. Le Guin and Marge Piercy.

Johnson, Charles. *Being and Race: Black Writing Since 1970.* Bloomington: Indiana University Press, 1988. Focuses on Samuel R. Delany in his discussion of black male writers. Argues that Delany is a part of the tradition in black writing that calls for diversity of subject matter and theme.

Peplow, Michael W., and Robert S. Bravard. *Samuel R. Delany: A Primary and Secondary Bibliography, 1962-1979.* Boston: G. K. Hall, 1980. An extremely useful compilation of material on Delany's writing to 1979. All of the major reviews, articles, and essays are included.

Philmus, Robert, ed. "On Triton and Other Matters: An Interview with Samuel R. Delany." *Science Fiction Studies* 3 (November, 1990): 295-324. Includes an interview conducted in 1986 in which Delany discusses the genesis of the *Triton* (1976) novel and his return to the more conventional science fiction form.

Stone-Blackburn, Susan. "Adult Telepathy: *Babel-17* and *The Left Hand of Darkness.*" *Extrapolation* 30 (Fall, 1989): 243-253. Extensive treatment of the phenomenon of telepathy in Delany's *Babel-17* (1966) and the comparison of that treatment to Ursula K. Le Guin's *The Left Hand of Darkness* (1969).

Charles P. Toombs

MUMBO JUMBO

Author: Ishmael Reed (1938-   )
Type of work: Novel
Type of plot: Satire
Time of plot: The 1920's
Locale: Harlem, New York
First published: 1972

> *Principal characters:*
> PAPA LABAS, a Neo-HooDoo detective living in Harlem at the
>   Mumbo Jumbo Kathedral with his family of assistants
> EARLINE, Papa LaBas' closest human confidante
> BERBELANG, a radical black revolutionary who leaves LaBas
>   because he believes that LaBas is obsessed with political
>   conspiracy theories
> ABDUL SUFI HAMID (JOHNNY JAMES), a Black Muslim critical of
>   PaPa LaBas as being too mystical and removed from real
>   problems
> HINCKLE VON VAMPTON, the white editor of the *Benign Monster*
>   and illegal owner of the Jes Grew Text
> BIFF MUSCLEWHITE, a former police commissioner of New York,
>   now a museum curator
> WOODROW WILSON JEFFERSON, a rural African American from
>   Re Mote Mississippi

The Novel

Mumbo Jumbo is an experimental novel that blends fiction and history. In it, Jes Grew, an epidemic of ecstasy originating in New Orleans, is rapidly taking over the United States, making people dance, laugh, and love life. It can be the blues, jazz, ragtime, or slang and black vernacular. Jes Grew needs its Text to survive, and apparently the Text exists somewhere in Manhattan.

The novel takes place in 1920's Harlem. PaPa LaBas' search for the Text and the murderer of Abdul Hamid is linked to the ancient past of Egypt. Reed gives a revisionary interpretation of the rise of Western civilization, one based on an Afrocentric worldview. The conflicts in the novel revolve around a basic split in human consciousness. Osiris, the Egyptian god, created a sect of life-affirming principles that resulted in Jes Grew. Set, his brother, instigated an antilife sect determined to destroy the world—the Atonists. Osiris' dances of fertility are recorded in The Book of Thoth, the original Text of Jes Grew. The lost Text was discovered in 1118 by the Knights Templar, a secret Christian society formed during the Crusades. Hinckle Von Vampton, an original member of the Knights Templar, steals the Text. In 1307,

Pope Clement outlaws the Knights Templar, and Von Vampton escapes with the Text. Wherever Von Vampton goes with the Text, there are spontaneous outbreaks of Jes Grew as people sense the nearness of the sacred book.

The latest outbreak of Jes Grew occurs during the 1920's in Harlem. This is the period of the Harlem Renaissance, a great flowering of African American arts and culture. The action of the novel is played out against historical events such as the U.S. Marine invasion and occupation of Haiti (1915-1934) and the politics of Warren Harding.

Von Vampton is an editor of the New York *Sun* and disperses the Text in installments to African Americans in Harlem. He makes a deal with the Atonists that he will turn over the text if they make the Knights Templar the leading eradicators of Jes Grew. The Text ends up in Abdul Hamid's hands. Von Vampton tries to get it back. When Abdul resists, he is killed.

PaPa LaBas discovers Abdul's body, his hand wrapped around a clue to the whereabouts of the Text. As a metaphysical detective, LaBas is intrigued by the philosophical implications the Text has for liberating African Americans. Concerned with protecting the ancient mysteries of Haitian hoodoo, LaBas is undergoing a crisis brought about by the defection of his assistants. He also has argued with Abdul Hamid, who urged a more pragmatic and stricter approach to African American organization and behavior.

Berbelang is a former assistant of LaBas. He and his gang of art snatchers, the *Mu'tafikah*, kidnap Biff Musclewhite, the former police commissioner. Musclewhite escapes and kills Berbelang, but the *Mu'tafikah* recover important pieces of ethnic art and deliver them to Benoit Battraville's ship. Battraville is a Haitian rebel fighting for freedom in the line of Toussaint L'Ouverture, who gained independence for Haiti.

LaBas and Black Herman arrest Von Vampton for the killing of Abdul. They also arrest Gould, another Knight Templar, who is in blackface acting as a talking black android urging African Americans to resist Jes Grew. They deliver the two for punishment to Battraville on his ship. Jes Grew begins to die out. LaBas and Black Herman dig up an ornate box, in which Abdul hid the Text, from under the Cotton Club. The Text is gone, and in a letter Abdul explains that he burned the Text because it would be a bad influence on African Americans.

In an epilogue, LaBas lectures students at a university in the 1960's. He predicts continued conflict between the Atonists and Jes Grew, a conflict in which Jes Grew will eventually triumph.

The Characters

The characters in *Mumbo Jumbo* suggest allegory rather than social realism. Each character represents a philosophical worldview, a composite of ideas from each side of the Atonist and Jes Grew conflict. There is little attempt by the author to flesh out the characters and give them the background, personal traits, and breadth of experience normally associated with characters in a novel. Rather than using real people, the novel outlines positions on African American concerns by placing its characters in unresolvable conflict.

Few of the characters change or develop from their initial depictions in the text. Woodrow Wilson Jefferson, the ignorant rural African American, never matures in his urban environment, and his naïve impressions seem forced by the end of the novel. Black Herman and Von Vampton are both occultists, but Black Herman strictly pursues positive African American values with his powers while Von Hampton is corrupt to the core. This strict duality of good and evil holds true for other characters in the text. Generally, the black characters represent a spectrum of African American attitudes and worldviews, while white characters each tend to reflect a single viewpoint.

On the personal level, the characters are easy marks for ridicule and satire because of their ideological rigidity. The satire also works on an abstract level because the characters stand for philosophical attitudes of a broader nature. Reed shows the hypocrisy and extremism of many aspects of both black and white life through this type of allegorical or representational character presentation.

PaPa LaBas and Earline are exceptions to the general presentation of types, in that their characters develop to some degree. Earline is in love with Berbelang, and her grief at his murder by Musclewhite is depicted in socially recognizable terms of sorrow and regret. Weakened and depressed by this human loss, she is overcome by Erzulie and enters a world of hallucination. She undergoes an exorcism by Black Herman that restores her human nature. Likewise, LaBas suffers a crisis of spirit when Berbelang and Charlotte leave the Mumbo Jumbo Kathedral. Even Earline questions LaBas' dedication to the HooDoo detective way of life. LaBas wonders if HooDoo can be relevant to the social changes and fragmented spirit of modern life. As a HooDoo detective, LaBas represents African American creativity and renewal through spiritual connection to the Afrocentric past. In his most positive aspects, LaBas gives structure and meaning to the novel. LaBas is one hundred years old in the 1960's and has not changed physically from the start of the book, when he was fifty years old.

Other characters, such as the white Hinckle Von Vampton and Biff Musclewhite, are obviously meant to be allegorical. Von Vampton is hundreds of years old, and Biff Musclewhite acts and thinks just as his name suggests. Characters such as these imply caricature or cartoon. These overblown and excessive personalities collide in the text, leaving mayhem and destruction in their wake. Other characters move magically through the text regardless of obstacles such as time or borders between countries. Thus, Benoit Battraville can appear in his large ship *The Black Plume* on the shores of Manhattan simply because Reed needs someone to represent the revolutionary aspect of Haitian life.

Consequently, the characters in the world of *Mumbo Jumbo* defy natural laws. They can live to extraordinary ages, survive catastrophic physical punishment, and ignore the normal boundaries of human frailty. Characters such as these exist to be made fun of or to defend a radical redefinition of the African American worldview.

Reed's satirical approach in this respect can at times by extremely humorous and revealing. At other times, the didacticism of the text intrudes on the narrative flow and seems perhaps too obvious. One final note in this regard concerns Reed's use of actual figures from the historical past, such as President Warren Harding and James Weldon Johnson, as characters in the text. The use of real characters in a fictional framework complicates and questions the accepted notions of how fiction is written and read. Overall, the characters in this novel have to be appreciated on the level of allegorical fantasy and cannot be expected to conform to the usual expectations of character development.

Themes and Meanings

As a novel of ideas and satirical criticism, *Mumbo Jumbo* works on a number of levels. Primarily, it is a postmodernist detective novel in the tradition of black detective fiction. It uses altered detective personas, black vernacular, double consciousness, and magic while parodying the detective form. *Mumbo Jumbo*'s metaphysical central mystery and its revisionist approach to history are additional indications of postmodern detective viewpoints.

On another level, it is a witty indictment of extreme behavior of all types. Characters representing many aspects of the ideological spectrum are shown to be buffoonish and narrow-minded. Abdul Hamid, sounding his clarion call of black power, is ridiculed in the end as a black puritan who burns the sacred text because it is, in his estimation, too lewd and scandalous.

On another level, the book suggests the ancient conflict between Eros and Thanatos. Put in its simplest terms, *Mumbo Jumbo* reflects humankind's constant war with itself. On one side lie love and life, affirming revitalization; on the other side lie hate and self-destruction. Reed seems to suggest that the intensity of the conflict heightened as the world moved into the twentieth century.

The social and political structure of Western civilization, based on a death-seeking ethos, is portrayed as contemptible. An example of this occurs when the chief Atonist is overjoyed to see that the watercress darter has become extinct, further proof that the Atonist cause is winning the fight for control of the planet.

The continuous conflict between different ideologies and groups in the novel suggests a society as well as a world in conflict. Berbelang is a black revolutionary fighting the racist practices of institutions such as museums. There is even division among ranks, as the Knights Templar quarrel with the death-dealing Wallflower Order. Amid this chaos, there seem to be few manifestations of sanity and continuity.

A broad condemnation of Western civilization is constructed through the eyes of an educated, sensitive African American. The novel posits a positive approach to African American consciousness based on Afrocentric, not Eurocentric, worldviews. Reed accomplishes this by reinterpreting the entire history of Western civilization, redefining its myths and reconstructing its gods.

"Mumbo jumbo" in common vernacular suggests something unintelligible or mysterious. Reed concentrates instead on the positive aspects of the African mother tongue. Within the text itself, "mumbo jumbo" is defined as coming from the Mandingo language and means a "magician who makes the troubled spirits of ancestors go away." Reed indicates by this example his intent to reconnect the African American community to African ancestors and to restore the African American identity by redefining the historical past.

Reed does this by creating, in this and other works, his own particular worldview, or Neo-HooDoo aesthetic, based on African American perception. Neo-HooDoo stresses the positive attributes of African American community and value systems. For example, PaPa LaBas is linked to the Haitian voodoo mysteries, since LaBas is a powerful Haitian spirit connected in turn to the ancient mysteries of African religion.

Reed's revisionist interpretation establishes the Osiris/Set conflict at the very origins of human consciousness. Africa's Egypt is seen in this sense as the progenitor of humankind, containing the seeds of both destruction and renewal. Jes Grew is Reed's Neo-HooDoo terminology for the positive revitalization of the African American spirit that possesses the power to save all of humankind from total destruction.

Positive attributes of African American culture are stressed through the repeated insertion of real figures from black history, black music, and black politics. Reed makes constant reference to the great writers of the Harlem Renaissance, such as James Weldon Johnson, Wallace Thurman, Langston Hughes, and Zora Neale Hurston. This affirmation of black personalities further extends Reed's notion of the Neo-HooDoo aesthetic.

By reconstructing black history and reconnecting it to the ancient past, Reed emphasizes the great strengths of African Americans. Their survival as a culture indicates the powers of an inherent Jes Grew ability to re-create spontaneously, adapting old forms to new methods of accomplishment. The book *Mumbo Jumbo* is a case in point.

Mumbo Jumbo is an experiment in form and style; it introduces innovative ideas as well. It breaks common assumptions about how a novel should be read by creating a colorful pastiche of narrative methods. Reed inserts photos, footnotes written by himself, passages from other books, and pictures to create a new type of text. Much like Jes Grew, it seems to spring spontaneously into being.

The structure of the novel follows no recognizable pattern, consisting of episodes of narrative interwoven in a pattern of interjections, footnotes, and illustrations. The linearity of the narrative is constantly under attack, suggesting the importance of circularity in time, another aspect of Afrocentric religions. The main body of the novel is preceded by a cinematic prologue. There is also an epilogue and a partial bibliography of historical and philosophical texts, giving the book a scholarly air. The novel is a blend of research, historical fact, and imagination.

By interrupting the flow of narrative, stressing historical asides, and positing positive African American worldviews, Reed seems to suggest that all texts must be examined closely for fabrication. Furthermore, history itself may be a fabrication that can be manipulated by whoever interprets supposed facts.

Critical Context

Mumbo Jumbo has been hailed as a revolutionary literary work and a masterpiece of literary imagination. As in his other satirical works of fiction, including *The Free-Lance Pallbearers* (1967) and *Yellow Back Radio Broke-Down* (1969), Reed takes broad swipes at Western civilization. *Mumbo Jumbo* is his most successful novel in its breadth of vision and stylistic innovations.

Reed's earlier novels have been criticized for the very elements that make *Mumbo Jumbo* so successful. The ludicrousness of his plots and the bizarre confrontations of allegorical characters have not always worked. In particular, Reed has been criticized for cardboard characterization that suggests to critics a furthering of stereotypes. Many feminist critics have taken offense at his depictions of female characters.

Reed's ability to juggle these contradictions is most successful in *Mumbo Jumbo*. Reed's confrontational style entertains while it instructs. Best of all, *Mumbo Jumbo* shows Reed at the top of his form in terms of scathing wit and humor.

The mingling of fact and fiction in *Mumbo Jumbo* works because it does not fall to either side. The politics of the novel resist propaganda, while the themes resist polemic. The central conceit of using a black HooDoo priest as a detective holds the novel together. It creates a narrative suspense often lacking in Reed's other fiction. Detective PaPa LaBas is a clever blend of ancient and modern consciousness.

Finally, *Mumbo Jumbo* is most strong in its depiction of the Neo-HooDoo aesthetic. Reed's philosophy of positive African American identity based on both the African past and the creative present is masterfully presented. *Mumbo Jumbo* continues the tradition of black detective fiction while showing the African American ability to create new forms out of old.

Bibliography

Byerman, Keith E. "Voodoo Aesthetics: History and Parody in the Novels of Ishmael Reed." In *Fingering the Jagged Grain: Tradition and Form in Recent Black Fiction.* Athens: University of Georgia Press, 1985. Focuses on Reed's use of parody and reworking of history. Analyzes six novels and traces the development of a new aesthetic of African American sensibility that Reed calls Neo-HooDoo art.

Cooke, Michael G. "Tragic and Ironic Denials of Intimacy: Jean Toomer, James Baldwin, and Ishmael Reed." In *Afro-American Literature in the Twentieth Century: The Achievement of Intimacy.* New Haven, Conn.: Yale University Press, 1984. Recognizes *Mumbo Jumbo* as a high-spirited satire but criticizes Reed for not developing the concept of the Jes Grew Text into something more positive for African Americans.

Fox, Robert Elliot. "Ishmael Reed: Gathering the Limbs of Osiris." In *Conscientious Sorcerers: The Black Postmodernist Fiction of Leroi Jones/Amiri Baraka, Ishmael Reed, and Samuel R. Delany.* New York: Greenwood Press, 1987. Fox studies in depth seven of Reed's novels and finds that each work builds on the previous one.

Gates, Henry Louis, Jr. "On 'The Blackness of Blackness': Ishmael Reed and a Critique of the Sign." In *The Signifying Monkey: A Theory of Afro-American Literary Criticism.* New York: Oxford University Press, 1988. Recognizes Reed's importance in the tradition of African American literature. Finds *Mumbo Jumbo* to be an elaboration on the detective novel and a postmodern text because of its use of intertextuality.

Martin, Reginald. *Ishmael Reed and the New Black Aesthetic Critics.* New York: St. Martin's Press, 1988. Martin closely analyzes Reed's evolving notion of Neo-HooDoo aesthetics and how it relates to black aesthetic critics such as Clarence Major, Houston Baker, Jr., Addison Gayle, Jr., and Amiri Baraka. Comes to the conclusion that Reed refuses to acknowledge any mode of criticism. Discusses *Mumbo Jumbo* as a satiric allegory that is in itself the Text that is searched for in the novel.

Whitlow, Roger. "Ishmael Reed." In *Black American Literature: A Critical History.* Chicago: Nelson-Hall, 1973. Covers the early work of Reed, including his poetry, and makes a strong argument for Reed's inclusion in the absurdist literary tradition. Whitlow sees many connections to the style and satiric content of such American writers as Joseph Heller, Norman Mailer, and J. D. Salinger. Finds Reed's work entertaining.

Stephen Soitos

MY AMPUTATIONS

Author: Clarence Major (1936-   )
Type of work: Novel
Type of plot: Picaresque
Time of plot: The 1980's
Locale: The United States, Europe, and Africa
First published: 1986

Principal characters:
MASON ELLIS, an African American man born in Georgia who
　　masquerades as the Author
CHIRO, Mason's father, a dark figure who leaves Mason a
　　complicated legacy
PAINTED TURTLE, a Native American woman who lived on a
　　reservation in New Mexico before meeting Mason in Georgia
JUDITH WILLIAMS, the wife of Mason Ellis and mother of their six
　　children
EDITH LEVINE, a white, college-educated actress who conspires
　　with Mason, Jesus, and Brad on a bank robbery
JESUS, a criminal
BRAD, a criminal friend of Mason
JOHN ARMEGURN, the director of Mason's fellowship money
THE AUTHOR, an unnamed and unspecified African American
　　writer who takes the name Clarence McKay

The Novel

　　My Amputations is a postmodernist experimental novel that combines picaresque
and *Bildungsroman* techniques in a story about Mason Ellis and his search for an
African American identity. Written in short episodes, the novel narrates the escapades
of Mason from child to Air Force serviceman to hoodlum and bank robber and then
to lecturer. His ultimate con is to receive $50,000 a year from the Magnan-Rockford
Foundation. The novel is a complex blend of Mason's past with his dreams and hallucinations. Fragments of his own novel are interjected into a narrative unreliably
presented by a nameless narrator. Mason's mental state suggests paranoid schizophrenia, as he constantly fears an unnamed conspiracy organized by the System.

　　Mason is the son of Melba, a light-skinned black woman, and Chiro, a hard-living
black man. Mason's youth in Chicago is troubled, and he has a fantasy existence
with his muse, Celt CuRoi, perhaps a derivation of his mother's partial Irish ancestry. Mason suffers episodes of racial bigotry in the service. His apprenticeship as a
writer starts conventionally, as he imitates white writers such as Charles Dickens,
Joseph Conrad, and Ernest Hemingway and black writers such as Richard Wright,
Chester Himes, and James Baldwin. After the service, Mason moves back to Chi-

cago's South Side, marries, has six children, and separates from his wife. Mason and a woman named Painted Turtle move to New York City and turn to a life of crime.

Mason claims that another man, possibly the Author, stole his manuscript. This same man has taken the name Clarence McKay to hide his identity. Mason kidnaps Clarence McKay and, with three others, robs a bank. After the robbery, Mason assumes the identity of the Author and claims the Author's fellowship money. The reader is never sure if this Author is Clarence McKay, Mason himself, or the author of the novel being read. Mason lectures at colleges and universities in the United States, Europe, and Africa. Lovers and friends from the past appear briefly in the second half of the novel, but only as hallucinations. Each episode describes drinking, eating, and sexual escapades connected to his lecture tour. At different lectures, Mason reads from his work in progress. Wherever Mason lectures, violence breaks out. In London, he escapes a bomb explosion in the tube station. In Berlin, people standing at a bus stop are blown to pieces. Later, in Berlin, he is kidnapped by a neo-Nazi group, and in Italy, he is arrested and beaten by the police for being an arsonist. In each instance, alcohol is involved, the actual facts of the incident are confused, and Mason is miraculously rescued by his friends.

In Nice, Mason becomes anxious about his great deception as the Author and fears a conspiracy against him. He goes to a detective fiction conference and voices questions about fog, confusion, and contradictions. These questions mirror others raised in the novel concerning truth, fiction, and the nature of reality. Mason's quest for his identity disintegrates into hallucination. He imagines that he sees old criminal friends from his past, and then Clarence McKay attacks him on the beach with a pistol. Mason is incapable of balancing his criminal past with his current masquerade as the black Author. He imagines that he is pursued by detectives sent by the mysterious foundation that funds his fellowship. Mason descends into paranoid frenzy as he travels through Italy and Greece. Finally, he is sent an envelope by the foundation and is told to deliver it to an African chieftain in Ghana. Mason locates the village and, in the middle of the night, wearing a mask, he is escorted into the presence of the chieftain, who tells him that he has come to the end of his running. The novel ends ambiguously, questioning the nature of discourse and leaving Mason in the dark.

The Characters

Mason Ellis is the focal point of the novel. The reader never really knows if Mason is hallucinating or is dreaming what has happened. The first part of the novel sketches Mason's youth and young manhood in a realistic mode, but as the novel progresses the text becomes more fantasy than reality. The possibility of Mason's schizophrenia is brought up early in the novel in relation to his fantasy episodes with Celt CuRoi. A strict reading of Mason's character as insane is too easy an interpretation of this complicated text. Certainly, the issue of Mason's criminality and his great hoax of masquerading as a well-known black Author is cloaked in ambiguity. The reader comes to believe that Mason is in fact a black author struggling with

844 *Masterplots II*

defining his identity and somehow feeling as if he is an impostor.

Mason's background as an African American contains many authentic touches and suggests a continuity of community that Mason seems incapable of accepting. References are made to black authors and aspects of the black vernacular and folk tradition. Black musicians such as Charlie Parker, Mississippi Fred McDowell, and the Platters pop up continuously in the text. Furthermore, the split in Mason's consciousness represented by his connection to the Irish-sounding Celt CuRoi and his search for authentic African American identity and African heritage may in part be responsible for the conflicts in the novel. Mason's criminality figures heavily in the first half of the novel, yet in the second part, he is able to talk to academic audiences all over the world, and his expertise is never brought into question. The two parts of his personality do not seem to connect in any meaningful way except on the hinge of his assumption of the black Author's identity. In the end, perhaps the reader is meant to see Mason's and the Author's identity as the same. The narrative then concerns the progressive disintegration of Mason's consciousness as he travels back to his African roots for rebirth and renewal.

This divorce in Mason's reality is reflected in the other characters in the novel. Mason's family history is well sketched. Readers recognize his light-skinned mother and his renegade father as two characters who have emotional range and depth. Mason's progression from childhood through his time in the Air Force to his disastrous marriage in Chicago also has the ring of verisimilitude. Mason's entry into the criminal world seems less substantive. With this descent, the novel's focus also begins to fragment. The characters of Edith, Jesus, and Brad, with whom Mason commits a bank robbery, are shadowy at best. Edith Levine is an academic who craves the excitement of the underworld. Jesus and Brad could be anybody as they become props in Mason's growing obsession with the Author.

Nebulous characterization is best represented by the Author. The reader is never given a clue about this character. He may be Clarence McKay, or he may be Mason Ellis, who imagines himself as an impostor masquerading as himself. As the narrative focuses more on Mason's wild hallucinations of pursuit, capture, and torture, other characters become only names who pop up in the text. This sketchy characterization becomes the norm as Mason travels (as the Author) through the United States, Europe, and Africa.

Readers are hazily informed of Mason's extracurricular activities, in which he continuously gets free meals, alcohol, and women. In Nice, his companion is an exchange student named Barbara Ann who may or may not be appearing in his bed at night chain-smoking cigarettes. In Berlin, it is a professor, Heiner Graf, with whom he spends a riotous evening ending in a mad bombing spree. In Italy, it is Vito and nameless women. In Greece, it is Zizi Kifissias, a painter, and Melina Karamanlis, a journalist. The catalog of minor characters continues to the end of the book, with no clear rationale for their existence ever established.

Overall, the characters in *My Amputations* revolve around the central character of Mason Ellis. Mason is the focal point of the narrative, and the characters in the first part of the book help to elucidate his early background. In the second part, the characters become whimsical and elusive. As Mason slips in and out of dreams and hallucinations, the characters may be people he meets or simply figments of his imagination.

Themes and Meanings

My Amputations is a metafictional novel questioning the nature of fiction and the perception of reality. It combines *Bildungsroman* techniques with the picaresque tradition of an episodic narrative about the travels and adventures of a rogue or criminal. *My Amputations* is also postmodern in its self-reflexive concern with the fictional depiction of reality. The novel experiments with characters, plot, and action by refusing to use realist or naturalistic techniques. Embedded in its surrealistic flow of disconnected episodes are references to the process of fiction, the conflict between truth and imagination, and the relation of the author to the text.

My Amputations is written in the third person by an unreliable narrator who refuses to conform to the dramatic verities of time, place, and action. Mason represents himself through his work in progress as an unreliable character whose dreams contradict the narrative presented in the main body of the text. Since readers have no idea who Mason is masquerading as, if he in fact is masquerading, the reader is often bewildered. The last half of the novel confirms Mason's growing despair at his quest for meaning and identity. Mason is self-educated and gives many lectures, yet readers know little about what he says or thinks or writes. His growing paranoia focuses on his fellowship agreement, his search for an impostor, and suspicion of the System. The abstract quality of his journey further questions the traditional linear narrative.

The portrait that emerges is of a very troubled African American man torn in two directions. His Anglo-Saxon muse, Celt CuRoi, represents half of the equation. Within her domain fall all the references to the Euro-Americentric world of Mason's imagination. She provided inspiration in youth, but when Mason starts his European search for African American roots, she can no longer help. Within the second half of the equation lies Mason's identity as a black man. His picaresque adventures attempt to reconcile these two worlds and reveal his African heritage. In Europe, Mason dreams continuously of being kidnapped, tortured, and attacked. He fears that his masquerade as the Author will be exposed, and he imagines himself about to be exterminated. He believes that the foundation controls him and that everybody he meets is part of the conspiracy. He drinks too much, blacks out frequently, and lives in a hazy world of fear.

This narrative conundrum frustrates the reader intentionally, bringing into question the nature of the text and questioning accepted modes of perception. Mason also disappoints the reader, particularly when he sidesteps intellectual conflict. This is aggravating in the African section, when Mason is asked important questions about black nationalism, Afrocentric identity, and the black writer's political position. The famous Author evades these important issues by lapsing into total blankness. His facile and confusing passage through Europe reads like a travelogue written by an ignorant tourist. The emptiness of Mason's character becomes truly frightening. Is this black man representative of his African American culture? If so, it is a strong indictment of the Euro-Americentric culture that it has helped to create such a confused individual. The reader is left with a distressing portrait of a paranoid black academic who teeters on the edge of total disintegration. As a series of fantastic episodes in the tradition of the picaresque, the metaphor becomes a further indictment of the dilemma of African American double consciousness. Mason's constant analysis of himself suggests incompleteness, fabricated on the mistaken notion that black identity must be modeled on white value systems. Even more distressing is Mason's inability to find his identity in black worldviews. In this sense, the ending of the novel holds out the most positive message. By stressing the self-reflexive nature of the narrative and the personal nature of discourse, Major seems to suggest that an individual can remake his or her reality. In Mason's case, an African rebirth in the consciousness of self, the sense of community, and the nature of language and discourse is still possible.

Critical Context

My Amputations fits well into Major's body of postmodernist writing. Major is perhaps best known for his novel *All-Night Visitors* (1969), which shares many of the themes surrounding African American male identity found in this novel. Major experiments with unusual narrative techniques, blending prose and poetry. He is also interested in creatively adapting genre forms, as in the detective novel *Reflex and Bone Structure* (1975). Major's background as a painter is often seen in his novels. *My Amputations* contains many references to European painters of the modern tradition.

Major is recognized as a leading experimenter in black writing and has been critically appraised as an innovative artist. In novels such as *All-Night Visitors*, *No* (1973), and *Emergency Exit* (1979), the author uses a combination of prose experiments to present an alternative view of the African American experience. His work is commonly appreciative of the black vernacular tradition. Through the daring use of sex, nonlinear plots, and unreliable narrators, Major confirms the postmodernist examination of fiction's accepted roles in society. Major's work rejects the assumption that language offers a logical means by which one might understand the world. In the end, the text represents nothing outside itself.

Major is an African American poet and editor of the *Dictionary of Afro-American Slang* (1970). He is often cited as one of the founding theoreticians of the 1960's new black aesthetic movement. As editor of a poetry anthology, *The New Black Poetry* (1969), Major stressed the importance of African American poetic identity in collectively attempting to revolutionize social and political relationships through creation of a brotherhood of black consciousness. This African American cultural emphasis and heightened sense of the positive black identity was shared by other black writers such as Amiri Baraka (LeRoi Jones), Addison Gayle, Jr., and Ishmael Reed.

Bibliography

Bell, Bernard W. "Modernism and Postmodernism." In *The Afro-American Novel and Its Tradition.* Amherst: University of Massachusetts Press, 1987. Places Major in the African American postmodern tradition of experimenting with language and form. Sees Major as parodying and extending genre forms while searching for new ways to express African American identity.

Black American Literary Forum 13, no. 2 (1979). This issue is devoted to Major and contains a number of interesting articles. Among these are "Towards a Primary Bibliography of Clarence Major," by Joe Weixlmann and Clarence Major, and "Major's *Reflex and Bone Structure* and the Anti-Detective Tradition," by Larry McCaffrey and Linda Gregory.

Klinkowitz, Jerome. "Chapter Eight: Clarence Major." In *The Life of Fiction.* Urbana: University of Illinois Press, 1977. Discusses the disruptive qualities of Major's work in relation to the postmodernist text. Sees Major as an instrumental African American writer who blends social and racial critique into experimental texts.

——————. *The Self-Apparent Word: Fiction as Language/Language as Fiction.* Carbondale: Southern Illinois University Press, 1984. Places Major in a postmodern tradition of writers including William S. Burroughs and John Barth. Considers Major an extremely clever writer confronting accepted narrative conventions.

Major, Clarence. *The Dark and Feeling: Black American Writers and Their Work.* New York: Third Press, 1974. A collection of varied essays, including Major's seminal essay on the black aesthetic titled "Black Criteria." Also includes a number of interviews, one of them a self-interview.

Stephen F. Soitos

MY LIFE WITH MARTIN LUTHER KING, JR.

Author: Coretta Scott King (1927-   )
Type of work: Autobiography
Time of work: 1927-1968
Locale: Boston, Massachusetts, and the American South
First published: 1969

Principal personages:

CORETTA SCOTT KING, the wife of civil rights leader Martin Luther King, Jr., and the founder of the Martin Luther King, Jr. Center for Nonviolent Social Change

DR. MARTIN LUTHER KING, JR., Coretta's husband, the founding president of the Southern Christian Leadership Conference

BERNICE MCMURRY SCOTT, Coretta's mother, a reserved and cautious woman

OBADIAH SCOTT, Coretta's father, an Alabama farmer of modest means

EDYTHE SCOTT (MRS. ARTHUR BAGLEY), Coretta's sister and confidante

REVEREND MARTIN LUTHER KING, SR., Coretta's father-in-law, the pastor of Ebenezer Baptist Church in Atlanta

YOLANDA DENISE (YOKI) KING, Coretta's daughter and first child

MARTIN LUTHER KING, III, Coretta's first son and second child

DEXTER KING, Coretta's second son and third child

BERNICE ALBERTINE (BUNNY) KING, Coretta's second daughter and fourth child

RALPH DAVID ABERNATHY, a close friend of the Kings and their associate in the Civil Rights movement

Form and Content

My Life with Martin Luther King, Jr. is more than Coretta Scott King's autobiography, more even than the story of her marriage. In key respects, it is also a mirror of the African American experience in the twentieth century. In seventeen chapters, an epilogue, and several appendices, Mrs. King surveys her background in Marion, Alabama, her education at Antioch College (Ohio), and her fifteen-year marriage that ended tragically with the assassination of her famous husband on April 4, 1968. In that sense, her book is personal and traditionally autobiographical. Yet its perspective is national and even international with regard to the mission that she identifies throughout as the *raison d'être* of the couple's public career.

Her account begins in October, 1964, when Martin Luther King, Jr., resting in a hospital, learns that he will receive the Nobel Prize for Peace. The Nobel Prize reception banquet in Oslo sets the tone for the book by establishing the moral foundations of the nonviolent movement, which the author interweaves with her personal story. King referred in Oslo to the "long road" that African Americans had traveled in their quest for equality.

From that imagery, Coretta Scott King drew the unifying theme of her autobiography. Not only had the road been long and hard for black Americans in general, and for Americans as a whole, but it had also been hard for her family as well. "No one who has not traveled it," she reflected, "could possibly envision how very long it was."

For her, it was a journey that began near Marion, Alabama, a rural setting that contrasted sharply with that of her husband's middle-class urban upbringing in Atlanta. Whereas Coretta's father, Obadiah (Obie) Scott, was a farmer, Martin's was the pastor of the prestigious Ebenezer Baptist Church on Auburn Avenue in Atlanta. Both, as it turned out, were in Boston in the early 1950's preparing for professions that at first seemed incompatible. Martin was preparing to be a church minister; Coretta dreamed of a career as a professional musician. After her graduation from Antioch College of Ohio, she was admitted to the New England Conservatory of Music, and Martin began his theological studies at Boston University. The last thing she was looking for in a husband, she admits, was a desire to be a preacher. As she met and fell in love with Martin, however, Coretta adjusted her plans and thus became linked with one of the most influential social movements in American history.

Vignettes and intimate glimpses of details otherwise not available make up much of *My Life with Martin Luther King, Jr.* The first seven of its seventeen chapters deal with the journey to Oslo and the development of Coretta's life with Martin from 1953 through the Montgomery, Alabama, bus boycott of 1955 and 1956. It is in her candid revelation of personal experiences and feelings, including her initial disappointment when she learned that Martin was planning to be a minister, that the reader sees Coretta emerge as a distinctive personality. She also shares her concerns about limiting her planned musical career by marrying and her reluctance to go back to the South, from which she had found some escape in Boston—where racial relations were at least formally less segregated.

It is not surprising that the Montgomery experience is central to her story. The Dexter Avenue Baptist Church in the capital of the old Confederacy was Martin's first pastorate, and it was there that Coretta learned to be a mother. Their first daughter, Yolanda, was born in November, 1955, just three weeks before Rosa Parks's historic refusal to give up her bus seat, the incident that triggered the bus boycott and sparked a new era in the American Civil Rights movement. Like her husband, Coretta viewed the Montgomery experience as pivotal in the emergence of a widespread nonviolent movement. "Montgomery was the soil in which the seed of a new theory of social action took root," she writes.

The second half of the book is devoted to events between 1957 and King's death in 1968. These were critical years in the movement's history. In January, 1957, the process of creating the Southern Christian Leadership Conference (SCLC) began at the Ebenezer Baptist Church at a moment when antiblack violence erupted again in Montgomery. In May, a national "Prayer Pilgrimage" in behalf of minority voting rights was held in Washington, D.C., and with it Martin Luther King, Jr., became an even more prominent national figure because of a rousing speech he delivered called "Give Us the Ballot."

Coretta recounts these events and then proceeds through the period of the first sit-ins and Freedom Rides (1960-1961), the campaigns in Albany, Birmingham, and Selma (1962-1965), and the difficult efforts to carry the nonviolent message northward into Chicago and other cities after the passage of the 1965 Voting Rights Act. That she remained at home during most of this period limits her treatment in one sense. Yet in another, her perspective is sharp and quite relevant. Through it, the reader can see the strains on the Kings' family life, Coretta's determination to support her husband's public efforts, and the weariness that inevitably resulted from almost impossible demands on Martin's time.

Chapter 14 has a distinctive place in the coverage because of its focus on the watershed period of 1964 and 1965. It was the time of the 1964 Civil Rights Act, the Nobel Prize award, and the beginnings of Coretta's Freedom Concert programs. She outlines the music she presented in the series, which underscored the religious foundations of the movement. She also discusses the pivotal importance of the Montgomery movement and describes the August, 1963, March on Washington that was the occasion for her husband's best-known speech, "I Have a Dream." This chapter also candidly portrays several painful experiences, including her own difficulties getting the King children into a segregated school in Atlanta. Coretta also relates Martin's burdensome effort to comfort the family of Jimmy Lee Jackson, a young black man shot to death by police as he tried to protect his family from raiding officers. She also gives some attention to the Black Power movement, an alternative proffered by Stokely Carmichael and other young blacks who did not share Martin's patient commitment to nonviolence.

The last section of the book focuses extensively on Martin's assassination, the details of his funeral, and the vast outpouring of sympathy by the city of Atlanta and by millions of people around the nation. Somehow, Coretta found in the affirmation of her husband's life and career the strength to go on with the work. She viewed *My Life with Martin Luther King, Jr.* as a major part of her own responsibility for keeping his dream alive.

Analysis

At the heart of *My Life with Martin Luther King, Jr.* is a pervasive emphasis upon the incompleteness of modern life, an emptiness caused chiefly by the materialism and social inequality that have accompanied the development of Western civilization. Even in the midst of the axial period of early Greek culture—when new heights of philosophy, religion, and democracy were attained—there was destructive inequality, the author argues. It continued in later centuries:

> Greece gave us noble philosophy and poetic insights, but her glorious cities were built on a foundation of slavery. Western civilization was also great, bequeathing to us glories of art and culture as well as the Industrial Revolution that was the beginning of

material abundance for man. But it was based on injustice and colonialism and allowed its material means to outdistance spiritual ends.

Her husband, she argues, had understood this analysis and its corollary: that individuals are also incomplete for much the same reason. Indeed, the recovery of completeness within the individual is the key to real hope for social fulfillment. Drawing heavily upon the imagery of Social Gospel theologian Walter Rauschenbusch, Martin had called for a "Beloved Community" informed by religious faith and permeated by a spirit of selfless service to mankind. "Set yourself earnestly to discover what you are made to do," he had challenged, "and then give yourself passionately to the doing of it." Both Coretta and her husband believed that only in that way could positive change come.

Implicit in this is a theme of service and a related response to providential guidance. Although not a religious book as such, *My Life with Martin Luther King, Jr.* returns frequently, through quotations, conversations, and personal reflections, to the theme of God's leadership. It first appears in a decisive way in Coretta's recollections of that moment in Boston when she and Martin decided to accept the pastorate in Montgomery:

> Though I had been opposed to going to Montgomery, I realize now that it was an inevitable part of a greater plan for our lives. Even in 1954 I felt that my husband was being prepared—and I too—for a special role about which we would learn more later. Each experience that we had was preparation for the next one.

Clearly, Coretta welcomed that role in the sense that she identified with the Christian nonviolent approach—both during and after her husband's life—and shared much of its content in her account. Particularly detailed and personal is her treatment of the assassination in Memphis and the subsequent parade and funeral in Atlanta. Stunned and shocked, she committed herself to keeping his memory and the movement alive. In one of her appendices, she quotes Dr. Benjamin E. Mays, the former president of Morehouse College, who had been a longtime supporter of Martin. "If we love Martin Luther King, Jr. and respect him," Mays insisted at the slain leader's funeral, "let us see to it that he did not die in vain."

Critical Context

An ever-enlarging body of literature on Martin Luther King, Jr., and the nonviolent Civil Rights movement has provided the reading public with a massive literature on civil rights history. The availability of King's papers at the King Center in Atlanta and other libraries and archives has made possible a wide variety of coverage. Most of this has been written by nonblack scholars working within the framework of academia or journalism. Coretta King's autobiographical account is different from much of this in three respects, and these features define the place of her work in the history of African American literature.

First, she is an African American. Her book reflects the soul-searching quest for personal identity of a young woman who, like her husband, had been forced early to learn the parameters of black Americans' participation in society. She knew first-hand about the necessity to be the best in order to have a fair chance to enter the prestigious institutions of higher learning or to carve out a career in a society where race loomed larger as a challenge than it did after the Civil Rights movement.

Second, Coretta Scott King was the wife of a man widely regarded as the most influential African American reform leader of the post-World War II period. That was surely not an easy role. She stayed home during most of the campaigns and was thus remote from the detail. Yet she had to keep up with what was going on, to intervene at times to help her husband, to keep up the image of a happy, strong family when pressures familiar to many African American families—such as enrolling children in schools that resisted integration—were making life difficult. Early in the history of the movement, when Martin was promoting his first book, *Stride Toward Freedom* (1958), he was nearly killed by a deranged black woman who plunged a letter opener into his chest. Frequently, Martin was arrested, harrassed, or injured, and ultimately he was murdered. Her typically calm and optimistic account thus stands in contrast to the negativism that might have characterized a wife's account of such events.

Third, *My Life with Martin Luther King, Jr.* is one of the earliest examples of an African American memoir based on experience with the nonviolent movement. Scholars have frequently drawn on such material to enlarge the scope of documents and other more conventional sources. Ralph Abernathy wrote such a book near the end of his life; others, including Clayborne Carson and Jo Ann Robinson, have also added to this literary-historical genre. The value of such works is their unique combination of historical reflection and personal involvement, without which other observers cannot fully comprehend the momentous days of the Civil Rights movement.

Bibliography

Abernathy, Ralph David. *And the Walls Came Tumbling Down: Ralph David Abernathy, An Autobiography.* New York: Harper & Row, 1989. Few people knew the Kings better than Ralph Abernathy, whose career in civil rights meshed with Martin's from Montgomery in 1955 until the assassination in Memphis in 1968. Abernathy's autobiography is thus essential, despite its subjective approach and questionable recollection on some matters.

Ansbro, John J. *Martin Luther King, Jr.: The Making of a Mind.* Maryknoll, N.Y.: Orbis Books, 1982. An intellectual history of Martin that complements Coretta's more personal account. Ansbro reinforces her emphasis upon Martin's morality-based social reform theory. Ansbro's is the best of the spiritual pilgrimage studies of Dr. King.

Garrow, David J. *Bearing the Cross: Martin Luther King, Jr. and the Southern Christian Leadership Conference.* New York: William Morrow, 1986. Although thin as an analysis of King and the SCLC, Garrow's account is essential because of its massive detail on the life of the famous civil rights leader. This Pulitzer Prize-winning journal of the King years was the first major work to expose King's personal life to a candid critique.

King, Coretta Scott. "He Had a Dream." *Life* 67 (September 12, 1969): 54-62. This compact, illustrated extract from the first edition offers a useful introduction to her historical biography.

Lewis, David Levering. *King: A Biography.* 2d ed. Urbana: University of Illinois Press, 1978. The first critical biography of King, Lewis' work is nevertheless both much milder in its analysis than recent studies and more valuable in clarifying the motives and goals of the nonviolent movement.

Peake, Thomas R. *Keeping the Dream Alive: A History of the Southern Christian Leadership Conference from King to the Nineteen-Eighties.* New York: Lang, 1987. The first comprehensive history of the SCLC, this work also includes extensive material on King's personal life, his relationship to the SCLC, and his theological perspective.

Thomas R. Peake

NARRATIVE OF THE LIFE OF FREDERICK DOUGLASS
An American Slave

Author: Frederick Douglass (Frederick Augustus Washington Bailey, 1817?-1895)
Type of work: Autobiography/slave narrative
Time of work: c. 1817-1841
Locale: Maryland and Massachusetts
First published: 1845

> *Principal personages:*
> FREDERICK BAILEY, later FREDERICK DOUGLASS, the slave narrator
> HARRIET BAILEY, the mother from whom Frederick is separated as an infant
> BETSEY BAILEY, the grandmother who nurtures Frederick until he is six years old
> AARON ANTHONY, Frederick's first master
> THOMAS AULD, Aaron Anthony's son-in-law, a cruel master
> HUGH AULD, the brother of Thomas Auld

Form and Content

In 1841, three years after Frederick Douglass escaped from slavery, he launched his career as an abolitionist. In Nantucket, Massachusetts, he spoke for the first time about his slave experiences before a white audience. Before that, he had told his story only to black gatherings. So impressive was his account that he was hired as a full-time antislavery lecturer by the Massachusetts Anti-Slavery Society.

By 1844, the society was becoming increasingly disturbed that many were doubting Douglass' authenticity. His critics saw him as being too refined and too erudite for a man who had escaped from slavery only six years previously. The leaders of the Anti-Slavery Society, therefore, urged Douglass to write his story.

The *Narrative of the Life of Frederick Douglass: An American Slave*, including a preface by William Lloyd Garrison and a letter from Wendell Phillips, was published in 1845. Its success was immediate. Thousands of copies were sold both in the United States and in Great Britain. The *Narrative* was even translated into French and Dutch.

Just as there were those who doubted Douglass' oral accounts of his experiences in slavery, there were those who declared the written version a hoax. Such an accusation was not as farfetched as it might at first seem. Many slave narratives were not only transcribed but also organized and revised by white abolitionists. The latter, however, were generally careful to indicate the extent of their assistance. They recognized that to do otherwise was to put the whole antislavery movement in jeopardy. The *Narrative*, for its part, is a notable exception. Frederick Douglass neither asked for nor received any help from white abolitionists.

The decision to divide the work into two main sections was his. The first part consists of nine chapters. These detail Douglass' experiences in slavery. The second section, with two chapters, is as long as the first and describes Douglass' escape. This organization seems to indicate that the first nine chapters form a kind of prelude to the main action—Douglass' escape from slavery.

Before this escape takes place, the reader is given a graphic account of slavery in pre-Civil War America. Douglass begins his narrative with his birth in Tuckahoe, Talbot County, Maryland. The second sentence states that he does not know his age. This is followed by other details about which the narrator is unsure. For example, although he knows that Harriet Bailey is his mother, he has very little communication with her. She dies when he is seven years old; before that, he sees her only four or five times. He lives with his grandmother, Betsey Bailey, on the outskirts of Edward Lloyd's plantation.

The young boy is introduced to the horrors of slavery when he witnesses the beating of his Aunt Hester by their master, Aaron Anthony, soon after Frederick begins living on the plantation. This beating is only the first of many at which the young Frederick is both observer and participant. Frederick later goes to Baltimore to live with Hugh and Sophia Auld. He considers this move providential, since it sets the stage for his eventual escape from slavery. Sophia Auld begins to teach him to read, and by the time her husband finds out and objects, it is already too late; the young slave has made the connection between literacy and freedom.

There is now no turning back for the city slave. Thus, when Frederick is sent to live with Thomas Auld because of a quarrel between the brothers, Thomas cannot control him. He sends him to Edward Covey, a "nigger-breaker." The stay at Covey's marks another pivotal point in the young slave's journey from bondage to freedom; when Covey attempts to beat Douglass, he defends himself and fights the older man to a standoff.

If Covey is the worst master Frederick has encountered, his next, William Freeland, is the best. With Freeland, Frederick with his eyes on freedom as never before, teaches a Sabbath school of more than forty slaves. Here, too, he plans an aborted escape. After the failed escape, Frederick is again returned to Hugh Auld in Baltimore. Auld oversees his training as a caulker. With this trade comes increasing independence and a small taste of freedom.

This taste of freedom prepares Douglass for his life after slavery. After a successful escape, Frederick keeps his past shrouded in mystery; he is afraid of unwittingly divulging any information to slaveholders.

Frederick Douglass, having discarded the name given him by the mother he hardly knew, settles in New Bedford, Massachusetts, with his new wife, Anna, and joins the abolitionist cause.

Analysis

To write autobiography is to assess the significance of one's life. Douglass' journey from "the peculiar institution" of slavery to freedom has both individual and societal importance. His narrative details the "dehumanizing" and "soul-killing" effects of slavery in language that is both formal and dispassionate.

As others have observed, the first page of the *Narrative* is replete with negatives: The slave narrator does not know his age; he is not allowed to ask about it; all he knows about his father is that he is white. This lack of identifying data is undoubtedly dehumanizing.

The brutality of the slaveholders provides other examples of the dehumanization of slavery. The beating of Aunt Hester by Aaron Anthony sets the stage for the many whippings to which Douglass is to be witness. Among the first of these is the incident of the two Barneys, father and son. They take care of Colonel Lloyd's horses, but it is clear that the horses are more valued than they are; their master whips them frequently and arbitrarily. Later, in the incident with Covey, the "nigger-breaker," Douglass decides that he has had enough. He fights Covey and declares that the encounter marks "the turning-point in my career as a slave."

The sexual nature of these beatings has been pointed out. In the case of Aunt Hester, this aspect is fairly explicit. Captain Anthony is enraged not so much because Aunt Hester has disobeyed him and gone out in the evening, but rather because she has been with Ned Roberts, another slave. Miscegenation is, of course, rife between slaveholders and their female slaves. The slaveholder who is both master and father to his slave is quite common. Conversely, where both beater and beaten are males, homosexuality has been suggested.

While such physical abuse undoubtedly leaves psychological scars, the custom of separating the slave infant from his mother is perhaps even more emotionally damaging. Douglass several times refers to this unnatural procedure. In fact, he receives the news of his own mother's death "with much the same emotions I should have probably felt at the death of a stranger."

The slave narrator, however, is no stranger to religion. References to it become increasingly specific. Early in the *Narrative*, the death of a cruel overseer is "regarded by the slaves as the result of a merciful providence." Similarly, Frederick Douglass describes his move to Baltimore as "a special interposition of divine Providence." Later, slaveholders such as Thomas Auld use religion to "sanction and support" their "slaveholding cruelty." Also, the final portion of the *Narrative* concerns itself with the incompatibility of Christianity and slavery. Douglass, therefore, by examining one life addresses issues that affect society as a whole.

The slave's sense of community is referred to at crucial points in the *Narrative*. Douglass plans his aborted escape with other slaves, and his autobiography ends with the hope that the book will increase awareness about "the American slave system." Such knowledge will, the slave narrator hopes, lead to emancipation. Similarly, when Douglass imagines his grandmother, it is her isolation that pains him most. She has been put out to pasture in utter loneliness.

The passage in which Douglass imagines his grandmother's loneliness is perhaps the most poignant in the *Narrative*, perhaps because Douglass is angry at himself for not being there when she needs him. Whatever the reason, the passage's tone is unlike the tone of the rest of the autobiography. "Dispassionate," "matter-of-fact," "detached" are words that come to mind when the tone of the *Narrative* is consid-

ered. Such distanced narration could be the detachment of the erudite adult abolitionist looking back; it might also be that the dehumanizing and soul-killing institution has taken its toll. Occasionally in the *Narrative*, Frederick Douglass mentions
his inability to write down his feelings. Is the slave narrator refusing to feel because
it is too painful to do so?

Feelings are perhaps not best served by a formal style, and some have described
Frederick Douglass' language as "high-flown." One cannot but admire, however, the
language of the apostrophe to the ships on the Chesapeake Bay beginning, "You are
loosed from your moorings, and are free; I am fast in my chains, and am a slave!"
There is also a wonderful chiasmus as Frederick Douglass is about to describe his
first confrontation with Covey: "You have seen how a man was made a slave; you
shall see how a slave was made a man."

The fight with Covey has symbolic value for Douglass. As Douglass sees it, the
slave-master who whips him in the future must be prepared to kill him. The autobiographer thus uses one incident to shed light on a larger issue, the brutality of
slaveholders. The beating of Aunt Hester also addresses this issue symbolically. As
the first of such beatings, it sets the stage for all the rest. In addition, the sexual
overtones make the whipping akin to rape and therefore more brutal. The inextricable link between slavery and the sexual cannot be denied.

So pervasive is the emphasis on community that there are critics who regard the
Narrative not as autobiography but as a personal history of American slavery. That
Douglass himself intended the work to be viewed as both is evidenced by the appendix. Here the slave narrator expands on a theme in the work—the incompatibility of
slavery and Christianity—at the same time as he signs his new name with a certain
pride and flourish. After all, the individual slave can truly be free only when slavery
as an institution is abolished.

Literacy, for Douglass, is the key to the slave's freedom. His epiphany occurs
when he witnesses Hugh Auld's anger at his wife's teaching Frederick, now eight
years old, to read. By the time he is twelve, the autobiographer is reading *The Co-
lumbian Orator*, with its strong antislavery arguments. He soon learns to write from
white street children. The ex-slave narrator is aware that true liberation can only be
achieved when both body and mind are free.

The actual writing of his autobiography may be regarded as the ultimate freeing
of the mind for Douglass. Given the therapeutic nature of the work, therefore, any
help from white abolitionists would have been inappropriate. When the ex-slave
signs his new name at the end of the *Narrative*, he is affirming both his literacy and
his identity.

Critical Context

Douglass' *Narrative* is as important to history as it is to literature; it speaks as
eloquently to blacks as it does to whites. Ultimately, the autobiography looks at a
timeless theme—man's inhumanity to man—through the lens of slavery.

Historically, the *Narrative* is a significant document in the pre-Civil War abolitionist movement. In fact, the last sentence of the appendix reminds the reader of the "sacred cause" for which the autobiography was written. Douglass earnestly hopes that his story, detailing the horrors of slavery, will hasten the end of "the peculiar institution."

Douglass' *Narrative* belongs to the genre of slave narratives, a popular literary mode from the end of the eighteenth century to the beginning of the American Civil War. Thousands were written during this period, and many were translated into several languages. Douglass' story epitomizes the best of the genre.

The ex-slave's story exists in three revised versions: *My Bondage and My Freedom* (1855) and two separate editions of *Life and Times of Frederick Douglass* (1881, 1892). The original version, however, has received the most critical acclaim. The 1845 rendition has been praised for its narrative skills, succinctness, and clarity.

Although the *Narrative* is Douglass' masterpiece, he was also a publisher and journalist. He launched this career after returning from England, where he had fled upon the publication of the *Narrative* to avoid being returned to slavery. His journalistic endeavors included the *North Star*, *Frederick Douglass Weekly*, *Frederick Douglass' Paper*, *Douglass' Monthly*, and the *New National Era*. Despite his prolific journalist output, Douglass' fame as a writer rests on the *Narrative*. It is a work that will continue to fascinate both the historian and the literary critic.

Bibliography

Huggins, Nathan Irvin. *Slave and Citizen: The Life of Frederick Douglass.* Boston: Little, Brown, 1980. Offers a succinct and lucid biography for the general reader; Huggins is a good storyteller.

McFeely, William S. *Frederick Douglass.* New York: W. W. Norton, 1991. Presents a comprehensive biography with an excellent bibliography. McFeely is particularly good in describing Douglass' relationship with family and friends.

O'Meally, Robert G. "Frederick Douglass' 1845 Narrative: The Text Was Meant to Be Preached." In *Afro-American Literature: The Reconstruction of Instruction*, edited by D. Fisher and R. Stepto. New York: Modern Language Association of America, 1979. Argues that the *Narrative* has recognizable affinities with the sermons of black preachers. The audience, according to O'Meally, is white, and "preacher" Douglass is exhorting them to end the abysmal institution of slavery.

Preston, Dickson J. *Young Frederick Douglass: The Maryland Years.* Baltimore: The Johns Hopkins University Press, 1980. Provides detailed descriptions of all important personages in the *Narrative*. Preston is in familiar territory, and his depiction of Douglass' relationship with those around him is illuminating.

Quarles, Benjamin. *Frederick Douglass.* New York: Atheneum, 1970. Presents an excellent first chapter that demonstrates how Douglass' years in slavery influenced his later life. The epigraphs that introduce each chapter, most of which are by Douglass, give a sense of the man and his age.

Sheila J. McDonald

A NARRATIVE OF THE LORD'S WONDERFUL DEALINGS WITH JOHN MARRANT, A BLACK

Author: John Marrant (1755-1791)
Type of work: Autobiography
Time of work: 1755-1785
Locale: South Carolina, the Atlantic Ocean, and England
First published: 1785

> *Principal personage:*
> JOHN MARRANT, an African American freeman who recounted his
> adventures in his highly popular narrative

Form and Content

On account of its author's freeman status at birth, John Marrant's autobiographical work is not, strictly speaking, a slave narrative. Yet because Marrant was a black man who experienced capture and enslavement at the hands of American Indians, most scholars place his work in the slave-narrative tradition. Another reason for classifying his work as a slave narrative is that Marrant was an influential figure in the development of that genre.

Marrant's narrative is both the story of his Indian captivity and a spiritual autobiography. The two sections of the narrative feature a three-part structure. In the religious work, the parts deal with a person's experiences of sin, conversion, and spiritual rebirth; the three sections of the Indian captivity account focus on Marrant's experiences when he is taken captive, the transformation that occurs in him during his exposure to Indian culture, and his attainment of a freedom that is marked by a deeper awareness of life.

Marrant relates the story of his experiences to the Reverend Mr. Aldridge, who serves as editor of the account; both men are primarily interested in communicating a spiritual message to the reader. At the beginning of his narrative, Marrant sets forth the religious purpose and tone of his work by stating that he hopes the example of his life will be useful in encouraging men and women to become stronger believers in the Christian faith.

Marrant recalls that he was born on June 15, 1755, in New York, but he does not relate his early experiences there. Neither does he say much about his later schooling in Florida and Georgia. Yet, he describes how his early youth was devoted to pleasure and drinking and how he loved to play the violin and French horn at all the balls and gatherings in town. Marrant describes himself as a slave to every vice until the age of thirteen. At that time, he is living in Charleston, South Carolina, where an event occurs that accidentally gives him the opportunity to hear the words of a great religious leader.

On that fateful day, Marrant and his wayward companions are passing a church when they decide to disrupt the services. Marrant's friends dare him to enter the church and blow his French horn during the delivery of the minister's sermon. The bold youth goes into the church and prepares to cause a commotion until he is struck by the sight of the famous George Whitefield, an English evangelical preacher known throughout the American colonies. As Marrant is about to blow his horn, he hears Whitefield pronouncing striking verses of Scripture from the pulpit. The words transfix Marrant; he listens to the sermon and becomes so moved and disturbed by it that he faints and collapses in the church.

Later, the stricken youth is restored to health by Whitefield, who visits him at home and prays with him until he recovers from his state of anxiety. Subsequently, Marrant abandons his sinful ways and seriously studies the Scriptures. His family members are not sympathetic to his new religious life, however, and thus he departs from them and goes into the Southern wilderness to sort things out. There he is captured by Cherokee Indians, who twice threaten him with execution. Both times he is spared when he utters aloud prayers containing powerful biblical passages. The Indians understand him because Marrant, miraculously, is able to speak their own language. They then ask him to pray over their king's daughter; as Marrant delivers the prayers that heal her, he experiences a mystical communion with the Lord. Soon after this marvelous event, the Cherokee king and his daughter ask Marrant to convert them to Christianity.

Subsequently, the grateful Indians allow the young captive to wander among them at will, and he uses his liberty to serve as a missionary to the tribes living in the forest. During the several years he spends trying to convert the Indians, Marrant adopts their style of dress. His garments are the skins of wild beasts, his hair is cut in the "savage" manner, and he carries a tomahawk on his side. He also becomes more fluent in the Indian language, and he develops a close friendship with the Cherokee king.

Finally, after meeting with little success in his efforts to convert the Indians, Marrant decides to return to his home in civilization. When he arrives in Charleston, he is unrecognized by all of his family members except his eleven-year-old sister.

Now Marrant sees himself as a newborn Christian who has undergone a chastening experience in the wilderness. In the rest of his narrative, he emphasizes his dedication to furthering the spiritual lives of men and women, and he illustrates his special providential role in this world. During the Revolutionary War, Marrant is impressed into the British naval service. In one harrowing episode at sea, he is washed overboard three times during a storm but manages to survive. Later, he is wounded during a fierce battle and is sent to England to recover. There, he continues his religious pursuits and eventually trains to become an ordained Methodist minister. His friends encourage him to engage in missionary work among the black population in Nova Scotia, and Marrant ends his narrative by entreating his Christian readers to pray for the success of his future religious efforts.

Analysis

Marrant depicts himself as a fascinating character. He is a young, almost picaresque person who abandons his errant ways after being converted to Christianity. Much of Marrant's narrative, however, suffers from a lack of believability. His zealous religious spirit makes him give everything a providential character. The biblically significant period of three days figures in everything that happens to him. He goes unharmed when he walks by the beasts in the forest, and he immediately knows how to speak to the Indians in their language. His prayers heal the king's daughter, and he is able to convert the Cherokee king and his daughter with little trouble.

The narrative also shows a lack of artistic design. The closing part of the account is especially weak. Marrant quickly runs through the latter facts of his life and abruptly ends his story. He says almost nothing about his impressment in the British navy, where he was a virtual slave for over six years, and he never mentions any of the prejudice that he must have encountered as an African American, despite his freeman status. Nevertheless, the story of his early adventures in the South, the absorbing picture of George Whitefield, who captures the youth's spirit for the Christian faith, and Marrant's marvelous experiences with the Indians in the wilderness make the narrative an appealing piece of prose.

What is also interesting about Marrant's work is that it is both an Indian captivity narrative and a spiritual autobiography. The spiritual pattern of sin, conversion, and rebirth appears alongside the Indian captivity's structural components of separation, transformation, and freedom. These elements can be seen in the sharply outlined parts of the story. After Marrant undergoes his conversion episode, he wanders into the forest, where he is captured by Indians who plan to kill him; however, he succeeds in saving himself and his newly acquired Christian faith while he is in captivity. In fact, his faith in God is strengthened and his commitment to a religious life is deepened by his experience with the Indians, who allow him to make attempts to convert them. After several years of living as an Indian, Marrant returns to the English world and dedicates himself to furthering his missionary work.

Unlike many Indian captivity narratives that depict Indians as superstitious demons, Marrant's work gives a balanced treatment of the Native Americans. He makes a point of mentioning the Indians who help him and extend their friendship to him during his captivity, and he sympathizes with them concerning their persecution at the hands of the white Americans. He is interested in the Indian culture, to the extent that he learns the Cherokee language and adopts the Indian style of dress and appearance.

The spiritual autobiographical elements in Marrant's narrative include his portrait of his sinful life prior to his spiritual awakening and his descriptions of listening to a sermon that affects him to the point of crisis, of becoming physically ill (symbolically representing his spiritual sickness), of undergoing a conversion that must be tested by an ordeal, and of the chastening quality of the ordeal experience, which enables him, once he is free, to attain a state of spiritual rebirth.

In addition, Marrant makes use of other spiritual autobiographical devices, such as stating that his purpose is to offer instruction to his readers, depicting his anxieties about backsliding to a sinful life, and describing his solitary meditations. He credits Providence for giving him protection from such dangers as Indians and wild animals and for helping him to survive storms and wrecks at sea that save him to do God's work.

In many parts of his narrative, Marrant depicts himself as following Christ's example. At times he almost casts himself in the role of a Christ figure, especially in the two events that occur when the Indians come close to executing him. When Marrant relates how he is nearly burned at the stake, he describes the episode in language similar to the language that is used in the Bible to describe Christ's crucifixion.

Critical Context

Marrant's autobiography appeared in London in 1785, and despite a derisive review, the work went through six editions in a short period of time. It was published in the United States in 1789 and became one of the three most celebrated Indian captivity narratives published in America (the others were a 1757 work by Peter Williamson and the narrative of Mary Jemison in 1824). Marrant's popular account was translated into several European languages and published in countries on both sides of the Atlantic; there was even a Welsh version printed in 1818. Editions of the narrative continued to appear well into the nineteenth century.

Many early African American writers knew Marrant's spiritual autobiography and were influenced by its themes and form. Strong evidence exists that Marrant's work was well known by Olaudah Equiano, who is credited with writing the first major slave autobiography, the prototype for the numerous nineteenth century fugitive-slave narratives. Equiano's two-volume work, *The Interesting Narrative of the Life of Olaudah Equiano, or Gustavus Vasa, the African*, appeared in 1789 and included references to other works that mention Marrant's story.

Marrant continued relating the story of his life after 1785 in the journal he kept of his missionary experiences in Canada and in New England. In 1790, Marrant's journal was published in London and was marked by the same spiritual tone and purpose as his earlier work.

Although Marrant's autobiographical accounts say little about matters concerning black men and women, the sermons he wrote and delivered as a minister include strong comments about racial prejudice and injustice. His sermons also stress the need for African Americans to learn about the contributions of great Africans in history and to feel proud of their African heritage.

Bibliography

Andrews, William L. *To Tell a Free Story: The First Century of Afro-American Autobiography, 1760-1865*. Urbana: University of Illinois Press, 1986. Chapter 2 provides a thorough study of several early slave narratives. Illustrates how the first narrators relied on captivity and conversion traditions to tell their first-person accounts to a white audience.

Costanzo, Angelo. *Surprizing Narrative: Olaudah Equiano and the Beginnings of*

Black Autobiography. Westport, Conn.: Greenwood Press, 1987. Explains and analyzes the slave-narrative tradition as it developed in the eighteenth century. Discusses the significance of the early black writers upon the form and structure of the slave narrative as a literary genre. Contains a detailed examination of Marrant's narrative, with a special emphasis on the portrayal of his character as a biblical type.

Foster, Frances Smith. *Witnessing Slavery: The Development of Ante-bellum Slave Narratives.* Westport, Conn.: Greenwood Press, 1979. Provides a study of the history, influences, development, plots, and racial myths of the slave narratives. Discusses the eighteenth century accounts that were the forerunners of the numerous slave works published by abolitionists just prior to the Civil War.

Kaplan, Sidney. *The Black Presence in the Era of the American Revolution, 1770-1800.* Greenwich, Conn.: New York Graphic Society, 1973. Describes Marrant's narrative and parts of his journal. Also deals with the rousing and inspiring content of the sermon Marrant preached in Boston in 1789, in which he attacked racism and summoned black men and women to develop pride in their African heritage.

Williams, Kenny J. *They Also Spoke: An Essay on Negro Literature in America, 1787-1930.* Nashville, Tenn.: Townsend Press, 1970. Emphasizes how Marrant credited divine providence for the success of his spiritual life. Chapter 3 provides a useful general account of the slave-narrative structure. Also deals with the melodramatic and didactic elements of slave works and their various religious and realistic prose styles.

Angelo Costanzo

A NARRATIVE OF THE UNCOMMON SUFFERINGS, AND SURPRIZING DELIVERANCE OF BRITON HAMMON, A NEGRO MAN

Author: Briton Hammon (fl. 1760)
Type of work: Autobiography
Time of work: 1747-1760
Locale: Coastal Florida, Cuba, the Atlantic Ocean, and London
First published: 1760

> *Principal personage:*
> BRITON HAMMON, an African American slave who is seized by
> Indians and subsequently rescued by a Spanish captain

Form and Content

Briton Hammon's narrative is the first known slave autobiography in American literature. Hammon dictated his factual story to a writer who probably recorded the account in almost the exact way Hammon delivered it. The narrative style is plain and straightforward and marked by many awkward and ungrammatical sentences.

The slave's story is only fourteen pages long and, as Hammon himself states, deals mostly with matters of fact. His story is interesting, however, because he describes exciting adventures resulting from his captivities at the hands of Indians and Spaniards. Furthermore, his work is related to spiritual autobiography and contains many biblical references and quotations. Hammon constantly thanks the Lord for delivering him from the dangers of captivity.

Published in Boston, Hammon's brief account covers his experiences from 1747 to 1760. With his master's consent, the loyal Hammon signs aboard a vessel bound for Jamaica. After loading up with wood in Jamaica, the ship heads back, but it soon meets with disaster when it is wrecked on a Florida reef. A boat with nine men aboard, including Hammon, is sent out to reach the shore, but a large band of Indians in twenty canoes surprises the sailors. The Indians capture them and then proceed to attack the ship and kill the captain and remaining crew members. Hammon, the sole survivor, is taken prisoner. The Indians treat him cruelly and threaten to roast him alive; but after five weeks of captivity, he is rescued by a Spanish captain who takes him to Havana, Cuba. There, Hammon becomes a slave in the governor's castle.

Hammon's service with the governor lasts for about a year. One day while walking on a street, Hammon is kidnapped by a press gang that wants to put him aboard a ship bound for Spain. When he refuses to serve, he is taken to a dungeon and confined there for four years and seven months. Hammon is released when his plight finally reaches the governor's attention through the efforts of an Englishwoman. His captivity continues, however, as he is placed again in the service of the governor, who later sends him to assist the bishop of the island. In the ensuing years, the despondent slave yearns for his freedom and makes three attempts to escape. The last one succeeds when Hammon is befriended by an English captain, who takes him on board a ship to Jamaica.

Thereafter, Hammon works mostly as a cook on various military vessels that engage in severe naval battles, in one of which Hammon is wounded. Finally, while in London recovering from a fever, Hammon finds himself impoverished and decides to sign up for service on a ship going to Africa. His sudden desire to return home causes him to change his mind, however, and he switches to a vessel leaving for Boston. By coincidence, his old master is sailing on the same ship, and Hammon describes how a happy reunion between master and slave takes place after a separation of thirteen years.

Analysis

Hammon's voyage begins on Christmas Day, thus signaling to the reader that a new life of temporary freedom and personal discovery is about to commence for the adventurous slave. Soon Hammon's experiences at sea reveal that his journey is one of harrowing transition from innocence to maturity, one in which, as he learns about himself and the world, he is tested for strength of character.

At the beginning of his story, Hammon illustrates his naïveté in the account of how he and his companions are easily deceived when they are stranded off the coast of Florida. Hammon is first fooled by the appearance of the Indian canoes, which look like rocks. Then, when the canoes begin to move, the shipwrecked men see the English colors hoisted in one of them, and they think that they are about to be rescued by friendly forces. The men advance and fall into the hands of the Indians.

To stress how his perilous adventures chasten him and test his character, Hammon graphically depicts the terrors of his Indian and Spanish captivities. The Indians threaten to roast him alive, and he lives in fear until he falls into the hands of the Spanish Catholics in Havana. During his years of captivity in Cuba, Hammon is able to withstand the threat to his Protestant faith posed by the Catholics. He gives some indication that he views their religion as being decadent and materialistic when he describes his service to the bishop. Hammon makes a point of mentioning how the bishop is carried about in a large chair lined with crimson velvet as he goes about the island confirming and baptizing people in exchange for huge sums of money.

Even though his life is comfortable in the governor's castle, Hammon makes several attempts to flee. When he finally succeeds in escaping, he enlists for service aboard various ships, where at times he is thrown in the midst of perilous sea battles. In depicting his dangerous experiences, Hammon is stressing the testing and strengthening effects upon both his character and his spiritual condition.

Although Hammon's short work can be termed a spiritual autobiography, it does not give a picture of a self-scrutinizing, conscience-stricken man looking inward for his soul's deliverance. Hammon is concerned with factual details and outward events. He sees such events as signs of God's plan for his soul's suffering and deliverance, and he accepts life and its vicissitudes (apparently including Hammon's own status as a slave) as events justifiably ordained by a purposeful God.

Hammon shares with his white masters the view that his Indian captors are ignoble, cruel savages, but he fails to see his white captors as almost equally evil. It must be remembered, however, that Hammon is telling his story while he is still enslaved and that he is directing his narrative to a white audience. These facts, coupled with his belief that Christianity is the true way to God, probably account for his cautiousness in displaying any other feelings about his own slave status. Eighteenth century Christianity taught Hammon and other slaves the acceptance of and resignation to their servant rank in life, and it impressed upon their minds the admonition from God that servants should obey their masters.

It is probable, then, that because he is telling his story while still in bondage, Hammon says nothing against his permanent slave status in America; however, he emphasizes the horrors of the other captivities that he undergoes on his journey. Hammon experiences captivity after captivity, and all are shown to be terrible and unjust. The fact that he does not criticize his initial captivity stands out, since he does depict graphically the terrors of his Indian captivity, his captivity under the governor of Cuba, and his kidnapping by the Spanish press gang and his subsequent incarceration. During all of his captivities, he describes how he always feels miserable and how he constantly seeks to escape to freedom.

Hammon mixes his account of his experiences with his views about their religious meaning. Thus, his narrative contains many passages that are meant to parallel passages from the Bible. He especially evokes the story of the deliverance of the Hebrews from captivity in Egypt and their terrible ordeals in the wilderness before they reached the Promised Land. Hammon's allusions also reveal how he identifies himself with the biblical hero David, who defeated the Philistine giant Goliath. While Hammon does not seem to think of himself as a deliverer, he does implicitly express the notion that he is acting heroically in withstanding the Indians and the Spanish Catholics.

Hammon's interpretive remarks are scarce and simple. As he states in his introductory address, he expects his readers to analyze the meaning of his sufferings under captivity. Hammon realizes that eighteenth century readers will believe that the workings of Providence generally explain all the events in a person's life, and he also knows that his audience will understand that other, deeper meanings can be derived from the slave's remarkable experiences.

This is why Hammon wisely invites his readers to make sense of his trials in a perilous world. Because of his slave status, he makes a point of presenting himself as a lowly, unlearned person who expects his readers to probe for themselves the depths of his experiences. By humbling himself and flattering his readers, he can command attention for his life story. After all, Hammon's narrative presents the first demonstration of a black slave expressing himself on a level of human and spiritual worth that white autobiographers had always assumed natural in their life experiences.

It is clear, then, that Hammon is aware of his daring enterprise in telling his story.

He certainly knows that white readers are going to find it difficult to believe the strange experiences of a black slave with claims to heroic qualities of human endurance. For this reason, Hammon casts himself in the figure of a simple person lacking overt interpretive abilities. He cleverly leaves it to his readers to analyze the narrative events, while he supposedly relates only the factual matters of his adventures.

Critical Context

Hammon's captivity narrative was not the only work of its kind. An Indian captivity tale by Thomas Brown also was published by another Boston printer in 1760. It was a popular work and went through two editions that same year. Hammon and Brown must have been aware of each other's works, because both their texts bear resemblances to each other that cannot be considered coincidental. As to which author borrowed from whom, it is impossible to tell. Hammon may have inspired Brown, or Brown may have influenced Hammon, but the relationships between the two narratives are certainly clear from the works. Hammon's and Brown's titles, prefatory remarks, and closing religious exhortations are practically the same word for word. Brown's tale also contains elements similar to those that appear in Hammon's work, such as accounts of Indian duplicities, captivity, danger of exposure to the alien faith of Roman Catholicism (in Brown, the French Canadians pose the threat), and kind acts by a governor and a woman. In addition, Brown and Hammon end their narratives with a religious plea taken from the same source in the Bible (Psalm 107).

Although it seems that Hammon's narrative is authentic mainly because of its ingenuous style and unique voice, the difference of tone in the short beginning and ending sections seems to indicate the work of another person. Most of the narrative, however, is presented as a plain and circumstantial account told directly by an unschooled religious person, and the consistency of language, feeling, and viewpoint supports the narrative's claim to veracity.

Hammon's description of his adventures is important for historical reasons, because it is the first autobiographical slave narrative produced in America. Although few scholars regard it as a great literary piece, Hammon's work unquestionably contributed to the development of the slave-narrative genre. The spiritual autobiographical elements, the biblical parallels, the heroic portrayal of the narrator, and the hidden subversive elements of the account are all techniques that appear in the more extended and developed slave narratives of the late eighteenth and mid-nineteenth centuries.

Little critical analysis of Hammon's narrative exists, but critics who have commented on the work have remarked on its lack of sophistication, its reliance on circumstantial detail, its contrived and coincidental nature, and its weighty religious ending. Yet many scholars agree that a consideration of Hammon's autobiographical account is important for a full understanding of the slave narrative's development in American literature. Furthermore, Hammon's unusual experiences provide the reader with an exciting adventure story.

Bibliography

Andrews, William L. "Voices of the First Fifty Years, 1760-1810." In *To Tell a Free Story: The First Century of Afro-American Autobiography, 1760-1865.* Urbana: University of Illinois Press, 1986. Discusses why Hammon found it necessary to defer to his white readers, and explains how this trait of deference characterizes early African American autobiography.

Costanzo, Angelo. "Black Autobiographers as Biblical Types." In *Surprizing Narrative: Olaudah Equiano and the Beginnings of Black Autobiography.* Westport, Conn.: Greenwood Press, 1987. Examines how Hammon portrays himself as a type of biblical hero. Also deals with the possibility of hidden meanings existing within Hammon's narrative account.

Foster, Frances Smith. *Witnessing Slavery: The Development of Ante-bellum Slave Narratives.* Westport, Conn.: Greenwood Press, 1979. Discusses Hammon's account as a precursor of the slave narrative. Stresses that Hammon concentrates on presenting himself as a black person with commendable religious and character attributes.

Starling, Marion Wilson. *The Slave Narrative: Its Place in American History.* Washington, D.C.: Howard University Press, 1988. Contains scattered comments on Hammon's work dealing with its appearance at a time when similar sensational accounts were being published and avidly read. Starling's investigative research into slave narrative literature, which she completed in 1946, was the first of its kind. She gives the reader a sense of where Hammon fits in the line of the slave narrative's development. Her liberal definition of what can be called a slave narrative, however, allows her to consider other kinds of slave texts, and thus Starling does not claim that Hammon's work is the first of its kind.

Williams, Kenny J. "A New Home in a New Land." In *They Also Spoke: An Essay on Negro Literature in America, 1787-1930.* Nashville, Tenn.: Townsend Press, 1970. Notes the loose construction, simple expression, and pervasive spiritual interpretation of Hammon's adventure story. Other chapters in the book deal extensively with the slave-narrative structure and prose style.

Angelo Costanzo

THE NARROWS

Author: Ann Petry (1908-   )
Type of work: Novel
Type of plot: Psychological realism
Time of plot: The 1950's
Locale: Monmouth, Connecticut
First published: 1953

> *Principal characters:*
> ABIGAIL CRUNCH, a seventy-year-old New England widow
> LINCOLN "LINK" WILLIAMS, the nephew of Abbie Crunch
> CAMILO TREADWAY SHEFFIELD, a rich white heiress

The Novel

The Narrows, set in the small New England town of Monmouth, Connecticut, focuses upon an ill-fated love affair between a handsome, well-educated young black man, Link Williams, and Camilo Sheffield, a rich white heiress to the Treadway munitions fortune. After being graduated from Dartmouth, Link returns home intent upon writing a history of America from an African American perspective. Yet when he meets and falls in love with Camilo, whom he believes to be Camilo Williams, a fashion photographer, Link abandons his writing project. Later, he learns of her deception and breaks off the affair. Camilo, hurt and humiliated, accuses Link of rape. After he is arrested, she drives away at a high speed, striking and seriously injuring a black child.

The treatment of both stories in the press leads Camilo's mother, Mrs. Treadway, and Camilo's husband, Captain Sheffield, to murder Link. In trying to dispose of Link's body in the river off the Dumble Street docks, however, the two are arrested for speeding, and the murder is discovered.

Although the action of the novel covers only three months prior to the death of Link Williams, the story covers about twenty years, chronicling the transition of a middle-class, ethnically mixed section of Monmouth to a poverty-ridden ghetto inhabited primarily by blacks. The story unfolds through a series of flashbacks and digressions, as certain incidents trigger the memories of the major characters.

As Abbie reflects upon the early days in Monmouth before the death of her husband, she recalls a quieter, cleaner, more peaceful place. Over the years, however, the neighborhood has steadily declined—so much so that it is now referred to variously as "The Narrows, The Eye of the Needle, The Bottoms, Little Harlem, Niggertown." Signs of the disintegration are everywhere apparent—in the pollution of the River Wye, in the drunks who loiter in the shade of the hangman's tree, and in places like the Moonbeam Cafe and the Last Chance Saloon.

Link's memories of the past, however, reveal Monmouth in quite a different light. During the time that he spends with Bill Hod after the Major's death, Link is taught respect for the culture of African American people as well as respect for himself as a black man. In fact, for most of Link's early life, Bill Hod and other Monmouth locals supervise Link's street education. Thus, despite the changes that so distress Abbie, Link views The Narrows and its people as a continuing source of nurture and support.

The thoughts of Malcolm Powther, a newcomer to The Narrows, reveal Monmouth in still another light; his reflections provide a glimpse into the world of the rich and powerful. His position as butler at Treadway Hall allows Powther access to this world and the secrets of its inhabitants. Through his observations and the servants' gossip, he acquires intimate knowledge of the Treadway family.

Woven into the story of the Camilo-Link love affair are stories of the white inhabitants of Monmouth. There is Peter Bullock, the editor, owner, and publisher of the *Monmouth Chronicle*, a newspaper that had once had a reputation for espousing the abolitionist cause. That reputation, however, has eroded in the face of Bullock's increasing concern with appeasing the rich and powerful in order to maintain his station. In contrast to Bullock is the free-lance photographer Jubine, who lives in a loft, rides a motorcycle, and chides Bullock for "having turned so many handsprings" to pay for his expensive possessions.

Finally, an interesting assortment of eccentrics people Petry's novel; their names generally reflect some behavior or physical condition: Weak Knees, Bug Eyes, the Writing Man (a shadowy figure who moves about the streets writing Bible verses on the sidewalks of Monmouth), and Cat Jimmie (a legless, armless grotesque who propels himself about on a cart and takes advantage of his position on the ground to look up women's skirts).

The Characters

Ann Petry has created her characters with the skill and deftness of the consummate artist. She draws her characters in such a manner as to reflect the diversity of African American society and the interrelationship between that society and American society in general. In carefully weaving together the lives of her characters, she emphasizes both the complexity and the interconnectedness of all human life. While the two dominant voices in the novel are those of Abigail Crunch and her adopted son, Link Williams (the two characters whose psychic depths are plumbed most thoroughly), there are always, in the background, a chorus of minor voices, deepening and enriching the narrative. Except for Malcolm Powther, however, these voices are subdued, and the characters may be viewed in terms of their relationships to Abbie or to Link.

In Abigail Crunch, Petry creates a character unique in African American fiction of the period—black, middle-class, strong—enduring many hardships but refusing to be defeated by them. A primary source of her strength lies in her ability to discount all but her own concept of reality. Forged in the cauldron of prejudice and racism, Abbie emerges as a typical New England matron, steeped in tradition and propriety, embracing her Anglo-Saxon Protestant heritage with a passion and eschewing every aspect of her African American heritage. She refuses to associate with the inhabitants of The Narrows, which is now predominantly black; and she views every aspect of it—its people, its haunts, its environs—as degraded and shameful. Despite the denial of her African American heritage, Abbie reveals certain aspects of that heritage in subtle ways—sometimes in mannerisms and sometimes in her reaction to other characters in the novel, as she measures them against her concept of the ideal.

Mamie Powther, for example, is held in low esteem by Abbie, who considers her loud, coarse, and vulgar. Ironically, however, Petry binds these two women together inextricably, both by place and circumstance (Mamie is Abbie's tenant) and by personality. In fact, Mamie serves as something of an alter ego to Abbie. While Abbie is reserved and solemn, Mamie is carefree and filled with the joy of living. Much of what Abbie considers vulgar—Mamie's blues singing, dancing, and ready laughter—is merely another side of Abbie's personality, that exuberance and vitality that Petry recognizes as essential to the African American character. The sense of rhythm so blatant in Mamie Powther is also apparent in Abbie—though more covert, less strident—and is expressed in the little verses and nonsense rhymes that she continually composes in her head as she goes about her daily activities.

Malcolm Powther, soft-spoken, well dressed, and hardworking, seems to fit Abbie's ideal, and she immediately accepts him. He moves easily between the black and white worlds, fantasizes about white women, and regales his sons with bedtime stories about blonde-haired fairy princesses. It seems an irony that this very proper, conservative gentleman could be so totally captivated by the earthy, sensuous Mamie. From the time of their first encounter, however, he pursues her relentlessly until she agrees to marry him; Mamie brings light and joy into his life, and without her he is incomplete. For Powther, as for Abbie, Mamie seems an alter ego, the vitality of the African American experience that cries out for recognition.

In Link Williams, Petry creates a character who functions as a visible "link" between the various elements of a changing society. As he moves between Number Six Dumble Street and the Last Chance Saloon, he attempts to link the traditional world of Abbie Crunch with the nontraditional world of Bill Hod. As he tries to establish and maintain an interracial relationship with Camilo Treadway, he attempts to link the traditional culture of upper-class white society and the iconoclastic ethnic culture of The Narrows. Neither Link's training as a historian nor his research of African American history affords him the necessary insight or strength to forge a bond between these two worlds. He discovers, unfortunately, that this knowledge isolates rather than bonds; the link does not hold, and the societies remain separate.

The other characters in the novel, both black and white, in one way or another reflect the traditional and nontraditional aspects of this changing community, irreparably separated by ignorance, prejudice, and hatred. Abigail Crunch, alone, acquires the double vision that allows her, ultimately, to see the connectedness of all human beings. In the end, she admits that appearances are unimportant and that everyone in the community must assume responsibility for Link's death. As she says, "We all reacted violently to . . . Link and that girl because he was colored and she was white."

Themes and Meanings

The Narrows is a complex novel, involving several subplots and a multiplicity of characters skillfully interwoven. Essentially, *The Narrows* is a New England novel: the characters are cast in the tradition of the New England Puritan ethic and may be viewed as conforming to or deviating from that tradition.

Both Abbie Crunch and her friend, Frances (F. K.) Jackson, the black woman undertaker of Monmouth, conform to this tradition. Despite her genteel manner and her aristocratic attitude, Abbie is hardworking and fiercely independent. Before her marriage to the Major, Abbie earned her living as a schoolteacher; after the death of her husband, realizing that she must supplement her income in order to care for herself and Link, she rents the top floor of her house. While the transition from housewife to landlady is not easy, it is necessary, and Abbie makes it without hesitation. F. K. Jackson, though different in appearance and demeanor, is much like Abbie. She has managed to graduate from Wellesley College in a period when matriculation at that institution was almost unheard of for a black woman. She relinquishes her dreams of becoming a doctor to take over her father's undertaking business in Monmouth, which she does quite successfully. Both Abbie and F. K. are highly intelligent, well-educated, hardworking business women, competing successfully in a world in which both their race and gender are prohibiting factors.

While Abbie and F. K. conform to the tradition, the other two women of importance in the novel, Mamie Powther (black and poor) and Camilo (white and rich) deviate from the tradition. Because neither has found productive work, each becomes bored, and that boredom leads them into destructive acts. In the case of Camilo, her cruising of Dock Street in The Narrows late at night leads ultimately to the physical destruction of Link Williams and to her own emotional destruction. In the case of Mamie Powther, her sexual escapades and her penchant for bar-hopping lead her to neglect both husband and children.

A major theme that Petry treats in *The Narrows* is the impact of the past on the present. At the outset of the novel, for example, as Abbie walks into Dumble Street, her eye is drawn to the River Wye, and her thoughts revert to a time long past—to the Monmouth of Link's childhood, when the river was unpolluted, the Last Chance Saloon did not exist, and drunks did not loiter under the hangman's tree. Focusing on the past, in some measure, enables Abbie to deal with present situations, to hold fast to a gentler way of life amid the forces of change that threaten to engulf her.

The impact of the past on the present is also revealed in Link's continuing interest in history. Not only does Link choose to major in history at Dartmouth, but he also searches his own cultural roots in an effort to identify himself and to understand his relationship to other people. In so doing, he discovers that African American history is a repository for the prejudice and racism that hold African Americans in bondage. Ironically, that same racism also holds whites in bondage. Camilo is held captive by a tradition that deems certain occupations to be unacceptable for persons of her social status. Captain Sheffield and Mrs. Treadway, on the other hand, are hostage to the racist tradition that forbids interracial relationships and places a death sentence upon any black man who engages in such a relationship.

Another important theme in the novel is that of guilt and its impact on the lives of individuals. After the death of her husband, for example, Abbie is consumed by guilt because she mistook his heart attack for drunkenness. This guilt affects every aspect of her life, and it is only at Link's funeral that she begins to come to terms with it. Also, Bill Hod attempts to make amends for a life of profligacy by trying to keep Link innocent, and Weak Knees—haunted by the memory of a murder that he committed years earlier—is often seen flailing his arms at an imaginary companion, muttering, "Get away, Eddie." Finally, Cesar the Writing Man's cryptic verses seem to hint at some nameless sin of which the whole town is guilty.

Finally, Petry's weaving of theme and symbol is apparent throughout the novel and is revealed in her naming of characters as well as places. Link Williams obviously provides a link between the white and black worlds portrayed in *The Narrows*, while the Last Chance Saloon seems to offer an escape, if only momentarily, from the world of reality. On the other hand, the imposing Treadway Hall, with its fleet of expensive cars, sits on the outskirts of Monmouth, its elegance and remoteness symbolizing the great gulf between the worlds of the poor and powerless and the rich and powerful.

Critical Context

When Ann Petry's novel *The Narrows* was first published, it was reviewed in prominent newspapers such as *The New York Times* and in well-known journals such as *Saturday Review*. Since that time, however, it has received little critical attention. Many critics consider Petry's first novel, *The Street* (1946), her best work and have frequently compared it to Richard Wright's *Native Son* (1940) because of its naturalistic elements. In *The Narrows*, though, Petry moves beyond the strictures of the naturalistic school of writers and probes the complexities of the human psyche, examining the myriad forces that influence it.

Aside from *The Narrows* and *The Street*, Ann Petry has produced one other adult novel, *Country Place* (1947). Her short stories have appeared in a number of journals and anthologies and were published in a volume entitled *Miss Muriel and Other Stories* in 1971. In the canon of Petry's works, however, *The Narrows* reveals the writer at her best. Her themes are universal, yet she is able to capture the many and varied nuances of the black experience. The novel is compelling in its psychological probing of character, its intricate interweaving of theme and symbol, and its remarkable prose style.

Bibliography

Bell, Bernard W. "Ann Petry's Demythologizing of American Culture and Afro-American Character." In *Conjuring: Black Women, Fiction, and the Literary Tradition*, edited by Marjorie Pryse and Hortense Spillers. Bloomington: Indiana University Press, 1985. Discusses the ways in which Petry's portrayal of characters in her fiction, especially *The Narrows*, "debunks" certain myths in American society. Innocence and virtue are not always indigenous to the small-town environment.

Hernton, Calvin C. *The Sexual Mountain and Black Women Writers.* New York: Anchor Press, 1987. Hernton devotes a chapter to Petry, whom he praises as an important pioneer.

McDowell, Margaret. "The Narrows: A Fuller View of Ann Petry." *Black American Literature Forum* 14 (1980): 135-141. Discusses *The Narrows* as one of Petry's most accomplished novels, focusing upon the skill with which the author interweaves character, theme, and symbol in the narrative.

Washington, Mary Helen, ed. *Invented Lives: Narratives of Black Women, 1860-1960.* Garden City, N.Y.: Doubleday, 1987. Examines Petry's development of female characters in her novels, with special attention to the character of Mamie Powther in *The Narrows.*

Weir, Sybil. "The Narrows: A Black New England Novel." *Studies in American Fiction* 15, no. 1 (Spring, 1987): 81-93. Examines *The Narrows* in light of the New England traditions that influence character development, focusing especially on the character of Abbie Crunch. Petry's novel reflects what Nathaniel Hawthorne saw as the chain of "dark necessity" from which people can rarely, if ever, extricate themselves.

Gladys J. Washington

NATIVE SON

Author: Richard Wright (1908-1960)
Type of work: Novel
Type of plot: Social criticism
Time of plot: The 1930's, during the Depression
Locale: Chicago
First published: 1940

Principal characters:

> BIGGER THOMAS, a twenty-year-old black man from Chicago's
> South Side
> MRS. THOMAS, Bigger's mother
> BUDDY THOMAS, Bigger's younger brother
> VERA THOMAS, Bigger's sister
> BESSIE MEARS, Bigger's girlfriend
> MR. DALTON, Bigger's landlord and employer
> MRS. DALTON, the blind wife of Mr. Dalton
> MARY DALTON, the daughter of Mr. and Mrs. Dalton
> JAN ERLONE, Mary Dalton's boyfriend
> BORIS MAX, Bigger's communist lawyer

The Novel

Native Son narrates the life and impending death of Bigger Thomas. The novel opens with the jarring sound of an alarm clock. The family's morning ritual is interrupted by a rat, which Bigger hysterically kills. This act marks the first instance of the fear and rage that pervade the novel.

The planned robbery of Blum's store also elicits fear and rage. Blum is white, and Bigger and his gang are used to preying on other blacks. He fights with Gus, a member of his gang, and calls the robbery off.

Bigger gets a job as the Daltons' chauffeur. His first assignment is to take Mary Dalton to the university. She, however, wants to meet her boyfriend, Jan. All three end up at Ernie's Kitchen Shack on the South Side of Chicago, and they get drunk. Mary is so drunk that Bigger has to carry her to her room. As he places her in bed, the ghostlike Mrs. Dalton enters. Panic-stricken, Bigger suffocates Mary with her pillow. He decapitates her so that her body will fit into the blazing furnace and returns home to sleep.

As the investigation into Mary's disappearance begins, Bigger implicates both Bessie and Jan. Mary's bones are eventually found in the furnace, and Bigger must murder Bessie, to whom he has confessed, for his own protection. He kills her with a brick while she is asleep after he has raped her. Bigger flees through abandoned buildings on the South Side of Chicago. He is finally captured atop a water tank and imprisoned.

The third part of the novel—the inquest and trial—is set in the Cook County Jail and its environs. Bigger faints at the inquest and is taken back to his cell, where he reads newspaper reports of himself as quintessential "nigger." While in his cell, he is also visited by all those who have influenced his life, including the Reverend Hammond, his mother's minister, who gives Bigger a wooden cross. Back at the inquest, Bigger is represented by Max, his communist lawyer.

Mary's bones and Bigger's signed confession are on display at the inquest. The deputy coroner elicits testimony from Mrs. Dalton and Jan; Max, for his part, questions Mr. Dalton. He points out that Mr. Dalton, as landlord of the rat-infested, one-room tenement in which Bigger and his family live, must bear a great deal of the responsibility for his daughter's death. As testimony continues, Bessie's mutilated corpse is brought in. The jury at the inquest decides that Bigger suffocated and strangled Mary while raping her. He must now be returned to jail to await trial.

Instead of being taken directly to Cook County Jail, Bigger is brought to Mary's room at the Daltons'. He is then told to show how he raped and murdered Mary. He insists that he did not rape her and refuses to do anything. As he is being returned to jail, he sees the burning cross of the Ku Klux Klan. On his return, he throws away the wooden cross given him by the Reverend Hammond and is visited by Max. Bigger tells him about his meaningless existence.

Bigger's trial begins. Max focuses on the causes of Bigger's behavior in his defense. Despite Max's eloquence, Bigger is convicted and sentenced to die in the electric chair. An appeal to the governor fails.

The Characters

Bigger Thomas is a paradox—a "bad nigger" sympathetically portrayed. Not only is his the only point of view in the novel, but he is also the axis around which the other characters revolve.

Bigger's relationship with his family is fraught with tension. He regards them all as "blind" and willing to accept the dehumanizing lot white society proffers. His mother, sister, and brother each has a way of succumbing. Mrs. Thomas finds comfort in religion. Vera, Bigger's sister, does what is expected. For her, sewing lessons at the "Y" provide a safe activity. Buddy, although he looks up to his older brother, is resolved to "stay in his place."

Bessie, Bigger's girlfriend, has her own way of succumbing to white society. She is an alcoholic who no longer finds even sex satisfying. Bigger gives her liquor in exchange for sex, and she allows him to steal from her employers. Eventually, Bigger must kill her because she knows too much. Bessie is a true victim.

Bigger and his gang—G. H., Jack, and Gus—are victims of their own fear, hate, and rage. They demonstrate these negative emotions toward both themselves and white society. They are too scared to carry out the planned robbery of Blum's store. Each, however, recognizes that the others are afraid because Blum is white. To rob Blum is to violate the white establishment.

A black man's killing of a white woman constitutes the ultimate taboo. Thus, when Bigger accidentally kills the young white liberal Mary Dalton, his fate is sealed.

Mary, however, plays a part in her own demise. She is too friendly toward the young black protagonist; she should have recognized his potential danger.

Mr. Dalton, Mary's father, is a seeming contradiction. He gives generously to black charities while at the same time owning the rat-infested tenement in which Bigger and his family live. Similarly, he provides table tennis for blacks but not decent housing.

Mrs. Dalton displays a kind of missionary zeal in her relationship with blacks. Her physical and psychological blindness, however, belie her actions. On first meeting Bigger, she speaks about him in his presence as though he were a textbook case. She is intent on doing what is best for him, as she sees it.

Jan Erlone, Mary Dalton's boyfriend, also wants to do what is best for Bigger. He tries to befriend him on their first meeting by shaking his hand and insisting that Bigger call him by his first name. The protagonist is understandably uncomfortable; he is not used to such behavior on the part of a white man. Later, when Bigger is in prison, Jan visits him and finds him a lawyer. It is perhaps to Jan's credit that Bigger's final request of his lawyer is that he "tell Jan hello."

Boris Max, Bigger's communist lawyer, is eloquent though ineffectual. As Max sees it, white society, not Bigger, is to be blamed for the protagonist's actions. Contrived though such a defense may seem, Max succeeds in gaining Bigger's trust.

All the characters, black and white, Bigger included, are, to a degree, stereotypes. Wright seems more interested in the message and less in the medium.

Themes and Meanings

Bigger Thomas, as his name suggests, is the stereotypical "nigger." As such, he is destined to end up in jail, and Bigger knows it. Very early in the novel, he admits "that the moment he allowed what his life meant to enter fully into consciousness, he would either kill himself or someone else." Living on Chicago's South Side in the 1930's, Bigger is trapped in a hostile environment. His every action is predicated on his obsessive fear of the white world.

His accidental killing of Mary and his murder of Bessie are both motivated by fear. It is because he is panic-stricken at the thought of Mrs. Dalton finding him in Mary's room that he suffocates Mary. Similarly, he murders Bessie because he is afraid she will give him away to the police.

After Mary's death, Bigger experiences feelings of power, equality, and freedom. In fact, he might even be said to have acquired an identity. So powerful is he that he no longer needs his knife and his gun. Also, he believes himself the equal of whites because he has destroyed their most prized possession. He can decide how much to tell the police about Mary's disappearance; for a while, the "dumb nigger" is in charge, and Bigger toys with the police. For the first time in his life, he is somebody—a murderer. The word "murderer" is appropriate, since Bigger convinces himself after Mary's accidental killing that he really intended to kill her.

Bessie is part of his limited environment, and he kills her because he feels he must. After he murders Bessie, Bigger's feelings of power, equality, and freedom, and his sense of an identity are all heightened.

In jail, Bigger is listless and apathetic. His lawyer becomes his confidant, and Bigger tries to sort out his feelings. His dubious epiphany seems to be that his only viable option is violence. The alternative, as he sees it, is dehumanizing submission to white society.

In Bigger's view, all the other blacks in the novel opt for submission to whites. His mother finds solace in religion; his brother unquestioningly accepts the status quo; his sister is excessively timid and believes in the tenets of the "Y"; Bessie, his girlfriend, turns to alcohol and ultimately does not even find sex satisfying. Bigger's friends, Gus, G. H., and Jack, are not willing to go all the way to rid themselves of white oppression.

The reader sees these characters through Bigger's eyes, and they seem like stereotypes; critics have commented adversely on this aspect of the novel. To some, stereotypical character portrayal is inherently faulty, and these critics find even the portrayal of Bigger unsatisfactory. Others, however, contend that Bigger's character, though stereotypical, is convincingly developed, whereas the other characters are mere stick figures.

Among these stick figures are the whites in the novel. Bigger's blanket response to all whites is fear, hate, rage, and shame, with two exceptions. In the case of Jan, Mary's boyfriend, Bigger's standard response gives way to bewilderment and later reluctant trust. As for Max, Bigger trusts him almost immediately; as a result, some commentators view the Bigger-Max relationship as contrived.

If the theme of trust comes late in the novel and causes skepticism, the same cannot be said of the major theme—fear. Not only do the killing of the rat and the fight with Gus foreshadow Mary's death, but they are also motivated by fear. Bigger fights with Gus to cover up his fear of robbing Blum's store. He and his friends are used to preying on other blacks, but to rob a white man's store is taboo. Thus, the killing of Mary demonstrates how Bigger's fear and its concomitant emotions of hate, rage, and shame culminate in increasing violence.

On a much larger scale, Richard Wright seems to be saying that the fate of blacks is determined by a hostile white environment. Determinism, then, is an important theme in *Native Son.* For the Bigger Thomases growing up on the South Side of Chicago in the 1930's, there is no escape; they will end up in jail. The only question is, for what crime? Other blacks are confronted with a Hobson's choice—dehumanizing submission.

Who is to blame for this state of affairs? For most of the novel, Wright seems to be insisting that it is white society that is at fault. As the novel approaches its end, however, the reader gets the sense that Bigger Thomas is the "native son" of all Americans, black and white. If Bigger belongs to all Americans, he is ultimately responsible for his actions and must be held accountable. By killing, Bigger has carved out an identity for himself; by destroying, he has created. Despite his meager choices, he has chosen violence over submission. Even Bigger recognizes this: "But what I killed for, I am!"

At the end of the novel, the reader is still trying to understand Bigger. The point of view is sympathetic. Wright manages to convince the reader that this black youth who has killed twice and begins to feel only after he has murdered is worthy of understanding and compassion.

Some critics insist that in the book's concluding section, the pace of the novel slows to a crawl. These critics regard the final section as a major flaw in the novel, viewing it as contrived and serving only to put forward Wright's communist views. Others concede that, although perhaps too didactic in tone, the concluding section is necessary to show the extent to which Bigger's life is fated. Still others argue that this material should have been integrated into the rest of the novel.

If critics are divided about the effectiveness of Wright's narrative structure, his symbolism is less controversial. The snowfalls and blizzards that occur throughout the novel represent a hostile white society. Similarly, Mrs. Dalton's physical blindness is indicative of the psychological blindness of the other characters. Time, too, has symbolic significance in the novel. Whether it be the cacophonous sound of the alarm clock in the opening line of the novel or the clock ticking at the head of Mary's bed, the references seem to represent Bigger's meaningless existence. Most critics grant a measure of effectiveness to these symbols. The wooden cross, however, does not fare so well. This is the cross that the Reverend Hammond, Bigger's mother's minister, gives Bigger when he visits him in prison. Those who bother to mention it regard it as too obvious. Bigger throws the cross away after seeing the burning cross of the Ku Klux Klan; he cannot absorb the differences between the two symbols. In discarding the wooden cross, however, he is rejecting his mother's religion and, ultimately, his mother.

Critical Context

When first published in 1940, *Native Son* was an immediate success. It was a Book-of-the-Month Club selection, and in three weeks 215,000 copies were sold.

Richard Wright was a prolific writer, and his other works include *Black Boy: A Record of Childhood and Youth* (1945), *Lawd Today* (written 1935, but not published until 1963), *Uncle Tom's Children* (1938), and *The Outsider* (1953).

As literature, *Native Son* employs the tenets of naturalism and existentialism to portray Bigger Thomas, the stereotypical "nigger." If, as the naturalist contends, human beings are the products of their environment, then the very title of the novel— *Native Son*—seems to indicate that Bigger responds to environmental forces. In true naturalistic fashion, Bigger does not understand these forces, and hence he cannot control them.

Wright is as true to existential tenets as he is to naturalism. The meaninglessness of Bigger's existence is at one with the existential philosophy. When, at the end of the novel, Bigger says, "But what I killed for, I am!" he is accepting responsibility for his actions—yet another attribute of existentialism.

Native Son is naturalistic and existential not because Wright is intent on adhering to particular philosophical systems but because, as some commentators have observed, he found black life in America both naturalistic and existential.

Since *Native Son* was published in 1940, it has disturbed the complacency of Americans, both blacks and whites. Bigger Thomas' raw rage cannot be ignored; the reader responds either negatively or positively to the novel. Wright kept the promise he made when he discovered that "even bankers' daughters could read and weep over and feel good about *Uncle Tom's Children.*" He vowed that his next book would be one that "no one would weep over." In fact, "it would be so hard and deep that they would have to face it without the consolation of tears." In this, Wright succeeded.

Bibliography

Kinnamon, Keneth, ed. *New Essays on "Native Son."* New York: Cambridge University Press, 1990. Presents a thorough examination of the genesis and background of *Native Son.* Kinnamon analyzes Wright's own essay "How 'Bigger' Was Born" along with letters, notes, manuscripts, and galley and page proofs to show how external forces influenced the writing of the novel.

Skerrett, Joseph T., Jr. "Composing Bigger: Wright and the Making of *Native Son.*" In *Modern Critical Interpretations: Richard Wright's "Native Son,"* edited by Harold Bloom. New York: Chelsea House, 1988. Offers an illuminating analysis of the biographical aspects of *Native Son.* Skerrett argues convincingly that Richard Wright and Bigger Thomas share many attributes.

Williams, John A. *The Most Native of Sons: A Biography of Richard Wright.* Garden City, N.Y.: Doubleday, 1970. Provides a solid biography for the general reader. Williams places Wright in his historical context both at home and abroad, giving a sense of the man and his times.

Wright, Richard. *Early Novels: Lawd Today! Uncle Tom's Children, Native Son.* Vol. 2 in *Works.* Edited by Arnold Rampersad. New York: Library of America, 1991. Reinstates significant cuts that were made in *Lawd Today!* and *Native Son.* The volume, however, also deserves attention for its detailed chronology, which reads like an excellent biography.

_____. "How 'Bigger' Was Born." In *Native Son,* by Richard Wright. Reprint. New York: Perennial Library, 1987. Details the genesis of *Native Son.* The author describes five Bigger Thomases, dating back to his childhood. Wright is his own best critic.

Sheila J. McDonald

NATIVES OF MY PERSON

Author: George Lamming (1927-   )
Type of work: Novel
Type of plot: Historical realism
Time of plot: The sixteenth century
Locale: The west coast of Africa and the Caribbean
First published: 1972

> *Principal characters:*
> THE COMMANDANT, the enigmatic master of the ship
>   *Reconnaissance*
> PINTEADOS, the ship's pilot
> SASHA, the ship's cabin boy
> THE BOATSWAIN, an experienced sailor
> BAPTISTE, one of the most vocal and militant of the ordinary
>   seamen

The Novel

Although *Natives of My Person* has a historical setting and deals with the voyage of the *Reconnaissance*, a vessel ostensibly engaged in the slave trade, a specific historical phenomenon, it is only partly accurate to describe it as a work of historical realism. Its realist component is not to be found in its fidelity to period costume, living conditions, or similar revealing detail. Instead of the veneer of verisimilitude that such usages provide, the novel locates its realism in the way in which it elaborately recapitulates an outlook.

In order to focus the reader's attention on this enactment of a mindset, there are no reliable geographical or historical bearings. Two powerful nations are mentioned, Lime Stone and Antarctica. Although they are traditionally enemies, their enmity derives from a common commitment to the type of exploration and exploitation that the slave trade brings into being. In Lime Stone, the nation to which the Commandant and the crew of the *Reconnaissance* supposedly owe allegiance, the ruling institution is known as the House of Trade and Justice. The titular head of this house is Gabriel Tate de Lysle, a name perhaps intended to evoke the firm of Tate and Lyle, a real-life British sugar company with substantial plantations in the Caribbean. Antarctica, on the other hand, is represented by the pilot, Pinteados, and an admiral, signifying its maritime interests. In both cases, the appearance of cohesiveness that these spheres of accomplishment provide is deceptive. The activities emerge as a kind of shadow-play, the manifestations of which are not material but psychological.

Similarly, the voyage of the *Reconnaissance* lacks geographical specificity and nautical detail. Nor is its purpose the traditional one of adding to the coffers of the House of Trade and Justice. Although mention is made of the Guinea coast, the customary West African source of slaves for the transatlantic trade, there is very little attempt to bring that environment to life. Moreover, no slaves are taken on board. As the *Reconnaissance* heads across the Atlantic in the general direction of the imaginary island of San Cristobal, the object of the voyage seems less to attain a new, rewarding landfall than to unveil the turbid spirit of nascent imperialism, and the emotional and spiritual squalor that lies beneath the arrogant mask of command. In *Natives of My Person*, much of the romance associated with going down to the sea in ships, with enduring hardship by no means other than raw courage, and with discovering new tropical paradises, is deprived of its hortatory simplemindedness and its ideologically suspect naïvete. The result is that Lamming presents a sustained critique of such one-dimensional verities. The courage depicted has no moral fiber. No heavenly landfall materializes. On the contrary, the voyage is inconclusive and unproductive, its payoff violent and chaotic.

This outcome is particularly telling because it issues from such an explicitly controlled and hierarchical world. Since the action is located on board a ship, elements of rank, order, integration, command, and purpose thus compose the fundamental lexicon of the reality that the characters share. So great is the emphasis placed upon such elements, and so widespread is the belief that this emphasis is in the service of an immutable, historically inscribed destiny, that it becomes inevitable that challenges to the structure of life on the *Reconnaissance* be identified and, if possible, extirpated. One of the most accomplished and explicit means by which the author evinces the inevitability of challenge and the inevitability of its suppression is in the characters' speech. Formal without being orotund, dramatic without being rhetorical, it is an instrument that reveals the probes and defenses used by the characters to substantiate their common reality.

Yet this common reality, fabricated in the name of the imperial ambitions of Lime Stone's ruling house and given direct impetus by the Commandant's own ambition, is less durable than the mixture of unhappy personal histories and dubious motivations that the individual crew members bring on board with them. These discrete narratives of humiliation and error all have a common root in sexuality, and all pertain to the Commandant's status both as captain of the *Reconnaissance* and as an intimate of the House of Trade and Justice. By seeing to it that there is no escaping the various forms of psychological enslavement that form the basis of the crew's personal reality, and by arranging the plot of *Natives of My Person* so that this inner bondage is the cause of the calamitous climax of the voyage, George Lamming exposes the mortal weakness of those who sought to impose their will on the world in the name of empire.

The Characters

From the point of view of character, the shipboard world of *Natives of My Person* is divided into two halves, the world of masters and the world of men. In the latter world, the characters have actual names such as Baptiste, Ivan, and Marcel. Considered collectively, the crew members' names resist the identification of Lime Stone with any specific imperial power. Many of the names have French associations. Of all the various empires to have made their marks on the Caribbean, the French was, arguably, the least prominent, so that the French emphasis becomes part of the structure of inversion upon which the novel is based.

The men, by virtue of their names, attain a certain individuality. Yet it is an attainment that they are not permitted to experience as empowerment. Such a condition of psychological disfranchisement is endemic to life at sea. The result is that, for all their colorfulness, the various skills of their trades, and the range of their differentiated backgrounds, the ordinary seamen are utterly dependent on the ebb and flow of surmise, rumor, and gossip that they trawl for indications of what lies in store for them. They are held captive both by the enigmatic Commandant and, more fundamentally, by a social structure that demands that they be kept in a state of lesser awareness than the officers. The effect of this dependence is that their individuality is purely nominal.

The manner in which the men are entrapped is largely social. In important respects, they are free of the sexual attachments that determine the fates of their superiors in rank, but this freedom is unable to assume a constructive form. There is no alternative available to the men to the command structure of the ship and the command economy that underlies and motivates it. Although they are implicated in the ways in which conditions develop on the *Reconnaissance*, they remain essentially outside the psychological penumbra that darkens the officers' inner lives. Despite their machismo and capacity for belligerence, the men are for all practical purposes innocent, as the Boatswain's story shows. This story, which tells of the intersection between the sailor's life and the officer's life, depicts the Boatswain attempting to redeem by means of sex the abjectness of a life spent unrewardingly in the service of the House of Trade and Justice. The story not only marks the beginning of the end of the voyage but also confirms the rigidity of the lines that control the social reality by which the characters are obliged to abide.

The situation of the officers is a mirror image of that of the men. They are known not by their names but by their professional occupations such as Priest, Surgeon, and Steward. These designations clearly obviate the characters' individuality. Yet their individuality, conceived in terms of marriage, private life, sexuality, thirst for power, and willingness to judge and punish, is what the officers cannot forego. The human cost of their service is what haunts and eventually destroys them. As with the men, but in a much more decisive manner that calls into question the hierarchical principles of the Lime Stone world, the officers are incapable of overcoming their attachment to the system in which they serve. Individuating elements are inadmissable in the world of the slave-traders.

What the Boatswain is with regard to the men, the Commandant is in connection with the officers. His attempts to personify for his own ends the ambitions of the House of Trade and Justice, and the fact that these attempts can be seen to be driven by a need to sublimate his sexual experiences in Lime Stone, bring to a critical, and untenable, juncture the conflicts between role and personality, between ego and id, between the amenities of land and the vicissitudes of sea. Both the Commandant and Boatswain embody to a problematic, and ultimately catastrophic, degree the tensions and contradictions to which the groups to which they belong are subject. Rather than developing a sense of the characters' individuality, *Natives of My Person* instead explores its moral landscape by showing the destructive resistance of type to individuality.

Themes and Meanings

In the burgeoning field of fiction and drama dealing with imperialism, colonialism, and their consequences, *Natives of My Person* is of particular significance not only for its stylization of the historical background but also for its treatment of its subject exclusively through the minds of the imperialists. Taking for its theme the moral and psychological strategies by which the avatars of empire articulate their moral natures, the novel dwells on the evasions, corruptions, sublimations, and impositions that are an unacknowledged but decisive force in the workings of those natures. In one sense, it is of little consequence that the voyage of the *Reconnaissance* to San Cristobal is abortive. What is at issue is not the conquest but the character of the would-be conquerors. Blind to their own human fallibility, they can hardly be expected to be alive to the humanity of those who seem different to them, whether the difference is in skin color or, as in the novel, in gender.

In one of the journal extracts that occur periodically throughout *Natives of My Person*, there is a rehearsal of some of the major tropes of racism. These include stereotypical assumptions regarding the untamed, indisciplined, sexually abandoned, and generally monstrous nature of those captured for enslavement. The inevitable conclusion is that such creatures are beyond the moral pale and must be considered alien to their captors' codes of civilization. Yet the plot of the novel subtly suggests that the same charges might well be leveled against these self-styled superior agents, not merely because of their racist views but also because of the way in which they treat their wives in Lime Stone. The consistently exploitative and punitive manner in which these women are treated is not only objectionable in itself but also contains the essence of what is morally repugnant in the world of the empire builders.

Desire for power on the domestic front is suggested to be the moral basis for the voyage. The manner in which the past haunts and threatens the officers is a demonstration of the abusive psychological economy to which they have become indentured. The women themselves, however, are not to be sentimentalized. They too are not beyond attempting to create their own power bases by exploiting their sexuality. This view reinforces the reciprocal nature of the novel's overview. Just as officers and men are complementary in their respective situations, so are husbands and wives. It is from this complementarity that the inescapable nature of the novel's moral universe derives.

Every facet of this universe has its own distinctive and persuasive part to play. Intimate interrogation in the captain's cabin or in the marriage bed has as forceful a determining role as exploration that spans oceans. Innocence ineluctably incriminates, while the guilty accidentally fall victim to what seems the moral equivalent of their just desserts. The voyage that fails, as that of the *Reconnaissance* does, is as instructive as the innumerable imperialist voyages that succeed. In its comprehensiveness, *Natives of My Person* embraces an immense swathe of fallible human behavior; as its title indicates, that swathe is embodied by each of the characters, each in a particular but unavoidably related manner. With his somewhat inaccessible title, the author may be suggesting that he is the inheritor of the world that the imperial mindset created, and that that world's bequest of a mindset is its primary and most problematic legacy.

Critical Context

The narrative strategy of assembling a cast of characters and sending them on a voyage can be traced at least as far back as the fifteenth century German poem *Das Narrenschiff* (1494; *The Ship of Folys of the Worlde*, 1509), and the representative nature of the characters of *Natives of My Person*, as well as its inevitable moral critique, align it with the tradition of such works. This tradition has connotations of plotting a course and envisaging a destination, as well as of foundering and losing one's bearings. These two sets of connotations continually interact in *Natives of My Person*.

Yet despite the work's allegorical potential deriving from its medieval prototype, the novel's main critical context is indebted to more modern works. Although *Natives of My Person* is conceived and executed on a much larger scale than Joseph Conrad's *Heart of Darkness* (1899), its thematic debt to that work is not difficult to discern. The thematic force of the journey as an event of more psychological than geographical interest is obviously present in both works, and the insistence on the corrupting effects of power, and on power conceived of in exclusively exploitative terms, are also aired in Conrad's story.

It is important also not to overlook the author's declaration of his own cultural allegiances. These are suggested in his partial dedication of the novel to the African American author Richard Wright and in the title's echo of Wright's most celebrated novel, *Native Son* (1940). Apart from the inherent interest in one writer's public homage to another, the dedication acts as a firm reminder that the issues raised in *Natives of My Person* have remained current, and that the human history that engendered these issues still requires the imaginative reconstruction and moral dissection to which George Lamming subjects it.

Bibliography

Boxhill, Anthony. "San Cristobal Unreached: George Lamming's Two Latest Novels." *World Literature Written in English* 12 (April, 1973): 16-28. Discusses Lamming's *Water with Berries* (1972) and *Natives of My Person*, examining in detail the latter's treatment of historical and colonial questions.

Campbell, Elaine. "West Indian Sea Fiction: George Lamming's *Natives of My Person*." *Commonwealth Novel in English* 3 (Spring/Summer, 1984): 56-65. Discusses the different nautical dimensions of *Natives of My Person* and relates them to the maritime tradition of the Caribbean novel.

McDonald, Avis G. " 'Within the Orbit of Power': Reading Allegory in George Lamming's *Natives of My Person." Journal of Commonwealth Literature* 22, no. 1 (1987): 73-86. An elaborate and complex reading of the novel's allegorical character, which is interpreted as, ultimately, a meditation on the consequences of power as a force for coherence in the world.

Munro, Ian. "George Lamming." In *West Indian Literature,* edited by Bruce King. London: Archon Books, 1979. A general introduction to Lamming's work, concentrating on his novels. The works' various treatments of emigration and colonialism are identified. The survey also indicates ways in which *Natives of My Person* can be considered the culmination of Lamming's fiction.

Paquet, Sandra Pouchet. *The Novels of George Lamming.* London: Heinemann, 1982. Contains a chapter on *Natives of My Person.* Provides a broad overview of the novel's economic, sociological, and historical underpinnings. Also has a substantial bibliography.

Peterson, Kirsten Holt. "Time, Timelessness, and the Journey Metaphor in George Lamming's *In the Castle of My Skin* and *Natives of My Person." In The Commonwealth Writer Overseas: Themes of Exile and Expatriation,* edited by Alastair Niven. Brussels: Marcel Didier, 1976. Highlights the journey theme in Lamming's works and considers the contribution made by the works in relation to the establishment of a specific West Indian mentality and culture.

George O'Brien

THE NEW NEGRO
An Interpretation

Author: Alain LeRoy Locke (1886-1954)
Type of work: Essays
First published: 1925

Form and Content

Edited by Alain Locke, a Howard University professor of philosophy, *The New Negro* was a compilation of poems, short fiction, essays, and illustrations. It celebrated the appearance of a new contingent of African American writers and artists, following the Great Migration of rural Southern blacks to Northern urban meccas in the early twentieth century. An expression of the creative energy and ferment of the postwar Jazz Age, the volume was both a collection of literary and visual artifacts and, in its ideological function as a racial manifesto, a cultural artifact in its own right. It hastened the emergence into public consciousness of the so-called Harlem Renaissance—Harlem was both its site and sometime subject—a phenomenon of spontaneous cultural combustion in this international capital of the "Negro" world.

The volume featured novelists, poets, playwrights, critics, scholars, and artists. Its contributors made up a who's who of black literati, with cameo appearances by representative white sympathizers. Of the thirty-eight contributors, eight were women, among them writer and folklorist Zora Neale Hurston and novelist Jessie Fauset, who was also the literary editor of *The Crisis*, the journal of the National Association for the Advancement of Colored People (NAACP). Alain Locke apart, the most notable male contributors to *The New Negro* were Jean Toomer, the author of *Cane* (1923), a book of vignettes of racial subject matter and formal inventiveness that had anticipated the Harlem Renaissance; the irascible West Indian poet Claude McKay, whose militant poem "If We Must Die" spoke for the younger generation; Countée Cullen, a poet more polished and conventional than the globe-trotting McKay; and the wordsmith Langston Hughes, in many respects the conscience of the younger artists. Among the elder statesmen represented were W. E. B. Du Bois, the chief editor of *The Crisis*; Kelly Miller, a professor at Howard University; the educator Robert R. Moton; and the widely esteemed racial diplomat James Weldon Johnson, coauthor of "Lift Every Voice and Sing," the "Negro national anthem." An intermediate generation was represented by the sociologists Charles S. Johnson and E. Franklin Frazier, the former already established, the latter soon to make his mark. The four white contributors were Albert C. Barnes, a wealthy connoisseur and collector whose taste for European impressionist paintings coexisted with an early appreciation of African and African American art; Paul U. Kellogg, director of the famous Pittsburgh Survey (1908-1914) and editor of *The Survey Graphic*, a progressive monthly journal; Melville J. Herskovits, a young anthropologist and pioneer Africanist, later to be celebrated and controversial for the suggestion that African American culture was marked by African survivals; and Winold Reiss, an Austrian illustrator and graphic artist who specialized in the delineation of folk types in Europe and the Americas.

For students of American intellectual history, *The New Negro* is noteworthy for the circumstances surrounding its appearance, its rhetorical purpose, and its editorial packaging, all of which are related. Appearing in 1925, *The New Negro* was an expanded version of a special Harlem issue of the magazine, *The Survey Graphic*. Underwritten in part by the Russell Sage Foundation, which had been established in 1907 to support progressive social initiatives, *The Survey Graphic* was the semiofficial journal of a multidimensional urban reform movement that had grown out of scientific charity and social settlement concerns. Those earlier movements were distinguished both by their attention to the so-called new immigrants from Southern and Eastern Europe and by their early recognition that rural Southern blacks were part of a population shift to urban centers that was changing the face of the United States. Thus, *The New Negro* had its genesis in a sympathetic interest in problems of black city life that characterized a growing number of educated men and women. Guest edited by Alain Locke, the March, 1925, issue of *The Survey Graphic* addressed a constituency of social reform professionals who were liberal on matters of race. Building on the magazine's nucleus, Locke fashioned for a wider audience a sweeping survey in book form of black cultural achievement. An ideological and cultural artifact, *The New Negro* was intended to make the case for a racial coming of age and, with it, a stronger claim for black participation in the collective making of a properly American civilization.

The book was organized in two parts. Following four introductory essays, the first three sections of part 1, "The Negro Renaissance," offered examples of new work by younger artists in fiction, poetry, and drama. In the following section, devoted to music, there were essays on Southern spirituals and on a controversial emerging musical form, urban jazz. The final section of part 1 featured "The Negro Digs Up His Past," an essay on the identity-building function of history by the Puerto Rican booklover and collector Arthur A. Schomburg; a discussion of African American folk literature by Arthur Huff Fauset, an acknowledged amateur authority; and a provocative essay by Locke on black music, poetry, and dance, supposedly the primary "ancestral arts" of the African diaspora. In retrospect, the most important aspects of part 1 of *The New Negro* were not the short contributions by younger artists but rather the introductory essays that framed the book as a whole and sharpened its ideological thrust.

Part 2, "The New Negro in a New World," provided useful snapshots of aspects of black life in the postwar era. Sociologist Charles S. Johnson, director of research and investigations for the National Urban League and editor of its journal *Opportunity*, discussed the Great Migration, the black population shift to the American urban frontier. James Weldon Johnson, composer, diplomat, and first black executive secretary of the NAACP, made Harlem itself his essay subject, reconstructing and celebrating its history as the black cultural capital. The young sociologist E. Franklin Frazier commented on middle-class life in Durham, North Carolina, an important site of black economic achievement. Robert Russa Moton, Booker T. Washington's successor as principal of Tuskegee Institute, and Kelly Miller, founding chairman of the Howard University department of sociology, contributed discussions of their respective educational institutions. In placing their essays side by side, Locke ratified the truce between supporters of industrial and higher education that had existed since Washington's death in 1915. The Jamaican journalist W. A. Domingo contributed a pioneering discussion of the cultural contributions of foreign-born blacks. In his essay, the West Indian spicing of the Harlem community received hearty acknowledgment. In a section on "The Negro and the American Tradition," three interesting essays were featured. Ironically—in view of the African "survivals" thesis with which he was later identified—Melville Herskovits argued the case for "The Negro's Americanism." This emphasis, however, fit well with Locke's conciliatory editorial strategy. Walter White, an NAACP official light-skinned enough to pass for white when investigating Southern lynchings, explored "The Paradox of Color." Elise Johnson McDougald, an educator, social investigator, and labor activist, offered an insightful analysis of the gendered lives of different classes of Harlem women.

Finally, the black predicament in the postwar world was seen in international terms. W. E. B. Du Bois brought issues of race, cultural autonomy, colonialism, and exploitative labor relations together under a single lens. He did so through a brief history of the pan-African conference movement of which he was the major architect.

The ideological purposes of *The New Negro* were reflected in all aspects of its construction, including the layout of the volume. Alain Locke commissioned Winold Reiss to do the cover design, decorative features, and illustrations. The result was successful, Locke indicated, because Reiss, "a folklorist of the brush and palette," did "not forc[e] an alien idiom upon nature or a foreign convention upon a racial tradition." Instead, Locke noted, "Concretely in his portrait sketches, abstractly in his symbolic designs, he has aimed to portray the soul and spirit of a people."

The terms of his praise suggest how Locke sought to frame *The New Negro* and how he read the significance of the Harlem Renaissance itself. The illustrator's success was due "as much to the philosophy of his approach as to his technical skill," Locke suggested. To demonstrate graphically the richness of Negro folk types as a source of material "both for the Negro artist and American art at large" was an indirect but effective way, Locke argued, of asserting that value of black culture itself.

The wide-ranging bibliographies that completed *The New Negro* were also essential to its purpose. Though not exhaustive, the listings led readers to useful information about important aspects of black life. Arthur A. Schomburg identified notable works by eighteenth and nineteenth century black authors. Arthur Huff Fauset provided titles on black folklore in the United States, Africa, and the West Indies, as well as references in several languages to aspects of African culture. Miscellaneous materials were grouped under the heading "The Negro in Literature." Listings of English, Continental, and American fiction joined bibliographies of black poetry, slave narratives, biographies, and autobiographies. Under the heading "Negro Drama," plays about black life and by black playwrights were identified. The richer listing of black music featured collections of black folk songs, commentaries on them, and collections and arrangements of black spirituals. The contributionist argument of *The New Negro* was implicit in the bibliography that followed, "A Selected List of Modern Music, Influenced by American Negro Themes or Idioms." Finally, Du Bois' magisterial hand was visible in the obligatory listings on "The Negro Problems" with which the volume closed.

Analysis

In *The New Negro*, three generations of black artists and intellectuals addressed questions raised by Du Bois two decades earlier in *The Souls of Black Folk* (1903). What does it mean to be both black and American? On what terms can African Americans participate in the making of a common national life in the United States without denying what is distinctive about themselves as members of a particular group? What is the relation of culture and politics? What is the relation of history, art, and racial identity?

Locke's opening essay, "The New Negro," is of enduring historical significance in this connection. His remarks on the politics of culture and the use of art for social purposes—specifically, on the exploitation of folk themes by middle-class artists as a form of racial lobbying—have stimulated decades of heated discussion and criticism. Responding to the tendency of sociologists to see black Americans primarily in light of the "Negro problem," Locke insisted instead that "the elements of truest social portraiture are found in artistic self-expression." So far as African Americans were culturally articulate, they were to speak for themselves.

The flowering of a new race spirit among African Americans was an example of movements of national self-determination around the world. As a large part of the peasant matrix of the American South, black Americans had made that region a gift of their folk temperament, contributing, Locke noted, a "leaven of humor, sentiment, imagination and tropic nonchalance." At the stage of cultural adolescence, the African American was now becoming a more conscious contributor to American civilization, as a younger generation moved "from the arid fields of controversy and debate to the productive fields of creative expression." The "forced radicalism" of an emphasis on race represented a unique social experiment, an attempt to build Americanism on race values, to turn a handicap into an advantage, and to anticipate and create a new democracy in American culture. At once therapeutic and tactical, the New Negro Movement looked within and without, Locke suggested. Internally, it sought to repair a damaged group psychology. Externally, it celebrated the paradox of ethnicity, the fact that the racialism of the Harlem Renaissance intended integration, not separatism; in Locke's words, the fullest racial self-expression was contingent upon "the fullest sharing of American culture and institutions." From this point of view, the cultural project was inevitably a political one. Admission to first-class citizenship on honorable terms turned on the revaluation of the African American's "cultural contributions, past and prospective."

Critical Context

The New Negro represented an African American intervention in debates about ethnicity, racial difference, cultural identity, and normative Americanism that were preoccupying the literate public. These issues shaped discussions of how the United States might deal with a rapidly changing population. In the face of Anglo-Saxon resentment that "model Americans" could not be made of the newer immigrants, social progressives countered that in diversity lay strength. In 1916, essayist and critic Randolph Bourne challenged the melting-pot model of Americanization. He urged that the ideal of a cosmopolitan federation of national cultures take its place. After the war, philosopher Horace Kallen weighed in with an equally cogent discussion of *Culture and Democracy in the United States* (1924). The emerging liberal consensus was consolidated with the Carnegie Corporation's monumental ten-volume series of books on "Americanization Studies" published from 1918 to 1924. Yet widespread nativist sentiment found political expression in the Immigration Act of 1924, which established entry quotas for less-favored foreign nationals.

Nevertheless, in the course of debating the incorporation of immigrant peoples on culturally equitable terms, a more flexible public language became available. American identity was reconceived as the composite product of multiple ethnic ingredients. Because pluralism was urged as an integral dimension of a forward-looking politics, a rhetorical and conceptual space was opened up for black thinkers to exploit. Making culture a language of social and political discourse might earn African Americans a seat at the national table, while preserving a collective identity still in the making.

Other factors also worked to encourage a cultural politics after World War I. An emerging interest in African motifs, famously instanced in the works of the painter Pablo Picasso, and a downward revaluation of Western abstract reason in favor of the emotional and the sensuous both helped to bring black themes within the ambit of an existing interest—artistic, anthropological, and linguistic—in "folk" peoples generally. Thus, Locke's framing of *The New Negro* project was both principled and politic. Locke, however, never addressed the tricky issue of exploiting stereotypes to combat stereotypes.

Beyond the confines of *The New Negro* itself, two classic perspectives on the Harlem Renaissance were staked out by the sociologist E. Franklin Frazier and by the poet Langston Hughes, both contributors to the volume. In "The Negro Artist and the Racial Mountain" (1926), an essay published in *The Nation*, Hughes spoke for the younger participants in the Harlem Renaissance. He embraced the zestful life of the lower classes as an unproblematic source of creative inspiration. His literary bohemianism and lack of concern with what middle-class audiences, white or black, might think, and his determination to pursue art for art's sake rather than for purposes of interracial diplomacy, distanced him from *The New Negro* line. In "Racial Self-Expression" (1927), Frazier adopted an outsider's stance, dispassionate and analytical. He discussed the dangers of a defensive and parochial nationalism that might ghettoize black culture, that might, in Locke's striking words, "encyst the Negro as a benign foreign body in the [American] body politic." From that day onward, discussions of the cultural strategy of the Harlem Renaissance have followed one of these two lines.

Bibliography

Garber, Eric. "A Spectacle in Color: The Lesbian and Gay Subculture of Jazz Age Harlem." In *Hidden from History: Reclaiming the Gay and Lesbian Past*, edited by Martin B. Duberman et al. New York: NAL Books, 1989. A pioneering discussion of a long-ignored but integral dimension of the lively club scene in 1920's Harlem.

Huggins, Nathan Irvin. *Harlem Renaissance.* New York: Oxford University Press, 1971. A useful, comprehensive discussion of the literary work of the major figures of the Harlem Renaissance. Notable for the author's concern to situate the texts in their American cultural context.

Hull, Gloria T. *Color, Sex, and Poetry: Three Women Writers of the Harlem Renaissance.* Bloomington: Indiana University Press, 1987. A representative act of literary "recovery," highlighting the important role played by women artists in the cultural ferment of the time.

Lewis, David Levering. *When Harlem Was in Vogue.* New York: Alfred A. Knopf, 1981. The single best evocation of the fascinating figures and kaleidoscopic world of the Harlem Renaissance. An important and immensely readable book.

Locke, Alain LeRoy. *The Critical Temper of Alain Locke: A Selection of His Essays on Art and Culture.* Edited by Jeffrey C. Stewart. New York: Garland, 1983. A useful way to unpack the cultural assumptions Locke brought to the task of editing *The New Negro.*

Meier, August. "The Social and Intellectual Origins of the New Negro." In *Negro Thought in America, 1880-1915.* Ann Arbor: University of Michigan Press, 1963. A classic interpretation of the historical background and social foundations of ideological currents in black communities in the early twentieth century. The "nationalist" stirrings and differing constituencies of the Marcus Garvey and Harlem Renaissance movements are perceptively compared.

Perry, Margaret. *The Harlem Renaissance: An Annotated Bibliography and Commentary.* New York: Garland, 1982. A useful starting point for further investigation of all aspects of the Harlem Renaissance. Highly recommended.

Paul Jefferson

1959

Author: Thulani Davis (1949-   )
Type of work: Novel
Type of plot: Social realism
Time of plot: 1959
Locale: The Chesapeake Bay area of Virginia
First published: 1992

Principal characters:

WILLIE TARRANT, the narrator, a bright twelve-year-old girl
DIXON TARRANT, Willie's father, a man who has slipped into
    complacency after the death of his activist wife
RALPH JOHNSON, Dixon's former college classmate
MAE TALIAFERRO, a teacher at Ida B. Wells Junior High
COLEMAN BOTELER, a tormented aspiring writer and teacher
MADDIE ALEXANDER, a distant cousin of the Tarrants and mother
    of Willie's best friend, Marian
HERMAN SHAW, a white supremacist member of the school board

The Novel

On the surface, *1959* recounts the rite of passage of Katherine "Willie" Tarrant. Through the use of a first-person narrator, Davis presents an evocative portrait of a young African American teenager living during the 1950's, an era beset by injustice and growing racial unrest.

The novel opens with the razing of Turner, Virginia. Above the sounds of bulldozers rumbling over what were once modest wooden bungalows, the adult Willie Tarrant muses over the history of the town. She imagines the arrival of an African woman three hundred years earlier. This woman, abandoned by a slaver because she is sick and therefore not a marketable commodity, has no name. Willie opts to call her "Gambia." A woman of immense dignity and fortitude, Gambia does not die. By her very survival, she becomes the progenitor of Turner's African American community. Subsequently, Willie regards Gambia as her spiritual kin. Although the town has been leveled and the mythical Gambia lives only in Willie's imagination, Willie the adult has returned in triumph. What follows is her story told in retrospect.

On the same day in July, 1959, Willie Tarrant turned twelve and Billie Holiday died. Willie's world is the world of most adolescents, one characterized by preoccupations with music, clothes, and the opposite sex. When her father, a college professor, tells her that twelve is the age of reason, Willie sees this as the opportunity to have her childish braids cut off in preparation for her first date.

Willie reveals that her interests transcend the teenage world of boys, clothes, and music. She is mesmerized by the exploits of prominent dictators in the news, among them Fulgencio Batista, Papa Doc Duvalier, and Fidel Castro. Willie's fascination with dictators and guerrillas stems from the white community's concern over Cuban affairs, which she equates with the furor over the civil rights struggle in Little Rock, Arkansas.

Interspersed within Willie's narrative is the story of Willie's dead Aunt Fannie. What Willie cannot glean from her father's family stories about Fannie, she imagines. Thus Fannie becomes a mythic figure within the novel. Fannie, Willie has learned, often sneaked out of the house to see minstrel shows, in defiance of her parents' wishes. Her niece shares her fascination with the Tambo/Mr. Interlocutor routines. Willie often begs her father to recount what his older sister had told him. Dixon is wary about re-creating the old routines for his precocious daughter. He does, however, tell her that the minstrel shows "were in a different language. It was a hungry language and all the words were a complicated code that grew more and more intricate. And all the words said, 'I'm a fool, but I'm not a fool,' or 'I'm just here and I don't understand but I know *exactly* what is going on.'"

The linguistic code of turn-of-the century minstrel shows becomes the code of the town when the school integration issue is raised. Many parents, including Dixon Tarrant, are concerned with what might happen if selected students from Ida B. Wells Junior High were to be sent to the all-white Patrick Henry Junior High. Fearing for their children's safety, the parents call a town meeting to discuss the issue. Eventually, they decide to send the top six students if the desegregation issue is forced. One of those students is Willie Tarrant.

Willie's remarkable teacher, Mae Taliaferro, rigorously prepares her students for the possible move. She refuses to teach the erroneous and biased material covered in the out-of-date textbooks that the all-white board of education has provided for the Wells students. One of the board members, Herman Shaw, is outraged by what he, a white supremacist, views as Mae's teaching of communist thought, and he calls for her dismissal. The African American community, however, stands behind Taliaferro, and Shaw's edict is dismissed.

That winter, eight African American college students openly oppose segregation laws when they sit at the lunch counter of the local Woolworth's. Jailed and beaten several times, the students do not give up and return daily to the counter. The African American community is galvanized by this event. Dixon Tarrant becomes the leading spokesperson for the desegregation movement. Other community members, heretofore apolitical and passive, engage in the fight. The changes affect all members of the community, particularly Willie. No longer is her world a pedestrian one. She has been exposed to the evils of racial injustice and becomes an activist. At the age of reason, Willie Tarrant becomes a tireless worker for civil rights, responding reasonably to an unreasonable system.

The Characters

The novel contains an interesting mixture of fictional and historical figures. Because it is Willie's story on a primary level, the changes in other characters, as well as in Willie herself, are filtered through the point of view of an adolescent. Davis captures the concerns and values of a twelve-year-old by interweaving the social and political issues of the time with popular culture. The music motif permeates the novel, beginning with the reference to Billie Holiday and sustained by references to jazz, rhythm and blues, and Willie's disdain for Pat Boone. The predominant music of the white culture seems empty to Willie, yet the songs of Billie Holiday are beyond her comprehension. The Willie Tarrant of the beginning of the novel does not have the life experience to appreciate the rich, painfully poignant music of Lady Day. The adult Willie Tarrant does. Willie's fascination with such figures as Papa Doc Duvalier and Fidel Castro is augmented by youthful romanticism. For example, she compares Castro to Dwight D. Eisenhower, finding Eisenhower wanting and Castro a Cuban version of Marlon Brando.

Much of the Tarrants' familial history is embellished by the creative Willie, especially the episodes dealing with Aunt Fannie and Gambia. Willie's romanticizing of her ancestors is her way of creating the strong, positive female role models she believes that her life is lacking, initially not realizing that the authoritative Mrs. Taliaferro and her frivolous Aunt Maddie are women of powerful character.

The male characters in the book are originally limned as passive, self-centered, or bitter. At first, in Willie's young eyes her father is old and staid, a reasonably accurate characterization for the first half of the novel. When he rises to the defense of the eight college students, Willie barely recognizes him. As the civil unrest begins to form and shape the lives of the adults, Willie is mystified by their behavior, not realizing that she is changing as well. When the Reverend Martin Luther King, Jr., comes to speak to the Turner community, Willie reaches an epiphany:

> I felt as if I had never known who I was or where I was living. And I felt good. And I felt full of power. I closed my eyes and soaked in a feast of spirit. When he finished, the chapel exploded in joy, touchable joy.
>
> Reverend King had made me angry and happy to be angry, really more happy than angry. He also made me feel that day that Negroes felt the same way about things, that the same kind of fire was in all of us.

The fire that lights Willie lights everyone. People who have led mundane, placid lives become activists. Ralph Johnson, the acerbic barber with an engineering degree, forsakes the solace his jazz records afford and becomes embroiled in the desegregation struggle. Coleman Boteler, a womanizing, self-indulgent writer and teacher, moves from his self-imposed periphery to the center of the movement. The lives of these people are thus irrevocably altered by the winds of change heralded by such leaders as Martin Luther King, Jr.

Themes and Meanings

Dixon Tarrant, when trying to convey to his young daughter the feelings within him during a meeting or a march, sums up the main themes of the novel: "Sometimes it's like when I hear spirituals I heard when I was a child. Kind of a consoling feeling. And sometimes, like the other day with the dogs, it's like standing in the middle of a storm, but it's not blowing around you, it's like it's coming from inside. Power, it's a feeling of power."

The movement from powerlessness and even despair to power and hope shapes the novel. Davis expands on this theme through the growing complexity of Willie's narrative, which eventually becomes a metanarrative for the African American community. The passage above concisely draws in the various devices and references deployed throughout the novel to emblazon the theme of power.

Within Willie's chronologically retold personal history are various family histories that deal with the national shames of slavery and Jim Crow laws. The elder Tarrants try to bury these histories, believing that to dredge up the darker aspects of the African American experience is harmful. For example, Dixon's father forbids the discussion of his parents' bondage, and Dixon is uneasy re-enacting the routines of minstrel shows. Ironically, Dixon finds some remnants of slavery, notably the singing of spirituals, to be comforting. The reluctant retelling of the Tarrant history serves as a caustic reminder of the legacy of slavery. This dark legacy is most effectively exemplified in the story of Ralph Johnson, the holder of a college degree in engineering who, because of his race, is unable to earn a living as an engineer and instead works as a barber.

The brutal killing of Jack Dempsey, a local black boy, explores the issue of racial injustice in the 1950's. Dempsey is shot in cold blood by a nervous white youth, but his murder is ignored by the justice system. Unlike the great white prizefighter for whom he was named, Jack Dempsey represents the powerlessness of humanity in an inhumane system. His story is one of despair, not of triumph.

The storm itself becomes the controlling metaphor in the novel. Many times Dixon Tarrant, an amateur meteorologist, takes his young son and daughter out to observe hurricanes. His matter-of-fact explanations of weather phenomena make the storms less threatening than interesting to Willie. Dixon correlates the natural storms that buffet the Virginia coast with the social storms raging throughout the town, particularly the confrontation of the police and their attack dogs with the peaceful women demonstrators. Because of the social storm surrounding these people, they have finally become empowered. Consequently, Willie and her family's activism makes the events swirling around the tiny community of Turner less frightening, as opposed to the novel's beginning, when just the thought of Little Rock and the desegregation issue makes the African American community uneasy. The cycle becomes complete when Willie, who as an adult has never forgotten the lessons of power and hope the Turner desegregation efforts of 1959 taught her, becomes a journalist and activist. As a survivor, she sees her role as being continually engaged in the struggle, lest others forget.

Critical Context

Thulani Davis is a respected journalist, dramatist, and poet. Her articles have appeared in such highly respected publications as *The New York Times*, *The Washington Post*, *The Village Voice*, and *American Film*. Her libretto for the opera *X:*

The Life and Times of Malcolm X and her adaptation of Bertolt Brecht's 1948 *The Caucasian Chalk Circle* have earned her widespread critical acclaim in operatic and theatrical circles. Her first novel was *1959.*

Overall, the novel has received positive reviews, being favorably compared with the works of James Baldwin and Carson McCullers. Critics have found correlations between Davis' first novel and the works of a more established contemporary writer, Toni Morrison. Both Morrison and Davis have chosen to address social issues by filtering them through events centered in small African American communities. These communities ultimately become microscosmic studies of national and social concerns.

In addition, *1959* is often praised for its fusion of the historic and the fictional. The use of the juvenile narrative voice places the novel within the tradition of the female *Bildungsroman.* Drawing upon her own experience as an African American who grew up in the era she is writing about, Davis has created a synthesis of autobiography, history, and fiction. As a work of fiction and as a social document, *1959* addresses a multitude of issues, including civil rights on a broad scale and the psychological implications inherent in the civil rights struggle on a more personal level.

Davis has presented an affirming view of the African American experience. The story of Willie Tarrant and her community serves as a testament to the power of the community that bands together. The endurance and fortitude of the people of whom Davis writes had been tested and tempered.

Bibliography
Burn, Gordon. "Review of *1959.*" *The Times Literary Supplement*, May 29, 1992, 21. Discusses the duality of the Willie Tarrant narrative and the broader implications of the civil rights experience, especially in the context of how the events set in motion transform the town.

Gates, David. "Review of *1959.*" *Newsweek* 119 (March 9, 1992): 60. Sees the civil rights activities in the novel as a microhistory of the Civil Rights movement and as an emblematic prophesy of the African American experience. Analyzes Davis' fictionalized account of how an African American community discovers its inherent power and the limits of that power from the standpoint of persuasive discourse.

Hull, Gloria T. "Review of *1959.*" *Women's Review of Books* (May, 1992): 6. Identifies the influences of Toni Morrison's works on Davis' novel. Views the novel as an affirmation of the spirit and dignity of people of the period described. Offers a brief analysis of Davis' employment of characterization, asserting that the revelation of character through situation is poetic. Overall, Hull deems *1959* to be an excellent first novel, one that is lively in tone and subject matter and evinces the author's talent.

Knight, Kimberly. "Thulani Davis: Writing the Untold Stories." *Essence* 23 (May, 1992): 60. Discusses how Davis has drawn upon her own life and family experiences in her writing of *1959.* Provides limited biographical information on Davis.

Levine, Beth. "Review of *1959.*" *The New York Times Book Review*, March 15, 1992, 18. Examines how the novel presents a moving testament of communal power, a power that ignited the Civil Rights movement in the 1960's. Points out how Davis' deft use of time and place, especially the function of the town's history and Fannie Tarrant's diary in the narrative, evokes that power.

Molesworth, Charles. "Culture, Power, and Society." In *Columbia Literary History of the United States*, edited by Emory Elliott. New York: Columbia University Press, 1988. Concisely deals with how contemporary American writers in general address and thereby illuminate the question of power. Considers the issue of social and political consciousness in the postwar era. Of particular interest is a discussion of the presence of adolescent sensibility in the contemporary novel, a device that allows postwar novelists to explore the notion of power versus powerlessness.

Anita M. Vickers

NOTES OF A NATIVE SON

Author: James Baldwin (1924-1987)
Type of work: Essays
First published: 1955

Form and Content

Notes of a Native Son is a collection of ten essays that James Baldwin published in magazines such as *Commentary, Harper's,* and *The Partisan Review* between 1948 and 1955. It also includes "Autobiographical Notes," written for this volume. Taken together, the essays reveal self-knowledge, cultural understanding, and articulateness that are astonishing when one considers that Baldwin wrote these essays without the benefit of a formal college education and before he was thirty years old. Baldwin makes clear in "Autobiographical Notes" that he was driven to be a writer, to use his imagination on his own experience, and thereby to create order out of chaos by facing his past and America's past fearlessly and honestly. To make himself into a writer, he had to become articulate, to understand and come to terms with his culture, and to know himself. The essays of *Notes of a Native Son* present the outlines of his quests and show what he had learned by 1955.

The book is divided into three sections. The three essays of the first section are cultural commentaries on representations of the African American in the arts. They show Baldwin's mature assessment of the complexity of his position as an African American intellectual. The three essays of the second part examine aspects of African American life during and shortly after World War II. These essays show Baldwin's origins, the home and the culture that he had to understand in order to become himself. The four essays of the third part discuss Baldwin's experiences living in Europe. These pieces reveal the crucial process by which Baldwin gained—through expatriation—the distance from his cultural history that allowed him to know and accept the identity from which he speaks in all the essays.

Although the outlines of Baldwin's quest to become a writer are apparent in this collection, and although certain concerns—such as identity and culture—pervade the essays, the topics are various. In "Everybody's Protest Novel," the opening piece, Baldwin notes that Harriet Beecher Stowe's *Uncle Tom's Cabin: Or, Life Among the Lowly* (1852) and Richard Wright's *Native Son* (1940) seem both to accept the American theology of white supremacy. This essay alienated Wright, who had befriended the younger man. The much more detailed discussion of *Native Son* in "Many Thousands Gone," the second piece, widened this rift rather than healing it. Baldwin did not change his thesis about *Native Son,* even though he was careful to discuss the importance of Wright's novel to African American writers. Critic Horace Porter believes that this essay, somewhat oddly written in the voice of a white liberal, was in part Baldwin's attempt to declare artistic independence from Wright, his literary father. Baldwin's title essay suggests that he is offering himself as a substitute for Wright's protagonist, Bigger Thomas, as the native son of the next generation of African American writers. In "Carmen Jones: The Dark Is Light Enough," Baldwin reviews *Carmen Jones* (1954), an Oscar Hammerstein II and Otto Preminger film updating Georges Bizet's opera, *Carmen* (1875), with a black cast and dubbed voices. Although the film was a popular success, Baldwin saw clear evidence of the pretense of acknowledging African Americans while remaining utterly ignorant about the reality of African American life and consciousness.

"The Harlem Ghetto," the first piece of the second set, offers a portrait of urban African American life and consciousness after World War II. The Harlem described is little different from the Depression era Harlem in which Baldwin grew up; therefore, the piece tells both about current conditions and about his background, with special attention to politics, media, religion, and especially anti-Semitism in Harlem. "Journey to Atlanta" discusses African American attitudes toward politics, using the story of his brother's exploitation by the Progressive Party during the 1948 election campaign. In the autobiographical "Notes of a Native Son," Baldwin tells mainly about his relationship with his stepfather, though he never in this piece explains that David Baldwin was his stepfather, that his own birth was illegitimate, and that he never knew his biological father's identity. Knowing this information, however, only increases the essay's power. In telling of David Baldwin's funeral on James Baldwin's nineteenth birthday, James acknowledges his deep ambivalence toward the man who seemed to show him so little love.

The four essays on Baldwin's early years in Europe return repeatedly to the theme of identity. "Encounter on the Seine: Black Meets Brown" discusses the associations of African Americans with one another and with African colonials in the postwar climate of Paris. "A Question of Identity" examines American students in Paris after the war and how they deal with the pressure that being in a foreign culture exerts on them to examine their own personal and cultural identities. "Equal in Paris" tells the story of Baldwin's mistaken arrest for the theft of a bedsheet, an incident that taught him that the protective laughter of whites that he so hated in the United States was, in fact, a universal phenomenon. Realization that his race was not uniquely the victim of such laughter began a phase of his liberating understanding of his native culture. "Stranger in the Village" relates Baldwin's experience of being the first black person ever seen in the remote Swiss village to which he retired to finish *Go Tell It on the Mountain* (1953). This visit gave him insight into how the American experience has changed African American and white identities since the first slaves were brought to America.

Analysis

In "The Creative Process," an essay that appears in *The Price of the Ticket* (1985), Baldwin says, "Societies never know it, but the war of an artist with his society is a lover's war, and he does, at his best, what lovers do, which is to reveal the beloved to himself and, with that revelation, to make freedom real." This quotation aptly describes one of the main threads of Baldwin's literary career, a thread that is clear in *Notes of a Native Son* as well as in the body of his fiction, drama, and prose. One main effect of this collection is to reveal the United States to itself from the special position Baldwin was able to occupy in the original publications, speaking to both white and African American magazine readers about African American life.

Baldwin ends "Autobiographical Notes" with this statement: "I want to be an honest man and a good writer." In this essay, he makes clear the main barriers he had to overcome in order to achieve these goals, barriers having mainly to do with race. Although much has been written about "the Negro problem," in fact very little is known about African American life and consciousness. The best way to reveal this little-known life is through works of art. To be an artist requires some distance from the arena of social reform and protest writing, but becoming an African American writer subjects one to a great pressure to be active in this arena. This situation occurs, in part, because the history of African American life is so painful that few want to look into it seriously, and those who study it become so angry that they rarely can attain the artistic distance necessary to create works of art. To be an honest man and to know who he was, Baldwin had to look seriously into the past, his own and America's. To become a good writer, he had to be able to stand back from the horrors of that history. In his later writings, Baldwin shows that he eventually concluded that in the process of learning to stand back from the pain of his personal and social history, he learned to accept suffering and to learn from suffering to love all of struggling humanity. Speaking on the same subjects in "The Creative Process," Baldwin said that in the particular aloneness of artistic creation and perception, "one discovers that life is tragic, and therefore unutterably beautiful."

"Notes of a Native Son" shows Baldwin moving through a cycle of this process as he contemplates the death of his stepfather. Several important events occur close together in the summer of 1943: his father's death, his youngest sister's birth, his father's funeral, his nineteenth birthday, and a race riot in Harlem. The coincidence of these events helps to make clear to Baldwin what sort of world he will have to make his way in and what resources he has available. He explains that his father reared him in a very protected environment, as separated as possible from white people, who represented to David Baldwin the evil of the outside world against which he preached in his small Harlem church. Although his father protected the children, he showed them little affection, and as he succumbed to mental illness, he tyrannized over and restricted them. When James leaves home after high school to work in a defense plant, he is ill-prepared to get along with the white people he then has to work among. He is used to associating with people on an equal footing, so he does not adjust easily to the attitudes and behaviors of inferiority. When he returns home for his father's death and sister's birth, he is filled with rage at his society for branding him and at his father for failing to love him. At the funeral, however, he begins to see some of the ways in which his father really had loved him, however imperfectly, and he realizes that despite his anger toward and even hatred of his father, he also loves the man. He learns that life and death matter, but color really does not. He learns that hatred always destroys the hater. He sees the paradox that he will have to hold in the mind forever two ideas which seemed to be in opposition. The first idea was acceptance . . . of life as it is, and men as they are: in the light of this idea, it goes without saying that injustice is a commonplace. But this did not mean that one could be complacent, for the second idea was of equal power: that one must never . . . accept these injustices as commonplace but must fight them with all one's strength.

He learns that this fight must be fought first in one's own heart by keeping it free of hatred and despair: "This intimation made my heart heavy and, now that my father was irrecoverable, I wished that he had been beside me so that I could have searched his face for the answers which only the future would give me now." These realizations complete perhaps the first important cycle of learning in Baldwin's artistic life, in which he begins to see how to step back from his ambivalent feelings for his father and accept them, learning in an important way how to love the terrible world about which he would write.

In addition to coming to terms with his personal history, Baldwin also had to come to terms with his social history, with the history of African Americans in the United States. He repeats in several essays that Americans, perhaps more than other people, are reluctant to know themselves as products of their history. They cultivate ignorance of their culture and history and so fail to know themselves. A major difference between white Americans and African Americans on this issue is that white Americans believe that their ancestors voluntarily surrendered their European backgrounds in order to become Americans, while African Americans believe their history was removed and hidden by force.

In "Stranger in the Village," one of his best-known essays, Baldwin offers a view of how the history of the United States has created unique cultural identities for whites and African Americans. His extended stay in an isolated Swiss village, where no one had ever before seen a black man, provides him with a base from which to measure how Europeans and Africans have changed during three centuries of living in North America. The Swiss villagers at first are filled with wonder at his physical differences from themselves. Their innocent behavior strikes him as culturally loaded because he is the product of the American experience. When children call him "Neger," they only announce the presence of this strange being, while in his memory the word "nigger" echoes with all of its cultural freight. When a kindly woman explains how their village "buys" Africans by giving money to the church for their missionary conversion, what seems a generous and sacred act to her reverberates with horrors for him. When he has remained longer, he sees evidence of their beginning to make use of him as a cultural other, to connect his color with the European mythology in which blackness is associated with evil, death, and hell.

The constant he sees between these "innocent" white Europeans and his fellow Americans is the idea of white, Christian superiority over black, African pagans: the foundation of white supremacy. The main difference he sees is that the fundamental morality of American democracy has always conflicted with the main

American consequence of white supremacy. The convenient beliefs that Africans were less than human and that they could be made slaves contradict the fundamental tenet of American political morality, that all people are created equal before God and the law. The trend in this long conflict of values has been toward honoring the ideals of democracy and abandoning, however violently and grudgingly, the ideas of white supremacy. One result of this uniquely American struggle has been the creation of "a new black man . . . and a new white man." Baldwin notes, "It is precisely this black-white experience which may prove of indispensable value to us in the world we face today. This world is white no longer, and it will never be white again." He sees the United States as destined either to realize a multiracial, multicultural civilization or to destroy itself. He believes the former to be more likely.

Written in the middle of the twentieth century and in Baldwin's youth, these essays seem mature and prescient in their understanding of Baldwin's self and culture. They show a young artist finding himself in his world, becoming an honest man and a good writer.

Critical Context
Fred Standley, in his obituary for James Baldwin, quotes literary figures from Irving Howe and Norman Mailer to Toni Morrison and Maya Angelou as affirming that Baldwin was among the foremost American intellectuals of the twentieth century and that his essays, like those of Ralph Waldo Emerson, Henry David Thoreau, Mark Twain, and H. L. Mencken, have contributed centrally to the self-understanding of the people of the United States.

Notes of a Native Son was Baldwin's second book. Together with *Go Tell It on the Mountain* and his regularly appearing short stories and essays in American magazines, this collection helped to establish Baldwin as a powerful and important voice in American culture. With this volume, Baldwin in effect claimed new territory for African American writers. Although he was not the first to call for freeing African Americans from having to write mainly about racial relations, he articulated an approach that he followed himself and that was taken up by younger writers, such as his friend Lorraine Hansberry. Fred Standley describes Baldwin's approach well: "Autobiography becomes transformed into frequently unforgettable expressions of image and insight that transcend the specifics of personal experience to become the means of providing situations and statements of universal applicability that are then inferred to possess even more relevant individual significance." This book was followed by several other important collections of his essays that elaborated and extended Baldwin's ideas and influenced—by example and provocation—many writers and thinkers in the United States and throughout the world: *Nobody Knows My Name: More Notes of a Native Son* (1961), *The Fire Next Time* (1963), and *The Price of the Ticket* (1985).

Bibliography
Campbell, James. *Talking at the Gates: A Life of James Baldwin.* New York: Viking,

1991. This full biography, by a man who knew Baldwin personally, is especially interesting because it draws on the Federal Bureau of Investigation files kept on Baldwin. Campbell deals frankly with Baldwin's bisexuality. Included are sixteen pages of photographs.

Kinnamon, Kenneth, ed. *James Baldwin: A Collection of Critical Essays.* Englewood Cliffs, N.J.: Prentice-Hall, 1974. In this selection of twelve essays and Kinnamon's introduction are discussions of several of Baldwin's major works. Langston Hughes's review of *Notes of a Native Son* praises and criticizes the book. F. W. Dupee's essay looks at Baldwin's development from *Notes of a Native Son* through *The Fire Next Time.* Also included is Eldridge Cleaver's discussion of Baldwin's essays from *Soul on Ice* (1968).

O'Daniel, Therman B. *James Baldwin: A Critical Evaluation.* Washington, D.C.: Howard University Press, 1977. This volume contains essays on Baldwin as novelist, as essayist, as short-story writer, as playwright, and as scenarist, as well as a section on his raps and dialogues and a bibliography. The secondary bibliography is extensive. There are four pieces on Baldwin's essays.

Porter, Horace A. *Stealing the Fire: The Art and Protest of James Baldwin.* Middletown, Conn.: Wesleyan University Press, 1989. Porter gives considerable attention to Baldwin's essays in order to study the development of his ideas about relating art and social protest. He devotes one chapter to Baldwin's relationship with Richard Wright.

Pratt, Louis H. *James Baldwin.* Boston: Twayne, 1978. A useful introduction to Baldwin's life and works. Chapters 1, 5, and 6 deal in various ways with Baldwin's essays, including an examination of their artistry. Contains a chronology and an annotated bibliography. Pratt believes that the essays are Baldwin's major contribution to American letters.

Standley, Fred L. "James Baldwin." In *Dictionary of Literary Biography Yearbook 1987.* Detroit: Gale Research, 1988. This obituary article provides an excellent introduction to Baldwin's career and writings, laying out concisely his major ideas and achievements and summarizing contemporary opinion about Baldwin's contributions to American literature.

Standley, Fred L., and Nancy V. Burt, eds. *Critical Essays on James Baldwin.* Boston: G. K. Hall, 1988. This volume is divided into sections including ones on fiction, nonfiction, and drama. The introduction surveys Baldwin's literary reputation, and the collection opens with a 1979 interview with Baldwin. There are ten essays in the nonfiction section, including pieces by Langston Hughes, Stephen Spender, and Julius Lester. In the general section appear several more essays on Baldwin's nonfiction work.

Terry Heller

OUR NIG

Author: Harriet E. Wilson (1808-c. 1870)
Type of work: Novel
Type of plot: Social criticism
Time of plot: The mid-1800's, before the Civil War
Locale: Boston, Massachusetts, and surrounding areas
First published: 1859

> *Principal characters:*
> FRADO, a pretty mulatto girl
> MRS. BELLMONT, the book's principal antagonist
> JAMES, the Bellmonts' son

The Novel

Our Nig is the story of an abandoned mulatto girl, Frado, who works from the age of six until she is eighteen as an indentured servant for a white, middle-class family in Boston. Before Frado's narrative moves forward, Harriet E. Wilson swiftly presents the background story, telling how Frado became an orphan. Next, she gives a full account of the protagonist's suffering at the hands of two cruel mistresses, and then she rapidly summarizes the sad events following Frado's arduous servitude: a bad marriage ending with desertion, single parenthood, and extreme poverty.

The reader first meets Frado's natural mother, the "lonely Mag Smith," a lower-class white woman who has been seduced and abandoned by an aristocratic white male. As a ruined woman, Mag enters into a relationship with a "kind-hearted African" named Jim, part owner of a coal-delivery business. Out of pity and a belief that marriage to a white woman, even one at the bottom of her world, can be a means for his upward mobility, Jim proposes to Mag; for her own financial security, Mag accepts. After the marriage, Jim becomes a devoted and dutiful husband. When Jim dies a few years later, Mag has two young mulatto daughters; the older one is Frado.

Widow Mag is courted by Jim's business partner. After a period of financial struggle, she is convinced that she needs a man's help, so she marries her second black suitor. The day comes when Mag and her new husband decide to leave the village to seek a better life. Since neither of them wishes to be saddled with two little girls, they slyly leave six-year-old, high-spirited Frado with a white, middle-class family, the Bellmonts. Thus begins Frado's life of misery and pain.

Mrs. Bellmont and her daughter Mary become Frado's chief tormentors. Day and night, they make the young girl's life miserable with their constant demands, beatings, and psychological assaults. To make matters worse, Mrs. Bellmont assigns Frado drab and unhealthy sleeping quarters. The good-hearted characters, Mr. Bellmont, Jack, James, Jane, and Aunt Abby, witness the abuse, but they are too preoccupied or passive to effect any substantial changes for the young servant. Frado saves herself eventually by realizing her own power to dictate limits to what she will endure.

The critical scene in which Frado learns to resist her chief enemy occurs after James, her favorite in the Bellmont household, dies. James is Mrs. Bellmont's son, but he is very different in temperament from his mean mother. He is more like his father in kindness; but, unlike Mr. Bellmont, he is more inclined, however ineffectively, to protect Frado.

Despite James's sympathy for Frado, he never suggests to her that she can stand up for herself. Not until after James dies does Mr. Bellmont tell Frado that she should not allow herself to be beaten when she does not deserve it. The first opportunity Frado has to apply this novel concept comes shortly thereafter. Mrs. Bellmont sends Frado for wood, and when Frado does not return soon enough for her, she walks out to Frado's woodpile, takes a stick, and strikes Frado over the head. To her surprise, Frado loudly refuses to be beaten again. In amazement, Mrs. Bellmont leaves the yard. From that moment on, Frado knows she is free. During the next and final year of her indenture, Frado receives her usual scoldings and a few whippings, but never again does Mrs. Bellmont threaten her with similar violence.

Frado's servitude ends when she is eighteen. She is sent out into the world with only one dress, a Bible, and a physical constitution too frail for hard work. Mrs. Moore, a kindly Christian woman, takes Frado in and teaches her to make straw hats. After a short apprenticeship, Frado uses her quickly acquired skill to support herself. This short period of autonomy for Frado ends when a black man named Samuel walks into her affection-starved world and sweeps her off her feet. Against Mrs. Moore's advice, Frado marries Samuel, a shifty orator who makes his living off abolitionists, giving "humbug" speeches about his life as a slave, although he has never been below the Mason-Dixon line.

After a few months, Frado's marriage goes awry, but by this time she is already pregnant. Because of her delicate condition and lack of money, she has to go to a poorhouse, where she gives birth to a son. At one point, Samuel, Frado's husband, reappears, giving her some respite from abject poverty, but he leaves again without warning. Later, she receives word that Samuel has died of a fever. Frado is forced to put her little boy in a foster home. Under these desperate circumstances, Frado starts to write her story. The story ends with Frado's hopeful vision that the book's sale will provide enough money to support herself and her child.

The Characters

Frado's basic impulses to laugh and to enjoy life's simple pleasures are not easily repressed by the cruel servitude she enters when her white mother, Mag, runs off and leaves her with the Bellmonts, a white family dominated by a cruel and bigoted matriarch.

Although life with the Bellmonts is exceedingly grim for Frado, the bright light of her humanity never completely dies. Indeed, Wilson writes, during the first three years of Frado's indenture, when she attends school, her constant "jollity" cannot "be quenched by whipping or scolding." Even after her formal education ends and life becomes creased by constant insults, the "spark of playfulness" manifests itself in the occasional "funny thing" she says to her sympathizers, in her performance of daring stunts, and in her amusements with animals.

Mrs. Bellmont, a fierce social climber, takes out her frustrations on Frado. Consequently, no matter what occurs to "ruffle" Mrs. Bellmont, "a few blows on Nig seemed to relieve her of a portion of ill-will."

Mrs. Bellmont is enthusiastically assisted in her efforts to break Frado's spirit by her equally willful and malcontent daughter, Mary, who advances in the practice of cruelty as she matures.

Constantly besieged by the two cruel Bellmont "ladies," Frado receives crumbs of kindness from three key family members: Mr. Bellmont, the father of the family, and Jack and James, his two sons. (Jane, a crippled daughter, and "Nabs," the elderly maiden aunt, live in the house and are kind to Frado, but they are too cowed by their states of dependency to speak out.)

Although Mr. Bellmont is consistently sympathetic toward Frado, his sympathy never translates into action. His refusal to exert his influence to stop the outrages against Frado shows that Mr. Bellmont's respect for white privilege outranks his sense of justice for blacks. Nevertheless, Mr. Bellmont does not have the stomach to watch Frado suffer. He avoids being a witness to her punishments by leaving the house at moments of crisis. Through his cowardice, which he mistakes for kindness, the attacks upon Frado, being uncensored, are prolonged.

As an adolescent, Jack saves Frado several times from undeserved suffering at the hands of his mother and sister. As Jack grows up, however, his outside interests and friendships begin to occupy his time and thoughts, and Frado's plight becomes only a small area of abrasion in his otherwise smooth life.

James, the oldest of the Bellmont children, is Frado's most effective protector, but even he fails to rescue Frado. James's failure is at first the result of his long absences from home during Frado's childhood; later, it is his marriage that keeps him separated from Frado. When James returns to his paternal home for good, Frado is nearly grown, and he is encumbered by a fatal illness. He no longer has the stamina to be a vigilant intercessor on Frado's behalf. Seeing the hopeless despair of Frado's earthly existence, James makes a concerted effort, in his last days, to convert her to Christianity. Despite his earnest entreaties, however, Frado cannot bring herself to worship the same God who, according to James, is the savior of her enemies.

Samuel, the "fine, straight negro" whom Frado finally marries after she frees herself from both the physical and psychological chains of servitude, proves to be a charlatan—a free-born black man who lectures as a former slave in the abolitionist cause. His maverick spirit causes him to leave Frado without a protector at the times when she needs him most, during her pregnancy and during her struggle to care for her child.

Themes and Meanings

Our Nig is the recently recovered first novel written by an African American woman.

It is also the first book to give an African American's view of the racial abuse and exploitation that defined the quality of life many "free" blacks experienced in the North.

On August 18, 1859, Mrs. Harriet E. Wilson went to the clerk's office of the District Court of Massachusetts and entered the copyright of her novel, *Our Nig: Or, Sketches from the Life of a Free Black, in a Two-Story White House, North. Showing That Slavery's Shadow Falls Even There.* At her own expense, one hundred fifty copies of the novel were made available for sale on September 5, 1859. This simple record marks the only notice her book received.

The public's apparent lack of interest in Wilson's book during the nineteenth century is still puzzling to current scholars, who continue to speculate about the slight this novel received during a time when evidence of black scholarship (especially writings) was enthusiastically noted as fuel for antislavery arguments. Henry Louis Gates, Jr., a literary theorist with a particular interest in the works of African American writers—and the person who actually recovered *Our Nig* from its literary graveyard in 1982, confirms that period historians, bibliophiles, and biographers alike neglected mentioning Wilson's literary effort. Gates could find only five scant references to the novel in the 124 years of criticism following its publication.

Confirming that her work was autobiographical, Wilson maintained that she had edited her story to minimize negative depictions of the condition of blacks living in the North so that the antislavery cause would not be threatened. In the book's preface, she wrote, "I have purposely omitted what would most provoke shame in our good anti-slavery friends at home."

Although Wilson maintained that she had suffered worse horrors than those she recorded in her book, she asserted that her book was not meant to be an attack on Northern whites. Hoping that she would not be misunderstood, Wilson rationalized her awful experiences by contending that her mistress "was imbued with southern principles."

Harriet E. Wilson's fear of being misinterpreted was indeed well founded. Not only was her appeal to whites to buy her book of no avail, but her appeal to the free Negro community for patronage was also ineffective.

Gates and other scholars suggest that bias against the themes and subject matter of *Our Nig* can explain the mysterious silence surrounding Wilson's work. Modern critics agree in their assessment that the fate of the book had nothing to do with its quality or literary merit. They point out that the dramatic power, clarity, and striking beauty of Wilson's language still recommend the novel highly.

Despite the novel's stock characters and sentimental plot, *Our Nig* remains remarkably readable, unlike the bulk of nineteenth century sentimental novels. Although Wilson utilized many of the formulas of the genre (an underdog heroine, an unfriendly environment, and absolutely good and evil characters, for example), she stretched the form and improvised in original ways to tell her own story. Gates has suggested that it was probably those innovations—the taboo themes and Afrocentric colorings—that supply the best explanation for the 124-year-long literary entombment of *Our Nig*. Indeed, depiction of Northern racism, of interracial marriage, and of phony escaped slaves duping abolitionists must have been unpopular even with the most liberal whites of the day as well as with free blacks, who probably did not wish to distance themselves from their benefactors.

Perhaps the highest offense Wilson may have given in offering the book to the public was her assignment of the novel's ironic title. She took a vile epithet, a cruel term used to demean her race, and reclaimed it. By boldly using the word "nig," a pet abbreviation for "nigger," Wilson may have sought to create a level ground where she could assert her own equality with the name caller, but such an innovative and startling device was probably misinterpreted by her intended audience. Those who were not embarrassed by the unusual use of the term may not have appreciated its sarcastic flavor or its empowering intent. It was probably a far more comfortable approach for the "liberal" reading audience of the day to ignore Wilson's problematic work, hoping it would go away.

Critical Context

Although the story of *Our Nig* ended on an optimistic note, Gates uncovered a sad finale to Wilson's true-life story. He found that the writer was disappointed in the precise ways she had hoped for success. The book did not create a source of income, and her precious son, for whom she undertook the task of writing a book, died of a fever at the age of seven. (Ironically, the recent discovery of an obituary notice for Wilson's son in a local paper supplied the most cogent evidence of Harriet E. Wilson's existence as a real person, and also confirmed her social classification as an African American.)

The ironic fate of Wilson and her book is a cruel yet a fitting finale to the saga, for Wilson's social vision was exceedingly advanced for her time, as was her expanded humanistic vision reflected in *Our Nig*. Certainly, the author herself recognized that the world probably was not ready for her story. In an unusual foreword to *Our Nig*, Wilson acknowledged the problem the subject matter of her book could pose for an important segment of her audience that she called "good anti-slavery friends."

Wilson nevertheless exposed how prejudiced people living in Massachusetts in the 1850's were abetted in their outrageous behaviors by the passivity of white liberals whose antislavery convictions were directed toward the South. She offered the pitiful story of her harsh life as an indentured servant in the North as proof.

Bibliography

Jefferson, Margo. "Down and Out in Black Boston." *The Nation* 236 (May 28, 1983): 675-677. Focuses on Wilson's ingenious use of irony and sarcasm as key elements distinguishing her book from other narratives written by antebellum blacks. Explores Wilson's sophistication in satirizing contemporary white women writers of the period through her careful selection of a title for her book.

Litwack, Leon F. *North of Slavery: The Negro in the Free States, 1790-1860.* Chicago: University of Chicago Press, 1961. Surveys the conditions of blacks in Northern states after those states abolished slavery and details the prejudices that circumscribed the lives of free blacks living in the North.

Starling, Marion Wilson. *The Slave Narrative: Its Place in American History.* Washington, D.C.: Howard University Press, 1988. A pioneering study of slave narratives. Provides a helpful context for assessing *Our Nig.*

Tate, Claudia. "Allegories of Black Female Desire; or Rereading Nineteenth-Century Sentimental Narratives of Black Female Authority." In *Changing Our Own Words: Essays on Criticism, Theory, and Writing by Black Women*, edited by Cheryl A. Wall. New Brunswick, N.J.: Rutgers University Press, 1989. Addresses the issue of why traditional African American scholarship has produced negative readings of *Our Nig* and other books written by nineteenth century black women.

Wilson, Harriet E. *Our Nig: Or, Sketches from the Life of a Free Black.* Edited, with an introduction, by Henry Louis Gates, Jr. 2d ed. New York: Random House, 1983. Gates's fifty-five-page introduction places *Our Nig* in its historical context. Gates summarizes the interesting and involved research used to authenticate the authorship of the novel, and he analyzes Wilson's narrative style, demonstrating how the writer used both the conventions of the sentimental novel and innovative devices to write her unique story.

Sarah Smith Ducksworth

THE OUTSIDER

Author: Richard Wright (1908-1960)
Type of work: Novel
Type of plot: Naturalism
Time of plot: 1951
Locale: Chicago, Illinois, and New York City
First published: 1953

> *Principal characters:*
> CROSS DAMON, the protagonist, age twenty-six, a black intellectual
> BOB HUNTER, a Pullman-car waiter and member of the
>   Communist Party
> ELY HOUSTON, a hunchbacked New York City district attorney
> GIL BLOUNT, a member of the Central Committee of the U.S.
>   Communist Party
> EVA BLOUNT, the young wife of Gil Blount, a painter
> JACK HILTON, a power-hungry, ruthless Communist
> HERNDON, a fascistic landlord

The Novel

Cross Damon's wintry search for meaningfulness and happiness falls into five stages, omnisciently narrated in books of the novel entitled "Dread," "Dream," "Descent," "Despair," and "Decision." By the time Cross reaches the fifth stage, no decision can stem the worsening of his life that is suggested by the first four titles.

When the story opens, Cross dreads everything about his intolerable life, which quickly comes to a crisis under pressure from his fifteen-year-old pregnant girlfriend, his abused wife, and his moralistic mother. Then the completely unexpected happens: He survives a subway accident and learns that a mangled victim has been identified as him. Cross takes this opportunity to create himself anew. Again, however, the unexpected happens; he is seen by a friend, and rather than return to a life made even worse, Cross kills him.

Cross's life is now dreamlike, because he carries in his mind a twenty-six-year identity that he is consciously denying. He is only early in the process of inventing what he believes will be a new personality, and therefore he is at the mercy of external circumstances. An accident in the dining car of a train causes him to meet two people who will haunt him like images in a dream that turns into a nightmare. Bob Hunter entangles him in the Communist Party, and Ely Houston is insightful enough to recognize him as a fellow outsider inclined to "ethical lawlessness." The style of Wright's narration in this part of the story is not dreamlike, however, as philosophical analysis plays a major role in his narration and characterization.

In New York, Cross meets Party members who claim to be rational, objective, and benevolent but whose only law is their purpose of domination. Cross, needing human contacts to give substance to his new identity, and believing that with his intelligence and existential freedom he is more than a match for anyone else, agrees to live with Gil and Eva Blount, in order to aid the Party's challenge to the racist practices of their landlord, Herndon. Increasingly for Cross, the flow of ideas is the believable and sustaining fabric of life. He believes that he actually is his idea of himself. Paradoxically, however, the more he intellectualizes life, the more he rationalizes his behavior with philosophical excuses, and the more he is driven by his own dread and compulsions.

Thus Cross's descent begins when, projecting ideas that threaten him onto other persons, he finds that those persons are, to his mind, ideas that offend him. Refusing existentially to go on living the bad faith of transcendental hope, he begins to share the Communists' and fascists' bad faith of exploitation through deception. Acting godlike, Cross appropriates absolute power, in the name of personal freedom and integrity, by killing Gil Blount and Herndon.

In despair over his discovery that, in exercising the freedom to create a new self, he has compulsively reenacted an ancient pattern of violent human behavior, Cross begins a love affair with Eva Blount, although he knows that she loves her image of him as an innocent victim. Ely Houston also prefers to think that Cross is innocent, rather than the kind of modern outlaw who would kill without need of transcendent justification for his act and without feeling transcendent judgment upon it. Yet a combative Cross cannot resist his compulsion to taunt Houston with the assertion that "humanity is nothing in particular" and that, therefore, a human may be anything at all. Another Communist, Hilton, now becomes offensive to Cross, intending to exercise moral ownership of him. Immediately before Cross kills him, Hilton expresses the non-Marxist personal philosophy that life is not justifiable, but merely exists for no particular reason. Individuals, he says, should make life whatever they want it to be. Cross counters that human suffering proves that life has meaning. Indeed Cross almost kills Eva to save her from the suffering that she is sure to feel if she learns that he is a murderer. He is stopped by his love for her, which causes him to feel hope and to commit himself to her.

In the last book, Houston confronts Cross with evidence of his guilt in the murders. Cross says nothing, and Houston sends him home. There Cross makes the decision to confess to Eva, hoping that she will somehow understand and forgive; instead, she loses all remaining trust and hope and leaps from a window to her death. Party thugs shoot Cross; on his deathbed, he confesses to Houston that his life has been horrible, all the more so because he has felt his existential innocence. He has, however, also learned that persons must not alienate themselves from humanity, which is, in essence, a promise that must not be broken.

The Characters

Cross Damon, as his name implies, is the embodiment of a complex idea. Wright conceived of a man who has been martyred by his Christian upbringing and by the institutionalization of values based on Christian and other Western mythologies that have been rendered obsolete by industrialism, but also a man whose existentialist attempt to create a new and free identity merely frees his egoistic compulsion to replace the defunct Godhead with his own godlike exercise of power. Thus he acts demonically, in the senses both of Satan and tormented demiurge. He is both driven and inspired to obliterate the enemies of human freedom, only to find that the more he defeats them, the more like them he becomes. He is a shockingly violent murderer who yet can claim to be innocent of transcendental and therefore societal guilt. Ironically, he re-creates himself as a heroic outsider, only to find that every other thoughtful person, law-abiding or not, is also an outsider.

As characters, these outsiders differ only inasmuch as the ideas that they embody differ. For example, the Communists are as free of traditional mythology, as violent, and as self-serving as is Cross, but their idea is to enslave, not to set free. Houston, the district attorney, is an "ethical criminal" like Cross, but any violence that he commits is within the law. Although Houston stands outside society in his personal and philosophical points of view, he chooses to conform to societal imperatives, because he knows that a sane human life requires community.

When Eva Blount experiences love and trust, she modifies her idea of meaningful art in the direction of community. It is through Cross's experience of love, and of betrayal of trust, that he learns the necessity of community and commitment. It is then that he is fully able to appreciate the horror of his life, in its mixture of dread, compulsion, betrayal, and innocence. Yet his deathbed confession of horror and hope seems as much the logical conclusion of his creator's theory as the result of a heartfelt change in personal perspective.

As Richard Lehan and others have pointed out, Wright's characterization repeats the naturalistic methods of his earlier fiction, especially *Native Son* (1940). Wright places Cross Damon in situations that illustrate Wright's ideas and that test and prompt his protagonist's thoughts. Cross's behavior then further illustrates Wright's analysis, which is conveyed by his omniscient narration or by Cross's self-analysis. At opportune times, Wright informs his readers of relevant ideas by having characters explain themselves or by having them confront Cross with questions, which he answers with lectures from his extensive reading. Actions that are not informed by philosophy are motivated by the most common creaturely drives. Cross tends, therefore, to career from one extreme to another, and this state is reinforced by Wright's imagery: The outer world is wintry, and the inner world, when aroused beyond dialectic, is like a furnace.

Nevertheless, the novel retains interest in spite of its artistic flaws because of the importance of its philosophical framework and struggle. Similarly, its characters are engaging because, although they are types, they are haunting in their representation of modern individuals, capable of—and even inclined toward—both petty and large destructions of life.

Themes and Meanings

Richard Wright wrote fiction as a way of pursuing his thoughts on an issue— usually racism. *The Outsider* is a "novel of ideas" in which he attempted to clarify, and perhaps contribute toward a solution for, an issue that he saw as larger than racism. He was concerned about the possibility of identity, meaningful action, and fulfillment in the modern world, in which judgments of good and evil (for example, of racism as practiced in America or Nazi Germany) cannot be made on the basis of faith in the existence of a transcendent being or scheme regarding the value of humanity.

Wright addressed this concern by accepting the challenge, and presenting his critique, of two modern lines of thought with which he had recently been engaged: Marxism, as he had observed its practice in the Communist Party of the U.S.A., and existentialism, in which he had read widely and which he had discussed in Paris with major existentialist thinkers and novelists. Marxism emphasizes the determination of history and individual lives by economic forces. Existentialism, however, emphasizes individual freedom to create unique selfhood and value. Both propose that traditional systems of meaning and value that include the existence of a transcendent creator are untrue and useless. There exists no covenant (promise) between a god and his creatures, and no divine judgment. Wright's strategy for examining these philosophies, as they would be lived, was to invent a protagonist who had found his entire life meaningless and revolting, but who possessed the intelligence and knowledge to analyze his predicament and seek an existential solution. In one winter of this protagonist's discontent, he learns lessons about Communism, existentialism, and his own personality, and he also learns a hopeful truth about humanity.

Book 1 of the novel is entitled "Dread," and Wright suggests throughout the novel that this state is shared by humanity in general. The epigraph, by the nineteenth century existentialist philosopher Søren Kierkegaard, characterizes dread as a psychological complex of simultaneous desire and fear, attraction and repulsion, toward every aspect of life. Cross Damon knows that the cause of his troubles is that he has broken promises; he also understands that what causes him to make promises that he cannot keep is dread. He believes that his dread results from his religious upbringing by his frightened and clinging mother, who uses the threat of God's punishment to control her son. Influenced by his readings in existentialism, Cross believes that he is suffering feelings of guilt in a world that is devoid of any reasonable basis for assigning individual guilt, since there is no God or other transcendent basis for values or for rules of behavior. Life is empty, but an individual is therefore free to fill the void.

An accident allows Cross to apply the idea that he can step outside history and all myths that have failed humanity and can create a self that satisfies him. He will make his own rules. He soon finds, however, not only that he is unable to avoid involvement with humanity (partly because accidents keep happening in life) but also that he requires involvement to confirm his sense of having an identity. Like Wright's earlier protagonist, *Native Son*'s Bigger Thomas, Cross learns that to successfully cry "I am," he must tell his story to someone other than himself, someone who will respond in kind. This becomes ironically important: Cross realizes that suffering is what gives meaning and value to human life (including his own), but he has compulsively become such an extreme source of suffering to others that he has isolated himself.

Ely Houston, the district attorney, wants to hear Cross's story, because Cross, as a black intellectual, is a rare individual who can understand Houston's own outsider point of view. To Cross, however, Houston represents societal judgment that will limit his freedom. Members of the Party ask for his story, promising to arrange for him to help them serve the cause of racial freedom; in fact, though, they cannot understand him and only want to own him. When they accuse him of "everything," he counters with a story of human history, focusing on the psychological and political damage done by industrialization. Like the ancients, Cross explains, modern humanity is driven by dread, but cannot assuage it through belief and hope. So humanity has placed its faith in absolutism, and therefore men have arisen who seek absolute freedom for themselves, and absolute, self-justifying power with which to control everyone else. These godlike men include leaders of the Party, whom Cross murders, thereby exercizing the same godlike power that he hates. Eventually, the party convicts and executes Cross. Eva Blount, the one person who loves Cross, wants to hear only the romantic story that she has imagined. Cross knows that she will judge him harshly if he tells her who he really is. Indeed, when he finally tells her his true story, she flees to her death.

By insisting on the nothingness of life and therefore the "anythingness" of any particular human, Cross steadily narrows his options, and his range of listeners, until he is reduced to nothing. At that point, realizing too late that humanity itself is a promise that must not be broken, but clinging to his sense of his existential innocence, Cross dies—ironically, both more outside and more inside humanity than he has ever been.

Critical Context

Critical and scholarly reception of *The Outsider* has largely focused on four areas of interest: its relation to American racism, its existentialist thought, its artistry, and its relation to Wright's life. Some reviewers and scholars have expressed disappointment that Wright, having abandoned his homeland for residence in Paris, seemed to lose touch with African American life and to betray his promise as a critic of racism. Wright does, in fact, make it clear in the novel that his protagonist has not thought of himself significantly in terms of color and does not intend to redefine himself in racial terms. His condition, Wright suggests, is the condition of all modern humanity. Racist stereotyping is only one manifestation of the larger modern malaise, the arrogation of power in an attempt to find meaning where positive, transcendent systems of value have failed. Yet in reducing racism to a symptom, perhaps Wright also reduced the contribution that he could make toward achieving freedom and justice for many people and instead set his imagination and his artistic powers adrift in European philosophical speculation.

Thus, some critics have faulted Wright for his inability to understand or contribute to existentialist thought, remarking that the novel appears to be existential in intent but actually contradicts that view of the human predicament. Others, however, have pointed out that the novel is actually Wright's portrayal of the failures of a philosophy that he had debated with his contemporaries in Paris, including Jean-Paul Sartre. Wright had already shown signs of interest in an existentialist protagonist when he created Bigger Thomas, but by the time he created Cross Damon, his thinking was moving beyond existentialism, as well as Marxism, to an interest in emerging African countries, in which he saw hope for a sane vision of humanity. Indeed, Wright's experience of American racism made it possible for him to understand both the insights and the shortcomings of existentialism.

Whether existentialist or not, the novel has been found engaging by many critics because of the significance of its social, psychological, and philosophical issues and because of the challenge presented by its protagonist. There is universal agreement among critics, however, that *The Outsider* became so much a novel of ideas that Wright's artistic control and effectiveness suffered.

Bibliography
Brignano, Russell Carl. *Richard Wright: An Introduction to the Man and His Works.* Pittsburgh: University of Pittsburgh Press, 1970. Claims that *The Outsider* gained attention because of interest in existentialist philosophy and literature, but that in fact the book, like Wright's late nonfiction, argues for reasoned cooperation in the creation of peaceful and free societies.
Davis, Allison. *Leadership, Love, and Aggression.* San Diego, Calif.: Harcourt Brace Jovanovich, 1983. This psychological study of Wright's personality and life, especially the childhood traumas caused by his "sadistic maternal family," illuminates many motifs in his fiction.
Fabre, Michel. *The Unfinished Quest of Richard Wright.* Translated by Isabel Barzun. 2d ed. Urbana: University of Illinois Press, 1993. Places *The Outsider* in the context of Wright's evolution from Marxism to existentialism, then discusses his critique of the latter as he turned his attention to the human potential that he saw in newly independent African nations.
Fishburn, Katherine. *Richard Wright's Hero: The Faces of a Rebel-Victim.* Metuchen, N.J.: Scarecrow Press, 1977. Wright created a protagonist who blends the innocence of the American Adam (but more alienated) with the dispossessed outsiders of European existentialism and nihilism (but more influenced by environment and history). Fishburn quotes important passages from existentialist works that Wright and his protagonist read.
Gayle, Addison. *Richard Wright: Ordeal of a Native Son.* Garden City, N.Y.: Doubleday, 1980. Preoccupied by the conflict between nihilism and freedom, Wright knew from experience that religious mores and political authoritarianism stimulate impulses to lawlessness that must be moderated by compassion and concern for the common good. Self-restrained persons, like the character Ely Houston, realize that freedom is not absolute but relative and in need of limits.

Lehan, Richard. "Existentialism in Recent American Fiction: The Demonic Quest." *Texas Studies in Literature and Language* 1 (Summer, 1959): 181-202. An extensive analysis of major American and French existential novels. Like the others, *The Outsider* presents a demonic hero whose quest for an autonomous identity leads him to overreach himself. Wright's naturalistic method of storytelling, however, contradicts existentialism.

Margolies, Edward. *The Art of Richard Wright.* Carbondale: Southern Illinois University Press, 1969. Wright tried to "reconcile his basically humanitarian and liberal beliefs with a profound feeling that man is fundamentally amoral and anarchistic." In the same way that his protagonist cannot reconcile freedom and order, however, Wright could not resolve the contradictions posed by the novel's ideas, and the result was serious artistic flaws.

Tom Koontz

OXHERDING TALE

Author: Charles Johnson (1948-   )
Type of work: Novel
Type of plot: Bildungsroman
Time of plot: 1838-1862
Locale: South Carolina
First published: 1982

> *Principal characters:*
> ANDREW HAWKINS, the novel's narrator, a light-skinned young
>   slave of mixed blood
> GEORGE HAWKINS, Andrew's father, a butler at the Cripplegate
>   plantation
> MATTIE HAWKINS, George's wife and Andrew's stepmother
> EZEKIEL SYKES-WITHERS, Andrew's tutor
> MINTY, a seamstress
> FLO HATFIELD, a middle-aged widow and farm owner
> REB THE COFFINMAKER, a hardworking carpenter
> HORACE BANNON, THE "SOULCATCHER," a sadistic manhunter
> PEGGY UNDERCLIFF, Andrew's white bride
> DR. GERALD UNDERCLIFF, a Spartanburg physician

The Novel

Oxherding Tale depicts the startling and varied adventures of Andrew Hawkins as he attempts to negotiate the perilous passage from slavery to freedom, crossing racial barriers and throwing his identity into crisis along the way. Born into slavery on a cotton plantation, Andrew at the same time becomes an exceptionally sophisticated thinker after being tutored by an intellectual from an early age. His status at Cripplegate, a plantation owned by Jonathan Polkinghorne, is deeply ambiguous; conceived by an enslaved butler, given birth by Polkinghorne's wife, well regarded by Polkinghorne, he attempts to exploit his unusual position to negotiate a path to freedom.

At twenty, having fallen in love with Minty, a seamstress of blossoming beauty, Andrew is emboldened to confront Polkinghorne, requesting a deed of manumission in order to earn money so that he might marry Minty. Polkinghorne sends Andrew to a widow's distant farm to work for wages and promises to sign the freedom papers only when Andrew returns with the money. Aflame with the possibilities, Andrew sets out to take responsibility for his future, to shape a destiny for himself and his loved ones.

The novel consists of two major parts. Part 1, entitled "House and Field," is devoted largely to Andrew's life at the Polkinghorne plantation and to his service at Flo Hatfield's farm. Most of Andrew's childhood and adolescence is presented in flashbacks; at the end of chapter 1, Andrew has received his assignment to the Hatfield farm, and his memories of Minty, George, Mattie, and Ezekiel are woven into the current action.

At the Hatfield farm, Andrew becomes a sexual servant to the beautiful Flo Hatfield, a sensuous woman in her forties who has made a habit of grooming at least one young servant for a pampered life in the house. Although Andrew enjoys with Flo the indulgences of opium and an erotic education, she evades the subject of his wages. Losing his temper, Andrew one day strikes Flo while they are making love and is immediately banished to the slave quarters; he is then sent with Reb to certain death at the mines. When they report to the Yellowdog mine with a group of other slaves, Andrew poses as a white employee of Flo's in order to engineer an escape to the North with Reb the Coffinmaker, a carpenter.

Part 2, "The White World," concerns the new life forged by Andrew. During their ride northward on stolen horses, Andrew and Reb are joined by Horace Bannon, a manhunter who pretends not to recognize his prey; his method is to wait until a runaway loses all hope before acting. Suffering from severe withdrawal from an addiction to opium, Andrew is taken by Bannon to a white doctor, Gerald Undercliff, in Spartanburg, South Carolina. Unable to pay for his treatment, he is forced to accept work under an assumed identity as a schoolteacher, with Reb posing as his manservant. All the philosophical and moral wherewithal that Andrew has acquired is put on trial when he is pressured into marriage with Peggy Undercliff, the doctor's daughter. Having achieved a modest security in his marriage and his new identity as a white man, Andrew one evening wanders into a slave auction and finds Minty on sale. Slavery has robbed her of her beauty; she is exhausted and diseased. Grief-stricken, Andrew buys her freedom and persuades Peggy to accept Minty into their home. Although he has achieved a measure of uneasy comfort, he accepts responsibility for Minty at the risk of his own life. At the novel's climax, Minty's death coincides with Andrew's final confrontation with Horace Bannon. Andrew learns that his father is dead but that his own identity as an escaped slave will be protected and his life spared.

The Characters

Andrew Hawkins, of course, is by far the most important and complex figure in *Oxherding Tale*. The characters of what might be called the supporting cast appear sequentially, often for a chapter or two at a time, each figure portrayed engagingly, wittily, but quickly, in the mode of a series of sketches. Yet the supporting cast cannot be said to consist simply of flat characters, for the author is interested in the intersubjective dimensions of identity, in the degree to which Andrew's selfhood is bound up in an ever-shifting web of relationships. This element is clearly marked in the novel's preoccupation with telepathy and transcendentalism, and it accounts in part for the novel's episodic yet unified plot structure.

The characterization of Andrew himself is achieved largely through the language of his first-person narrative. Andrew's discursive perspective is wryly authoritative and urbanely observational, a frank departure from the tone of most picaresque narratives of youth. Such novels often attribute to their youthful protagonists a charming naïveté, improvisational verbal dexterity, and, underlying all else, an innocent, unspoiled wisdom. Johnson partakes of this tendency only to the extent that he deploys a protagonist whose utterances within the novel's dialogue are dextrous, capable of trickster-like dissembling. Andrew's narrative voice, though, rarely betrays a naïvete concerning his circumstances.

In a uniquely existential perspective on whirlwind, life-threatening adventures, Andrew's tone as narrator is musing, detached, and skeptical. His propensity for interiorized reflection—amidst a plot line comparable to those of nineteenth century melodramatic narratives—contributes an ironic counterpoint to suspenseful, dramatic exterior action and thickens the linguistic texture of the novel.

Ezekiel is typical of the characters of the supporting cast in the sense that his importance long outlasts his actual appearance within the plot. In fact, many of the stories of Ezekiel, George, and Minty are told in lengthy flashbacks and reminiscences after Andrew has left Polkinghorne. Andrew's relations to the supporting cast members are dialectical and always shifting, with many ongoing effects in the characters' absences.

A certain intermingling of identity occurs among Andrew's three dark-skinned elders: George Hawkins, Reb the Coffinmaker, and the Soulcatcher. Eventually, these figures each demonstrate a patronizing but affectionate indulgence for Andrew, and each finds his life to be clearly altered because of Andrew. As a triumvirate of African American male strength, they come to seem crucial figures in the story of Andrew's attempt to negotiate his identity. After George has forsaken his father's urgent advice by passing for white in order to make his escape, he carries a burden of guilt. In fact, Andrew had described George as something of an object of satire: a belligerent "Race Man" unaware of the nuances of Andrew's experiences, a meat-lover comically forced to eat vegetables. Yet this relation is resolved to an extent through the nexus of George, Reb, and the Soulcatcher. Through the mystical capacities of Reb and, especially, the Soulcatcher, the relationship between Andrew and George is redeemed, when the father metaphysically "saves" his son's life.

Themes and Meanings

Oxherding Tale is a richly textured work that uses the first-person viewpoint to portray the complex sensibilities of Andrew Hawkins and of the novel's central characters, none of whom is a stock type. Andrew is characterized chiefly through the language of his narration itself; the prose style, learned, graceful, philosophic, and reflective, bespeaks a genuinely searching character who is open to all manner of perception and who sees deeply into the lives of his acquaintances. Johnson's method of presenting Andrew's early life through several flashbacks allows the reader to learn about characters piecemeal, through interwoven series of events that thicken a sense of the density and immediacy of Andrew's experience and yearnings. Although Andrew's mature point of view is sometimes ironic and comic, he sees himself as a butt of humor as often as he ridicules others.

The problem of identity is the novel's central theme. Andrew is uniquely positioned as a character who, light-skinned, refined, and eloquent, can traverse the boundary of race. As he desperately finagles a limited degree of autonomy, he must acknowledge the moral nature of his actions.

Oxherding Tale resists easy categorization because of its experimentation with different forms and traditions of writing. In one sense, the novel joins with the tradition of picaresque novels to which Mark Twain's *The Adventures of Tom Sawyer* (1876) belongs, novels whose structures are episodic rather than tightly integrated. Andrew is flung from one situation into another; he careens like a pinball through the novel's action, achieving what little control he can over his destiny through his superior wits. The novel makes use of the picaresque tradition to the degree that Andrew cleverly improvises language and tactics to meet each new challenge. In this connection, the novel makes use of the trickster-figure tradition of African American folktales exemplified by such characters as Brer Rabbit and the Signifying Monkey.

Further, the picaresque hero rarely displays any radical development of character through his succession of adventures. Andrew is so mature in his views and language from an early age that his story often seems to be less about personal development or coming of age than about the exploits of an already sensitive and precocious character in an absurd world. The picaresque hero is often carefree and happy-go-lucky, however, and in this sense the novel represents a revision of the form. The adventures of Andrew—first a slave, later a runaway slave, and finally a man with an assumed identity—are sometimes comic, but they do not allow for an entirely light-hearted tone.

In another sense, Johnson uses the form of the *Bildungsroman*, the novel of formation or novel of education. Such novels usually begin with an account of the circumstances into which their hero is born and follow the hero's growth into early adulthood and into a discovery of identity and purpose in life. Johnson's use of this form is underlined by the novel's first scene, a largely comic account of the bizarre night on which Andrew is conceived by George Hawkins and Anna Polkinghorne. The opening of the novel with a humorous account of the narrator-hero's own conception, leaving the reader to wonder how these events are known to the narrator, is also a feature of *Tristram Shandy* (1759-1767), Laurence Sterne's eighteenth century *Bildungsroman*. *Oxherding Tale* is not focused centrally on the extraordinary development of Andrew Hawkins, which is presented as already achieved, but the novel crucially raises questions of identity and of life's purpose as its hero enters adulthood.

The form of writing to which *Oxherding Tale* is perhaps most importantly connected is the nineteenth century slave narrative. Johnson makes explicit reference to these writings in his novel. Slave narratives are nonfictional, first-person accounts written by former slaves, often tracing a movement from slavery to freedom and from South to North; the most famous examples of this form are *Narrative of the Life of Frederick Douglass: An American Slave* (1845) and Harriet Jacobs' *Incidents in the Life of a Slave Girl* (1861). With *Oxherding Tale*, Johnson invents a fictional slave narrative that imparts a sense of the density of lived experience upon the form. Rather than portray his characters as good or evil stock types, Johnson renders the sensibilities of his fictional slaves and slaveholders as complex, three-dimensional, and ambiguous.

The language of the novel varies considerably, sometimes using contemporary slang alongside the Southern vernacular of the nineteenth century. By using modern as well as antiquated language in a novel about slavery, Johnson suggests the difficulty of comprehending the past, the timelessness of the themes of identity and responsibility, and the influence of the past over the present. Like a jazz musician improvising upon standard melodies, Johnson creates a freehand mix of styles and literary modes of expression in order to provide an imaginatively rich, magnanimous, and immediate sense of his characters.

Oxherding Tale is a virtuoso performance that incorporates many linguistic and narrative strategies into a re-exploration of the tangled problem of how slavery can be understood from the perspective of the twentieth century. There is some affiliation between the transcendentalist teachings of Ezekiel and the movement of the novel itself: The narrative scope extends beyond narrow limitations, platitudes, or stereotypes toward a full, imaginatively rich vision.

Critical Context

Oxherding Tale received favorable notice in periodicals when it was published in 1982; it was admired by reviewers for *The New York Times*, *The Village Voice*, *Publishers Weekly*, and *The New Yorker*, among others. The novel, however, did not immediately receive the scholarly critical attention that it was due.

The second of Johnson's novels (his first was 1974's impressive *Faith and the Good Thing*), *Oxherding Tale* won for Johnson a widening readership that continued to expand. In 1988, he published a collection of short fiction, *The Sorcerer's Apprentice*, and in 1990 he published *Middle Passage*, which extended his improvisations to seafaring stories. *Middle Passage* won the National Book Award, the first time that honor had been awarded to an African American male since Ralph Ellison won for *Invisible Man* (1952).

Bibliography

Davis, Arthur P. "Novels of the New Black Renaissance, 1960-1977: A Thematic Survey." *College Language Association Journal* 21 (June, 1978): 457-491. Analyzes the work of twenty-four modern black writers, including Johnson. A useful introduction to the major African American fiction of the period.

Harris, Norman. "The Black Universe in Contemporary Afro-American Fiction." *College Language Association Journal* 30 (1986): 1-13. Claims that Johnson, like Ishmael Reed and Toni Morrison, moves beyond the naturalism and realism that characterized earlier African American fiction.

Johnson, Charles. *Being and Race: Black Writing Since 1970.* Bloomington: Indiana

University Press, 1988. Johnson discusses the development of African American literature and his own theories of fiction. He asserts that the best literature is a blend of imagination, invention, and interpretation.

——————————. "Reflections on Fiction, Philosophy, and Film: An Interview with Charles Johnson." *Callaloo* 1 (October, 1978): 118-128. A wide-ranging discussion of the author's varied areas of interest.

Shultz, Elizabeth. "The Heirs of Ralph Ellison." *College Language Association Journal* 22 (December, 1978): 101-122. Useful for gauging Johnson's significance in the context of post-World War II African American literature.

James Knippling

PAINTED TURTLE
Woman with Guitar

Author: Clarence Major (1936-   )
Type of work: Novel
Type of plot: Experimental
Time of plot: The 1930's to the 1980's
Locale: Arizona, Colorado, New Mexico
First published: 1988

> *Principal characters:*
> PAINTED TURTLE, a Zuni woman singer and guitar player
> BALDWIN "BALDY" SAIYATACA, the narrator, Painted Turtle's lover
>   and musical partner
> OLD GCHACHU, the father of Painted Turtle's clan
> GRANDMA WILHELMINA, Painted Turtle's grandmother
> WALDO ETAWA, Painted Turtle's father
> MARELDA ETAWA, Painted Turtle's mother

The Novel

   Painted Turtle: Woman with Guitar is an experimental novel in the fable tradition that traces the moral, personal, psychological, and spiritual development of Clarence Major's principal character, Mary Etawa, called "Painted Turtle." Born into a traditional Zuni family on December 17, 1938, Painted Turtle gets her nickname because she crawls on all fours and raises her head like a turtle. In some ways, this name comes to define her position to everyone and for everything outside her own life. She tries to shut out the traditions of her family and the realities of her ancestry, much like a turtle in its shell. She exists in a place between actual reality, dreams, mystical experiences, and the construction of her autobiography, as told through the "voice" of her lover, Baldy. In many ways, this story is a poetic statement on alienation and transformation, the misunderstanding inherent in the dynamics of multicultural interaction, pride and prejudice, sexism and racism, and the known and unknown spaces that exist between the traditional roles of men and women.

   The novel begins with Baldy's explanation of how he came to know Painted Turtle. It ends with their riding through the barren landscapes of the Southwest as a committed team in both music and love. In between is the story of many people who inhabit Painted Turtle's world as children, ghosts, parents, relations, relatives, and spirits. All these relationships are complicated by the demands of tradition fighting against Painted Turtle's desire for identity and independence. Painted Turtle's life is difficult and confusing because she defies traditional mores and dares to disagree with authority. As if unconscious and in a trance, Painted Turtle wanders through her life as much an observer as an active participant. She does what she wants to do, needs to do, has to do, not quite knowing why or how. She knows that the "old ways" keep her in a state of agitation, and therefore she rebels against what appears to be a fixed position in life. She does not fit into the social and cultural systems of the reservation, nor does she accept the demands of motherhood. Her defiance, as well as her rape and bearing of twins, make her an unacceptable bride; her lack of conventionality forces her to leave the Zuni reservation to escape its restrictions. Moreover, her desire to go beyond the ordinary means that her life cannot be like that of her mother, who by making pottery out of clay follows the traditional static path of females.

After attempting to drown the twins, Painted Turtle is placed in the Gallup Indian Medical Center. Released after a few months, she returns to the reservation but soon realizes that she can no longer live there. This begins her quest for identity. She takes a few odd jobs; after being arrested for prostitution, she finally picks up her guitar again and finds the space where her life has meaning. In a series of trips away from the reservation and on visits back to bury the dead and observe rituals, she discovers that she is more fulfilled, even as a very proud and conscious Zuni, away from the reservation. Thus, time on the cantina circuit takes on a life of its own; she meets Baldy and allows him to travel with her. Familiarity grows into love and mutual respect into a partnership. The story ends as they ride to their first job together.

The Characters

Painted Turtle's alienation from her culture allows her to transcend reality through her music. Early in her life, she yearns to be a boy and experience the freedom of her father's sphere; however, she must learn the confining ways of the worlds of her mother and grandmother. When she is raped at age thirteen and gives birth to twins, most of the Zuni interpret this as a curse, and their attitude gives meaning to the lifelong distance and discomfort she always feels for the demands and expectations placed upon her by gender and culture. To escape, she goes to a mental hospital and later becomes an unsuccessful barmaid and prostitute; eventually, she becomes a nightclub performer. She finally realizes that her childhood guitar can offer her not only an escape from reality but also an escape from a dreaded life on the reservation. Thus, she travels to third-rate clubs, bars, and hotels, singing for tips while sleeping in flophouses and hour-rated motels, until she meets Baldy.

Baldy, the narrator in the story, peers into Painted Turtle's life across actual time and mythic distance; his own story becomes woven into hers. He initially meets Painted Turtle on "the grimy cantina circuit" when he is sent to hear her perform by their mutual agent, Peter Inkpen. Baldy's task is to transform Painted Turtle into a more commercially appealing singer by suggesting that she switch to the electric guitar; instead, she unwittingly transforms him, and he joins her act when he trades in his prized electric guitar for an acoustic one. Being the son of a Hopi mother and a Navajo father makes him emblematic of the story; he, like Painted Turtle, must walk between two worlds. He represents the historic conflict that has always existed between different people. Throughout the novel, Baldy remains a distant figure and a stilted voice, telling little of Painted Turtle's life and even less about his own. He is seen through her eyes as the narrative reveals her life to the world.

Old Gchachu, the father of the clan, is the human incarnation of the old ways. The collective memory—culture, custom, folklore, and history—is represented in his being; while she is in his presence, Painted Turtle is never sure if her experiences are dreams or reality. He prophesies when she is young that she will marry a wise priest, become famous for her traditional cooking skills, and become legendary for her love of children and family. When these beliefs do not come true, he reminds her that the soul of a Zuni dies if it strays too far from home.

Grandma Wilhelmina, Painted Turtle's grandmother, represents both the sanctity of the past, as she embodies the traditional female role of healer and caretaker, and the options of the future, as she produces fine jewelry and sells it in stores all over the Southwest. Without saying much, she validates Painted Turtle's independent spirit and sanctions her movement away from the traditional life.

Waldo Etawa, Painted Turtle's father, symbolizes both the traditional father figure and the erosion of the Native American way of life. On one hand, he drinks; on the other, he teaches his daughter male tasks and helps her develop skills usually not taught to women. He fuels her independence by treating her like a son. Though successful, he lets the family's material and social status slip as he fails to keep white society and modernization from altering the "old ways."

Marelda Etawa, Painted Turtle's mother, represents the stability of hearth and home and the probability of continuation. She remains at home, caretaker to both an older and younger generation as well as keeper of the family lore, its customs, and traditions; she rears the two grandsons in Painted Turtle's absence.

Themes and Meanings

Painted Turtle is an emotionally complex yet psychologically distant character. In some ways, she represents no one but herself; in others, she is everyone. To some extent, she is the eternal poet, always searching for herself in a lyric, always revealing herself in a song. While Major wants the reader to see Painted Turtle as a character representative of Native American culture in general and Zuni culture in particular, Painted Turtle is not sufficiently developed; thus, the other characters are utilized to display the dynamic ways in which earth, wind, fire, and air connect to sustain life. The stereotypes and minor characters in this novel all serve functions necessary to an understanding of the story. An example of this is Baldy's Aunt Franny, who represents the stereotype of the "drunken Indian" but who also symbolizes what happens to women who leave their ancestral home and forsake the old ways. Her presence evokes more shame than pity. As she eats with Painted Turtle and Baldy, the rose Franny puts in Painted Turtle's hair serves more to anoint her own independence of spirit and defiance of tradition than it does to recognize the beauty of her nephew's friend. Aunt Franny is drunk because she lost her soul by marrying an "anglo." Thus, the message is clear: Step outside the acceptable boundaries of the culture and invite disgrace and misfortune.

This point is made quite clearly when Old Gchachu, as patriarch and senior mystic, tells Painted Turtle that if she ventures from the clan her soul will die. A Zuni soul cannot live too far from home. His words have power, yet she continues to defy his wishes. In one instance, when he and Painted Turtle are alone in his home, he seeks to engage her sexually; she refuses, and he summons evil spirits. They come and dance around her; she refuses their advances also, and they possess her. She has no power to fend them off. Painted Turtle awakens in her own bed only to realize that perhaps this was all just a bad dream. Yet the point has been made: To be disobedient is to crave punishment.

The interaction that Painted Turtle has with her Grandma Wilhelmina is never frightening, harsh, or unpleasant; it is, however, very complex. Grandma Wilhelmina says little, listens a great deal, and renders few opinions. This is the comfortable and special relationship that can only exist between a grandmother and her granddaughter; in this context, Painted Turtle does not feel alien, nor does she feel uncomfortable. With the resignation that only aging can bring, Grandma Wilhelmina has a calming and soothing effect upon her contentious grandchild. It is only with Grandma Wilhelmina as reference that Painted Turtle feels a part of the Zuni nation. In the presence of her grandmother, Painted Turtle does not chafe under the conformity demanded on the reservation. While her parents fulfill their respective roles, Painted Turtle enjoys being with her father more than with her mother. She likes the outdoors and the activities that males are expected to perform. She finds the world of women too closed, the actions too predictable, the tasks too monotonous. Men lead active lives full of different tasks and are always anticipating something new and exciting to happen. In the interactions with her immediate family Painted Turtle finds the most pain; it is their desire to make her conform to her role in their society that she must escape. Painted Turtle refuses to accept the sacred traditions her family holds dear, and this refusal and failure to compromise force her on the road.

Critical Context

Painted Turtle is a continuation of Major's incursion into what is called experimental fable. This short book examines the birth, childhood, and adult life of a character, Painted Turtle, whom Major first introduced as an older woman in *My Amputations* (1986). It continues his interest in metafictional characters and issues that transcend both time and space. Indeed, reality and mysticism are as prominent in this work as they are in the interesting and engaging *Such Was the Season* (1987) and his long poem "Observations of a Stranger at Zuni in the Latter Part of the Twentieth Century" (1990). Some critics suggest that this is one of Major's most accessible works, and it represents a significant model for the emerging genre of multicultural literature in the United States. In some ways, *Painted Turtle* allows Major to break completely away from the self-consciousness of his earlier work and to demonstrate that the spaces that exist between class, ethnicity, gender, and race do not prevent serious writers from transcending their own realities to delve in interesting and respectful ways into those of others. The frequent use of undefined or unexplained terms in the Zuni, Hopi, Navajo, and Spanish languages lends a certain distance and intrigue to this work. It is there on the printed page but slightly inaccessible; it is readable but somewhat incomprehensible. The barrier of language becomes a metaphor for the barriers of difference. In this short novel, Major presents an example of a new aesthetic devoid of the personal social reality that is common among black writers. To accomplish this, he uses random allusions, incomplete textual development, lyrical poetry, and disjointed rhythms in an attempt to step beyond himself to create a new direction in fiction.

Bibliography
Bell, Bernard W. "Modernism and Postmodernism." In *The Afro-American Novel and Its Tradition.* Amherst: University of Massachusetts Press, 1987. Places Major in the postmodern tradition of experimentation with language and form.
Cagidemetrio, Alide. "The Real Thing: Notes on an American Strategy." In *Critical Angles: European Views of Contemporary American Literature*, edited by Marc Chénetier. Carbondale: Southern Illinois University Press, 1986. Discusses Major's writing as a response to the need and desire to break away from the confines of race-specific literature. Notes that some of Major's earlier themes that find ultimate expression in *Painted Turtle* reflect a style that is deliberately disjointed, random, and confused.
Major, Clarence. *The Dark and Feeling: Black American Writers and Their Work.* New York: Third Press, 1974. Includes an important essay by Major on the "Black Aesthetic" and several interviews, including a self-interview.
_____. "Necessary Distance: Afterthoughts on Becoming a Writer." *Black American Literature Forum* 23 (Summer, 1989): 197-212. Asks whether or not the writer can separate the literary from the personal and to what extent all writing is somewhat autobiographical. Major reflects on innovation and on time and space in the process of writing. He notes that writing *Painted Turtle* caused him to go beyond the narrow confines of experience and to delve into mysticism.
Martin, Reginald. *Ishmael Reed and the New Black Aesthetic Critics.* New York: St. Martin's Press, 1988. Identifies Major as one of the writers who has done much to translate the metaphysical nature of blackness into a major literary genre. Martin looks at Major, Reed, and others as having found and utilized the revolutionary potential of black literature.

Alphine W. Jefferson

PASSING

Author: Nella Larsen (1891-1964)
Type of work: Novel
Type of plot: Psychological realism
Time of plot: The 1920's
Locale: New York City and Chicago, Illinois
First published: 1929

Principal characters:
> IRENE WESTOVER REDFIELD, the protagonist, a respected member of the black middle class of Harlem
> CLARE KENDRY (MRS. JOHN BELLEW), Irene's childhood friend, orphaned as a young teenager
> BRIAN REDFIELD, Irene's husband, a successful black physician who longs for the opportunity to practice medicine in an environment free of racial discrimination
> JOHN BELLEW, Clare's wealthy white husband
> GERTRUDE MARTIN, a childhood friend of Irene and Clare; she also passes for white
> ZULENA and LIZA, Irene's maids

The Novel

Passing explores the psychological and social costs of racial passing on two women, Irene Redfield and Clare Kendry. Although Irene does not, except on occasions when it is convenient, pass as white, Clare's passing and subsequent decision to reenter parts of the black experience through her friendship with Irene disrupt the life-style Irene has fought so hard to maintain, doing so with tragic consequences for both women.

Larsen pays special attention to the emotional bonds that connect the two women. The opening chapter begins with Irene musing over a letter she receives from Clare. Irene's emotional state is made obvious in her reflection on what the letter's contents might mean. She focuses on the letter's more personal message. Clare writes about how lonely she is and how she must see Irene, as though Irene is the only person in the world who might alleviate her loneliness.

The next chapter emphasizes the emotional connection between the two women. It depicts their meeting two years previously. They had not seen each other since they were teenagers. Irene has temporarily decided to pass because it is hot and humid in Chicago, where she is visiting her father and shopping for her two sons. She has tea at the top of the Drayton Hotel and meets Clare. At first, Irene is simply fascinated with the woman's beauty and is curious as to why the woman keeps staring at her. Her first thought is that the woman might suspect that she is passing. Before long, the bold Clare makes her identity known. The women begin discussing old times and, briefly, new ones. During tea, Irene notes the rage she feels toward

Clare, who has done the despicable in denying her race, but she also notes Clare's beauty, thinking of Clare as a lovely creature. Clare wants Irene to come to her house for tea, and although Irene knows that she should not do it, because Clare's husband is white, she agrees, almost as if compelled.

Two years later, Irene is in the same predicament. Clare has requested another meeting, and in spite of knowing that she should not meet with her, Irene agrees. She knows that more is at risk this time because Clare, being in New York City, is on Irene's turf. Anything outrageous or scandalous that happens will have immediate consequences on Irene's life.

Irene and Clare meet. Clare tells Irene of her plan to spend time with black people, to become reacquainted with the black experience. Against her better judgment, Irene agrees to help Clare in her plan. The novel next showcases a number of parties, racial uplift meetings, and dinners that the two women attend in Harlem.

Most people are charmed with Clare, and everything seems to be working fine until Clare's visits to the Redfield home become more frequent. Irene notes the attraction Brian has for Clare. Added to Irene's growing jealousy is the complication of Clare's husband, who returns from a business trip. His presence makes Clare's getting away to be among black people more difficult and dangerous.

The novel is divided into three major sections, entitled "Encounter," "Re-Encounter," and "Finale." Larsen advances her story by detailing Irene's responses to the changes in her life that Clare's "newfound" blackness brings. At various times, Irene either hates or loves Clare, feels sorry for her or feels contempt, and wants Clare near her or banished to another part of the world. It becomes clear to Irene that Clare's attention to Brian may be all he needs to make a decision to leave Harlem, costing Irene the material and social comfort she has worked hard to get. Irene resolves that Clare must leave her life. Irene often hopes that something will happen to remove Clare from the Redfields' social circle.

The novel's ending, which includes Clare's death, is ambiguous. Irene wanted Clare out of her life, but the narrative does not make it clear if Clare accidentally fell from an apartment window, jumped, or was pushed by John Bellew or by Irene. In any event, Irene is relieved that Clare is dead.

The Characters

Larsen uses a third-person omniscient narrator who is always close to Irene Redfield's thoughts and feelings. Most of the novel's meaning depends on Irene's character. Irene, Clare, and Brian are the most fully realized of the characters, though several relatively undeveloped characters are present, including Gertrude Martin, John Bellew, Zulena, Hugh Wentworth, and Felise Freeland.

Irene is a complicated character whose exterior conventionality masks a woman who wants adventure and excitement and whose reinvolvement with Clare gives her vicarious outlets for feelings she has denied. Irene is an inauthentic woman. By disclosing her thoughts, feelings, and life choices, Larsen highlights not only the extent of this inauthenticity but also how it creates a woman more dangerous in her denial of self than Clare is in her overt risk-taking.

Irene has groomed herself to be a model of black middle-class respectability. She marries a physician, has two sons, lives in a respectable Harlem brownstone, associates with the right people, and supports the right social causes, such as the Negro Welfare League. On the surface, she has it all. Beneath the surface, Larsen shows the price Irene pays to live a fraudulent life.

When Irene reflects on her relationship with Brian and the constant tension she has to quell to keep him from moving to Brazil and disrupting her life, she understands that she does not love him and never has. She thinks that if he were to die, she would only look askance at his photograph. She and Brian even sleep in separate bedrooms. She remains in her marriage for the financial security and social standing it provides. When Clare poses a risk to her security, Irene decides to do something about it. Most of her activity is relegated to an ever-increasing series of thoughts, first centering on how nice it would be if Clare disappeared from their circle of friends and then proceeding to visions of Clare's death.

Irene is also inauthentic in her role of mother. She makes sure that her sons are dressed, are fed well, and are doing their homework, but she takes no real interest in their lives other than wanting them not to be hurt by racism. She will not discuss racism or human sexuality with them because she thinks that if these topics are not discussed, then they do not exist.

In other words, Irene "passes" as a wife and mother. Both guises make her angry and irritable just beneath the surface. Another Irene lurks deeper inside, one craving the very danger she objects to in Clare's life. Larsen presents this part of Irene's character through a detailing of Irene's oscillating thoughts and feelings about Clare. In her thoughts, Irene often hates Clare, seeing her as a despicable black woman and mother, but in her actions she always lets Clare have her way, at least until the final pages of the novel. Psychologically, Irene is fascinated with Clare, with her vitality, her risk-taking, her doing what she wants to do. Irene is always preoccupied with Clare.

Clare Kendry is not so preoccupied with Irene. From the beginning of the novel, Clare is presented as someone who has always taken risks to get what she wants. Her decision to pass and then to marry a white man is her most significant risk, for she can have no control over the color of any children she might have. When she meets Irene in Chicago and invites Irene and Gertrude to meet her husband, John, she is again taking risks. He might suspect not only that her friends are black but also that she is too. Reentering the black experience through Irene's contacts is yet one more risk Clare takes. Her risks are taken with little thought as to how negative consequences might affect others, for example her child and her black friends. In this sense, Clare is willful, selfish, and daring. More important, unlike Irene, Clare makes the choices to live as she wants to, not as others might expect her to. Her decision to rejoin black people is not presented in any noble way. She does not seem to want to reidentify with black people. Her intention is to have experiences that satisfy her. The price for her choices is her death.

Themes and Meanings

Passing develops many issues that converge on the novel's larger theme of the consequences and nuances of racial passing in the 1920's. Larsen extends her understanding of passing to more than its obvious racial considerations. In her extended coverage of the phenomenon of passing, her focus is on those who do not live authentically. To Larsen, living inauthentically is a human tragedy. This idea is advanced most directly in her scrutiny of the Redfields, particularly Irene.

Larsen critiques racial passing from the position that racial uniqueness, which in the United States includes a historical and cultural African American tradition, is not something that one should dismiss. Even as she details Clare's reasons for passing, which include economic and social opportunity and sometimes peace of mind, Larsen suggests that these do not take the place of one's racial culture. Clare's reasons for wanting to reenter the black experience make the point. In spite of the wealth and leisure she has in her marriage to John Bellew, Clare misses her people. Although she is not always sincere in her determination to be a part of black people's lives, Clare is sincere when she tells Irene how much she misses black people.

The price individuals pay when they choose to pass racially is high. Many remain trapped in their new white world, forever geographically and socially separated from their people, but always spiritually connected in some way. If, as in Clare's case, they choose to return to their people, dire consequences threaten, as evinced by John Bellew's reaction to the knowledge that Clare is black and more poignantly by Clare's mysterious death.

Larsen's critique of the other kinds of passing is no less severe. In her close attention to Irene's psychology, Larsen emphasizes that living inauthentically by adhering to cultural scripts of conventionality and material possession, even within one's race, is dangerous and damaging to the human spirit. Irene is a shell of a woman. She is intelligent and creative, but those traits are wasted in maintaining a marriage to a husband she does not love. She persists in the marriage only because she wants the upper-class life-style that it affords.

Wanting to believe that Clare's intrusion into her life is a threat to her marriage, Irene does all she can to destroy a friendship that provides her only real living. Irene's change from doing whatever Clare says to finding ways to sever their friendship accompanies her recognition that her marriage to Brian, indeed her entire adult life, is a fraud. Rather than accept this growing understanding, Irene denies it. She thinks that if only Clare were out of the way, all else would return to normal.

At the novel's end, Larsen makes it clear that Irene's relief at Clare's death is temporary. At Clare's death, Irene is faced with the knowledge that her life is empty. Her passing, like Clare's passing, has come to naught.

Critical Context

Larsen's *Passing*, like her first and more ambitious novel *Quicksand* (1928), explores black middle-class milieus and the lack of choices and alternatives available to women who are a part of them. Although on a surface reading the women in

Passing appear to have choices, a closer scrutiny of the text suggests that they have few real options available to them. For those such as Clare who chose to pass, a white middle-class life-style, with its restrictions on possibilities for women, is offered. For women such as Irene, the same choices are present, only couched within middle-class respectability. In *Quicksand*, Helga Crane, the protagonist, travels across the United States and then to Europe in search of a place where she can live an authentic life. She spends much time complaining about the limited choices available to black middle-class women. For many of them, being respectable and good, which often means marrying a professional black man and having his children, are the only acceptable roles. In both novels, Larsen demonstrates the toll such limited choices take on her protagonists, who are both psychologically defeated.

Larsen's novels, furthermore, examine black middle-class women's lives from a different and more aesthetically challenging position than those of her contemporary, Jessie Fauset. Fauset usually had her protagonists not only acquiesce to marriage but also enjoy the subservience of it. Larsen's novels, when compared to Fauset's, present a more in-depth treatment of black middle-class subject matter.

Larsen's novels look forward to a time when black female writers would be able to explore a wider range of subject matter and include even more options for black female characters. Deborah E. McDowell, for example, in the introduction to the 1986 America Women Writers reissue of *Quicksand* and *Passing*, suggests that Larsen proposed the alternative of lesbian sexual expression in her creation of the friendship of Irene and Clare. Black women writers of the 1980's and 1990's have freedom that Larsen did not have in creating character, subject matter, and theme.

With two slim novels and a short story as a record of her creative production, Nella Larsen is considered by most critics of African American literature to be of seminal importance in presenting the black female character's way of viewing the world in the 1920's. Such acclaim began appearing in the late 1970's, when black feminist critics looked at Larsen's work anew and resurrected it from a critical tradition that had denied it any authority.

Bibliography

Carby, Hazel V. *Reconstructing Womanhood: The Emergence of the Afro-American Woman Novelist.* New York: Oxford University Press, 1987. Considers Nella Larsen to be one of the most important novelists to emerge from the Harlem Renaissance. Focuses on Larsen's aesthetic issues and on her political and social critiques.

Christian, Barbara T. *Black Women Novelists: The Development of a Tradition, 1892-1976.* Westport, Conn.: Greenwood Press, 1980. An important discussion of black female writers that helped to bring about a new assessment of their fiction. Significant analysis of Nella Larsen, the integrity of her fiction, and the forward-looking quality of her vision.

Davis, Thadious M. "Nella Larsen's Harlem Aesthetic." In *The Harlem Renaissance: Revaluations*, edited by Amritjit Singh, William S. Shiver, and Stanley Brodwin.

New York: Garland, 1989. Argues that Larsen's aesthetic faithfully captures the spirit of her times. Emphasizes the tension Larsen evokes between the social and the personal.

McDowell, Deborah E. Introduction to *"Quicksand and Passing."* New Brunswick, N.J.: Rutgers University Press, 1986. Excellent discussion of both novels that places them in a number of critical and historical contexts to elucidate their meaning. Reads *Passing* as a novel with obvious lesbian suggestions.

Shockley, Ann Allen. *Afro-American Women Writers, 1746-1933.* New York: Meridian, 1988. Presents a general and useful overview of black female writers. Has a specific discussion of Larsen's life and her major works.

Charles P. Toombs

PHILADELPHIA FIRE

Author: John Edgar Wideman (1941-   )
Type of work: Novel
Type of plot: Social criticism
Time of plot: The 1960's and the 1980's
Locale: Primarily Philadelphia, Pennsylvania
First published: 1990

Principal characters:

CUDJOE, a would-be writer working as a barman on the Greek
island of Mykonos; he returns to Philadelphia

SIMBA MINTU (SIMMIE), a young boy orphaned as a result of the
police attack on the MOVE compound

MARGARET JONES, Cudjoe's sole direct link to the fire and
therefore to Simba

JOHN AFRICA (JAMES BROWN), the charismatic leader of the
MOVE organization, the "dirtiest man" Margaret Jones
ever saw

SAM, a successful writer and editor, Cudjoe's mentor and
surrogate father

TIMBO, a friend of Cudjoe from the 1960's

JOHN EDGAR WIDEMAN, a novelist and, in the second of the
book's three parts, the narrator

J. B., a strange figure who plays a prominent but decidedly
ambiguous part in the novel's final section

The Novel

After learning of the 1985 police attack on the Philadelphia headquarters of John
Africa's MOVE organization, an attack that destroyed fifty-three houses and killed
eleven people, Cudjoe, a once-promising black novelist, leaves the Greek island where
he has been living since his divorce and returns to Philadelphia. There he hopes to
find some explanation for this seemingly senseless tragedy, and then, like Wideman,
to write about it. First he must locate Simba, the child who escaped the fire at the
MOVE compound. Simba, orphaned as a result of the fire, stands for all the novel's
lost children, including Cudjoe's biracial children now living with their mother; Wideman's imprisoned son, who along with Wideman figures prominently in the second
of the novel's three parts; the inner-city youths whom Cudjoe taught before abandoning them in order to pursue his own higher education; and finally the younger
Cudjoe, who sought to escape both his identity and his responsibility as an African
American.

At the sparsely attended funeral service for the eleven victims of the fire, "White
college kids riff and scat an elegy for four voices." *Philadelphia Fire* is itself an
elegy for multiple voices written by an author who, although not himself white, has,

like Cudjoe, gained entrance to the white world and enjoyed the "Power Money Things" coveted by Kaliban's Kiddie Korps (KKK), the youths that Cudjoe had taught earlier in his life and who now communicate through graffiti and violence. The novel mourns the eleven direct victims of the fire along with the child Simba, living but lost, for all practical purposes one of the KKK; Wideman's son; Cudjoe's children; and more generally the idealism of the 1960's that resulted in so few changes in the lives of so many black Americans. Bringing a "riff and scat" style to bear on so conservative and conventional a literary form as the elegy poses considerable difficulties for both the writer and especially the reader, who may well assume that elegy, social criticism, and narrative innovation should remain separate. Formidable as these difficulties may be, they are central to the novel's purpose.

Divided into three progressively shorter parts, *Philadelphia Fire* is written in a prose that is at once elliptical and densely packed, filled with social detail and mythic resonance. There is little plot as such and even less linear development. The novel's multiple narratives probe the interior lives of its characters, dropping them and the reader into a nightmarish reality vaguely reminiscent of that earliest (and most Gothic) of Philadelphia fictions, Charles Brockden Brown's *Arthur Mervyn: Or, Memoirs of the Year 1793* (part 1, 1799; part 2, 1800) set, like Wideman's short story "Fever," during the scarlet fever epidemic of 1793. Ultimately, *Philadelphia Fire* is no more gothic than it is conventionally elegiac. "Maybe this is a detective story," Cudjoe wonders at one point. If it is, then it is a convoluted one, one that even in its final paragraph chooses to compound the mystery rather than resolve it: "Cudjoe hears footsteps behind him. A mob howling his name. Screaming for blood. Words come to him, cool him, stop him in his tracks. He'd known them all his life. Never again. Never again. He turns to face whatever it is rumbling over the stones of Independence Square."

Whatever Cudjoe is about to discover is left unclear, as unclear as the identity of the enigmatic J. B., who figures prominently yet ambiguously in the novel's concluding section. The only certainty is that Cudjoe has stopped running. He is now willing to face all that he once sought to evade and that, since he heard of the fire and returned to Philadelphia, has evaded him, especially as a novelist. "Words fail me," Wideman writes midway through the novel, "because there are no words for what's happening. I am a witness." He is witness chiefly to his own perplexity, which also belongs to Cudjoe and even to the reader, who must negotiate a novel the form of which is complex and vehemently nontraditional. *Philadelphia Fire* recounts several parallel stories, each reflecting the others as if in some surreal funhouse.

The Characters

The visual metaphor of the novel as a hall of mirrors has its verbal equivalent in Wideman's relay of narrative voices. Cudjoe, for example, plays the part of the Pied Piper. Magician and musician, he is also the one who writes and the one about whom is written. "Why this Cudjoe, then?" Wideman (now as narrator) asks. "This airy other floating into the shape of my story. Why am I him when I tell certain parts? Why am I hiding from myself? Is he mirror or black hole?" The novel serves as both mirror and black hole, reflecting and devouring, shedding light (wisdom) and preventing its escape, its real subject being an absence (Simba, for example) detectable only by virtue of the bodies (planetary or human) caught in its gravitational pull. Wideman's characters are similarly constructed. They are mirrors and voids rather than stable subjects: shifting, shapeless, voiceless (insofar as they have no voice of their own), and disembodied. Having no (one) voice of its own, the novel, like its characters, speaks in an amazing multiplicity of ventriloquized voices and interpolated styles and forms: nursery rhymes, biblical echoes, the radio monologue of a rapper, a dialogue between two mayors (one black, one white), and passages from William Shakespeare's *The Tempest* (1611) and other texts. It also uses more conventional narrative devices such as dialogue, description, indirect discourse, letters, and a notebook passage. Cudjoe's thinking and remembering often takes the form of editing, and much of Margaret Jones's story takes the highly mediated form of a tape recording that Cudjoe plays and fast forwards at will. The narrative discontinuity reflects and echoes the discontinuity of the characters' (especially Cudjoe's and Wideman's) lives as well as a postmodern conception of the human subject and the part narrative plays in its formation.

The second part of the novel, for example, begins by forgoing even the minimal continuity evident in the novel's opening section, intruding a second narrative presence that both merges with and diverges from Cudjoe. It opens with a brief objective description of the May 13, 1985, police attack on the MOVE headquarters in West Philadelphia. The next paragraph begins, "Pretend for a moment that none of this happened. . . . Pretend we can imagine our events into existence. . . . Imagine our fictions imagining us." A later paragraph quotes from the *Annals of Philadelphia* for 1850, while the next section quotes in part from, and retrospectively comments on, a telephone conversation that Wideman has with his imprisoned son. The next section, longer still, recounts how Wideman and his wife watched live television coverage of the Philadelphia fire, an account made strange by the fact that it starts out in the second person ("push button scanning of all available channels, flipping, clicking, twenty-nine cable options and none satisfactory so you choose them all and choose none, cut and paste images, you are the director, driver, pilot, boss hoss, captain, the switch is in your hand") only itself to "switch" in mid-paragraph to first person.

Wideman develops, or structures, his characters in much the same way that he structures the novel's plot and establishes its setting, the city that is virtually a character in its own right. Nowhere is this mode of characterization more apparent than in Wideman's handling of the enigmatic J. B., who figures prominently in the novel's concluding section. J. B. seems less a character than a composite sketch, the "Everyman" of medieval allegories. J. B. is, however, an Everyman who has no hope of reaching the Celestial City, for he finds himself not in an allegory but in a labyrinth of race and poverty, in the city of brotherly love transmogrified into the inner city of "brothelly" love. Literally a black derelict, J. B. is also John Africa, born James

Brown, escaped (like Simba) from the Osage Street fire. He is a version of Simba but also one of Hitler escaped from his bunker, Christ risen from his tomb, and the legendary phoenix reborn from its own ashes. Among other things, J. B. is a Caribbean trying to find work in order to buy the freedom of his wife and children who are being held hostage (although they may already be dead), perhaps in the Dominican Republic or neighboring Haiti, where Cudjoe's former wife, now remarried, lives with her and Cudjoe's children. J. B. is also someone who, like Cudjoe but unlike many inner-city African American men, did not fight in Vietnam. That appears to be the only suffering that this black version of Archibald MacLeish's J. B. from *J. B.: A Play in Verse* (1958), a rendering of the biblical Job, has been spared. Wideman's J. B. is both Job and a God weary of having to tame the light every morning and of "playing father son and holocaust to the kids running wild in the streets and vacant lots," presumably the same KKK that sets the sleeping J. B. on fire one morning. J. B. is also singer James Brown, singer of the blues that reflect the lives of African Americans, whose fate is to be both anonymous and demonized.

Themes and Meanings

Philadelphia Fire begins its meditation on the origins and meanings of the holocaust on Osage Avenue with William Penn's instructions for the placement of houses in the middle of grass plats to ensure that the city would always be green and wholesome and "never be burnt." It ends with the memorial service for those who died in the fire. The memorial program offers hope, but the poor attendance leads the narrator to comment, "Yes, there's a party. Problem is, looks like Philadelphia ain't coming." The collective failure of the largely white city to mourn the deaths of eleven of its citizens or to acknowledge its responsibility for their tragic fate is merely the last in a series of betrayals and abandonments, both public and private. Between Cudjoe's guilt over his children and Wideman's anguish over the fate of his son and over the mayor's handling of MOVE as an urban renewal problem, the novel offers various images of a society that has become the antithesis of the one William Penn envisioned three centuries earlier.

The local university dismantles its school of social work on the grounds that its city-centered approach runs counter to the university's newly defined "international" mission. As the narrator explains, "The forces at work in the University mirrored those in the larger society." There are more private visions of the horror, including Cudjoe's dream in which, cut off at the knees, he becomes the helpless witness to "a boy lynched from the rim" of a basketball hoop.

Philadelphia Fire is Wideman's version of Charles Dickens' *A Tale of Two Cities* (1859) and Marcel Proust's *Remembrance of Things Past* (1913-1927) combined into one narrative. It explores the deepening of racial and socioeconomic divisions and the threat of forgetting that hangs over the Osage Street fire. Wideman, in his role as narrator/character, realizes that he must write his son's story and that "not dealing with it may be causing the forgetfulness" he experiences, a forgetfulness that contributes to the novel's troubling but purposeful discontinuity. To remember means both to recall and to reassemble a dismembered whole. As witness, Cudjoe/Wideman sees but does not claim to understand the "moral" of the scene before him any more than he claims to know exactly where and when the metaphorical fire in fact began (with Jackie Robinson, he wonders, or with William Penn?). If "looking backward" leads to uncertainty, then looking ahead leads to a form of qualified despair or, alternatively, a minimalist hope. Thus comes Wideman's advice to his son, "Hold on," and J. B.'s advice to himself, "On with it."

Philadelphia Fire offers a succession of failures to do just that, to get "on with it." These include the ambitious production of *The Tempest* that Cudjoe's ten- and eleven-year-old inner-city students rehearse but never have the chance to perform. Offering a set of variations on a Shakespearean theme, the novel retells *The Tempest* in a double sense: telling again and telling differently. Cudjoe's version is first rained out and then abandoned when Cudjoe leaves teaching to pursue his own higher education. In succeeding where the students fail, Cudjoe and Wideman in effect become prosperous (or even Prosperos), at least for a time.

Critical Context

Robert Bone, author of the seminal study *The Negro Novel in America* (1958), has called Wideman "perhaps the most gifted black novelist of his generation." Wideman began his writing career showing little interest in the African American tradition. He seemed more interested in and aware of the tradition that began with the eighteenth century English novel, which was the subject of his doctoral dissertation. Wideman has cited Daniel Defoe, Henry Fielding, and Laurence Sterne as major influences on his work. His dense style, stream-of-consciousness technique, and formal experimentation, all of which derive from that tradition as transformed by writers such as James Joyce, set him apart still further from his African American heritage and more particularly the influential Black Arts movement of the 1960's and 1970's. The black literary movement has come to exert a powerful, if belated, influence on Wideman's writing, particularly after his agreement, after some initial reluctance, to establish a black studies program at the University of Pennsylvania in the early 1970's, shortly after his years in England as a Rhodes scholar. Beginning with *The Lynchers* (1973) and, after an eight-year "silence," continuing with his highly acclaimed *The Homewood Trilogy* (1985: includes *Damballah*, 1981; *Hiding Place*, 1981; and *Sent for You Yesterday*, 1983), Wideman's work began to show the results of his immersion in a literary tradition that was at once foreign to him and yet his own. His books have also been increasingly personal. They include his thoughts on his return to the Homewood section of Pittsburgh where he grew up; a nonfiction account of himself and his brother, a convicted murderer serving a life sentence without parole (*Brothers and Keepers*, 1984); and *Philadelphia Fire*.

"In America, especially if you're black," Wideman has said, "there is a temptation to buy a kind of upward mobility. One of the requirements is to forget. Eventually I felt impoverished by that act." Forgetfulness and impoverishment are the twin themes upon which *Philadelphia Fire* plays its disturbing variations. Combining trenchant social criticism and postmodern narrative techniques, *Philadelphia Fire* is, like Cudjoe's planned production of *The Tempest*, a work of great daring, impassioned artistry, and exceptional courage. It is also a novel that, in risking so much, risks being misread. The same year that *Middle Passage* (1990)—another densely (but playfully) intertextual novel about racial divisions—won the National Book Award, its author, Charles Johnson, summed up *Philadelphia Fire*, winner of the PEN/Faulkner Award for Fiction, this way: "And there you have it: a novel in which we learn nothing new about the MOVE incident, a book brimming over with brutal, emotional honesty and moments of beautiful prose lyricism . . . but by no means a page turner." In a novel that combines so many literary traditions and covers so much ground, encouraging the turning of pages no longer seems quite the virtue in a novel that Johnson believes it to be.

Bibliography
Bell, Bernard W. *The Afro-American Novel and Its Tradition*. Amherst: University of Massachusetts Press, 1987. An excellent, although brief, introduction to Wideman's writing through *The Homewood Trilogy*. Bell's discussion of Wideman's shift from a Eurocentric to an African American tradition is particularly good.
Coleman, James W. *Blackness and Modernism: The Career of John Edgar Wideman*. Jackson: University Press of Mississippi, 1989. This highly sympathetic study traces Wideman's movement "from an uncritical acceptance of the forms and themes of mainstream modernism as practiced by white literary masters to a black voicing of modernism and postmodernism that is consistent with Afro-American perspectives and reflects a commitment to the needs of the black community." Concludes with an interview of Wideman conducted in 1988.
O'Brien, John. *Interviews with Black Writers*. New York: Liveright, 1973. In an early but important interview, Wideman discusses the modernist influence on his first three novels and the importance of myths and "racial memories," particularly in *The Lynchers*.
Pinckney, Darryl. " 'Cos I'm a So-o-oul Man: The Back-Country Blues of John Edgar Wideman." *Times Literary Supplement*, August 23, 1991, 19-20. Pinckney reviews *Fever* (1989) and *Philadelphia Fire* in the contexts of Wideman's career and the larger cultural shift that has made Wideman's return to his African American roots both explicable and predictable. Although he praises *Fever* for its range of characters and "carefully realized" situations, Pinckney finds *Philadelphia Fire* to be marred by Wideman's penchant for profundity. Overall, "Wideman suffers from a wish to prove that he can be both poetic and funky."
Rowell, Charles H. "An Interview with John Edgar Wideman." *Callaloo* 13 (Winter, 1990): 47-61. Wideman discusses his background, his earliest interest in writing, the impact of his return to the United States in 1967 following his Rhodes scholarship, and use of "public history" in *The Lynchers*, *Fever*, and *Philadelphia Fire*.

Robert A. Morace

A PHOTOGRAPH
Lovers in Motion

Author: Ntozake Shange (Paulette Williams, 1948-   )
Type of work: Play
Type of plot: Psychological realism
Time of plot: The late twentieth century
Locale: San Francisco, California
First produced: 1977, at the New York Shakespeare Festival under the title *A Photograph: A Still Life with Shadows/ A Photograph: A Study in Cruelty*; in present form, 1979 at the Equinox Theatre in Houston, Texas
First published: 1981

> *Principal characters:*
> SEAN DAVID, the protagonist, an amoral, struggling photographer
> MICHAEL, Sean's female live-in lover, a dancer who listens to his artistic ambitions
> EARL, an attorney and longtime friend of Sean who serves as a liaison between Sean and the women who cluster around him
> NEVADA, a wealthy attorney and patron for Sean
> CLAIRE, a hedonistic model used by Sean in his photographs

The Play

A *Photograph: Lovers in Motion* details the complex relationship between artistic creation, sex, and love in the life of photographer Sean David. Largely enacted within his San Francisco flat, the play traces his evolving relationship with a boyhood friend, an artistic patron, a model, and his current lover. The constant touchstones are his artistic ambitions and his developing commitment to Michael, his lover.

In involved discussions, Sean explains his aggressive artistic philosophy to Michael. In an early scene, as he shows her his photographs, he states his goals. "i'm gonna go ona rampage . . . this camera's gonna get em." His art, as he explains, is a means of re-creating the world "in my image." Photography, for Sean, is a tool for filling the holes in his life; he tells Michael, "give me a camera & i cd get you anything you wanted."

For Sean and Michael, artistic creation is inextricably connected to their daily lives. Because their discussions often take place on their bed, the focus naturally shifts to sex and relationships. Both reject any "normal" romantic conception of heterosexual love. Michael explains to Sean why she is attracted to him. She tells him "i've kept a lover/ who waznt all-american/ who didnt believe/ wdnt straighten up. . . . i loved yr bitterness and hankered after that space in you where you are outta control."

Sean's conversations with Michael are interrupted periodically by Earl, Nevada, and Claire. Each wants a piece of Sean, for each sees his or her life as interwoven with Sean's art. Sean controls their wishes and actions, thus revealing the ability of his artistic vision to corrupt.

Sex and sensuality are never far from the surface of the play. The selfish and decadent implications of Sean's goals are revealed in earthy scenes with Claire, his model. The first modeling session portrays Claire and Sean moving, in a well-oiled dance of lust and desire, from abuse to sex. Sean encourages the willing Claire to pour whiskey over herself and speak of her sexual accomplishments as a prelude to sex.

Although Sean delights in Claire's actions, she is not a passive victim. Like each of the characters, she has a philosophy that dictates her actions. Her "artistic" vision is vitally connected to the need to be desired. In a later scene, she explains that the foundations for her actions emanate from advice from her father. "yr body is the blood & the flesh/ god gave his only daughter/ to save alla his sons. . . . give a man exactly what he wants & he wants you/ simple as that."

Sean uses Earl and Nevada just as brazenly. Seeing themselves as the architects of Sean's development, they often discuss their role as collaborators. Since in their eyes, Sean is an unfinished work of art they can influence, Earl and Nevada "know" what the photographer needs. Referring to their material success and social status, Earl explains to Nevada that Sean must attain "what you & i have." Sean "needs some sense of his future."

Although Earl and Nevada, both attorneys flush in middle-class comfort, are confident in prescribing what Sean lacks, they are far from being "free." Both speak often about the freedom they possess, yet in their continued involvement with Sean, both encourage new forms of enslavement. Earl passively accepts verbal abuse and helplessly watches Sean engage in sexual acts with his former girlfriend, Claire. Nevada, Sean's wealthy patron, persistently tries to buy Sean's affection, even as she is rejected and ridiculed. As she recounts how Earl and Sean once "let" her "be wild" after she passed her bar exam, she reveals that her money cannot buy her vision of a romantic relationship in which she is dependent on a dominant man. Sean rejects her attempts to "give him some part of me like in the bar."

Discussions about freedom and enslavement appear in a number of overlapping scenes. As each character recounts incidents from the past, the specter of oppression becomes a haunting, ever-present image. Each feels the lingering effects of various forms of enslavement. In contrast to Earl and Nevada, who seem eager to forget their African American heritage and join a mainstream culture, Claire never lets the others forget the effects of racial identity. She reminds the others that Alexandre Dumas (Sean's spiritual hero) was a "niggah." Ignoring their soaring ambitions for his art, Claire suggests that Sean, like Dumas, still retains this "acrid stench."

The effects of this shared African American heritage permeate the play, though each character reacts to it differently. Sean, in particular, is haunted by his past. As the play fades back to scenes of Michael and Sean discussing their relationship, a portrait of Sean's childhood with an absent, drug-abusing father emerges. The new form of slavery he has inherited entails an impulse toward self-destruction and an inability to love. Unable to form commitments, he aggressively demands that others allow him to take what he "needs." Thus, even as he tells Michael that she is the driving force in his life, he insists that he needs other women to fuel his art.

Michael responds to these demands with an independence that the other women do not possess. Rejecting a relationship built upon subservience, she tells Sean "i'm physically incapable of chasing & arguing abt a man." As the play progresses, it becomes evident that Michael possesses a strength and vision that the others gravitate toward. Both Sean and Claire attack this strength. Michael counters Claire's attempts to seduce her, and unlike the others, remains unmoved by Sean's contrived and brutal photographs. She draws on a heritage of strong women who held families together when the men were destroyed by white culture. Unlike Sean's family, her "people took care of themselves." She tells him "dont nobody own history/ cant nobody make ours but us." The ability to "rewrite" her history daily is the foundation of her art. The poetic song that accompanies her dance is a powerful refrain that echoes her strength.

> i can move
> be free in time/ a moment is mine always. . . .
> i'm a rustling of dead leaves
> collections of ol women by the weddin
> the legs of a cotton club queen . . .
> i'm gonna dance/ for all of us. . . .
> i can always remember
> make it come again

Her independence and the force of her vision draw Sean to her. By the end of the play, she demands a commitment of love from him as well as his rejection of other women. She denounces his desire to harden and kill, in both his art and his relationships, and forces him to confront his racial heritage. She asks him, "if not now when." Ultimately, she demands that he find "treasures" that will make art and life resonate.

Themes and Meanings

Relationships between friends and lovers inevitably are complex. When they are complicated further by ambitions, the effects of artistic aims, racial heritage, class structure, and gender identity, the complexity is often overwhelming. Ntozake Shange, building upon African American and feminist traditions, argues for life-sustaining sources of art and for relationships based on honesty, independence, and a sense of community.

In *A Photograph: Lovers in Motion*, the characters reveal the complex sides of their African American heritage. Sean and Earl symbolize what some would suggest are the troubles of many black men. Sean perpetrates the neglect, self-abuse, and inability to nurture learned from his father. Unwilling to commit to a relationship or to conceive of a friendship not based upon exploitation, he exists as a stagnant and destructive force. Devoid of "healthy" male role models, Sean and Earl construct their present out of the chaos of the past.

Only Michael is able to use the past as a healthy tool for constructing the present. Her links to strong matriarchal black women who held families together and fought adversity when men were rendered helpless contrast with the past offered to Sean and Earl. Her heritage is filled with examples of self-sacrificing, independent women able to take care of themselves and others. While Sean allows his past to tear him down, Michael embraces the experiences of women who preceded her and uses these as a foundation of strength.

Shange also illustrates the dangers for both men and women of blindly accepting romantic gender roles. Claire and Nevada are uncritical victims, dependent on dominating male figures. Because she accepts her father's image of women as objects of desire, Claire falls into debauchery, loneliness, and ultimate despair. Nevada also is a victim of role conditioning. Despite her economic independence and social status, she still seeks the "enslavement" of subservience. In this regard, Michael again stands in contrast, as an independent woman who demands honesty and commitment in a relationship, whose "life's work" can exist without the "prop" of a man to serve.

The dialogue between Sean and Michael explores how art can serve as a constructive force in both the artist's life and the larger culture. Based on an aggressive ambition and a lust for exploitation, Sean's art is frozen and static. Michael's art, the dance, is fluid and alive, tied intimately to the earthy "dance" of women who nurtured her. In contrast to Sean's art, which denies the reality of his past, Michael's dance re-creates and "rewrites" the heritage that created her.

Rejection of values that hinder loving relationships is a central theme. Thus, Earl and Nevada's reliance on materialism and status and Claire's hedonism and street sensuality are rejected. Also rejected are confining sex roles for both men and women as well as attempts to deny the influences of race, culture, and history. Shange's poetic dialogue, her fluid transitions within scenes, and her rejection of standard English and conventional punctuation connect her prose to the dance and to the tradition of vibrant storytellers. Shange's rejection of traditional forms mirrors her rejection of conventional explanations and conclusions.

Critical Context

Drawing directly on stylistic concerns of an African American heritage, *A Photograph: Lovers in Motion* has been praised for its insights into romantic relationships, for its portrayal of the African American middle class, and for its critical look at the sources of artistic expression. Although the play depicts uniquely American characters and themes, Shange herself has suggested that her influences reach beyond the American experience. Her poems, plays, novels, and essays build upon poetry, jazz, and traditional oral traditions from Latin American, African, and African American sources. Scholar and critic Paul Carter Harrison includes Shange among black writers from many countries who use a common "iconography." Harrison suggests that building upon traditional forms and rhythms exposes a communal memory that can help produce "the critical insights required to deal with profound feelings of alienation." Learning to deal with the self-hatred produced by alienation from the dominant white culture is a central theme in this play and in other key works by female African American writers from Zora Neale Hurston to Alice Walker.

Editor and essayist Cheryl Wall argues that Shange and other black female writers have established a new literary tradition that cannot be evaluated without taking into account gender, race, and women's sexuality. The themes reflected in Shange's poetry, plays, and novels reveal these multiple contexts at work.

Distinguished editor Mary Helen Washington sees Shange as a pioneer in demystifying female sexuality. Along with other feminist critics, Washington suggests that by placing women as strong solitary figures, artists can undermine culturally ingrained roles for women in romantic plots. When characters such as Michael reject "male-dominated forms," they can then begin the work of re-creating the future.

Because Shange consistently depicts contemporary themes and portrays African American culture as complex and diverse, her work often has been controversial. Some critics argue that Shange harshly portrays the black male experience and devalues traditional heterosexual relationships. Because, as Mary Helen Washington suggests, Shange often "locates much of women's oppression in the sexual arena," this controversy will follow her work.

Bibliography

Betsko, Kathleen, and Rachel Koenig, eds. *Contemporary Women Playwrights.* New York: William Morrow, 1987. A collection of interviews exploring the sources of inspiration for contemporary female playwrights. Shange's interview connects writing to the rhythmic and visceral world of dance. Shange explores political and cultural links to Latin American and Third World writers and discusses the effects of performance art on her writing.

Harrison, Paul Carter, ed. *Totem Voices: Plays from the Black World Repertory.* New York: Grove Press, 1989. A collection of plays from eminent African American, African, and Afro-Caribbean writers. The introduction links Shange and other writers to the social, political, and cultural roots of the black world repertory. The heart of this tradition is a connection to ritualized roots, non-Western rhythms, and culturally ingrained improvisation. Links to the black church, to poetry, to jazz, and to oral traditions are fully realized in Shange's writing.

Tate, Claudia. *Black Women Writers at Work.* New York: Continuum, 1983. Portraits of contemporary writers. Includes a thorough and fascinating look at Shange's artistic development.

Wall, Cheryl A., ed. *Changing Our Own Words: Essays on Criticism, Theory, and Writing by Black Women.* New Brunswick, N.J.: Rutgers University Press, 1989. A collection of essays from academic feminist critics committed to black female writers. The introduction emphasizes the need to rethink the concept of tradition as it applies to Shange and other contemporary black female writers and argues for evaluating these writers in multiple contexts. Connects Shange to feminist, cultural, and political concerns.

Washington, Mary Helen, ed. *Black-Eyed Susans/Midnight Birds: Stories by and About Black Women*. New York: Anchor Books, 1989. A diverse collection of works by contemporary black female writers. In a preface to Shange's stories, Washington connects Shange's stories, poems, and plays to feminist concerns with heterosexual relations and suggests that creating women who are strong solitary figures undermines the traditional romantic plot. Shange's rejection of standard English reflects her insistence on independence from male-dominated forms.

Mark Vogel

THE PIANO LESSON

Author: August Wilson (1945-   )
Type of work: Play
Type of plot: Representational
Time of plot: 1937
Locale: Pittsburgh
First produced: 1987, at the Yale Repertory Theatre, New Haven, Connecticut
First published: 1990

Principal characters:
>BOY WILLIE CHARLES, a brash thirty-year-old man with an infectious grin and a boyish charm
>BERNIECE, Boy Willie's sister, a thirty-five-year-old widow
>DOAKER CHARLES, the brother of Boy Charles, who was the father of Berniece and Boy Willie
>LYMON, Boy Willie's companion, twenty-nine years old
>AVERY, a suitor of Berniece
>WINNING BOY, Doaker's brother
>MARETHA, Berniece's eleven-year-old daughter
>GRACE, a woman who comes home with Boy Willie and later with Lymon

The Play

All the action of the play takes place in the kitchen and parlor of Doaker Charles's house, which, though sparsely furnished, has an old upright piano in the parlor. The piano's legs are covered with mask-like figures, artfully carved in the manner of African sculpture.

When the play begins, it is five o'clock in the morning and Boy Willie is at the front door banging and shouting. Doaker admits Boy Willie and Lymon, who have just arrived from the South with a truckload of watermelons. Boy Willie soon informs Doaker that Sutter, a descendant of the white family that once owned the Charles family, has died, that Sutter's brother wants to sell Boy Willie the remaining one hundred acres of Sutter's farm, and that he, Boy Willie, intends to sell the piano as a means of helping him buy the land. Doaker calmly tells him that Berniece "ain't gonna sell that piano."

After Berniece is heard screaming from upstairs because she has seen Sutter's ghost, Maretha comes downstairs, greets Boy Willie, and plays a song for him on the piano. Soon, Avery Brown arrives and tells the story of how he has been called to preach. By scene's end, Boy Willie confronts Berniece with his intention of selling the piano, to which Berniece rejoins that if he has come to Pittsburgh to sell the piano, he "done come up here for nothing." As the scene ends, Boy Willie announces that "I'm gonna cut it in half and go on and sell my half."

Scene 2 begins three days later, with Doaker and Winning Boy sitting around drinking and reminiscing about their lives. Boy Willie and Lymon enter, and, in a crucial scene, Doaker tells Lymon the story of how his grandmother, also named Berniece, and her little boy, who grew up to become Doaker's father, were traded by their owner, Robert Sutter, to another white man for a piano that Sutter wished to give to his wife, Miss Sophie, on their wedding anniversary. Because Miss Sophie started missing her slaves and could not get them back, Sutter ordered pictures of Berniece and her son to be carved into the piano by one of his slaves, who also added pictures of other members of the family as well as of important family events. After Miss Sophie's death, Doaker's father, Boy Charles, became obsessed with the idea that he must take the piano away from Sutter. When he did and was found hiding in a railroad boxcar along with four hobos, the boxcar was set on fire. Not long afterward, the suspected murderers started falling down wells, and the legend was created that it was the ghosts of the boxcar who were doing the pushing. When Boy Willie and Lymon try to move the piano, the sound of Sutter's ghost is heard, and then Maretha from upstairs screams at the sight of Sutter's ghost.

In the first scene of act 2, Doaker tells Winning Boy that he too has seen Sutter's ghost in the house. Boy Willie and Lymon come home to announce that they have had good luck selling the watermelons, Winning Boy convinces Lymon to buy his old but fancy clothes, and Lymon prepares to go out with Boy Willie to find some women.

In scene 2, Avery arrives to tell Berniece that he has found a place for his church and that what he now needs is a wife. Berniece tries to get Avery to rid the house of Sutter's ghost by blessing it. Meanwhile, Avery tries to persuade Berniece to donate her piano to his new church, where she could play it and even start a choir.

Later on that night, in scene 3, Boy Willie arrives with Grace, a woman he has just met, but Berniece chases them both away. Lymon then arrives and, after complaining about his luck with women, offers perfume to Berniece, kisses her, and is rebuffed by her.

In scene 4, Boy Willie wakes up Lymon to tell him he has been offered eleven hundred and fifty dollars for the piano. Together they try, but fail, to move the piano, which elicits the sound of Sutter's ghost, while Doaker informs Boy Willie that they are not taking the piano anywhere until Berniece comes home. Boy Willie leaves, telling Doaker that he is going to get some rope and wheels and that nobody is going to stop him from taking the piano.

In scene 5, Boy Willie sits attaching casters to a board in preparation for moving the piano while he makes one last defense of his need to make his way in the world with a farm; Berniece challenges him by mentioning her gun. Soon, Avery enters with his Bible, Lymon arrives with the rope, Boy Willie tries to move the piano, Winning Boy comes in and sits down to play the piano, and Grace, who has been waiting for Lymon in his truck outside, tries to get Lymon to leave. Amid all the confusion, Sutter's ghost appears. Avery begins an exorcism and sprinkles the place with water, while Boy Willie engages in a struggle with the ghost itself. Berniece suddenly sits down at the piano and begins to play with rousing intensity until a calm settles over the house. Boy Willie, realizing Berniece's triumph, urges her to keep playing and leaves to catch a train. Berniece, who has been enlisting the aid of her ancestors in her song, expresses her gratitude for the peace that has returned to her life.

Themes and Meanings

The Piano Lesson deals with the historical phenomenon of the African American migration from the Southern, agrarian way of life to the large industrial cities of the North in search of freedom, dignity, and economic opportunities. As such, the play has two settings, the onstage setting of Doaker's house, located in a black neighborhood in Pittsburgh in the present, and the setting of the past in the South from which all the characters in the play have come. It is through the collective memories of the characters that the Southern, offstage setting is brought to life by talk of shared experiences, acquaintances, and family relations.

The sparsely furnished setting, "lacking in warmth and vigor," of Doaker's house captures the quality of life of those African Americans who have migrated to the North, where they are cut off from their family roots and history. Their life is stark, cold, and often lonely, and they live a life of grim necessity, hard work, and poverty. It is contrasted with life in the South, where, even though prejudice abounds, blacks live close to the earth and their familial homes, close to the struggle, the suffering, and the meager triumphs of their ancestors, from which they draw spiritual sustenance.

The temporal location of the play is the year 1937, a time when the black migration northward was gaining momentum. Wilson is intrigued by this phenomenon and has said that he believes that it was a mistake for blacks to leave the South, where they could have eventually gained economic power by owning the land. Instead, in the North they still encountered prejudice and found themselves huddled in squalid neighborhoods and working in menial jobs.

The conflict of *The Piano Lesson* is classic in its naturalistic simplicity. Two people are obsessed with conflicting desires: Boy Willie is determined to sell the piano, Berniece is equally determined that he will not. At the heart of the play is the piano itself, which evolves into a rich symbol as well as a powerful dramatic device. To Berniece, the piano, with its carved faces of family members and events, represents the history of the pain and oppression of their family, including their father's own death. To Boy Willie, the piano represents opportunity for the future; by selling it for cash, he hopes to buy the land on which their ancestors were slaves. Berniece, who has moved to the North and is cut off from her family roots, sees the piano as her connection with her past and her own personal identity. Boy Willie, who has stayed close to his family roots in the South, views the piano as a means of gaining equality with the white landowners, which would also mean achieving dignity and personhood.

As a dramatic device, the piano is a catalyst for much of the action. Not only do

Berniece and Boy Willie create dramatic tension by fighting about the piano, but also the whole suspense of the climactic scene is built as Boy Willie makes elaborate preparations for moving the piano while Berniece gets her gun to stop him. Moreover, it is by means of the piano that much of the family history is brought forth. Berniece, who has not touched the piano in many years because of the cruel memories that it contains for her, begins to play the piano in the last scene and thereby invokes the spiritual power of their ancestors through its music. The "piano lesson" of the title is not a lesson in how to play the piano but a lesson in what the piano means.

Another powerful dramatic device that is also rich with symbolic value is the ghost of the white landowner, Sutter, which symbolizes the memory of the enslavement and oppression of blacks by whites. The drive of the play is toward the liberation of these people from that history, which can only come about through a sense of self-worth, which is what both Berniece and Boy Willie seek. Although the piano belonged to the Sutters, the Charles family believed that it belonged to them, not only because their grandfather had carved their family history on it, but also because it was paid for with their flesh and redeemed by their blood. After her father's death, Berniece's mother made her play the piano because she understood that it was a form of possessing it. When Berniece is about to lose the piano through Boy Willie's scheme, she repossesses it by playing on it and thus exorcises Sutter's ghost. Boy Willie gives up his plan because he then understands that the family has its identity and pride intact, and he does not need land to gain those qualities.

Critical Context

The Piano Lesson is another addition to August Wilson's projected cycle of plays that portray the black experience in America in the twentieth century. The first play in this series was the Tony Award-winning *Ma Rainey's Black Bottom* (pr. 1984), which dealt with jazz musicians in the 1920's who were exploited by white entrepreneurs. *Fences* (pr. 1985), which won a Pulitzer Prize, takes place in the 1950's and dramatizes the effects of the exclusion of black baseball players from professional baseball. *Joe Turner's Come and Gone* (pr. 1986) takes place in 1911 and portrays the anguish of those who had fled the enforced labor gangs of the South and suffered the destruction of their families and the tribulations of a migratory existence. Wilson's commitment is to write a history of blacks and of how they have been denied participation in American life. Wilson has said that blacks are "leftovers from history," meaning that when free labor was needed, blacks were valuable, but as the world moved into the industrial age and the computer age, "we're no longer needed." *The Piano Lesson* is a vivid documentation of history in the process of expelling blacks and of the African American's struggle to retain dignity, pride, and personhood by clinging to the symbols of history.

Bibliography

Henry, William. "Exorcising the Demons of Memory." *Time*, April 11, 1989, 77-78.

A profile of August Wilson, his life, his work, and his beliefs. Surveys his work to this date.

Migler, Rachael. "An Elegant Duet." *Gentleman's Quarterly* 60, no. 4 (April, 1990): 114-144. Wilson and Lloyd Richards, the director of Wilson's plays, are profiled. They discuss their effort on *The Piano Lesson*. Biographical information on each is given.

Savran, David. "August Wilson." In *In Their Own Words: Contemporary American Playwrights*. New York: Theatre Communication Group, 1988. A probing interview of Wilson conducted by Savran on March 13, 1987, at the West Bank Cafe in New York City. Wilson talks freely about his beginnings in theater, his work, his experiences, and his political, social, and historical views.

"Two-Timer." *Time*, April 18, 1990, 99. A discussion of Wilson on the occasion of his second Pulitzer Prize for *The Piano Lesson*. He has transcended the label of "black" playwright, but comparisons with Eugene O'Neill may be premature.

Wilson, August. "August Wilson's American: A Conversation with Bill Moyers." Interview by Bill Moyers. *American Theatre* 6, no. 3 (June, 1989): 12-17, 54. Interview focusing mainly on Wilson's view of history, American society, blacks' position in that society, and the way in which Wilson's views relate to his work.

Tony J. Stafford

PLATITUDES

Author: Trey Ellis (1962-   )
Type of work: Novel
Type of plot: Parody
Time of plot: The mid-1980's and the 1930's
Locale: New York City and rural Georgia
First published: 1988

> *Principal characters:*
> DEWAYNE WELLINGTON, a recently divorced and depressed middle-aged black writer
> ISSHEE AYAM, a successful middle-aged black feminist writer who criticizes Dewayne's work-in-progress as sexist and outside black folk tradition
> EARLE TYNER, the protagonist of Dewayne's story, a pudgy, awkward, and romantic middle-class black boy
> DOROTHY LAMONT, a young waitress at her mother's Harlem diner who cultivates a friendship with Earle that grows into a satisfying romantic relationship
> DARCELLE LAMONT, Dorothy's mother, owner of a Harlem diner specializing in country-style black cooking
> JANEY ROSEBLOOM, a pretty, socially popular friend of Dorothy and white schoolmate of Earle
> CAPTAIN NAT MEE, a New York City police precinct captain who dates Earle's mother
> STEVIE, an elderly janitor and caretaker
> RICHARD, an elegant and rich white male model

The Novel

Platitudes is a novel within a novel that tells two parallel love stories. The first story concerns the romance of high schoolers Earle Tyner and Dorothy LaMont. The second story is about the growing attraction of authors Dewayne Wellington and Isshee Ayam. The romance of the two authors develops while Dewayne is writing the story of Earle and Dorothy, called *Platitudes.* These two stories are periodically interrupted by parodies of aptitude test questions, menus, song lyrics, and different comic lists.

At the beginning of their story, Earle and Dorothy attend different private schools in New York City and have not met. Both black students try in different ways to fit in at their mostly white schools. Earle excels in computer class and associates with computer buffs Donald and Andy. Together they call themselves "Trinary." They are looked down upon by the other students, who call them "Nerd One, Two, and Three." Dorothy divides her time between the wild social life of her wealthy friends at school and the dull work at her mother's Harlem home-cooking restaurant.

After introducing these characters, author Dewayne interrupts the story of Earle and Dorothy to confess that he is having trouble writing and to ask for assistance. He receives a sharply worded response from Isshee Ayam, who criticizes what Dewayne has written as sexist and offers her version of Earle and Dorothy's story. In Isshee's first chapter "Rejoice!," Earle is a respectful child of a poor but honest rural black family struggling for survival against a heartless creditor, Mr. Wyte.

Dewayne continues to write about Earle in a sexist way. Earle and his friends are frustrated in relationships and take an interest in sex. Earle begins to develop a relationship with a white classmate, Janey Rosebloom, after he helps her in computer class. She invites Trinary to a party, where they feel foolish and out of place. Later, when they are both feeling depressed about relationships, Earle and Janey spend a romantic evening together.

Earle begins to develop a relationship with Dorothy after they meet at her mother's Harlem restaurant. Dorothy admires Earle's work for black mayoral candidate Al Robinson and begins to see him as not just another computer nerd. They spend romantic time together. Earle's life seems to be coming together all at once. He is having success with registering voters, losing weight, and getting close to Dorothy. While Earle gets closer to Dorothy, Dewayne gets closer to Isshee. Though still critical of *Platitudes*, she approves of the continued development of Dorothy and Earle from stereotypes into believable characters. Dewayne and Isshee agree to meet at a writers' convention in New York.

Isshee misses her date with Dewayne because a former boyfriend, the famous writer Richard Johnson, comes to see her. Dewayne feels so betrayed by Isshee and becomes so depressed that he decides to write an unhappy ending for *Platitudes.* Earle is betrayed in both love and work. When Earle accidentally finds Dorothy in bed with a successful male model, Richard, he loses faith in her. Police captain Nat Mee accuses Al Robinson of stealing money from his mayoral campaign.

This unhappy ending is turned around when Isshee recognizes how much she has hurt Dewayne and decides to make a special trip to New York to see him. To cheer him up, she writes a happy ending, in Dewayne's sexually explicit style, to her version of *Platitudes.* In her version, Earle bravely defends Dorothy from the lecherous Mr. Wyte. During his long-awaited night with Isshee, Dewayne suffers from impotence, which he cures by writing his own happy ending to the story, in which Dorothy explains to Earle the conflict between her social status and her love for him. "You're too pure. And sometimes I didn't need pure; I didn't have all the time for pure and ice skating and Coney island because I am not that way. . . . Who wanted to fall in love with a fat nerd."

The Characters

Like the other important characters in *Platitudes*, Dewayne Wellington develops from a stereotype into a full-bodied person. Although the story he writes is not explicitly autobiographical, he uses it to resolve some of the tensions in his personal and creative lives. His early focus on sex and the power of women to hurt men reflects his own feelings of loneliness and betrayal after his divorce.

Unlike Dewayne, Isshee is confident of her ability as a writer and happy with her identity as a woman and an African American. She is a successful author of well-known works of black folk life and is frequently invited to lecture around the country. While she helps Dewayne to rise out of his depression with her challenging criticism of both his work and his view of women, she gains new insight from him and comes to an understanding that there is more than one way to write about African American romance.

Dewayne expresses his anxiety through his creation, Earle Tyner. As Dewayne grows in confidence and in understanding of Isshee's black feminist perspective, Earle goes beyond his original role of a computer nerd interested in pornography. He gains confidence in himself while working in the voter registration drive that allows him to finally talk to women. In the end, he outgrows his boyish view of women as either objects of low sexual desire or high romance and comes to see Dorothy as a loving but fallible human being, both a friend and a lover.

The fast social and sexual life of white New York young people appeals to Dorothy because she admires its freedom. She yearns to escape the suffocating atmosphere of her mother's Harlem diner and live as a liberated middle-class woman. She looks forward to the day when she will earn a good salary in a high-powered business position. Although she is an extremely popular girl, Dorothy finds common ground with Earle as a fellow member of the new black middle class in a largely white world.

Despite their race, Earle and Dorothy successfully integrate into private-school life. Earle is known not primarily as an African American but as a computer buff and member of "Trinary," along with white Andy and "beige" Donald. Although she lives in Harlem, Dorothy attempts to leave down-home family life behind in her fast-lane partying with rich white friends such as the exclusive Janey Rosebloom or the charming model Richard.

Like Dorothy, Earle comes in contact with characters of different races and classes. A favorite of white computer instructor Commander Considine, Earle also learns about city racial politics from the elderly janitor Stevie.

The characters in Isshee's version of the story stand in stark contrast to Dewayne's Earle and Dorothy. In Lowdnes County, Georgia, there is a simple distinction between the positive and productive lives of the poor-but-happy families of Earle and Dorothy and the uncaring materialism of the landlord Mr. Wyte and his agent, the race traitor I. Corinthians.

Themes and Meanings

Trey Ellis, like Dewayne Wellington, attempts to write a new kind of fiction about African Americans. Ellis himself calls this style the "New Black Aesthetic," an attempt to refine and revise the African American view of art. He also takes his characters into a world where mingling across class and race boundaries is nothing new. *Platitudes* builds on the foundation laid by earlier black writing to express a vision of a black urban life that is as comfortable with black tradition as with mainstream ideas of achievement and success.

Earle and Dorothy are urban African Americans who happily exist integrated with mainstream urban society. Although not ashamed of their race, they both pursue success as defined by mainstream values, Earle looking toward the prestigious Massachusetts Institute of Technology and Dorothy toward business school and a well-paid executive position. They move effortlessly between the black world of their families and the mixed-race milieu of the private-school scene.

Another way that Ellis tries to create a new kind of black novel is by using experimental writing techniques. Ellis takes his narrative beyond the traditional realistic form and style of black fiction into a playful and eclectic postmodernism. Along with the romance of Earle and Dorothy comes the second-level encounter of authors Dewayne and Isshee, which complicates the realism of Earle's story. In addition, Ellis uses various satirical lists only marginally connected with the story, from aptitude test questions to menus and even a love poem that Earle ordered from Dewayne himself. These techniques add a self-consciousness to the romance stories that constantly reminds the reader that this is fiction.

Key to Ellis' experimental style is the way he connects the lives of the two authors to the story of Earle and Dorothy. Throughout the novel, the ideas and feelings of Dewayne and Isshee are expressed through their different versions of the story they each write. As Dewayne comes out of his depression, Earle learns how to succeed with women. When Isshee wants to apologize to Dewayne, she makes Earle the brave hero in her version of the story.

A theme central to both stories is that self-confidence is necessary to recover from betrayal and disappointment. Feeling betrayed by his recent divorce, Dewayne learns to trust Isshee and to value her criticism when she begins to appreciate his talent. Even after she misses their planned meeting, Dewayne is willing to accept her apology. Likewise, though Dorothy has hurt him through her affair with Richard, Earle shows his new maturity by allowing Dorothy to make it up to him. Presumably the whole black community will have to recover from the betrayal of traitors such as the embezzling mayoral candidate Al Robinson and bill collector I. Corinthians.

The conclusions of both unlikely romances express the supreme power of romantic love. Love has the power to reconcile the great differences between Dewayne's sexism and Isshee's feminism. It also brings together the shy computer nerd Earle and the outgoing clubhopper Dorothy, despite all the force of high-school opinion against their friendship. Once he discovers the "real thing" in his passion for Dorothy, Earle "wonders how he had ever lived so long without it."

Critical Context

Platitudes has been called a call for peace between black feminist writers and those who criticize them. Parodying both the writing of sexual freedom favored by male authors and the emphasis on folk culture and family solidarity of female writers, Ellis suggests synthesis and the inadequacy of each style when practiced in isolation.

Dewayne Wellington is reminiscent of African American male writers such as novelist, poet, and social critic Ishmael Reed. Reed has criticized black feminist writers for their negative portrayals of black men as sexist. His own satirical fiction is known for its portrayal of a conspiracy against African American men, as in his novel *Reckless Eyeballing* (1986). Reed's narrative style relies on experimental techniques that blend black folk culture with material from white American culture in a playful postmodern style.

One of the female writers criticized by Reed is Pulitzer Prize-winning author Alice Walker. Like Isshee Ayam, Walker is a well-known novelist and feminist critic. Her best-selling novel *The Color Purple* (1982) focuses on the warmth and vitality of black folk and family life in the rural South, where black people are protected from the corrupting values of white society. Isshee's version of the story of Earle and Dorothy is a broad parody of the folkloric style of Walker's fiction.

Ellis believes that each of these traditions by itself risks falling into stereotypes, or, as the novel's title suggests, meaningless platitudes. For him, both the experimentalism of Reed and the tradition represented by Walker are necessary for a vibrant African American literature. In his article "The New Black Aesthetic" (1989), Ellis argues for a new style of African American literature and a new kind of African American artist, the "cultural mulatto." This new black artist playfully combines elements of traditional black culture with materials from both mainstream mass culture and serious art.

In *Platitudes*, romantic love is a metaphor for the positive intentions that the new black artist uses to bring together different cultural, class, and racial traditions. Just as romantic love resolves the stark differences between Dewayne and Isshee and between Earle and Dorothy, an honest and open appreciation of diverse kinds of artistic material, taken from both black and white creators, will serve as a model for cultural desegregation and rejuvenation.

Bibliography
Ellis, Trey. "The New Black Aesthetic." *Callaloo* 12 (Winter, 1989): 233-246. The current younger generation of black writers, artists, and musicians is creating a new kind of black culture that combines traditional African American elements with material from mainstream white culture. The creations of the new "cultural mulattos" will be just as vibrant as those of the 1920's Harlem Renaissance or the 1960's Black Arts movement.
Gates, Henry Louis, Jr. *The Signifying Monkey: A Theory of Afro-American Literary Criticism.* New York: Oxford University Press, 1988. African American writing is organized around the figure of the "signifying monkey," a trickster in West African folk tales known for his quick wit. This influence of the vernacular trickster tradition is examined in the work of major African American authors including Ishmael Reed and Alice Walker.

Hunter, Tera. "'It's a Man's Man's World': Specters of the Old Re-newed in Afro-American Culture and Criticism." *Callaloo* 12 (Winter, 1989): 247-249. Hunter criticizes Ellis' "The New Black Aesthetic" as a return of sexism.

Lott, Eric. "Hip Hop Fiction." *The Nation* 247 (December 19, 1988): 691-692. Ellis' novel is seen as a young writer's plea for a truce between male and female black writers. *Platitudes* parodies both the folklore style of such feminist writers as Alice Walker and the experimental style of such postmodernist male writers as Ishmael Reed in an attempt to bring the two styles together. In the end, though, Ellis himself comes out far closer to Reed than to Walker.

Reed, Ishmael. *Reckless Eyeballing.* New York: St. Martin's Press, 1986. An experimental postmodernist novel that explores Reed's idea that black men are the victim of a widespread conspiracy against them and that criticizes Alice Walker's *The Color Purple.*

Tate, Greg. "Cult-Nats Meet Freaky-Deke: The Return of the New Black Aesthetic." *Voice Literary Supplement* (December, 1986): 7. African American writing, art, and music have revived the energy of cultural nationalism and placed it in the new context of 1980's popular culture.

Walker, Alice. *The Color Purple.* New York: Washington Square Press, 1982. Reprint. New York: Harcourt Brace Jovanovich, 1992. Walker's novelistic affirmation of the vitality of rural black life and criticism of black men for replaying the role of plantation owner in their oppression of black women.

Erik D. Curren

PLUM BUN

Author: Jessie Redmon Fauset (1884?-1961)
Type of work: Novel
Type of plot: Bildungsroman
Time of plot: 1900 to the 1920's
Locale: Philadelphia, Pennsylvania, and New York City
First published: 1928

> *Principal characters:*
> ANGELA MURRAY, a beautiful mulatto girl who learns that she can
>   "pass" as white
> VIRGINIA (JINNY) MURRAY, Angela's beloved younger sister
> ROGER FIELDING, a well-meaning but feckless white playboy
> ANTHONY CROSS, a talented painter whom Angela meets while
>   attending art classes
> JUNIUS MURRAY and MATTIE MURRAY, the parents of Angela and
>   Virginia
> RACHEL POWELL, a young black woman
> RALPH ASHLEY, a young, white, aristocratic New Yorker

The Novel

Plum Bun is a *Bildungsroman*, or coming-of-age novel, about Angela Murray, whose romantic illusions about the advantages of "passing" as white are shattered by a succession of cruel experiences. The format of the novel is based on the old nursery rhyme "To Market, to Market/ To buy a Plum Bun;/ Home again, Home again,/ Market is done." The "plum bun" represents all the advantages Angela hopes to obtain by using her charm and talent to enter the upper-class white world.

In the first section, entitled "Home," sixteen-year-old Angela is introduced, along with her sister Virginia and their parents. The family lives in a poor but respectable black neighborhood in Philadelphia. Junius and Mattie Murray are hardworking, thrifty, religious-minded parents who have tried to teach their daughters the highest moral standards. Virginia is happy in this humble domestic setting, but the restless, ambitious Angela can hardly wait to be old enough to escape to New York, where she hopes to use her talents as an artist to find a more stimulating life, even if this means denying her own race forever.

"Market," the second section, deals with Angela's early experiences in New York in the 1920's, after both her parents have died, leaving her enough money to move to the big city. "Plum Bun," the third section, deals with Angela's affair with the white playboy Roger Fielding, who represents all the comfort, security, prestige, and sophistication she desires. Fielding, who believes Angela to be pure white, falls in love with her but is afraid to propose marriage, because his domineering father will only permit him to marry a woman with wealth and family background. The charismatic Fielding persuades Angela to go against all her moral and religious training and become his mistress. She hopes this illicit affair will lead to marriage, but Fielding becomes tired of her, and they break up after a nasty quarrel.

In the meantime, Virginia has moved to New York to pursue her own career as a musician. Because of her color, she has no chance of entering the white world, nor does she wish to do so. She moves to a segregated neighborhood and becomes involved in the Harlem Renaissance, meeting many talented and interesting black people. In "Home Again," the longest section of the book, the thoroughly disillusioned Angela tries to establish meaningful relationships with men and women of both races, including her estranged sister Virginia. She discovers that there are many gifted black people who feel no need to be recognized by white society; she also meets some progressive whites who have risen above the bigotry of the time.

The man to whom Angela is most strongly attracted is a young portrait painter named Anthony Cross. Ironically, Cross is also "passing" and does not feel that he can aspire to Angela's affections, because he takes her to be white. Instead, Cross becomes emotionally involved with Virginia; he is ignorant of the fact that she is Angela's sister, since the two young women have kept their relationship a secret.

In the final section, "Market Is Done," the many deceptions are unraveled. Angela is outraged when a fellow art student, Rachel, is denied a scholarship because she is black. This prompts Angela to reveal her own racial identity, with the result that she too is barred from enjoying the benefits of a scholarship. She sails to Paris to study art on her own resources, assisted by loans from some of her true friends of both races. She is still heartbroken over her loss of Anthony Cross; in a rather implausible ending, however, Cross breaks up with Virginia and comes to Paris to join Angela in matrimony and an exciting new creative life.

Angela has learned two lessons about life. One is that it is a mistake to lie about one's true ethnic background or to use deceit in any other way for personal advancement; the other is that it is a mistake for a woman to marry for any reason except love. Although *Plum Bun* is subtitled "A Novel Without a Moral," it might not be unfair to say that the implicit moral can be found in the New Testament: "What profiteth a man if he gaineth the whole world and loseth his own soul?"

The Characters

The most important character in this novel is Angela Murray, since the entire story is about her intellectual, artistic, and moral development. Every incident and every other character is described from Angela's point of view, although the narration is in the third person. This literary device has the effect of making Angela seem extremely perceptive and sensitive, as she is intended to be. She analyzes the people she meets with unerring accuracy; however, she generally keeps her own counsel, and her observations and conclusions are conveyed to the reader through the dispassionate third-person narrator.

Angela's character evolves in the face of the disillusioning experiences she undergoes during the thirteen years spanned by the novel. Fauset highlights these experiences with significant scenes that strike directly at the reader's emotions. For example, when Virginia first comes to New York, Angela is at the train depot to meet her. Just before the train arrives, Roger Fielding suddenly appears by chance and stands talking to Angela, who wants him to believe she is white and dreads having him discover that the dark-skinned Virginia is her sister. When Virginia comes forward to greet her beloved sister after a long period of separation, Angela makes the bitter decision to pretend she does not know her. This moving scene, more than any other in the novel, makes Angela realize how much she had changed. The memory keeps coming back to haunt her.

Another significant scene occurs when Angela and Fielding are having dinner at a fashionable restaurant and three well-dressed, well-mannered black people ask to be seated at a table. Fielding is outraged by the idea of "colored people" wanting to eat with whites. The spoiled, headstrong playboy makes a terrible scene and has the blacks ejected. Angela understands their feelings perfectly; she thinks that the three people might easily have been her own mother, father, and sister. Angela must keep up her masquerade, and Fielding, ironically, thinks that her obvious emotion was caused by the fact that black people wanted to eat in the same room with her. In this scene, Angela first realizes that crossing over into the white world will force her to share in its bigotry.

Virginia Murray, the book's second most important character, serves as a foil to her older sister. Virginia does not have grandiose ambitions; she is happy associating with people of her own race, and she would never consider sacrificing her integrity for the sake of wealth or fame. Since these two young women are so close, they are often able to discuss their character development directly with each other.

Roger Fielding is the most important male character in the story, and he is presented mainly through Angela's point of view. At first she considers him to be the embodiment of all the things she wants, including wealth, sophistication, and social position. As their relationship becomes more intimate, however, she realizes his shortcomings, including his bigotry, selfishness, snobbishness, and contempt for women. Fielding's character is presented through several dramatic scenes that involve Angela either as a participant or as a spectator. The most significant scene occurs when the two break up; Fielding reveals that he has lost his respect for Angela simply because she allowed him to seduce her.

The other characters in the book are of minor importance, and they seem to exist primarily to serve as object lessons for Angela. Anthony Cross goes through a process of self-realization that parallels that undergone by Angela; both recognize the futility of pretending to be something they are not. The miscellaneous white characters exist primarily to exemplify white attitudes toward blacks. Angela's parents appear only in the first short section and function mainly to illustrate the virtues of industry, integrity, and conjugal fidelity, virtues that Angela is in serious danger of forgetting once she moves to New York.

Themes and Meanings

Plum Bun is a didactic novel containing several messages to the reader, all of which are imparted through Angela Murray's life experiences from adolescence to mature adulthood. The dominant theme throughout the novel is the moral that blacks should be themselves and should stop imitating whites. The novel was written at a time when African Americans were so submerged in the dominant culture that they were virtually "invisible," to use the striking metaphor coined by the African American author Ralph Ellison in his 1952 novel *Invisible Man*. It was natural for many blacks of the time, consciously and unconsciously, to adopt white values, including white ideals of physical beauty. Jessie Redmon Fauset, like many other writers and artists of the Harlem Renaissance, was deeply concerned with persuading African Americans to recognize their own beauty, values, and racial heritage.

Fauset creates an African American protagonist who happens to look white. This device not only creates many suspenseful scenes, making the novel read a bit like a spy story, but it also poses a question in a provocative way: If Angela herself cannot find happiness in adopting white cultural values, what chance does the ordinary African American have of doing so? By pretending to be white, Angela involves herself in one unpleasant experience after another. She becomes the kept mistress of a white playboy, and she eventually finds herself alienated from her beloved sister. She is unable to marry the one man she truly loves because, ironically, he is of black descent and believes that she is white.

Another message in the novel is that women should not sell themselves for financial security or social prestige. This is directly related to the message that African Americans should be true to themselves. Women, too, should be true to themselves and refuse to deceive themselves or others for gain. Angela's relations with men are unsatisfactory until she arrives at the decision to be herself, both as an African American and as a woman. Once she makes this courageous decision, she is able to achieve a reconciliation with her sister, marry the man she loves, and find her true vocation as an artist.

Critical Context

Plum Bun received mostly favorable reviews when it first appeared in 1929, although many of the reviews by white critics tended to be somewhat patronizing. Fauset's novels enjoyed modest success both in America and Great Britain, but she was nearly forgotten after the publication of her last novel, *Comedy, American Style*, in 1933. The Great Depression of the 1930's largely eclipsed the interest in African American writers begun with the Harlem Renaissance.

The 1950's saw an entirely different attitude toward African Americans and toward race relations in general. In *The Negro Novel in America* (1958), Robert Bone labeled Fauset an old-fashioned, "Victorian" writer. In 1962, the militant playwright and activist LeRoi Jones (Amiri Baraka) dismissed middle-class African American writers such as Fauset in his essay "The Myth of a 'Negro Literature'." Baraka argued that most such writers had attempted "to prove to America, and recently to the world at large, that they were not really who they were, i.e., Negroes."

Later criticism has tended to take a more generous view of Fauset's work. *Plum*

Bun is regarded as Fauset's best novel; its strengths are seen as the author's characterization of the protagonist and her shrewd observations of white middle-class life. Its weaknesses are viewed as its old-fashioned sentimentality and its portrayal of African Americans as essentially no different from whites in any important respect. The unrealistic dialogue, too, is often pointed to as a glaring defect; there is no slang, no dialect, and the characters often sound impossibly intellectual or idealistic. Moreover, Fauset seems reluctant to express strong feelings about injustices suffered by African Americans; in *Plum Bun*, she frequently refers to outrageously discriminatory practices as merely "silly." Yet with the rise of feminist criticism, Fauset's achievements as a novelist grappling with both racism and sexism have come to seem increasingly impressive.

Bibliography
Berzon, Judith R. *Neither White nor Black: The Mulatto Character in American Fiction.* New York: New York University Press, 1978. A study of the historical, sociological, and scientific backgrounds of American novels about the problems of mulattos, with frequent references to the works of Fauset. Berzon analyzes the "crisis experience" common to many of these novels and the modes of adjustment to the experience.

Christian, Barbara. *Black Women Novelists: The Development of a Tradition, 1892-1976.* Westport, Conn.: Greenwood Press, 1980. This historical study emphasizes the common themes in novels by black women writers, beginning with Frances Ellen Watkins Harper's *Iola LeRoy: Or, Shadows Uplifted* (1892). Fauset's works are evaluated in relation to those of other black women novelists.

Johnson, Abby Arthur. "Literary Midwife: Jessie Redmon Fauset and the Harlem Renaissance." *Phylon* 39 (June, 1978): 143-153. Summarizes Fauset's career as a writer and editor and attempts to evaluate her significance in African American literature. As the title of the article suggests, the author considers Fauset important mainly for her influence on her contemporaries and successors.

Sato, Hiroko. "Under the Harlem Shadow: A Study of Jessie Fauset and Nella Larsen." In *The Harlem Renaissance Remembered*, edited by Arna Bontemps. New York: Dodd, Mead, 1972. A discussion of Fauset's life and work, with special reference to her role in the Harlem Renaissance. Contains photographs of prominent members of the Harlem Renaissance and many other interesting articles about Fauset's contemporaries.

Sylvander, Carolyn Wedin. *Jessie Redmon Fauset, Black American Writer.* Troy, N.Y.: Whitson Publishing, 1981. A full-length study of Fauset's life and works. Argues that Fauset was a more important author than generally acknowledged and that she has been unfairly accused of denying her own racial values in favor of those of middle-class whites. Sylvander's study was originally undertaken as a doctoral dissertation and contains an exhaustively researched bibliography.

Bill Delaney

THE POETRY OF AI

Author: Ai (Florence Anthony, 1947-   )
Type of work: Poetry
First published: Cruelty, 1973; *Killing Floor,* 1979; *Nothing But Color* (audiotape),
  1981; *Sin,* 1986; *Cruelty/Killing Floor,* 1987 (reprint); *Fate,* 1991

Few American poets have achieved the establishment of such a distinct voice as
has Ai, and in less than twenty years. Some commentators on American poetry believe her pseudonym to be the sound of a cry, such as those uttered by many of her
personae; critic Hayden Carruth suggests that her name means "love" in Japanese
(Ai has indeed described herself as one-half Japanese). In one important sense, she
does not fall within the canon of traditional African American writers. Her subjects
transcend their concerns, and her style, as it has developed, incorporates a flat,
almost emotionless tone, regardless of her subject matter, no matter how beautiful or
how hideous.

Ai awakened critics to her work in 1973 with poems that treat such subjects as
murder, suicide, sexual and physical violence, whoring, and simple lusts. She presents her subjects usually through first-person voices that are flat and atonal. Indeed,
the experience of listening to her early poems on the audiotape *Nothing But Color*
adds to a sense that there is a terrible rhythm to the cruelties of the world and that
she has tapped into that rhythm. She reads in a flat but still lyrical voice; all of her
poems sound the same, as if she were in a trance while reading the work of some
other poet. The experience is at once delightful and unsettling.

All the poems on the tape but two are from *Killing Floor.* A different version of
her "Blue Suede Shoes," titled "Blue Suede Shoes: A Fiction" is included in *Sin,* as
is "The Mother's Tale."

Ai adds a terrible beauty in her reading to the brutal poem "The Kid," in which
she takes on the persona of a fourteen-year-old boy who murders his entire family.
No reason is given for the murders, for the breaking of the father's skull with a rod,
for the beating of the mother on the spine with the same rod, for the shooting of the
little sister in the backyard. After it is all done, Ai ends the poem: "Then I go
outside and cross the fields to the highway./ I'm fourteen. I'm a wind from nowhere./ I can break your heart."

The first two books pose the world as a mechanistic, terrible accident in which
horrors are to be expected. Ai's device is always the voice of the person speaking, of
the person brutalized, of the person drawn down to a level of bestiality and shame.
In her poem "Prostitute," from *Cruelty,* Ai's first-person narrator first goes to the
trouble to pretend that her latest customer is her "husband," whom she shoots. Then
she robs him and considers the possibilities. After all, she never cost much in the
past, but now, with two combs in her hair and a gun in her belt, who knows what she
can do?

As Ai's poetry develops, she shows an interest in an understanding of the human mind, particularly in the relationship between what people say and what they do. The poems in the first two books present one-dimensional characters, but the later personae are more complex. Her ability to take time to study extensively and her success as an American poet seem to have given her an opportunity to draw out, in her most recent books, what she only started in the first two.

In 1975, Ai was awarded a Guggenheim Fellowship and a Radcliffe Fellowship, providing her with invaluable time to spend on her art. In 1976, she received a fellowship from the Massachusetts Arts and Humanities Foundation. Awards quickly followed. *Killing Floor* was the 1978 Lamont Selection of the Academy of American Poets, and Ai received the first of two fellowships from the National Endowment for the Arts (NEA) in 1980. The second came in 1985. The writing of *Sin* was further augmented by receipt of an Ingram Merrill Foundation grant and an Emergency Fund for Writers award from the International Association of Poets, Playwrights, Editors, Essayists, and Novelists. Finally, *Sin* was awarded the American Book Award from the Before Columbus Foundation.

Few African American writers who have had such short careers can boast such an impressive list of grants, awards, and fellowships. Though Ai eschews the African American classification, she will be remembered as one of the most important African American writers and as one of the leading voices in contemporary poetry.

Before embarking on the road that would take her to *Sin* and *Fate*, Ai was asked to read her work at the Martin Luther King, Jr., Library in Washington, D.C. Part of that reading is included on *Nothing But Color*, the title of which does indicate at least some interest in ethnic heritage.

Ai's poetry, particularly as it develops, can be disturbing, so much so that debates have raged about her writing a kind of pornography, a pornography of pain and extremity, raising the question of why the reader participates. Clearly, Ai is skillful at manipulating words and at drawing readers into poems about a multiplicity of subjects. Do readers, however, participate primarily because of a perverse pleasure in watching others in the throes of pain, or because they marvel at the ability of the poet to so capture the fringes of human emotion, emotion to which any reader can relate, even in such a disturbed manner?

The poems in *Sin* are longer and more meditative than the poems in the first two books. Where the early poems posed a kind of disorder and dismemberment in the social fabric, these longer poems explore human consciousness through the poetic medium, as if primal acts are those intended for the most basic understandings. Does she identify with her speakers? That is hard to say. Certainly her dispassionate readings indicate a split in her approach to the work, but she suggests herself in some of the poems that to give oneself up to another completely—by voice, by body, by relationship, by poetry—is in itself a kind of suicide.

"The Resurrection of Elvis Presley," from *Fate*, presents a man who cannot be Elvis Presley, a man who knows Vaslav Nijinsky in life and Ernest Hemingway in death, a man who becomes the embodiment of appetite: another pill, another woman, another television set, another show to perform. Yet Ai's Presley is not resurrected;

rather, he exists in a purgatory in which he must do what Hemingway says—including not sing—for reasons that remain unclear. The time that they share is seen as better than the ice-encrusted world of heaven.

The difference between this poem, and others like it, and the early poems is that the later poems develop an ontology, or an attempt at one. The early poems are death, despair, suicide, murder. The later poems are an investigation into the necessity for such conditions, the possibility that it need not be like this, and that through the voices of (often) famous people, a reader can learn lessons to prevent similar occurrences in the future. If lessons are to be learned, however, they are not guaranteed. Ai's "Two Brothers," about John and Robert Kennedy, is a long conversation between the two dead men, who commiserate and remember and wish certain things had not been. All of their reasoning and wishing, though, is seen as a complicated riddle; the Kennedy name was what the people wanted, and it was what the people got, even in the brothers' deaths. Similarly, "The Testimony of J. Robert Oppenheimer" presents a man fooled by the world in which he was reared, a man who believed that William Blake had been right about the relationship between art and science, a man who believed as a boy in science as an investigation fraught not with values or ethics but whole truths, truths that must be discovered and presented to the world. Of course, he never suspected what he was to learn, what was to be attributed to his name. "I was always motivated/ by a ferocious need to know," he says, and like a good scientist, he discovers that the "truth" is always changing; perhaps he did not have to learn the terrible secrets of atomic fission after all. Regardless, his lesson is that humankind is on a relentless search after annihilation and has finally stumbled upon the mechanism for it.

In these poems, Ai takes on big questions that govern the world. Her definition of human potential almost always is negative, but one never gets the feeling that that is her fault. Rather, that is the nature of what she has discovered for and about the world. Ai seems to understand that single events of human history, whether involving John Kennedy or a nameless prostitute, are the hinges upon which the world turns, and are thereby possibilities for the heart to turn in a different direction. No matter how bleak her observations may appear, there is another side to what one must do with those observations.

In some ways, Ai acts like a seer in classical Greek drama. She presents what she knows, what is true. A reader, like the audience of a Greek play, must determine whether her vision is also right; the gods (world order) are neither necessarily right or just.

Ai sees in her personae the possibility of presenting universal tendencies and effects of both the living and the dead, the living for their mistakes, the dead for their contemplation of what they would do if given another chance. Ai builds her poems from book to book from monstrous acts by unnamed characters to similar acts by people very familiar to the reader. The point is that it makes no difference, that one fools oneself if one decides that the Pope is any different from any other man, or that Marilyn Monroe had something that other women lack. That is the cosmic joke that the living keep alive; the dead are able to look over the world and say that it is not so. This movement of the poet develops from seeing, to real vision, to meditations on those visions, to possible suggestions for change.

Ai is not interested in heroes; she is interested in survivors, for only the living are capable of any kind of real epiphany. Ai's larger agenda, of course, has been her realization of how little one person can affect the world—except perhaps for people such as Oppenheimer. She is interested in raising the consciousness of a social order that has become collectively anaesthetized to the brutalities of the human condition as it has come to be known. Ai moves from private, personal myth to a public myth that may have the capacity for salvation.

Ai's style may seem straightforward, but if it were so simple, then someone would long ago have done what she has done so masterfully. Critics such as Hayden Carruth commend her passion; reviewers such as G. E. Murray admire her authority. Her passion, her authority, even her seeming dispassion all come from the development of a clean, largely unpunctuated free-verse line. Of course, the use of personae, literally masks, is paramount in her work. There is, however, a modulation present in the control of the poet that resounds with rhythms of the living, with the breath line of modern American poetry, with the chanting of a more primal element in all humanity. Fastidious, disciplined, organized, chastened: All these words have come to characterize Ai's writing. She is not enamored of figurative language, but she utilizes it much more in the later work than in the earlier. Certainly, she will experiment with her verse line as she continues to develop in complexity.

Not every commentator on Ai's poetry likes it. Several question the need for such brutality. Some wonder at the very issue of dispassion, and at least one critic has questioned her distortion of facts to fit her own presentation of what is indeed factual. To her credit, she subtitles many of her poems "a fiction," as if to implore the reader to accept a mythic version of what has been seen as a "real" event. Her intention is very clear, especially in her poem "Evidence: From a Reporter's Notebook": Ai does not trust the "real" accounts as they have been given to the world. She trusts the voices of her created and mythic personae more. The world knows versions of the Kennedys, knows versions of what happened to Elvis Presley, knows versions of the stories about Lyndon Johnson, Jimmy Hoffa, George Armstrong Custer, and James Dean, but the world does not know the truth about these people and the events that surround them. Her versions may as well be that truth. It is in that light that one must read Ai's poetry.

As one reviewer noted, dying does not end anything. For Ai, though, there is a truth in the final act of life that cannot be denied, and she has taken it upon herself to render that truth as vividly, as eerily, as voluptuously, and as terrifyingly as any poet can.

Bibliography
Albers, Randall. "Ai's *Killing Floor.*" *Chicago Review* 30, no. 4 (Spring, 1979): 119-122. An in-depth critical reaction to Ai's early poetry.

Carruth, Hayden. "Impetus and Invention: Poetic Tradition and the Individual Talent." *Harper's* 258, no. 1548 (May, 1979): 88-90. Carruth places Ai in the poetic tradition from which she springs and attempts to explain her idiosyncratic style.

Forché, Carolyn. "Sentenced to Despair." *The Washington Post Book World*, March 11, 1979, F2. The author comes face to face with the subjects of Ai's work: rape, sodomy, death, drowning, all in relation to the contemporary world.

Morris, John N. "Making More Sense Than Omaha." *The Hudson Review* 27, no. 1 (Spring, 1974): 107-108. Examines Ai's biographical roots and compares them to the subjects of her poems.

Murray, G. E. "Book Notes: *Killing Floor.*" *The Nation* 228, no. 19 (May 19, 1979): 578. Another early view of the idiosyncrasies of Ai's poetry by a well-known Chicago columnist and book reviewer.

Walker, Alice. "'Like the Eye of a Horse.'" *Ms.* 2 (June, 1974): 41. Walker uses a line from the poet to show the distance that Ai utilizes in describing potentially subjective events from an objective viewpoint.

Yenser, Stephen. "New Books in Review: *Killing Floor.*" *The Yale Review* 68, no. 4 (Summer, 1979): 566-569. Still another attempt to explain Ai's excesses so that they might fit in the contemporary canon.

John Jacob

THE POETRY OF MAYA ANGELOU

Author: Maya Angelou (Marguerite Johnson, 1928-   )

Type of work: Poetry

First published: Just Give Me a Cool Drink of Water 'Fore I Diiie, 1971; *Oh Pray My Wings Are Gonna Fit Me Well,* 1975; *And Still I Rise,* 1978; *Shaker, Why Don't You Sing?,* 1983; *Now Sheba Sings the Song* (1987; written for Tom Feelings' drawings of black women); *I Shall Not Be Moved,* 1990; "On the Pulse of Morning," 1993

The televised reading of her poem "On the Pulse of Morning" at the inauguration ceremony of President William Clinton in January, 1993, represented a crowning moment for Maya Angelou, who had already received many honorary degrees and awards during her multifaceted career. The broadcast also reminded her readers that Angelou, although better known as an autobiographer, is first and foremost a poet.

Angelou's poetry occupies a special position in her development as a writer. As a child, Angelou went through five years of self-imposed silence after she was raped at the age of seven by a Mr. Freeman, who was subsequently kicked to death by her uncles. The loss of her voice was a result of the trauma, which made her imagine that her voice could kill. Thanks to her teacher, Bertha Flowers, Angelou started writing poetry and overcame her trauma. Poetry thus played an essential part in the recovery of her voice, which in turn signaled the success of the healing process.

Angelou's commitment to be a writer began about at the age of thirty. By the time she started publishing, she had gone through a number of dramatic turns in her personal and social life. The pattern emerging from those events is that of a person's struggle to establish, as Dolly A. McPherson says of Angelou's autobiographies, "order out of chaos," a struggle to relate her personal experience to the general condition of African Americans, so that the individual's chaotic life is given order through the awareness of its being related to the communal experience. Angelou's poetry also bears out this struggle, which Pricilla Ramsey characterizes as the transformation of "the elements of a stultifying and personal, social, political and historical milieu into a sensual and physical refuge."

Just Give Me a Cool Drink of Water 'Fore I Diiie (1971) is typical of Angelou's poetry in that the poems employ two related voices to address individual as well as communal issues, so that eventually the personal voice (for example, the lover's) merges with, and becomes indistinguishable from, the communal voice (for example, the social critic's). The communal voice, in other words, transcends the personal at the end of the struggle. The two voices are evident from the two divisions of the book.

Part 1, "Where Love Is a Scream of Anguish," focuses on various kinds of male-female relationships and employs the "I" persona. Some of these relationships are love affairs filled with bittersweet emotions, as in "Remembering" and "Tears." Even at the most tender and most intimate moments, the shadow of insecurity and loss looms large, as in "After." The shadow is especially prominent in relationships that are somewhat abnormal, as in the case of a prostitute and her transient clients in "They Went Home" and that of a woman and a "lover-boy" who has turned to a younger woman in "No Loser, No Weeper." At times, the woman even indulges in the morose premonition of her own demise, as in "Mourning Grace." Despite the gloom that dominates in part 1, there is nevertheless a poem that signals the persona's desire to transcend the impasse. In "On Diverse Deviations," the persona, out of exasperation, expresses her wish to be carried off "To a shore,/ Where love is the scream of anguish/ And no curtain drapes the door." The poem also serves as a transitional link to the next section, which can be understood as the other "shore."

Part 2, "Just Before the World Ends," deals with communal, social, and political issues. Despite the greater variety of subject matter here, the poems are unified by their social realism and criticism with regard to the predicament of African Americans, exemplified by "Times-Square-Shoeshine-Composition" and "When I Think About Myself." Social realism is inseparable from social satire, which can be directed at white society, as in "The Calling of Names," or at the black community, as in "Sepia Fashion Show." At times, satire gives way to sarcastic protest. In "My Guilt," for example, the persona declares in bitterness that her guilt is making music out of slavery's chains, her crime is being alive to tell of heroes, dead and gone, and her sin is hanging from a tree without screaming aloud.

At her best, Angelou is able to combine satire and protest into a powerful indictment. One remarkable example is "Miss Scarlett, Mr. Rhett and Other Latter-Day Saints," in which the lynching of blacks on a plantation colludes with a grotesquely surrealistic Christian ritual in which victims turn out to be Jesus and Ku Klux Klan members serve as priests for King Kotton as God. The ritual is even complete with a "little Eva" as the Virgin Mary of Dixie who, in order to guard the relics of her intact hymen, plays a part in "daily putting to death,/ into eternity,/ The stud, his seed." Angelou's relentless indictments come close to the apocalyptic vision when given the occasion. In "Riot: 60's," we get a glimpse of "Lighting: a hundred Watts/ Detroit, Newark and New York," in which African Americans are shot by nervous National Guards. In "No No No No," which contains the line responsible for the volume's title, the colonial, racial, and global violence perpetuated by the West compels the persona to deny the possibility of love and forgiveness. The hint of nihilism in this kind of bitterness is accentuated by the threat of a nuclear war, the subject of "On a Bright Day, Next Week." The subtitle of part 2 comes from this poem.

The two parts of the book are tied together antithetically: The poignant emotions and personal sufferings of part 1 are juxtaposed with the activist militancy and critical reflections of part 2, as if to suggest that the individual's failures and distresses in life and love ought to be understood and measured in the context of the community's historical and social conditions. The framework of the book is closely related to the title of the volume itself, which, Angelou has said, refers to her "belief that we as individuals in a species are still so innocent that we could ask our murderer just before he puts the final wrench upon the throat, 'Would you please give me a cool drink of water?'" Symbolically, it is the innocence—and the courage—to ask for such a "cool drink of water" that allows the communal persona in part 2 to voice its understanding and critique of the anguishes and tribulations of the individual persona in part 1. The black woman may have suffered, both as an individual and as a collective persona, but as "The Mothering Blackness" suggests, Angelou's interest is in highlighting her return to the mother's waiting arms "blameless," "black," and "tall as was Sheba's daughter."

In *Oh Pray My Wings Are Gonna Fit Me Well* (1975), which was inspired by a song (the tune from "a slave holler" and the words from a nineteenth century spiritual), Angelou's purpose was "to put all the things bothering me—my heavy load—in that book, and let them pass." The book continues the pattern of ordering chaos by merging the individual and the communal voices, but there is an increasing amount of humor, wit, tenderness, and meditation. The first two parts, which deal with love in its various guises ranging from consolation ("Conceit") to frustration ("Poor Girl"), are intensely personal. The success of these poems lies mainly in their drama: Moments of moodiness are captured lyrically ("Passing Time") along with temperamental outbursts ("The Telephone") to suggest a special type of romance that an early-middle-aged black woman (see "On Reaching Forty") finds herself getting into, only to realize that instead of romantic leaves and birds and snows and nights, "I need to write/ of lovers false/ and hate/ and hateful wrath/ quickly" ("Art Pose").

The personal drama in this volume once again is enacted against the backdrop, in parts 3 through 5, of historical and contemporary realities, including the alienation of the poor ("Alone"), the abandonment of the underprivileged ("Request"), the sexist victimization of women ("Chicken-Licken"), and various other social injustices ("Southeast Arkansas"). This sense of heaviness is directly related to the failure of the American Dream for African Americans. Angelou's emphasis here is not so much to condemn America as to rediscover the real America ("America") and, as an antidote, to appreciate the New Africa emerging from colonialism and to learn about African civilization itself ("Africa"). Linking the two continents by means of space (the ocean) and time (history), Angelou comes to terms with her identity and ethnicity in a series of carefully crafted poems including "Child Dead in Old Seas," "Song for the Old Ones," and "Elegy." Mysteriously, these poems are characterized by a combination of poignancy and triumph, thus indicating the poet's belief that her race has never been broken.

And Still I Rise (1978) further develops Angelou's pattern of turning chaos into order, and order dominates. Part 1, "Touch Me, Life, Not Softly," consists of poems about love in many guises. Here Angelou treats it as a subject of study and critique rather than as an experience to indulge in. For example, in "A King of Love, Some Say" and in "Men," she addresses the issue of abusive relationships; in "Where You Belong: A Duet" and "Just for a Time," she portrays types of men who "fool around" and regard women as possessions. Because the poet frequently assumes the persona of a man, the voice in these poems is not only a lover's but also an actor's or a director's. In part 2, "Traveling," the analytical mind is also brought into play, in case-study portraits of various types of personages including drug addicts ("The

Lesson"), pretentious philanthropists ("Lady Luncheon Club"), self-righteous welfare mothers ("Momma Welfare Roll"), happy-go-lucky tricksters ("Willie"), menial laborers ("Woman Work"), and hypocritical politicians ("Through the Inner City to the Suburbs"). In these vignettes, Angelou's clinical observations of society and her mockery of reality are also infused with a strong sense of compassion, as if to prepare the reader for the next section.

The subtitle of part 3, "And Still I Rise," is taken from the first poem of the section; this title is not only the namesake of the volume but also the title of a 1977 play based on the poem. "And Still I Rise" is indeed one of the most important aphorisms by which Angelou's poetry can be understood. The poem opens with a mundane but powerful simile: "You may write me down in history/ With your bitter, twisted lies,/ You may trod me in the very dirt/ But still, like dust, I'll rise." The poem then continues in a proud, even haughty, tone, which through a series of stanzas rises steadily in pitch, in dauntless challenge to the history and reality of oppression, and in self-congratulatory celebration of dignity, strength, and survival. The kind of bitterness found in earlier volumes is conspicuously absent, indicating that perhaps a process of sublimation and transcendence has taken place upon the triumphant close of the Civil Rights era. Indeed, in some of her most lighthearted moments, Angelou can even afford to sound clownishly funny. In "Ain't That Bad?," a carnivalesque poem with festive dance rhythms, after giving the audience a rundown of a dozen or so black celebrities ranging from Stevie Wonder and Jesse Jackson to Muhammad Ali and Andrew Young, the poet jests comically: "Now ain't they bad?/ An' ain't they Black?" There are also serene moments when the poet turns meditative, contemplating God but without feeling obligated to be submissive, for she now sees God as the God who has made a pact with Job and given His Word, the Word that the poet can "step out on" ("Just Like Job"). Appropriating Christianity and reinventing the religion for African Americans, Angelou declares in the concluding poem of the volume that her God is "Brown-skinned,/ Neat Afro,/ Full lips,/ A little goatee./ A Malcolm,/ Martin,/ DuBois" ("Thank You, Lord").

As a poet, Angelou reached maturity with the publication of *And Still I Rise* because she had found her voice, her self, her history, her race, and her God; order is coming into shape out of the chaos of her life and of her world. The volumes that follow are in general further attempts to adumbrate and reinforce this order along the trajectory traced above, but each volume contains some new elements.

In *Shaker, Why Don't You Sing?* (1983; the title is taken from a John Henry song), the persona is often a black woman. Besides being assertive and assured of herself ("Weekend Glory"), she is afflicted by the blues ("Good Woman Feeling Blue") and becomes nostalgic ("A Georgia Song"), insomnious ("Insomniac"), and even depressed ("The Last Decision"). In the sentimental but suggestive title poem, "Shaker, Why Don't You Sing?," the persona asks a bedmate, the "Shaker," in the middle of the night why the Shaker does not sing. The reader is mystified as to why the Shaker has "withdrawn/ your music and lean inaudibly/ on the quiet slope of memory." If the turn taken by Angelou in *Shaker, Why Don't You Sing?* is a sentimental one, then

Now Sheba Sings the Song (1987) can be seen as a turn toward sensuality, but in a feminist way. Angelou has commented that the work is "a play on the Song of Solomon. We never heard Sheba's song." The book is dedicated to all her "sisters," by which Angelou refers to "all my brown, black, beige, yellow, red and white sisters." Taking advantage of Tom Feelings' monochrome drawings of black women in various poses, Angelou boldly celebrates the beauty of the sexuality and spirituality of black womanhood: "From the columns of my thighs/ I take the strength to hold the world aloft/ Standing, too often, with a cloud of loneliness/ Forming halos for my head." The volume is perhaps the most emblematic of Angelou's poetic achievement, thanks to the mythmaking image of Sheba as a black woman of beauty in body and in spirit.

Because Angelou's stature as a public figure has been enhanced by her connections with presidents Gerald Ford, Jimmy Carter, and William Clinton, her poetry has taken yet another turn, namely toward the construction of a civic culture conducive to the democracy of the United States. She may be perceived as being didactic in many poems, including "On the Pulse of Morning," but since she has courageously taken up the burden of a public mission, these poems ought to be understood in the context of the rage toward order to which Angelou has devoted her entire life.

The drive toward the great order of the nation is evident from many poems in *I Shall Not Be Moved* (1990). The title of the volume is derived from the refrain of "Our Grandmothers," a composite portrait of the historical role of black women. It also reminds readers of a popular song that declares, "On our way to freedom, we shall not be moved." Evidently, Angelou cannot bear to see the chaos of an individual like herself expanded to a national or even global scale; as she writes in "These Yet to Be United States," that country's awesome power is the source of suffering at home and abroad. This statement is, however, a patriotic one because Angelou's ultimate concern is how the wounds can be healed. Risking didacticism, she explains that "In minor ways we differ,/ in major we're the same. . . . We are more alike, my friends,/ than we are unalike" ("Human Family"). She then goes on to denounce bigotry in "Main Bigot," call for the morality of forgiveness in "Forgive," and sing of equality in "Equality." In her vision, the Savior is one who practices sacrifice out of *agape*, or the love of humanity ("Savior"), and paradise is a place "where families are loyal/ and strangers are nice,/ where the music is jazz/ and the season is fall" ("Preacher, Don't Send Me"). All these themes culminate in her optimistic outlook in the inaugural poem, "On the Pulse of Morning," in which multiculturalism is offered as a viable solution to the problems of American society, a blueprint for creating supreme order out of the devastating chaos of history and the world.

Because Angelou's poems make use of the voice and are meant for the ear and the heart rather than the eye, they can be deceptively simple to some of her readers. Borrowing Nathaniel Hawthorne's notion that "Easy reading is damn hard writing," she has said that a simple style can contain "deep talk," that is, meanings that go deep beneath the surface of language. In Angelou's poetry, the "deep talk" is the talk of the world through a nation, the talk of the nation through a race, the talk of the race through a black woman, and the talk of the black woman through a human being. As lyrical statements of this talk of humanism, her poems resonate with such a vital pulse that chaos must give way to order. Although she once thought that her voice could kill, it is in fact life-giving by virtue of this transcendence.

Bibliography

Angelou, Maya. *Conversations with Maya Angelou.* Edited by Jeffrey M. Elliot. Jackson: University Press of Mississippi, 1989. A handy collection of thirty-two interviews conducted at different times. Contains many comments by Angelou on her own poetry.

McPherson, Dolly A. *Order Out of Chaos: The Autobiographical Works of Maya Angelou.* New York: Peter Lang, 1990. Provides theoretical insights into Angelou's writings.

Plimpton, George. "Maya Angelou." In *Writers at Work: The Paris Review Interviews.* 8th ser. New York: Penguin Books, 1988. An interview in which Angelou discusses the concept of "deep talk," which sheds light on her poetry.

Ramsey, Pricilla R. "Transcendence: The Poetry of Maya Angelou." In *Current Bibliography on African Affairs,* 17, no. 2 (1984-1985): 139-153. A rare article focusing on Angelou as a poet; proposes the idea of transcendence in her poetry.

Tate, Claudia, ed. *Black Women Writers at Work.* New York: Continuum, 1983. Contains an interview with Maya Angelou (reprinted in *Conversations with Maya Angelou*). This collection also puts Angelou in the context of contemporary black women's writing.

Balance Chow

THE POETRY OF AMIRI BARAKA

Author: Amiri Baraka (Everett LeRoi Jones, 1934-   )
Type of work: Poetry
First published: Preface to a Twenty Volume Suicide Note, 1961; *The Dead Lecturer,* 1964; *Black Magic: Sabotage—Target Study—Black Art: Collected Poetry, 1961-1967,* 1969; *It's Nation Time,* 1970; *In Our Terribleness: Some Elements and Meaning in Black Style,* 1970; *Spirit Reach,* 1972; *Hard Facts,* 1975; *Selected Poetry of Amiri Baraka/LeRoi Jones,* 1979; *Reggae or Not!,* 1981; *The LeRoi Jones/Amiri Baraka Reader* (edited by William J. Harris), 1991

While Amiri Baraka (LeRoi Jones) is a leading African American poet, his poetry accounts for only one part of his literary career. He has also written essays, short stories, a novel, a major study of American jazz, plays, a musical drama, and an autobiography. He has founded the Black Arts Repertory Theater-School, edited seminal anthologies and journals of avant-garde and African American writing, received major scholarly fellowships and awards, taught at several major American universities, and been an influential political and cultural leader in the African American community. Baraka's life, achievements, and writing have reflected—and have often helped to determine—the evolution of African American thought in the last half of the twentieth century. The philosophical and political developments in Baraka's thinking have resulted in four distinct poetical periods: a 1950's and 1960's involvement with the Greenwich Village "Beat" scene; an early 1960's quest for personal identity and community; a phase connected with black nationalism and the Black Arts movement; and a Marxist-Leninist period.

Everett LeRoi Jones was born in Newark, New Jersey, in 1934. His father was a postal worker; his mother was a college dropout who became a social worker. Graduated with honors from Barringer High School in 1951, Jones first attended Rutgers University on scholarship and transferred to Howard University in Washington, D.C., in 1952, only to be expelled in 1954 for failing grades. He immediately joined the U.S. Air Force, reaching the rank of sergeant, but was discharged "undesirably" in 1957 for having sent some of his poems to purportedly communist publications. Upon his release, Jones moved to Greenwich Village, became friends with such avant-garde poets as Allen Ginsberg, Frank O'Hara, and Charles Olson, and married Hettie Cohen, with whom he edited a literary journal. In 1960, he—along with several other important "Negro writers"—was invited to visit Cuba, where he met Fidel Castro. Jones witnessed Cuba's socialist infancy firsthand and realized how political poetry could be. The success of his play *Dutchman* (1964) and the murder of Malcolm X in 1965 convinced Jones that Greenwich Village's white Beat poetry scene and his white Jewish wife contradicted his interests in the African American community and issues. Consequently, he moved initially to Harlem and then back to Newark. During this period, Jones—along with Larry Neal, Hoyt Fuller, Don L.

Lee, and others—initiated the Black Arts movement, a cultural embodiment of black nationalism. He also married Sylvia Robinson (Amina Baraka) and in 1967 changed his name to Imamu (meaning "spiritual leader," a name he later dropped) Ameer (meaning "Prince," a name he later changed to Amiri) Baraka (meaning "blessed"). Throughout the 1960's and into the 1970's, Baraka's major interests were the Black Power movement, Black Muslim philosophy and politics, Maulana Ron Karenga's Kawaida cultural revolutionary doctrine, and pan-Africanism. In 1974, however, Baraka became convinced that the "cultural nationalist positions" were too narrow in their concerns and that class, not race, determines the social, political, and economic realities of people's lives. For this reason, he shifted his focus in writing and politics to Marxist-Leninist thought.

Post-World War II avant-garde Greenwich Village poetry represented a break with what Baraka considered the impersonal, academic poetry of T. S. Eliot and the poetry published in *The New Yorker*. When Baraka read Allen Ginsberg's 1956 poem "Howl," it was a turning point in his poetic life. Baraka says "Howl" moved him because "it talked about a world I could identify with and relate to. . . . I now knew poetry could be about some things that I was familiar with. That it did not have to be about suburban birdbaths and Greek mythology." In "How You Sound??," Baraka wrote: "MY POETRY is whatever I think I am. . . . I CAN BE ANYTHING I CAN. I make a poetry with what I feel is useful & can be saved out of all the garbage of our lives." He believed not only that any observation, experience, or object is appropriate for poetry, but also that, "There must not be any preconceived notion or *design* for what the poem *ought* to be. . . . I'm not interested in writing sonnets, sestinas or anything . . . only poems."

What interests Baraka is his own experience, popular American culture, and the struggle between the seemingly contradictory black and white worlds in which he dwells. A number of Baraka's early poems published in *Preface to a Twenty Volume Suicide Note* express a yearning for a more orderly and meaningful world that he associated with radio, a yearning he calls "A maudlin nostalgia/ that comes on/ like terrible thoughts about death." In "In Memory of Radio," he compares the wisdom of Bishop Fulton J. Sheen and the Shadow to his own lack of insight into the evil that "lurks in the hearts of men," while "Look for You Yesterday, Here You Come Today" contrasts the certainty of radio's imagined worlds to the real world, where, he realizes, "nobody really gives a damn" and "All the lovely things I've known have disappeared." Almost despairingly, he wonders, "Where is my space helmet, I sent for it/ 3 lives ago . . . when there were box tops. . . . THERE MUST BE A LONE RANGER!!!" Neither the Lone Ranger nor his radio companions come to the rescue. The poet is left alone and forlorn, "My silver bullets all gone/ My black mask trampled in the dust."

In making popular culture the focus of his poetry, Baraka reflects the poetic shift from mythological and literary icons (which he considered bourgeois, academic, and dead) to the vitality of the everyday. Baraka and his circle looked to Walt Whitman, William Carlos Williams, Ezra Pound, the French poet Guillaume Apollinaire, and the Surrealist painters to help them create a new American poetic tradition. The personal "I" so important to the whole body of Baraka's poetic works also began to develop during this period, which is characterized by direct and even confessional poems such as "Preface to a Twenty Volume Suicide Note": "Lately, I've become accustomed to the way/ The ground opens up and envelopes me/ Each time I go out to walk the dog." This personal voice clearly expresses the confusion the poet feels living in both the black and white worlds. "Hymn for Lanie Poo" juxtaposes images from 1950's New York to images from Africa and laments the poet's schoolteacher sister's capitulation to white values. She is, he says at the end of the poem, happy in "the huge & loveless/ white-anglo sun/of/ benevolent step/ mother America." In the volume's final poem, "Notes for a Speech," Baraka writes, "African blues/ does not know me." Though he is not white like his bohemian friends, he also feels alienated from his racial heritage: "They shy away. My own/ dead souls, my, so called/ people. Africa/ is a foreign place. You are/ as any other sad man here/ american." He thus ends *Preface to a Twenty Volume Suicide Note* on a note of confusion over his identity, his place, his voice.

Such confusion contributed to Baraka's split with his wife, his move from Greenwich Village to Harlem and eventually to Newark, and his quest for personal and racial identity captured in his second book of poetry, *The Dead Lecturer*, a struggle Baraka describes as "trying to puncture fake social relationships and gain some clarity about what I really felt about things." In his autobiography, Baraka remarks of the poems of this period, "again and again they speak of this separation, this sense of being in contradiction with my friends and peers." In "A Poem for Willie Best" (who was a Hollywood minstrel stereotype), Baraka wrestles with his estrangement in the world: "A face sings, alone/ at the top/ of the body. All/ flesh, all song aligned. For hell is silent/ . . . It was your own death/ you saw." Forced to act in a way contrary to his nature, to dance a dance that "punishes speech" and to speak words that are not his own, Willie Best is able "to provoke/ some meaning, where before there was only hell," so that those who come after him may "Hear," as the last line of the poem insists. Baraka also creates Crow Jane in this poetry collection, a "white Muse appropriated by the black experience." She embodies for Baraka a rejection of the white Western aesthetic. Baraka describes her as "Dead virgin/ of the mind's echo. Dead lady/ of thinking, back now, without/ the creak of memory"; in the last poem of the series, he implores, "Damballah, kind father,/ sew up/ her bleeding hole." Transformed by African culture and the African American experience, the muse may live again. During this period of racial and political unrest, Baraka says, "I was struggling to be born. . . . I was in a frenzy, trying to get my feet solidly on the ground, of reality," a fact that rings out in poems such as "I Substitute for the Dead Lecturer." He asks, "What kindness/ What wealth/ can I offer? Except/ what is, for me/ ugliest. What is/ for me, shadows, shrieking phantoms." Somehow, he feels destined to speak a new "lecture" of the horrors of American reality: "The Lord has saved me/ to do this" despite his fear of failure. He invokes in another poem "black dada nihilismus," a black god, to destroy all vestiges of white culture and to assume its own righteous power. During this second period, then, Baraka poses tough questions regarding identity, integrity, and society without knowing the answers. He negates what is but is hard-pressed to offer positive alternatives. He searches for his self, though he is not sure who that will be. As he says in "The Liar," "When they say, 'It is Roi/ who is dead?' I wonder/ who will they mean?" He does not know.

Not until he involved himself with the Black Power movement, the Nation of Islam, the West Coast Kawaida revolution, and the Black Arts movement did Baraka come to see himself and his art clearly. In Cuba, Baraka had come to see that politics and poetry could work together, and in his black nationalist period, he successfully joins the two. In his essay "The Legacy of Malcolm X, and the Coming of the Black Nation," Baraka declares, "The Black artist . . . is desperately needed to change the images his people identify with, by asserting Black feeling, Black mind, Black judgment"; in "State/meant," he says: "The Black Artist must draw out of his soul the correct image of the world." In the poem "Black Art," he insists that the function of art is to be intimately connected with the real world, not to be an exercise in abstraction. Art must reflect and change that world: "We want 'poems that kill.'/ Assassin poems, Poems that shoot/ guns." In the final stanza, he writes: "We want a black poem./ And a/ Black World." It is a poetry that calls for separatist black nationalism. In "Return of the Native," he imagines a completely African American world "where we may see ourselves/ all the time." His tribute to Malcolm X, "A Poem for Black Hearts," celebrates the contributions of the "black god of our time" and looks to his memory to transform those who follow. "Poem for HalfWhite College Students" is a warning to black students whose words, gestures, and values are compromised by the white academic world. "Ka'Ba" honors the beauty of blackness: "We are beautiful people/ with african imaginations/ full of masks and dances and swelling chants." He calls for African tradition evoked by black nationalism to supply meaning, self-affirmation, and order in an alien land.

Baraka has observed that "all nationalism finally, taken to any extreme, has got to be oppressive to the people who are not in that nationality." This constrictive view of the world led Baraka to adopt a Marxist-Leninist perspective. Baraka has attributed the change in his thinking to his realization that "skin color was not determinant of political content." Furthermore, he has stated, "I see art as a weapon, and a weapon of revolution. It's just now that I define revolution in Marxist terms." In his poem "When We'll Worship Jesus," for example, Baraka criticizes Christian America for its failure to help people in any substantive way: "he cant change the world/ we can change the world." He insists, "throw/ jesus out yr mind. Build the new world out of reality, and new vision." In "A New Reality Is Better than a New Movie!," Baraka envisions the old unequal capitalist world consumed in an inferno. What is captured on film pales in comparison to the revolutionary reality to come: "The real terror of nature is humanity enraged, the true/ technicolor spectacle that/ hollywood/ cant record." Such outrage will lead, Baraka predicts, to a demand for "the new socialist reality . . . the ultimate tidal/ wave" that will change the world. In poems such as

"The Dictatorship of the Proletariat" and "Das Kapital," Baraka presents a poetic articulation of socialist ideology. In his 1982 poem "In the Tradition," Baraka moves beyond strict Marxist concerns to African American culture, providing a tribute to the contributors to that tradition: "We are the composers, racists & gunbearers/ We are the artists." He wants American history and culture to "get out of europe/ come out of europe if you can." Were scholars to look for truly American culture, he maintains, "nigger music's almost all/ you got, and you find it/ much too hot." Baraka's series of poems entitled *Why's/Wise* also focuses on the life and history of African Americans, though Baraka is still committed to his Marxist vision.

The poetry of Amiri Baraka is clearly wide-ranging in content and style. He continues to work, to grow, and to influence those who come after him. As critic Gerald Early observes, Amiri Baraka has been "the most influential black person of letters over the last twenty years, particularly influential among young blacks," and he has had "a striking ability to communicate to people who [have] never read his books. It is not likely that any black writer or intellectual will generate a similar power any time in the near or foreseeable future."

Bibliography

Berry, Jay R., Jr. "Poetic Style in Amiri Baraka's *Black Art.*" *College Language Association Journal* 32 (December, 1988): 225-234. Insists that though his attention in *Black Art* is primarily political, Baraka shows great concern for poetic style and structure also.

Harris, William J. *The Poetry and Poetics of Amiri Baraka: The Jazz Aesthetic.* Columbia: University of Missouri Press, 1985. Comprehensive examination of Baraka's thought and work from his bohemian stage through black nationalism to Marxism, with particular emphasis on the influence of jazz upon him.

Melhern, D. H. "Revolution: The Constancy of Change: An Interview with Amiri Baraka." *Black American Literature Forum* 16, no. 3 (Fall, 1982): 87-105. Baraka discusses the development of his politics, philosophy, and art.

Miller, James A. "'I Investigate the Sun': Amiri Baraka in the 1980's." *Callaloo* 9 (Winter, 1986): 184-192. Miller maintains that, despite some critics' claims to the contrary, Baraka's poetry has not deteriorated since his "conversion" to Marxist-Leninism.

Phillips, Marilynn J. "LeRoi Jones/Amiri Baraka: A Study in Creolization." *MAWA Review* 2 (June, 1986): 8-10. Claims that creolization, the incorporation and mingling of the vocabulary and grammar of two or more language groups, marks Baraka's poetry. Baraka uses "all language varieties available to him" to express his ideas.

Sollors, Werner. *Amiri Baraka/LeRoi Jones: The Quest for a "Populist Modernism."* New York: Columbia University Press, 1978. Argues that two ideas unify Baraka's works and ideas through all of their various stages: popularism and modernism.

Laura Weiss Zlogar

THE POETRY OF EDWARD KAMAU BRATHWAITE

Author: Edward Kamau Brathwaite (1930-   )
Type of work: Poetry
First published: Panda No. 349, 1969; *The Arrivants: A New World Trilogy,* 1973 (contains *Rights of Passage,* 1967; *Masks,* 1968; *Islands,* 1969); *Other Exiles,* 1975; *Days and Nights,* 1975; *Black + Blues,* 1976; *Mother Poem,* 1977; *Soweto,* 1979; *Word Making Man: A Poem for Nicólas Guillèn,* 1979; *Sun Poem,* 1982; *Third World Poems,* 1983; *Jah Music,* 1986; *X/Self,* 1987; *Sappho Sakyi's Meditations,* 1989; *Shar,* 1990; *Middle Passages,* 1992

Born in 1930 in Barbados, a British colony until 1966, Edward Kamau Brathwaite is a prolific poet of international stature. Employing Afro-Caribbean cultural forms such as myths, cults, rituals, music, dance, speech, and creolized expressions to explore themes ranging from the middle passage and exile to national identity and the Third World's struggle for freedom, his poetic works are central to the emerging canon of West Indian literature. Also recognized as a critic, story writer, playwright, editor, historian, professor, and educator, he has a long list of publications reflecting his efforts toward the establishment of a national culture for the West Indies.

Brathwaite started publishing poems during the 1950's, when he was a student on scholarship at the University of Cambridge. While in England, Brathwaite realized that the Western culture imposed on him as a black man in a British colony would be denied to him once he presumed to call it his own. Such a sense of rootlessness led him on a quest for cultural identity in Africa, where he served as an education officer in Ghana (1955-1962) under Kwame Nkrumah. The African connection proved to be a turning point in his career. Reassuring him of a cultural home in Africa and inspiring him to unearth the African heritage in the Caribbean upon his return in 1962, it shaped his vision of a national culture. The encounter had a definite impact on his poetry, scholarship, and literary criticism. In particular, African cultural forms such as rituals and oral performances gave him insights into the type of holistic poetry he would need to write in order to overcome the problems of fragmentation with which West Indians were burdened.

Throughout his career, Brathwaite developed a series of cultural concepts that shed important light on his poetry. The most important one is the notion of fragmentation, by which he refers to the geographical, historical, cultural, political, ethnic, and linguistic realities of the West Indies. To deal with fragmentation, the West Indian writer's mission is to establish political and ethnic unification by means of a national culture. Connected to fragmentation is the idea of "the submerged," by which Brathwaite refers to the "base" of the fragments preserved in the racial memory of Amerindians and Afro-Caribbeans. This submerged culture, similar to the geographical formation that connects the individual Caribbean islands at the base of the ocean, is a potential force for the sea change of unification. Brathwaite sometimes personifies the submerged as the untamable and uncolonizable Sycorax (Caliban's mother, from William Shakespeare's *The Tempest*, 1611); on other occasions he calls it *nam*, which he defines as "secret name, soul-source, connected with *nyam* (eat), *yam* (root food), *nyame* (name of god)"; *nam* is "the heart of our *nation-language* which comes into conflict with the cultural imperial authority." As the "core" inside the protective mask, *nam* represents the survivability and spirituality of the Afro-Caribbean.

In literary terms, to overcome fragmentation by means of the submerged entails the conscious effort to develop what Brathwaite calls the "creole aesthetic" to counteract the "missile," or Eurocentric, aesthetic. For Brathwaite, creolization is an organic process that involves imitation (regarded as initiation) and invention. Because creolized cultural forms, such as the jazz novel, are creative appropriations rooted in folk tradition, it is through the creole aesthetic that Caribbean artists and writers can create, or "possess," their national culture. As he writes in an editorial titled "Timehri," "the recognition of an ancestral relationship with the folk or aboriginal culture involves the artist and participant in a journey into the past and hinterland which is at the same time a movement of possession into present and future." He states that "through this movement of possession we become ourselves, truly our own creators, discovering word for object, image for the Word." Integral to Brathwaite's creole aesthetic is the idea of possession, which he explains in terms of kinetic energy: "in Africa, the more energy you can accumulate and express, the nearer you will come to God. . . . I'm using the concept of kinesis to make us aware of the things that we do possess, and the people who write the poetry of kinesis do actually in themselves enact a religious process whereby they become aware of certain omens and icons that are vital to themselves." Practicing what he preaches, Brathwaite has employed a great variety of creolized cultural forms, such as rasta, reggae, limbo, calypso, ska, jazz, blues, the yard theater, and the drum, in his poetry in order to achieve the condition of possession. As the culmination of the aesthetic-religious experience, this would allow the West Indian to come to terms with "dispossession" and other problems associated with the legacy of colonialism and slavery.

Of the more than a dozen books of poetry by Brathwaite, the most important ones are the New World trilogy and the Bajan trilogy. Because both works share Brathwaite's search for identity as an Afro-Caribbean, they can be regarded as an autobiographical record of the poet's inner experience. Insofar as they also exemplify his efforts to establish, or "possess," a national culture for the West Indies, they can be seen as the epic of a nation as well. This duality is by no means a dichotomy, because the personal "I" and the communal "I" found interspersed in these two works constitute a united rather than a divided consciousness. Sometimes known as the collective voice of the African diaspora, this consciousness is developed into an archetypal voice with mythical implications. On the whole, Brathwaite's works follow this pattern.

Brathwaite started working on the first trilogy upon his return to the Caribbean in 1962. It was published in England while he was pursuing a doctoral degree in history at the University of Sussex (1965-1968). The three parts, *Rights of Passage* (1967),

Masks (1968), and *Islands* (1969), were republished in 1973 collectively as *The Arrivants: A New World Trilogy*. This new edition is preceded by a quotation from the Kumina Queen of Jamaica, in Creole, about the "arrivance" of her ancestors as "arrivants" from Africa. The quote sums up concisely the theme of the trilogy in that the narrator not only acknowledges her African heritage but also asserts her West Indian identity in the present. This discourse of acknowledgment and assertion constitutes a double movement between past and present, between Africa and the West Indies, between personal experience and communal history, and between dispossession and possession.

The double movement of the New World trilogy is immediately evident from the title of the first book, *Rights of Passage*. "Passage" refers not only to the middle passage of African slaves in the past but also to the exile of West Indians in the present. "Rights," a pun on "rites," refers not only to the "rites of passage" marking the growth of a person and a people through ritualistic ordeals but also to the "rights" of "possession" to be gained through such a ritual. The title hence encapsulates the main theme of the collection, the individual poems of which deal with major aspects of the double movement and the rights/rites of passage of the Afro-Caribbean. The double movement is also structured into the four divisions of *Rights of Passage*, the overall action of which begins in Africa, shifts to the Americas, and then bounces circuitously through Europe, back to Africa, and then to the New World.

Masks, the second part of the trilogy, continues the double movement, but the action lingers at the pivotal point of Africa, in particular, Ghana, home of the Akan. The title, *Masks*, also implies *nam*, or the core behind the mask. The collection opens with an Akan proverb, "Only the fool points at his origins with his left hand," thus making explicit that the subject is the quest for one's ancestral origins in Africa and that the search itself has to be conducted with the deepest reverence. All the poems deal with aspects of African culture, such as myths, cults, rituals, ancestors, and heroes, which in turn are all "masks" behind which is to be found the African identity. The overall action of this collection, following the pattern of a rite of passage, also involves a journey. The journey takes place in Africa itself and culminates in a return to, and arrival at, the cultural home.

In *Islands*, the double movement comes full circle as yet another sort of middle passage. The poet focuses on the Afro-Caribbean's physical and spiritual return to the West Indies equipped with a new sense of home and belonging that makes the possession of a national culture possible. In a way paralleling the concept of *nam* that is central to the theme of *Masks*, the poems in *Islands*, by dealing with the colonial experience as well as the racial memories and cultural practices shared among Caribbeans, also point to the submerged formation that is the common core of the West Indian community. Although the cycle is complete, the epigraph from James Baldwin's *Tell Me How Long the Train's Been Gone* (1968) makes it clear that the double movement has to be reenacted if necessary.

Although the three books of *The Arrivants* are best read together, each exhibits a character of its own and contains a variety of points of interest peculiar to its design and locale. In *Rights of Passage*, the predicament of black people in the United States prior to and after emancipation is given much attention. The portrayal of Uncle Tom is especially poignant. He is endowed with a psychological depth that evokes both pity and compassion; despite his sufferings, he is given colossal qualities reminiscent of Job in the Old Testament. The angry Negro of contemporary times, as a counterpoint to Uncle Tom, is portrayed vividly as a self-exiled Odysseus who, upon the discovery of Rastafarianism, begins to jive in dance and song.

Whereas *Rights of Passage* is characterized by its lively sociohistorical drama, African cultural forms dominate in *Masks*, to the extent that the whole collection resembles a re-created ceremony replete with libations, invocations, incantations, sacrifices, drum rhythms, and other related rituals, all of which contribute to the religious and performative qualities of the book. In *Islands*, the primordial past and the colonial past exist alongside the present, when the postcolonial nation is still a fragile thing in its cradle. There is obviously an impulse to synthesize the religious and performative qualities of *Masks* and the sociohistorical drama of *Rights of Passage*. This synthesis is best epitomized by the poems dealing with the limbo dance, for example "Caliban." Said to be derived from physical exercises Africans conducted in the crowded space of slave ships, the limbo is symbolic of not only the brutal experience of the middle passage but also the African's desire and strength to rise above such humilities. Furthermore, as if to suggest that the national culture of the West Indies must be derived from the African tradition as rejuvenated by the West Indian, *Islands* is populated with an entire pantheon of African deities, whom the poet both invokes and transforms in order to counteract the myths of the Greco-Roman and Judeo-Christian traditions.

Brathwaite's New World trilogy has demonstrated eloquently to skeptics, including his Caribbean compatriots, that it is possible to create something out of the apparent nothingness of West Indian culture. Because the myth-making project started in *The Arrivants* offers promises of a national culture that Afro-Caribbeans can call their own, it came to be regarded as some sort of prelude to the second, or Bajan, trilogy, which attracted attention even before it was completed. "Bajan" means "Barbadian," so the trilogy is apparently meant to have national significance. Comprising *Mother Poem* (1977), *Sun Poem* (1982), and *X/Self* (1987), the Bajan trilogy focuses on the national character of the black Bajan as it is shaped by the social, historical, cultural, and anthropological forces of the Caribbean, Africa, and the West.

Barbados as the mother-island is epitomized by the figure of the subjugated woman in the text, in which readers see her conduct daily chores, undergo various ordeals, and harbor uncertain hopes with regard to the future of herself and her children. The futility of most of her efforts is symbolized by the "rock seed" that fails to germinate. The reason Brathwaite focuses on such a downtrodden figure is that slavery had extremely debilitating effects on what he calls "the manscape," the character of the Caribbean man who, while being a victim of slavery and colonialism, also contributes to the victimization of the black woman. Nevertheless, the woman survives in spite of the hardships because of her *nam*, thus making it possible for the new generation to emerge.

As a counterpoint to the geological symbolism and feminine realism of *Mother Poem*, the focus in *Sun Poem* is astronomical and masculine. The figure of the black male is rendered as the sun, which is both the son of creation (Adam) and the father-sun, as opposed to the mother-island. The sun is also connected with the rainbow, the agent that joins the earth and the sky. The poem is organized ingeniously so that the action is structured according to the cyclical trajectory of the sun, from dawn through dusk to dawn. Each of the episodes also links a certain human action to the cosmic action. For example, "The Crossing" refers both to the movement of the sun toward the meridian and to "the Middle Passage in reverse," whereas "Return of the Sun" refers both to the reemergence of the sun (after an eclipse) and to the return of the prodigal son. *Sun Poem* hence reenacts the double movement of *The Arrivants*, but it goes further by recasting it in cosmic terms. This cosmic dimension of the poem also turns the poet into a godlike creator.

With parental archetypes thus set up by the mythical framework of *Mother Poem* and *Sun Poem*, the last third of the trilogy, *X/Self*, is designed to complete the project with a portrayal of the offspring. Interestingly, in this puzzling poem such an offspring turns out to be a transhistorical figure called "X/Self," whose name may designate a crossed-out self, an ex-self, an exoself, or a creolized self. In the poem, X/Self, not unlike the visionary Tiresias, has witnessed many episodes in history. These historical events are mostly concerned with the conflict and interplay between the descendants of the Roman Empire—the white race—and the nonwhite races. The lines "rome burns/ and our slavery begins" serve as a leitmotif throughout and point to the dynamics of history that led to the rise and fall of civilizations and empires. Although the poem's action centers on Europe, the main thrust is anti-Eurocentric because the mission of X/Self, a voice representing the postcolonial consciousness of the Third World, is to offer a relentless critique of Western ideology. The poem that concludes the book, in which X/Self invokes Xango ("Pan African god of thunder, lightning, electricity and its energy, sound systems, the locomotive engine and its music"), celebrates the triumph of the mission.

The Bajan trilogy embodies the major themes that Brathwaite has been exploring throughout his career. In it, he achieved a formidable level of complexity and depth appropriate for his myth-making task. Brathwaite's capacity as a scholar played a prominent role in this tremendous project, but at the same time the poems are impressive as being intensely personal. Not unlike the first trilogy, the personal voice and the communal voice converge into a collective voice, but because of the mythological design of the work, on top of the collective voice emanating from the human characters and the personified landscape, a sacred voice also emerges that belongs to the cosmic process of creation.

The New World trilogy and the Bajan trilogy, because of their epic proportions, have rightfully established Brathwaite as one of the most prominent poets not only of the West Indies but also of the Third World. In his poetry as well as in his other writings, by focusing on the reconnection of the West Indies' submerged African heritage with the indigenous traditions still alive in postcolonial Africa, Brathwaite has created an idiom and a vocabulary that allow not only himself but also other writers to address and redress the problems of dispossession and fragmentation resulting from slavery and colonization. Brathwaite's contribution, in this light, is exemplary in that it goes beyond poetry per se and enters the realm of history itself.

Bibliography

Breiner, Laurence. "The Other West Indian Poet." In *Partisan Review* 56 (Spring, 1989): 316-320. A review of *X/Self.*

Dash, Michael. "Edward Brathwaite." In *West Indian Literature*, edited by Bruce King. Hamden, Conn.: Archon Books, 1979. One of the best earlier studies of Brathwaite's poetry.

Gowda, H. H. Anniah. "Edward Kamau Brathwaite: A Profile." In *Literary Half-Yearly* 23 (July, 1982): 40-46. Encapsulates the most important aspects of Brathwaite's career.

Martini, Jürgen. "Literary Criticism and Aesthetics in the Caribbean, I: E. K. Brathwaite." In *World Literature Written in English* 24 (Autumn, 1984): 373-383. Discusses the major aspects of Brathwaite's cultural position.

Pattanayak, Chandrabhanu. "Brathwaite: Metaphors of Emergence." In *The Literary Criterion* 17, no. 3 (1982): 60-68. A report based on Brathwaite's lectures given at the University of Mysore. Concise and excellent introduction to his poetry.

Thomas, Sue. "Sexual Politics in Edward Brathwaite's *Mother Poem* and *Sun Poem.*" In *Kunapipi* 9, no. 1 (1987): 33-43. A feminist critique of the visionary voice in the two poems.

Balance Chow

THE POETRY OF GWENDOLYN BROOKS

Author: Gwendolyn Brooks (1917-   )
Type of work: Poetry
First published: A Street in Bronzeville, 1945; *Annie Allen,* 1949; *Bronzeville Boys and Girls,* 1956 (children); *The Bean Eaters,* 1960; *Selected Poems,* 1963; *In the Mecca,* 1968; *Riot,* 1969; *Family Pictures,* 1970; *Aloneness,* 1971; *Beckonings,* 1975; *Primer for Blacks,* 1980; *To Disembark,* 1981; *The Near-Johannesburg Boy and Other Poems,* 1986; *Blacks,* 1987; *Gottschalk and the Grand Tarantelle,* 1988; *Winnie,* 1988

However the canon of African American poetry is to be construed—from Phillis Wheatley to Paul Laurence Dunbar, Countée Cullen to Langston Hughes, Amiri Baraka to Michael Harper, Robert Hayden to Haki Madhubuti—there can be no way of diminishing, or sidelining, the wholly singular achievement of Gwendolyn Brooks. Quite simply, she has ranked as a prime American imagination since her first collection, *A Street in Bronzeville.* Black by birthright, consciously or not "womanist" (in Alice Walker's term), she has shown the ability to range from a modernist experimentalism (Wallace Stevens, T. S. Eliot, and Countée Cullen being key influences) to a "down-home" intimacy of idiom drawn from blues, spirituals, jazz, and rap, and, from the start, the example of Langston Hughes. Even so, and despite the Pulitzer Prize that deservedly came her way in 1950 for *Annie Allen,* she remains seriously undervalued, a writer whose virtuosity only lately has begun to receive anything like its due.

Kansas-born but reared and educated in the Chicago of Hyde Park and the South Side, she attended in turn Hyde Park High School, the all-black Wendell Phillips High School, and Englewood High School before being graduated from Wilson Junior College in 1935. The "Bronzeville," or black Chicago, of her poems thus draws upon a lived familiarity.

Brooks is also a deeply committed family woman, and the strength of her relationship with her parents, David and Keziah Brooks, would readily carry over to her brother Raymond, to her husband and fellow poet, Henry Blakely, and to her two children, Henry, Jr., and Nora. Yet to Brooks "family" has long meant more, namely black "family" or "community" oneness. That attitude has shown in her poetry from the start, whether in "the old marrieds," from the 1940's, with its lovely cadence of "But in the crowding darkness not a word did they say," or in "The Last Quatrain of the Ballad of Emmett Till," from the 1960's, with its imagistic, affecting "She kisses her killed boy./ And she is sorry./ Chaos in windy grays/ through a red prairie," or in "Paul Robeson," from the 1980's, with its insistence "that we are each other's/ harvest:/ we are each other's/ business:/ we are each other's/ magnitude and bond." In each of these poems, as in most of her poetry, the colloquialism is subtle, a complex, highly wrought simplicity.

She has, moreover, never given way to polemic; the particularity of her poetry's voice and imagery guard against any inclination simply to lecture or harangue. In her teasingly reflexive "The Egg Boiler," as if to set a marker, she says of her "egg-boiler," "You come upon it as an artist should,/ With rich-eyed passion, and with straining heart." Similarly, in "The Chicago Picasso," she urges "We must . . . style ourselves for Art." In "To Don at Salaam," she writes approvingly of her great friend and fellow-poet, Don L. Lee (Haki Madhubuti), "Your voice is the listened-for music./ **Your** act is the consolation."

For all her insistence upon the private crafting of poetry, she has not shunned the American institutional domain or failed to bring her "Bronzeville" into a more public hearing. She has been a Guggenheim Fellow (1946); an invitee at the Library of Congress Poetry Festival (1962); an Honorary Doctor of Humane Letters in 1964 at Columbia College, Chicago; a participant in Fisk University's Second Black Writers' Conference (1967), from which she dates her "awakening" into the Black Arts movement and the thinking of the Black Aesthetic; Poet Laureate of Illinois (1969); recipient of *To Gwen with Love* (1971), a dedicatory volume written mainly by Chicago's Organization of Black American Culture; and poetry consultant to the Library of Congress (1985). In all these, her own insistence on her work as a form of ceremonial, an outgoing gift of the personal, has been paramount.

As synoptic a comment as any on the plenitude she has found in African American life can be met with in the opening of her five-part "Another Preachment to Blacks" in *Beckonings*:

> Your singing,
> your pulse, your ultimate booming in
> the not-so-narrow temples of your Power—
> call all that, that is your poem, AFRIKA.

Brooks's own "poem," or rather her own lifetime's "poem," begins with *A Street in Bronzeville*, her gallery of beautifully nuanced soliloquies and portraits. She evokes, for example, in "kitchenette building," the tenants whose "dream" must persist "through onion fumes" and "yesterday's garbage"; in "the mother," a woman who cannot forget her abortions; in "when Mrs. Martin's Booker T.," a woman whose son has "ruined Rosa Brown" and whose only wish is to see him "take that gal/ And get her decent wed"; in "The Sundays of Satin-Legs Smith" the zoot-suited Romeo whose dandyism barely compensates for his essential aloneness; in "Queen of the Blues," the shake-dancing, sad "Mame," alone and, for all her singing, thought of as no more than a figure out of cheap burlesque; and in "Gay Chaps at the Bar," and the accompanying sonnets, the death-threatened soldiers shortly off to war. All these "street" types she invokes as if slightly displaced, a community seen, and as it were heard, precisely, from an oblique angle of observation.

An equally elliptical, symbolist imagery energizes the poems that make up *Annie Allen*, the story of a "chocolate," acquiescent, brown-skinned girl whose dreams of romance die as tenement city life constricts and, finally, nearly buries her. The book's central component, "The Anniad," with its Homeric echo, is a cautionary tale against unused, unfulfilled womanhood. Even so, the Annie who arrives late to adult, feminine consciousness can say "Open my rooms, let in the light and air." Always dense in its racial and emotional imagery ("Harried sods dilate, divide,/ Suck her sorrowfully inside," as Brooks describes Annie in a Stevensesque turn of phrase at one point), *Annie Allen* as a sequence belongs in the company of James Joyce's *Dubliners* (1914) or Sherwood Anderson's *Winesburg, Ohio* (1919) as a small masterpiece of "the buried life." The redemption it offers lies in a shared, black, womanly maturity. Appropriately, Brooks concludes the section she entitles "The Womanhood" with the command "Rise./ Let us combine."

The Bean Eaters contains some of Brooks's best-honed poems, preeminent among them "In Honor of David Anderson Brooks, My Father," an exquisite memorial, with its opening Eliotesque quatrain: "A dryness is upon the house/ My father loved and tended./ Beyond his firm and sculptured door/ His light and lease have ended." Likewise, the collection's title poem calls upon memory, the intimate, unspoken remembrances of an "old yellow pair" amid "their rented back room that is full of beads and receipts and dolls and cloths, tobacco crumbs, vases and fringes." So lyric a poem plays against the staccato, imitatively laid-back youth talk of "We Real Cool," or the hard-hitting, satiric slap at white, middle-class patronage in "The Lovers of the Poor," which ends "They allow their lovely skirts to graze no wall,/ Are off at what they manage of a canter,/ And, resuming all the clues of what they were,/ Try to avoid inhaling the laden air." Brooks has never been short on variety.

Again, too, Brooks displays throughout a controlled impressionism, a poetry whose technical skills of free verse, of assonance, and of an inventive, unpredictable rhetoric of likeness in difference belie any apparent simplicity of theme. In this respect, the ending of "The *Chicago Defender* Sends a Man to Little Rock" bears out the point to perfection:

> And true, they are hurling spittle, rock,
> Garbage and fruit in Little Rock.
> And I saw coiling storm a-writhe
> On bright madonnas. And a scythe
> Of men harassing brownish girls.
> (The bows and barrettes in the curls
> And braids declined away from joy.)
>
> I saw a bleeding brownish boy. . . .
>
> The lariat lynch-wish I deplored.
>
> The loveliest lynchee was our Lord.

This poem, too, points the way to the radical change that came about for Brooks in the 1960's: her response, as one virtually reborn, to the call of Black Power. In each of her subsequent main collections, "Blackness" becomes a more explicit dynamic.

As she writes in "To Kereoapetse Kgositsile (Willie)," from *Family Pictures*, "Blackness is a going to essences and unifyings." In "Boys. Black," from *Beckonings*, she speaks from another vantage point, that of a motherly, custodial presence encouraging "Black Boys" to "Take my Faith./ Make of my Faith an engine./ Make of my Faith/ a Black Star. I am Beckoning."

One major impetus for this changed direction lay in her writerly association with Madhubuti, Baraka, and their fellow nationalists. Then, too, she reacted admiringly to the clenched-fist militancy of the Black Panthers, the Black Muslims, and other groups. She especially felt at one with the rest of black America in her reaction to the assassination of Martin Luther King, Jr., in 1968, and, on her home turf, with the ensuing "Chicago disturbances" under the regime of Mayor Richard Daley. Not least in her "awakening," was the pilgrimage she took to East Africa in 1971. So, in her *Report from Part One: An Autobiography* (1972), she could say engagingly:

> I—who have "gone the gamut" from an almost angry rejection of my dark skin by some of my brainwashed brothers and sisters to a surprised queenhood in the new black sun—am qualified to enter at least the kindergarten of new consciousness now. New consciousness and trudge-towards progress.
>
> I have hopes for myself.

In the Mecca, in its first part of the same name, portrays black Chicago as a multiverse, a polyglot, mosaical city of both high culture and vernacular African American memory and voices. Deservingly, it has been compared with Hart Crane's *The Bridge* (1930), another myth of urban America. In its second part, "After Mecca," Brooks can thus write both of "The Chicago Picasso" ("Art hurts. Art urges voyages") and of "The Blackstone Rangers" ("There they are./ Thirty at the corner./ Black, raw, ready./ Sores in the city/ that do not want to heal."), double-tokens of a citied, metropolitan America as a kind of living tableau. *Primer for Blacks* assumes a speaking voice even more direct: "Blackness/ is a title,/ is a preoccupation,/ is a commitment Blacks/ are to comprehend—/ and in which you are/ to perceive your Glory." She goes on, with not a little irony, to address the poem to "you proper Blacks,/ you half-Blacks, you wish-I-weren't Blacks." This same lack of solemnity, though with a ready affection, applies in her following poem, "To Those Sisters Who Kept Their Naturals." She writes "You never worshiped Marilyn Monroe./ You say: Farrah's hair is hers./ You have not wanted to be white," and, concluding, insists, "Your hair is Celebration in the world!"

Her "black" self-awakening, her "new black sun," continues over even more emphatically into *Beckonings*. Prefaced by an elegy to her recently dead brother, Raymond Melvin Brooks, *Beckonings* contains poems of high drama ("The Boy Died in My Alley"), a memorial to John Oliver Killens ("You were a mender/ You were a sealer of tremblings and long trepidations."), and, in "A Black Wedding Song," a kind of richly patterned anthem to black rebirth and strength ("I wish you jewels of black love"). The same inflection expresses itself, with a symptomatically deft indirection, in "Elegy in a Rainbow":

When I was a little girl
    Christmas was exquisite.
    I didn't touch it.
    I didn't look at it too closely.
    To do that
    might nullify the shine.

Thus with a Love
    that has to have a Home
    like the Black Nation,
    like the Black Nation
    defining its own Roof
    that no one else can see.

To Disembark contains the three-part "Riot," which is prefaced with Martin Luther King, Jr.'s, observation that "A riot is the language of the unheard," and which moves from a pioneer's negrophobia through a Chicago political shoot-out to a community back at one with itself ("On the street we smile"). The title poem, in turn, of *The Near-Johannesburg Boy and Other Poems* opens upon Soweto and the voice of a child coming to the embrace of, and the coming victory of, his own blackness:

Tonight I walk with
    a hundred of playmates to where
    the hurt Black of our skin is forbidden.
    There, in the dark that is our dark, there,
    a-pulse across earth that is our earth, there,
    there exulting, there Exactly, there redeeming, there
    Roaring Up. . . .
    we shall forge with the Fist-and-the-Fury:
    we shall flail in the Hot Time:
    we shall
    we shall

Chicago's South Side to Africa, "Bronzeville" to "Near-Johannesburg," Stevens or Cullen to Madhubuti or Baraka: The journey, in imagination as in life, has been a remarkable one for Gwendolyn Brooks. It has undeniably been uniquely her own, that of an American writer, an African American writer, at poetry's leading edge.

Bibliography

Evans, Mari, ed. *Black Women Writers, 1950-1980: A Critical Evaluation.* Garden City, N.Y.: Anchor Press/Doubleday, 1983. Reprints an extract from Brooks's autobiography, together with essays by Addison Gayle on black self-awareness in Brooks and by George Kent on the range of styles and voice in her poetry.

Kent, George E. *A Life of Gwendolyn Brooks.* Lexington: University Press of Kentucky, 1990. The most authoritative biography. Contains an excellent account of her Chicago upbringing and literary life, a full set of readings of the poetry and fiction, and a helpful placing of Brooks as a leading African American writer.

Madhubuti, Haki R., ed. *Say That the River Turns: The Impact of Gwendolyn Brooks.* Chicago: Third World Press, 1987. A timely celebration of Brooks both for her writings and her example as role model.

Mootry, Maria K., and Gary Smith, eds. *A Life Distilled: Gwendolyn Brooks, Her Poetry and Fiction.* Chicago: University of Illinois Press, 1987. Eighteen essays covering the entire range of Brooks's writing. Contains important essays by Houston A. Baker (on Brooks's overall achievement), George E. Kent (on Brooks's aesthetics), Gayl Jones (on "Community and Voice"), and Barbara Christian (on *Maud Martha*). The bibliography is especially helpful.

Shaw, Harry B. *Gwendolyn Brooks.* Boston: Twayne, 1980. Dutiful (if at times contentious) life-and-works overview. Annotated bibliography.

Tate, Claudia, ed. *Black Women Writers at Work.* New York: Continuum, 1983. Includes a revealing interview on Brooks's move toward black nationalism.

A. Robert Lee

THE POETRY OF STERLING BROWN

Author: Sterling Brown (1901-1989)
Type of work: Poetry
First published: Southern Road, 1932; *The Last Ride of Wild Bill and Eleven Narrative Poems,* 1975; *The Collected Poems of Sterling A. Brown,* 1980

Born into an educated, middle-class African American family, Sterling Allen Brown was the last of six children and the only son of Adelaide Allen Brown and the Reverend Sterling Nelson Brown. His father had taught in the School of Religion at Howard University since 1892, and the year Brown was born, his father also became the pastor of Lincoln Temple Congregational Church. The person who encouraged Brown's literary career and admiration for the cultural heritage of African Americans, however, was his mother, who had been born and reared in Tennessee and graduated from Fisk University. Brown also grew up listening to tales of his father's childhood in Tennessee, as well as to accounts of his father's friendships with noted leaders such as Frederick Douglass, Blanche K. Bruce, and Booker T. Washington.

Brown attended public schools in Washington, D.C., and was graduated from the well-known Dunbar High School, noted for its distinguished teachers and alumni; among the latter were many of the nation's outstanding black professionals. Brown's teachers at Dunbar included literary artists such as Angelina Weld Grimké and Jessie Redmon Fauset. Moreover, Brown grew up on the campus of Howard University, where there were many outstanding African American scholars, such as historian Kelly Miller and critic and philosopher Alain Locke.

Brown received his A.B. in 1922 from Williams College (Phi Beta Kappa) and his M.A. in 1923 from Harvard University. Brown then began a teaching career that took him to Virginia Seminary and College, Lincoln University in Missouri, and Fisk University before he settled at Howard University in 1929. He remained at Howard until his retirement in 1969, and died in Takoma Park, Maryland, on January 13, 1989.

The poetry of Sterling Brown is imbued with the folk spirit and culture of African Americans. For Brown there was no wide abyss between his poetry and the spirit inherent in slave poetry; indeed, his works evidence a continuity of racial spirit from the slave experience to the African American present and reflect his deep understanding of the multitudinous aspects of the African American personality and soul.

The setting for Brown's poetry is primarily the South, through which he traveled to listen to the folktales, songs, wisdom, sorrows, and frustrations of his people, and where the blues and ballads were nurtured. Brown respected traditional folk forms and employed them in the construction of his own poems; thus he may be called "the poet of the soul of his people."

Brown's first published collection of poems, *Southern Road,* was critically acclaimed by his peers and colleagues James Weldon Johnson and Alain Locke because of its rendering of the living speech of the African American, its use of the raw material of folk poetry, and its poetic portrayal of African American folk life and thought. Later critics such as Arthur P. Davis, Jean Wagner, and Houston Baker have continued to praise Brown's poetry for its creative and vital use of folk motifs. Some of the characters in Brown's poetry, such as Ma Rainey, Big Boy Davis, and Mrs. Bibby, are based on real people. Other characters such as Maumee Ruth, Sporting Beasley, and Sam Smiley seem real because of Brown's dramatic and narrative talent. He is also highly skilled in the use of poetic techniques such as the refrain, alliteration, and onomatopoeia, and he employs several stanzaic forms with facility. Brown's extraordinary gift for re-creating the nuances of folk speech and idiom adds vitality and authenticity to his verse.

Brown is successful in drawing upon rich folk expressions to vitalize the speech of his characters through the cadences of Southern speech. Though his poems cannot simply be called "dialect poetry," Brown does imitate Southern African American speech, using variant spellings and apostrophes to mark dropped consonants. He uses grunts and onomatopoeiac sounds to give a natural rhythm to the speech of his characters. These techniques are readily seen in a poem that dramatizes the poignant story of a "po los boy" on a chain gang. This poem follows the traditional folk form of the work song to convey the convict's personal tragedy.

Brown's work may be classed as protest poetry influenced by poets such as Carl Sandburg and Robert Frost; he is able to draw upon the entire canon of English and American poetry as well as African American folk material. Thus he is fluent in the use of the sonnet form, stanzaic forms, free-verse forms, and ballad and blues forms.

In *Southern Road*, several themes express the essence of the Southern African American's folk spirit and culture. Recurring themes and subjects in Brown's poetry include endurance, tragedy, and survival. The theme of endurance is best illustrated in one of his most anthologized poems, "Strong Men," which tells the story of the unjust treatment of black men and women from the slave ship, to the tenant farm, and finally to the black ghetto. The refrain of "Strong Men" uses rhythmic beats, relentlessly repeating an affirmation of the black people's ability and determination to keep pressing onward, toward freedom and justice. The central image comes from a line of a Carl Sandburg poem, "The strong men keep comin on." In "Strong Men," Brown praises the indomitable spirit of African Americans in the face of racist exploitation. With its assertive tone, the rhythm of this poem suggests a martial song.

Some of the endurance poems express a stoic, fatalistic acceptance of the tragic fate of the African American, as can be seen in "Old Man Buzzard," "Memphis Blues," and "Riverbank Blues." Another important aspect of the endurance theme as portrayed by Brown is the poetic characters' courage when they are confronted with tragedy and injustice. In the poem "Strange Legacies," the speaker gives thanks to the legendary Jack Johnson and John Henry for their demonstration of courage.

Brown's poems reflect his understanding of the often tragic destinies of African Americans in the United States. No poet before Brown had created such a comprehensive poetic dramatization of the lives of black men and women in America.

Brown depicts black men and women as alone and powerless, struggling nevertheless to confront an environment that is hostile and unjust. In this tragic environment,
African American struggles against the schemes of racist whites are seen in "The
Last Ride of Wild Bill," published in 1975 as the title poem of a collection. A black
man falls victim to the hysteria of a lynch mob in "Frankie and Johnnie," a poem
that takes up a familiar folktale and twists it to reflect a personal tragedy that occurs
as a result of an interracial relationship. Brown emphasizes that in this story the only
tragic victim is the black man. The retarded white girl, Frankie, reports her sexual
experience with the black man, Johnnie, to her father and succeeds in getting her
black lover killed; she laughs uproariously during the lynching. "Southern Cop"
narrates the mindless killing of a black man who is the victim of the panic of a
rookie police officer.

Yet Brown's poems show black people not only as victims of whites but also as
victims of the whole environment that surrounds them, including natural forces of
flood and fire as well as social evils such as poverty and ignorance. Rural blacks'
vulnerability to natural disasters is revealed in "Old King Cotton," "New St. Louis
Blues," and "Foreclosure." In these poems, if a tornado does not come, the Mississippi River rises and takes the peasant's arable land and his few animals, and even
kills his children. These poems portray despairing people who are capable only of
asking futile questions in the face of an implacable and pitiless nature. The central
character of "Low Down" is sunk in poverty and loneliness. His wife has left and
his son is in prison; he is convinced that bad luck is his fate and that in the workings
of life someone has loaded the dice against him. In "Johnny Thomas," the title
character is the victim of poverty, abuse by his parents and society, and ignorance.
(He attempts to enroll in a one-room school, but the teacher throws him out.) Johnny
ends up on a chain gang, where he is killed. The poem that most strongly expresses
African American despair of the entire race is "Southern Road," a convict song
marked by a rhythmic, staccato beat and by a blues line punctuated by the convict's
groaning over his accursed fate:

> My ole man died—hunh—
> Cussin' me;
> Old lady rocks, bebby,
> huh misery.

The African American's ability to survive in a hostile world by mustering humor,
religious faith, and the expectation of a utopian afterlife is portrayed in poems depicting the comical adventures of Slim Greer and in one of Brown's popular poems,
"Sister Lou." The series of Slim Greer poems, "Slim Greer," "Slim Lands a Job,"
"Slim in Atlanta," and "Slim in Hell," reveal Brown's knowledge of the life of the
ordinary black people and his ability to laugh at the weaknesses and foolishness of
blacks and whites alike. With their rich exaggerations, these poems fall into the tall-
tale tradition of folk stories. They show Slim in Arkansas passing for white although
he is quite dark, or Slim in Atlanta laughing in a "telefoam booth" because of a law

that keeps blacks from laughing in the open. In "Slim Lands a Job," the poet mocks the ridiculous demands that Southern employers make on their black employees. Slim applies for a job in a restaurant. The owner is complaining about the laziness of his black employees when a black waiter enters the room carrying a tray on his head, trays in each hand, silver in his mouth, and soup plates in his vest, while simultaneously pulling a red wagon filled with other paraphernalia. When the owner points to this waiter as one who is lazy, Slim makes a quick exit. In "Slim in Hell," Slim discovers that Hell and the South are very much alike; when he reports this discovery to Saint Peter, the saint reprimands him, asking where he thought Hell was if not the South.

In "Sister Lou," one of his well-known poems, Brown depicts the simple religious faith that keeps some blacks going. After recounting all the sorrows in Sister Lou's life, the poem pictures Heaven as a place where Sister Lou will have a chance to allow others to carry her packages, to speak personally to God without fear, to rest, and most of all to take her time. In "Cabaret," however, Brown shows the everyday reality that belies the promises God made to his people: The black folk huddle, mute and forlorn, in Mississippi, unable to understand why the Good Lord treats them this way. Moreover, in poems such as "Maumee Ruth," religion is seen as an opium that feeds people's illusions. Maumee Ruth lies on her deathbed, ignorant of the depraved life led by her son and daughter in the city, and needing the religious lies preached to her in order to attain a peaceful death.

Sterling Brown's poems embrace themes of suffering, oppression, and tragedy yet always celebrate the vision and beauty of African American people and culture. One such deeply moving piece is "Remembering Nat Turner," a poem in which the speaker visits the scene of Turner's slave rebellion, only to hear an elderly white woman's garbled recollections of the event; moreover, the marker intended to call attention to Turner's heroic exploits, a rotting signpost, has been used by black tenants for kindling. A stoic fatalism can be seen in the poem "Memphis Blues," which nevertheless praises the ability of African Americans to survive in a hostile environment because of their courage and willingness to start over when all seems lost: "Guess we'll give it one more try." In the words of Sterling Brown, "The strong men keep a-comin' on/ Gittin' stronger. . . ."

Bibliography
Davis, Arthur P. "Sterling Brown." In *From the Dark Tower: Afro-American Writers (1900 to 1960)*. Washington, D.C.: Howard University Press, 1974. A comprehensive study by the dean of African American critics. Davis knew Brown personally and taught with him at Howard University. Includes an extensive bibliography.

Huggins, Nathan. *Harlem Renaissance*. New York: Oxford University Press, 1971. An overall discussion of the Harlem Renaissance authors that views them in terms of their general historical and literary significance. Brown's work is considered alongside that of his literary contemporaries, and an overview of his major themes and concerns is given.

Redding, J. Saunders. *To Make a Poet Black.* Chapel Hill: University of North Carolina Press, 1939. This pioneering study gives an effective overview of the intellectual and literary influences on African American poets of the time. Although it includes only a few pages on Brown himself, it is essential background reading.

Redmond, Eugene B. *Drumvoices: The Mission of Afro-American Poetry, a Critical History.* Garden City, N.Y.: Anchor Press, 1976. Redmond treats the historical importance of the poet as well as his themes, images, language, and his use of the African American folk traditions and dialect. Redmond also discusses Brown's role as a critic.

Wagner, Jean. "Sterling Brown." In *Black Poets of the United States: From Paul Laurence Dunbar to Langston Hughes.* Translated by Kenneth Douglas. Urbana: University of Illinois Press, 1973. A comprehensive and insightful study of the poetry of Brown.

Betty Taylor-Thompson

THE POETRY OF LUCILLE CLIFTON

Author: Lucille Clifton (1936-   )
Type of work: Poetry
First published: Good Times, 1969; *Good News About the Earth,* 1972; *An Ordinary Woman,* 1974; *Two-Headed Woman,* 1980; *Good Woman: Poems and a Memoir, 1969-1980,* 1987; *Next: New Poems,* 1987; *Ten Oxherding Pictures,* 1989; *Quilting: Poems, 1987-1990,* 1991

Lucille Clifton's first collection of poems was published during the year after the assassination of Martin Luther King, Jr., and in the year of her father's death. She was thirty-three years old, and her mother had died eleven years earlier, at the age of forty-four. Yet in the book's title poem she admonishes readers to "think about the good times." The tough spirit of that practical wisdom, accepting, forgiving, determined, and celebratory, is the predominant tone of her artistry.

The voice that speaks this wisdom throughout Clifton's poetry is the voice of an empowered and empowering woman, and specifically a black woman whose identity has been molded by memories within a family that was given its genesis by American slavery. Yet through the figure of its female progenitor, Caroline Sayle, a midwife who was born eight years before her enslavement and died long after the Emancipation, these memories and Clifton's art sing about freedom symbolized by Africa and about a future symbolized especially by daughter-mothers yet to be born. In the perspective of Clifton's black American "Song of Myself," then, while she suffers grievous losses, her story echoes Walt Whitman's affirmation that "there is really no death,/ And if ever there was, it led forward life."

The members of Clifton's family play large roles in her poetry, and she has presented details and moving commentary on her family history in *Generations: A Memoir* (1976). The poet's father, Samuel Louis Sayles, Sr., recounted that his greatgrandmother was brought into slavery from Dahomey, West Africa, in 1822, when she was eight years old. She walked in a coffle to Virginia, where she was sold, away from her mother, to the Donald family, who named her Caroline. When she was a young woman, she was purchased by a neighboring plantation owner, who gave her in marriage to his slave Sam Louis Sale (1777-1860). She lived to 1910, a powerful figure in the region, a highly respected midwife to blacks and whites alike, with at least six children of her own. One of her daughters, Lucille (Lucy), bore a son, Gene Sayle (the "y" having been added after the Emancipation to distinguish the family from the former slaveholders), whose father was Harvey Nichols, a married carpetbagger. For killing Nichols with a rifle, Lucy was hanged. Gene and his wife, Georgia, had four children, including Clifton's father (who added the pluralizing "s" to the family name) and her Aunt Lucille. When Samuel's first wife died at age twentyone, leaving him with their infant daughter, Josephine, he married Thelma Moore, with whom he had a daughter, Thelma Lucille (the poet, born in 1936), and a son, Samuel, Jr. Lucille married Fred Clifton, with whom she parented—while becoming a writer of children's books and poetry—a family of four daughters and two sons; but Thelma Moore Sayles died, at age forty-four, one month before the birth of her first grandchild.

Five of Clifton's book titles suggest awareness of the lives of women, and indeed womanhood is a major presence in her art. As she wrote in 1987, "this is the tale/ i keep on telling/ trying to get it right." A long "line/ of black and going on women" in her poems reject and rediscover their blackness, endure cold, make mistakes, grieve, blame and dream, hunger and feed, bleed, break and break through, love and defend, "trust the Gods," expend their bodies, and perform with daily magic the making of families and homes. Although individuals sometimes fail or are destroyed, together they are the survivors through whom black America keeps pushing on. They "know how long and strong life is" and they know "what to do." In many poems, the history and fate of the family is presented in the form of a mother-daughter dialectic of the same but different self. To the mother, the daughter is "my more than me." The daughter "puts on a dress called woman," but does not forget. "Lucy/ is the history of/ her girls/ are the place where/ lucy/ was going."

Yet the good and the bad times in the lives of families are associated with men also. Men have the power to "murder it or/ marry it." Fathers may be frightening and haunting, may have to be forgiven their debts, but often they also love their families and provide. Men are gardeners who plant and who bloom in their own ways. The stunning beauty of black sons causes people to ask, "What is the meaning of this?" Black men suffer the annihilating power of racism, and Clifton's poems show some who waste to nil; but more "walk manly" and "don't stumble/ even in the lion's den." They bless blackness with the beauty of their ordinary comings and goings. Some become national leaders, imprisoned or assassinated, and a black man named Jesus brought the promise that "Men will be gods/ if they want it." Clifton's father was a griot who taught her the power of history; and her husband brought a saving and triumphant wholeness to her life and family history. In her poem "the message of fred clifton," Lucille's husband teaches from his fatal illness that "the only mercy/ is memory,/ . . . the only hell/ is regret."

Regret is rarely expressed in Clifton's writing, perhaps because memory has been such a strong feature of her artistry. As she wrote in *Generations*, "Who remembers the names of the slaves? Only the children of slaves." The bones of the black poet, she says, remember the soul of the African homeland, as the name, Lucille, remembers the ancestors of her African bloodline. She calls herself a "two-headed woman" who looks both outward and inward; while looking back along the way that her people and family have come, she looks ahead in the promise of constant renewal. History, then, is a garden ripe with living and cherishing memory, as in the exchange of "Do you remembers" while rocking on the porch, or in the giving and regiving of names.

Related to memory, naming is a feature of Clifton's understanding of her art, for in such acts the essential realities of persons are released: "we are lost from the field/ of flowers, we become/ a field of flowers." The job of the poet, Clifton explains in "the making of poems," is to try to give true names, and to accept the inevitable failures (or half-successes) of a being of flesh, since the rightful names, the true identities of persons and things, exist in the realm of pure spirit beyond life, while poems are made of "the blood that clots on your tongue." Nevertheless, as Clifton suggests in "my dream about time," without these attempts, persons would face the nightmare of a world for which they had no language, like a room full of clocks that all "strike/ NO."

So Clifton's art demands that she speak plainly and directly of the spiritual meaning and value of the ordinary human experiences that are held in common by all persons who are not blind to universal humanity. Clifton, herself, has overcome whatever racist stereotyping she has experienced in the black community; but often the whites whom she presents in poems are representative of those persons whom she has met or observed who are blinded by color prejudice, and much of the quality of American culture seems to her to reflect their weaknesses. She suggests, for example, that white New Englanders might view their rural landscape as a sign of a long past, but without responding to it as regenerative history. Therefore they become exploitative or, at best, careless, so that "the land is in ruins/ no magic, no anything." After all, though, their living history includes the stories of the Trail of Tears and the Middle Passage. The white men and women in those stories have faces that blacks, too, need to forget. In her early collections, whites are depicted as being spiritually and socially underdeveloped, pitiable creatures. They are lost souls who would not know what to do in really hard times. The ways of white men are the ways of death, killing their own trees, cities, and even children ("Kent State"). To Clifton, the resulting fear and loneliness of their alienation in time seems like the "final Europe" of the mind.

Africa, in contrast, is an idea of life unfettered by slavery and undistorted by preoccupation with racism. In such a life, persons grow into the selves of their natural design and responsible inclination, with respect for all humans and all species of life. It is "the life thing in us/ that will not let us die." The other name of that place is love.

The Dahomey women from whom Clifton is descended were warrior women who represent power and promise. To be descended from them is to know that one is free, even within the "temporary thing" of slavery. It is to know that one is under historical orders to fight for the truth and that one has the resources to carry on that struggle until the promised victory. It is also to know that to be a woman is to be the vessel of the magical power of the life-force itself. As Clifton writes in the poem "female": "there is an amazon in us/ she is the secret we do not/ have to learn./ . . . birth is our birthright."

Lucille means "light," and ten poems at the end of *Two-Headed Woman* tell of "the light that came to lucille clifton" and the voices of her ancestors that populated that light. Hearing them, in a room that was empty except for the poet, was an extraordinary experience of a kind that lent itself to sympathetic misinterpretation as madness. It shattered the poet's old verities and radically altered her perspective. Yet like the Zen enlightenment of satori, in its full effect it was as natural and ordinary as walking becomes for those who once were lame.

In "speaking of loss," Clifton says that she is "left with plain hands and/ nothing to give you but poems." She would suffer more losses, but the song of herself that began in the 1960's has continued to expand into a song beyond herself, just as the daughter begins in the mother but lives beyond her mother's identity and life.

Clifton's great-great-grandmother Caroline said to her daughter, also named Lucille, "Get what you want, you from Dahomey women." What Clifton's poems want, get, and give is life—the mysterious power that living offers to all who will accept its conditions, with tough good humor, and assert its truths.

Bibliography

Clifton, Lucille. "A Simple Language." In *Black Women Writers, 1950-1980: A Critical Evaluation*, edited by Mari Evans. Garden City, N.Y.: Anchor Press/Doubleday, 1983. A statement about being a black woman poet.

Lazer, Hank. "Blackness Blessed: The Writings of Lucille Clifton." *The Southern Review* 25, no. 3 (July, 1989): 760-770. Because the primary purpose of Clifton's poetry is to help African Americans to know themselves, her uses of language fuse political and aesthetic concerns.

McCluskey, Audrey T. "Tell the Good News: A View of the Works of Lucille Clifton." In *Black Women Writers, 1950-1980: A Critical Evaluation*, edited by Mari Evans. Garden City, N.Y.: Anchor Press/Doubleday, 1983. Notes that in her poetry and children's books, Clifton writes with realism and the strength to say "yes" to life.

Madhubuti, Haki. "Lucille Clifton: Warm Water, Greased Legs, and Dangerous Poetry." In *Black Women Writers, 1950-1980: A Critical Evaluation*, edited by Mari Evans. Garden City, N.Y.: Anchor Press/Doubleday, 1983. An interpretation by noted African American poet of the importance of Clifton's poetry for African Americans.

Rushing, Andrea Benton. "Lucille Clifton: A Changing Voice for Changing Times." In *Coming to Light: American Women Poets in the Twentieth Century*, edited by Diane Wood Middlebrook and Marilyn Yalom. Ann Arbor: University of Michigan Press, 1985. The major influence on Clifton's poetry was the Black Arts movement of the 1960's and 1970's, with its emphasis upon political, sexual, and spiritual liberation, black speech and music, the intuited truths of black experience, and a black audience. Clifton has found her own voice in writing about women's issues, the psychic tensions in the complex lives of modern women, her family heritage, and her religious experience.

Scarupa, Harriet Jackson. "Lucille Clifton: Making the World 'Poem-Up'." *Ms.* 5, no. 4 (October, 1976): 118, 120, 123. A visit to Clifton's home reveals the relationship between her life experiences and themes in her poetry.

Tom Koontz

THE POETRY OF WANDA COLEMAN

Author: Wanda Coleman (1946-   )
Type of work: Poetry
First published: Art in the Court of the Blue Fag, 1977; *Mad Dog Black Lady,* 1979; *Imagoes,* 1983; *Heavy Daughter Blues: Poems and Stories, 1968-1986,* 1987; *The Dicksboro Hotel and Other Travels,* 1989; *African Sleeping Sickness: Stories and Poems,* 1990.

Born and reared in the slums of Los Angeles, Wanda Coleman writes passionately about her life as a member of the dispossessed and downtrodden in that city, re-creating its outrageous banalities, mundane sufferings, and quotidian tragedies not only as an eyewitness but also as a player of the drama. She is best known for the anger in her poetry, which she has sometimes read to audiences dramatically by getting on all fours and barking like a mad dog. Largely neglected by literary circles and academia beyond the Pacific Coast, Coleman, who knows firsthand what it means to be a welfare mother, a typist, a waitress, an editor for a soft-core pornographic magazine, and a medical clerk, is a grass-roots poet whose outcry comes straight from the hearts of a largely silent majority of marginalized "minorities."

Coleman's anger is inseparable from her day-to-day experience of poverty, racism, and sexism, but concomitant with the anger is her love for the community that has defined the meaning of her life. As Coleman reveals in an interview, "I have one desire—to write. And, through writing, control, destroy, and create social institutions. I want to wield the power that belongs to the pen." The racial riot in Watts in 1965 led Coleman to participate in community service for young blacks, thus preparing her for a writing career. Fighting against tremendous odds, she ventured into experimental theater and dance and then took up scriptwriting. Although she later went on to win an Emmy Award (for an episode of the soap opera "Days of Our Lives") in 1976, she was disillusioned by Hollywood and began to concentrate on writing poetry and short fiction.

Coleman's poetry is informed by black speech and the blues tradition; her background in drama and scriptwriting also has an impact on her poetry. What sets her apart, however, are her writing habits, which are closely tied to the chores and burdens of her quotidian life. Speaking to her interviewers, Coleman describes herself as a "catch-as-catch-can" writer: "I write poems while I'm standing in line at the supermarket, while the car is getting fixed. When you are poor, you spend a lot of time waiting. I never wanted to waste that time, so I always had a book or notebook handy, something I could work on." Her notes she turns into poems, and if they do not come out right, she will keep them for future use. Because of these habits, she has developed what may be described as an "accumulative notebook style." A Coleman poem often comes into being when enough notes on a certain topic are gathered, and now and then a new poem under a previously used title will emerge when additional notes are collected.

Coleman's first book, *Art in the Court of the Blue Fag*, contains examples characteristic of her poetry. Focusing on the goings-on in a pornographic film studio and the inner thoughts of the producer, his associates, and the actors and actresses, the three title poems exemplify Coleman's application of the scriptwriting technique to poetry, with scenes fading and zooming in and out according to the shifting of perspectives. More significant, furthermore, is her treatment of sexual exploitation as a theme, here allegorized by means of the "court" of the "blue fag" and his associates, a murderously calculating and apathetic clique.

With regard to *Mad Dog Black Lady*, the book by which Coleman's reputation was established, she has explained that "being a mad dog . . . was one image I had for myself in terms of my response to racism. I had to be either cured or killed. And there is no cure for rabies. . . . 'Mad Dog' is also slang for Mogen David 20/20, a 'rot gut' favored by winos." Many poems in the book contain powerful, if shocking, expressions that bespeak her anger. For example, the persona in "Where I Live" claims that she lives "at the lip of a big black vagina/ birthing nappy headed pickaninnies every hour on the hour," and goes on to state that "the country is her pimp and she can turn a trick/ swifter than any bitch ever graced this earth/ she's the baddest piece of ass on the west coast/ named black los angeles." In the slum-scape typified by "Somewhere" and many other poems, Coleman depicts such characters as a man dropping to his death from the top of a building to avoid his debt-collector ("Untitled"), a waitress slipping out "to give/ pussy to cute yellow don" in order to get extra tips ("At the Stop"), a number of prostitutes, including a teenage male ("Dear Little Boy"), cannibals ("Woman Eater"), and so forth. The injustices of society, as epitomized by these characters, have driven the poet to compare herself to an African warrior who, though dripping blood, must fight against the white wolf (racism) that "has a fetish for black meat" ("Doing Battle with the Wolf").

Apart from autobiographical poems where the poetic persona and Coleman are identical (such as the clerks in "Doctor Spider," "Drone," and "Accounts Payable"), one of the most important personas in the book is the black woman, who as a composite figure voices her protests against her society. In "A Black Woman's Hole," she complains how, after she has struggled to transform her "hole" of an apartment into a paradise, "if the world knew it would put her hole up for sale and turn her out." Unmistakably, the black woman's protests are often couched in terms of the economics and politics of sex. For example, in "Sweet Mama Wanda Tells Fortunes for a Price," the persona is a prostitute who calls herself happy in strictly economic terms; in "No Woman's Land," the black woman condemns "love politics" as "a legislature of pricks." The black woman, represented as the object of many seductions ("The Deuce of Cups"), is constantly scared of being hurt and abandoned ("Wanda in Worryland"). She curses and threatens the "bourgeois nigger bitch" who has jilted her ("The Red Queen"), muses on how in order to survive "you have to sort out all the shit life keeps/ dishing into your bowl" ("An Overdose of Lovers"), and advises that a woman judge a man by his silences ("You Judge a Man by the Silence He Keeps"). Sexuality, then, is one of the most important figures of speech in Coleman's imagination; it has a positive role to play in the black woman's protests as well as in the poet's project of self-definition in the autobiographical poems. Along with race and gender, it constitutes Coleman's rhetoric of "doing battle with the wolf" as a "mad dog black lady."

Imagoes continues the major tendencies of *Mad Dog Black Lady*, but a new trend also begins to emerge. As Coleman has explained to interviewers, the book's title refers not only to the "sexually mature state of insect larvae" (of butterflies and moths) but also to the "idealized state of self" and "images." "Imagoes" as a term hence signals the evolution of Coleman's self-identity as a developing artist. In the title poem, the poet transposes her meditation on imagoes to a mediation of self ("white birds do not eat them/ they taste bitter"), and confronts her phobia of moths and butterflies until, through a semiconscious state induced by the sexual ecstasy of the present and the dreamlike memory of her ancestry, she is transformed in such a way that "*in my soul winged beings flutter.*" The poem can be regarded as emblematic of Coleman's self-fashioning maneuvers in the book, the main concern of which is her quest, through the perfection of expressive language, for a sexually and spiritually mature (or idealized) self.

Coleman's quest is evident from the first two poems in *Imagoes.* "In Search of the Mythology of Do Wah Wah" rewrites Greco-Roman civilization in terms of the melodrama of racist America: "oedipus, spawned on the breeding plantations of civil war america/ slays his white father and covets his black mother." "Daddyboy," a sketch of her father's life, is the poet's poignant recognition of her own identity through her father's; when the family's children address their father as "daddyboy," an affectionate nickname, he reacts angrily, and the family's mother must explain that "your father's black. white people/ disrespect black men by calling them boy/ call him anything but." Having thus established the Africanness of her being, Coleman moves on to a series of three poems about a "radical revolutionary red neck" from Georgia who became a civil rights fighter and who married a black woman in Watts (the "Jerry" poems). The interracial marriage undergoes various ordeals and concludes on a tragic note: "history lay between them/ love did not survive injustice." The failure of this interracial relationship, apparently followed by other unsuccessful relationships (in "Mama's Man" and "Men Lips"), leads the poet to reflect bitterly: "men come and go/ i whisper to my shadow, 'there's a qualitative/ difference between a love and a fuck'" ("Diagnosis").

Sexuality is once again employed as a figure of speech, in this case to exemplify how the black woman's fashioning of the self entails the maturity not only of the spiritual being but of her sexual being as well. This quest is traced skillfully in part 2 of *Imagoes*, where the poet explores a full range of the black woman's experience of sexuality, including pregnancy, childbirth, motherhood, family life, household chores, domestic conflicts, separation, sexual escapades, single-parenting, unemployment, and welfare life. In these poems, Coleman registers the ontological difference of the black woman in urban America as a person marginalized not only by race but also by gender and economics. This ontological difference, which some feminist critics have come to recognize as the hallmark of black women's writings, is best captured in "Rape," a tour de force dramatizing how a woman raped during a burglary is subjected to multiple levels of victimization by the rapists, the police, and even her husband. Realistic vignettes such as "Rape" make clear that, in Coleman's poetry, sexuality has come to mean sexual politics as well. Accordingly, her quest for maturity in spiritual and sexual being is also an allegory for the struggle of African American women in society and in history.

In *Imagoes*, Coleman is noticeably in better command of her poetic idioms. She has started polishing her language; it is less cryptic and disjointed, more fluent and pliant. The poet can afford the luxury of wry humor ("Dinner with a Friend") or even an occasionally playful gesture of complacency ("Pigging Out"). Indeed, Coleman's anger now serves as an undertone rather than as the dominant melody. This change is epitomized by a poem in which the previous book's "mad dog" reappears under a different guise: "blue bruise my thigh i won the fight . . . / blue bruise my thigh after fight/ . . . / blue day he came got his clothes left the key/ . . . / blue monday street rife with hustle muscle and winos/ sipping blue grape mad dog 20/20" ("Blue"). The mad dog, no longer a dog but the slang term for a kind of liquor, is not so much a metaphor for anger as an agent of the blues, a form that Coleman begins to favor from this volume on.

Heavy Daughter Blues is a showcase of Coleman's literary art in the lyric, dramatic, and narrative modes. Here, although the poet is covering familiar ground, the storytelling impulse is stronger, and third-person perspectives begin to dominate. Frequently, the poetic self seems to disappear from the text, particularly in character studies ("Mother Taylor" and "Mister Clark") and blues poems ("Trouble on My Doorsteps Blues" and "Bottom Out Blues"). An important hint about the character of this volume can be found in "Walking Paper Blues," where the figure of the "mad dog" for which Coleman is known is used in the context of the blues: "if'n yo don't fire me soon/ i'm leavin' he-ah today/ . . . / mah soul nevah been he-ah/ mah heart been gone fo days/ got me a fifth o mad dog/ to celebrate this day." Here, the emphasis has shifted from anger and helplessness to celebratory defiance, thus signaling the self-sufficiency characteristic of the mature self. Because the poetic self is quietly in control rather than submerged, the volume demonstrates Coleman's success in achieving the maturity that she sought earlier in *Imagoes*.

In *African Sleeping Sickness*, Coleman continues to excel in her regular repertoire ("Notes of a Cultural Terrorist," "Starved for Affection Blues," "In the Kitchen My Potatoes Are Polemical," "Self-Immolation," and others), but has expanded it to include a discourse on acquired immune deficiency syndrome (AIDS), in "Current Events," "The Educational Lab Counselor," "A Late 80s Party," "Obituaries," "A Civilized Plague," "The Article in the Newspaper," and "Nesomania (2)." Also apparent are Coleman's attempts to enhance her expressiveness by experimenting with form ("American Sonnet" and "Koan") and language in order to address the issues of the American Dream more effectively. The two title poems, which are rather obscure, employ medical metaphors to illustrate a black woman's experience of feelings of inauthenticity, distintegration, and loss of self, a complex syndrome that, in turn, signifies the dysfunctionality of African American communities as a consequence of slavery, racism, oppression, and mistreatment. In the first "African Sleeping Sickness" poem, the disease is associated with the persona's insistence on memory, language, dreaming, and becoming; in the second, the disease is related to the persona's sexuality. In both poems, the persona implores the implied listener to sing to her of rivers, an allusion to Langston Hughes's "The Negro Speaks of Rivers." Significantly, Coleman does not stop at hinting that the American Dream is the general issue; at the end of the second poem, by announcing that "between my thighs runs the river whiskey and he—he is a divin' duck," the persona also reiterates Coleman's rhetoric of sexuality, linking the American Dream to gender issues.

A closer examination of some other poems in *African Sleeping Sickness* reveals that Coleman's rhetoric of sexuality also begins to focus on the reproductive aspect of the central motif. An important example is the first poem of the book, "Black Madonna," in which the poet characterizes the archetypal black woman as the "night of nights" and "victim of victims," with legions of children tearing at her breasts and partaking of her flesh, thus calling into question the relevance of the crucifixion. Rejecting Christianity as a religion oppressive to blacks, the poet turns to the Egyptian goddess Isis to celebrate her procreative fertility ("Black Isis"). Another telling example is "Baby I've Got the Reds," where the poet transforms the language of the blues into a discourse about the inherent relationship between abortion and poverty. As a counterpoint, in "Art in the Court of the Blue Fag (9)," the persona's surrealistic, abortionlike childbirth is associated with wealth-generating exploitation. The language of reproduction begins to permeate Coleman's poetry to the extent that even menstruation begins to play the role of poetics: When a male poet asks his wife whether she likes his poems, "she took off the sanitary napkin she was wearing/ and plopped it on the page/ 'needs more blood in it'/ and went back to the kitchen" ("Ars Poetica"). This reproductive rhetoric boldly reiterates Coleman's persistent concern with how the social role of the black woman is governed by sexual politics; by reinstating reproduction as an integral part of the black woman's sexuality, Coleman has in effect challenged the politics that has sought, through distorted and reified notions of sexuality, to reduce black women to "the victim of victims."

If Wanda Coleman's poetry strikes readers as being polemical and quarrelsome in intention and graphic and grotesque in expression, it is because she has succeeded in a clinically candid and esthetically unique representation of America as a pathological society. As she has said to interviewers, "The body politic of America is gangrenous"; and what she tries to do, she says, is to get diagnostic studies underway, to "cut open the flesh and see that sepsis"—which is, of course, not pretty, but which is nevertheless real. Because the issues that she addresses are relevant to so many, her poetic voice demands urgent attention.

Bibliography
Coleman, Wanda. "Clocking Dollars." In *African Sleeping Sickness: Stories and*

Poems. Santa Rosa, Calif.: Black Sparrow Press, 1990. An important position statement by the poet about the impact of poverty on her writing; also shows how Coleman, as a marginalized author, differs from other black writers sanctioned by the establishment.

—————————. "Sweet Mama Wanda Tells Fortunes: An Interview with Wanda Coleman." Interview by Tony Magistrale and Patricia Ferreira. *Black American Literature Forum* 24, no. 3 (Fall, 1990): 491-507. A lengthy, comprehensive interview. Essential reading for Coleman scholars.

Goldstein, Laurence. "Looking for Authenticity in Los Angeles." *Michigan Quarterly Review* 30, no. 4 (Fall, 1991): 717-731. Contains a review of *African Sleeping Sickness* and discusses Coleman's work in the ethnic and cultural context of Los Angeles.

Magistrale, Tony. "Doing Battle with the Wolf: A Critical Introduction to Wanda Coleman's Poetry." *Black American Literature Forum* 23, no. 3 (Fall, 1989): 539-554. An indispensable in-depth study of Coleman's poetry.

Williams, Sherley Anne. "The Blues Roots of Contemporary Afro-American Poetry." In *Afro-American Literature: The Reconstruction of Instruction*, edited by Dexter Fisher and Robert B. Stepto. New York: Modern Language Association, 1979. Shows how African American women poets are inspired by the blues tradition.

Balance Chow

THE POETRY OF JAYNE CORTEZ

Author: Jayne Cortez (1936-   )
Type of work: Poetry
First published: Pissstained Stairs and the Monkey Man's Wares, 1969; *Festivals and Funerals,* 1971; *Scarifications,* 1973; *Mouth on Paper,* 1977; *Firespitter,* 1982; *Coagulations: New and Selected Poems,* 1984

Jayne Cortez is a poet of anger who utilizes urban scenes of violence and dehumanization. Her poetry is a volatile mixture of major trends in both the art and the politics of the twentieth century. She is a social revolutionary, passionately interested in the plight of downtrodden people everywhere, and she is a seeker of African roots and bases of morality who uses the techniques of free verse, borrowing artistic concepts from surrealism. Hers is a prophetic voice that uses jazz rhythms and relates existentialist philosophy. Her insistence on discovering the origins of African moral concepts and her use of a voice that has the overtones of Old Testament prophecy indicate that she is also very much aware of the uses of the past.

Jean-Paul Sartre, the great twentieth century French existential writer, named authors who write out of their revolt against colonialism as the *mauvaise foi,* or those of bad faith. His study of the work of Leon Damas, a black novelist and poet originally from French Guiana, brought to light the elements that enabled Sartre to make his analysis. Damas and his friend Leopold Senghor of Senegal were important writers in Paris in the 1930's and early 1940's. These two, along with their friend Aimé Césaire of Martinique, went on to develop the concept of Negritude, an aesthetic and ideological affirmation of Negro culture. The first mention of this concept occurs in a line in a poem by Césaire written in 1939. The ideas of these three writers obviously have influenced Jayne Cortez. There is no doubt that she is in revolt against a racist society and its norms, which she sees as exploitive and destructive. There is another facet to her poetry, however, in her celebratory poems about black and African themes and people, whom she affirms.

Cortez's revolt against the society in which she finds herself centers on the city, specifically New York City, where she lives. One of her most powerful poems bears its name, "I Am New York City." It was originally collected in *Scarifications*; in the later *Coagulations: New and Selected Poems,* she gave it the first page. In many ways it is emblematic of her work. She anthropomorphizes the city, using street language. Her metaphors are violent and often repulsive, and she relies heavily on bodily parts and functions, especially scatological functions.

Like much of her work, the poem has literary antecedents. It cannot help but call to the reader's mind Carl Sandburg's poem "Chicago," written in 1914. In Sandburg's poem, there is a celebration of raw power and untamed insolence. His city is masculine, powerful, and young. Sandburg does mention the negative side of Chicago but gives it only three lines, admitting that in Chicago he has seen "painted women . . . luring the farm boys," that the city is "crooked," that its "gunmen kill and go free to kill again." His third negative line admits that the city is brutal and that the narrator has seen the marks of "wanton hunger" on women and children's faces. After this brief unfavorable notice, Sandburg goes back to affirming his obviously robust and masculine town. Sandburg's city is of the working class, but it is young and strong; it hopes to rise in life through strength and "cunning."

Jayne Cortez's poem does not celebrate New York. Rather, it dissects the city. Sandburg's city was definitely masculine; her city appears to be feminine. In early stanzas, the city appears to be exploited and old, a woman with "legs apart" who has her "contraceptives." She is not proud of her profession, however, and says in the next line, "look at my pelvis blushing." If New York is a painted woman, she is not pretty, desirable, or even healthy. She has only half an ankle and half an elbow, and she wears a "rat tail wig." This city presents a character completely different from Sandburg's. Sandburg sees "wanton hunger" on the faces of women and children; the reader may wonder if the slut depicted by Cortez is sluttish because of this very real physical hunger. Sandburg has names and metaphors for Chicago; Cortez gives a physical description of the city-woman who sports "my marquee of false nipples/ my sideshow of open beaks/ in my nose of soot." Sandburg portrays his town as laughing and bragging, but Cortez's will "piss/ into the bite of our handshake." She ends her description by inviting its citizens to "break wind with me."

This poem introduces Jayne Cortez's anger at a society that allows such filth, such waste, and such disregard for decent human values. She blames the economic and political system, laying out her premises quite baldly in "There It Is," a poem addressed to black people. In this poem she insists that the "ruling class" will try to exploit, absorb, confine, disconnect, isolate, or kill to preserve its privileges. She sees drugs as tools used by white society to "ossify" black society. Her solution is for members of the black community to fight, resist, organize, unify, and control their own lives. She warns that if they do not, the "dehumanized look of fear" and the "decomposed look of repression" will be theirs forever.

Sandburg gives women and children a mere mention, but Cortez is terribly concerned about what happens to them, particularly black women and children, in the city. In her poem "Give Me the Red on the Black of the Bullet," she asks for the bullet that hit Claude Reece, Jr., a fourteen-year-old shot accidentally or otherwise by New York City police. She wants to make a statue, wants to make an "explosion of thunder," wants to make a "cyclone of protest." She insists that she wants the bullet to make power for "the blackness called pent-up frustration/ called unidentified negro/ called nigger revolutionary."

In Cortez's city, black children are shot and women are raped. "Rape" is about the situations faced by Inez Garcia and Joanne Little, who were victims of this crime in the 1970's. Cortez equates the violence of the act of rape with the violence of the act of war. Inez Garcia's rapist "carved a combat zone between her breasts." Then he expected her to "lick crabs from his hairy ass/ kiss every pimple on his butt." After the rape, when the three-hundred-pound man started coming at her again with a knife, she was able to grab a rifle and started "doing what a defense department will do in times of war." Another victim, Joanne Little, killed a policeman with an ice pick when he attempted to rape her. Cortez asks what Little was supposed to do: "choke on his clap trap balls/ squeeze on his nub of rotten maggots"? Cortez ends the poem in a celebratory mode, saying "from coast to coast/ house to house/ we celebrated the day of the dead rapist punk/ and just what the fuck else were we supposed to do."

Sandburg personifies his city as a strong, young worker who embodies hope because he can work and because he has jobs. Many black people find that there is no way that they can get jobs, no way that they can hope to be part of the mainstream. In "Blood Suckers," she shows her concern for what happens to people of color both in the United States and elsewhere. She rails against those forces of politics and economics that literally siphon off the lifeblood of the people. She sees corrupt officials in Miami "resucking/ the dried mutilated scalps of a Seminole nation." Their corruption is not limited to people—they destroy animals and the environment as well. She finds them "grunting and chewing and pissing" on stuffed alligators. They are sucking in "little Pretoria" and in the dumps of Love Canal, the city built on a toxic dump, and Liberty City, the section of Miami torn by black rioters.

The combination of capitalism and exploitation knows no national boundaries, and in Jayne Cortez's poems, it knows no moral boundaries. In *Firespitter* (1982), she includes a poem entitled "Nigerian/American Relations." It has only two lines, repeated to fill a page: "They want the oil/ But they don't want the people." She is equally explicit in "Expenditures: Economic Love Song 1," which appears in the section of new poems in *Coagulations*. In that poem, she writes entirely in capital letters. The poem consists of two two-line stanzas that are repeated to fill almost two pages. They read:

> MILITARY SPENDING HUGE PROFITS &
> DEATH
>
> MILITARY SPENDING HUGE PROFITS &
> DESTRUCTION

In "Firespitters," a poem about an African city, Cortez's tone changes. She attended the Second World Black and African Festival of Arts and Culture (FESTAC) in Lagos, Nigeria. This experience served to heighten her interest in African politics and gave her insights into her African roots. The city of Lagos has the element of hope that the reader finds in Sandburg's Chicago. Although Cortez recognizes the problems in Lagos, the city calls up images of both her father and her mother. She sees the firespitters in her poem of that name, their "lips spreading like/ stripes and medals from the chest of my father." She also sees "torches gleaming like/ the gold tooth of my mother." Here she finds a homeland that is both beautiful and ugly, but it teems with energy just as Sandburg's Chicago did. She finds "painted skins swiveling pupils gut blasting moans and/ the supersonic sound of invisible orchestras." Although Lagos is not a perfect city, as she travels past the city dumps on the outskirts she feels an exhilaration at the "dark puree of flesh in a mask of spinning mirrors." She encourages the city, like a dancer, to "shake everything in your beautiful nasty self/ we're here."

Although Sandburg merely mentions singing in "Chicago," he was interested in music and traveled across the country to collect folk songs. Jayne Cortez's interest in music also goes deep. She often reads her poetry with musical accompaniment, and she has made several recordings of her poetry. At many of her readings throughout the United States, the Caribbean, and Europe, she has used a background of music. She also has written a number of celebratory poems about people, especially black musicians. These include "Rose Solitude (For Duke Ellington)," and "So Many Feathers," for Josephine Baker, the famous singer, dancer, and entertainer who found fame in Paris and worked in the resistance movement in World War II, winning the Legion of Honor for her dangerous activities. Baker later adopted numerous orphans.

In Sandburg's poem about Chicago, there is only one mention of art. His city is "singing so proud to be alive and coarse and strong and cunning." Music is far more important to Cortez. She invokes it and its artists often, frequently referring to jazz. In "Tapping," from *Scarifications*, she calls up a "Johnny Hodges like" theme, "Charlie Parker riffs," a "Coltrane yelp," "a Satchmo pitch," and "Ma Rainey Blues." She is especially interested in drums and invokes them and their percussive sounds in several poems. One of these is "If the Drum Is a Woman." She repeats several phrases in this work, using the title line a number of times as well as repeating "why are you" and "your drum is not." She ends the poem with the drumbeat sounds of "don't abuse your drum/ don't abuse your drum/ don't abuse your drum." Different kinds of drums occur in "I See Chano Pozo," all of which have marvelous sounds in their names: Atamo, Mpebi, Donno, Obonu Atumpan, Mpintintoa, Ntenga, Siky Akkua, Bata, and Fontomfrom. Cortez's drum names are also drum sounds of great subtlety.

With or without mention of music and musicians, her celebratory poems often use words or syllables that emulate drumbeats. "The Red Pepper Poet (For Leon Damas)" is one of these. At the end of almost every line, she uses "ah," "a," "uh-huh," or "uh-hun." The final stanza incorporates "ah," placing that word next to "I." This use of single syllables detached from the syntax produces a percussive effect that adds emphasis to Cortez's tribute to a poet whose work embodies many of her own major concerns. Damas' work reflects his influences: the French surrealist painters, the literature and music of the Harlem Renaissance, and the speech of working-class people. These influences are also Cortez's, although her criticism of colonial concepts and racism is excoriation rather than protest.

This use of extra syllables at line endings occurs in another significant celebratory poem, "For the Poets (Christopher Okigbo & Henry Dumas)." Both of these young black men were killed early in their careers. Henry Dumas, an extremely talented short-story writer who was active in the Civil Rights movement, was killed by a New York City subway policeman, ostensibly in a case of mistaken identity. Christopher Okigbo, a young African poet who served as a major in the Biafran army during the Nigerian civil war, was killed in action. In this poem, Cortez celebrates their lives, making a "delta praise for the poets," and lashes out at the killers and at white officials who support black intertribal warfare "Because they'll try and shoot us/ like they shot Henry Dumas huh/ because we massacre each other/ and Christopher Okigbo is dead uh-huh/ because i can't make the best of it uh-hun/ because i'm not a bystander uh-hun." Cortez is not a bystander. She is a fighter, and she urges others to stand up and fight.

Even poetic form is a matter of principle with her. Both Sandburg and Cortez utilize the forms of free verse, Sandburg being one of its early pioneers. For Cortez, its use is a matter both of aesthetics and of politics. In "Plain Truth," she refers to a "They" that can only be the same "They" of "Bloodsuckers." In this poem, one of the new poems in *Coagulations*, she says, "They want you/ to hate yourself" and "Suck/ their national standard/ of/ dead metrical feet/ and free-base into/ refugee camp. . . ." This line indicates that Cortez equates the old metrical forms with oppression. Like Adrienne Rich and other contemporary poets, she sees free verse as not only form but also substance.

Both poets also use repetition. Sandburg slightly rephrases his opening stanza and uses all of its ideas in his closing stanza of "Chicago." This is a technique that Cortez uses frequently. A number of her poems repeat the first stanza or variations of it in the last stanza. Her "I Am New York City" does this, making the parallels with Sandburg unmistakable. Her opening line, "i am new york city," is also the opening line of her last stanza.

In addition to repetition and the sounds from music, Cortez uses the shock value of scatological language and vivid images of degradation. Her metaphors are often unusual to the point of obscurity, although they may at times represent some in-group knowledge. All of her work appears in free verse, but in the later poems in *Coagulations* she experiments with various shapes on the page.

Her early work often used short lines to describe subjects and locales of the United States. In her later poetry, her lines lengthened and her subject matter became universal, but her anger, which was her first hallmark, did not abate. Her voice in her poetry is so strong that the reader is confident that it is also the voice in her life. She confronts, battles, and exhorts others to take their lives in their own hands, to make their destinies by their own actions. She does not depend on any *deus ex machina*, any intervention from heaven. She lives and writes about the world in which she lives, and she is determined to work with what is available in the here and now in a revolutionary existential approach.

If her work is polemic and didactic, and if sometimes her politics supersedes her poetry, her outrage against the conditions in New York City and in the world are justified. The poet is not called to be popular or diplomatic. Jayne Cortez is very much aware of this as she fulminates in the manner of an Old Testament prophet. She cares enough about the women and children who are victims to bring their grisly situations to the attention of her readers. She is telling the truth about the conditions of people of color around the world. If her metaphors sometimes seem severe, contrived, or contorted, if she relies too much on the four-letter words of the street, it is because of the rage that she feels.

Sandburg's 1914 Chicago now looks tame compared to Cortez's violent and filthy New York. Sandburg was active in the labor movement and was a champion of the common people. He often quoted, with admiration, one of Rudyard Kipling's characters: "I will be the word of the people. Mine will be the bleeding mouth from which the gag is snatched. I will say anything." Jayne Cortez has snatched the rag from the bleeding mouth, letting her city and her times speak.

Bibliography

Addison, Gayle. *The Black Aesthetic.* Garden City, N.Y.: Doubleday, 1971. Brief mention of Cortez's work. Emphasis is on her background in music, especially bop, boogie, and the blues.

Frazier, Vernon. "The Poetry-Jazz Fusion." *Poets and Writers Magazine* 20 (March 1, 1992): 26. Describes how Cortez's work carries on a tradition that dates back to Homer and Sappho of marrying music and verse.

Melhem, D. H. *Heroism in the New Black Poetry.* Lexington: University Press of Kentucky, 1990. Describes six writers, Cortez among them, who have extended the concept of leadership and thus are heroes. Each essay is clearly written and provides good introduction to a writer's work. Contains primary bibliographies.

Redmond, Eugene B. *Drumvoices: The Mission of Afro-American Poetry.* Garden City, N.Y.: Anchor Press, 1976. Contains two brief mentions of Cortez's work. Notes her affinity to music as an aspect of form. Says of *Festivals and Funerals* that it embodies the fast pace of black life that is necessary because of prejudice and oppression but results in an enormous number of deaths.

Wilmer, Val. "Jayne Cortez—The Unsubmissive Blues: The Great Poet." *Coda* 230 (February 1, 1990): 16. An interview with Jayne Cortez.

Ann Struthers

THE POETRY OF COUNTÉE CULLEN

Author: Countée Cullen (Countée Porter, 1903-1946)
Type of work: Poetry
First published: Color, 1925; *Copper Sun*, 1927; *The Ballad of the Brown Girl: An Old Ballad Retold*, 1927; *The Black Christ, and Other Poems*, 1929; *The Medea, and Some Poems*, 1935; *The Lost Zoo (A Rhyme for the Young, But Not Too Young)*, 1940; *On These I Stand: An Anthology of the Best Poems of Countée Cullen*, 1947

The contributions of Countée Cullen to African American literature are well established. He was one of the most important figures of the Harlem Renaissance—he is sometimes labeled its poet laureate—and in fact most of his major poetry was written during the 1920's. In his day, Cullen was the most popular African American poet since Paul Laurence Dunbar, but since that time, his works have been viewed as too derivative and too locked into white, bourgeois perceptions of art—a criticism often launched against Dunbar as well.

There is a certain simplicity in the lyricism of Cullen, showing his indebtedness to William Wordsworth's "language of the common man." His poetry is also shaped by his admiration of John Keats and Percy Bysshe Shelley, other significant British Romantics. His diction is sometimes imprecise, sometimes sentimental and unoriginal. Nevertheless, at his best, Countée Cullen is an outstanding poet worthy of admiration and deserving of much more serious critical attention than he has received. While Cullen's poetry is derived from the Western lyrical heritage, it raises a number of important and interesting questions about the poet and about race, spirituality, the outcasts of society, and the meaning of Africa for African Americans. Critics consider his most important poems those that reflect his own experiences as an African American, though he wrote many poems that have little or nothing to do with race. These poems deal with love, friendship, and conventional poetic themes such as nature and death. In some of his greatest poems, he contrasts paganism with Christianity, recognizing his own "pagan" inclinations, which he cannot quite overcome despite his commitment to a Christian worldview. As he got older, he was ready to embrace a Christ who was "black" and reject the images of white religion that he, like so many of his fellow African Americans, had embraced during times of their bondage.

Born Countée Porter on May 30, 1903, he at the age of eleven or thirteen (biographers are not sure which) became the adopted son of the Reverend Frederick A. Cullen and his wife, Carolyn Bell Mitchell, who were associated with the African Methodist Episcopal Church. Cullen's upbringing was a rigid one; the Reverend Cullen was a fundamentalist who instilled in Countée a deep sense of guilt while at the same time inspiring in him a love of learning. Until he was adopted by the Cullens, he lived with his maternal grandmother.

At the height of the Harlem Renaissance, Cullen published his first collection of poetry, *Color*, which is still considered his finest work. The central theme of the collection, race, reflects the "race consciousness" generally associated with the Harlem Renaissance. Included in the collection is the frequently anthologized and important poem "Yet Do I Marvel." This poem uses the sonnet form for which Cullen is best known and introduces two central and interconnected themes of Cullen's work: the theme of race and the theme of spirituality. The speaker of the poem, presumably Cullen himself, ponders a series of questions concerning the nature of God. Using a rather Blakean and Romantic mode, Cullen raises questions about the motivation God might have had in making "a poet black" and bidding "him sing" in a world that is fundamentally racist and that does not readily accept the creative work of African Americans. His conclusion is that God is too complex for the human mind to comprehend, though he raises questions about whether God is indeed "good, well-meaning, kind" in making the world as it is and making an African American poet.

Another important poem in this collection, "A Brown Girl Dead," reflects on the ambiguity and irony of dressing a dead African American girl in the colors of her oppressors: "With two white roses on her breasts,/ White candles at head and feet,/ Dark Madonna of the grave she rests;/ Lord Death has found her sweet." Her mother has to sell her wedding ring in order to see to it that her daughter is dressed in white, and the poet writes that the girl would be proud to see herself in this attire were she alive to do so. She is a "Dark Madonna" in that she represents childhood innocence and purity that were not destroyed by a racist society. Ironically, she died perhaps believing, like her mother, that white is superior. To the poet, however, it is clear that the girl and her mother fail to recognize the degree to which they have allowed the white, racist society to alter their perceptions of themselves.

"Black Magdalens" perhaps influenced such later poets as Gwendolyn Brooks to write about social outcasts, including prostitutes. It deals with the inverse of the white Madonna figure of Western culture symbolized by the Virgin Mary. Rather than allow their human dignity to be destroyed by those who judge them, the "black Magdalens" hide their pain and "wrap their wounds in pride." Unlike Mary Magdalene, they do not have Christ to defend them against the self-righteous, judgmental "chaste clean ladies," so they must fend for themselves. Nevertheless, those who consider themselves worthy of Christ's kingdom find it easy to "cast the first hard stone." This poem, like many other Cullen works, demonstrates his sympathy and identification with the outcast and his criticism of judgmental and provincial Christians.

In the poem "Tableau," Cullen addresses the homoerotic friendship between a white and a black boy. Although Cullen was married twice, biographers have concluded that Cullen, like his adopted father, was largely a homosexual. Although hidden and repressed from his works as a whole, in this particular poem a homoerotic undercurrent is evident in the relationship between the two boys. Primarily concerned with the reactions of the community, like the previous poem, the boys walk "arm in arm" through both the "golden splendor of the day" and the "sable pride of night," a line that suggests their intimate relationship. At the same time, the poet uses metaphor to equate the white boy with day and the black boy with night. The implication is that they complement each other, but the community itself is appalled by the relationship, not so much because it has elements of homoeroticism (of which they are probably not conscious) but because the racist and segregated society of the time forbade such closeness and interaction. While the community watches behind the blinds and talks about the boys, the friends do, however, achieve a certain sense of personal freedom not shared by those locked into the conventions of society. They are "Oblivious to look and word." Here again, Cullen identifies with the outcast and suggests there is a certain freedom in violating the conventions of society. The poem closes with an unusual image: "They pass, and see no wonder/ That lightning brilliant as a sword/ Should blaze the path of thunder." The phallic sword is connected with the symbol of power and rebellion against convention, the thunder, and these two images together suggest the unconventional relationship between the two boys. Perhaps, also, Cullen indicates that in violating social codes the friends run the risk of disrupting the provincial society of which they are a part.

In the simple, often-anthologized lyric poem "Incident," Cullen reflects on a boy's first experience with overt racism. The speaker, a man looking back on a trip he took to Baltimore as an eight-year-old, comments on how he so innocently expected his trip to be an ideal experience. Ironically, he first sees himself as an alien being on the trip, for a white boy, who was "no whit bigger" than the speaker, called him the pejorative "nigger." Though he spent much more time in Baltimore, he can recall nothing else about the experience there. In this poem, Cullen demonstrates the effects of a painful experience involving the loss of innocence and indicates that human beings have a tendency to remember the worst rather than the best occurrences in their lives. He also shows the effects of racism on the self-esteem and growth of the individual African American.

"Heritage," which is dedicated to Cullen's intimate friend Harold Jackman, concerns a common theme of Cullen's work: Africa. This poem is considered by some to be the greatest poem of the Harlem Renaissance. It demonstrates the poet's ambivalence about his African heritage but argues against the inferiority imposed by the white and Western culture. Searching for a God who is black rather than the color of his oppressor, the speaker calls on Africa to inspire him to reconcile himself to God. Cullen associates Africa with the sensual side of the self that the Western culture of which he is a part has taught him to deny. Cullen's conflict between paganism and Western religion is evident through these lines: "My conversion came high-priced;/ I belong to Jesus Christ,/ Preacher of humility;/ Heathen gods are naught to me." Critic Jean Wagner considers the poem a commentary on the "inner struggle" of Cullen over his sexual orientation, his race, and his heavily religious (and orthodox Christian) nature. Darwin Turner has commented that "Heritage" concerns "the lyric cry of a civilized mind which cannot silence the memories of Africa that thrill the blood, of a heart which responds to rain and which, prostrate before the Christian altar, yearns for a black god who might comprehend suffering as no white god can." A comparable poem in the same collection is "The Shroud of Color," which reveals Cullen's spiritual struggle as well.

Cullen's second collection, *Copper Sun*, which appeared in the same year as the long poem "The Ballad of the Brown Girl," did not receive the acclaim his first one did. Mark Van Doren, a friend, warned Cullen not to publish a second collection so soon after the first, but he ignored the advice. Admittedly, few poems in this collection are of major importance, and some have argued that this is because only seven poems in the collection deal with race. The collection does, however, include one of Cullen's best and most influential poems, "From the Dark Tower." After receiving a bachelor's degree from New York University in 1925 and a master's degree from Harvard University in 1926, Cullen wrote a column on literary criticism for *Opportunity* entitled "The Dark Tower" for nearly two years. In the poem, one of his greatest sonnets, he reflects on the experience of African Americans and suggests that the time has come for them to stop suffering: "We were not made eternally to weep." In some sense, the poem can be labeled a protest poem, with apocalyptic overtones suggesting the possibility that African Americans will no longer stand by as they are abused and exploited. Nevertheless, they do "hide the heart that bleeds,/ And wait, and tend our agonizing seeds." These last lines indicate the effects of living in a world where African Americans are outcasts, forced to mask their pain and wait for the day when complete liberation of the mind and spirit will come through overcoming racial barriers. The masking motif common to much African American literature implies that the pain is hidden as an attempt to triumph over the oppression of racist whites.

In "Threnody for a Brown Girl," another memorable poem from *Copper Sun*, Cullen again employs a racial theme. The poet raises questions about the ways in which white society is responsible for the death of the girl and implies that the girl's mother should not purchase a tombstone of white marble: "Lay upon her no white stone/ From a foreign quarry;/ Earth and sky be these alone/ Her obituary." To cover her grave with such a symbol of white oppression would be inappropriate. As Jean Wagner has commented, "White, here, is the symbol of a commitment, of a racial and spiritual allegiance, and the use of white would mean doing violence, in the first place, to the deeper meaning of the dead girl's existence."

In the same year as *Copper Sun*, Cullen published, in pamphlet form, *The Ballad of the Brown Girl: An Old Ballad Retold*, a retelling of an earlier Western ballad that adds the element of interracial marriage and changes the brown-haired girl of the earlier versions to an African American woman. The poem is more than two hundred lines long. Many people, including the influential scholar George Lyman Kittredge, praised the poem as an excellent example of the ballad. In the poem, an aristocratic young man, Lord Thomas, marries a black woman for her land and gold, but he loves another woman, who is white. Attacking the idea of white female virtue so well established in the South, Cullen suggests that the white race triumphs over the oppressed African American woman. The black woman stabs her rival and is in turn stabbed by her husband. In death she is also an outcast, for her husband and the white woman are buried next to each other. Through this poem, Cullen again points out the alien status of African Americans and their exploitation and abuse by white Americans.

In 1928, Cullen received a Guggenheim Fellowship and went to Paris, where he remained for almost two years. Meanwhile, his marriage to Yolande Du Bois, the daughter of W. E. B. Du Bois, one of the inspirers of the Harlem Renaissance, failed, ending in 1929. After returning to the United States in 1929, Cullen taught French at Frederick Douglass Junior High School in New York City until his death. His second marriage, to Ida Mae Robertson, occurred in 1940. In 1932, he published his only novel, *One Way to Heaven*, which concerns the role of the church in the African American community. A children's book in verse form, *The Lost Zoo (A Rhyme for the Young, But Not Too Young)*, appeared in 1940. Critics and biographers are uncertain as to why Cullen wrote little new poetry after the 1920's, but some have speculated that his reduced output was a result of his commitment to teaching.

Cullen's next collection, *The Black Christ and Other Poems*, which was published in 1929, contains few memorable poems except for the title poem. By this point, Cullen had begun to move closer to his traditional Christian upbringing and to a large degree away from his pagan inclinations. "The Black Christ" demonstrates his commitment to a Western religious heritage at the same time it illustrates his desire for reconciliation with his African self. Concerned with the lynching of a black man, the poet again shows his propensity to protest racial oppression. Jim, the main character in this narrative poem, rebels against God and clashes with his mother, who blindly follows her Western religious (and Christian) heritage. While superficially the poem concerns a lynching, a number of critics, most notably Jean Wagner, see it as "a masterly reconstruction of the poet's inner drama," the conflict between disbelief and faith. Wagner argues that the poem reflects Cullen's own reconciliation with Christianity. Jim dies but is resurrected, like Christ, and he is portrayed as a Christ figure. There are many parallels with the Passion story of Christ as well. The poem illustrates Cullen's movement toward Christian mysticism, and some critics have argued that therein lies its major weakness.

Cullen's last collection, other than his collected poems, was entitled *The Medea, and Some Poems*. It includes a retelling of the classical Euripides tragedy *Medea* (431 B.C.); Cullen emphasizes the racial differences of Medea and her alien status. The poems most memorable in this collection are "Medusa" and "Scottsboro, Too, Is Worth Its Song." In the former work, Cullen, who often uses allusions to Greek mythology (an aspect of his paganism), addresses in sonnet form the mythic figure of Medusa. Unlike most of the poems for which he is known, "Medusa" does not concern race but reflects Cullen's fascination with Greek mythology. The poem's speaker expresses his undying curiosity concerning the Medusa figure: "But I was never one to be subdued/ By any fear of aught not reason-bred,/ And so I mocked the ruddy word, and stood/ To meet the gold-envenomed dart instead." Unlike the Medusa of Greek mythology, however, this one does not destroy the speaker when he looks upon her but instead blinds him: "I know it was a lovely face I braved."

"Scottsboro, Too, Is Worth Its Song," is a protest poem, the only one in the collection dealing directly with the issue of race and social injustice. The title refers to the Scottsboro, Alabama, trial of nine black men accused of raping two white girls. After the conviction, one girl recanted her previous accusation, but after the case was heard in the Supreme Court, four men were convicted to life imprisonment. Cullen sees this event as similar to the injustice involving the Sacco-Vanzetti case of the 1920's. Nicola Sacco and Bartolomeo Vanzetti were accused and convicted of armed robbery and murder in April, 1920, even though they had witnesses verifying they could not have possibly been at the scene of the crime. Eventually, they were executed, despite the discovery that a gang of robbers had been responsible for the crime. Cullen uses this case and the Scottsboro incident to attack the American system for condemning those of ethnic and minority groups and devaluing their existence. The speaker expects poets, to whom the poem is dedicated, to see the Scottsboro case as an inspiration for their art. The racial element of the poem is especially evident in these lines: "Here too's a cause divinely spun/ For those whose eyes are on the sun,/ Here in epitome/ Is all disgrace/ And epic wrong,/ Like wine to brace/ The minstrel heart, and blare it into song." In referring to the "minstrel," Cullen condemns American racism, which has reduced blacks and other minorities to mere masks of humanity. As the poem ends, Cullen points out the irony in the fact that poets should have been inspired to write by the Scottsboro case as they were by the Sacco-Vanzetti trial, but they were unwilling to protest injustice against African Americans.

In 1947, Cullen's *On These I Stand: An Anthology of the Best Poems of Countée Cullen* appeared. He had selected the poems for inclusion just before his death, which was caused by complications from high blood pressure in 1946. This collection includes major poems from previous collections as well as half a dozen previously unpublished poems. These new poems, while maintaining the style and content for which Cullen is noted, add nothing to his literary reputation; critics consider them lesser poems than most of the earlier poems. Though most of the poems for which Cullen is known deal with the subject of race and were written during the 1920's, his literary reputation as a significant American poet is stable. As Houston Baker has written, Cullen "never achieved the 'Vision Splendid.' He can be classified as a minor poet whose life and poetry raise major problems."

Bibliography

Baker, Houston A., Jr. *A Many-Colored Coat of Dreams: The Poetry of Countee Cullen*. Detroit: Broadside Press, 1974. In this important but brief study, Baker emphasizes Cullen's Romantic heritage and places him within the context of African American poetry up through the Harlem Renaissance. There are useful analyses of individual poems, especially those from *Color*. The notes and bibliography, though somewhat dated, may be useful for finding other materials on Cullen.

Davis, Arthur P. *From the Dark Tower: Afro-American Writers (1900 to 1960)*. Washington, D.C.: Howard University Press, 1974. A general but useful overview of the life and career of Cullen. Davis emphasizes the dual nature of Cullen as both pagan and Christian and suggests that he seems to have reconciled himself to his Christian side after his first volume of poetry. A select bibliography of primary and secondary material is included.

Redding, J. Saunders. *To Make a Poet Black*. Chapel Hill: University of North Carolina Press, 1939. Although Redding's book concentrates on African American poetry before the Harlem Renaissance, his perceptive remarks concerning Cullen, though brief, may be of use even today. Redding calls Cullen the "Ariel of Negro poets" and mentions Cullen's reluctance to be labeled a Negro poet and his confusion about race. Nevertheless, to Redding, Cullen is best when writing about racial issues.

Turner, Darwin T. *In a Minor Chord: Three Afro-American Writers and Their Search for Identity*. Carbondale: Southern Illinois University Press, 1971. A short but useful discussion of Cullen's life and work. Turner stresses that Cullen was a Romantic poet who allowed his emotional inclinations to interfere with his intellectual abilities; as a result, Turner argues, Cullen was a failure after his first collection of poetry. A select bibliography, mostly containing articles on Cullen, is included.

Wagner, Jean. *Black Poets of the United States: From Paul Laurence Dunbar to Langston Hughes*. Translated by Kenneth Douglas. Urbana: University of Illinois Press, 1973. By far the most complete and excellent discussion of Cullen's life and career, this work includes biographical information not included elsewhere and offers analyses of Cullen's spiritual and racial poetry. Includes an effective section on Cullen's use of Africa in his works and a lengthy analysis of "The Black Christ." There is a useful bibliographical appendix and a bibliographical supplement.

D. Dean Shackleford